AMERICAN PHILOSOPHY
IN THE TWENTIETH CENTURY

This book, together with its companion volume, *American Thought Before 1900*, is part of a series, Classics in the History of Thought, prepared under the general editorship of Crane Brinton and Paul Edwards.

American Philosophy in the Twentieth Century

A Sourcebook

FROM PRAGMATISM TO PHILOSOPHICAL ANALYSIS

Edited, with an Introductory Survey, Notes, and Bibliographies, by **PAUL KURTZ**

THE MACMILLAN COMPANY, NEW YORK

COLLIER-MACMILLAN LTD., LONDON

The Macmillan Company, New York

Collier-Macmillan Canada Ltd., Toronto, Ontario

PRINTED IN THE UNITED STATES OF AMERICA

Fourth Printing, 1968

Grateful acknowledgment is hereby made for permission to reprint in this volume material from:

Collected Papers of Charles Sanders Peirce, Vols. V, VI, ed. by Charles Hartshorne and Paul Weiss. Reprinted by permission of the publishers. Cambridge, Mass.: The Belknap Press of Harvard University Press, Copyright, 1931, 1960 by the President and Fellows of Harvard College.

A Pluralistic Universe, by William James. Copyright © 1909. Reprinted by permission of Paul R. Reynolds & Son, 599 Fifth Avenue, New York 17, New York.

Experience and Nature, by John Dewey. Copyright 1925 and 1929. The Open Court Publishing Co. By permission of the publishers.

Essays in Experimental Logic, by John Dewey, by permission of The University of Chicago Press. Copyright 1916 by The University of Chicago.

Logic: The Theory of Inquiry, by John Dewey. Copyright © 1938, Holt, Rinehart and Winston, Inc. By permission of the publishers.

"The Logic of Judgments of Practice" by John Dewey in *The Journal of Philosophy*, Vol. XII, No. 19 (1916). "The Future of Liberalism" by John Dewey, in *The Journal of Philosophy*, Vol. XXXII (1935). Reproduced by permission of the Editors and by permission of Mrs. John Dewey.

Democracy and Education by John Dewey. Reprinted with permission of the publisher. Copyright 1916 by The Macmillan Company, renewed 1944 by John Dewey.

Skepticism and Animal Faith by George Santayana. Copyright 1923, Constable & Co. Ltd., and *Realms of Being*, Copyright 1927. By permission of the executor and the publishers.

Process and Reality by Alfred North Whitehead. Reprinted by permission of the publisher. Copyright 1929 by The Macmillan Company.

Modes of Thought by Alfred North Whitehead. Reprinted by permission of the publisher. Copyright 1938 by The Macmillan Company.

Mind, Self, and Society by George Herbert Mead by permission of The University of Chicago Press. Copyright 1934 by The University of Chicago.

"The Program and First Platform of Six Realists" by E. B. Holt, W. T. Marvin, W. P. Montague, R. B. Perry, W. B. Pitkin, and E. G. Spaulding, in *The Journal of Philosophy*, Vol. VII, No. 15 (1910). By permission.

ACKNOWLEDGMENTS 5

Essays in Critical Realism by D. Drake, A. O. Lovejoy, J. B. Pratt, A. K. Rogers, G. Santayana, R. W. Sellars, C. A. Strong. Copyright 1920, Macmillan & Co. Ltd. (London). By permission.

"Realism in Retrospect" by Ralph Barton Perry and "Realism, Naturalism and Humanism" by Roy Wood Sellars in *Contemporary American Philosophy*. Vol. II, ed. by G. P. Adams and W. P. Montague. Copyright 1930. George Allen & Unwin Ltd., London. By permission.

General Theory of Value by Ralph Barton Perry. Reprinted by permission of the publishers. Cambridge, Mass.: Harvard University Press, Copyright 1926 by the President and Fellows of Harvard College. Copyright 1954 by Ralph Barton Perry.

The Revolt Against Dualism by Arthur O. Lovejoy. Copyright 1930. The Open Court Publishing Co. By permission.

"A Humanist Manifesto" in *The New Humanist* (May-June, 1933). *The Humanist* (March-April, 1953). Copyright, The American Humanist Association, Yellow Springs, Ohio. By permission.

Reason and Nature, by Morris R. Cohen. Reprinted with permission of the estate of Morris R. Cohen and with permission of The Free Press of Glencoe. Copyright 1931 by Morris R. Cohen, renewed 1959 by Leonora Cohen Rosenfield.

"A Pragmatic Conception of the *A Priori*" by C. I. Lewis in *The Journal of Philosophy*, Vol. XX:7 (1923). By permission.

An Analysis of Knowledge and Valuation by C. I. Lewis. Copyright 1946. The Open Court Publishing Co. By permission.

"Empiricism, Semantics and Ontology" by Rudolf Carnap in *Revue internationale de philosophie*, Vol. XI (1950). By permission.

"The Nature of Ethical Disagreement" by Charles Stevenson in *Sigma*, Vols. 1-2 (1947-48). By permission.

"Speaking of Objects" by W. V. O. Quine in *Proceedings and Addresses of The American Philosophical Association,* Vol. XXXI (1957-58). By permission.

"Language and Reality" by Max Black in *Proceedings and Address of The American Philosophical Association,* Vol. XXXII (1958-59). By permission.

Reason and Analysis by Brand Blanshard. Copyright 1962. The Open Court Publishing Co., and Allen & Unwin Ltd., London. By permission.

Philosophy of the Future: The Quest of Modern Materialism, ed. by R. W. Sellars, V. J. McGill, and M. Farber. Reprinted with permission of the publisher. Copyright 1949 by The Macmillan Company.

"Existential Philosophy" by Paul J. Tillich, Copyright by and printed originally in *The Journal of the History of Ideas*, Volume V (January 1944), pp. 44-70. By permission of its Board of Editors and the author.

"Pragmatism and the Tragic Sense of Life" by Sidney Hook in *Proceedings and Addresses of the American Philosophical Association,* Vol. XXXII (1959-60). By permission.

"Naturalism and First Principles" by Sidney Hook. Reprinted by permission of the publisher from *American Philosophers at Work*, ed. by Sidney Hook (New York: 1959). Copyright © 1959 by Criterion Books Inc.

"Naturalism Reconsidered" by Ernest Nagel in *Proceedings and Addresses of The American Philosophical Association,* Vol. XXVIII (1954-55). By permission.

for Sidney Hook

Contents

PART TWO:
THE CONTEMPORARY PHILOSOPHICAL SCENE

Preface

American Philosophy in the Twentieth Century: A Sourcebook from Pragmatism to Philosophical Analysis and *American Thought Before 1900: A Sourcebook from Puritanism to Darwinism* are companion volumes, which may be used separately or together. *American Philosophy in the Twentieth Century* is devoted specifically to the development of philosophical ideas in the United States from the latter part of the nineteenth century until the present day. It should be useful not only to students of American philosophy but to American studies students and to the general reader who is interested in recent and current philosophical thinking. *American Thought Before 1900* is designed for a wide range of readers in the fields of American studies and American philosophy. Inasmuch as intellectual expression in the United States before the twentieth century is continuous with the social context, the term "thought" rather than "philosophy" is more applicable, and readers of history, literature, religion and politics, as well as those interested in philosophy, should find that book useful.

My special thanks in preparing these volumes go to Paul Edwards for his wise counsel and assistance. I also wish to acknowledge my appreciation to Herbert W. Schneider and Harold Larrabee for their valuable suggestions, especially in the preparation of *American Thought Before 1900*. The following were also helpful in selecting appropriate pieces or in providing important information, especially for *American Philosophy in the Twentieth Century*: Sidney Hook, Brand Blanshard, the late C. I. Lewis, Rudolf Carnap, Paul Tillich, Max Black, Horace L. Friess, Bernard Perry, and Edward Boring. I wish to thank those of my students on whom I have tested portions of this manuscript, and the library staffs of Union College and Vassar College for bibliographical assistance. The Ford Foundation Public Affairs Program and the Union College Social Science Research Center are responsible for providing a grant to defray some of the costs involved in research for these books. I am grateful to my wife for her constant inspiration and devotion.

PAUL KURTZ

Introduction

An American philosophical renaissance occurred at the end of the nineteenth century, and it continues in full force down to the present. If the de Tocqueville of 1835 could return to the United States today, he might be surprised to find that, contrary to his time, in almost no country in the world is *more* attention being paid to technical philosophy than in the United States.

There are many tangible signs of this remarkable increase of interest in philosophy. First, there has been a sharp rise in the publication of new philosophy journals and books. *The International Journal of Ethics* was founded in 1890, *The Philosophical Review* in 1892, and *The Journal of Philosophy, Psychology and Scientific Methods* in 1904. Today there are over forty philosophy journals in the United States, and over 600 books in the field of philosophy are published annually. Second, during this century numerous philosophical societies have been established. The American Philosophical Association was founded in 1901, and there are now over 80 societies devoted to philosophical inquiry in the United States. Third, the serious introduction of philosophy as a subject into liberal arts colleges and graduate schools and the steady expansion of higher education is a major factor in this growth of interest. Before the Civil War American colleges and universities were primarily sectarian and denominational. As a result, they produced few original philosophers of first rate importance. A decided change occurred when appointments to faculties of philosophy were no longer filled by college presidents or those whose primary qualifications were pastoral piety, but were awarded instead to those who qualified by philosophical training and competence. The liberation of philosophy from sterility and stupor was also made possible by the introduction of advanced graduate study at Johns Hopkins (1876) and elsewhere. (Philosophy within *academia*, however, was not entirely autonomous. Some highly competent thinkers were excluded from college faculties on arbitrary grounds by conservative administrations and trustees, and "radicals" are still frequently looked upon with disfavor. This was, for example, the fate of Charles Peirce, Chauncey Wright and Thomas Davidson.)

A mere increase in the number of students or publications does not of course insure a higher quality in the work that is done. However, in the United States, growth of interest in philosophy coincided with the emergence of a remarkable number of original thinkers and fresh movements. The period of roughly 1880 to 1940 has sometimes, not inappropriately, been called "The Golden Age of American Philosophy"; the first half of the present volume is devoted to the work of the outstanding philosophers of this period. The most important figures of the "Golden Age" were Peirce, James, Dewey, Royce, Santayana and Whitehead; the most significant movements were pragmatism, realism and naturalism.

Before sketching the main characteristics of these three movements, it may be helpful to say a few words about the philosophy against which all of them were, in one way or another, rebelling. This was the idealism which dominated much of American thought in the second half of the 19th century and which was still very influential in the opening years of the 20th century. Selections from Royce, the outstanding American representative of this tendency, are included in the companion book, *American Thought Before 1900*, but several of his most famous works were published during the period covered by the present volume, and his influence continued to be felt for many years after his death in 1916. Furthermore, although it is unquestionably true that idealists have generally been on the defensive since the beginning of the century and that their numbers have been constantly diminishing, it must also be pointed out that philosophers of considerable standing have continued until the present day to advocate one or another of the basic theories associated with idealism.

The following three propositions would probably have been endorsed by most of the idealists of the late 19th and early 20th century: (1) Mind is in some sense the fundamental reality—everything that exists can on analysis be seen to be mental or, if not itself mental, at any rate dependent on mind; (2) Reality is an organic whole in which everything is logically or internally connected with everything else; (3) Value and purpose are not merely features of the human scene, but are of cosmic significance. Most, though not all, idealists were defenders of some form of traditional religion, and even those who were not nevertheless had obvious affinities with the outlook of rationalistic theology.

Pragmatism

The ideas subsequently associated with the school of pragmatism were first discussed by the members of the "Metaphysical Society" in Cambridge in the 1870's. These included Chauncey Wright, Charles Peirce, William James and John Fiske. For Charles Peirce (1839–

1914), pragmatism was primarily a method of clarifying ideas and concepts by clearing away metaphysical and other confusions. Peirce explicitly defined the word "pragmatism" in print in 1902 when he contributed an article to Baldwin's *Dictionary of Philosophy and Psychology*, but his basic ideas had already been formulated in several essays over twenty years earlier, especially in the article "How to Make Our Ideas Clear," which appeared in the *Popular Science Monthly* in 1878. "Consider what effects, that might conceivably have practical bearings, we conceive the object of our conception to have," wrote Peirce; "then, our conception of these effects is the whole of our conception of the object." Peirce made it clear that the method was to be used chiefly to ascertain the meaning of "hard words" and "abstract concepts." Indeed, he later pointed out that he was not concerned with all ideas, but only with "intellectual concepts." The meaning of ideas is properly stated in hypothetical form. Their experimental consequences *are* their meaning. To say that something is "brittle" means that "if we were to strike it, it would shatter." To understand the meaning of our idea we do not actually have to perform such experiments, but we must be able to conceive of experimental consequences if our ideas are to mean anything at all. Peirce's theory here clearly foreshadows the later Verification Principle of logical positivism and the operationalism of P. W. Bridgman.

Peirce's published ideas lay virtually dormant until William James (1842–1910) popularized them in a lecture entitled "Philosophical Conceptions and Practical Results," which he delivered in 1898 at the University of California. Some leanings in the same direction had already been noticeable in some of James' earlier writings, such as "The Will to Believe" (1896). When James spoke of pragmatism, he meant *both* the pragmatic method as advocated by Peirce *and* a new theory about the nature of truth which he thought to be implicit in the pragmatic method. There are several striking passages in which James tried to bring out the main point in his new theory. "The true," he wrote in one place, "is only the *expedient* in the way of our thinking, just as 'the right' is only the expedient in the way of our behaving. Expedient in almost any fashion; and expedient in the long run and on the whole of course." Elsewhere we are told that the only thing that different true statements or beliefs have in common is that they "pay." In another much-quoted passage James says of the expressions "It is useful because it is true" and "It is true because it is useful" that they "mean exactly the same thing." James was accused, not unjustly, by many of his critics, including Bertrand Russell and A. O. Lovejoy, of using the words "useful," "pay," and "expedient" in a thoroughly ambiguous fashion. When we say that a scientific theory is useful in the sense of allowing us to derive certain predictions, we obviously do not mean the same as when we say that a belief is useful, and mean that it is emotionally satisfying. It may not perhaps be too implausible to maintain that if a statement is useful in the former sense, this implies that it is true; but it seems preposterous to maintain that a statement is true because it is useful in the second sense. Yet James undoubtedly did mean to say just this when he came to his justification of religion. Although James was an empiricist and suspicious of metaphysical speculations about a transcendent reality, he was also a champion of religion, and thought it was possible to provide a new empiricistic justification for the basic tenets of traditional religion. "On pragmatic principles," he wrote, "we cannot reject any hypothesis if concepts useful to life flow from it. . . . If the hypothesis of God works satisfactorily in the widest sense of the word, it is true. Now . . . experience shows that it certainly does work."

None of the other leaders of American pragmatism could bring themselves to accept this theory of truth. Peirce was naturally hostile to the subjectivistic tenor of this theory, which he maintained was not implied by the pragmatic method. His criterion was framed in the light of public tests of laboratory science. This does not mean that Peirce was uninterested in a theory of truth. Indeed, he defended the "method of science" as the most effective way of resolving doubt and fixing belief. But he insisted that there were limitations to the use of the pragmatic criterion. Not only did it not apply to subjective consequences, it had little to say about applied consequences of "pure" science. To dissociate himself from James' version of pragmatism, he rechristened his own theory "pragmaticism"—a word which, he said, was so ugly that it was safe from kidnappers.

John Dewey (1859–1952) shared James' opposition to the traditional correspondence and coherence theories of truth, but, unlike James, he had no wish to offer a new justification of traditional religion and he found the subjectivistic implications of James' pragmatism quite objectionable. Unlike Peirce, however, he wished to extend the pragmatic criterion to the broader aspects of life. For Dewey, the term "pragmatic" meant only "the rule of referring all thinking, all reflective consideration, to consequences for final meaning and test"; but he preferred to label his theory "instrumentalism," to avoid the earlier connotations of "pragmatism." Dewey developed views on both "meaning" and "truth." The key point of his theory of meaning is that language is an instrument which transforms raw experience in accordance with the purposes of human beings. The meaning of an idea refers to a "set of operations" to be performed, the "consequences" produced by a thing or event. Dewey recognized different functions of language—scientific language focuses on prediction and control, and aesthetic language is expressive and consummatory—but he claimed that all language is prescriptive, in that it is related to problems of conduct.

The idea of a "situation" is central to Dewey's philosophy, and especially to his theory of inquiry. Inquiry is initiated by conflicts which arise within immediate experience ("primary experience"), and the function of reflective thinking ("secondary experience") is to resolve the problematic situation. Inquiry is the "controlled or directed transformation of an indeterminate situation into one that is so determinate in its constituent distinctions and relations—as to convert the elements of the original situation into a unified whole." Ideas which are arrived at in the course of an inquiry are interpreted as hypotheses; they are plans of action and are tested by their experimental consequences. "That which satisfactorily terminates inquiry is, by definition, knowledge," or, as Dewey prefers to call it, "warranted assertion." A "true" idea, then, resolves a situation, a false idea does not. In answer to the charge that here is another form of subjectivism, Dewey maintained that this was the method of science, (which was continuous with common sense); he asserted that it applied not to subjective states, but to *existential* situations.

Central to Dewey's pragmatism was the development of a "biological" theory of experience, which in many ways resembles the later theories of the behaviorists and Gilbert Ryle. Such a biological interpretation of thought and experience had already been implicit in Peirce and in some chapters of James' *The Principles of Psychology* (1890). Thinking was conceived by Dewey as a mode of adapting to the challenges of the environment. "Mind" or "consciousness" do not exist as separate entities, but must be regarded as functions and transactions of the living organism. Dewey's pragmatism also presupposed a social theory of experience. George Herbert Mead (1863–1931), another important pragmatist, attempted to extend the social interpretation of mind. "Mind" and "self," he held, develop only out of the process of social communication. Society is basically a set of social habits developed in man's attempt to control his environment. We become selves only in so far as we can assimilate these social habits. Through the use of language, or significant symbols, the individual acquires the common attitudes of others, so that he takes the same attitude as the society toward himself. Through this process, the self is formed.

The net effect of pragmatism was that it contributed to the destruction of traditional conceptions of metaphysics and to the reconstruction of philosophy. Peirce, James and Dewey were not hostile to metaphysics in every sense of the word, but they thought that, like the sciences, any defensible metaphysics would have to be empirical and tentative in character. Accordingly, all notions of Absolute Being or ultimate certainty such as the idealists espoused were rejected. Peirce was ingenious in his formulation of metaphysical ideas —phenomenological, realistic, and evolutionary—though at times these seem hardly to conform with the pragmatic criterion. James outlined several novel ideas, such as a metaphysics of pure experience, and radical empiricism, and Dewey advanced a naturalistic metaphysics allegedly descriptive of the generic traits of nature and based upon human experience.

The influence of pragmatism was not confined to academic philosophy. It soon began to be felt in new theories that were propounded in the social sciences, and behavioral scientists from Bentley and Lasswell to Skinner and Lundberg are identified with its program. Pragmatism generally has given impetus to the ideals of liberalism, democracy and freedom. Sociological jurisprudence and legal realism were espoused by pragmatic jurists, such as Roscoe Pound and Oliver Wendell Holmes, Jr.; legal decisions were treated not as formal structures, but as related to actual social needs. Many consider Dewey's pragmatism more important for its theory of "progressive education" than for its contributions to technical philosophy. His educational theory emphasized learning by doing, and he ceased to regard the child as merely a passive recipient of information. But here Dewey was only applying a basic principle of pragmatism as it developed in America: ideas must be related to practical consequences and be responsive to the broader problems of civilization.

Realism

The realistic revolt against idealism in the early decades of this century was by no means confined to the United States. In England, the leaders of the rebellion were Bertrand Russell and G. E. Moore. In Germany, realistic doctrines were advocated by Husserl and the phenomenologists, and in Belgium and elsewhere the Neo-Thomists propagated a realist theory of knowledge. However, realism was perhaps nowhere more influential or widespread than in the United States, and it was only here that anything approaching organized movements existed. Peirce, James, and even Whitehead were sympathetic to aspects of realism, but it appears to owe its development mostly to two schools, known respectively as the "New" and the "Critical" Realists. Although the realists differed on many matters of importance, they agreed on certain basic epistemological issues. They all denied the idealistic premise that physical objects are reducible to "ideas" and denied equally that the objects of experience exist only when we experience them. The fact that we know something makes no difference to the object known. In more technical language: the relation between knowing and the object known is an "external" and not an "internal" relation.

Numerous articles and books by new realists appeared during the first decade of the century. As an organized movement, however, the new realism was launched in 1910 with the publication in the *Journal of Philosophy* of "The Program and First Platform of Six Realists," reprinted in the present volume. The authors of this manifesto were Ralph B. Perry, William P. Montague, E. B. Holt, E. G. Spaulding, W. T. Marvin and W. B. Pitkin. The same authors subsequently published an influential volume, *The New Realism* (1912). Several other philosophers of this period, including F. J. E. Woodbridge, E. B. McGilvary, M. R. Cohen, J. Lowenberg and J. E. Boodin were also sympathetic to this outlook.

Ralph Barton Perry (1876–1957), in an influential article, "The Ego-Centric Predicament," laid the groundwork for the platform of the realists. "The Ego-Centric Predicament" points to the fact that whatever is known is related to the consciousness of some knower. The ontological idealists maintain that everything that exists (T) bears some relationship to the consciousness R^c of some ego (E). But we are not entitled on the basis of this predicament, said Perry, to argue for ontological idealism, or to claim that what exists (T) is identical with or dependent upon its relation to (E).

In opposition to subjectivism, the "new realists" maintained the independence of things known. Realism, according to Montague, accepted the premise of naïve realism: "Some particulars of which we are conscious exist when we are not conscious of them." But it went beyond the common sense doctrine by asserting "the subsistence of essences or universals," a form of Platonic realism. The new realists also maintained an epistemological monism, which contrasted with the epistemological dualism of Descartes and Locke. Montague interpreted this epistemological monism to mean that the particulars and universals that are real "are apprehended directly rather than indirectly through copies or mental images." The "new realists," in answer to the dualists, did not deny knowledge by intermediaries, but they made it subordinate to direct or presentative knowledge.

The "new realists" also offered a program of reform for philosophy itself—quite similar to many features of recent analytic philosophy. They attacked speculative system building and mystical philosophy. They sought to dissociate philosophical research from the history of philosophy, and to relate it to the special sciences. They insisted that philosophers be scrupulous in the use of words, and that they define their terms carefully. They advocated the use of logic and the method of analysis as the model for doing philosophy, the careful and systematic approach to philosophical problems. It was essential, they thought, that philosophers deal with one problem at a time. In this way they hoped that philosophers might find some agreement, or at least come to know where they agreed and disagreed.

For awhile there seemed to be a genuine coalition among the new realists, but it proved to be short-lived. Although the new realists were united in their general view that external physical objects exist, they differed on many other issues. They disagreed, for example, in their theories of mind. Holt and Perry were sympathetic to functional and behavioristic psychology, whereas Montague was sympathetic to a form of materialism which held mind to be potential energy. The most fundamental dispute concerned the nature of error. A staff appears bent in water, or at least it presents itself as such, but is it really? How explain the differences between veridical and false presentations? Holt and Perry were led to the curious view that errors, illusions, and hallucinations exist objectively. Holt maintained that, if consciousness is not in the skull but "out there," and if percepts in consciousness are equivalent to their immediate objects, then an identity must also apply to "false" percepts, which are likewise "real." Montague agreed that false percepts subsist—"subsistence is an actual or possible object of thought, be it ideal or real"—though he denied that they had causal force. This seemed to lead to the contradictory conclusion that a staff in water is both straight and bent at the same time.

As already noted, the "critical realists," like the new realists, were anxious to vindicate the ordinary man's beliefs in the independent reality of material objects. However, arguments such as the above convinced them that what is directly given in perception is never the physical object itself, but a datum which, while providing the perceiver with evidence for the existence of the object, is not in any sense a part or characteristic of it. Physical objects, in other words, are known by inference and not directly.

Critical realism, because of its distinction between the datum and the object, may be regarded as a form of "epistemological dualism." The critical realists, in brief, maintained that the world contained *at least* two sets of entities: (a) material things and (b) mental states, ideas or essences, and that it is only the latter which are given or presented directly to consciousness. The given is not the same as the existent object. Moreover, our sense qualities exist at a time later than that of the events in the object that cause them. This theory, it was thought, had the advantage of enabling us to explain error by attributing it to the psychological state of the knower.

Several of the leading exponents of this position—George Santayana, Arthur O. Lovejoy, Roy Wood Sellars, C. P. Strong, James B.

Pratt, Durant Drake, and Arthur K. Rogers—collaborated in the publication of *Essays in Critical Realism* (1920), which was in effect a manifesto sketching the common doctrines and aims of the group. From the start, there was one question on which the critical realists strongly disagreed among themselves. This concerned the status of the data that are immediately given in perception.

The critical realists eventually divided into two camps. Drake, Strong, and Santayana held that in knowledge we affirm the presence of abstract "essences," which are the logical characteristics of the object. These objective essences are independent both of the object and of the mental states which entertain them. When we know an object, we assign a certain essence to some reality which exists independently of the process of knowing. Santayana, like Plato, considered essences to be eternal. Lovejoy, Sellars, and Pratt on the other hand denied the doctrine of essences and said that what is given is the character complex of the mental existent of the moment —a particular sense datum, not an independent entity.

This led to the question which has plagued epistemological dualists since the days of Locke and Descartes: if the object is never given in experience, how do we ever get to it? How do we know that there is an object and, assuming that there is one, how can we know what characteristics it has? Is not the knower confined to the datum, and if so can he ever know the existence of that which he affirms and claims to know? If the new realists were faced with the problem of error, the critical realists had to contend with the problem of truth. Moreover, they seemed to be confronted with still another form of the ego-centric predicament.

George Santayana (1863–1952) in *Skepticism and Animal Faith* (1923) maintained that we can never prove by rational means the nature of the external object. But we can and do bridge the gap by means of "animal faith" and instinct. Man is a doer, and he has a dynamic relation to objects as well as a passive, knowing or perceiving relationship. Arthur O. Lovejoy (1873–1962) in *The Revolt Against Dualism* (1930) maintained that, if you are to believe in a real physical world, you must be a dualist, since the datum is never identical with the object known. He admitted that the existence of physical objects cannot be "proven," yet he affirmed their existence as an assumption which the man of common sense makes, and which no one can deny. The ordinary man, he argued, realizes full well that objects persist and do not stop existing when he stops noticing them, that they have a spatial and temporal externality, and a causal independence.

Realism ceased to be a significant influence in American philosophy after the mid-30's. This was not, in all likelihood, because of the logical difficulties besetting both forms of the theory, but because of the shift of interest among young philosophers to other problems. Very few philosophers after 1935 were in the least inclined to doubt or deny the independent reality of physical objects, and in that regard at least, realism may be said to have triumphed. However, under the impact of logical positivism, British analytic philosophy, and Dewey's naturalism, most of the younger philosophers became concerned with issues which they took to be more fundamental than disputes about the independence of physical objects and the status of sense-data. Nonetheless, in deflating pretensions to system-building and in emphasizing a careful and rigorous approach to philosophical questions, the realistic revolt has had a continuing effect on present-day philosophy.

Naturalism

In a broad sense of the term "naturalism," any philosophy may be regarded as naturalistic if it maintains that all phenomena can in principle be explained in terms of natural causes or principles. In this sense, a number of philosophies of past centuries are also "naturalistic." This is undoubtedly true of most materialistic systems. It is true of Hume, who may too—at least in certain parts of his work—be classified as a naturalist. The naturalism which became influential in philosophy during the present century is, however, in certain respects markedly different from most earlier varieties.

The philosopher most responsible for its development was John Dewey, in whose later works, especially his book *Experience and Nature* (1925), the main theories of the new naturalism were forcefully presented. Because of Dewey's intimate connection with the rise of pragmatism, there has been a tendency among some historians to identify naturalism with pragmatism or instrumentalism, but any such identification is highly misleading. There is no logical connection between the key doctrines of the new naturalism and any pragmatic theory of truth; in fact, many leading naturalists were not at all sympathetic to pragmatism. Several of the philosophers mentioned above were naturalists in addition to being realists. Santayana's early work, *The Life of Reason* (1905–06), may be regarded as a general statement of a naturalistic outlook. Among the other realists who were also naturalists, we may mention Roy Wood Sellars, F. J. E. Woodbridge, M. R. Cohen, W. P. Montague, R. B. Perry, and D. Drake. An important collection of essays by leading naturalists, entitled *Naturalism and the Human Spirit*, was published in 1944. The contributors included John Dewey, Ernest Nagel, Sidney Hook, H.

W. Schneider, J. H. Randall, Jr., Abraham Edel, Harold Larrabee, H. T. Costello, George Boas, Sterling P. Lamprecht, and others. Several of these writers would not wish to be regarded as pragmatists.

Because of its connection with John Dewey and Santayana, it has been convenient to treat naturalism as one of the movements belonging to the "Golden Age of American Philosophy." This should not be taken to imply that naturalism is a thing of the past, for quite unlike pragmatism and realism it is one of the most influential philosophies on the American scene today.

Like the older brands of naturalism, American naturalism regards the logico-empirical method of science as the only proper procedure for establishing cognitive claims. Knowledge in any area, it is emphasized, does not depend on any esoteric capacity for discovering "higher truths." Nor is there anything mysterious about the scientific method itself; it is continuous with the same operations of thought used in the ordinary affairs of life. Intuitions and mystical experiences, whatever their moral or aesthetic value, are not means of arriving at any kind of truth. The scientific method is adequate to the study of everything there is, including human consciousness and social phenomena. It is clear that naturalists are opposed not only to transcendent metaphysics, but also to the widespread opinion, shared by such diverse thinkers as Dilthey and contemporary existentialists, that a special method is required to deal with human, as opposed to other kinds of phenomena.

One respect in which the new naturalism markedly differs from all previous forms is its vigorous "anti-reductionism." This feature was stated with great emphasis and clarity by Ernest Nagel in an article published in 1947. The new naturalism, he writes, maintains

> that the world contains at least as many qualitatively distinct features as are disclosed in human experience, and not a fewer number of them. The widespread view exemplified in such claims as that the playing of a Bach *Chaconne* is "nothing but" a scraping of horsehair across catgut, or that the human scene is "nothing but" an aggregation of certain allegedly "ultimate" elements, is therefore rejected as resting upon patent confusions. Modern physics and modern biopsychology are taken seriously by contextualistic naturalists, and current theories concerning the electrical structure of matter and the biophysical basis of human action are assumed to be well-grounded in competent evidence. But they fail to see any merit in the argument according to which, simply because complex organizations of the elementary particles of modern physics constitute the conditions for the occurrence of familiar events and processes, the characteristic behaviors of such complex wholes are indistinguishably identical with the behaviors of their differently organized parts.

Closely connected with this anti-reductionism is the "contextual-ism" emphasized by many of the American naturalists. They em-phatically reject the blanket distinction between appearance and a reality behind "the world of appearances." A distinction between ap-pearance and reality makes sense only in a given context, and in terms of the aims of a given inquiry. There is, to quote Ernest Nagel once again, "no absolutely privileged context. . . . Every quality and event is a genuine occurrence in some complex process or con-text, and possesses ascertainable relations and functions in that con-text." A quality, say, like sweetness, which depends for its occurrence upon certain physiological conditions, is in this context no less a constituent of nature than the qualities with which physical science concerns itself.

The American naturalists always emphasized that they were not denying the occurrence of novel features in the world or the unique-ness of the human race. While the conditions of man's life are con-tinuous with the rest of nature, he possesses, in Nagel's words, "the apparently unique gift of an inquiring mind . . . which enables him to direct his impulses and to master many of the forces in his en-vironment." However, this inquiring mind, as already noted, is not beyond the scope of scientific investigation. Most, though not all, American naturalists have favored some form of materialism, but here they once again insist that their position is not a form of re-ductionism. Consciousness and conscious processes are not, as some previous materialists have maintained, identical with occurrences in the brain or the nervous system or with the actual and potential physical reactions of human organisms. However, while not identical with material occurrences, all conscious processes are causally de-pendent on such occurrences and hence, as Nagel puts it, "there is no place for the operation of disembodied forces, no place for an im-material spirit directing the course of events, no place for the survival of the personality after the corruption of the body which exhibits it."

It is obvious that naturalists cannot endorse the claims of tradi-tional religion, and many of them have been among the most out-spoken critics of religion in American life. However, it would be inaccurate to say that naturalists have without exception been anti-religious. Religious experiences, according to Dewey and some of his followers, may be of inestimable value, although it is a mistake to re-gard them as evidence for the existence of a supernatural reality. Dewey distinguished "religion" from the "religious" quality of experi-ence, and he asserted that it is the latter which is significant: a re-ligious experience is a consummatory experience, in which we become aware of our highest ideals and aspirations. Indeed "God," for Dewey, may be taken to refer to "the ideal ends that at a given time and place one acknowledges as having authority over his volitions and emotions," the values to which one is "supremely devoted."

It should be evident from what has just been said that naturalists —while they do not endorse the theology of traditional theistic religions—are far from oblivious to the needs and aspirations which traditional religion or religions have attempted to satisfy. Religions are to be judged first and foremost not by their alleged truth claims, but by their functions, whether moral and social (Dewey) or aesthetic and expressive (Santayana). Most naturalists reject traditional supernaturalism and would describe themselves as "humanists," in the sense that the center of value is man and the things that he cherishes and prizes. *The Humanist Manifesto,* which is reprinted in this book, expresses the rather widespread religious sentiments of many American philosophers. A religion is naturalistic and humanistic if it concentrates upon empirically ascertainable goals, and if it uses a scientific approach to knowledge. Even positivists such as Herbert Feigl have found much in common with scientific humanism as so defined.

Naturalists have written extensively on the subject of the nature of moral problems and the meaning and function of moral judgments. They have focused, however, on the wider problem of value and valuation rather than on moral value alone. Perry in his *General Theory of Value* (1926) provided a naturalistic definition of value as "the object of any interest," and C. I. Lewis (1883–1964) in *An Analysis of Knowledge and Valuation* (1946) asserted that valuation judgments are in principle confirmable in the same way as other empirical judgments. The function of valuation judgments, according to Dewey and his followers, cannot be understood except in the context of the problems which they are supposed to resolve, and these problems always arise in concrete situations whose structure is determined by human needs and preferences. Moral problems are for the most part concerned with the adjustment of competing needs and preferences and they are completely misunderstood by philosophers who profess to explore some transcendental realm of values.

Writing for the most part after the publication of G. E. Moore's *Principia Ethica* and its criticisms of the "naturalistic fallacy," American naturalists have found it necessary to take issue with Moore's arguments. They agree that Moore was probably on sound ground in insisting that ethical terms cannot be defined along the lines suggested by such 19th century naturalists as Mill and Spencer, but they maintain that this did not amount to a refutation of naturalism *as such.* There is no *one* constant meaning of moral judgments, if only because moral problems are plural and always specific—and any attempt to give a simple analysis is bound to fail. However, this does

not mean that we cannot in concrete situations analyze moral judgments along naturalistic lines. It seems clear, naturalists would argue,
that in a great many, if not all, moral disputes it is antecedently
agreed that certain empirical facts are, and that certain others are
not, relevant to the settlement of the dispute, in much the way that
certain parts are antecedently agreed to in the case of scientific disputes. They would go further and assert that it makes perfectly good
sense to speak of some moral judgments as "well supported" and
others as "unsupported" by the evidence. Of course, this does not
mean that it is usually easy to obtain the relevant empirical information. This is certainly a very attractive theory, since it would do away
with the need to appeal to any special moral faculty as well as avoiding the necessity of relegating moral judgments to the status of
purely emotive utterances. It is interesting to note that, in spite of
the great influence of G. E. Moore, some English writers have very
recently come out in favor of naturalism in ethics, at least to the
extent of allowing that, while most moral predicates are not simply
descriptive, many moral judgments are objectively supportable.

Idealism and Rationalism

It was pointed out at the beginning of this introduction that although idealism has acquired the status of only a minority school in
our time, it does not lack some respected champions. One of the
most interesting idealists of recent years was Edgar Sheffield Brightman, the leader of a school known as "personalism," which is still
currently active. According to Brightman, "In the broadest sense, Personalism is a way of thinking that makes personality the key to all
philosophical problems," including value, epistemology and metaphysics. In the broadest sense, too, Brightman would claim that most
idealists and theists are personalists. Personalism has an affinity to
idealism because "all being is defined as personal consciousness. To
be is to be a person or self, or some act of person or self." Among
other writers who have defended various theories traditionally associated with idealism are James E. Creighton, William E. Hocking,
and Wilbur Urban.

Brand Blanshard does not like to be described as an "idealist," but
in his very widely read work, *The Nature of Thought* (1939), and
more recently in *Reason and Analysis* (1962), he has vigorously defended two of the most cherished doctrines supported by both idealists and rationalists: the coherence theory of truth, and the view that
phenomena in the world are connected by logical necessity. Morris
R. Cohen (1880–1947), although a naturalist and realist, was also a
champion of rationalism in that he regarded reason—in the sense in

which this term is used by rationalists—as the key to the understanding of nature (*Reason and Nature,* 1931). Alfred North Whitehead (1861–1947), is the foremost defender of rationalistic speculative philosophy, though he admittedly eludes strict classification. An Anglo–American philosopher, first influenced by analytic philosophy at Cambridge and co-author with Russell of the monumental *Principia Mathematica* (1910–13), Whitehead spent his later years at Harvard. There he attempted to develop a comprehensive cosmic system, containing elements of naturalism, realism and even idealism. Questioning the assumptions of the Newtonian world-view, Whitehead constructed a new cosmology based on organismic categories. He is perhaps the last of the great system-builders of the Golden Age, one who now has almost no influence in Great Britain, and whose major influence in the United States is among metaphysicians and theologians.

II. THE CONTEMPORARY PHILOSOPHICAL SCENE

It would be absurd to try to assign a precise year for the end of the period we have been calling "The Golden Age of American Philosophy." Not a few of the theories which were first widely discussed in the early years of the present century are still being vigorously debated at the present time. Still, anyone studying philosophical publications of the last twenty years would immediately notice certain significant differences as to both the problems at the center of discussion and the kinds of answers likely to receive serious attention.

Marxism and Neo-Thomism

Few observers would deny that philosophical analysis, i.e., logical positivism and what is called "linguistic analysis," has been the dominant philosophical tendency in America in recent years. Any reasonably complete survey, however, should also take note of certain other less influential theories. Some attention must be given, for instance, to Marxist philosophy. Many American intellectuals were attracted to Marxism during the depression years of the 1930's, including a number of academic philosophers, who were, however, sympathetic to the political recommendations and the analysis of historical change found in Marx and Engels rather than to the "laws of the dialectic" and the other Hegelian apparatus. Probably the best known American philosopher strongly influenced by Marxism is Sidney Hook, whose books, *From Hegel to Marx* (1936) and *Towards the Understanding of Karl Marx* (1933) are widely regarded as classics of critical Marxist scholarship. Among other American philosophers sympathetic to Marxism, mention should be made of Abraham Edel, Lewis Feuer, Vernon Venable, John Somerville and V. G. McGill. In 1949, several Marxists joined forces with other materialists and produced the book, *Philosophy for the Future: The Quest of Modern Materialism.* The editors of that book in a selection reprinted below, claim that materialists are more willing than naturalists "to set forth a synoptic view of man and the universe implicit in the sciences at their present stage of development." Generally, however, American philosophers who have shown interest in Marxist materialism have avoided the "dialectical" side of dialectical materialism. In recent years there has been considerable discussion (partly because of the spread of existentialism) of Marx's views on "alienation." Some writers—especially the psychoanalyst Erich Fromm—have tended to interpret Marx in a metaphysical vein, but naturalists like Sidney Hook have objected that this interpretation is mistaken.

Neo-Thomism has had very much less influence in the United States than in most countries of continental Europe. The writings of Jacques Maritain and Etienne Gilson are widely read, and Gilson especially is greatly admired for his historical scholarship, but not many philosophers outside the Catholic universities have found anything in neo-Thomism that is new or inspiring. In very recent years, attempts have been made to establish some kind of "dialogue" between neo-Thomists and American philosophers belonging to other schools. For example, James Collins of St. Louis University has made efforts in this direction, and his work *God in Modern Philosophy* (1959) discusses at some length skeptical and empirical philosophies. The visits to the United States of the Polish Dominican, I. N. Bochenski, who is noted for his broad sympathies and interests, have also done much to establish some meaningful contacts between Catholic and non-Catholic philosophers. Yet all in all a gulf still remains in American philosophy between Thomistic Catholic philosophers and most others.

Philosophical Analysis: Logical Positivism and Linguistic Analysis

The term "Logical Positivism" has a relatively precise meaning—considerably more precise than most of the other labels which designate philosophical movements. It refers to the standpoint worked out by a number of philosophers and scientists in the 1920's who were known as the Vienna Circle. Some of their ideas can doubtless be traced back to the British empiricists, especially Hume, but the philosophers who most influenced the members of the Vienna Circle were Bertrand Russell and Ludwig Wittgenstein. Wittgenstein, especially in his later years, did not himself approve of all the aims and theories of the logical positivists, but no single work had as profound an impact on the Vienna group as his *Tractatus Logico-Philosophicus*, which was published in 1921. Several of the doctrines unique to logical positivism are contained in this book, although their more detailed and "official" formulations are to be found in the writings of Schlick, Carnap, Reichenbach, and Neurath.

The theories of these men rapidly became widely known in the United States. Schlick visited the United States twice before his death in 1936, and Herbert Feigl, who had been Schlick's assistant at the University of Vienna, moved to this country in 1930. In 1931 he published, together with A. E. Blumberg, in the *Journal of Philosophy*, the very influential article, "Logical Positivism, a New Movement in European Philosophy." Ernest Nagel visited the leading positivists in 1934 and 1935, and was particularly impressed with Carnap's work. He recounted his experiences in his widely read two-part article entitled "Impressions and Appraisals of Analytic Philosophy in Europe," *Journal of Philosophy* (1936). Carnap emigrated to the United States in 1935 and, as the Nazis took over country after country in Europe, he was followed by other distinguished members of the group, including Reichenbach, Philipp Frank, Richard von Mises, Carl Hempel, and the famous logician, Alfred Tarski. Attempts to keep up some kind of organized movement proved futile, largely because of the outbreak of the war, although they did result in the publication in Chicago of an interesting series of brochures entitled the *International Encyclopedia of Unified Science*. In any event, the presence of so many important representatives of this standpoint could not help but have significant repercussions on the American philosophical scene.

This is not the place for a detailed presentation or evaluation of the theories of the logical positivists. However, it is impossible to convey an adequate idea of the changes they wrought in the American philosophical climate without saying at least a few words about some of their doctrines. Probably the most controversial of the new theories is the so-called Verifiability Principle and the condemnation of metaphysics as "nonsense," which is based on it. Stated in very summary fashion, the Verifiability Principle says that a sentence is cognitively (or descriptively) meaningful only if it is empirically verifiable. When this view is combined with the logical positivists' other key doctrine—namely that the sentences of logic and pure mathematics, and indeed all sentences expressing necessary propositions, are tautological—it follows that metaphysical pronouncements are literally devoid of sense. They are not empirically verifiable nor can they be considered to be purely formal sentences. Even if they were so considered, this would not be adequate, since tautologies "say nothing," being compatible with anything whatsoever. The logical positivists concluded that many of the most cherished philosophical theories of the past—all claims about the Absolute, about the forms in The World of Being, about transcendent values, material and spiritual substances, things-in-themselves, about Being and "the Nothing," and also about God—must be dismissed as meaningless. The sentences of the metaphysician may indeed have "emotive" meaning in the sense of expressing his feelings and they also usually have "pictorial" meaning in that they naturally arouse certain images in speaker and hearer alike, but they fail to express genuine propositions. This rejection of metaphysics is far more radical than that of earlier "skeptics" like Hume or Comte. The earlier opponents of metaphysics had not really questioned the meaningfulness of metaphysical questions, but had simply considered human understanding too weak to deal with such ultimate and profound issues. The logical positivists in effect deny that there are any such questions to be answered.

Not surprisingly, the older generation of philosophers did not take kindly to these views, and the philosophical journals of the late 30's and early 40's are filled with articles exposing their alleged errors. Many younger philosophers, however, found the new theories challenging and even liberating. It should be remembered that, although the language of the logical positivists was a great deal more violent, their ideas were really not so different from those expressed by Peirce and James when they proposed their pragmatic theory of meaning. Moreover, largely in independence of the developments in Vienna, the American philosopher C. I. Lewis and the Nobel Prize-winning physicist, P. W. Bridgman, had developed strikingly similar theories in America. In his book, *The Mind and the World Order* (1929), C. I. Lewis had advocated a pragmatic theory about the nature of logical and mathematical statements which was quite in line with the views of Wittgenstein and Schlick, and Bridgman's "Operationalism" bears a very strong resemblance to the Verifiability Principle, at least in some of its forms. It is difficult to say with certainty whether many philosophers in the United States ever wholeheartedly accepted the Verifiability Principle and the condemnation of metaphysics as "nonsense." However, the work of the logical positivists unquestionably produced a far more critical and suspicious attitude towards any kind of speculative philosophy, and it focused attention on questions woefully neglected by previous generations about the conditions of meaningful discourse.

The general outlook of logical positivism has obviously much in common with that of the American naturalists. One similarity is particularly worth noting, in view of the recent popularity of so-called "existential psychiatry," and the claims of certain writers that history and sociology can never be properly scientific disciplines. Logical positivists and American naturalists are equally opposed to the theory that there is a radical difference in aim and method between the natural sciences and the "human studies" or so-called *Geisteswissenschaften*. Both groups are equally insistent that there is no essential difference in aim or method—that in both areas alike it is the business of the investigator to formulate hypotheses which must then be subjected to the test of observation. This position has been forcefully defended by Hempel in his well-known article, "The Function of General Laws in History" (1942), and it has been wholeheartedly endorsed by various writers, including a number (Ernest Nagel and Sidney Hook, for instance) usually classified as "naturalists."

It was the rather extreme position which many logical positivists took in regard to moral judgments—the so-called "emotive theory"—that provoked the greatest outcry from American philosophers. According to the emotive theory, moral judgments cannot be properly called true or false at all; they do not assert the existence of any facts of any kind—neither mysterious facts about some transcendent realm of values, nor observable facts about happiness, consequences, or the state of mind of the speaker. Their function is expressive and persuasive, not descriptive. They serve to express the speaker's attitude and to arouse attitudes in the hearer. On this view, naturalists no less than intuitionists fail to perceive the most distinctive feature of moral judgments, their "dynamic" character.

There were already suggestions of the emotive theory in one of Carnap's early papers, but its full development was largely the work of English and American philosophers. The most celebrated statements are to be found in Ayer's *Language, Truth and Logic* (1936) and in several articles published in the late 1930's by the American philosopher, C. L. Stevenson. Stevenson subsequently devoted an entire book to the exposition and defense of the emotive theory (*Ethics and Language*, 1944). In this book he added a number of important qualifications to his original formulations, and this later version is not as far removed from naturalism as the earlier versions. Yet the emotive theory has been bitterly attacked by naturalists otherwise sympathetic to logical positivism. They maintain that the emotive theory fails to do justice to the cognitive character of moral judgments. It is not infrequently added that the theory ultimately implies some kind of nihilism. Moreover, most philosophers of other schools also disapprove of what they consider the unduly restrictive attitude of the logical positivists, in their insistence that the philosopher, qua philosopher, must confine himself to the analysis of ethical judgments and the nature of ethical argument, and must not himself engage in moral recommendations. The outlook of the logical positivists, it is said, trivializes moral philosophy and deprives it of what has always been its chief function.

The charge of turning philosophy into a series of trivial verbal exercises has been even more generally leveled against the representatives of what is called "linguistic analysis." This label does not have nearly as precise a meaning as "logical positivism." It refers to a number of somewhat heterogenous philosophical tendencies associated with the work of G. E. Moore, the later Wittgenstein, and several influential Oxford philosophers, notably Gilbert Ryle and John Austin. Max Black, Norman Malcolm, Alice Ambrose, Morris Lazerowitz, and O. K. Bouwsma are among the best-known American writers who would be classified as "linguistic analysts" rather than logical positivists, although the line is not always easy to draw. One of the main differences between the linguistic analysts and the logical positivists concerns their respective attitudes towards metaphysics. Like the logical positivists, Wittgenstein and his followers do not practice metaphysics nor do they advocate that philosophers should engage in metaphysics. At the same time, however, they do not call it nonsense. There is something admittedly "queer" about most metaphysical theories, but they always have a point of some kind. If they are simply dismissed as nonsense and no attempt is made to find out what led to the introduction and development of these queer theories, some valuable insight, usually into the way or ways in which our language functions in certain areas, would be missed.

The different linguistic analysts appear to have little in the way of common doctrine. Some, for example, favor determinism, while others oppose it; some strongly incline to a behavioristic analysis of psychological statements, while others favor some form of dualism; perhaps most interestingly, some, though admittedly a minority, argue that linguistic analysis is perfectly compatible with religious belief. The one thing that all these writers do seem to have in common is a special interest in ordinary language, a belief that by studying the ways in which words are used we can shed a great deal of light on philosophical problems and in many instances avoid becoming the victims of "pseudo-problems." Most of these writers would agree, for example, that the traditional problem of induction is a bogus problem and that if one were clear about the various uses of such words as "reason" or "evidence," there would be no need to raise the issue at all. "Problems" of this kind have, strictly speaking, no solution, but they can be "dissolved," in the sense that, once certain confusions are brought into the open, any temptation to ask the question disappears.

Unlike Russell and Carnap, the linguistic analysts have little confidence in the use of symbolic logic as an instrument for clarifying philosophical problems, and they are completely opposed to the view, which they attribute to the logical positivists, that language is a kind of calculus. In their view there is, for example, no simple answer to the question, "What is the meaning of 'cause'?" Any simple formula will at best call attention to one of many functions of the word. To throw light on a problem like this, it is necessary to study a multitude of cases in which we use the word, together with the reasons which make us use it. Similar considerations would apply to a great many other philosophical questions—e.g., "What is probability?" or "What is consciousness?" The construction of formal, axiomatic systems, whatever other uses they may have, can hardly help us in a properly philosophical solution of these problems. It should be added that, although this "informal" approach to philosophical questions is probably more widespread than any other, among young American philosophers two of the most influential and original contemporary American philosophers, W. V. O. Quine and Nelson Goodman, strongly favor the more "formal" approach associated with the work of Russell and Carnap.

In emphasizing the differences between the logical positivists and the linguistic analysts, one should not lose sight of the similarities in their aims, which are more significant than their differences. In the *Tractatus*, Wittgenstein had said, "The object of philosophy is the logical clarification of thoughts." Although they may disagree about the best methods for attaining this end, all of the philosophers discussed in this section would probably subscribe to this dictum and they would all be opposed to the bombast and mystification which has so often passed and still continues to pass as profundity.

Existentialism and Phenomenology

The philosophical movement that has unquestionably been most widely discussed among the general public in the years since World War II is existentialism. The works of Kierkegaard, Sartre and Camus, and even Heidegger and Jaspers, have had a remarkably large circulation, although one may wonder how much of their content is intelligible to the ordinary reader. The impact of existentialism on academic philosophy in the United States has not been nearly so great as public curiosity might lead one to expect. Many American philosophers are repelled by what they take to be the irrationalism implicit in certain existentialist doctrines, especially Kierkegaard's view that "truth is subjectivity." Moreover, they believe that the existentialists are reviving all kinds of doctrines that were exploded long ago by critical philosophers, such as the view that existence is a characteristic, or that there is a mysterious reality called "Nothingness" or "The Nothing."

Nevertheless, existentialism has had a far greater influence even on academic philosophy than any other recent movement in the speculative tradition. It has appealed particularly to those who believe that philosophy should concern itself with basic human problems and who accuse positivists and linguistic analysts of reducing philosophy to trivial games of words. It can hardly be denied that existentialists have written interestingly about such topics as the "alienation" of modern man, his anxieties and the "inauthentic" mode of his life. It should also be noted that the humanistic ethic advocated by both Sartre and Camus is not very different from the moral outlook of most naturalists and positivists, and this side of existentialism has had a friendlier reception among American philosophers than the obscure pronouncements about the nature of Being and Nothingness.

Sartre's defense of free will is in some respects similar to doctrines advocated in the Anglo-American world by writers like C. A. Campbell. It is similar in some respects also to the contention of some analytic philosophers that rational action is in principle unpredictable, and that motive explanations are not a species of causal explanations. None of these latter, however, would endorse the extreme form of indeterminism Sartre champions, and indeed it does seem to be plainly at variance with what we know about the large measure of regularity in human conduct and our actual predictive capacities. Similarly, the doctrine put forward by Sartre and other existentialists, that man has no "essence," appears—if it can be given any operational meaning—to be in conflict with the results obtained in the behavioral sciences. Mention should be made of the fact that in recent years more effort has gone into the development of the social and behavioral sciences in the United States than in any other country in the world. It is small wonder, then, that the existentialist disavowal of the scientific approach to man, and its emphasis instead on philosophical anthropology, frequently finds an unreceptive audience in America.

American philosophers who have been sympathetic to the existentialist (and phenomenological) outlook include John Wild, William Barrett, George Schrader, James Edie, Maurice Natanson, and Robert G. Olson. However, the most influential existentialist in the United States has undoubtedly been Paul Tillich, a theologian, and indeed the impact of existentialism has been very great on Protestant theology in the entire English-speaking world. Strongly influenced by Heidegger and Kierkegaard, Tillich is opposed to any attempts to "prove" theological statements. While the traditional arguments for the existence of God do, in Tillich's opinion, have a certain value, they altogether fail to establish their conclusions, as has been correctly pointed out by such critics as Hume and Kant. Tillich has also strenuously opposed any kind of anthropomorphic theology or, as he ironically terms it, "monarchic monotheism." To conceive of God as a kind of omnipresent policeman, as have so many traditional theologians, is merely to play into the hands of unbelievers. There is no omnipresent policeman, but Tillich insists that it does not follow from this that there is no God in the true, non-anthropomorphic sense. Tillich has also proposed a redefinition of what it is to be religious. In his new sense, a person is religious so long as he has some object of "ultimate concern." A scientist, for example, whose ultimate concern in life is the extension of human knowledge, would quite properly be regarded as a religious person even if he should call himself an atheist.

Another philosophical movement which is extremely influential on the European continent but which, until very recently has had relatively little impact on the American scene, is Husserl's phenomenology. Since the foundation of the journal *Philosophy and Phenomenological Research*, under the editorship of Marvin Farber, in 1939, there has been a forum in the United States for the presentation of phenomenological theories. This journal has published much valuable material dealing with the history of phenomenology, but it is instructive to note that the great bulk of the material it prints has no immediate connection with phenomenology and, furthermore, that many of the articles dealing with phenomenology are written by Germans and Frenchmen and not by Americans.

The term "phenomenology" achieved prominence in philosophy for the first time in the work of Edmund Husserl (1859–1939), a professor of philosophy at Göttingen and Freiburg. Husserl wished to refute "psychologism," which reduces the subject matter of logic and mathematics to psychological generalizations. As against this psychological outlook, Husserl proposed a phenomenological account of our mental "approaches," in the logico-mathematical and other fields. This phenomenological account is not concerned with actual states of mind, for which there is empirical evidence, but instead deals abstractly and intuitively with the experiences in which certain kinds of objects are set before us. It seeks to analyze such directed, or "intentional," experiences and to discover their relationships to their objects and to other experiences. Such a phenomenological analysis of our mental approaches also involves examination of the different kinds of objects toward which our mental approaches are directed.

The phenomenologist is not concerned, however, with the actual existence or real character of such objects, but only with their status as phenomena for consciousness. Therefore an abstract, merely possible, or even impossible object is as important for his research as one that is actual.

Phenomenology requires that one suspend all naïve, commonsense beliefs about the natural–empirical world, thereby disclosing a vast, entirely unsuspected field of research. In this transcendental suspension of conviction, or *epoché*, consciousness itself becomes highlighted, the mere appearance of objects being equivalent to one's awareness of them. Once consciousness has in this way been made manifest to our inner perception, it can then be subjected to the same generalizing process of abstraction and examination of essence that have been applied to its objects. Husserl's later work contained certain theses which seem to abandon his original *epoché* and involve a surrender to metaphysical idealism. He came to believe that the natural–empirical objects of acts of consciousness exist only for consciousness.

Recently, phenomenology has had a certain influence on some American thinkers through its connection with existentialism. Heidegger was a student of Husserl, and Heidegger, Sartre and Merleau-Ponty employ, or claim to employ, the phenomenological method. Many of those who use the phenomenological method accept it broadly as a means of explaining the *Lebenswelt* (life world), a way of studying in depth the conscious world of concrete and lived experience—of art, morality, religion and all phases of the inner life. John Wild maintains that there are some parallels between phenomenology, the study of language by linguistic philosophers, and the Jamesian approach to the immediacies of pure experience. If this is the case, the phenomenological approach is in contrast to the speculative methods the existentialists generally seem to employ. Neither phenomenologists nor existentialists usually describe themselves as metaphysicians, but the remaining metaphysicians on the American philosophical scene tend to regard them as allies in the battles against positivism and linguistic analysis.

Metaphysics, in the sense of speculation about a reality transcending the empirical world, is no longer fashionable, but a number of philosophers engage in work which can with perfect propriety be called "metaphysics." In this regard, *The Review of Metaphysics*, edited by Paul Weiss, has attempted to keep alive the spirit of metaphysical inquiry, and a wide variety of studies in metaphysics are printed in its pages. It should be added, perhaps, that some naturalists are also quite willing to be described as "metaphysicians." What they mean by "metaphysics," however, is a far cry from what was meant by this term in the heyday of Hegelian idealism, and it is not at all the kind of thing the positivists are anxious to discredit.

Philosophy East-West

The great amount of interest in Asian philosophy in recent years deserves brief mention. The work of several philosophers, including W. T. Stace, F. S. C. Northrop, J. B. Pratt, A. E. Burtt, and Charles A. Moore, shows the influence of Eastern thought. The journal *Philosophy East-West* is primarily devoted to efforts at a rapprochement between the two cultures, and several "East-West Philosophers' Conferences" have been organized for the same purpose. Books on Zen Buddhism are widely read in America, and a number of philosophers have seen merits in this particular outlook. Van Meter Ames, for example, in his *Zen in American Thought* (1962) writes in defense of Zen and asserts that he sees significant affinities between it and American philosophy, especially in the emphasis by such writers as Mead, James and Dewey on the immediacy of "pure experience." It is very difficult, however, to appraise this development and to determine whether it is a passing fashion or something of more permanent significance.

If any single generalization can be made of present-day philosophy in America, it is that pluralism is characteristic of the outlook of most American philosophers. In spite of an apparent prevalence of "naturalism" ("naturalism," that is, in the broad sense that includes all schools critical of transcendental metaphysical speculation), and an undercurrent of pragmatism, there is, nevertheless, a tolerance and receptiveness to various points of view, and there are few movements of thought that are not sympathetically studied. Although representatives of virtually all philosophical positions on the contemporary world scene can be found in the United States, most American philosophers seem to be uninterested in identification with dogmatic schools, isms, or ideological labels. Rather, the tendency is to draw upon a variety of philosophical traditions and to consider philosophy an ongoing cooperative enterprise in which all philosophers may participate and make some contribution.

A NOTE ON THE SELECTIONS

The following pages are intended to be a guide to some of the men and movements in American philosophy of the 20th century. Space limitations have unfortunately made it impossible to include selections from a number of important contemporaries. Moreover, it has been necessary, in some instances, to use a selection which is too brief to do full justice to the philosopher's entire thought. Finally, only major philosophical schools are represented.

It should be added that, in the preparation of this volume, the word "American" has been understood in a rather broad sense. Whitehead, Carnap and Tillich are included, although none of them was born in America, and although all of them became famous long before their emigration to the United States. However, much of their most important work was done here, and their influence has probably been greater in this country than anywhere else.

PART ONE

The Golden Age of American Philosophy

Charles S. Peirce

[1839-1914]

Charles Peirce is probably the most profound and creative philosopher that America has produced. Though his writings are often obscure and disorganized, they are brilliant in their philosophical virtuosity. Peirce had a direct influence upon James, Dewey, Royce, Mead, and Schiller in his own day, and his ideas continue to exert a powerful influence. He is most noted in American philosophy as the originator of pragmatism, but he was also a major force in America in the development of contemporary symbolic logic. He made major contributions to semiotics, the theory of signs and symbols. In addition, he contributed to an understanding of the methodology of the experimental sciences, and was in his own right a conceiver of new metaphysical systems.

Peirce's career in American philosophy was unfortunate, in that he was able neither to locate a commercial publisher for any of his proposed philosophic books, nor to obtain an academic position in a college or university (save for relatively few years), being unappreciated even at his *alma mater*, Harvard. His behavior was considered "eccentric" and his marital life apparently raised eyebrows. Peirce criticized the conservatism and conventionality of the colleges; he observed that "wher-

ever there is a large class of academic professors who are provided with good incomes and looked up to as gentlemen, scientific inquiry must languish."[1] Thus one of the richest minds that America has produced had to suffer in silence and obscurity. His influence in his own day was largely confined to the few scholars who appreciated him, and he died in poverty.

Born in Cambridge, Massachusetts, Peirce was the son of the famous mathematician Benjamin Peirce, who tutored him carefully. He graduated from Harvard College in 1859 and spent most of his life in the U.S. Coast and Geodetic Survey (1861–1887). Indeed, he made original and internationally recognized contributions to geodetic research. Peirce lectured at Harvard for brief periods (1864–65, 1869–71), and delivered the Lowell Lectures in 1903; he also lectured at Johns Hopkins (1879–84). His main philosophical influence during his lifetime was as a writer of articles and reviews, which appeared in magazines such as the *Nation, North American Review, Journal of Speculative Philosophy, Scientific Monthly,* and in the *Century Dictionary* and the *Dictionary of Philosophy and Psychology.*

Peirce was persistently concerned with problems now classified as be-

[1] *Collected Papers of Charles Sanders Peirce,* ed. by C. Hartshorne and P. Weiss. Cambridge: Harvard University Press, 1931, Vol. I, p. 22.

longing to the "philosophy of science." In *The Fixation of Belief* (1877), reprinted below, Peirce criticized the notion of unlimited Cartesian doubt. Beliefs, he maintained, guide actions, and they arise in response to dissatisfaction and doubt from which we struggle to free ourselves by means of inquiry. But how are we to fix beliefs, asks Peirce? Not by tenacity or authority, nor by *a priori* methods, but by the method of science. Science is the most effective way of resolving doubt, largely because it is the method most in accord with "real objects." Moreover, it is not the exclusive affair of individuals in isolation, but of a community of inquirers. Elsewhere Peirce labeled the method used to formulate hypotheses in science "abduction" and he defended the principle of "fallibilism," i.e., the view that beliefs are provisional or probable.

Peirce began to suggest, in his early papers and reviews, and in his extended discussions with his friends in the Metaphysical Society at Cambridge, the central ideas that were later to be called "pragmatism." But it was William James in 1898 who first gave official credit to Peirce as the founder of pragmatism. Peirce's most famous article, *How to Make Our Ideas Clear* (1878), is reprinted below. In this Peirce suggests pragmatism as a principle or method of clarification: the meaning of an idea is to be discovered by reference to its conceivable practical bearings. Peirce's definition of pragmatism is again stated in *Pragmatic and Pragmatism*, a short piece he wrote for the *Dictionary of Philosophy and Psychology* (1902), and also reproduced below. His brand of pragmatism was conceptually rigorous; it

looked to the experimental sciences as its model. When "pragmatism" was extended by James beyond what Peirce intended, Peirce renamed his own theory "pragmaticism." He considered his philosophy to be a form of "critical common sensism," a discussion of which is seen in the piece, *Pragmaticism* (1905), reprinted below.

There is, however, another aspect to Peirce's philosophy—the attempt at metaphysical system-building—and this in spite of Peirce's view that the pragmatic method is a technique for dissipating metaphysical abstractions. Peirce constantly suggested new and novel ideas, ideas which he frequently did no more than introduce or outline without full explication. Later commentators have taken up and developed many of his ideas. Thus under the influence of evolutionary categories, Peirce suggested the role of *tychism* (chance), *synechism* (continuity), and *agapism* (evolutionary love) in the universe. And in his article, *The Doctrine of Necessity Examined* (1892), reprinted below, he questioned the need for determinism as a postulate of science and suggested instead the possibility of indeterminacy—years before the problem was to come into sharp focus in physics. (Peirce frequently described his metaphysical position as a form of "scholastic realism." He also suggested a phenomenology of the given, a categorical scheme of "Firstness," "Secondness" and "Thirdness.")

The range of Peirce's thought (best seen in the many-volumed, posthumously published *Collected Papers*) makes it possible for many different kinds of philosophers to look to him for inspiration and guidance. Logical positivists, pragmatists, naturalists, and others have all found much of value in Peirce, and the strength of his originality has left its enduring mark on American philosophy.

THE FIXATION OF BELIEF [2]

I

Few persons care to study logic, because everybody conceives himself to be proficient enough in the art of reasoning already. But I observe that this satisfaction is limited to one's own ratiocination, and does not extend to that of other men.

We come to the full possession of our power of drawing inferences the last of all our faculties, for it is not so much a natural gift as a long and difficult art. The history of its practice would make a grand subject for a book. The mediæval schoolman, following the Romans, made logic the earliest of a boy's studies after grammar, as being very easy. So it was as they understood it. Its fundamental principle, according to them, was that all knowledge rests on either authority or reason; but that whatever is deduced by reason depends ultimately on a premise derived from authority. Accordingly, as soon as a boy was perfect in the syllogistic procedure, his intellectual kit of tools was held to be complete.

To Roger Bacon, that remarkable mind who in the middle of the thirteenth century was almost a scientific man, the schoolmen's conception of reasoning appeared only an obstacle to truth. He saw that experience alone teaches anything—a proposition which to us seems easy to understand, because a distinct conception of experience has been handed down to us from former generations; which to him also seemed perfectly clear, because its difficulties had not yet unfolded themselves. Of all kinds of experience, the best, he thought, was interior illumination, which teaches many things about nature which the external senses could never discover, such as the transubstantiation of bread.

Four centuries later, the more celebrated Bacon, in the first book of his *Novum Organum*, gave his clear account of experience as something which must be opened to verification and re-examination.

[2] First published in *Popular Science Monthly*, vol. XII, 1877, pp. 1–15. Reprinted in *Collected Papers of Charles Sanders Peirce*, ed. Charles Hartshorne and Paul Weiss. Cambridge, Mass.: The Belknap Press of Harvard University Press, 1934. Vol. V, pp. 223–47.

But, superior as Lord Bacon's conception is to earlier notions, a modern reader who is not in awe of his grandiloquence is chiefly struck by the inadequacy of his view of scientific procedure. That we have only to make some crude experiments, to draw up briefs of the results in certain blank forms, to go through these by rule, checking off everything disproved and setting down the alternatives, and that thus in a few years physical science would be finished up—what an idea! "He wrote on science like a Lord Chancellor,"[3] indeed, as Harvey, a genuine man of science, said.

The early scientists, Copernicus, Tycho Brahe, Kepler, Galileo, Harvey, and Gilbert, had methods more like those of their modern brethren. Kepler undertook to draw a curve through the places of Mars;[4] and his greatest service to science was in impressing on men's minds that this was the thing to be done if they wished to improve astronomy; that they were not to content themselves with inquiring whether one system of epicycles was better than another but that they were to sit down by the figures and find out what the curve, in truth, was. He accomplished this by his incomparable energy and courage, blundering along in the most inconceivable way (to us), from one irrational hypothesis to another, until, after trying twenty-two of these, he fell, by the mere exhaustion of his invention, upon the orbit which a mind well furnished with the weapons of modern logic would have tried almost at the outset.

In the same way, every work of science great enough to be remembered for a few generations affords some exemplification of the defective state of the art of reasoning of the time when it was written; and each chief step in science has been a lesson in logic. It was so when Lavoisier and his contemporaries took up the study of Chemistry. The old chemist's maxim had been *Lege, lege, lege, labora, ora, et relege*. Lavoisier's method was not to read and pray, not to dream that some long and complicated chemical process would have a certain effect, to put it into practice with dull patience, after its inevitable failure to dream that with some modification it would have another result, and to end by publishing the last dream as a fact: his way was to carry his mind into his laboratory, and to make of his alembics and cucurbits instruments of thought, giving a new conception of reasoning as something which was to be done with one's eyes open, by manipulating real things instead of words and fancies.

The Darwinian controversy is, in large part, a question of logic.

[3] Cf. J. Aubrey's *Brief Lives*. Oxford, 1898. Vol. I, p. 299.
[4] Not quite so, but as nearly as can be told in a few words.

Mr. Darwin proposed to apply the statistical method to biology.[5] The same thing has been done in a widely different branch of science, the theory of gases. Though unable to say what the movement of any particular molecule of gas would be on a certain hypothesis regarding the constitution of this class of bodies, Clausius and Maxwell were yet able, by the application of the doctrine of probabilities, to predict that in the long run such and such a proportion of the molecules would, under given circumstances, acquire such and such velocities; that there would take place, every second, such and such a number of collisions, etc.; and from these propositions they were able to deduce certain properties of gases, especially in regard to their heat-relations. In like manner, Darwin, while unable to say what the operation of variation and natural selection in every individual case will be, demonstrates that in the long run they will adapt animals to their circumstances. Whether or not existing animal forms are due to such action, or what position the theory ought to take, forms the subject of a discussion in which questions of fact and questions of logic are curiously interlaced.

II

The object of reasoning is to find out, from the consideration of what we already know, something else which we do not know. Consequently, reasoning is good if it be such[6] as to give a true conclusion from true premises, and not otherwise. Thus, the question of validity is purely one of fact and not of thinking. A being the premises and B being the conclusion, the question is, whether these facts are really so related that if A is, B is. If so, the inference is valid; if not, not. It is not in the least the question whether, when the premises are accepted by the mind, we feel an impulse to accept the conclusion also. It is true that we do generally reason correctly by nature. But that is an accident; the true conclusion would remain true if we had no impulse to accept it; and the false one would remain false, though we could not resist the tendency to believe in it.

We are, doubtless, in the main logical animals, but we are not perfectly so. Most of us, for example, are naturally more sanguine and hopeful than logic would justify. We seem to be so constituted that in the absence of any facts to go upon we are happy and self-satisfied; so that the effect of experience is continually to counteract our

---

[5] We now know what was authoritatively denied when I first suggested it, that he took a hint from Malthus' book on population. [Note added in 1903.]

[6] I.e., be denominated by such a habit as generally to give. [1903.]

hopes and aspirations. Yet a lifetime of the application of this corrective does not usually eradicate our sanguine disposition. Where hope is unchecked by any experience, it is likely that our optimism is extravagant. Logicality in regard to practical matters is the most useful quality an animal can possess, and might, therefore, result from the action of natural selection; but outside of these it is probably of more advantage to the animal to have his mind filled with pleasing and encouraging visions, independently of their truth; and thus, upon unpractical subjects, natural selection might occasion a fallacious tendency of thought.[7]

That which determines us, from given premises, to draw one inference rather than another is some habit of mind, whether it be constitutional or acquired. The habit is good or otherwise, according as it produces true conclusions from true premises or not; and an inference is regarded as valid or not, without reference to the truth or falsity of its conclusion specially, but according as the habit which determines it is such as to produce true conclusions in general or not. The particular habit of mind which governs this or that inference may be formulated in a proposition whose truth depends on the validity of the inferences which the habit determines; and such a formula is called a *guiding principle* of inference. Suppose, for example, that we observe that a rotating disk of copper quickly comes to rest when placed between the poles of a magnet, and we infer that this will happen with every disk of copper. The guiding principle is that what is true of one piece of copper is true of another. Such a guiding principle with regard to copper would be much safer than with regard to many other substances—brass, for example.

A book might be written to signalize all the most important of these guiding principles of reasoning. It would probably be, we must confess, of no service to a person whose thought is directed wholly to practical subjects, and whose activity moves along thoroughly beaten paths. The problems which present themselves to such a mind are matters of routine which he has learned once for all to handle in learning his business. But let a man venture into an unfamiliar field, or where his results are not continually checked by experience, and all history shows that the most masculine intellect will ofttimes lose his orientation and waste his efforts in directions which bring him no nearer to his goal, or even carry him entirely astray. He is like a ship on the open sea, with no one on board who understands the rules of navigation. And in such a case some general study of the guiding principles of reasoning would be sure to be found useful.

---

[7] Let us not, however, be cocksure that natural selection is the only factor of evolution. [1903.]

The subject could hardly be treated, however, without being first limited; since almost any fact may serve as a guiding principle. But it so happens that there exists a division among facts, such that in one class are all those which are absolutely essential as guiding principles, while in the other are all those which have any other interest as objects of research. This division is between those which are necessarily taken for granted in asking whether a certain conclusion follows from certain premises, and those which are not implied in that question. A moment's thought will show that a variety of facts are already assumed when the logical question is first asked. It is implied, for instance, that there are such states of mind as doubt and belief—that a passage from one to the other is possible, the object of thought remaining the same, and that this transition is subject to some rules which all minds are alike bound by. As these are facts which we must already know before we can have any clear conception of reasoning at all, it cannot be supposed to be any longer of much interest to inquire into their truth or falsity. On the other hand, it is easy to believe that those rules of reasoning which are deduced from the very idea of the process are the ones which are the most essential; and, indeed, that so long as it conforms to these it will, at least, not lead to false conclusions from true premises. In point of fact, the importance of what may be deduced from the assumptions involved in the logical question turns out to be greater than might be supposed, and this for reasons which it is difficult to exhibit at the outset. The only one which I shall here mention is that conceptions which are really products of logical reflections, without being readily seen to be so, mingle with our ordinary thoughts, and are frequently the causes of great confusion. This is the case, for example, with the conception of quality. A quality as such is never an object of observation. We can see that a thing is blue or green, but the quality of being blue and the quality of being green are not things which we see; they are products of logical reflections. The truth is that common sense, or thought as it first emerges above the level of the narrowly practical, is deeply imbued with that bad logical quality to which the epithet *metaphysical* is commonly applied; and nothing can clear it up but a severe course of logic.

III

We generally know when we wish to ask a question and when we wish to pronounce a judgment, for there is a dissimilarity between the sensation of doubting and that of believing.

But this is not all which distinguishes doubt from belief. There is a practical difference. Our beliefs guide our desires and shape our actions. The Assassins, or followers of the Old Man of the Mountain, used to rush into death at his least command, because they believed that obedience to him would insure everlasting felicity. Had they doubted this, they would not have acted as they did. So it is with every belief, according to its degree. The feeling of believing is a more or less sure indication of there being established in our nature some habit which will determine our actions. Doubt never has such an effect.

Nor must we overlook a third point of difference. Doubt is an uneasy and dissatisfied state from which we struggle to free ourselves and pass into the state of belief;[8] while the latter is a calm and satisfactory state which we do not wish to avoid, or to change to a belief in anything else.[9] On the contrary, we cling tenaciously, not merely to believing, but to believing just what we do believe.

Thus, both doubt and belief have positive effects upon us, though very different ones. Belief does not make us act at once, but puts us into such a condition that we shall behave in a certain way, when the occasion arises. Doubt has not the least effect of this sort, but stimulates us to action until it is destroyed. This reminds us of the irritation of a nerve and the reflex action produced thereby; while for the analogue of belief, in the nervous system, we must look to what are called nervous associations—for example, to that habit of the nerves in consequence of which the smell of a peach will make the mouth water.

IV

The irritation of doubt causes a struggle to attain a state of belief.[10] I shall term this struggle *inquiry*, though it must be admitted that this is sometimes not a very apt designation.

The irritation of doubt is the only immediate motive for the struggle to attain belief. It is certainly best for us that our beliefs should

[8] In this, it is like any other stimulus. It is true that just as men may, for the sake of the pleasures of the table, like to be hungry and take means to make themselves so, although hunger always involves a desire to fill the stomach, so for the sake of the pleasures of inquiry, men may like to seek out doubts. Yet for all that, doubt essentially involves a struggle to escape it. [1903.]

[9] I am not speaking of secondary effects occasionally produced by the interference of other impulses.

[10] Doubt, however, is not usually hesitancy about what is to be done then and there. It is anticipated hesitancy about what I shall do hereafter, or a feigned hesitancy about a fictitious state of things. It is the power of making believe we hesitate, together with the pregnant fact that the decision upon the make-believe dilemma goes toward forming a bona fide habit that will be operative in a real emergency. It is these two things in conjunction that constitute us intellectual beings. [Added in 1893.]

be such as may truly guide our actions so as to satisfy our desires; and this reflection will make us reject any belief which does not seem to have been so formed as to insure this result. But it will only do so by creating a doubt in the place of that belief. With the doubt, therefore, the struggle begins, and with the cessation of doubt it ends. Hence, the sole object of inquiry is the settlement of opinion. We may fancy that this is not enough for us, and that we seek not merely an opinion, but a true opinion. But put this fancy to the test, and it proves groundless; for as soon as a firm belief is reached we are entirely satisfied, whether the belief be false or true. And it is clear that nothing out of the sphere of our knowledge can be our object, for nothing which does not affect the mind can be a motive for a mental effort. The most that can be maintained is that we seek for a belief that we shall *think* to be true. But we think each one of our beliefs to be true, and, indeed, it is mere tautology to say so.[11]

That the settlement of opinion is the sole end of inquiry is a very important proposition. It sweeps away, at once, various vague and erroneous conceptions of proof. A few of these may be noticed here.

1. Some philosophers have imagined that to start an inquiry it was only necessary to utter or question or set it down on paper, and have even recommended us to begin our studies with questioning everything! But the mere putting of a proposition into the interrogative form does not stimulate the mind to any struggle after belief. There must be a real and living doubt, and without all this, discussion is idle.

2. It is a very common idea that a demonstration must rest on some ultimate and absolutely indubitable propositions. These, according to one school, are first principles of a general nature; according to another, are first sensations. But, in point of fact, an inquiry, to have that completely satisfactory result called demonstration, has only to start with propositions perfectly free from all actual doubt. If the premises are not in fact doubted at all, they cannot be more satisfactory than they are.[12]

3. Some people seem to love to argue a point after all the world is fully convinced of it. But no further advance can be made. When doubt ceases, mental action on the subject comes to an end; and, if it did go on, it would be without a purpose, except that of self-criticism.

[11] For truth is neither more nor less than that character of a proposition which consists in this, that belief in the proposition would, with sufficient experience and reflection, lead us to such conduct as would tend to satisfy the desires we should then have. To say that truth means more than this is to say that it has no meaning at all. [1903.]

[12] Doubts about them may spring up later; but we can find no propositions which are not subject to this contingency. [1903.]

V

If the settlement of opinion is the sole object of inquiry, and if belief is of the nature of a habit, why should we not attain the desired end, by taking any answer to a question, which we may fancy, and constantly reiterating it to ourselves, dwelling on all which may conduce to that belief, and learning to turn with contempt and hatred from anything which might disturb it? This simple and direct method is really pursued by many men. I remember once being entreated not to read a certain newspaper lest it might change my opinion upon free-trade. "Lest I might be entrapped by its fallacies and misstatements" was the form of expression. "You are not," my friend said, "a special student of political economy. You might, therefore, easily be deceived by fallacious arguments upon the subject. You might, then, if you read this paper, be led to believe in protection. But you admit that free-trade is the true doctrine; and you do not wish to believe what is not true." I have often known this system to be deliberately adopted. Still oftener, the instinctive dislike of an undecided state of mind, exaggerated into a vague dread of doubt, makes men cling spasmodically to the views they already take. The man feels that if he only holds to his belief without wavering, it will be entirely satisfactory. Nor can it be denied that a steady and immovable faith yields great peace of mind. It may, indeed, give rise to inconveniences, as if a man should resolutely continue to believe that fire would not burn him, or that he would be eternally damned if he received his *ingesta* otherwise than through a stomach-pump. But then the man who adopts this method will not allow that its inconveniences are greater than its advantages. He will say, "I hold steadfastly to the truth and the truth is always wholesome." And in many cases it may very well be that the pleasure he derives from his calm faith overbalances any inconveniences resulting from its deceptive character. Thus, if it be true that death is annihilation, then the man who believes that he will certainly go straight to heaven when he dies, provided he have fulfilled certain simple observances in this life, has a cheap pleasure which will not be followed by the least disappointment. A similar consideration seems to have weight with many persons in religious topics, for we frequently hear it said, "Oh, I could not believe so-and-so, because I should be wretched if I did." When an ostrich buries its head in the sand as danger approaches, it very likely takes the happiest course. It hides the danger, and then calmly says there is no danger; and, if it feels perfectly sure there is none, why should it raise its head to see? A man may go through life, systematically keeping out of view all that might cause a change in his opinions, and if he only succeeds—basing his method, as he does, on two fundamental psychological laws—I do not see what can be said against his doing so. It would be an egotistical impertinence to object that his procedure is irrational, for that only amounts to saying that his method of settling belief is not ours. He does not propose to himself to be rational, and indeed, will often talk with scorn of man's weak and illusive reason. So let him think as he pleases.

But this method of fixing belief, which may be called the method of tenacity, will be unable to hold its ground in practice. The social impulse is against it. The man who adopts it will find that other men think differently from him, and it will be apt to occur to him in some saner moment that their opinions are quite as good as his own, and this will shake his confidence in his belief. This conception, that another man's thought or sentiment may be equivalent to one's own, is a distinctly new step, and a highly important one. It arises from an impulse too strong in man to be suppressed, without danger of destroying the human species. Unless we make ourselves hermits, we shall necessarily influence each other's opinions; so that the problem becomes how to fix belief, not in the individual merely, but in the community.

Let the will of the state act, then, instead of that of the individual. Let an institution be created which shall have for its object to keep correct doctrines before the attention of the people, to reiterate them perpetually, and to teach them to the young; having at the same time power to prevent contrary doctrines from being taught, advocated, or expressed. Let all possible causes of a change of mind be removed from men's apprehensions. Let them be kept ignorant, lest they should learn of some reason to think otherwise than they do. Let their passions be enlisted, so that they may regard private and unusual opinions with hatred and horror. Then, let all men who reject the established belief be terrified into silence. Let the people turn out and tar-and-feather such men, or let inquisitions be made into the manner of thinking of suspected persons, and, when they are found guilty of forbidden beliefs, let them be subjected to some signal punishment. When complete agreement could not otherwise be reached, a general massacre of all who have not thought in a certain way has proved a very effective means of settling opinion in a country. If the power to do this be wanting, let a list of opinions be drawn up, to which no man of the least independence of thought can assent, and let the faithful be required to accept all these propositions, in order to segregate them as radically as possible from the influence of the rest of the world.

This method has, from the earliest times, been one of the chief means of upholding correct theological and political doctrines, and of preserving their universal or catholic character. In Rome, especially, it has been practiced from the days of Numa Pompilius to those of Pius Nonus. This is the most perfect example in history; but wherever there is a priesthood—and no religion has been without one—this method has been more or less made use of. Wherever there is an aristocracy, or a guild, or any association of a class of men whose interests depend or are supposed to depend on certain propositions, there will be inevitably found some traces of this natural product of social feeling. Cruelties always accompany this system; and when it is consistently carried out, they become atrocities of the most horrible kind in the eyes of any rational man. Nor should this occasion surprise, for the officer of a society does not feel justified in surrendering the interests of that society for the sake of mercy, as he might his own private interests. It is natural, therefore, that sympathy and fellowship should thus produce a most ruthless power.

In judging this method of fixing belief, which may be called the method of authority, we must, in the first place, allow its immeasurable mental and moral superiority to the method of tenacity. Its success is proportionally greater; and in fact it has over and over again worked the most majestic results. The mere structures of stone which it has caused to be put together—in Siam, for example, in Egypt, and in Europe—have many of them a sublimity hardly more than rivaled by the greatest works of nature. And, except the geological epochs, there are no periods of time so vast as those which are measured by some of these organized faiths. If we scrutinize the matter closely, we shall find that there has not been one of their creeds which has remained always the same; yet the change is so slow as to be imperceptible during one person's life, so that individual belief remains sensibly fixed. For the mass of mankind, then, there is perhaps no better method than this. If it is their highest impulse to be intellectual slaves, then slaves they ought to remain.

But no institution can undertake to regulate opinions upon every subject. Only the most important ones can be attended to, and on the rest men's minds must be left to the action of natural causes. This imperfection will be no source of weakness so long as men are in such a state of culture that one opinion does not influence another—that is, so long as they cannot put two and two together. But in the most priest-ridden states some individuals will be found who are raised above that condition. These men possess a wider sort of social feeling; they see that men in other countries and in other ages have held to very different doctrines from those which they themselves have been brought up to believe; and they cannot help seeing that it is the mere accident of their having been taught as they have, and of their having been surrounded with the manners and associations they have, that has caused them to believe as they do and not far differently. And their candor cannot resist the reflection that there is no reason to rate their own views at a higher value than those of other nations and other centuries; and this gives rise to doubts in their minds.

They will further perceive that such doubts as these must exist in their minds with reference to every belief which seems to be determined by the caprice either of themselves or of those who originated the popular opinions. The willful adherence to a belief, and the arbitrary forcing of it upon others, must, therefore, both be given up and a new method of settling opinions must be adopted, which shall not only produce an impulse to believe, but shall also decide what proposition it is which is to be believed. Let the action of natural preferences be unimpeded, then, and under their influence let men conversing together and regarding matters in different lights, gradually develop beliefs in harmony with natural causes. This method resembles that by which conceptions of art have been brought to maturity. The most perfect example of it is to be found in the history of metaphysical philosophy. Systems of this sort have not usually rested upon observed facts, at least not in any great degree. They have been chiefly adopted because their fundamental propositions seemed "agreeable to reason." This is an apt expression; it does not mean that which agrees with experience, but that which we find ourselves inclined to believe. Plato, for example, finds it agreeable to reason that the distances of the celestial spheres from one another should be proportional to the different lengths of strings which produce harmonious chords. Many philosophers have been led to their main conclusions by considerations like this; but this is the lowest and least developed form which the method takes, for it is clear that another man might find Kepler's [earlier] theory, that the celestial spheres are proportional to the inscribed and circumscribed spheres of the different regular solids, more agreeable to *his* reason. But the shock of opinions will soon lead men to rest on preferences of a far more universal nature. Take, for example, the doctrine that man only acts selfishly—that is, from the consideration that acting in one way will afford him more pleasure than acting in another. This rests on no fact in the world, but it has had a wide acceptance as being the only reasonable theory.

This method is far more intellectual and respectable from the point of view of reason than either of the others which we have noticed. But its failure has been the most manifest. It makes of inquiry something similar to the development of taste; but taste, unfortunately, is always more or less a matter of fashion, and accordingly, metaphysicians have never come to any fixed agreement, but the pendulum has swung backward and forward between a more material and a more spiritual philosophy, from the earliest times to the latest. And so from this, which has been called the *a priori* method, we are driven, in Lord Bacon's phrase, to a true induction. We have examined into this *a priori* method as something which promised to deliver our opinions from their accidental and capricious element. But development, while it is a process which eliminates the effect of some casual circumstances, only magnifies that of others. This method, therefore, does not differ in a very essential way from that of authority. The government may not have lifted its finger to influence my convictions; I may have been left outwardly quite free to choose, we will say, between monogamy and polygamy, and appealing to my conscience only, I may have concluded that the latter practice is in itself licentious. But when I come to see that the chief obstacle to the spread of Christianity among a people of as high culture as the Hindoos has been a conviction of the immorality of our way of treating women, I cannot help seeing that, though governments do not interfere, sentiments in their development will be very greatly determined by accidental causes. Now, there are some people, among whom I must suppose that my reader is to be found, who, when they see that any belief of theirs is determined by any circumstance extraneous to the facts, will from that moment not merely admit in words that that belief is doubtful, but will experience a real doubt of it, so that it ceases in some degree at least to be a belief.

To satisfy our doubts, therefore, it is necessary that a method should be found by which our beliefs may be caused by nothing human, but by some external permanency—by something upon which our thinking has no effect. Some mystics imagine that they have such a method in a private inspiration from on high. But that is only a form of the method of tenacity, in which the conception of truth as something public is not yet developed. Our external permanency would not be external, in our sense, if it was restricted in its influence to one individual. It must be something which affects, or might affect, every man. And, though these affections are necessarily as various as are individual conditions, yet the method must be such that the ultimate conclusion of every man shall be the same, or would be the same if inquiry were sufficiently persisted in. Such is the method of science. Its fundamental hypothesis, restated in more familiar language, is this: There are real things, whose characters are entirely independent of our opinions about them; those realities affect our senses according to regular laws, and, though our sensations are as different as our relations to the objects, yet, by taking advantage of the laws of perception, we can ascertain by reasoning how things really are, and any man, if he have sufficient experience and reason enough about it, will be led to the one true conclusion. The new conception here involved is that of reality. It may be asked how I know that there are any realities. If this hypothesis is the sole support of my method of inquiry, my method of inquiry must not be used to support my hypothesis. The reply is this: (1) If investigation cannot be regarded as proving that there are real things, it at least does not lead to a contrary conclusion; but the method and the conception on which it is based remain ever in harmony. No doubts of the method, therefore, necessarily arise from its practice, as is the case with all the others. (2) The feeling which gives rise to any method of fixing belief is a dissatisfaction at two repugnant propositions. But here already is a vague concession that there is some *one* thing to which a proposition should conform. Nobody, therefore, can really doubt that there are realities, or, if he did, doubt would not be a source of dissatisfaction. The hypothesis, therefore, is one which every mind admits. So that the social impulse does not cause men to doubt it. (3) Everybody uses the scientific method about a great many things, and only ceases to use it when he does not know how to apply it. (4) Experience of the method has not led us to doubt it, but, on the contrary, scientific investigation has had the most wonderful triumphs in the way of settling opinion. These afford the explanation of my not doubting the method or the hypothesis which it supposes; and not having any doubt, nor believing that anybody else whom I could influence has, it would be the merest babble for me to say more about it. If there be anybody with a living doubt upon the subject, let him consider it.

To describe the method of scientific investigation is the object of this series of papers. At present I have only room to notice some points of contrast between it and other methods of fixing belief.

This is the only one of the four methods which presents any distinction of a right and a wrong way. If I adopt the method of tenacity and shut myself out from all influences, whatever I think necessary to doing this is necessary according to that method. So with the method of authority: the state may try to put down heresy by means which, from a scientific point of view, seem very ill-calculated to accomplish its purposes; but the only test *on that method* is what the state thinks, so that it cannot pursue the method wrongly. So with the *a priori* method. The very essence of it is to think as one is inclined to think. All metaphysicians will be sure to do that, however they may be inclined to judge each other to be perversely wrong. The Hegelian system recognizes every natural tendency of thought as logical, although it is certain to be abolished by counter-tendencies. Hegel thinks there is a regular system in the succession of these tendencies, in consequence of which, after drifting one way and the other for a long time, opinion will at last go right. And it is true that metaphysicians get the right ideas at last; Hegel's system of Nature represents tolerably the science of his day; and one may be sure that whatever scientific investigation has put out of doubt will presently receive *a priori* demonstration on the part of the metaphysicians. But with the scientific method the case is different. I may start with known and observed facts to proceed to the unknown; and yet the rules which I follow in doing so may not be such as investigation would approve. The test of whether I am truly following the method is not an immediate appeal to my feelings and purposes, but, on the contrary, itself involves the application of the method. Hence it is that bad reasoning as well as good reasoning is possible; and this fact is the foundation of the practical side of logic.

It is not to be supposed that the first three methods of settling opinion present no advantage whatever over the scientific method. On the contrary, each has some peculiar convenience of its own. The *a priori* method is distinguished for its comfortable conclusions. It is the nature of the process to adopt whatever belief we are inclined to, and there are certain flatteries to one's vanities which we all believe by nature, until we are awakened from our pleasing dream by rough facts. The method of authority will always govern the mass of mankind; and those who wield the various forms of organized force in the state will never be convinced that dangerous reasoning ought not to be suppressed in some way. If liberty of speech is to be untrammeled from the grosser forms of constraint, then uniformity of opinion will be secured by a moral terrorism to which the respectability of society will give its thorough approval. Following the method of authority is the path of peace. Certain non-conformities are permitted; certain others (considered unsafe) are forbidden. These are different in different countries and in different ages; but, wherever you are let it be known that you seriously hold a tabooed belief, and you may be perfectly sure of being treated with a cruelty no less brutal but more refined than hunting you like a wolf. Thus, the greatest intellectual benefactors of mankind have never dared, and dare not now, to utter the whole of their thought; and thus a shade of *prima facie* doubt is cast upon every proposition which is considered essential to the security of society. Singularly enough, the persecution does not all come from without; but a man torments himself and is oftentimes most distressed at finding himself believing propositions which he has been brought up to regard with aversion. The peaceful and sympathetic man will, therefore, find it hard to resist the temptation to submit his opinions to authority. But most of all I admire the method of tenacity for its strength, simplicity, and directness. Men who pursue it are distinguished for their decision of character, which becomes very easy with such a mental rule. They do not waste time in trying to make up their minds to what they want, but, fastening like lightning upon whatever alternative comes first, they hold to it to the end, whatever happens, without an instant's irresolution. This is one of the splendid qualities which generally accompany brilliant, unlasting success. It is impossible not to envy the man who can dismiss reason, although we know how it must turn out at last.

Such are the advantages which the other methods of settling opinions have over scientific investigation. A man should consider well of them; and then he should consider that, after all, he wishes his opinions to coincide with the fact, and that there is no reason why the results of those first three methods should do so. To bring about this effect is the prerogative of the method of science. Upon such considerations he has to make his choice—a choice which is far more than the adoption of any intellectual opinion, which is one of the ruling decisions of his life, to which when once made he is bound to adhere. The force of habit will sometimes cause a man to hold on to old beliefs after he is in a condition to see that they have no sound basis. But reflection upon the state of the case will overcome these habits, and he ought to allow reflection full weight. People sometimes shrink from doing this, having an idea that beliefs are wholesome which they cannot help feeling rest on nothing. But let such persons suppose an analogous though different case from their own. Let them ask themselves what they would say to a reformed Mussulman who should hesitate to give up his old notions in regard to the relations of the sexes; or to a reformed Catholic who should still shrink from the Bible. Would they not say that these persons ought to consider the matter fully, and clearly understand the new doctrine, and then ought to embrace it in its entirety? But, above all, let it be considered that what is more wholesome than any particular belief is integrity of belief; and that to avoid looking into the support of any belief from a fear that it may turn out rotten is quite as immoral as it is disadvantageous. The person who confesses that there is such a thing as truth, which is distinguished from falsehood simply by this, that if acted on it should, on full consideration, carry us to the point we aim at and not astray, and then, though convinced of this, dares not know the truth and seeks to avoid it, is in a sorry state of mind, indeed.

Yes, the other methods do have their merits: a clear logical conscience does cost something—just as any virtue, just as all that we cherish, costs us dear. But, we should not desire it to be otherwise. The genius of a man's logical method should be loved and reverenced as his bride, whom he has chosen from all the world. He need not condemn the others; on the contrary, he may honor them deeply, and in doing so he only honors her the more. But she is the one that he has chosen, and he knows that he was right in making that choice. And having made it, he will work and fight for her, and will not complain that there are blows to take, hoping that there may be as many and as hard to give, and will strive to be the worthy knight and champion of her from the blaze of whose splendors he draws his inspiration and his courage.

HOW TO MAKE OUR IDEAS CLEAR [13]

Whoever has looked into a modern treatise on logic of the common sort, will doubtless remember the two distinctions between *clear* and *obscure* conceptions, and between *distinct* and *confused* conceptions. They have lain in the books now for nigh two centuries, unimproved and unmodified, and are generally reckoned by logicians as among the gems of their doctrine.

A clear idea is defined as one which is so apprehended that it will be recognized wherever it is met with, and so that no other will be mistaken for it. If it fails of this clearness, it is said to be obscure.

This is rather a neat bit of philosophical terminology; yet, since it is clearness that they were defining, I wish the logicians had made their definition a little more plain. Never to fail to recognize an idea, and under no circumstances to mistake another for it, let it come in how recondite a form it may, would indeed imply such prodigious force and clearness of intellect as is seldom met with in this world. On the other hand, merely to have such an acquaintance with the idea as to have become familiar with it, and to have lost all hesitancy in recognizing it in ordinary cases, hardly seems to deserve the name of clearness of apprehension, since after all it only amounts to a subjective feeling of mastery which may be entirely mistaken. I take it, however, that when the logicians speak of "clearness," they mean nothing more than such a familiarity with an idea, since they regard the quality as but a small merit, which needs to be supplemented by another, which they call *distinctness*.

A distinct idea is defined as one which contains nothing which is

[13] From *Popular Science Monthly*, Vol. XII (1878), pp. 286–302. Reprinted in *Collected Papers of Charles Sanders Peirce*, ed. Charles Hartshorne and Paul Weiss. Cambridge, Mass.: The Belknap Press of Harvard University Press, 1934. Vol. V, pp. 248–71.

not clear. This is technical language; by the *contents* of an idea logicians understand whatever is contained in its definition. So that an idea is *distinctly* apprehended, according to them, when we can give a precise definition of it, in abstract terms. Here the professional logicians leave the subject; and I would not have troubled the reader with what they have to say if it were not such a striking example of how they have been slumbering through ages of intellectual activity, listlessly disregarding the enginery of modern thought, and never dreaming of applying its lessons to the improvement of logic. It is easy to show that the doctrine that familiar use and abstract distinctness make the perfection of apprehension, has its only true place in philosophies which have long been extinct; and it is now time to formulate the method of attaining to a more perfect clearness of thought, such as we see and admire in the thinkers of our own time.

When Descartes set about the reconstruction of philosophy, his first step was to (theoretically) permit skepticism and to discard the practice of the schoolmen of looking to authority as the ultimate source of truth. That done, he sought a more natural fountain of true principles, and professed to find it in the human mind; thus passing, in the directest way, from the method of authority to that of apriority, as described in my first paper [*The Fixation of Belief*]. Self-consciousness was to furnish us with our fundamental truths, and to decide what was agreeable to reason. But since, evidently, not all ideas are true, he was led to note, as the first condition of infallibility, that they must be clear. The distinction between an idea *seeming* clear and really being so, never occurred to him. Trusting to introspection, as he did, even for a knowledge of external things, why should he question its testimony in respect to the contents of our own minds? But then, I suppose, seeing men, who seemed to be quite clear and positive, holding opposite opinions upon fundamental principles, he was further led to say that clearness of ideas is not sufficient, but that they need also to be distinct, i.e., to have nothing unclear about them. What he probably meant by this (for he did not explain himself with precision) was that they must sustain the test of dialectical examination; that they must not only seem clear at the outset, but that discussion must never be able to bring to light points of obscurity connected with them.

Such was the distinction of Descartes, and one sees that it was precisely on the level of his philosophy. It was somewhat developed by Leibniz. This great and singular genius was as remarkable for what he failed to see as for what he saw. That a piece of mechanism could not do work perpetually without being fed with power in some form, was a thing perfectly apparent to him; yet he did not understand that the machinery of the mind can only transform knowledge, but never originate it, unless it be fed with facts of observation. He thus missed the most essential point of the Cartesian philosophy, which is, that to accept propositions which seem perfectly evident to us is a thing which, whether it be logical or illogical, we cannot help doing. Instead of regarding the matter in this way, he sought to reduce the first principles of science to formulas which cannot be denied without self-contradiction, and was apparently unaware of the great difference between his position and that of Descartes.[14] So he reverted to the old formalities of logic, and, above all, abstract definitions played a great part in his philosophy. It was quite natural, therefore, that on observing that the method of Descartes labored under the difficulty that we may seem to ourselves to have clear apprehensions of ideas which in truth are very hazy, no better remedy occurred to him than to require an abstract definition of every important term. Accordingly, in adopting the distinction of *clear* and *distinct* notions, he described the latter quality as the clear apprehension of everything contained in the definition; and the books have ever since copied his words. There is no danger that his chimerical scheme will ever again be overvalued. Nothing new can ever be learned by analyzing definitions. Nevertheless, our existing beliefs can be set in order by this process, and order is an essential element of intellectual economy, as of every other. It may be acknowledged, therefore, that the books are right in making familiarity with a notion the first step toward clearness of apprehension, and the defining of it the second. But in omitting all mention of any higher perspicuity of thought, they simply mirror a philosophy which was exploded a hundred years ago. That much-admired "ornament of logic"—the doctrine of clearness and distinctness—may be pretty enough, but it is high time to relegate to our cabinet of curiosities the antique *bijou*, and to wear about us something better adapted to modern uses.

The very first lesson that we have a right to demand that logic shall teach us is how to make our ideas clear; and a most important one it is, depreciated only by minds who stand in need of it. To know what we think, to be masters of our own meaning, will make a solid foundation for great and weighty thought. It is most easily learned by those whose ideas are meagre and restricted; and far happier they than such as wallow helplessly in a rich mud of conceptions. A nation, it is true, may, in the course of generations, overcome the disadvantage of an excessive wealth of language and its natural concomitant, a vast, unfathomable deep of ideas. We may

---

[14] He was, however, above all, one of the minds that grow; while at first he was an extreme nominalist, like Hobbes, and dabbled in the nonsensical and impotent *Ars Magna* of Raymond Lully, he subsequently embraced the law of continuity and other doctrines opposed to nominalism. I speak here of his early views. [1903].

see it in history, slowly perfecting its literary forms, sloughing at length its metaphysics, and, by virtue of the untirable patience which is often a compensation, attaining great excellence in every branch of mental acquirement. The page of history is not yet unrolled which is to tell us whether such a people will or will not in the long run prevail over one whose ideas (like the words of their language) are few, but which possesses a wonderful mastery over those which it has. For an individual, however, there can be no question that a few clear ideas are worth more than many confused ones. A young man would hardly be persuaded to sacrifice the greater part of his thoughts to save the rest; and the muddled head is the least apt to see the necessity of such a sacrifice. Him we can usually only commiserate, as a person with a congenital defect. Time will help him, but intellectual maturity with regard to clearness comes rather late, an unfortunate arrangement of nature, inasmuch as clearness is of less use to a man settled in life, whose errors have in great measure had their effect, than it would be to one whose path lies before him. It is terrible to see how a single unclear idea, a single formula without meaning, lurking in a young man's head, will sometimes act like an obstruction of inert matter in an artery, hindering the nutrition of the brain, and condemning its victim to pine away in the fullness of his intellectual vigor and in the midst of intellectual plenty. Many a man has cherished for years as his hobby some vague shadow of an idea, too meaningless to be positively false; he has, nevertheless, passionately loved it, has made it his companion by day and by night, and has given to it his strength and his life, leaving all other occupations for its sake, and in short has lived with it and for it, until it has become, as it were, flesh of his flesh and bone of his bone; and then he has waked up some bright morning to find it gone, clean vanished away like the beautiful Melusina of the fable, and the essence of his life gone with it. I have myself known such a man; and who can tell how many histories of circle-squarers, metaphysicians, astrologers, and what not, may not be told in the old German story?

II

The principles set forth in the first of these papers lead, at once, to a method of reaching a clearness of thought of a far higher grade than the "distinctness" of the logicians. We have there found that the action of thought is excited by the irritation of doubt, and ceases when belief is attained; so that the production of belief is the sole function of thought. All these words, however, are too strong for my purpose. It is as if I had described the phenomena as they appear under a mental microscope. Doubt and Belief, as the words are commonly employed, relate to religious or other grave discussions. But here I use them to designate the starting of any question, no matter how small or how great, and the resolution of it. If, for instance, in a horsecar, I pull out my purse and find a five-cent nickel and five coppers, I decide, while my hand is going to the purse, in which way I will pay my fare. To call such a question Doubt, and my decision Belief, is certainly to use words very disproportionate to the occasion. To speak of such a doubt as causing an irritation which needs to be appeased, suggests a temper which is uncomfortable to the verge of insanity. Yet, looking at the matter minutely, it must be admitted that, if there is the least hesitation as to whether I shall pay the five coppers or the nickel (as there will be sure to be, unless I act from some previously contracted habit in the matter), though irritation is too strong a word, yet I am excited to such small mental activity as may be necessary to deciding how I shall act. Most frequently doubts arise from some indecision, however momentary, in our action. Sometimes it is not so. I have, for example, to wait in a railway station, and to pass the time I read the advertisements on the walls, I compare the advantages of different trains and different routes which I never expect to take, merely fancying myself to be in a state of hesitancy, because I am bored with having nothing to trouble me. Feigned hesitancy, whether feigned for mere amusement or with a lofty purpose, plays a great part in the production of scientific inquiry. However the doubt may originate, it stimulates the mind to an activity which may be slight or energetic, calm or turbulent. Images pass rapidly through consciousness, one incessantly melting into another, until at last, when all is over—it may be in a fraction of a second, in an hour, or after long years—we find ourselves decided as to how we should act under such circumstances as those which occasioned our hesitation. In other words, we have attained belief.

In this process we observe two sorts of elements of consciousness, the distinction between which may best be made clear by means of an illustration. In a piece of music there are the separate notes, and there is the air. A single tone may be prolonged for an hour or a day, and it exists as perfectly in each second of that time as in the whole taken together; so that, as long as it is sounding, it might be present to a sense from which everything in the past was as completely absent as the future itself. But it is different with the air, the performance of which occupies a certain time, during the portions of which only portions of it are played. It consists in an orderliness in the succession of sounds which strike the ear at different times; and to perceive it there must be some continuity of consciousness which makes the events of a lapse of time present to us. We certainly only perceive the air by hearing the separate notes; yet we cannot be said to directly hear it, for we hear only what is present at the instant, and an orderliness of succession cannot exist in an instant. These two sorts of objects, what we are *immediately* conscious of and what we are *mediately* conscious of, are found in all consciousness. Some elements (the sensations) are completely present at every instant so long as they last, while others (like thought) are actions having beginning, middle, and end, and consist in a congruence in the succession of sensations which flow through the mind. They cannot be immediately present to us, but must cover some portion of the past or future. Thought is a thread of melody running through the succession of our sensations.

We may add that just as a piece of music may be written in parts, each part having its own air, so various systems of relationship of succession subsist together between the same sensations. These different systems are distinguished by having different motives, ideas, or functions. Thought is only one such system; for its sole motive, idea, and function is to produce belief, and whatever does not concern that purpose belongs to some other system of relations. The action of thinking may incidentally have other results. It may serve to amuse us, for example, and among *dilettanti* it is not rare to find those who have so perverted thought to the purposes of pleasure that it seems to vex them to think that the questions upon which they delight to exercise it may ever get finally settled; and a positive discovery which takes a favorite subject out of the arena of literary debate is met with ill-concealed dislike. This disposition is the very debauchery of thought. But the soul and meaning of thought, abstracted from the other elements which accompany it, though it may be voluntarily thwarted, can never be made to direct itself toward anything but the production of belief. Thought in action has for its only possible motive the attainment of thought at rest; and whatever does not refer to belief is no part of the thought itself.

And what, then, is belief? It is the demi-cadence which closes a musical phrase in the symphony of our intellectual life. We have seen that it has just three properties: first, it is something that we are aware of; second, it appeases the irritation of doubt; and, third, it involves the establishment in our nature of a rule of action, or, say for short, a *habit*. As it appeases the irritation of doubt, which is the motive for thinking, thought relaxes, and comes to rest for a moment when belief is reached. But, since belief is a rule for action, the application of which involves further doubt and further thought, at the same time that it is a stopping-place, it is also a new starting-place for thought. That is why I have permitted myself to call it thought at rest, although thought is essentially an action. The *final* upshot of thinking is the exercise of volition, and of this thought no longer forms a part; but belief is only a stadium of mental action, an effect upon our nature due to thought, which will influence future thinking.

The essence of belief is the establishment of a habit, and different beliefs are distinguished by the different modes of action to which they give rise. If beliefs do not differ in this respect, if they appease the same doubt by producing the same rule of action, then no mere differences in the manner of consciousness of them can make them different beliefs, any more than playing a tune in different keys is playing different tunes. Imaginary distinctions are often drawn between beliefs which differ only in their mode of expression—the wrangling which ensues is real enough, however. To believe that any objects are arranged among themselves as in Fig. 1, and to believe that they are arranged as in Fig. 2, are one and the same belief; yet it is conceivable that a man

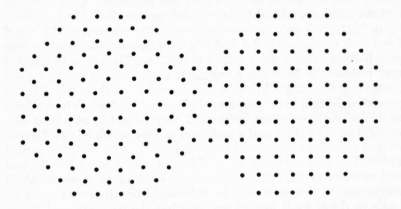

should assert one proposition and deny the other. Such false distinctions do as much harm as the confusion of beliefs really different, and are among the pitfalls of which we ought constantly to beware, especially when we are upon metaphysical ground. One singular deception of this sort, which often occurs, is to mistake the sensation produced by our own unclearness of thought for a character of the object we are thinking. Instead of perceiving that the obscurity is purely subjective, we fancy that we contemplate a quality of the object which is essentially mysterious; and if our conception be afterward presented to us in a clear form we do not recognize it as the same, owing to the absence of the feeling of unintelligibility. So long as this deception lasts, it obviously puts an impassable barrier in the way of perspicuous thinking; so that it equally interests the opponents of rational thought to perpetuate it, and its adherents to guard against it.

Another such deception is to mistake a mere difference in the grammatical construction of two words for a distinction between the ideas they express. In this pedantic age, when the general mob of writers attend so much more to words than to things, this error is common enough. When I just said that thought is an *action*, and that it consists in a *relation*, although a person performs an action but not a relation, which can only be the result of an action, yet there was no inconsistency in what I said, but only a grammatical vagueness.

From all these sophisms we shall be perfectly safe so long as we reflect that the whole function of thought is to produce habits of action; and that whatever there is connected with a thought, but irrelevant to its purpose, is an accretion to it, but no part of it. If there be a unity among our sensations which has no reference to how we shall act on a given occasion, as when we listen to a piece of music, why we do not call that thinking. To develop its meaning, we have, therefore, simply to determine what habits it produces, for what a thing means is simply what habits it involves. Now, the identity of a habit depends on how it might lead us to act, not merely under such circumstances as are likely to arise, but under such as might possibly occur, no matter how improbable they may be. What the habit is depends on *when* and *how* is causes us to act. As for the *when*, every stimulus to action is derived from perception; as for the *how*, every purpose of action is to produce some sensible result. Thus, we come down to what is tangible and practical as the root of every real distinction of thought, no matter how subtile it may be; and there is no distinction of meaning so fine as to consist in anything but a possible difference of practice.

To see what this principle leads to, consider in the light of it such a doctrine as that of transubstantiation. The Protestant churches generally hold that the elements of the sacrament are flesh and blood only in a tropical sense; they nourish our souls as meat and the juice of it would our bodies. But the Catholics maintain that they are literally just that, meat and blood; although they possess all the sensible qualities of wafer-cakes and diluted wine. But we can have no conception of wine except what may enter into a belief, either—

1. That this, that, or the other, is wine; or,

2. That wine possesses certain properties.

Such beliefs are nothing but self-notifications that we should, upon occasion, act in regard to such things as we believe to be wine according to the qualities which we believe wine to possess. The occasion of such action would be some sensible perception, the motive of it to produce some sensible result. Thus our action has exclusive reference to what affects the senses, our habit has the same bearing as our action, our belief the same as our habit, our conception the same as our belief; and we can consequently mean nothing by wine but what has certain effects, direct or indirect, upon our senses; and to talk of something as having all the sensible characters of wine, yet being in reality blood, is senseless jargon. Now, it is not my object to pursue the theological question; and having used it as a logical example I drop it, without caring to anticipate the theologian's reply. I only desire to point out how impossible it is that we should have an idea in our minds which relates to anything but conceived sensible effects of things. Our idea of anything *is* our idea of its sensible effects; and if we fancy that we have any other we deceive ourselves, and mistake a mere sensation accompanying the thought for a part of the thought itself. It is absurd to say that thought has any meaning unrelated to its only function. It is foolish for Catholics and Protestants to fancy themselves in disagreement about the elements of the sacrament, if they agree in regard to all their sensible effects, here or hereafter.

It appears, then, that the rule for attaining the third grade of clearness of apprehension is as follows: consider what effects, which might conceivably have practical bearings, we conceive the object of our conception to have. Then, our conception of these effects is the whole of our conception of the object.

III

Let us illustrate this rule by some examples; and, to begin with the simplest one possible, let us ask what we mean by calling a thing *hard*. Evidently that it will not be scratched by many other substances. The whole conception of this quality, as of every other, lies in its conceived effects. There is absolutely no difference between a hard thing and a soft thing so long as they are not brought to the test. Suppose, then, that a diamond could be crystallized in the midst of a cushion of soft cotton, and should remain there until it was finally burned up. Would it be false to say that that diamond was soft? This seems a foolish question, and would be so, in fact, except in the realm of logic. There such questions are often of the greatest utility as serving to bring logical principles into sharper relief than real discussions ever could. In studying logic we must not put them aside with hasty answers, but must consider them with attentive care, in order to make out the principles involved. We may, in the present case, modify our question, and ask what prevents us from saying that all hard bodies remain perfectly soft until they are touched, when their hardness increases with the pressure until they are scratched. Reflection will show that the reply is this: there would be no *falsity* in such modes of speech. They would involve a modification of our present usage of speech with regard to the words "hard" and "soft," but not of their meanings. For they represent no fact to be different from what it is; only they involve arrangements of facts which would be exceedingly maladroit. This leads us to remark that the question of what would occur under circumstances which do not actually arise is not a question of fact, but only of the most perspicuous arrangement of them. For example, the question of free-will and fate in its simplest form, stripped of verbiage, is something like this: I have done something of which I am ashamed; could I, by an effort of the will, have resisted the temptation, and done otherwise? The philosophical reply is that this is not a question of fact, but only of the [possible] arrangement of facts. Arranging them so as to exhibit what is particularly pertinent to my question—namely, that I ought to blame myself for having done wrong—it is perfectly true to say that, if I had willed to do otherwise than I did, I should have done otherwise. On the other hand, arranging the facts so as to exhibit another important consideration, it is equally true that when a temptation has once been allowed to work, it will, if it has a certain force, produce its effect, let me struggle how I may. There is no objection to a contradiction in what would result from a false supposition. The *reductio ad absurdum* consists in showing that contradictory results would follow from a hypothesis which is consequently judged to be false. Many questions are involved in the free-will discussion, and I am far from desiring to say that both sides are equally right. On the contrary, I am of opinion that one side [determinism] denies important facts, and that the other does not. But what I do say is that the above single question was the origin of the whole doubt; that, had it not been for this question, the controversy would never have arisen; and that this question is perfectly solved in the manner which I have indicated.

Let us next seek a clear idea of Weight. This is another very easy case. To say that a body is heavy means simply that, in the absence of opposing force, it will fall. This (neglecting certain specifications of how it will fall, etc., which exist in the mind of the physicist who uses the word) is evidently the whole conception of weight. It is a fair question whether some particular facts may not *account* for gravity; but what we mean by the force itself is completely involved in its effects.

This leads us to undertake an account of the idea of Force in general. This is the great conception which, developed in the early part of the seventeenth century from the rude idea of a cause, and, constantly improved upon since, has shown us how to explain all the changes of motion which bodies experience, and how to think about all physical phenomena; which has given birth to modern science, and changed the face of the globe; and which, aside from its more special uses, has played a principal part in directing the course of modern thought, and in furthering modern social development. It is, therefore, worth some pains to comprehend it. According to our rule, we must begin by asking what is the immediate use of thinking about force; and the answer is that we thus account for changes of motion. If bodies were left to themselves, without the intervention of forces, every motion would continue unchanged both in velocity and in direction. Furthermore, change of motion never takes place abruptly; if its direction is changed, it is always through a curve without angles; if its velocity alters, it is by degrees. The gradual changes which are constantly taking place are conceived by geometers to be compounded together according to the rules of the parallelogram of forces. If the reader does not already know what this is, he will find it, I hope, to his advantage to endeavor to follow the following explanation; but if mathematics are insupportable to him, pray let him skip three paragraphs rather than that we should part company here.

A *path* is a line whose beginning and end are distinguished. Two paths are considered to be equivalent, which, beginning at the same point, lead to the same point. Thus the two paths, A B C D E and A F G H E (Fig. 3), are equivalent. Paths which do *not* begin at the same point are considered to be equivalent, provided that, on moving either of them without turning it, but keeping it always parallel to its original position, [so that] when its beginning coincides with that of the other path, the ends also coincide. Paths are considered as geometrically added together, when one begins where the other ends; thus the path A E is conceived to be a sum of A B, B C, C D, and D E. In the parallelogram of Fig. 4 the diagonal A C is the sum of A B and B C; or, since A D is geometrically equivalent to B C, A C is the geometrical sum of A B and A D.

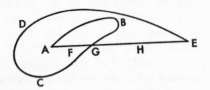
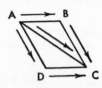

All this is purely conventional. It simply amounts to this: that we choose to call paths having the relations I have described equal or added. But, though it is a convention, it is a convention with a good reason. The rule for geometrical addition may be applied not only to paths, but to any other things which can be represented by paths. Now, as a path is determined by the varying direction and distance of the point which moves over it from the starting-point, it follows that anything which from its beginning to its end is determined by a varying direction and a varying magnitude is capable of being represented by a line. Accordingly, *velocities* may be represented by lines, for they have only directions and rates. The same thing is true of *accelerations*, or changes of velocities. This is evident enough in the case of velocities; and it becomes evident for accelerations if we consider that precisely what velocities are to positions—namely, states of change of them—that accelerations are to velocities.

The so-called "parallelogram of forces" is simply a rule for compounding accelerations. The rule is, to represent the accelerations by paths, and then to geometrically add the paths. The geometers, however, not only use the "parallelogram of forces" to compound different accelerations, but also to resolve one acceleration into a sum of several. Let $A B$ (Fig. 5) be the path which represents a certain acceleration—say, such a change in the motion of a body that at the end of one second the body will, under the influence of that change, be in a position different from what it would have had if its motion had continued unchanged, such that a path equivalent to $A B$ would lead from the latter position to the former. This acceleration may be considered as the sum of the accelerations represented by $A C$ and $C B$. It may also be considered as the sum of the very different accelerations represented by $A D$ and $D B$, where $A D$ is almost the opposite of $A C$. And it is clear that there is an immense variety of ways in which $A B$ might be resolved into the sum of two accelerations.

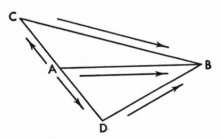

After this tedious explanation, which I hope, in view of the extraordinary interest of the conception of force, may not have exhausted the reader's patience, we are prepared at last to state the grand fact which this conception embodies. This fact is that if the actual changes of motion which the different particles of bodies experience are each resolved in its appropriate way, each component acceleration is precisely such as is prescribed by a certain law of Nature, according to which bodies in the relative positions which the bodies in question actually have at the moment[15] always receive certain accelerations, which, being compounded by geometrical addition, give the acceleration which the body actually experiences.

This is the only fact which the idea of force represents, and whoever will take the trouble clearly to apprehend what this fact is perfectly comprehends what force is. Whether we ought to say that a force *is* an acceleration, or that it *causes* an acceleration, is a mere question of propriety of language, which has no more to do with our real meaning than the difference between the French idiom "*Il fait froid*" and its English equivalent "*It is cold.*" Yet it is surprising to see how this simple affair has muddled men's minds. In how many profound treatises is not force spoken of as a "mysterious entity," which seems to be only a way of confessing that the author despairs of ever getting a clear notion of what the word means! In a recent, admired work on *Analytic Mechanics* [by Kirchhoff] it is stated that we understand precisely the effect of force, but what force itself is we do not understand! This is simply a self-contradiction. The idea which the word "force" excites in our minds has no other function than to affect our actions, and these actions can have no reference to force otherwise than through its effects. Consequently, if we know what the effects of force are, we are acquainted with every fact which is implied in saying that a force exists, and there is nothing more to know. The truth is, there is some vague notion afloat that a question may mean something which the mind cannot conceive; and when some hair-splitting philosophers have been confronted with the absurdity of such a view, they have invented an empty distinction between positive and negative conceptions, in the attempt to give their non-idea a form not obviously nonsensical. The nullity of it is sufficiently plain from the considerations given a few pages back; and, apart from those considerations, the quibbling character of the distinction must have struck every mind accustomed to real thinking.

IV

Let us now approach the subject of logic, and consider a conception which particularly concerns it, that of *reality*. Taking clearness in the sense of familiarity, no idea could be clearer than this. Every child uses it with perfect confidence, never dreaming that he does

[15] Possibly the velocities also have to be taken into account.

not understand it. As for clearness in its second grade, however, it would probably puzzle most men, even among those of a reflective turn of mind, to give an abstract definition of the real. Yet such a definition may perhaps be reached by considering the points of difference between reality and its opposite, fiction. A figment is a product of somebody's imagination; it has such characters as his thought impresses upon it. That those characters are independent of how you or I think is an external reality. There are, however, phenomena within our own minds, dependent upon our thought, which are at the same time real in the sense that we really think them. But though their characters depend on how we think, they do not depend on what we think those characters to be. Thus, a dream has a real existence as a mental phenomenon, if somebody has really dreamt it; that he dreamt so and so, does not depend on what anybody thinks was dreamt, but is completely independent of all opinion on the subject. On the other hand, considering, not the fact of dreaming, but the thing dreamt, it retains its peculiarities by virtue of no other fact than that it was dreamt to possess them. Thus we may define the real as that whose characters are independent of what anybody may think them to be.

But, however satisfactory such a definition may be found, it would be a great mistake to suppose that it makes the idea of reality perfectly clear. Here, then, let us apply our rules. According to them, reality, like every other quality, consists in the peculiar, sensible effects which things partaking of it produce. The only effect which real things have is to cause belief, for all the sensations which they excite emerge into consciousness in the form of beliefs. The question, therefore, is, how is true belief (or belief in the real) distinguished from false belief (or belief in fiction). Now, as we have seen in the former paper, the ideas of truth and falsehood, in their full development, appertain exclusively to the scientific method of settling opinion. A person who arbitrarily chooses the propositions which he will adopt can use the word truth only to emphasize the expression of his determination to hold on to his choice. Of course, the method of tenacity never prevailed exclusively; reason is too natural to men for that. But in the literature of the Dark Ages we find some fine examples of it. When Scotus Erigena is commenting upon a poetical passage in which hellebore is spoken of as having caused the death of Socrates, he does not hesitate to inform the inquiring reader that Helleborus and Socrates were two eminent Greek philosophers, and that the latter having been overcome in argument by the former took the matter to heart and died of it! What sort of an idea of truth could a man have who could adopt and teach, without the qualification of a "perhaps," an opinion taken so entirely at random? The real spirit of Socrates, who I hope would have been delighted to have been "overcome in argument," because he would have learned something by it, is in curious contrast with the naïve idea of the glossist, for whom (as for the "born missionary" of today) discussion would seem to have been simply a struggle. When philosophy began to awake from its long slumber, and before theology completely dominated it, the practice seems to have been for each professor to seize upon any philosophical position he found unoccupied and which seemed a strong one, to intrench himself in it, and to sally forth from time to time to give battle to the others. Thus, even the scanty records we possess of those disputes enable us to make out a dozen or more opinions held by different teachers at one time concerning the question of nominalism and realism. Read the opening part of the *Historia Calamitatum* of Abélard, who was certainly as philosophical as any of his contemporaries, and see the spirit of combat which it breathes. For him, the truth is simply his particular stronghold. When the method of authority prevailed, the truth meant little more than the Catholic faith. All the efforts of the scholastic doctors are directed toward harmonizing their faith in Aristotle and their faith in the Church, and one may search their ponderous folios through without finding an argument which goes any further. It is noticeable that where different faiths flourish side by side, renegades are looked upon with contempt even by the party whose belief they adopt; so completely has the idea of loyalty replaced that of truth-seeking. Since the time of Descartes, the defect in the conception of truth has been less apparent. Still, it will sometimes strike a scientific man that the philosophers have been less intent on finding out what the facts are than on inquiring what belief is most in harmony with their system. It is hard to convince a follower of the *a priori* method by adducing facts; but show him that an opinion he is defending is inconsistent with what he has laid down elsewhere, and he will be very apt to retract it. These minds do not seem to believe that disputation is ever to cease; they seem to think that the opinion which is natural for one man is not so for another, and that belief will, consequently, never be settled. In contenting themselves with fixing their own opinions by a method which would lead another man to a different result, they betray their feeble hold of the conception of what truth is.

On the other hand, all the followers of science are fully persuaded that the processes of investigation, if only pushed far enough, will give one certain solution to each question to which they can be applied. One man may investigate the velocity of light by studying the transits of Venus and the aberration of the stars; another by the oppositions of Mars and the eclipses of Jupiter's satellites; a third by the method of Fizeau; a fourth by that of Foucault; a fifth by the motions of the curves of Lissajoux; a sixth, a seventh, an eighth, and a ninth, may follow the different methods of comparing the measures of statical and dynamical electricity. They may at first obtain different results, but, as each perfects his method and his processes, the results will move steadily together toward a destined center. So with all scientific research. Different minds may set out with the most antagonistic views, but the progress of investigation carries them by a force outside of themselves to one and the same conclusion. This activity of thought by which we are carried, not where we wish, but to a foreordained goal, is like the operation of destiny. No modification of the point of view taken, no selection of other facts for study, no natural bent of mind even, can enable a man to escape the predestinate opinion. This great law is embodied in the conception of truth and reality. The opinion which is fated[16] to be ultimately agreed to by all who investigate is what we mean by the truth, and the object represented in this opinion is the real. That is the way I would explain reality.

But it may be said that this view is directly opposed to the abstract definition which we have given of reality, inasmuch as it makes the characters of the real depend on what is ultimately thought about them. But the answer to this is that, on the one hand, reality is independent, not necessarily of thought in general, but only of what you or I or any finite number of men may think about it; and that, on the other hand, though the object of the final opinion depends on what that opinion is, yet what that opinion is does not depend on what you or I or any man thinks. Our perversity and that of others may indefinitely postpone the settlement of opinion; it might even conceivably cause an arbitrary proposition to be universally accepted as long as the human race should last. Yet even that would not change the nature of the belief, which alone could be the result of investigation carried sufficiently far; and if, after the extinction of our race, another should arise with faculties and disposition for investigation, that true opinion must be the one which they would ultimately come to. "Truth crushed to earth shall rise again," and the opinion which would finally result from investigation does not depend on how anybody may actually think. But the reality of that which is real does depend on the real fact that investigation is destined to lead, at last, if continued long enough, to a belief in it.

---

16 Fate means merely that which is sure to come true, and can nohow be avoided. It is a superstition to suppose that a certain sort of events are ever fated, and it is another to suppose that the word "fate" can never be freed from its superstitious taint. We are all fated to die.

But I may be asked what I have to say to all the minute facts of history, forgotten never to be recovered, to the lost books of the ancients, to the buried secrets.

> Full many a gem of purest ray serene
> The dark, unfathomed caves of ocean bear;
> Full many a flower is born to blush unseen,
> And waste its sweetness on the desert air.

Do these things not really exist because they are hopelessly beyond the reach of our knowledge? And then, after the universe is dead (according to the prediction of some scientists), and all life has ceased forever, will not the shock of atoms continue though there will be no mind to know it? To this I reply that, though in no possible state of knowledge can any number be great enough to express the relation between the amount of what rests unknown to the amount of the known, yet it is unphilosophical to suppose that, with regard to any given question (which has any clear meaning), investigation would not bring forth a solution of it, if it were carried far enough. Who would have said, a few years ago, that we could ever know of what substances stars are made whose light may have been longer in reaching us than the human race has existed? Who can be sure of what we shall not know in a few hundred years? Who can guess what would be the result of continuing the pursuit of science for ten thousand years, with the activity of the last hundred? And if it were to go on for a million, or a billion, or any number of years you please, how is it possible to say that there is any question which might not ultimately be solved?

But it may be objected, "Why make so much of these remote considerations, especially when it is your principle that only practical distinctions have a meaning?" Well, I must confess that it makes very little difference whether we say that a stone on the bottom of the ocean, in complete darkness, is brilliant or not—that is to say, that it *probably* makes no difference, remembering always that that stone *may* be fished up tomorrow. But that there are gems at the bottom of the sea, flowers in the untraveled desert, etc., are propositions which, like that about a diamond being hard when it is not pressed, concern much more the arrangement of our language than they do the meaning of our ideas.

It seems to me, however, that we have, by the application of our rule, reached so clear an apprehension of what we mean by reality, and of the fact which the idea rests on, that we should not, perhaps, be making a pretension so presumptuous as it would be singular, if we were to offer a metaphysical theory of existence for universal acceptance among those who employ the scientific method of fixing belief. However, as metaphysics is a subject much more curious than useful, the knowledge of which, like that of a sunken reef, serves chiefly to enable us to keep clear of it, I will not trouble the reader with any more Ontology at this moment. I have already been led much further into that path than I should have desired; and I have given the reader such a dose of mathematics, psychology, and all that is most abstruse, that I fear he may already have left me, and that what I am now writing is for the compositor and proofreader exclusively. I trusted to the importance of the subject. There is no royal road to logic, and really valuable ideas can only be had at the price of close attention. But I know that in the matter of ideas the public prefer the cheap and nasty; and in my next paper I am going to return to the easily intelligible, and not wander from it again. The reader who has been at the pains of wading through this paper shall be rewarded in the next one by seeing how beautifully what has been developed in this tedious way can be applied to the ascertainment of the rules of scientific reasoning.

We have, hitherto, not crossed the threshold of scientific logic. It is certainly important to know how to make our ideas clear, but they may be ever so clear without being true. How to make them so, we have next to study. How to give birth to those vital and procreative ideas which multiply into a thousand forms and diffuse themselves everywhere, advancing civilization and making the dignity of man, is an art not yet reduced to rules, but of the secret of which the history of science affords some hints.

PRAGMATIC AND PRAGMATISM [17]

. . . The opinion that metaphysics is to be largely cleared up by the application of the following maxim for attaining clearness of apprehension: 'Consider what effects, that might conceivably have practical bearings, we conceive the object of our conception to have. Then, our conception of these effects is the whole of our conception of the object.'

This maxim was first proposed by C. S. Peirce in the *Popular Science Monthly* for January, 1878 (xii. 287); and he explained how it was to be applied to the doctrine of reality. The writer was led to the maxim by reflection upon Kant's *Critic of the Pure Reason*. Sub-

---

[17] From *Dictionary of Philosophy and Psychology,* ed. James Baldwin. N. Y.: Macmillan, 1902, Vol. 2, p. 322.

stantially the same way of dealing with ontology seems to have been practised by the Stoics. The writer subsequently saw that the principle might easily be misapplied, so as to sweep away the whole doctrine of incommensurables, and, in fact, the whole Weierstrassian way of regarding the calculus. In 1896 William James published his *Will to Believe*, and later his *Philos. Conceptions and Pract. Results*, which pushed this method to such extremes as must tend to give us pause. The doctrine appears to assume that the end of man is action—a stoical axiom which, to the present writer at the age of sixty, does not recommend itself so forcibly as it did at thirty. If it be admitted, on the contrary, that action wants an end, and that that end must be something of a general description, then the spirit of the maxim itself, which is that we must look to the upshot of our concepts in order rightly to apprehend them, would direct us towards something different from practical facts, namely, to general ideas, as the true interpreters of our thought. Nevertheless, the maxim has approved itself to the writer, after many years of trial, as of great utility in leading to a relatively high grade of clearness of thought. He would venture to suggest that it should always be put into practice with conscientious thoroughness, but that, when that has been done, and not before, a still higher grade of clearness of thought can be attained by remembering that the only ultimate good which the practical facts to which it directs attention can subserve is to further the development of concrete reasonableness; so that the meaning of the concept does not lie in any individual reactions at all, but in the manner in which those reactions contribute to that development. Indeed, in the article of 1878, above referred to, the writer practised better than he preached; for he applied the stoical maxim most unstoically, in such a sense as to insist upon the reality of the objects of general ideas in their generality.

A widely current opinion during the last quarter of a century has been that reasonableness is not a good in itself, but only for the sake of something else. Whether it be so or not seems to be a synthetical question, not to be settled by an appeal to the principle of contradiction—as if a reason for reasonableness were absurd. Almost everybody will now agree that the ultimate good lies in the evolutionary process in some way. If so, it is not in individual reactions in their segregation, but in something general or continuous. Synechism is founded on the notion that the coalescence, the becoming continuous, the becoming governed by laws, the becoming instinct with general ideas, are but phases of one and the same process of the growth of reasonableness. This is first shown to be true with mathematical exactitude in the field of logic, and is thence inferred to hold good metaphysically. It is not opposed to pragmatism in the manner in which C. S. Peirce applied it, but includes that procedure as a step.

PRAGMATICISM [18]

After awaiting in vain, for a good many years, some particularly opportune conjuncture of circumstances that might serve to recommend his notions of the ethics of terminology, the writer has now, at last, dragged them in over head and shoulders, on an occasion when he has no specific proposal to offer nor any feeling but satisfaction at the course usage has run without any canons or resolutions of a congress. His word "pragmatism" has gained general recognition in a generalized sense that seems to argue power of growth and vitality. The famed psychologist, James, first took it up, seeing that his "radical empiricism" substantially answered to the writer's definition of pragmatism, albeit with a certain difference in the point of view. Next, the admirably clear and brilliant thinker, Mr. Ferdinand C. S. Schiller, casting about for a more attractive name for the "anthropomorphism" of his *Riddle of the Sphinx*, lit, in that most remarkable paper of his on *Axioms as Postulates*, upon the same designation "pragmatism," which in its original sense was in generic agreement with his own doctrine, for which he has since found the more appropriate specification "humanism," while he still retains "pragmatism" in a somewhat wider sense. So far all went happily. But at present, the word begins to be met with occasionally in the literary journals, where it gets abused in the merciless way that words have to expect when they fall into literary clutches. Sometimes the manners of the British have effloresced in scolding at the word as ill-chosen—ill-chosen, that is, to express some meaning that it was rather designed to exclude. So then, the writer, finding his bantling "pragmatism" so promoted, feels that it is time to kiss his child good-by and relinquish it to its higher destiny; while to serve the precise purpose of expressing the original definition, he begs to announce the birth of the word "pragmaticism," which is ugly enough to be safe from kidnappers. . . .

Let us now hasten to the exposition of pragmaticism itself. Here it will be convenient to imagine that somebody to whom the doctrine is new, but of rather preternatural perspicacity, asks questions of a

[18] From "What Pragmatism Is," *The Monist*, XV (1905), pp. 161–81.

pragmaticist. Everything that might give a dramatic illusion must be stripped off, so that the result will be a sort of cross between a dialogue and a catechism, but a good deal liker the latter—something rather painfully reminiscent of Mangnall's *Historical Questions*.

Questioner: I am astounded at your definition of your pragmatism, because only last year I was assured by a person above all suspicion of warping the truth—himself a pragmatist—that your doctrine precisely was "that a conception is to be tested by its practical effects." You must surely, then, have entirely changed your definition very recently.

Pragmaticist: If you will turn to Vols. VI and VII of the *Revue Philosophique*, or to the *Popular Science Monthly* for November 1877 and January 1878, you will be able to judge for yourself whether the interpretation you mention was not then clearly excluded. The exact wording of the English enunciation (changing only the first person into the second) was: "Consider what effects that might conceivably have practical bearing you conceive the object of your conception to have. Then your conception of those effects is the WHOLE of your conception of the object."

Questioner: Well, what reason have you for asserting that this is so?

Pragmaticist: That is what I specially desire to tell you. But the question had better be postponed until you clearly understand what those reasons profess to prove.

Questioner: What, then, is the *raison d'être* of the doctrine? What advantage is expected from it?

Pragmaticist: It will serve to show that almost every proposition of ontological metaphysics is either meaningless gibberish—one word being defined by other words, and they by still others, without any real conception ever being reached—or else is downright absurd; so that all such rubbish being swept away, what will remain of philosophy will be a series of problems capable of investigation by the observational methods of the true sciences—the truth about which can be reached without those interminable misunderstandings and disputes which have made the highest of the positive sciences a mere amusement for idle intellects, a sort of chess—idle pleasure its purpose, and reading out of a book its method. In this regard, pragmaticism is a species of prope-positivism. But what distinguishes it from other species is, first, its retention of a purified philosophy; secondly, its full acceptance of the main body of our instinctive beliefs; and thirdly, its strenuous insistence upon the truth of scholastic realism (or a close approximation to that, well-stated by the late Dr. Francis Ellingwood Abbot in the Introduction to his *Scientific Theism*). So, instead of merely jeering at metaphysics, like other prope-positivists, whether by long-drawn-out parodies or otherwise, the pragmaticist extracts from it a precious essence, which will serve to give life and light to cosmology and physics. At the same time, the moral applications of the doctrine are positive and potent; and there are many other uses of it not easily classed. On another occasion, instances may be given to show that it really has these effects.

Questioner: I hardly need to be convinced that your doctrine would wipe out metaphysics. Is it not as obvious that it must wipe out every proposition of science and everything that bears on the conduct of life? For you say that the only meaning that, for you, any assertion bears is that a certain experiment has resulted in a certain way: Nothing else but an experiment enters into the meaning. Tell me, then, how can an experiment, in itself, reveal anything more than that something once happened to an individual object and that subsequently some other individual event occurred?

Pragmaticist: That question is, indeed, to the purpose—the purpose being to correct any misapprehensions of pragmaticism. You speak of an experiment in itself, emphasizing *"in itself."* You evidently think of each experiment as isolated from every other. It has not, for example, occurred to you, one might venture to surmise, that every connected series of experiments constitutes a single collective experiment. What are the essential ingredients of an experiment? First, of course, an experimenter of flesh and blood. Secondly, a verifiable hypothesis. This is a proposition relating to the universe environing the experimenter, or to some well-known part of it and affirming or denying of this only some experimental possibility or impossibility. The third indispensable ingredient is a sincere doubt in the experimenter's mind as to the truth of that hypothesis.

Passing over several ingredients on which we need not dwell, the purpose, the plan, and the resolve, we come to the act of choice by which the experimenter singles out certain identifiable objects to be operated upon. The next is the external (or quasi-external) ACT by which he modifies those objects. Next, comes the subsequent *reaction* of the world upon the experimenter in a perception; and finally, his recognition of the teaching of the experiment. While the two chief parts of the event itself are the action and the reaction, yet the unity of essence of the experiment lies in its purpose and plan, the ingredients passed over in the enumeration.

Another thing: in representing the pragmaticist as making rational meaning to consist in an experiment (which you speak of as an event in the past), you strikingly fail to catch his attitude of mind. Indeed, it is not in an experiment, but in *experimental phenomena,* that rational meaning is said to consist. When an experimentalist speaks of a *phenomenon,* such as "Hall's phenomenon," "Zeemann's phenomenon" and its modification, "Michelson's phenomenon," or "the chessboard phenomenon," he does not mean any particular event that did happen to somebody in the dead past, but what *surely will* happen to everybody in the living future who shall fulfill certain conditions. The phenomenon consists in the fact that when an experimentalist shall come to *act* according to a certain scheme that he has in mind, then will something else happen, and shatter the doubts of sceptics, like the celestial fire upon the altar of Elijah.

And do not overlook the fact that the pragmaticist maxim says nothing of single experiments or of single experimental phenomena (for what is conditionally true *in futuro* can hardly be singular), but only speaks of *general kinds* of experimental phenomena. Its adherent does not shrink from speaking of general objects as real, since whatever is true represents a real. Now the laws of nature are true.

The rational meaning of every proposition lies in the future. How so? The meaning of a proposition is itself a proposition. Indeed, it is no other than the very proposition of which it is the meaning: it is a translation of it. But of the myriads of forms into which a proposition may be translated, what is that one which is to be called its very meaning? It is, according to the pragmaticist, that form in which the proposition becomes applicable to human conduct, not in these or those special circumstances, nor when one entertains this or that special design, but that form which is most directly applicable to self-control under every situation, and to every purpose. This is why he locates the meaning in future time; for future conduct is the only conduct that is subject to self-control. But in order that that form of the proposition which is to be taken as its meaning should be applicable to every situation and to every purpose upon which the proposition has any bearing, it must be simply the general description of all the experimental phenomena which the assertion of the proposition virtually predicts. For an experimental phenomenon is the fact asserted by the proposition that action of a certain description will have a certain kind of experimental result; and experimental results are the only results that can affect human conduct. No doubt, some unchanging idea may come to influence a man more than it had done; but only because some experience equivalent to an experiment has brought its truth home to him more intimately than before. Whenever a man acts purposively, he acts under a belief in some experimental phenomenon. Consequently, the sum of the experimental phenomena that a proposition implies makes up its entire bearing upon human conduct. Your question, then, of how a pragmaticist can attribute any meaning to any assertion other than that of a single occurrence is substantially answered.

Questioner: I see that pragmaticism is a thorough-going phenomenalism. Only why should you limit yourself to the phenomena of experimental science rather than embrace all observational science? Experiment, after all, is an uncommunicative informant. It never expatiates: it only answers "yes" or "no"; or rather it usually snaps out "No!", or at best only utters an inarticulate grunt for the negation of its "no." The typical experimentalist is not much of an observer. It is the student of natural history to whom nature opens the treasury of her confidence, while she treats the cross-examining experimentalist with the reserve he merits. Why should your phenomenalism sound the meagre jew's-harp of experiment rather than the glorious organ of observation?

Pragmaticist: Because pragmaticism is not definable as "thoroughgoing phenomenalism," although the latter doctrine may be a kind of pragmatism. The *richness* of phenomena lies in their sensuous quality. Pragmaticism does not intend to define the phenomenal equivalents of words and general ideas, but, on the contrary, eliminates their sential element, and endeavours to define the rational purport, and this it finds in the purposive bearing of the word or proposition in question.

Questioner: Well, if you choose so to make Doing the Be-all and the End-all of human life, why do you not make meaning to consist simply in doing? Doing has to be done at a certain time upon a certain object. Individual objects and single events cover all reality, as everybody knows, and as a practicalist ought to be the first to insist. Yet, your meaning, as you have described it, is *general*. Thus, it is of the nature of a mere word and not a reality. You say yourself that your meaning of a proposition is only the same proposition in another dress. But a practical man's meaning is the very thing he means. What do you make to be the meaning of "George Washington"?

Pragmaticist: Forcibly put! A good half dozen of your points must certainly be admitted. It must be admitted, in the first place, that if pragmaticism really made Doing to be the Be-all and the End-all of life, that would be its death. For to say that we live for the mere sake of action, as action, regardless of the thought it carries out, would be to say that there is no such thing as rational purport. Secondly, it must be admitted that every proposition professes to be true of a certain real individual object, often the environing universe. Thirdly, it must be admitted that pragmaticism fails to furnish any translation or meaning of a proper name, or other designation of an individual object. Fourthly, the pragmaticistic meaning is undoubtedly general; and it is equally indisputable that the general is of the nature of a word or sign. Fifthly, it must be admitted that individuals alone exist; and sixthly, it may be admitted that the very meaning of a word or significant object ought to be the very essence of reality of what it signifies. But when those admissions have been unreservedly made, you find the pragmaticist still constrained most earnestly to deny the force of your objection, you ought to infer that there is some consideration that has escaped you. Putting the admissions together, you will perceive that the pragmaticist grants that a proper name (although it is not customary to say that it has a *meaning*) has a certain denotative function peculiar, in each case, to that name and its equivalents; and that he grants that every assertion contains such a denotative or pointing-out function. In its peculiar individuality, the pragmaticist excludes this from the rational purport of the assertion, although *the like* of it, being common to all assertions, and so, being general and not individual, may enter into the pragmaticistic purport. Whatever exists, *ex-sists*, that is, really acts upon other existents, so obtains a self-identity, and is definitely individual. As to the general, it will be a help to thought to notice that there are two ways of being general. A statue of a soldier on some village monument, in his overcoat and with his musket, is for each of a hundred families the image of its uncle, its sacrifice to the Union. That statue, then, though it is itself single, represents any one man of whom a certain predicate may be true. It is *objectively* general. The word "soldier," whether spoken or written, is general in the same way; while the name, "George Washington," is not so. But each of these two terms remains one and the same noun, whether it be spoken or written, and whenever and wherever it be spoken or written. This noun is not an existent thing: it is a *type*, or *form*, to which objects, both those that are externally existent and those which are imagined, may *conform*, but which none of them can exactly be. This is subjective generality. The pragmaticistic purport is general in both ways.

As to reality, one finds it defined in various ways; but if that principle of terminological ethics that was proposed be accepted, the equivocal language will soon disappear. For *realis* and *realitas* are not ancient words. They were invented to be terms of philosophy in the thirteenth century, and the meaning they were intended to express is perfectly clear. That is *real* which has such and such characters, whether anybody thinks it to have those characters or not. At any rate, that is the sense in which the pragmaticist uses the word. Now, just as conduct controlled by ethical reason tends toward fixing certain habits of conduct, the nature of which (as to illustrate the meaning, peaceable habits and not quarrelsome habits) does not depend upon any accidental circumstances, and *in that sense* may be said to be *destined*; so, thought, controlled by a rational experi-

mental logic, tends to the fixation of certain opinions, equally destined, the nature of which will be the same in the end, however the
perversity of thought of whole generations may cause the postponement of the ultimate fixation. If this be so, as every man of us virtually
assumes that it is, in regard to each matter the truth of which he
seriously discusses, then, according to the adopted definition of "real,"
the state of things which will be believed in that ultimate opinion is
real. But, for the most part, such opinions will be general. Consequently, *some* general objects are real. (Of course, nobody ever
thought that *all* generals were real; but the scholastics used to assume that generals were real when they had hardly any, or quite
no, experiential evidence to support their assumption; and their fault
lay just there, and not in holding that generals could be real.) One
is struck with the inexactitude of thought even of analysts of power,
when they touch upon modes of being. One will meet, for example,
the virtual assumption that what is relative to thought cannot be
real. But why not, exactly? *Red* is relative to sight, but the fact that
this or that is in that relation to vision that we call being red is not
itself relative to sight; it is a real fact.

Not only may generals be real, but they may also be *physically
efficient*, not in every metaphysical sense, but in the common-sense
acception in which human purposes are physically efficient. Aside
from metaphysical nonsense, no sane man doubts that if I feel the
air in my study to be stuffy, that thought may cause the window to
be opened. My thought, be it granted, was an individual event. But
what determined it to take the particular determination it did, was
in part the general fact that stuffy air is unwholesome, and in part
other *Forms*, concerning which Dr. Carus has caused so many men
to reflect to advantage—or rather, *by* which, and the general truth
concerning which Dr. Carus's mind was determined to the forcible
enunciation of so much truth. For truths, on the average, have a
greater tendency to get believed than falsities have. Were it otherwise, considering that there are myriads of false hypotheses to account for any given phenomenon, against one sole true one (or if
you will have it so, against every true one), the first step toward
genuine knowledge must have been next door to a miracle. So,
then, when my window was opened, because of the truth that stuffy
air is *malsain*, a physical effort was brought into existence by the
efficiency of a general and non-existent truth. This has a droll sound
because it is unfamiliar; but exact analysis is with it and not against
it; and it has besides, the immense advantage of not blinding us to
great facts—such as that the ideas "justice" and "truth" are, notwithstanding the iniquity of the world, the mightiest of the forces that

move it. Generality is, indeed, an indispensable ingredient of reality; for mere individual existence or actuality without any regularity whatever is a nullity. Chaos is pure nothing.

That which any true proposition asserts is *real*, in the sense of being as it is regardless of what you or I may think about it. Let this proposition be a general conditional proposition as to the future, and it is a real general such as is calculated really to influence human conduct; and such the pragmaticist holds to be the rational purport of every concept.

Accordingly, the pragmaticist does not make the *summum bonum* to consist in action, but makes it to consist in that process of evolution whereby the existent comes more and more to embody those generals which were just now said to be *destined*, which is what we strive to express in calling them *reasonable*. In its higher stages, evolution takes place more and more largely through self-control, and this gives the pragmaticist a sort of justification for making the rational purport to be general.

There is much more in elucidation of pragmaticism that might be said to advantage, were it not for the dread of fatiguing the reader. It might, for example, have been well to show clearly that the pragmaticist does not attribute any different essential mode of being to an event in the future from that which he would attribute to a similar event in the past, but only that the practical attitude of the thinker toward the two is different. It would also have been well to show that the pragmaticist does not make Forms to be the *only* realities in the world, any more than he makes the reasonable purport of a word to be the only kind of meaning there is. These things are, however, implicitly involved in what has been said. . . .

THE DOCTRINE OF NECESSITY EXAMINED [19]

. . . I propose here to examine the common belief that every single fact in the universe is precisely determined by law.

. . . The proposition in question is that the state of things existing at any time, together with certain immutable laws, completely determine the state of things at every other time (for a limitation to *future* time is indefensible). Thus, given the state of the universe

---

[19] First published in *The Monist*, II (1892), pp. 321–37. Reprinted in *Collected Papers of Charles Sanders Peirce*, ed. Charles Hartshorne and Paul Weiss. Cambridge, Mass.: The Belknap Press of Harvard University Press, 1935, Vol. VI, pp. 28–45.

in the original nebula, and given the laws of mechanics, a sufficiently powerful mind could deduce from these data the precise form of every curlicue of every letter I am now writing.

Whoever holds that every act of the will as well as every idea of the mind is under the rigid governance of a necessity co-ordinated with that of the physical world, will logically be carried to the proposition that minds are part of the physical world in such a sense that the laws of mechanics determine everything that happens according to immutable attractions and repulsions. In that case, that instantaneous state of things from which every other state of things is calculable consists in the positions and velocities of all the particles at any instant. This, the usual and most logical form of necessitarianism, is called the mechanical philosophy.

When I have asked thinking men what reason they had to believe that every fact in the universe is precisely determined by law, the first answer has usually been that the proposition is a "presupposition" or postulate of scientific reasoning. Well, if that is the best that can be said for it, the belief is doomed. Suppose it be "postulated": that does not make it true, nor so much as afford the slightest rational motive for yielding it any credence. It is as if a man should come to borrow money, and when asked for his security, should reply he "postulated" the loan. To "postulate" a proposition is no more than to hope it is true. There are, indeed, practical emergencies in which we act upon assumptions of certain propositions as true, because if they are not so, it can make no difference how we act. But all such propositions I take to be hypotheses of individual facts. For it is manifest that no universal principle can in its universality be comprised in a special case or can be requisite for the validity of any ordinary inference. To say, for instance, that the demonstration by Archimedes of the property of the lever would fall to the ground if men were endowed with free-will, is extravagant; yet this is implied by those who make a proposition incompatible with the freedom of the will the postulate of all inference. Considering, too, that the conclusions of science make no pretense to being more than probable, and considering that a probable inference can at most only suppose something to be most frequently, or otherwise approximately, true, but never that anything is precisely true without exception throughout the universe, we see how far this proposition in truth is from being so postulated.

But the whole notion of a postulate being involved in reasoning appertains to a by-gone and false conception of logic. Non-deductive, or ampliative inference, is of three kinds: induction, hypothesis, and analogy. If there be any other modes, they must be extremely unusual and highly complicated, and may be assumed with little doubt to be of the same nature as those enumerated. For induction, hypothesis, and analogy, as far as their ampliative character goes, that is, so far as they conclude something not implied in the premises, depend upon one principle and involve the same procedure. All are essentially inferences from sampling. Suppose a ship arrives at Liverpool laden with wheat in bulk. Suppose that by some machinery the whole cargo be stirred up with great thoroughness. Suppose that twenty-seven thimblefuls be taken equally from the forward, midships, and aft parts, from the starboard, center, and larboard parts, and from the top, half depth, and lower parts of her hold, and that these being mixed and the grains counted, four-fifths of the latter are found to be of quality A. Then we infer, experientially and provisionally, that approximately four-fifths of all the grain in the cargo is of the same quality. I say we infer this *experientially* and *provisionally*. By saying that we infer it *experientially*, I mean that our conclusion makes no pretension to knowledge of wheat-in-itself, our *alétheia*, as the derivation of that word implies, has nothing to do with *latent* wheat. We are dealing only with the matter of possible experience—experience in the full acceptation of the term as something not merely affecting the senses but also as the subject of thought. If there be any wheat hidden on the ship, so that it can neither turn up in the sample nor be heard of subsequently from purchasers—or if it be half-hidden, so that it may, indeed, turn up, but is less likely to do so than the rest—or if it can affect our senses and our pockets, but from some strange cause or causelessness cannot be reasoned about—all such wheat is to be excluded (or have only its proportional weight) in calculating that true proportion of quality A, to which our inference seeks to approximate. By saying that we draw the inference *provisionally*, I mean that we do not hold that we have reached any assigned degree of approximation as yet, but only hold that if our experience be indefinitely extended, and if every fact of whatever nature, as fast as it presents itself, be duly applied, according to the inductive method, in correcting the inferred ratio, then our approximation will become indefinitely close in the long run; that is to say, close to the experience *to come* (not merely close by the exhaustion of a finite collection) so that if experience in general is to fluctuate irregularly to and fro, in a manner to deprive the ratio sought of all definite value, we shall be able to find out approximately within what limits it fluctuates, and if, after having one definite value, it changes and assumes another, we shall be able to find that out, and in short, whatever may be the variations of this ratio in experience, experience indefinitely extended will enable us to detect them, so as to predict rightly, at last, what its ultimate value may be, if it have any ultimate value, or what the ultimate law of succession of values may be, if there be any such ultimate law, or that it ultimately fluctuates irregularly within certain limits, if it do so ultimately fluctuate. Now our inference, claiming to be no more than thus experiential and provisional, manifestly involves no postulate whatever.

For what is a postulate? It is the formulation of a material fact which we are not entitled to assume as a premise, but the truth of which is requisite to the validity of an inference. Any fact, then, which might be supposed postulated, must either be such that it would ultimately present itself in experience, or not. If it will present itself, we need not postulate it now in our provisional inference, since we shall ultimately be entitled to use it as a premise. But if it never would present itself in experience, our conclusion is valid but for the possibility of this fact being otherwise than assumed, that is, it is valid as far as possible experience goes, and that is all that we claim. Thus, every postulate is cut off, either by the provisionality or by the experientiality of our inference. For instance, it has been said that induction postulates that if an indefinite succession of samples be drawn, examined, and thrown back each before the next is drawn, then in the long run every grain will be drawn as often as any other, that is to say, postulates that the ratio of the numbers of times in which any two are drawn will indefinitely approximate to unity. But no such postulate is made; for if, on the one hand, we are to have no other experience of the wheat than from such drawings, it is the ratio that presents itself in those drawings and not the ratio which belongs to the wheat in its latent existence that we are endeavoring to determine; while if, on the other hand, there is some other mode by which the wheat is to come under our knowledge, equivalent to another kind of sampling, so that after all our care in stirring up the wheat, some experiential grains will present themselves in the first sampling operation more often than others in the long run, this very singular fact will be sure to get discovered by the inductive method, which must avail itself of every sort of experience; and our inference, which was only provisional, corrects itself at last. Again, it has been said, that induction postulates that under like circumstances like events will happen, and that this postulate is at bottom the same as the principle of universal causation. But this is a blunder, or *bévue*, due to thinking exclusively of inductions where the concluded ratio is either 1 or 0. If any such proposition were postulated, it would be that under like circumstances (the circumstances of drawing the different samples) different events occur in the same proportions in all the different sets—a proposition which is false and even absurd. But in truth no such thing is postulated, the experiential character of the inference reducing the condition of validity to this, that if a certain result does not occur, the opposite result will be manifested, a condition assured by the provisionality of the inference. But it may be asked whether it is not conceivable that every instance of a certain class destined to be ever employed as a datum of induction should have one character, while every instance destined not to be so employed should have the opposite character. The answer is that in that case, the instances excluded from being subjects of reasoning would not be experienced in the full sense of the word, but would be among these *latent* individuals of which our conclusion does not pretend to speak.

To this account of the rationale of induction I know of but one objection worth mention: it is that I thus fail to deduce the full degree of force which this mode of inference in fact possesses; that according to my view, no matter how thorough and elaborate the stirring and mixing process had been, the examination of a single handful of grain would not give me any assurance, sufficient to risk money upon, that the next handful would not greatly modify the concluded value of the ratio under inquiry, while, in fact, the assurance would be very high that this ratio was not greatly in error. If the true ratio of grains of quality A were 0.80 and the handful contained a thousand grains, nine such handfuls out of every ten would contain from 780 to 820 grains of quality A. The answer to this is that the calculation given is correct when we know that the units of this handful and the quality inquired into have the normal independence of one another, if for instance the stirring has been complete and the character sampled for has been settled upon in advance of the examination of the sample. But in so far as these conditions are not known to be complied with, the above figures cease to be applicable. Random sampling and predesignation of the character sampled for should always be striven after in inductive reasoning, but when they cannot be attained, so long as it is conducted honestly, the inference retains some value. When we cannot ascertain how the sampling has been done or the sample-character selected, induction still has the essential validity which my present account of it shows it to have.

I do not think a man who combines a willingness to be convinced with a power of appreciating an argument upon a difficult subject can resist the reasons which have been given to show that the principle of universal necessity cannot be defended as being a postulate of reasoning. But then the question immediately arises whether it is not proved to be true, or at least rendered highly probable, by observation of nature.

Still, this question ought not long to arrest a person accustomed to reflect upon the force of scientific reasoning. For the essence of the necessitarian position is that certain continuous quantities have certain exact values. Now, how can observation determine the value of such a quantity with a probable error absolutely *nil?* To one who is behind the scenes, and knows that the most refined comparisons of masses, lengths, and angles, far surpassing in precision all other measurements, yet fall behind the accuracy of bank accounts, and that the ordinary determinations of physical constants, such as appear from month to month in the journals, are about on a par with an upholsterer's measurements of carpets and curtains, the idea of mathematical exactitude being demonstrated in the laboratory will appear simply ridiculous. There is a recognized method of estimating the probable magnitudes of errors in physics—the method of least squares. It is universally admitted that this method makes the errors smaller than they really are; yet even according to that theory an error indefinitely small is indefinitely improbable; so that any statement to the effect that a certain continuous quantity has a certain exact value, if well-founded at all, must be founded on something other than observation.

Still, I am obliged to admit that this rule is subject to a certain qualification. Namely, it only applies to continuous[20] quantity. Now, certain kinds of continuous quantity are discontinuous at one or at two limits, and for such limits the rule must be modified. Thus, the length of a line cannot be less than zero. Suppose, then, the question arises how long a line a certain person had drawn from a marked point on a piece of paper. If no line at all can be seen, the observed length is zero; and the only conclusion this observation warrants is that the length of the line is less than the smallest length visible with the optical power employed. But indirect observations—for example, that the person supposed to have drawn the line was never within fifty feet of the paper—may make it probable that no line at all was made, so that the concluded length will be strictly zero. In like manner, experience no doubt would warrant the conclusion that there is absolutely *no* indigo in a given ear of wheat, and absolutely *no* attar in a given lichen. But such inferences can only be rendered valid by positive experiential evidence, direct or remote, and cannot rest upon a mere inability to detect the quantity in question. We have reason to think there is no indigo in the wheat, because we have remarked that wherever indigo is produced it is produced in considerable quantities, to mention only one argument. We have reason to think there is no attar in the lichen, because essential oils seem to be in general peculiar to single species. If the question had

---

[20] *Continuous* is not exactly the right word, but I let it go to avoid a long and irrelevant discussion.

been whether there was iron in the wheat or the lichen, though chemical analysis should fail to detect its presence, we should think some of it probably was there, since iron is almost everywhere. Without any such information, one way or the other, we could only abstain from any opinion as to the presence of the substance in question. It cannot, I conceive, be maintained that we are in any *better* position than this in regard to the presence of the element of chance or spontaneous departures from law in nature.

Those observations which are generally adduced in favor of mechanical causation simply prove that there is an element of regularity in nature, and have no bearing whatever upon the question of whether such regularity is exact and universal, or not. Nay, in regard to this *exactitude*, all observation is directly *opposed* to it; and the most that can be said is that a good deal of this observation can be explained away. Try to verify any law of nature, and you will find that the more precise your observations, the more certain they will be to show irregular departures from the law. We are accustomed to ascribe these, and I do not say wrongly, to errors of observation; yet we cannot usually account for such errors in any antecedently probable way. Trace their causes back far enough, and you will be forced to admit they are always due to arbitrary determination, or chance.

But it may be asked whether if there were an element of real chance in the universe it must not occasionally be productive of signal effects such as could not pass unobserved. In answer to this question, without stopping to point out that there is an abundance of great events which one might be tempted to suppose were of that nature, it will be simplest to remark that physicists hold that the particles of gases are moving about irregularly, substantially as if by real chance, and that by the principles of probabilities there must occasionally happen to be concentrations of heat in the gases contrary to the second law of thermodynamics, and these concentrations, occurring in explosive mixtures, must sometimes have tremendous effects. Here, then, is in substance the very situation supposed; yet no phenomena ever have resulted which we are forced to attribute to such chance concentration of heat, or which anybody, wise or foolish, has ever dreamed of accounting for in that manner.

In view of all these considerations, I do not believe that anybody, not in a state of case-hardened ignorance respecting the logic of science, can maintain that the precise and universal conformity of facts to law is clearly proved, or even rendered particularly probable, by any observations hitherto made. In this way, the determined advocate of exact regularity will soon find himself driven to *a priori* reasons to support his thesis. These received such a sockdolager from Stuart Mill in his Examination of Hamilton, that holding to them now seems to me to denote a high degree of imperviousness to reason; so that I shall pass them by with little notice.

To say that we cannot help believing a given proposition is no argument, but it is a conclusive fact if it be true; and with the substitution of "I" for "we," it is true in the mouths of several classes of minds, the blindly passionate, the unreflecting and ignorant, and the person who has overwhelming evidence before his eyes. But that which has been inconceivable today has often turned out indisputable on the morrow. Inability to conceive is only a stage through which every man must pass in regard to a number of beliefs—unless endowed with extraordinary obstinacy and obtuseness. His understanding is enslaved to some blind compulsion which a vigorous mind is pretty sure soon to cast off.

Some seek to back up the *a priori* position with empirical arguments. They say that the exact regularity of the world is a natural belief, and that natural beliefs have generally been confirmed by experience. There is some reason in this. Natural beliefs, however, if they generally have a foundation of truth, also require correction and purification from natural illusions. The principles of mechanics are undoubtedly natural beliefs; but, for all that, the early formulations of them were exceedingly erroneous. The general approximation to truth in natural beliefs is, in fact, a case of the general adaptation of genetic products to recognizable utilities or ends. Now, the adaptations of nature, beautiful and often marvelous as they verily are, are never found to be quite perfect; so that the argument is quite *against* the absolute exactitude of any natural belief, including that of the principle of causation.

Another argument, or convenient commonplace, is that absolute chance is *inconceivable*. (This word has eight current significations. The *Century Dictionary* enumerates six.) Those who talk like this will hardly be persuaded to say in what sense they mean that chance is inconceivable. Should they do so, it would easily be shown either that they have no sufficient reason for the statement or that the inconceivability is of a kind which does not prove that chance is nonexistent.

Another *a priori* argument is that chance is unintelligible; that is to say, while it may perhaps be conceivable, it does not disclose to the eye of reason the how or why of things; and since a hypothesis can only be justified so far as it renders some phenomenon intelligible, we never can have any right to suppose absolute chance to enter into the production of anything in nature. This argument may be considered in connection with two others. Namely, instead of going so far as to say that the supposition of chance can *never* properly be used to explain any observed fact, it may be alleged merely that no facts are known which such a supposition could in any way help in explaining. Or again, the allegation being still further weakened, it may be said that since departures from law are not unmistakably observed, chance is not a *vera causa*, and ought not unnecessarily to be introduced into a hypothesis.

These are no mean arguments, and require us to examine the matter a little more closely. Come, my superior opponent, let me learn from your wisdom. It seems to me that every throw of sixes with a pair of dice is a manifest instance of chance.

"While you would hold a throw of deuce-ace to be brought about by necessity?" (The opponent's supposed remarks are placed in quotation marks.)

Clearly one throw is as much chance as another.

"Do you think throws of dice are of a different nature from other events?"

I see that I must say that *all* the diversity and specificalness of events is attributable to chance.

"Would you, then, deny that there is any regularity in the world?"

That is clearly undeniable. I must acknowledge there is an approximate regularity, and that every event is influenced by it. But the diversification, specificalness, and irregularity of things I suppose is chance. A throw of sixes appears to me a case in which this element is particularly obtrusive.

"If you reflect more deeply, you will come to see that *chance* is only a name for a cause that is unknown to us."

Do you mean that we have no idea whatever what kind of causes could bring about a throw of sixes?

"On the contrary, each die moves under the influence of precise mechanical laws."

But it appears to me that it is not these *laws* which made the die turn up sixes; for these laws act just the same when other throws come up. The chance lies in the diversity of throws; and this diversity cannot be due to laws which are immutable.

"The diversity is due to the diverse circumstances under which the laws act. The dice lie differently in the box, and the motion given to the box is different. These are the unknown causes which produce the throws, and to which we give the name of chance; not the mechanical law which regulates the operation of these causes. You see you are already beginning to think more clearly about this subject."

Does the operation of mechanical law not increase the diversity?

"Properly not. You must know that the instantaneous state of a system of particles is defined by six times as many numbers as there are particles, three for the co-ordinates of each particle's position, and three more for the components of its velocity. This number of numbers, which expresses the amount of diversity in the system, remains the same at all times. There may be, to be sure, some kind of relation between the coordinates and component velocities of the different particles, by means of which the state of the system might be expressed by a smaller number of numbers. But, if this is the case, a precisely corresponding relationship must exist between the coordinates and component velocities at any other time, though it may doubtless be a relation less obvious to us. Thus, the intrinsic complexity of the system is the same at all times."

Very well, my obliging opponent, we have now reached an issue. You think all the arbitrary specifications of the universe were introduced in one dose, in the beginning, if there was a beginning, and that the variety and complication of nature has always been just as much as it is now. But I, for my part, think that the diversification, the specification, has been continually taking place. Should you condescend to ask me why I so think, I should give my reasons as follows:

(1) Question any science which deals with the course of time. Consider the life of an individual animal or plant, or of a mind. Glance at the history of states, of institutions, of language, of ideas. Examine the successions of forms shown by paleontology, the history of the globe as set forth in geology, of what the astronomer is able to make out concerning the changes of stellar systems. Everywhere the main fact is growth and increasing complexity. Death and corruption are mere accidents or secondary phenomena. Among some of the lower organisms, it is a moot point with biologists whether there be anything which ought to be called death. Races, at any rate, do not die out except under unfavorable circumstances. From these broad and ubiquitous facts we may fairly infer, by the most unexceptionable logic, that there is probably in nature some agency by which the complexity and diversity of things can be increased; and that consequently the rule of mechanical necessity meets in some way with interference.

(2) By thus admitting pure spontaneity or life as a character of the universe, acting always and everywhere though restrained within narrow bounds by law, producing infinitesimal departures from law continually, and great ones with infinite infrequency, I account for all the variety and diversity of the universe, in the only sense in which the really *sui generis* and new can be said to be accounted for. The ordinary view has to admit the inexhaustible multitudinous variety of the world, has to admit that its mechanical law cannot account for this in the least, that variety can spring only from spontaneity, and yet denies without any evidence or reason the existence

of this spontaneity, or else shoves it back to the beginning of time and supposes it dead ever since. The superior logic of my view appears to me not easily controverted.

(3) When I ask the necessitarian how he would explain the diversity and irregularity of the universe, he replies to me out of the treasury of his wisdom that irregularity is something which from the nature of things we must not seek to explain. Abashed at this, I seek to cover my confusion by asking how he would explain the uniformity and regularity of the universe, whereupon he tells me that the laws of nature are immutable and ultimate facts, and no account is to be given of them. But my hypothesis of spontaneity does explain irregularity, in a certain sense; that is, it explains the general fact of irregularity, though not, of course, what each lawless event is to be. At the same time, by thus loosening the bond of necessity, it gives room for the influence of another kind of causation, such as seems to be operative in the mind in the formation of associations, and enables us to understand how the uniformity of nature could have been brought about. That single events should be hard and unintelligible, logic will permit without difficulty: we do not expect to make the shock of a personally experienced earthquake appear natural and reasonable by any amount of cogitation. But logic does expect things *general* to be understandable. To say that there is a universal law, and that it is a hard, ultimate, unintelligible fact, the why and wherefore of which can never be inquired into, at this a sound logic will revolt; and will pass over at once to a method of philosophizing which does not thus barricade the road of discovery.

(4) Necessitarianism cannot logically stop short of making the whole action of the mind a part of the physical universe. Our notion that we decide what we are going to do, if as the necessitarian says, it has been calculable since the earliest times, is reduced to illusion. Indeed, consciousness in general thus becomes a mere illusory aspect of a material system. What we call red, green, and violet are in reality only different rates of vibration. The sole reality is the distribution of qualities of matter in space and time. Brain-matter is protoplasm in a certain degree and kind of complication—a certain arrangement of mechanical particles. Its feeling is but an inward aspect, a phantom. For, from the positions and velocities of the particles at any one instant, and the knowledge of the immutable forces, the positions at all other times are calculable; so that the universe of space, time, and matter is a rounded system uninterfered with from elsewhere. But from the state of feeling at any instant, there is no reason to suppose the states of feeling at all other instants are thus exactly calculable; so that feeling is, as I said, a mere frag-

mentary and illusive aspect of the universe. This is the way, then, that necessitarianism has to make up its accounts. It enters consciousness under the head of sundries, as a forgotten trifle; its scheme of the universe would be more satisfactory if this little fact could be dropped out of sight. On the other hand, by supposing the rigid exactitude of causation to yield, I care not how little—be it but by a strictly infinitesimal amount—we gain room to insert mind into our scheme, and to put it into the place where it is needed, into the position which, as the sole self-intelligible thing, it is entitled to occupy, that of the fountain of existence; and in so doing we resolve the problem of the connection of soul and body.

(5) But I must leave undeveloped the chief of my reasons, and can only adumbrate it. The hypothesis of chance-spontaneity is one whose inevitable consequences are capable of being traced out with mathematical precision into considerable detail. Much of this I have done and find the consequences to agree with observed facts to an extent which seems to me remarkable. But the matter and methods of reasoning are novel, and I have no right to promise that other mathematicians shall find my deductions as satisfactory as I myself do, so that the strongest reason for my belief must for the present remain a private reason of my own, and cannot influence others. I mention it to explain my own position; and partly to indicate to future mathematical speculators a veritable gold mine, should time and circumstances and the abridger of all joys prevent my opening it to the world.

If now I, in my turn, inquire of the necessitarian why he prefers to suppose that all specification goes back to the beginning of things, he will answer me with one of those last three arguments which I left unanswered.

First, he may say that chance is a thing absolutely unintelligible, and, therefore, that we never can be entitled to make such a supposition. But does not this objection smack of naïve impudence? It is not mine, it is his own conception of the universe which leads abruptly up to hard, ultimate, inexplicable, immutable law, on the one hand, and to inexplicable specification and diversification of circumstances on the other. My view, on the contrary, hypothesizes nothing at all, unless it be hypothesis to say that all specification came about in some sense, and is not to be accepted as unaccountable. To undertake to account for anything by saying boldly that it is due to chance would, indeed, be futile. But this I do not do. I make use of chance chiefly to make room for a principle of generalization, or tendency to form habits, which I hold has produced all regularities. The mechanical philosopher leaves the whole specification of the world utterly unaccounted for, which is pretty nearly as bad as to boldly attribute it to chance. I attribute it altogether to chance, it is true, but to chance in the form of a spontaneity which is to some degree regular. It seems to me clear at any rate that one of these two positions must be taken, or else specification must be supposed due to a spontaneity which develops itself in a certain and not in a chance way, by an objective logic like that of Hegel. This last way I leave as an open possibility, for the present; for it is as much opposed to the necessitarian scheme of existence as my own theory is.

Secondly, the necessitarian may say there are, at any rate, no observed phenomena which the hypothesis of chance could aid in explaining. In reply, I point first to the phenomenon of growth and developing complexity, which appears to be universal, and which though it may possibly be an affair of mechanism perhaps, certainly presents all the appearance of increasing diversification. Then, there is variety itself, beyond comparison the most obtrusive character of the universe: no mechanism can account for this. Then, there is the very fact the necessitarian most insists upon, the regularity of the universe which for him serves only to block the road of inquiry. Then, there are the regular relationships between the laws of nature —similarities and comparative characters, which appeal to our intelligence as its cousins, and call upon us for a reason. Finally, there is consciousness, feeling, a patent fact enough, but a very inconvenient one to the mechanical philosopher.

Thirdly, the necessitarian may say that chance is not a *vera causa*, that we cannot know positively there is any such element in the universe. But the doctrine of the *vera causa* has nothing to do with elementary conceptions. Pushed to that extreme, it at once cuts off belief in the existence of a material universe; and without that necessitarianism could hardly maintain its ground. Besides, variety is a fact which must be admitted; and the theory of chance merely consists in supposing this diversification does not antedate all time. Moreover, the avoidance of hypotheses involving causes nowhere positively known to act—is only a recommendation of logic, not a positive command. It cannot be formulated in any precise terms without at once betraying its untenable character—I mean as rigid rule, for as a recommendation it is wholesome enough.

I believe I have thus subjected to fair examination all the important reasons for adhering to the theory of universal necessity, and have shown their nullity. I earnestly beg that whoever may detect any flaw in my reasoning will point it out to me, either privately or publicly; for if I am wrong, it much concerns me to be set right speedily. If my argument remains unrefuted, it will be time, I think, to doubt the absolute truth of the principle of universal law; and when once such a doubt has obtained a living root in any man's mind, my cause with him, I am persuaded, is gained.

BIBLIOGRAPHY

PEIRCE, Charles Sanders. *Collected Papers of Charles Sanders Peirce*. Vols. I–VI, edited by Charles Hartshorne and Paul Weiss, Vols. VII–VIII, edited by A. W. Burks. Cambridge: Harvard U. Press, 1931–58.

———, *Chance, Love, and Logic*. Edited with Introduction by Morris R. Cohen. N.Y.: Harcourt, Brace, 1923. Reprinted: N.Y.: George Braziller, 1956.

———, *The Philosophy of Peirce; Selected Writings*. Justus Buchler, ed. N.Y.: Harcourt, Brace, 1940.

———, *Charles S. Peirce: Essays in the Philosophy of Science*. Vincent Tomas, ed. N.Y.: Liberal Arts Press, 1957.

———, *Values in a Universe of Chance*. Philip P. Wiener, ed. Stanford: Stanford U. Press, 1958.

BUCHLER, Justus. *Charles Peirce's Empiricism*. N.Y.: Harcourt, Brace, 1939.

FEIBLEMAN, James. *An Introduction to Peirce's Philosophy*. N.Y.: Harpers, 1946.

FREEMAN, Eugene. *The Categories of Charles Peirce*. Chicago: The U. of Chicago Libraries, 1937.

GALLIE, W. B. *Peirce and Pragmatism*. Harmondsworth-Middlesex: Penguin Books, 1952.

GOUDGE, Thomas Anderson. *The Thought of C. S. Peirce*. Toronto: U. of Toronto Press, 1950.

MOORE, Edward C. and ROBIN, Robin, eds. *Studies in the Philosophy of Charles Sanders Peirce*, Second Series. Amherst, Mass.: University of Massachusetts Press, 1964.

MURPHY, Murray G. *The Development of Peirce's Philosophy*. Cambridge: Harvard U. Press, 1961.

THOMPSON, M. H. *The Pragmatic Philosophy of C. S. Peirce*. Chicago: U. of Chicago Press, 1953.

WIENER, Philip P. and YOUNG, Frederick H., eds. *Studies in the Philosophy of Charles Sanders Peirce*. Cambridge: Harvard U. Press, 1952.

William James

[1842–1910]

William James was one of the first Americans invited to the University of Edinburgh at the beginning of the twentieth century to deliver the famous "Gifford Lectures." This led him to remark: "To us Americans, the experience of receiving instructions from . . . European scholars, is very familiar. . . . It seems the natural thing for us to listen whilst the Europeans talk. The contrary habit, of talking whilst the Europeans listen, we have not yet acquired; and in him who first makes the adventure it begets a certain sense of apology being due for so presumptuous an act." [1] But Europeans did listen to James and he became the first American philosopher to be read seriously throughout the world. Le Breton said of James: "Il a pu passer en Amérique pour le plus cosmopolite et en Europe pour le plus Américain des philosophes." ("He was able to pass in America for the most cosmopolitan of philosophers and in Europe for the most American.")

James had a great facility for expressing his ideas in literary form, and as his fame spread so did his influence. He had deep intellectual humility and a toleration for a wide variety of ideas. To James, philosophy was not a cloistered affair; it was to be lived and acted upon. James, a liberal in his political and social

sentiments, was a civil service reformer, a pacifist, and an anti-imperialist, and he was sympathetic to some sort of "socialistic equilibrium." On occasion, he criticized the policies of his former student, Theodore Roosevelt. In his widely read pamphlet, *The Moral Equivalent of War* (1910), he argued that, if war was ever to be eliminated, some substitute outlets must be discovered for the energies that go into war. He suggested that nations attempt to develop the qualities of devotion and duty, but for pacific purposes. Thus he recommended the conscription of the whole youthful population for a number of years in a war against nature and the injustices of life.

Born in New York City in 1842, the son of Henry James, Sr., a man of considerable philosophical and intellectual talents, William enjoyed a cosmopolitan background and education. His brother Henry became a successful novelist. William James, however, was erratic in his career; he went through a period of psychological depression, and was unable, until relatively late in his life, to "find himself." He attended school in New York City, studied with tutors in Europe, took up painting and for a while thought he might become an artist. He entered Lawrence Scientific School and Harvard Medical

[1] *The Varieties of Religious Experience: A Study in Human Nature*, N. Y., Collier Books, 1961, p. 21.

School, joined a scientific expedition with Louis Agassiz in Brazil, and finally took his M.D. from Harvard in 1869, though he never practiced medicine.

James' first academic position was as instructor of anatomy and physiology at Harvard in 1873, but he went on to teach psychology in 1875 and finally, in 1879, philosophy. In appraising his own career, James stated: "I originally studied medicine in order to be a physiologist, but I drifted into psychology and philosophy from a sort of fatality. I never had any philosophical instruction; the first lecture on psychology I ever heard being the first I ever gave."

James' philosophical interests were wide. His pragmatic ideas were suggested to him early in his career at the meetings of The Metaphysical Society in Cambridge. On August 26, 1898, he delivered a talk at the University of California, *Philosophical Conceptions and Practical Results,* in which he gave full credit to Peirce. The lecture did not become influential until 1904 when it was republished in revised form in *The Journal of Philosophy, Psychology, and Scientific Methods* as "The Pragmatic Method." In the original lecture, which is reprinted below, James judges the differences between materialism and theism by their practical effects on our lives, and he attacks abstract intellectualism. His ideas on pragmatism reached clearer formulation in his article "Pragmatism's Conception of Truth," which appeared in 1907 in *The Journal of Philosophy* and was later in that year published in slightly revised form in his book, *Pragmatism: A New Name for Some Old Ways of Thinking.* The original version of this piece also appears below. James modified Peirce's rigorous definition of "pragmatism" (a criterion of meaning which employed scientific and laboratory standards), and he extended it to a theory of truth, which allowed for particular individual and subjective consequences as the test of an idea, thus making room for religious and moral ideas. Here notions concerning the "cash value," "utility," and "expedience" of ideas were stated.

James' essay, *The Will to Believe* (1896), perhaps his most popular (reprinted below), set forth James' notion that beliefs are justified by their wider consequences. Although James accepted Peirce's scientific criteria for beliefs and considered himself to be "tough minded," generally he nonetheless held that in those areas, such as religion, where scientific proofs are not available either way and where the option to believe is "forced," "momentous," and "alive," we have the "will" or "right" (as he later said) to believe, if our belief is justified by its effect upon our lives. James further developed his pragmatic and liberal approach to religion in his "Gifford Lectures" (*The Varieties of Religious Experience*—1902), an analysis of the psychology of religious experience. James' ethical theory reveals him as a voluntarist, who emphasizes the practical character of moral ideals. In the essays *The Dilemma of Determinism* (1884) and *Is Life Worth Living?* (1895) he argues for the practical necessity of free will and the activist basis of moral choice. Value is ultimately related to the demands and interests of the individual; and social harmony is to be achieved by the reconciliation of individual interests.

James' influence on psychology was considerable, and he is frequently credited with having established the first psychological laboratory in

America. His great work, *The Principles of Psychology* (1890), which took fourteen years to complete, is still considered a classic. Under the influence of Darwin, James developed a biological and functional psychology. His view that consciousness was a "function," not an "entity" or "stuff," contributed to the growth of behaviorism. Some of these ideas are contained in the first part of his article *Does "Consciousness" Exist?* (1904) which is reprinted below.

James espoused what he called a "radical empiricism." His own account of radical empiricism, from the preface to *The Meaning of Truth*, was as follows:

"Radical empiricism . . . consists first of a postulate, next of a statement of fact, and finally of a generalized conclusion. . . . The postulate is that the only things that shall be debatable among philosophers shall be things definable in terms drawn from experience. . . . The statement of fact is that the relations between things, conjunctive as well as disjunctive, are just as much matter of direct particular experience, neither more so nor less so, than the things themselves. . . . The generalized conclusion is that therefore the parts of experience hold together from next to next by relations that are themselves parts of experience. The directly apprehended universe needs, in short, no extraneous transempirical connective support, but possesses in its own right a concatenated or continuous structure." (pp. xii–xiii).

Portions of the second part of *Does "Consciousness" Exist?* and of the article *A World of Pure Experience* (1904) are reprinted below. These two pieces contain his main ideas on radical empiricism, and were later published in his books, *The Meaning of Truth* (1909) and *Essays in Radi-cal Empiricism* (1912). In these writings James discusses the relation of cognition to its object, the role of concepts and percepts, the problem of relations, the sense in which two minds can be said to have the same object, feeling, the mind-body relation, causal activity and efficacy, and the nature of truth. It is here that James maintains that relations are given as real, not merely disconnected individuals. He also sets forth the idea of "pure or neutral experience." Reality is not made of one stuff, but of neutral experience, out of which different relations may be composed. Hence there is no "thought-stuff" different from "thing-stuff," but the same identical piece of "pure experience" can stand for a "fact of consciousness" or a "physical fact," depending upon whether it is taken in one context or another. James points out that pragmatism and radical empiricism are logically distinct; that by accepting one of these theories, one is not automatically committed to accept the other.

Another feature of James' philosophy was his pluralism. Teaching at Harvard at the same time as Royce, and learning a great deal from him, he nonetheless opposed what he considered to be Royce's absolute and monistic "block universe." Instead, James was sympathetic to the conception of the universe as pluralistic, diverse, restless, and free. In *A Pluralistic Universe* (1909), a portion of which is reprinted below, he argued that "Reality . . . *may* exist in distributive form and in the shape not of an all, but of a set of eaches." That is, there are many different kinds of things which exist, not simply one kind. Moreover, the universe may be indeterminate, not fixed, determined, and closed.

Although James' pragmatic theory of truth, which, of all his philosophical theories, attracted the most attention in his own lifetime, is very generally repudiated at the present time and does indeed seem to be quite untenable, his works are full of suggestive and original ideas. James undoubtedly deserves to be ranked as one of the outstanding philosophers of the last 100 years.

PHILOSOPHICAL CONCEPTIONS AND PRACTICAL RESULTS [2]

I will seek to define with you merely what seems to be the most likely direction in which to start upon the trail of truth. Years ago this direction was given to me by an American philosopher whose home is in the East, and whose published works, few as they are and scattered in periodicals, are no fit expression of his powers. I refer to Mr. Charles S. Peirce, with whose very existence as a philosopher I dare say many of you are unacquainted. He is one of the most original of contemporary thinkers; and the principle of practicalism—or pragmatism, as he called it, when I first heard him enunciate it at Cambridge in the early '70's—is the clue or compass by following which I find myself more and more confirmed in believing we may keep our feet upon the proper trail.

Peirce's principle, as we may call it, may be expressed in a variety of ways, all of them very simple. In the *Popular Science Monthly* for January, 1878, he introduces it as follows: The soul and meaning of thought, he says, can never be made to direct itself towards anything but the production of belief, belief being the demicadence which closes a musical phrase in the symphony of our intellectual life. Thought in movement has thus for its only possible motive the attainment of thought at rest. But when our thought about an object has found its rest in belief, then our action on the subject can firmly and safely begin. Beliefs, in short, are really rules for action; and the whole function of thinking is but one step in the production of habits of action. If there were any part of a thought that made no difference in the thought's practical consequences, then that part would be no proper element of the thought's significance. Thus the same thought may be clad in different words; but if the different words suggest no different conduct, they are mere outer accretions, and have no part in the thought's meaning. If, however, they determine conduct differently, they are essential elements of the signif-

[2] Address before the Philosophical Union of the University of California, August 26, 1898. Later reprinted in *The Journal of Philosophy, Psychology and Scientific Methods;* Vol. I (1904), as "The Pragmatic Method."

icance. "Please open the door," and, "*Veuillez ouvrir la porte*," in French, mean just the same thing; but "D——n you, open the door," although in English, *means* something very different. Thus to develop a thought's meaning we need only determine what conduct it is fitted to produce; that conduct is for us its sole significance. And the tangible fact at the root of all our thought-distinctions, however subtle, is that there is no one of them so fine as to consist in anything but a possible difference of practice. To attain perfect clearness in our thoughts of an object, then, we need only consider what effects of a conceivably practical kind the object may involve—what sensations we are to expect from it, and what reactions we must prepare. Our conception of these effects, then, is for us the whole of our conception of the object, so far as that conception has positive significance at all.

This is the principle of Peirce, the principle of pragmatism. I think myself that it should be expressed more broadly than Mr. Peirce expresses it. The ultimate test for us of what a truth means is indeed the conduct it dictates or inspires. But it inspires that conduct because it first foretells some particular turn to our experience which shall call for just that conduct from us. And I should prefer for our purposes this evening to express Peirce's principle by saying that the effective meaning of any philosophic proposition can always be brought down to some particular consequence, in our future practical experience, whether active or passive; the point lying rather in the fact that the experience must be particular, than in the fact that it must be active.

To take in the importance of this principle, one must get accustomed to applying it to concrete cases. Such use as I am able to make of it convinces me that to be mindful of it in philosophical disputations tends wonderfully to smooth out misunderstandings and to bring in peace. If it did nothing else, then, it would yield a sovereignly valuable rule of method for discussion. So I shall devote the rest of this precious hour with you to its elucidation, because I sincerely think that if you once grasp it, it will shut your steps out from many an old false opening, and head you in the true direction for the trail.

One of its first consequences is this. Suppose there are two different philosophical definitions, or propositions, or maxims, or what not, which seem to contradict each other, and about which men dispute. If, by supposing the truth of the one, you can foresee no conceivable practical consequence to anybody at any time or place, which is different from what you would foresee if you supposed the truth of the other, why then the difference between the two propositions is no difference,—it is only a specious and verbal difference, unworthy of further contention. Both formulas mean radically the same thing, although they may say it in such different words. It is astonishing to see how many philosophical disputes collapse into insignificance the moment you subject them to this simple test. There can be no difference which doesn't make a difference—no difference in abstract truth which does not express itself in a difference of concrete fact, and of conduct consequent upon the fact, imposed on somebody, somehow, somewhere, and somewhen. It is true that a certain shrinkage of values often seems to occur in our general formulas when we measure their meaning in this prosaic and practical way. They diminish. But the vastness that is merely vagueness is a false appearance of importance, and not a vastness worth retaining. The x's, y's, and z's always do shrivel, as I have heard a learned friend say, whenever at the end of your algebraic computation they change into so many plain a's, b's, and c's; but the whole function of algebra is, after all, to get them into that more definite shape; and the whole function of philosophy ought to be to find out what definite difference it will make to you and me, at definite instants of our life, if this world-formula or that world-formula be the one which is true.

If we start off with an impossible case, we shall perhaps all the more clearly see the use and scope of our principle. Let us, therefore, put ourselves, in imagination, in a position from which no forecasts of consequence, no dictates of conduct, can possibly be made, so that the principle of pragmatism finds no field of application. Let us, I mean, assume that the present moment is the absolutely last moment of the world, with bare nonentity beyond it, and no hereafter for either experience or conduct.

Now I say that in that case there would be no sense whatever in some of our most urgent and envenomed philosophical and religious debates. The question is, "Is matter the producer of all things, or is a God there too?" would, for example, offer a perfectly idle and insignificant alternative if the world were finished and no more of it to come. Many of us, most of us, I think, now feel as if a terrible coldness and deadness would come over the world were we forced to believe that no informing spirit or purpose had to do with it, but it merely accidentally had come. The actually experienced details of fact might be the same on either hypothesis, some sad, some joyous; some rational, some odd and grotesque; but without a God behind them, we think they would have something ghastly, they would tell no genuine story, there would be no speculation in those eyes that they do glare with. With the God, on the other hand, they would grow solid, warm, and altogether full of real significance. But I say that such an alternation of feelings, reasonable enough in a consciousness that is prospective, as ours now is, and whose world is partly yet to come, would be absolutely senseless and irrational in a purely retrospective consciousness summing up a world already past. For such a consciousness, no emotional interest could attach to the alternative. The problem would be purely intellectual; and if un-aided matter could, with any scientific plausibility, be shown to cipher out the actual facts, then not the faintest shadow ought to cloud the mind, of regret for the God that by the same ciphering would prove needless and disappear from our belief.

For just consider the case sincerely, and say what would be the *worth* of such a God if he *were* there, with his work accomplished and his world run down. He would be worth no more than just that world was worth. To that amount of result, with its mixed merits and defects, his creative power could attain, but go no farther. And since there is to be no future; since the whole value and meaning of the world has been already paid in and actualized in the feelings that went with it in the passing, and now go with it in the ending; since it draws no supplemental significance (such as our real world draws) from its function of preparing something yet to come; why then, by it we take God's measure, as it were. He is the Being who could once for all do *that*; and for that much we are thankful to him, but for nothing more. But now, on the contrary hypothesis, namely, that the bits of matter following their "laws" could make that world and do no less, should we not be just as thankful to them? Wherein should we suffer loss, then, if we dropped God as an hypothesis and made the matter alone responsible? Where would the special deadness, "crassness," and ghastliness come in? And how, experience being what it is once for all, would God's presence in it make it any more "living," any richer in our sight?

Candidly, it is impossible to give any answer to this question. The actually experienced world is supposed to be the same in its details on either hypothesis, "the same, for our praise or blame," as Brown-ing says. It stands there indefeasibly; a gift which can't be taken back. Calling matter the cause of it retracts no single one of the items that have made it up, nor does calling God the cause augment them. They are the God or the atoms, respectively, of just that and no other world. The God, if there, has been doing just what atoms could do—appearing in the character of atoms, so to speak—and earning such gratitude as is due to atoms, and no more. If his presence lends no different turn or issue to the performance, it surely can lend it no increase of dignity. Nor would indignity come to it were he absent, and did the atoms remain the only actors on the stage. When a play is once over, and the curtain down, you really make it no better by claiming an illustrious genius for its author, just as you make it no worse by calling him a common hack.

Thus if no future detail of experience or conduct is to be deduced from our hypothesis, the debate between materialism and theism becomes quite idle and insignificant. Matter and God in that event mean exactly the same thing—the power, namely, neither more nor less, that can make just this mixed, imperfect, yet completed world —and the wise man is he who in such a case would turn his back on such a supererogatory discussion. Accordingly most men instinctively—and a large class of men, the so-called positivists or scientists, deliberately—do turn their backs on philosophical disputes from which nothing in the line of definite future consequences can be seen to follow. The verbal and empty character of our studies is surely a reproach with which you of the Philosophical Union are but too sadly familiar. An escaped Berkeley student said to me at Harvard the other day—he had never been in the philosophical department here—"Words, words, words, are all that you philosophers care for." We philosophers think it all unjust; and yet, if the principle of pragmatism be true, it is a perfectly sound reproach unless the metaphysical alternatives under investigation can be shown to have alternative practical outcomes, however delicate and distant these may be. The common man and the scientist can discover no such outcomes. And if the metaphysician can discern none either, the common man and scientist certainly are in the right of it, as against him. His science is then but pompous trifling; and the endowment of a professorship for such a being would be something really absurd.

Accordingly, in every genuine metaphysical debate some practical issue, however remote, is really involved. To realize this, revert with me to the question of materialism or theism; and place yourselves this time in the real world we live in, the world that has a future, that is yet uncompleted whilst we speak. In this unfinished world the alternative of "materialism or theism?" is intensely practical; and it is worth while for us to spend some minutes of our hour in seeing how truly this is the case. . . .

Theism and materialism, so indifferent when taken retrospectively, point when we take them prospectively to wholly different practical consequences, to opposite outlooks of experience. For, according to the theory of mechanical evolution, the laws of redistribution of matter and motion, though they are certainly to thank for all the good hours which our organisms have ever yielded us and for all the ideals which our minds now frame, are yet fatally certain to undo their work again, and to redissolve everything that they have once evolved. You all know the picture of the last foreseeable state of the dead universe, as evolutionary science gives it forth. I cannot state it better than in Mr. Balfour's words: "The energies of our system will decay, the glory of the sun will be dimmed, and the earth, tideless and inert, will no longer tolerate the race which has for a moment disturbed its solitude. Man will go down into the pit, and all his thoughts will perish. The uneasy consciousness which in this obscure corner has for a brief space broken the contented silence of the universe, will be at rest. Matter will know itself no longer. 'Imperishable monuments' and 'immortal deeds,' death itself, and love stronger than death, will be as if they had not been. Nor will anything that is, be better or worse for all that the labor, genius, devotion, and suffering of man have striven through countless ages to effect."[3]

That is the sting of it, that in the vast driftings of the cosmic weather, though many a jewelled shore appears, and many an enchanted cloud-bank floats away, long lingering ere it be dissolved—even as our world now lingers, for our joy—yet when these transient products are gone, nothing, absolutely *nothing* remains, to represent those particular qualities, those elements of preciousness which they may have enshrined. Dead and gone are they, gone utterly from the very sphere and room of being. Without an echo; without a memory; without an influence on aught that may come after, to make it care for similar ideals. This utter final wreck and tragedy is of the essence of scientific materialism as at present understood. The lower and not the higher forces are the eternal forces, or the last surviving forces within the only cycle of evolution which we can definitely see. Mr. Spencer believes this as much as any one; so why should he argue with us as if we were making silly æsthetic objections to the "grossness" of "matter and motion,"—the principles of his philosophy, —when what really dismays us in it is the disconsolateness of its ulterior practical results?

No, the true objection to materialism is not positive but negative. It would be farcical at this day to make complaint of it for what it *is*, for "grossness." Grossness is what grossness *does*—we now know *that*. We make complaint of it, on the contrary, for what it is *not*—not a permanent warrant for our more ideal interests, not a fulfiller of our remotest hopes.

The notion of God, on the other hand, however inferior it may be in clearness to those mathematical notions so current in mechanical philosophy, has at least this practical superiority over them, that it guarantees an ideal order that shall be permanently preserved. A world with a God in it to say the last word, may indeed burn up or

[3] *The Foundations of Belief*, p. 30.

freeze, but we then think of Him as still mindful of the old ideals
and sure to bring them elsewhere to fruition; so that, where He is,
tragedy is only provisional and partial, and shipwreck and dissolu-
tion not the absolutely final things. This need of an eternal moral
order is one of the deepest needs of our breast. And those poets,
like Dante and Wordsworth, who live on the conviction of such an
order, owe to that fact the extraordinary tonic and consoling power
of their verse. Here then, in these different emotional and practical
appeals, in these adjustments of our concrete attitudes of hope and
expectation, and all the delicate consequences which their differences
entail, lie the real meanings of materialism and theism—not in hair-
splitting abstractions about matter's inner essence, or about the metaphysical attributes of God. Materialism means simply the denial that
the moral order is eternal, and the cutting off of ultimate hopes;
theism means the affirmation of an eternal moral order and the
letting loose of hope. Surely here is an issue genuine enough, for any
one who feels it; and, as long as men are men, it will yield matter
for serious philosophic debate. Concerning this question, at any rate,
the positivists and pooh-pooh-ers of metaphysics are in the wrong.

But possibly some of you may still rally to their defence. Even
whilst admitting that theism and materialism make different prophe-
cies of the world's future, you may yourselves pooh-pooh the difference as something so infinitely remote as to mean nothing for a
sane mind. The essence of a sane mind, you may say, is to take
shorter views, and to feel no concern about such chimæras as the
latter end of the world. Well, I can only say that if you say this, you
do injustice to human nature. Religious melancholy is not disposed
of by a simple flourish of the word "insanity." The absolute things,
the last things, the over-lapping things, are the truly philosophic
concern; all superior minds feel seriously about them, and the mind
with the shortest views is simply the mind of the more shallow man.

However, I am willing to pass over these very distant outlooks
on the ultimate, if any of you so insist. The theistic controversy can
still serve to illustrate the principle of pragmatism for us well enough,
without driving us so far afield. If there be a God, it is not likely
that he is confined solely to making differences in the world's latter
end; he probably makes differences all along its course. Now the
principle of practicalism says that the very meaning of the conception of God lies in those differences which must be made in our
experience if the conception be true. God's famous inventory of perfections, as elaborated by dogmatic theology, either means nothing,
says our principle, or it implies certain definite things that we can
feel and do at particular moments of our lives, things which we
could not feel and should not do were no God present and were the

business of the universe carried on by material atoms instead. So far as our conceptions of the Deity involve no such experiences, so far they are meaningless and verbal,—scholastic entities and abstractions, as the positivists say, and fit objects for their scorn. But so far as they do involve such definite experiences, God means something for us, and may be real.

Now if we look at the definitions of God made by dogmatic theology, we see immediately that some stand and some fall when treated by this test. God, for example, as any orthodox text-book will tell us, is a being existing not only *per se*, or by himself, as created beings exist, but *a se*, or from himself; and out of this "aseity" flow most of his perfections. He is for example, necessary; absolute; infinite in all respects; and single. He is simple, not compounded of essence and existence, substance and accident, actuality and potentiality, or subject and attributes, as are other things. He belongs to no genus; he is inwardly and outwardly unalterable; he knows and wills all things, and first of all his own infinite self, in one indivisible eternal act. And he is absolutely self-sufficing, and infinitely happy. Now in which one of us practical Americans here assembled does this conglomeration of attributes awaken any sense of reality? And if in no one, then why not? Surely because such attributes awaken no responsive active feelings and call for no particular conduct of our own. How does God's "aseity" come home to *you*? What specific thing can I do to adapt myself to his "simplicity"? Or how determine our behavior henceforward if his "felicity" is anyhow absolutely complete? In the '50's and '60's Captain Mayne Reid was the great writer of boys' books of out-of-door adventure. He was forever extolling the hunters and field-observers of living animals' habits, and keeping up a fire of invective against the "closet-naturalists," as he called them, the collectors and classifiers, and handlers of skeletons and skins. When I was a boy I used to think that a closet-naturalist must be the vilest type of wretch under the sun. But surely the systematic theologians are the closet-naturalists of the Deity, even in Captain Mayne Reid's sense. Their orthodox deduction of God's attributes is nothing but a shuffling and matching of pedantic dictionary-adjectives, aloof from morals, aloof from human needs, something that might be worked out from the mere word "God" by a logical machine of wood and brass as well as by a man of flesh and blood. The attributes which I have quoted have absolutely nothing to do with religion, for religion is a living practical affair. Other parts, indeed, of God's traditional description do have practical connection with life, and have owed all their historic importance to that fact. His omniscience, for example, and his justice. With the one he sees us in the dark, with the other he rewards and punishes what he sees. So do his ubiquity and eternity and unalterability appeal to our confidence, and his goodness banish our fears. Even attributes of less meaning to this present audience have in past times so appealed. One of the chief attributes of God, according to the orthodox theology, is his infinite love of himself, proved by asking the question, "By what but an infinite object can an infinite affection be appeased?" An immediate consequence of this primary self-love of God is the orthodox dogma that the manifestation of his own glory is God's primal purpose in creation; and that dogma has certainly made very efficient practical connection with life. It is true that we ourselves are tending to outgrow this old monarchical conception of a Deity with his "court" and pomp—"his state is kingly, thousands to his bidding speed," etc.—but there is no denying the enormous influence it has had over ecclesiastical history, nor, by repercussion, over the history of European states. And yet even these more real and significant attributes have the trail of the serpent over them as the books on theology have actually worked them out. One feels that, in the theologians' hands, they are only a set of dictionary-adjectives, mechanically deduced; logic has stepped into the place of vision, professionalism into that of life. Instead of bread we get a stone; instead of a fish, a serpent. Did such a conglomeration of abstract general terms give really the gist of our knowledge of the Deity, divinity-schools might indeed continue to flourish, but religion, vital religion, would have taken its flight from this world. What keeps religion going is something else than abstract definitions and systems of logically concatenated adjectives, and something different from faculties of theology and their professors. All these things are after-effects, secondary accretions upon a mass of concrete religious experiences, connecting themselves with feeling and conduct that renew themselves *in saecula saeculorum* in the lives of humble private men. If you ask what these experiences are, they are conversations with the unseen, voices and visions, responses to prayer, changes of heart, deliverances from fear, inflowings of help, assurances of support, whenever certain persons set their own internal attitude in certain appropriate ways. The power comes and goes and is lost, and can be found only in a certain definite direction, just as if it were a concrete material thing. These direct experiences of a wider spiritual life with which our superficial consciousness is continuous, and with which it keeps up an intense commerce, form the primary mass of direct religious experience on which all hearsay religion rests, and which furnishes that notion of an ever-present God, out of which systematic theology thereupon proceeds to make capital in its own unreal pedantic way. What the word "God" means is just those passive and active experiences of your life. Now, my friends, it is quite immaterial to my purpose whether you yourselves enjoy and venerate these experiences, or whether you stand aloof, and, viewing them in others, suspect them of being illusory and vain. Like all other human experiences, they too certainly share in the general liability to illusion and mistake. They need not be infallible. But they are certainly the originals of the God-idea, and theology is the translation; and you remember that I am now using the God-idea merely as an example, not to discuss as to its truth or error, but only to show how well the principle of pragmatism works. That the God of systematic theology should exist or not exist is a matter of small practical moment. At most it means that you may continue uttering certain abstract words and that you must stop using others. But if the God of these particular experiences be false, it is an awful thing for you, if you are one of those whose lives are stayed on such experiences. The theistic controversy, trivial enough if we take it merely academically and theologically, is of tremendous significance if we test it by its results for actual life.

I can best continue to recommend the principle of practicalism to you by keeping in the neighborhood of this theological idea. I reminded you a few minutes ago that the old monarchical notion of the Deity as a sort of Louis the Fourteenth of the Heavens is losing nowadays much of its ancient prestige. Religious philosophy, like all philosophy, is growing more and more idealistic. And in the philosophy of the Absolute, so called, that post-Kantian form of idealism which is carrying so many of our higher minds before it, we have the triumph of what in old times was summarily disposed of as the pantheistic heresy,—I mean the conception of God, not as the extraneous creator, but as the indwelling spirit and substance of the world. I know not where one can find a more candid, more clear, or, on the whole, more persuasive statement of this theology of Absolute Idealism than in the addresses made before this very Union three years ago by your own great Californian philosopher (whose colleague at Harvard I am proud to be), Josiah Royce. His contributions to the resulting volume, *The Conception of God*, form a very masterpiece of popularization. Now you will remember, many of you, that in the discussion that followed Professor Royce's first address, the debate turned largely on the ideas of unity and plurality, and on the question whether, if God be One in All and All in All, "One with the unity of a single instant," as Royce calls it, "forming in His wholeness one luminously transparent moment," any room is left for real morality or freedom. Professor Howison, in particular, was earnest in urging that morality and freedom are relations between a manifold of selves, and that under the régime of Royce's monistic Absolute Thought "no true manifold of selves is or can be provided for." I will not go into any of the details of that particular discussion, but just ask you to consider for a moment whether, in general, any discussion about monism or pluralism, any argument over the unity of the universe, would not necessarily be brought into a shape where it tends to straighten itself out, by bringing our principle of practical results to bear.

The question whether the world is at bottom One or Many is a typical metaphysical question. Long has it raged! In its crudest form it is an exquisite example of the *loggerheads* of metaphysics. "I say it is one great fact," Parmenides and Spinoza exclaim. "I say it is many little facts," reply the atomists and associationists. "I say it is both one and many, many in one," say the Hegelians; and in the ordinary popular discussions we rarely get beyond this barren reiteration by the disputants of their pet adjectives of number. But is it not first of all clear that when we take such an adjective as "One" absolutely and abstractly, its meaning is so vague and empty that it makes no difference whether we affirm or deny it? Certainly this universe is not the mere number One; and yet you can number it "one," if you like, in talking about it as contrasted with other possible worlds numbered "two" and "three" for the occasion. What exact thing do you *practically* mean by "One," when you call the universe One, is the first question you must ask. In what ways does the oneness come home to your own personal life? By what difference does it express itself in your experience? How can you act differently towards a universe which is one? Inquired into in this way, the unity might grow clear and be affirmed in some ways and denied in others, and so cleared up, even though a certain vague and worshipful portentousness might disappear from the notion of it in the process.

For instance, one practical result that follows when we have one thing to handle, is that we can pass from one part of it to another without letting go of the thing. In this sense oneness must be partly denied and partly affirmed of our universe. Physically we can pass continuously in various manners from one part of it to another part. But logically and psychically the passage seems less easy, for there is no obvious transition from one mind to another, or from minds to physical things. You have to step off and get on again; so that in these ways the world is not one, as measured by that practical test.

Another practical meaning of oneness is susceptibility of collection. A collection is one, though the things that compose it be many. Now, can we practically "collect" the universe? Physically, of course we cannot. And mentally we cannot, if we take it concretely in its details. But if we take it summarily and abstractly, then we collect it mentally whenever we refer to it, even as I do now when I fling the term "universe" at it, and so seem to leave a mental ring around it. It is plain however, that such abstract noetic unity (as one might call it) is practically an extremely insignificant thing.

Again, oneness may mean generic sameness, so that you can treat all parts of the collection by one rule and get the same results. It is evident that in this sense the oneness of our world is incomplete, for in spite of much generic sameness in its elements and items, they still remain of many irreducible kinds. You can't pass by mere logic all over the field of it.

Its elements have, however, an affinity or commensurability with each other, are not wholly irrelevant, but can be compared, and fit together after certain fashions. This again might practically mean that they were one *in origin*, and that, tracing them backwards, we should find them arising in a single primal causal fact. Such unity of origin would have definite practical consequences, would have them for our scientific life at least.

I can give only these hasty superficial indications of what I mean when I say that it tends to clear up the quarrel between monism and pluralism to subject the notion of unity to such practical tests. On the other hand, it does but perpetuate strife and misunderstanding to continue talking of it in an absolute and mystical way. I have little doubt myself that this old quarrel might be completely smoothed out to the satisfaction of all claimants, if only the maxim of Peirce were methodically followed here. The current monism on the whole still keeps talking in too abstract a way. It says the world must be either pure disconnectedness, no universe at all, or absolute unity. It insists that there is no stopping-place half way. Any connection whatever, says this monism, is only possible if there be still more connection, until at last we are driven to admit the absolutely total connection required. But this absolutely total connection either means nothing, is the mere word "one" spelt long; or else it means the sum of all the partial connections that can possibly be conceived. I believe that when we thus attack the question, and set ourselves to search for these possible connections, and conceive each in a definite practical way, the dispute is already in a fair way to be settled beyond the chance of misunderstanding, by a compromise in which the Many and the One both get their lawful rights.

But I am in danger of becoming technical; so I must stop right here, and let you go.

I am happy to say that it is the English-speaking philosophers who first introduced the custom of interpreting the meaning of conceptions by asking what difference they make for life. Mr. Peirce has only expressed in the form of an explicit maxim what their sense for reality led them all instinctively to do. The great English way of investigating a conception is to ask yourself right off, "What is it *known as?* In what facts does it result? What is its *cash-value*, in terms of particular experience? and what special difference would come into the world according as it were true or false?" Thus does Locke treat the conception of personal identity. What you mean by it is just your chain of memories, says he. That is the only concretely verifiable part of its significance. All further ideas about it, such as the oneness or manyness of the spiritual substance on which it is based, are therefore void of intelligible meaning; and propositions touching such ideas may be indifferently affirmed or denied. So Berkeley with his "matter." The cash-value of matter is our physical sensations. That is what it is known as, all that we concretely verify of its conception. That therefore is the whole meaning of the word "matter"—any other pretended meaning is mere wind of words. Hume does the same thing with causation. It is known as habitual antecedence, and tendency on our part to look for something definite to come. Apart from this practical meaning it has no significance whatever, and books about it may be committed to the flames, says Hume. Stewart and Brown, James Mill, John Mill, and Bain, have followed more or less consistently the same method; and Shadworth Hodgson has used it almost as explicitly as Mr. Peirce. These writers have many of them no doubt been too sweeping in their negations; Hume, in particular, and James Mill, and Bain. But when all is said and done, it was they, not Kant, who introduced "the critical method" into philosophy, the one method fitted to make philosophy a study worthy of serious men. For what seriousness can possibly remain in debating philosophic propositions that will never make an appreciable difference to us in action? And what matters it, when all propositions are practically meaningless, which of them be called true or false?

The shortcomings and the negations and baldnesses of the English philosophers in question come, not from their eye to merely practical results, but solely from their failure to track the practical results completely enough to see how far they extend. Hume can be corrected and built out, and his beliefs enriched, by using Humian principles exclusively, and without making any use of the circuitous and ponderous artificialities of Kant. It is indeed a somewhat pathetic matter, as it seems to me, that this is not the course which the actual history of philosophy has followed. Hume had no English successors of adequate ability to complete him and correct his negations; so it happened, as a matter of fact, that building out of critical philosophy has mainly been left to thinkers who were under the influence of Kant. Even in England and this country it is with Kantian catch-words and categories that the fuller view of life is pursued, and in our universities it is the courses in transcendentalism that kindle the enthusiasm of the more ardent students, whilst the courses in English philosophy are committed to a secondary place. I cannot think that this is exactly as it should be. And I say this not out of national jingoism, for jingoism has no place in philosophy; or out of excitement over the great Anglo-American alliance against the world, of which we nowadays hear so much—though heaven knows that to that alliance I wish a Godspeed. I say it because I sincerely believe that the English spirit in philosophy is intellectually, as well as practically and morally, on the saner, sounder, and truer path. Kant's mind is the rarest and most intricate of all possible antique bric-a-brac museums, and connoisseurs and dilettanti will always wish to visit it and see the wondrous and racy contents. The temper of the dear old man about his work is perfectly delectable. And yet he is really—although I shrink with some terror from saying such a thing before some of you here present—at bottom a mere curio, a "specimen." I mean by this a perfectly definite thing: I believe that Kant bequeaths to us not one single conception which is both indispensable to philosophy and which philosophy either did not possess before him, or was not destined inevitably to acquire after him through the growth of men's reflection upon the hypotheses by which science interprets nature. The true line of philosophic progress lies, in short, it seems to me, not so much *through* Kant as *round* him to the point where now we stand. Philosophy can perfectly well outflank him, and build herself up into adequate fulness by prolonging more directly the older English lines.

PRAGMATISM'S CONCEPTION OF TRUTH [4]

When Clerk-Maxwell was a child it is written that he had a mania for having everything explained to him, and that when people put him off with vague verbal accounts of any phenomenon he would interrupt them impatiently by saying, "Yes; but I want you to tell me the *particular go* of it!" Had his question been about truth, only a pragmatist could have told him the particular go of it. I believe that our contemporary pragmatists, especially Messrs. Schiller and Dewey, have given the only tenable account of this subject. It is a very ticklish subject, sending subtle rootlets into all kinds of crannies, and hard to treat in the sketchy way that alone befits a public lec-

[4] The sixth of a course of eight lectures on "Pragmatism" delivered at the Lowell Institute, Boston, November–December, 1906. Reprinted in *The Journal of Philosophy, Psychology and Scientific Methods*, Vol. IV, No. 6, (1907) pp. 141–155.

ture. But the Schiller-Dewey view of truth has been so ferociously attacked by rationalistic philosophers, and so abominably misunderstood, that here, if anywhere, is the point where a clear and simple statement should be made.

I fully expect to see the pragmatist view of truth run through the classic stages of a theory's career. First, you know, a new theory is attacked as absurd; then it is admitted to be true, but obvious and insignificant; finally it is seen to be so important that its adversaries claim that they themselves discovered it. Our doctrine of truth is at present in the first of these three stages, with symptoms of the second stage having begun in certain quarters. I wish that this lecture might help it beyond the first stage in the eyes of many of you.

Truth, as any dictionary will tell you, is a property of certain of our ideas. It means their "agreement," as falsity means their disagreement, with "reality." Pragmatists and intellectualists both accept this definition as a matter of course. They begin to quarrel only after the question is raised as to what may precisely be meant by the term "agreement," and what by the term "reality," when reality is taken as something for our ideas to agree with.

In answering these questions the pragmatists are more analytic and painstaking, the intellectualists more offhand and irreflective. The popular notion is that a true idea must copy its reality. Like other popular views, this one follows the analogy of the most usual experience. Our true ideas of sensible things do indeed copy them. Shut your eyes and think of yonder clock on the wall, and you get just such a true picture or copy of its dial. But your idea of its "works" (unless you are a clock-maker) is much less of a copy, yet it passes muster, for it in no way clashes with the reality. Even though it should shrink to the mere word "works," that word still serves you truly; and when you speak of the "time-keeping function" of the clock, or of its spring's "elasticity," it is hard to see exactly what your ideas can copy.

You perceive that there is a problem here. Where our ideas can not copy definitely their object, what does agreement with that object mean? A Berkeleian idealist might say that they are true whenever they are what God means that we ought to think about that object. But transcendental idealism holds the copy-view all through. Its doctrine is that our ideas possess truth just in proportion as they approach to being copies of the absolute's eternal way of thinking.

These views, you see, invite pragmatistic discussion. But the great assumption of the intellectualists is that truth means essentially an inert static relation. When you've got your true idea of anything, there's an end of the matter. You're in possession; you *know*; you've fulfilled your thinking destiny. You are where you ought to be mentally; you have obeyed your categorical imperative; and nothing more need follow on that climax of your rational destiny. Epistemologically you are in equilibrium.

Pragmatism, on the other hand, asks its usual question. "Grant an idea or belief to be true," it says, "what concrete difference will its being true make in any one's actual life? How will the truth be realized? What experiences will be different from those which would obtain if the belief were false? What, in short, is the truth's cash value in experiential terms?"

The moment pragmatism asks this question, it sees the answer: *True ideas are those that we can validate, corroborate and verify. False ideas are those that we can not.* That is the practical difference it makes to us to have true ideas; that, therefore, is the meaning of truth, for it is all that truth is known as.

This thesis is what I have to defend. The truth of an idea is not a stagnant property inherent in it. Truth *happens* to an idea. It *becomes* true, is *made* true by events. Its verity *is* in fact an event, a process, the process, namely, of its verifying itself, its veri-*fication*. Its validity is the process of its valid-*ation*.

This trivial-sounding thesis has results which it will take the rest of my hour to explain.

Let me begin by reminding you of the fact that the possession of true thoughts means everywhere the possession of invaluable instruments of action; and that our duty to gain truth, so far from being a blank command from out of the blue, or a "stunt" self-imposed by our intellect, can account for itself by excellent practical reasons.

The importance to human life of having true beliefs about matters of fact is a thing too notorious. We live in a world of realities that can be infinitely useful or infinitely harmful. Ideas that tell us which of them to expect count as the true ideas in all this primary sphere of verification, and the pursuit of such ideas is a primary human duty. The possession of truth, so far from being here an end in itself, is only a preliminary means towards other vital satisfactions. If I am lost in the woods and starved, and find what looks like a cow-path, it is of the utmost importance that I should think of a human habitation at the end of it, for if I do so and follow it, I save myself. The true thought is useful here because the house which is its object is useful. The practical value of true ideas is thus primarily derived from the practical importance of their objects to us. Their objects are, indeed, not important at all times. I may on another occasion have no use for the house; and then my idea of it, however verifiable, will be practically irrelevant, and had better remain latent. Yet since almost any object may some day become temporarily important, the advantage of having a general stock of *extra* truths, of ideas that shall be true of merely possible situations, is obvious. We store such extra truths away in our memories, and with the overflow we fill our books of reference. Whenever such an extra truth becomes practically relevant to one of our emergencies, it passes from cold-storage to do work in the world, and our belief in it grows active. You can say of it then either that "it is useful because it is true" or that "it is true because it is useful." Both these phrases mean exactly the same thing, namely, that here is an idea that gets fulfilled and can be verified. Truth is the name for what starts the verification-process, use is the name for what completes it. True ideas would never have been singled out as such, would never have acquired a class-name, least of all a name suggesting value, unless they had been useful from the outset.

From this simple cue pragmatism gets her general notion of truth as something essentially bound up with the way in which one moment in our experience may lead us towards other moments which it will be worth while to have been led to. Primarily, and on the common-sense level, the truth of a state of mind means this function of *a leading that is worth while*. When a moment in our experience of any kind whatever inspires us with a thought that is true, that means that sooner or later we dip by that thought's guidance into the particulars of experience again and make advantageous connection with them. This is a vague enough statement, but I beg you to retain it, for it is essential.

Our experience meanwhile is all shot through with regularities. One bit of it can warn us to get ready for another bit, can "intend" or be "significant of" that remoter object. The object's advent is the significance's verification. Truth, in these cases, meaning nothing but eventual verification, is manifestly incompatible with waywardness on our part. Woe to him whose beliefs play fast and loose with the order which realities follow in his experience: They will lead him nowhere or else make false connections.

By "realities" or "objects" here, we mean either "things" of common sense, sensibly present, or else common-sense relations, such as dates, places, distances, kinds, activities. Following our mental image of a house along the cow-path, we actually come to see the house; we get the image's full verification. Such simply verified leadings are certainly the originals and prototypes of the truth-process. Experience offers indeed other forms of truth-process, but they are all conceivable as primary verifications arrested, multiplied or substituted one for another.

Take, for instance, yonder object on the wall. You and I consider it to be a "clock," although no one of us has seen the hidden works that make it one. We let our notion pass for true without attempting to verify. If truth mean verification-process essentially, ought we then to call such unverified truths as this abortive? No, for they form the overwhelmingly large number of the truths we live by. Indirect as well as direct verifications pass muster. Where circumstantial evidence is sufficient, we can go without eye-witnessing. Just as we here assume Japan to exist without ever having been there, because it *works* to do so, everything we know conspiring with the belief, and nothing interfering, so we assume that thing to be a clock. We *use* it as a clock, regulating the length of our lecture by it. The verification of the assumption here means its leading to no frustration or contradiction. Verifi*ability* of wheels and weights and pendulum is as good as verification. For one truth-process completed there are a million in our lives that function in this state of nascency. They turn us *towards* direct verification; lead us into the surroundings of the objects they envisage; and then, if everything runs on harmoniously, we are so sure that verification is possible that we omit it, and are usually justified by all that happens.

Truth lives, in fact, for the most part on a credit system. Our thoughts and beliefs "pass" so long as nothing challenges them, just as bank notes pass so long as nobody refuses them. But this all points to direct face-to-face verifications somewhere, without which the fabric of truth collapses like a financial system with no cash basis whatever. You accept my verification of one thing, I yours of another. We trade on each other's truth. Beliefs verified concretely by *somebody* are the posts of the whole superstructure.

Another great reason for waiving complete verification in the usual business of life is that all things exist in kinds and not singly. Our world is found once for all to have that peculiarity. So that when we have once directly verified our ideas about one specimen of a kind, we consider ourselves free to apply them to other specimens without verification. A mind that habitually discerns the kind of thing before it, and acts by the law of the kind immediately, without pausing to verify, will be a "true" mind in ninety-nine out of a hundred emergencies, proved so by its conduct fitting everything it meets, and getting no refutation.

Indirectly or only potentially verifying processes may thus be true as well as full verification-processes. They work as true processes would work, give us the same advantages, and claim our recognition for the same reasons. All this on the common-sense level of matters of fact, which we are alone considering.

But matters of fact are not our only stock in trade. *Relations among ideas* form another sphere where true and false beliefs obtain, and here the beliefs are absolute, or unconditional. When they are true they bear the name either of definitions or of principles. It is either a principle or a definition that 1 and 1 make 2, that 2 and 1 make 3, and so on; that white differs less from gray than it does from black; that when the cause begins to act the effect also commences. Such propositions hold of all possible "ones," of all conceivable "whites" and "grays" and "causes." The objects here are mental objects. Their relations are obvious at a glance, and no sense-verification is necessary. Moreover, once true, always true, of those same mental objects. Truth here has an "eternal" character. If you can find a concrete thing anywhere that is "one" or "white" or "gray," or an "effect," then your principles will everlastingly apply to it. The only risk is in the finding. It is but one more case of ascertaining the kind, and applying the law of its kind to the particular object. You are sure to get truth if you can but name the kind rightly, for your principles hold good of everything of that kind without exception. If they failed to obtain concretely, you would say that you had classed your objects wrongly.

In this realm of mental relations, truth again is an affair of leading. We pass from one abstract idea to another, framing in the end great systems of logical and mathematical truth, under the respective terms of which the sensible facts of experience eventually arrange themselves, so that our eternal truths hold good of realities also. This marriage of fact and theory is endlessly useful. What we say is here already true in advance of special verification, if we have subsumed our objects rightly. Our ready-made ideal framework for all sorts of possible objects follows from the very structure of our thinking. We can no more play fast and loose with these abstract relations than we can do so with our sense-experiences. They coerce us; we must treat them consistently, whether or not we like the results. The rules of addition apply to our debts as rigorously as to our assets. The hundredth decimal of π is pre-determined ideally now, though no one may have computed it. If we should ever need the figure in our dealings with an actual circle we should need to have it given rightly, calculated by the usual rules; for it is the same kind of truth that those rules elsewhere calculate.

Between the coercions of the sensible order and those of the ideal order, our mind is thus wedged tightly. Our ideas must agree with realities, be such realities concrete or abstract, be they facts or be they principles, under penalty of endless inconsistency and frustration.

So far, intellectualists can raise no protest. They can only say that we have barely touched the skin of the matter.

Realities mean, then, either concrete facts, or abstract kinds of things, and relations perceived intuitively between them. But what now does "agreement" with such realities mean?—to quote again the definition of truth that is current.

Here it is that pragmatism and intellectualism begin to part company. Primarily, no doubt, to agree means to copy, but we saw that the mere word "clock" would do instead of a mental picture of its works, and that of many realities our ideas can only be symbols and not copies. "Past time," "power," "spontaneity,"—how can our mind copy such realities?

To "agree" in the widest sense with a reality, *can only mean to be guided either straight up to it or into its surroundings, or to be put into such working touch with it as to handle either it or something connected with it better than if we disagreed.* Better either intellectually or practically! And often agreement will only mean the negative fact that nothing contradictory from the quarter of that reality comes to interfere with the way in which our ideas guide us elsewhere. To copy a reality is, indeed, one way of agreeing with it, but it is far from being essential. The essential thing is the process of being guided. Any idea that helps us to deal with either the reality or its belongings, that doesn't entangle our progress in frustrations, that *fits*, in fact, and adapts our life to the reality's whole setting, will agree sufficiently to meet the requirement. It will hold true of that reality.

Thus, *names* are just as "true" or "false" as definite mental pictures are. They set up similar verification-processes, and lead to fully equivalent practical results.

All human thinking gets discursified; we exchange ideas; we lend and borrow verifications, get them from one another by means of social intercourse. All truth thus gets verbally built out, stored up, and made available for every one. Hence, we must *talk* consistently just as we must *think* consistently; for both in talk and thought we deal with kinds. Names are arbitrary, but once understood, they must be kept to. We mustn't now call Abel "Cain" or Cain "Abel." If we do, we ungear ourselves from the book of Genesis, and from all its connections with the universe of speech and fact down to the present time. We throw ourselves out of whatever truth that whole system may embody.

The overwhelming majority of our true ideas admit of no direct or face-to-face verification—those of past history, for example, as of Cain and Abel. The stream of time can be remounted only verbally, or verified indirectly by the present prolongations or effects of what the past harbored. Yet if they agree with these verbalities and effects, we can know that our ideas of the past are true. *As true as past time itself was,* so true was Julius Cæsar, so true were ante-diluvian monsters, all in their proper dates and settings. That past time itself was, is guaranteed by its coherence with everything that's present. True as the present *is,* the past *was* also.

Agreement thus turns out to be essentially an affair of leading—leading that is useful because it is into quarters that contain objects that are important. True ideas lead us into useful verbal and conceptual quarters as well as directly up to useful sensible termini. They lead to consistency, stability and flowing human intercourse. They lead away from eccentricity and isolation, from foiled and barren thinking. The untrammeled flowing of the leading-process, its general freedom from clash and contradiction, passes for its indirect verification; but all roads lead to Rome, and in the end, and eventually, all true processes must lead to the face of directly verifying sensible experiences *somewhere.*

Such is the large loose way in which the pragmatist interprets the word agreement. He treats it altogether practically. He lets it cover any process of conduction from a present idea to a future terminus, provided only it run prosperously. It is only thus that "scientific" ideas, flying as they do beyond common sense, can be said to agree with their realities. It is *as if* reality were made of ether, atoms or electrons, but we mustn't think so literally. The term "energy" doesn't even pretend to stand for anything "objective." It is only a way of measuring the surface of phenomena so as to *string* their changes on a simple formula.

Yet in the choice of these man-made formulas we can not be capricious any more than we can be capricious on the common-sense practical level. We must find a theory that will *work;* and that means something extremely difficult; for our theory must mediate between all previous truths and certain new experiences. It must derange common sense and previous belief as little as possible, and it must lead to some sensible terminus or other that can be verified exactly. To "work" means both these things; and the squeeze is so tight that there is little loose play for any theory. They are wedged and controlled as nothing else is. Yet sometimes alternative theoretic formulas are equally compatible with all the truths we know, and then we choose between them for subjective reasons. We choose the kind of theory to which we are already partial; we follow "elegance" or "economy." Clerk-Maxwell somewhere says it would be "poor scientific taste" to choose the more complex of two equally well-evidenced conceptions; and you will all agree with him. Truth here is what gives us the maximum possible sum of satisfactions, taste included, but consistency both with previous truth and with novel fact is always the most imperious claimant.

I have led you through a very sandy desert. But now, if I may be allowed so vulgar an expression, we begin to taste the milk in the cocoanut. Our rationalist critics here discharge their batteries upon us, and to reply to them will take us out from all this dryness into full sight of a momentous philosophical alternative.

Our account of truth is an account of truths in the plural, of processes of leading, realized *in rebus*, and having only this quality in common, that they *pay*. They pay by guiding us into or towards some part of a system that dips at numerous points into sense-percepts, which we may copy mentally or not, but with which at any rate we are now in the kind of commerce vaguely designated as verification. Truth for us is simply a collective name for verification-processes, just as health, wealth, strength, etc., are names for other processes connected with life, and also pursued because it pays to pursue them. Truth is *made*, just as health, wealth and strength are made, in the course of experience.

Here rationalism is instantaneously up in arms against us. I can imagine a rationalist to talk as follows:

"Truth is not made," he will say; "it absolutely obtains, being a unique relation that does not wait upon any process, but shoots straight over the head of experience, and hits its reality every time. Our belief that yon thing on the wall is a clock is true already, although no one in the whole history of the world should verify it. The abstract quality of standing in that transcendent relation is what makes any thought true that possesses it, whether or not there be verification. You pragmatists put the cart before the horse in making truth's being reside in verification-processes. These are merely signs of its being, merely our lame ways of ascertaining, after the fact, which of our ideas already has possessed the wondrous quality. The quality itself is timeless, like all essences and natures. Thoughts partake of it directly, as they partake of falsity or of irrelevancy. It can't be analyzed away into pragmatic consequences."

The whole plausibility of this rationalist tirade is due to the fact to which we have already paid so much attention. In our world, namely, abounding as it does in things of similar kinds and similarly associated, one verification serves for others of its kind, and one great use of knowing things is to be led not so much to them as to their associates, especially to human talk about them. The quality of truth, obtaining *ante rem*, pragmatically means, then, the fact that in such a world innumerable ideas work better by their indirect or possible than by their direct and actual verification. Truth *ante rem* means only verifiability, then; or else it is a case of the stock rationalist delusion of treating the *name* of a concrete phenomenal reality as an independent metaphysical entity, and placing it behind the reality as its explanation. Professor Mach quotes somewhere an epigram of Lessing's:

Sagt Hänschen Schlau zu Vetter Fritz,
"Wie kommt es, Vetter Fritzen,
Dass grad' die reichsten in der Welt,
Das meiste Geld besitzen?"

Hänschen Schlau here treats the principle "wealth" as something distinct from the facts denoted by the man's being rich. It antedates them; the facts become only a sort of secondary coincidence with the rich man's essential nature.

In the case of "wealth" we all see the fallacy. We know that wealth is but a name for concrete processes that certain men's lives play a part in, and not a natural excellence found in Messrs. Rockefeller and Carnegie, but not in the rest of us.

Like wealth, health also lives *in rebus*. It is a name for processes, as digestion, circulation, sleep, etc., that go on happily, though in this instance we are more inclined to think of it as a principle and say the man digests and sleeps so well because he is so healthy.

With "strength" we are, I think, more rationalistic still, decidedly inclined to treat it as an excellence preexisting in the man and explanatory of the herculean performances of his muscles.

With "truth" most people go over the border entirely, and treat the rationalistic account as self-evident. But really all these words in *th* are exactly similar. Truth exists *ante rem* just as much and as little as the other things do.

The scholastics made much of the distinction between habit and act. Health *in actu* means, among other things, good sleeping and digesting. But a healthy man need not always be sleeping, or always digesting, any more than a wealthy man need be always handling money, or a strong man always lifting weights. All such qualities sink to the status of "habits" between their times of exercise; and similarly truth becomes a habit of certain of our ideas and beliefs in their intervals of rest from verifying activity. But that activity is the root of the whole matter, and the condition of there being any habit to exist in the intervals.

"The true," to put it very briefly, is only the expedient in the way of our thinking, just as "the right" is only the expedient in the way of our behaving. Expedient in almost any fashion; and expedient in the long run and on the whole, of course; for what meets expediently all the experience in sight won't necessarily meet all farther experiences equally satisfactorily. Experience, as we know, has ways of *boiling over*, and making us correct our present formulas.

The "absolutely" true, meaning what no further experience will ever alter, is that ideal vanishing-point towards which we imagine that all our temporary truths will some day converge. It runs on all fours with the perfectly wise man, and with the absolutely complete experience; and, like these other ideals, it may never fully eventuate or materialize. We have to live to-day by what truth we can get to-day, and be ready to-morrow to call it falsehood. Ptolemaic astronomy, Euclidean space, Aristotelian logic, scholastic metaphysics, were expedient for centuries, but human experience has boiled over those limits, and we now call these things only relatively true, or true within those borders of experience. "Absolutely" they are false; for we know that those limits were casual, and might have been transcended by past theorists just as they are by present thinkers.

When new experiences lead to retrospective judgments, using the past tense, what these judgments utter *was* true, even though no past thinker had been led there. We live forwards, a Danish thinker has said, but we understand backwards. The present sheds a backward light on the world's previous processes. They may have been truth-processes for the actors in them. They are not so for one who knows the later revelations of the story.

This regulative notion of a potential better truth to be established later, possibly to be established some day absolutely, and having powers of retroactive legislation, turns its face, like all pragmatist notions, towards concreteness of fact and towards the future. Like the half-truths, the absolute truth will have to be *made*, made as a relation incidental to the growth of a mass of verification-experience, to which the half-true ideas are all along contributing their quota.

I have already insisted on the fact that truth is made largely out of previous truths. Men's beliefs at any time are so much experience *funded*. But they are themselves parts of the sum total of the world's experience, and become matter, therefore, for the next day's funding operations. So far as reality means experienceable reality, both it and the truths men gain about it are everlastingly in process of mutation —mutation towards a definite goal, it may be—but still mutation.

Mathematicians can solve problems with two variables. On the Newtonian theory, for instance, acceleration varies with distance, but distance also varies with acceleration. In the realm of truth-processes facts come independently and determine our beliefs provisionally. But these beliefs make us act, and as fast as they do so, they bring new facts into sight which redetermine the beliefs accordingly. So the whole coil and ball of truth, as it rolls up, is the product of a double influence. Truths emerge from facts; but they dip forward into facts again and add to them; which facts again create or reveal new truth (the word is indifferent) and so on *ad infinitum*. The facts themselves meanwhile are not true. They simply *are*. Truth is the function of beliefs that start and terminate among them.

The case is like a snowball's growth, due, as it is, to the distribution of the snow on the one hand, and to the direction of the boy's successive pushes on the other, with these factors codetermining each other incessantly.

The most fateful point of difference between being a rationalist and being a pragmatist is now fully in sight. Experience is in mutation, and our psychological ascertainments of truth are in mutation —so much rationalism will allow; but never that either reality itself or truth itself is mutable. Reality stands complete and ready-made from all eternity, rationalism insists, and the agreement of our ideas with it is that unique and timeless virtue in them of which she has already told us. As that intrinsic excellence, their truth has nothing to do with our experiences. It adds nothing to the content of experience. It makes no difference to reality itself; it is supervenient, inert, static, a reflection merely. It doesn't *exist*, it *holds* or *obtains*; it belongs to another dimension from that of facts and fact-relations, belongs, in short, to the epistemological dimension—and with that big word rationalism closes the discussion.

Thus, just as pragmatism faces forward to the future, so does rationalism here again face backward to a past eternity. True to her inveterate habit, rationalism reverts to "principles," and thinks that when an abstraction once is named, we own a solution.

The tremendous pregnancy in the way of consequences for life of this radical difference of outlook will only become apparent in my later lectures. I wish meanwhile to close this lecture by showing that rationalism's sublimity does not save it from inanity.

When, namely, you ask rationalists, instead of accusing pragmatism of desecrating the notion of truth, to define it themselves by saying exactly what *they* understand by it, the only positive attempts I can think of are these two:

1. "Truth is the system of propositions which have an unconditional claim to be recognized as valid."[5]

2. "Truth is a name for all those judgments which we find ourselves under obligation to make by a kind of imperative duty."[6]

The first thing that strikes one in such definitions is their unutter-

[5] A. E. Taylor, *Philosophical Review*, Vol. XIV., p. 288.
[6] H. Rickert, *Der Gegenstand der Erkenntnis*, chapter on "Die Urtheilsnothwendigkeit."

able triviality. They are absolutely true, of course, but absolutely insignificant until you handle them pragmatically. What do you mean by "claim" here, and what do you mean by "duty"? As summary names for the concrete reasons why thinking in true ways is overwhelmingly expedient and good for mortal men, it is all right to talk of claims on reality's part to be agreed with, and of obligations on our part to agree. We feel both the claims and the obligations, and we feel them for just those reasons.

But the rationalists who talk of claim and obligation expressly say that they have nothing to do with our practical interests or personal reasons. Our reasons for agreeing are psychological facts, they say, relative to each thinker, and to the accidents of his life. They are his evidence merely, they are no part of the life of truth itself. That life transacts itself in a purely logical or epistemological, as distinguished from a psychological, dimension, and its claims antedate and exceed all personal motivations whatsoever. Though neither man nor God should ever *ascertain* truth, the word would still have to be defined as that which *ought* to be ascertained and recognized.

There never was a more exquisite example of an idea abstracted from the concretes of experience and then used to oppose and negate what it was abstracted from.

Philosophy and common life abound in similar instances. The "sentimentalist fallacy" is to shed tears over abstract justice and generosity, beauty, etc., and never to know these qualities when you meet them in the street, because the circumstances make them vulgar. Thus I read in the privately printed biography of an eminently rationalistic mind: "It was strange that with such admiration for beauty in the abstract, my brother had no enthusiasm for fine architecture, for beautiful painting, or for flowers." And in almost the last philosophic work I have read, I find such passages as the following: "Justice is ideal, solely ideal. Reason conceives that it ought to exist, but experience shows that it can not. . . . Truth, which ought to be, can not be. . . . Reason is deformed by experience. As soon as reason enters experience, it becomes contrary to reason."

The rationalist's fallacy here is exactly like the sentimentalist's. Both extract a quality from the muddy particulars of experience, and find it so pure when extracted that they contrast it with each and all its muddy instances as an opposite and higher nature. All the while it is *their* nature. It is the nature of truths to be validated, verified. It pays for our ideas to be validated. Our obligation to seek truth is part of our general obligation to do what pays. The payments true ideas bring are the sole *why* of our duty to follow them. Identical whys exist in the case of wealth and health.

Truth makes no other kind of claim and imposes no other kind of ought than health and wealth do. All these claims are conditional; the concrete benefits we gain are what we mean by calling the pursuit a duty. In the case of truth, untrue beliefs work as perniciously in the long run as true beliefs work beneficially. Talking abstractly, the quality "true" may thus be said to grow absolutely precious, and the quality "untrue" absolutely damnable. The one may be called good, the other bad, unconditionally. We ought to think the true, we ought to shun the false, imperatively.

But if we treat all this abstraction literally and oppose it to its mother soil in experience, see what a preposterous position we work ourselves into.

We can not then take a step forward in our actual thinking. When shall I acknowledge this truth and when that? Shall the acknowledgment be loud?—or silent? If sometimes loud, sometimes silent, which *now*? When may a truth go into cold-storage in the encyclopedia? and when shall it come out for battle? Must I constantly be repeating the truth "twice two are four" because of its eternal claim on recognition? or is it sometimes irrelevant? Must my thoughts dwell night and day on my personal sins and blemishes, because I truly have them?—or may I sink and ignore them in order to be a decent social unit, and not a mass of morbid melancholy and apology?

It is quite evident that our obligation to acknowledge truth, so far from being unconditional, is tremendously conditioned. Truth, with a big T, and in the singular, claims abstractly to be recognized, of course; but concrete truths in the plural need be recognized only when their recognition is expedient. A truth must always be preferred to a falsehood when both relate to the situation; but when neither does, truth is as little of a duty as falsehood. If you ask me what o'clock it is and I tell you that I live at 95 Irving Street, my answer may indeed be true, but you don't see why it is my duty to give it. A false address would be as much to the purpose.

With this admission that there are conditions that limit the application of the abstract imperative, the pragmatistic treatment of truth sweeps back upon us in its fullness. Our duty to agree with reality is seen to be grounded in a perfect jungle of concrete expediencies.

When Berkeley had explained what people meant by matter, people thought that he denied matter's existence. When Messrs. Schiller and Dewey now explain what people mean by truth, they are accused of denying *its* existence. These pragmatists destroy all objective standards, critics say, and put foolishness and wisdom on one level. A favorite formula for describing Mr. Schiller's doctrines and mine is that we are persons who think that by saying whatever you find it pleasant to say and calling it truth you fulfill every pragmatistic requirement.

I leave it to you to judge whether this be not an impudent slander. Pent in, as the pragmatist, more than any one else, sees himself to be, between the whole body of funded truths squeezed from the past, and the coercions of the world of sense about him, who so well as he feels the immense pressure of objective control under which our minds perform their operations? We have heard much of late of the uses of the imagination in science. It is high time to urge the use of a little imagination in philosophy. The unwillingness of some of our critics to read any but the silliest and stupidest of possible meanings into our statements is as discreditable to their imaginations as anything I know in recent philosophic history. Schiller says the true is that which "works." Thereupon he is treated as one who limits verification to the lowest material utilities. Dewey says truth is what gives "satisfaction." He is treated as one who believes in calling everything true which, if it were true, would be pleasant.

Our critics certainly need more imagination of realities. I have honestly tried to stretch my own imagination and to read the best possible meaning into the rationalist conception, but I have to confess that it still completely baffles me. The notion of a reality calling on us to "agree" with it, and that for no reasons, but simply because its claim is "unconditional" or "transcendent," is one that I can make neither head nor tail of. I try to imagine myself as the sole reality in the world, and then to imagine what more I would "claim" if I were allowed to. When you suggest the possibility of my claiming that a mind should come into being from out of the void inane and stand and copy me, I can indeed imagine what the copying might mean, but I can conjure up no motive. What good it would do me to be copied, or what good it would do that mind to copy me, if practical consequences are expressly and in principle ruled out as motives for the claim (as they are by our rationalist authorities) I can not fathom. And when we get beyond copying, and fall back on unnamed forms of agreeing that are expressly denied to be either copyings or leadings or fittings, or any other processes pragmatically definable, the *what* of the "agreement" claimed becomes as unintelligible as the why of it. Neither content nor motive can be imagined for it. It is an absolutely meaningless abstraction.[7]

[7] I am not forgetting that Professor Rickert long ago gave up the notion of truth being founded on agreement with reality. Reality, according to him, is whatever agrees with truth, and truth is founded solely on our primal duty. This fantastic flight, together with Mr. Joachim's candid confession of failure in his book "The Nature of Truth," seem to me to mark the bankruptcy of rationalism when dealing with this subject. Naturally I could not, in a popular lecture, pursue my subject into such intricacies.

Surely in this field of truth it is the pragmatists and not the rationalists who are the more genuine defenders of the universe's rationality.

THE WILL TO BELIEVE[8]

In the recently published Life by Leslie Stephen of his brother, Fitz-James, there is an account of a school to which the latter went when he was a boy. The teacher, a certain Mr. Guest, used to converse with his pupils in this wise: "Gurney, what is the difference between justification and sanctification?—Stephen, prove the omnipotence of God!" etc. In the midst of our Harvard freethinking and indifference we are prone to imagine that here at your good old orthodox College conversation continues to be somewhat upon this order; and to show you that we at Harvard have not lost all interest in these vital subjects, I have brought with me tonight something like a sermon on justification by faith to read to you,—I mean an essay in justification *of* faith, a defence of our right to adopt a believing attitude in religious matters, in spite of the fact that our merely logical intellect may not have been coerced. "The Will to Believe," accordingly, is the title of my paper.

I have long defended to my own students the lawfulness of voluntary adopted faith; but as soon as they have got well imbued with the logical spirit, they have as a rule refused to admit my contention to be lawful philosophically, even though in point of fact they were personally all the time chock-full of some faith or other themselves. I am all the while, however, so profoundly convinced that my own position is correct, that your invitation has seemed to me a good occasion to make my statements more clear. Perhaps your minds will be more open than those with which I have hitherto had to deal. I will be as little technical as I can, though I must begin by setting up some technical distinctions that will help us in the end.

Let us give the name of *hypothesis* to anything that may be proposed to our belief; and just as the electricians speak of live and dead wires, let us speak of any hypothesis as either *live* or *dead*. A live hypothesis is one which appeals as a real possibility to him to whom it is proposed. If I ask you to believe in the Mahdi, the notion makes no electric connection with your nature,—it refuses to scintil-

[8] "The Will to Believe," published in *The New World*, June 1896. Later reprinted in *The Will to Believe*, N. Y.: Longmans, Green, 1896.

late with any credibility at all. As an hypothesis it is completely dead. To an Arab, however (even if he be not one of the Mahdi's followers), the hypothesis is among the mind's possibilities: it is alive. This shows that deadness and liveness in an hypothesis are not intrinsic properties, but relations to the individual thinker. They are measured by his willingness to act. The maximum of liveness in an hypothesis means willingness to act irrevocably. Practically, that means belief; but there is some believing tendency wherever there is willingness to act at all.

Next, let us call the decision between two hypotheses an *option*. Options may be of several kinds. They may be—1, *living* or *dead*; 2, *forced* or *avoidable*; 3, *momentous* or *trivial*; and for our purposes we may call an option a *genuine* option when it is of the forced, living, and momentous kind.

1. A living option is one in which both hypotheses are live ones. If I say to you: "Be a theosophist or be a Mohammedan," it is probably a dead option, because for you neither hypothesis is likely to be alive. But if I say: "Be an agnostic or be a Christian," it is otherwise: trained as you are, each hypothesis makes some appeal, however small, to your belief.

2. Next, if I say to you: "Choose between going out with your umbrella or without it," I do not offer you a genuine option, for it is not forced. You can easily avoid it by not going out at all. Similarly, if I say, "Either love me or hate me," "Either call my theory true or call it false," your option is avoidable. You may remain indifferent to me, neither loving nor hating, and you may decline to offer any judgment as to my theory. But if I say, "Either accept this truth or go without it," I put on you a forced option, for there is no standing place outside of the alternative. Every dilemma based on a complete logical disjunction, with no possibility of not choosing, is an option of this forced kind.

3. Finally, if I were Dr. Nansen and proposed to you to join my North Pole expedition, your option would be momentous; for this would probably be your only similar opportunity, and your choice now would either exclude you from the North Pole sort of immortality altogether or put at least the chance of it into your hands. He who refuses to embrace a unique opportunity loses the prize as surely as if he tried and failed. *Per contra*, the option is trivial when the opportunity is not unique, when the stake is insignificant, or when the decision is reversible if it later prove unwise. Such trivial options abound in the scientific life. A chemist finds an hypothesis live enough to spend a year in its verification: he believes in it to that extent. But if his experiments prove inconclusive either way, he is quit for his loss of time, no vital harm being done.

It will facilitate our discussion if we keep all these distinctions well in mind. . . .

The thesis I defend is, briefly stated, this: *Our passional nature not only lawfully may, but must, decide an option between propositions, whenever it is a genuine option that cannot by its nature be decided on intellectual grounds; for to say, under such circumstances, "Do not decide, but leave the question open," is itself a passional decision,—just like deciding yes or no,—and is attended with the same risk of losing the truth.* The thesis thus abstractly expressed will, I trust, soon become quite clear. . . .

And now, after all this introduction, let us go straight at our question. I have said, and now repeat it, that not only as a matter of fact do we find our passional nature influencing us in our opinions, but that there are some options between opinions in which this influence must be regarded both as an inevitable and as a lawful determinant of our choice.

I fear here that some of you my hearers will begin to scent danger, and lend an inhospitable ear. Two first steps of passion you have indeed had to admit as necessary,—we must think so as to avoid dupery, and we must think so as to gain truth; but the surest path to those ideal consummations, you will probably consider, is from now onwards to take no further passional step.

Well, of course, I agree as far as the facts will allow. Wherever the option between losing truth and gaining it is not momentous, we can throw the chance of *gaining truth* away, and at any rate save ourselves from any chance of *believing falsehood*, by not making up our minds at all till objective evidence has come. In scientific questions, this is almost always the case; and even in human affairs in general, the need of acting is seldom so urgent that a false belief to act on is better than no belief at all. Law courts, indeed, have to decide on the best evidence attainable for the moment, because a judge's duty is to make law as well as to ascertain it, and (as a learned judge once said to me) few cases are worth spending much time over: the great thing is to have them decided on *any* acceptable principle, and got out of the way. But in our dealings with objective nature we obviously are recorders, not makers, of the truth; and decisions for the mere sake of deciding promptly and getting on to the next business would be wholly out of place. Throughout the breadth of physical nature facts are what they are quite independently of us, and seldom is there any such hurry about them that the risks of being duped by believing a premature theory need be faced. The questions here are always trivial options, the hypotheses are hardly living (at any rate not living for us spectators), the choice between believing truth or falsehood is seldom forced. The attitude of sceptical balance is therefore the absolutely wise one if we would escape mistakes. What difference, indeed, does it make to most of us whether we have or have not a theory of the Röntgen rays, whether we believe or not in mind-stuff, or have a conviction about the causality of conscious states? It makes no difference. Such options are not forced on us. On every account it is better not to make them, but still keep weighing reasons *pro et contra* with an indifferent hand.

I speak, of course, here of the purely judging mind. For purposes of discovery such indifference is to be less highly recommended, and science would be far less advanced than she is if the passionate desires of individuals to get their own faiths confirmed had been kept out of the game. See for example the sagacity which Spencer and Weismann now display. On the other hand, if you want an absolute duffer in an investigation, you must, after all, take the man who has no interest whatever in its results: he is the warranted incapable, the positive fool. The most useful investigator, because the most sensitive observer, is always he whose eager interest in one side of the question is balanced by an equally keen nervousness lest he become deceived.[9] Science has organized this nervousness into a regular *technique*, her so-called method of verification; and she has fallen so deeply in love with the method that one may even say she has ceased to care for truth by itself at all. It is only truth as technically verified that interests her. The truth of truths might come in merely affirmative form, and she would decline to touch it. Such truth as that, she might repeat with Clifford, would be stolen in defiance of her duty to mankind. Human passions, however, are stronger than technical rules. "Le coeur a ses raisons," as Pascal says, "que la raison ne connaît pas"; and however indifferent to all but the bare rules of the game the umpire, the abstract intellect, may be, the concrete players who furnish him the materials to judge of are usually, each one of them, in love with some pet "live hypothesis" of his own. Let us agree, however, that wherever there is no forced option, the dispassionately judicial intellect with no pet hypothesis, saving us, as it does, from dupery at any rate, ought to be our ideal.

The question next arises: Are there not somewhere forced options in our speculative questions, and can we (as men who may be interested at least as much in positively gaining truth as in merely

[9] Compare Wilfrid Ward's Essay, "The Wish to Believe," in his *Witnesses to the Unseen*, Macmillan & Co., 1893.

escaping dupery) always wait with impunity till the coercive evidence shall have arrived? It seems *a priori* improbable that the truth should be so nicely adjusted to our needs and powers as that. In the great boarding-house of nature, the cakes and the butter and the syrup seldom come out so even and leave the plates so clean. Indeed, we should view them with scientific suspicion if they did.

Moral questions immediately present themselves as questions whose solution cannot wait for sensible proof. A moral question is a question not of what sensibly exists, but of what is good, or would be good if it did exist. Science can tell us what exists; but to compare the *worths*, both of what exists and of what does not exist, we must consult not science, but what Pascal calls our heart. Science herself consults her heart when she lays it down that the infinite ascertainment of fact and correction of false belief are the supreme goods for man. Challenge the statement, and science can only repeat it oracularly, or else prove it by showing that such ascertainment and correction bring man all sorts of other goods which man's heart in turn declares. The question of having moral beliefs at all or not having them is decided by our will. Are our moral preferences true or false, or are they only odd biological phenomena, making things good or bad for *us*, but in themselves indifferent? How can your pure intellect decide? If your heart does not *want* a world of moral reality, your head will assuredly never make you believe in one. Mephistophelian scepticism, indeed, will satisfy the head's play-instincts much better than any rigorous idealism can. Some men (even at the student age) are so naturally cool-hearted that the moralistic hypothesis never has for them any pungent life, and in their supercilious presence the hot young moralist always feels strangely ill at ease. The appearance of knowingness is on their side, of *naïveté* and gullibility on his. Yet, in the inarticulate heart of him, he clings to it that he is not a dupe, and that there is a realm in which (as Emerson says) all their wit and intellectual superiority is no better than the cunning of a fox. Moral scepticism can no more be refuted or proved by logic than intellectual scepticism can. When we stick to it that there *is* truth (be it of either kind), we do so with our whole nature, and resolve to stand or fall by the results. The sceptic with his whole nature adopts the doubting attitude; but which of us is the wiser, Omniscience only knows.

Turn now from these wide questions of good to a certain class of questions of fact, questions concerning personal relations, states of mind between one man and another. *Do you like me or not?*—for example. Whether you do or not depends, in countless instances, on whether I meet you half-way, am willing to assume that you must like me, and show you trust and expectation. The previous faith on my part in your liking's existence is in such cases what makes your liking come. But if I stand aloof, and refuse to budge an inch until I have objective evidence, until you shall have done something apt, as the absolutists say, *ad extorquendum assensum meum*, ten to one your liking never comes. How many women's hearts are vanquished by the mere sanguine insistence of some man that they *must* love him! he will not consent to the hypothesis that they cannot. The desire for a certain kind of truth here brings about that special truth's existence; and so it is in innumerable cases of other sorts. Who gains promotions, boons, appointments, but the man in whose life they are seen to play the part of live hypotheses, who discounts them, sacrifices other things for their sake before they have come, and takes risks for them in advance? His faith acts on the powers above him as a claim, and creates its own verification.

A social organism of any sort whatever, large or small, is what it is because each member proceeds to his own duty with a trust that the other members will simultaneously do theirs. Wherever a desired result is achieved by the co-operation of many independent persons, its existence as a fact is a pure consequence of the precursive faith in one another of those immediately concerned. A government, an army, a commercial system, a ship, a college, an athletic team, all exist on this condition, without which not only is nothing achieved, but nothing is even attempted. A whole train of passengers (individually brave enough) will be looted by a few highwaymen, simply because the latter can count on one another, while each passenger fears that if he makes a movement of resistance, he will be shot before any one else backs him up. If we believed that the whole car-full would rise at once with us, we should each severally rise, and train-robbing would never even be attempted. There are, then, cases where a fact cannot come at all unless a preliminary faith exists in its coming. *And where faith in a fact can help create the fact,* that would be an insane logic which should say that faith running ahead of scientific evidence is the "lowest kind of immorality" into which a thinking being can fall. Yet such is the logic by which our scientific absolutists pretend to regulate our lives!

In truths dependent on our personal action, then, faith based on desire is certainly a lawful and possibly an indispensable thing.

But now, it will be said, these are all childish human cases, and have nothing to do with great cosmical matters, like the question of religious faith. Let us then pass on to that. Religions differ so much in their accidents that in discussing the religious question we must make it very generic and broad. What then do we now mean by the religious hypothesis? Science says things are; morality says some things are better than other things; and religion says essentially two things.

First, she says that the best things are the more eternal things, the overlapping things, the things in the universe that throw the last stone, so to speak, and say the final word. "Perfection is eternal," —this phrase of Charles Secrétan seems a good way of putting this first affirmation of religion, an affirmation which obviously cannot yet be verified scientifically at all.

The second affirmation of religion is that we are better off even now if we believe her first affirmation to be true.

Now, let us consider what the logical elements of this situation are *in case the religious hypothesis in both its branches be really true.* (Of course, we must admit that possibility at the outset. If we are to discuss the question at all, it must involve a living option. If for any of you religion be a hypothesis that cannot, by any living possibility be true, then you need go no farther. I speak to the "saving remnant" alone.) So proceeding, we see, first, that religion offers itself as a *momentous* option. We are supposed to gain, even now, by our belief, and to lose by our non-belief, a certain vital good. Secondly, religion is a *forced* option, so far as that good goes. We cannot escape the issue by remaining sceptical and waiting for more light, because, although we do avoid error in that way *if religion be untrue,* we lose the good, *if it be true,* just as certainly as if we positively chose to disbelieve. It is as if a man should hesitate indefinitely to ask a certain woman to marry him because he was not perfectly sure that she would prove an angel after he brought her home. Would he not cut himself off from that particular angel-possibility as decisively as if he went and married some one else? Scepticism, then, is not avoidance of option; it is option of a certain particular kind of risk. *Better risk loss of truth than chance of error,* —that is your faith-vetoer's exact position. He is actively playing his take as much as the believer is; he is backing the field against the religious hypothesis, just as the believer is backing the religious hypothesis against the field. To preach scepticism to us as a duty until "sufficient evidence" for religion be found, is tantamount therefore to telling us, when in presence of the religious hypothesis, that to yield to our fear of its being error is wiser and better than to yield to our hope that it may be true. It is not intellect against all passions, then; it is only intellect with one passion laying down its law. And by what, forsooth, is the supreme wisdom of this passion warranted? Dupery for dupery, what proof is there that dupery through hope is so much worse than dupery through fear? I, for one, can see no proof; and I simply refuse obedience to the scientist's command to imitate his kind of option, in a case where my own stake is important enough to give me the right to choose my own form of risk. If religion be true and the evidence for it be still insufficient, I do not wish, by putting your extinguisher upon my nature (which feels to me as if it had after all some business in this matter), to forfeit my sole chance in life of getting upon the winning side,— that chance depending, of course, on my willingness to run the risk of acting as if my passional need of taking the world religiously might be prophetic and right.

All this is on the supposition that it really may be prophetic and right, and that even, to us who are discussing the matter, religion is a live hypothesis which may be true. Now, to most of us religion comes in a still further way that makes a veto on our active faith even more illogical. The more perfect and more eternal aspect of the universe is represented in our religions as having personal form. The universe is no longer a mere *It* to us, but a *Thou*, if we are religious; and any relation that may be possible from person to person might be possible here. For instance, although in one sense we are passive portions of the universe, in another we show a curious autonomy, as if we were small active centres on our own account. We feel, too, as if the appeal of religion to us were made to our own active good-will, as if evidence might be forever withheld from us unless we met the hypothesis halfway. To take a trivial illustration: just as a man who in a company of gentlemen made no advances, asked a warrant for every concession, and believed no one's word without proof, would cut himself off by such churlishness from all the social rewards that a more trusting spirit would earn,—so here, one who should shut himself up in snarling logicality and try to make the gods extort his recognition willy-nilly, or not get it at all, might cut himself off forever from his only opportunity of making the gods' acquaintance. This feeling, forced on us we know not whence, that by obstinately believing that there are gods (although not to do so would be so easy both for our logic and our life) we are doing the universe the deepest service we can, seems part of the living essence of the religious hypothesis. If the hypothesis *were* true in all its parts, including this one, then pure intellectualism, with its veto on our making willing advances, would be an absurdity; and some partici-pation of our sympathetic nature would be logically required. I, therefore, for one, cannot see my way to accepting the agnostic rules for truth-seeking, or wilfully agree to keep my willing nature out of the game. I cannot do so for this plain reason, that *a rule of think-ing which would absolutely prevent me from acknowledging certain kinds of truth if those kinds of truth were really there, would be an irrational rule.* That for me is the long and short of the formal logic of the situation, no matter what the kinds of truth might materially be.

I confess I do not see how this logic can be escaped. But sad experience makes me fear that some of you may still shrink from radically saying with me, *in abstracto*, that we have the right to believe at our own risk any hypothesis that is live enough to tempt our will. I suspect, however, that if this is so, it is because you have got away from the abstract logical point of view altogether, and are thinking (perhaps without realizing it) of some particular religious hypothesis which for you is dead. The freedom to "believe what we will" you apply to the case of some patent superstition; and the faith you think of is the faith defined by the schoolboy when he said, "Faith is when you believe something that you know ain't true." I can only repeat that this is misapprehension. *In concreto*, the freedom to believe can only cover living options which the intellect of the individual cannot by itself resolve; and living options never seem absurdities to him who has them to consider. When I look at the religious question as it really puts itself to concrete men, and when I think of all the possibilities which both practically and theoretically it involves, then this command that we shall put a stopper on our heart, instincts, and courage, and *wait*—acting of course meanwhile more or less as if religion were *not* true[10]—till doomsday, or till such time as our intellect and senses working together may have raked in evidence enough,—this command, I say, seems to me the queerest idol ever manufactured in the philosophic cave. Were we scholastic absolutists, there might be more excuse. If we had an infallible intellect with its objective certitudes, we might feel ourselves disloyal to such a perfect organ of knowledge in not trusting to it exclusively, in not waiting for its releasing word. But if we are empiricists, if we believe that no bell in us tolls to let us know for certain when truth is in our grasp, then it seems a piece of idle fantasticality to preach so solemnly our duty of waiting for the bell. Indeed we *may* wait if we will,—I hope you do not think that I am denying that,—but if we do so, we do so at our peril as much as

---

[10] Since belief is measured by action, he who forbids us to believe religion to be true, necessarily also forbids us to act as we should if we did believe it to be true. The whole defence of religious faith hinges upon action. If the action required or inspired by the religious hypothesis is in no way different from that dictated by the naturalistic hypothesis, then religious faith is a pure superfluity, better pruned away, and controversy about its legitimacy is a piece of idle trifling, unworthy of serious minds. I myself believe, of course, that the religious hypothesis gives to the world an expression which specifically determines our reactions, and makes them in a large part unlike what they might be on a purely naturalistic scheme of belief.

if we believed. In either case we *act*, taking our life in our hands. No one of us ought to issue vetoes to the other, nor should we bandy words of abuse. We ought, on the contrary, delicately and profoundly to respect one another's mental freedom: then only shall we bring about the intellectual republic; then only shall we have that spirit of inner tolerance without which all our outer tolerance is soulless, and which is empiricism's glory; then only shall we live and let live, in speculative as well as in practical things.

I began by a reference to Fitz-James Stephen; let me end by a quotation from him. "What do you think of yourself? What do you think of the world? . . . These are questions with which all must deal as it seems good to them. They are riddles of the Sphinx, and in some way or other we must deal with them. . . . In all important transactions of life we have to take a leap in the dark. . . . If we decide to leave the riddles unanswered, that is a choice; if we waver in our answer, that, too, is a choice: but whatever choice we make, we make it at our peril. If a man chooses to turn his back altogether on God and the future, no one can prevent him; no one can show beyond reasonable doubt that he is mistaken. If a man thinks otherwise and acts as he thinks, I do not see that any one can prove that *he* is mistaken. Each must act as he thinks best; and if he is wrong, so much the worse for him. We stand on a mountain pass in the midst of whirling snow and blinding mist, through which we get glimpses now and then of paths which may be deceptive. If we stand still we shall be frozen to death. If we take the wrong road we shall be dashed to pieces. We do not certainly know whether there is any right one. What must we do? 'Be strong and of a good courage.' Act for the best, hope for the best, and take what comes. . . . If death ends all, we cannot meet death better."[11]

DOES "CONSCIOUSNESS" EXIST?[12]

"Thoughts" and "things" are names for two sorts of object, which common sense will always find contrasted and will always practically oppose to each other. Philosophy, reflecting on the contrast, has varied in the past in her explanations of it, and may be expected to vary in the future. At first, "spirit and matter," "soul and body," stood for a pair of equipollent substances quite on a par in weight

[11] *Liberty, Equality, Fraternity*, p. 353, 2d edition. London, 1874.
[12] From *The Journal of Philosophy, Psychology and Scientific Methods*, Vol. I (1904), pp. 477–486, 490–491.

and interest. But one day Kant undermined the soul and brought in the transcendental ego, and ever since then the bipolar relation has been very much off its balance. The transcendental ego seems nowadays in rationalist quarters to stand for everything, in empiricist quarters for almost nothing. In the hands of such writers as Schuppe, Rehmke, Natorp, Münsterberg—at any rate in his earlier writings, Schubert-Soldern and others, the spiritual principle attenuates itself to a thoroughly ghostly condition, being only a name for the fact that the "content" of experience *is known*. It loses personal form and activity—these passing over to the content—and becomes a bare *Bewusstheit* or *Bewusstsein überhaupt*, of which in its own right absolutely nothing can be said.

I believe that "consciousness," when once it has evaporated to this estate of pure diaphaneity, is on the point of disappearing altogether. It is the name of a nonentity, and has no right to a place among first principles. Those who still cling to it are clinging to a mere echo, the faint rumor left behind by the disappearing "soul" upon the air of philosophy. During the past year, I have read a number of articles whose authors seemed just on the point of abandoning the notion of consciousness[13] and substituting for it that of an absolute experience not due to two factors. But they were not quite radical enough, not quite daring enough in their negations. For twenty years past I have mistrusted "consciousness" as an entity; for seven or eight years past I have suggested its non-existence to my students, and tried to give them its pragmatic equivalent in realities of experience. It seems to me that the hour is ripe for it to be openly and universally discarded.

To deny plumply that "consciousness" exists seems so absurd on the face of it—for undeniably "thoughts" do exist—that I fear some readers will follow me no farther. Let me then immediately explain that I mean only to deny that the word stands for an entity, but to insist most emphatically that it does stand for a function. There is, I mean, no aboriginal stuff or quality of being, contrasted with that of which material objects are made, out of which our thoughts of them are made; but there is a function in experience which thoughts perform, and for the performance of which this quality of being is invoked. That function is *knowing*. "Consciousness" is supposed necessary to explain the fact that things not only are, but get reported, are known. Whoever blots out the notion of consciousness from his list of first principles must still provide in some way for that function's being carried on.

[13] Articles by Baldwin, Ward, Bawden, King, Alexander and others. Dr. Perry is frankly over the border.

I

My thesis is that if we start with the supposition that there is only one primal stuff or material in the world, a stuff of which everything is composed, and if we call that stuff "pure experience," then knowing can easily be explained as a particular sort of relation towards one another into which portions of pure experience may enter. The relation itself is a part of pure experience; one of its "terms" becomes the subject or bearer of the knowledge, the knower,[14] the other becomes the object known. This will need much explanation before it can be understood. The best way to get it understood is to contrast it with the alternative view; and for that we may take the recentest alternative, that in which the evaporation of the definite soul-substance has proceeded as far as it can go without being yet complete. If neo-Kantism has expelled earlier forms of dualism, we shall have expelled all forms if we are able to expel neo-Kantism in its turn.

For the thinkers I call neo-Kantian, the word consciousness to-day does no more than signalize the fact that experience is indefeasibly dualistic in structure. It means that not subject, not object, but object-plus-subject is the minimum that can actually be. The subject-object distinction meanwhile is entirely different from that between mind and matter, from that between body and soul. Souls were detachable, had separate destinies; things could happen to them. To consciousness as such nothing can happen, for, timeless itself, it is only a witness of happenings in time, in which it plays no part. It is, in a word, but the logical correlative of "content" in an Experience of which the peculiarity is that *fact comes to light* in it, that *awareness of content* takes place. Consciousness as such is entirely impersonal—"self" and its activities belong to the content. To say that I am self-conscious, or conscious of putting forth volition, means only that certain contents, for which "self" and "effort of will" are the names, are not without witness as they occur.

Thus, for these belated drinkers at the Kantian spring, we should have to admit consciousness as an "epistemological" necessity, even if we had no direct evidence of its being there.

But in addition to this, we are supposed by almost every one to have an immediate consciousness of consciousness itself. When the world of outer fact ceases to be materially present, and we merely recall it in memory, or fancy it, the consciousness is believed to stand out and to be felt as a kind of impalpable inner flowing, which, once

[14] In my *Psychology* I have tried to show that we need no knower other than the "passing thought."

known in this sort of experience, may equally be detected in presentations of the outer world. "The moment we try to fix our attention upon consciousness and to see *what*, distinctly, it is," says a recent writer, "it seems to vanish. It seems as if we had before us a mere emptiness. When we try to introspect the sensation of blue, all we can see is the blue; the other element is as if it were diaphanous. Yet it can be distinguished, if we look attentively enough, and know that there is something to look for."[15] "Consciousness" (*Bewusstheit*), says another philosopher, "is inexplicable and hardly describable, yet all conscious experiences have this in common that what we call their content has this peculiar reference to a center for which 'self' is the name, in virtue of which reference alone the content is subjectively given, or appears. . . . While in this way consciousness, or reference to a self, is the only thing which distinguishes a conscious content from any sort of being that might be there with no one conscious of it, yet this only ground of the distinction defies all closer explanations. The existence of consciousness, although it is the fundamental fact of psychology, can indeed be laid down as certain, can be brought out by analysis, but can neither be defined nor deduced from anything but itself."[16]

"Can be brought out by analysis," this author says. This supposes that the consciousness is one element, moment, factor—call it what you like—of an experience of essentially dualistic inner constitution, from which, if you abstract the content, the consciousness will remain revealed to its own eye. Experience, at this rate, would be much like a paint of which the world pictures were made. Paint has a dual constitution, involving, as it does, a menstruum[17] (oil, size or what not) and a mass of content in the form of pigment suspended therein. We can get the pure menstruum by letting the pigment settle, and the pure pigment by pouring off the size or oil. We operate here by physical subtraction; and the usual view is, that by mental subtraction we can separate the two factors of experience in an analogous way—not isolating them entirely, but distinguishing them enough to know that they are two.

II

Now my contention is exactly the reverse of this. *Experience, I believe, has no such inner duplicity; and the separation of it into*

[15] G. E. Moore: *Mind*, Vol. XII, N. S., p. 450.

[16] Paul Natorp: *Einleitung in die Psychologie*, 1888, pp. 14, 112.

[17] "Figuratively speaking, consciousness may be said to be the one universal solvent or menstruum, in which the different kinds of psychic acts and facts are contained, whether in concealed or in obvious form." G. T. Ladd: *Psychology, Descriptive and Explanatory*, 1894, p. 30.

consciousness and content comes, not by way of subtraction, but by way of addition—the addition, to a given concrete piece of it, of other sets of experiences, in connection with which severally its use or function may be of two different kinds. The paint will also serve here as an illustration. In a pot in a paint-shop, along with other paints, it serves in its entirety as so much saleable matter. Spread on a canvas, with other paints around it, it represents, on the contrary, a feature in a picture and performs a spiritual function. Just so, I maintain, does a given undivided portion of experience, taken in one context of associates, play the part of a knower, of a state of mind, of "consciousness"; while in a different context the same undivided bit of experience plays the part of a thing known, of an objective "content." In a word, in one group it figures as a thought, in another group as a thing. And, since it can figure in both groups simultaneously we have every right to speak of it as subjective and objective both at once. The dualism connoted by such double-barrelled terms as "experience," "phenomenon," "datum," "*Vorfindung*" —terms which, in philosophy at any rate, tend more and more to replace the single-barrelled terms of "thought" and "thing"—that dualism, I say, is still preserved in this account, but reinterpreted, so that, instead of being mysterious and elusive, it becomes verifiable and concrete. It is an affair of relations, it falls outside, not inside, the single experience considered, and can always be particularized and defined.

The entering wedge for this more concrete way of understanding the dualism was fashioned by Locke when he made the word "idea" stand indifferently for thing and thought, and by Berkeley when he said that what common sense means by realities is exactly what the philosopher means by ideas. Neither Locke nor Berkeley thought his truth out into perfect clearness, but it seems to me that the conception I am defending does little more than consistently carry out the "pragmatic" method which they were the first to use.

If the reader will take his own experiences, he will see what I mean. Let him begin with a perceptual experience, the "presentation," so called, of a physical object, his actual field of vision, the room he sits in, with the book he is reading as its center; and let him for the present treat this complex object in the common-sense way as being "really" what it seems to be, namely, a collection of physical things cut out from an environing world of other physical things with which these physical things have actual or potential relations. Now at the same time it is just *those self-same things* which his mind, as we say, perceives; and the whole philosophy of perception from Democritus's time downwards has been just one long wrangle over the paradox that what is evidently one reality should be in two places at once, both in outer space and in a person's mind. "Representative" theories of perception avoid the logical paradox, but on the other hand they violate the reader's sense of life, which knows no intervening mental image but seems to see the room and the book immediately just as they physically exist.

The puzzle of how the one identical room can be in two places is at bottom just the puzzle of how one identical point can be on two lines. It can, if it be situated at their intersection; and similarly, if the "pure experience" of the room were a place of intersection of two processes, which connected it with different groups of associates respectively, it could be counted twice over, as belonging to either group, and spoken of loosely as existing in two places, although it would remain all the time a numerically single thing.

Well, the experience is a member of diverse processes that can be followed away from it along entirely different lines. The one self-identical thing has so many relations to the rest of experience that you can take it in disparate systems of association, and treat it as belonging with opposite contexts. In one of these contexts it is your "field of consciousness"; in another it is "the room in which you sit," and it enters both contexts in its wholeness, giving no pretext for being said to attach itself to consciousness by one of its parts or aspects, and to outer reality by another. What are the two processes, now, into which the room-experience simultaneously enters in this way?

One of them is the reader's personal biography, the other is the history of the house of which the room is part. The presentation, the experience, the *that* in short (for until we have decided *what* it is it must be a mere *that*) is the last term of a train of sensations, emotions, decisions, movements, classifications, expectations, etc., ending in the present, and the first term of a series of similar "inner" operations extending into the future, on the reader's part. On the other hand, the very same *that* is the *terminus ad quem* of a lot of previous physical operations, carpentering, papering, furnishing, warming, etc., and the *terminus a quo* of a lot of future ones, in which it will be concerned when undergoing the destiny of a physical room. The physical and the mental operations form curiously incompatible groups. As a room, the experience has occupied that spot and had that environment for thirty years. As your field of consciousness it may never have existed until now. As a room, attention will go on to discover endless new details in it. As your mental state merely, few new ones will emerge under attention's eye. As a room, it will take an earthquake, or a gang of men, and in any case a certain amount of time, to destroy it. As your subjective state, the closing of your eyes, or any instantaneous play of your fancy will suffice. In the real world, fire will consume it. In your mind, you can let fire play over it without effect. As an outer object, you must pay so much a month to inhabit it. As an inner content, you may occupy it for any length of time rent-free. If, in short, you follow it in the mental direction, taking it along with events of personal biography solely, all sorts of things are true of it which are false, and false of it which are true if you treat it as a real thing experienced, follow it in the physical direction, and relate it to associates in the outer world.

III

So far, all seems plain sailing, but my thesis will probably grow less plausible to the reader when I pass from percepts to concepts, or from the case of things presented to that of things remote. I believe, nevertheless, that here also the same law holds good. If we take conceptual manifolds, or memories, or fancies, they also are in their first intention mere bits of pure experience, and, as such, are single *thats* which act in one context as objects, and in another context figure as mental states. By taking them in their first intention, I mean ignoring their relation to possible perceptual experiences with which they may be connected, which they may lead to and terminate in, and which then they may be supposed to "represent." Taking them in this way first, we confine the problem to a world merely "thought-of" and not directly felt or seen. This world, just like the world of percepts, comes to us at first as a chaos of experiences, but lines of order soon get traced. We find that any bit of it which we may cut out as an example is connected with distinct groups of associates, just as our perceptual experiences are, that these associates link themselves with it by different relations,[18] and that one forms the inner history of a person, while the other acts as an impersonal "objective" world, either spatial and temporal, or else merely logical or mathematical, or otherwise "ideal."

The first obstacle on the part of the reader to seeing that these non-perceptual experiences have objectivity as well as subjectivity will probably be due to the intrusion into his mind of *percepts*, that third group of associates with which the non-perceptual experiences have relations, and which, as a whole, they "represent," standing to them as thoughts to things. This important function of the non-perceptual experiences complicates the question and confuses it; for, so used are we to treat percepts as the sole genuine realities that, unless we keep them out of the discussion, we tend altogether to

[18] Here as elsewhere the relations are of course *experienced* relations, members of the same originally chaotic manifold of non-perceptual experience of which the related terms themselves are parts.

overlook the objectivity that lies in non-perceptual experiences by themselves. We treat them, "knowing" percepts as they do, as through and through subjective, and say that they are wholly constituted of the stuff called consciousness, using this term now for a kind of entity, after the fashion which I am seeking to refute.[19]

Abstracting, then, from percepts altogether, what I maintain is, that any single non-perceptual experience tends to get counted twice over, just as a perceptual experience does, figuring in one context as an object or field of objects, in another as a state of mind: and all this without the least internal self-diremption on its own part into consciousness and content. It is all consciousness in one taking; and, in the other, all content.

I find this objectivity of non-perceptual experiences, this complete parallelism in point of reality between the presently felt and the remotely thought, so well set forth in a page of Münsterberg's *Grundzüge*, that I will quote it as it stands.

"I may only think of my objects," says Professor Münsterberg; "yet, in my living thought they stand before me exactly as perceived objects would do, no matter how different the two ways of apprehending them may be in their genesis. The book here lying on the table before me, and the book in the next room of which I think and which I mean to get, are both in the same sense given realities for me, realities which I acknowledge and of which I take account. If you agree that the perceptual object is not an idea within me, but that percept and thing, as indistinguishably one, are really experienced *there, outside,* you ought not to believe that the merely thought-of object is hid away inside of the thinking subject. The object of which I think, and of whose existence I take cognizance without letting it now work upon my senses, occupies its definite place in the outer world as much as does the object which I directly see.

"What is true of the here and the there, is also true of the now and the then. I know of the thing which is present and perceived, but I know also of the thing which yesterday was but is no more, and which I only remember. Both can determine my present conduct, both are parts of the reality of which I keep account. It is true that of much of the past I am uncertain, just as I am uncertain of much of what is present if it be but dimly perceived. But the interval of time does not in principle alter my relation to the object, does not transform it from an object known into a mental state. . . . The things in the room here which I survey, and those in my distant home of which I think, the things of this minute and those of my

---

[19] Of the representative function of non-perceptual experience as a whole, I will say a word in a subsequent article: it leads too far into the general theory of knowledge for much to be said about it in a short paper like this.

long-vanished boyhood, influence and decide me alike, with a reality which my experience of them directly feels. They both make up my real world, they make it directly, they do not have first to be introduced to me and mediated by ideas which now and here arise within me. . . . This not-me character of my recollections and expectations does not imply that the external objects of which I am aware in those experiences should necessarily be there also for others. The objects of dreamers and hallucinated persons are wholly without general validity. But even were they centaurs and golden mountains, they still would be 'off there,' in fairy land, and not 'inside' of ourselves."[20]

This certainly is the immediate, primary, naïf, or practical way of taking our thought-of world. Were there no perceptual world to serve as its "reductive," in Taine's sense, by being "stronger" and more genuinely "outer" (so that the whole merely thought-of world seems weak and inner in comparison), our world of thought would be the only world, and would enjoy complete reality in our belief. This actually happens in our dreams, and in our day-dreams so long as percepts do not interrupt them.

And yet, just as the seen room (to go back to our late example) is *also* a field of consciousness, so the conceived or recollected room is *also* a state of mind; and the doubling-up of the experience has in both cases similar grounds.

The room thought-of, namely, has many thought-of couplings with many thought-of things. Some of these couplings are inconstant, others are stable. In the reader's personal history the room occupies a single date—he saw it only once perhaps, a year ago. Of the house's history, on the other hand, it forms a permanent ingredient. Some couplings have the curious stubbornness, to borrow Royce's term, of fact; others show the fluidity of fancy—we let them come and go as we please. Grouped with the rest of its house, with the name of its town, of its owner, builder, value, decorative plan, the room maintains a definite foothold, to which, if we try to loosen it, it tends to return, and to reassert itself with force.[21] With these associates, in a word, it coheres, while to other houses, other towns, other owners, etc., it shows no tendency to cohere at all. The two collections, first of its cohesive, and, second, of its loose associates, inevitably come to be contrasted. We call the first collection the system of external realities, in the midst of which the room, as "real," exists; the other we call the stream of our internal thinking, in which,

[20] *Grundzüge der Psychologie*, Vol. I, p. 48.
[21] Cf. A. L. Hodder: *The Adversaries of the Skeptic*, N. Y., 1899, pp. 94-99.

as a "mental image," it for a moment floats.[22] The room thus again gets counted twice over. It plays two different rôles, being *Gedanke* and *Gedachtes*, the thought-of-an-object, and the object-thought-of, both in one; and all this without paradox or mystery, just as the same material thing may be both low and high, or small and great, or bad and good, because of its relations to opposite parts of an environing world.

As "subjective" we say that the experience represents; as "objective" it is represented. What represents and what is represented is here numerically the same; but we must remember that no dualism of being represented and representing resides in the experience *per se*. In its pure state, or when isolated, there is no self-splitting of it into consciousness and what the consciousness is "of." Its subjectivity and objectivity are functional attributes solely, realized only when the experience is "taken," *i.e.*, talked-of, twice, considered along with its two differing contexts respectively, by a new retrospective experience, of which that whole past complication now forms the fresh content.

The instant field of the present is at all times what I call the "pure" experience. It is only virtually or potentially either object or subject as yet. For the time being, it is plain, unqualified actuality or existence, a simple *that*. In this *naïf* immediacy it is of course *valid*; it is *there*, we *act* upon it; and the doubling of it in retrospection into a state of mind and a reality intended thereby, is just one of the acts. The "state of mind," first treated explicitly as such in retrospection, will stand corrected or confirmed, and the retrospective experience in its turn will get a similar treatment; but the immediate experience in its passing is always "truth,"[23] practical truth, *something to act on*, at its own movement. If the world were then and there to go out like a candle, it would remain truth absolute and objective, for it would be "the last word," would have no critic, and no one would ever oppose the thought in it to the reality intended.[24]

[22] For simplicity's sake I confine my exposition to "external" reality. But there is also the system of ideal reality in which the room plays its part. Relations of comparison, of classification, serial order, value, also are stubborn, assign a definite place to the room, unlike the incoherences of its places in the mere rhapsody of our successive thoughts.

[23] Note the ambiguity of this term, which is taken sometimes objectively and sometimes subjectively.

[24] In the *Psychological Review* for July of this year, Dr. R. B. Perry has published a view of Consciousness which comes nearer to mine than any other with which I am acquainted. At present, Dr. Perry thinks, every field of experience is so much "fact." It becomes "opinion" or "thought" only in retrospection, when a fresh experience, thinking the same object, alters and corrects it. But the corrective experience becomes itself in turn corrected, and thus experience as a whole

I think I may now claim to have made my thesis clear. Consciousness connotes a kind of external relation, and does not denote a special stuff or way of being. *The peculiarity of our experiences, that they not only are, but are known, which their "conscious" quality is invoked to explain, is better explained by their relations—these relations themselves being experiences—to one another.*

RADICAL EMPIRICISM [25]

I. RADICAL EMPIRICISM

I give the name of "radical empiricism" to my *Weltanschauung*. Empiricism is known as the opposite of rationalism. Rationalism tends to emphasize universals and to make wholes prior to parts in the order of logic as well as in that of being. Empiricism, on the contrary, lays the explanatory stress upon the part, the element, the individual, and treats the whole as a collection and the universal as an abstraction. My description of things, accordingly, starts with the parts and makes of the whole a being of the second order. It is essentially a mosaic philosophy, a philosophy of plural facts, like that of Hume and his descendants, who refer these facts neither to Substances in which they inhere nor to an Absolute Mind that creates them as its objects. But it differs from the Humian type of empiricism in one particular which makes me add the epithet radical.

To be radical, an empiricism must neither admit into its constructions any element that is not directly experienced, nor exclude from them any element that is directly experienced. For such a philosophy, *the relations that connect experiences must themselves be experienced relations, and any kind of relation experienced must be accounted as "real" as anything else in the system.* Elements may indeed be redistributed, the original placing of things getting corrected, but a real place must be found for every kind of thing experienced, whether term or relation, in the final philosophic arrangement.

Now, ordinary empiricism, in spite of the fact that conjunctive and disjunctive relations present themselves as being fully coordinate

---

is a process in which what is objective originally forever turns subjective, turns into our apprehension of the object. I strongly recommend Dr. Perry's admirable article to my readers.

parts of experience, has always shown a tendency to do away with the connections of things, and to insist most on the disjunctions. Berkeley's nominalism, Hume's statement that whatever things we distinguish are as "loose and separate" as if they had "no manner of connection," James Mill's denial that similars have anything "really" in common, the resolution of the causal tie into habitual sequence, John Mill's account of both physical things and selves as composed of discontinuous possibilities, and the general pulverization of all Experience by association and the mind-dust theory, are examples of what I mean.

The natural result of such a world-picture has been the efforts of naturalism to correct its incoherencies by the addition of transexperiential agents of unification, substances, intellectual categories and powers, or Selves; whereas, if empiricism had only been radical and taken every thing that comes without disfavor, conjunction as well as separation, each at its face value, the results would have called for no such artificial correction. *Radical empiricism*, as I understand it, *does full justice to conjunctive relations*, without, however, treating them as rationalism always tends to treat them, as being true in some supernal way, as if the unity of things and their variety be·longed to different orders of truth and vitality altogether.

II. CONJUNCTIVE RELATIONS

Relations are of different degrees of intimacy. Merely to be "with" one another in a universe of discourse is the most external relation that terms can have, and seems to involve nothing whatever as to farther consequences. Simultaneity and time-interval come next, and then space-adjacency and distance. After them, similarity and difference, carrying the possibility of many inferences. Then relations of activity, tying terms into series involving change, tendency, resistance, and the causal order generally. Finally, the relation experienced between terms that form states of mind, and are immediately conscious of continuing each other. The organization of the Self as a system of memories, purposes, strivings, fulfilments or disappointments, is incidental to this most intimate of all relations, the terms of which seem in many cases actually to compenetrate and suffuse each other's being.

Philosophy has always turned on grammatical particles. With, near, next, like, from, towards, against, because, for, through, my—these words designate types of conjunctive relation arranged in a roughly ascending order of intimacy and inclusiveness. *A priori*, we can imagine a universe of withness but no nextness; or one of nextness but no likeness, or of likeness with no activity, or of activity with no purpose, or of purpose with no ego. These would be universes, each with its own grade of unity. The universe of human experience is, by one or another of its parts, of each and all these grades. Whether or not it possibly enjoys some still more absolute grade of union does not appear upon the surface.

Taken as it does appear, our universe is to a large extent chaotic. No one single type of connection runs through all the experiences that compose it. If we take space-relations, they fail to connect minds into any regular system. Causes and purposes obtain only among special series of facts. The self relation seems extremely limited and does not link two different selves together. *Prima facie*, if you should liken the universe of absolute idealism to an aquarium, a crystal globe in which goldfish are swimming, you would have to compare the empiricist universe to something more like one of those dried human heads with which the Dyaks of Borneo deck their lodges. The skull forms a solid nucleus; but innumerable feathers, leaves, strings, beads, and loose appendices of every description float and dangle from it, and save that they terminate in it, seem to have nothing to do with one another. Even so my experiences and yours float and dangle, terminating, it is true, in a nucleus of common perception, but for the most part out of sight and irrelevant and unimaginable to one another. This imperfect intimacy, this bare relation of *withness* between some parts of the sum total of experience and other parts, is the fact that ordinary empiricism overemphasizes against rationalism, the latter always tending to ignore it unduly. Radical empiricism, on the contrary, is fair to both the unity and the disconnection. It finds no reason for treating either as illusory. It allots to each its definite sphere of description, and agrees that there appear to be actual forces at work which tend, as time goes on, to make the unity greater.

The conjunctive relation that has given most trouble to philosophy is *the co-conscious transition*, so to call it, by which one experience passes into another when both belong to the same self. About the facts there is no question. My experiences and your experiences are "with" each other in various external ways, but mine pass into mine, and yours pass into yours in a way in which yours and mine never pass into one another. Within each of our personal histories, subject, object, interest and purpose *are continuous or may be continuous*.[26] Personal histories are processes of change in time, and *the change itself is one of the things immediately experienced*. "Change"

[26] The psychology books have of late described the facts here with approximate adequacy. I may refer to the chapters on "The Stream of Thought" and on the Self in my own *Principles of Psychology*, as well as to S. H. Hodgson's *Metaphysic of Experience*, Vol. I, Chap. VII, and VIII.

in this case means continuous as opposed to discontinuous transition. But continuous transition is one sort of a conjunctive relation; and to be a radical empiricist means to hold fast to this conjunctive relation of all others, for this is the strategic point, the position through which, if a hole be made, all the corruptions of dialectics and all the metaphysical fictions pour into our philosophy. The holding fast to this relation means taking it at its face value, neither less nor more; and to take it at its face value means first of all to take it just as we feel it, and not to confuse ourselves with abstract talk *about* it, involving words that drive us to invent secondary conceptions in order to neutralize their suggestions and to make our actual experience again seem rationally possible.

What I do feel simply when a later moment of my experience succeeds an earlier one is that though they are two moments, the transition from the one to the other is *continuous*. Continuity here is a definite sort of experience; just as definite as is the *discontinuity-experience* which I find it impossible to avoid when I seek to make the transition from an experience of my own to one of yours. In this latter case I have to get on and off again, to pass from a thing lived to another thing only conceived, and the break is positively experienced and noted. Though the functions exerted by my experience and by yours may be the same (*e.g.*, the same objects known and the same purposes followed), yet the sameness has in this case to be ascertained expressly (and often with difficulty and uncertainty) after the break has been felt; whereas in passing from one of my own moments to another the sameness of object and interest is unbroken, and both the earlier and the later experience are of things directly lived.

There is no other *nature*, no other whatness than this absence of break and this sense of continuity in that most intimate of all conjunctive relations, the passing of one experience into another when they belong to the same self. And this whatness is real empirical "content" just as the whatness of separation and discontinuity is real content in the contrasted case. Practically to experience one's personal continuum in this living way is to know the originals of the ideas of continuity and of sameness, to know what the words stand for concretely, to own all that they can ever mean. But all experiences have their conditions; and over-subtle intellects, thinking about the facts here, and asking how they are possible, have ended by substituting a lot of static objects of conception for the direct perceptual experiences. "Sameness," they have said, "must be a stark numerical identity; it can't run on from next to next. Continuity can't mean mere absence of gap; for if you say two things are in immediate contact, *at* the contact how can they be two? If, on the other hand, you put a relation of transition between them, that it-self is a third thing, and needs to be related or hitched to its terms. An infinite series is involved," and so on. The result is that from difficulty to difficulty, the plain conjunctive experience has been dis-credited by both schools, the empiricists leaving things permanently disjoined, and the rationalists remedying the looseness by their Ab-solutes or Substances, or whatever other fictitious agencies of union they may have employed. From all which artificiality we can be saved by a couple of simple reflections: first, that conjunctions and separations are, at all events, coordinate phenomena which, if we take experiences at their face value, must be accounted equally real; and second, that if we insist on treating things as really separate when they are given as continuously joined, invoking, when union is required, transcendental principles to overcome the separateness we have assumed, then we ought to stand ready to perform the converse act. We ought to invoke higher principles of *dis*union also, to make our merely experienced *dis*junctions more truly real. Failing thus, we ought to let the originally given continuities stand on their own bottom. We have no right to be lopsided or to blow capriciously hot and cold. . . .

A PLURALISTIC UNIVERSE[27]

Pragmatically interpreted, pluralism or the doctrine that it is many means only that the sundry parts of reality *may be externally related.* Everything you can think of, however vast or inclusive, has on the pluralistic view a genuinely "external" environment of some sort or amount. Things are "with" one another in many ways, but nothing includes everything, or dominates over everything. The word "and" trails along after every sentence. Something always escapes. "Ever not quite" has to be said of the best attempts made anywhere in the universe at attaining all-inclusiveness. The pluralistic world is thus more like a federal republic than like an empire or a kingdom. However much may be collected, however much may report itself as present at any effective centre of consciousness or action, some-thing else is self-governed and absent and unreduced to unity.

Monism, on the other hand, insists that when you come down to reality as such, to the reality of realities, everything is present to *everything* else in one vast instantaneous co-implicated completeness —nothing can in *any* sense, functional or substantial, be really absent

[27] From *A Pluralistic Universe*, N. Y.: Longmans, Green, 1909, pp. 321–328.

from anything else, all things interpenetrate and telescope together in the great total conflux.

For pluralism, all that we are required to admit as the constitution of reality is what we ourselves find empirically realized in every minimum of finite life. Briefly it is this, that nothing real is absolutely simple, that every smallest bit of experience is a *multum in parvo* plurally related, that each relation is one aspect, character, or function, way of its being taken, or way of its taking something else; and that a bit of reality when actively engaged in one of these relations is not *by that very fact* engaged in all the other relations simultaneously. The relations are not *all* what the French call *solidaires* with one another. Without losing its identity a thing can either take up or drop another thing, like the log I spoke of, which by taking up new carriers and dropping old ones can travel anywhere with a light escort.

For monism, on the contrary, everything, whether we realize it or not, drags the whole universe along with itself and drops nothing. The log starts and arrives with all its carriers supporting it. If a thing were once disconnected, it could never be connected again, according to monism. The pragmatic difference between the two systems is thus a definite one. It is just thus, that if *a* is once out of sight of *b* or out of touch with it, or, more briefly, "out" of it at all, then, according to monism, it must always remain so, they can never get together; whereas pluralism admits that on another occasion they may work together, or in some way be connected again. Monism allows for no such things as "other occasions" in reality—in *real* or absolute reality, that is.

The difference I try to describe amounts, you see, to nothing more than the difference between what I formerly called the each-form and the all-form of reality. Pluralism lets things really exist in the each-form or distributively. Monism thinks that the all-form or collective-unit form is the only form that is rational. The all-form allows of no taking up and dropping of connexions, for in the all the parts are essentially and eternally co-implicated. In the each-form, on the contrary, a thing may be connected by intermediary things, with a thing with which it has no immediate or essential connexion. It is thus at all times in many possible connexions which are not necessarily actualized at the moment. They depend on which actual path of intermediation it may functionally strike into: the word "or" names a genuine reality. Thus, as I speak here, I may look ahead *or* to the right *or* to the left, and in either case the intervening space and air and ether enable me to see the faces of a different portion of this audience. My being here is independent of any one set of these faces.

If the each-form be the eternal form of reality no less than it is the form of temporal appearance, we still have a coherent world, and not an incarnate incoherence, as is charged by so many absolutists. Our "multiverse" still makes a "universe"; for every part, tho it may not be in actual or immediate connexion, is nevertheless in some possible or mediated connexion, with every other part however remote, through the fact that each part hangs together with its very next neighbors in inextricable interfusion. The type of union, it is true, is different here from the monistic type of *alleinheit*. It is not a universal co-implication, or integration of all things *durcheinander*. It is what I call the strung-along type, the type of continuity, contiguity, or concatenation. If you prefer Greek words, you may call it the synechistic type. At all events, you see that it forms a definitely conceivable alternative to the through-and-through unity of all things at once, which is the type opposed to it by monism. You see also that it stands or falls with the notion I have taken such pains to defend, of the through-and-through union of adjacent minima of experience, of the confluence of every passing moment of concretely felt experience with its immediately next neighbors. The recognition of this fact of coalescence of next with next in concrete experience, so that all the insulating cuts we make there are artificial products of the conceptualizing faculty, is what distinguishes the empiricism which I call "radical," from the bugaboo empiricism of the traditional rationalist critics, which (rightly or wrongly) is accused of chopping up experience into atomistic sensations, incapable of union with one another until a purely intellectual principle has swooped down upon them from on high and folded them in its own conjunctive categories.

Here, then, you have the plain alternative, and the full mystery of the difference between pluralism and monism, as clearly as I can set it forth on this occasion. It packs up into a nutshell:—Is the manyness in oneness that indubitably characterizes the world we inhabit, a property only of the absolute whole of things, so that you must postulate that one-enormous-whole indivisibly as the *prius* of there being any many at all—in other words, start with the rationalistic block-universe, entire, unmitigated, and complete?—or can the finite elements have their own aboriginal forms of manyness in oneness, and where they have no immediate oneness still be continued into one another by intermediary terms—each one of these terms being one with its next neighbors, and yet the total "oneness" never getting absolutely complete?

The alternative is definite. It seems to me, moreover, that the two horns of it make pragmatically different ethical appeals—at least they *may* do so, to certain individuals. But if you consider the pluralistic horn to be intrinsically irrational, self-contradictory, and absurd, I can now say no more in its defence. Having done what I could in my earlier lectures to break the edge of the intellectualistic *reductiones ad absurdum*, I must leave the issue in your hands. Whatever I may say, each of you will be sure to take pluralism or leave it, just as your own sense of rationality moves and inclines. The only thing I emphatically insist upon is that it is a fully co-ordinate hypothesis with monism. This world *may*, in the last resort, be a block-universe; but on the other hand it *may* be a universe only strung-along, not rounded in and closed. Reality *may* exist distributively just as it sensibly seems to, after all. On that possibility I do insist. . . .

BIBLIOGRAPHY

JAMES, William, *The Principles of Psychology.* 2 vols. N.Y.: Henry Holt, 1890.

———, *The Will to Believe and Other Essays in Popular Philosophy.* N.Y.: Longmans, Green, 1896.

———, *The Varieties of Religious Experience: A Study in Human Nature.* N.Y.: Longmans, Green, 1902.

———, *Pragmatism: A New Name for Some Old Ways of Thinking.* N.Y.: Longmans, Green, 1907.

———, *The Meaning of Truth: A Sequel to "Pragmatism."* N.Y.: Longmans, Green, 1909.

———, *A Pluralistic Universe.* N.Y.: Longmans, Green, 1909.

———, *Some Problems of Philosophy: A Beginning of an Introduction to Philosophy.* N.Y.: Longmans, Green, 1911.

———, *Memories and Studies.* N.Y.: Longmans, Green, 1911.

———, *Essays in Radical Empiricism.* N.Y.: Longmans, Green, 1912.

———, *Collected Essays and Reviews.* N.Y.: Longmans, Green, 1920.

———, *Selected Letters,* ed. with an introduction by Elizabeth Hardwick, N.Y.: Farrar, Straus and Cudahy, 1961.

JAMES, Henry, ed. *The Letters of William James.* 2 vols. N.Y.: Longmans, Green, 1920.

Essays Philosophical and Psychological in Honor of William James. N.Y.: Longmans, Green, 1908.

In Commemoration of William James, 1842–1942. N.Y.: Columbia U. Press, 1942.

William James the Man and the Thinker. Madison: U. of Wisconsin Press, 1942.

BAUM, Maurice. "The Development of James's Pragmatism Prior to 1879," *Journal of Philosophy,* Vol. 30 (1933), pp. 43–51.

BLAU, Théodore. *William James; sa théorie de la connaissance et la vérité.* Paris, Jouve et Cie, 1933.

DEWEY, John, "The Vanishing Subject in the Psychology of James," *Journal of Philosophy*, Vol. 37 (1940), pp. 589–99.

FLOURNOY, Theodore. *The Philosophy of William James*. Translated by E. B. Holt and Wm. James, Jr., N.Y.: Henry Holt, 1917.

GRATTAN, C. Hartley. *The Three Jameses; a Family of Minds, Henry James, Sr., William James, Henry James*. N.Y.: Longmans, Green, 1932.

KALLEN, Horace M. *William James and Henri Bergson*. Chicago: U. of Chicago Press, 1914.

KNIGHT, Margaret, ed. William James. *A Selection From His Writings on Psychology*. Harmondsworth, Middlesex: Penguin Books, 1950.

MEAD, George H. "The Philosophies of Royce, James and Dewey in their American Setting," *International Journal of Ethics*, Vol. 40 (1929–30), pp. 211–31.

MOORE, G. E. *Philosophical Studies*. N.Y.: Harcourt, Brace, 1922, pp. 97–146.

MORRIS, Lloyd R. *William James: The Message of a Modern Mind*. N.Y.: Charles Scribner's, 1950.

PERRY, Ralph Barton. *Annotated Bibliography of the Writings of William James*. N.Y.: Longmans, Green, 1920.

————, *The Thought and Character of William James: Revealed in Unpublished Correspondence and Notes, Together with His Published Writings*. 2 vols. Boston: Little, Brown, 1935.

————, *In the Spirit of William James*. New Haven: Yale U. Press, 1938.

————, *Present Philosophical Tendencies*. N.Y.: Longmans, Green, 1912. (Appendix: "The Philosophy of William James").

ROBACK, A. A. *William James, His Marginalia, Personality and Contribution*. Cambridge, Mass.: Sci–Art Publishers, 1942.

ROYCE, Josiah. *William James and Other Essays on the Philosophy of Life*. N.Y.: Macmillan, 1911.

SABIN, Ethel E. *William James and Pragmatism*. Lancaster, Pa., 1916.

SANTAYANA, George. *Character and Opinion in the United States; with Reminiscences of William James and Josiah Royce and Academic Life in America*. N.Y.: Charles Scribner's, 1920 (Ch. III).

SCHILLER, F. C. S. "William James and the Making of Pragmatism," *Personalist*, Vol. 8 (1927), pp. 81–93.

————, "William James and Empiricism," *Journal of Philosophy*, Vol. 25 (1928), pp. 155–62.

WAHL, Jean. *The Pluralist Philosophies of England and America* (trans. Fred Rothwell), London: Open Court, 1925 (Bk. III).

John Dewey

[1859–1952]

John Dewey is probably the most generally influential American philosopher of the twentieth century. A pragmatist, instrumentalist and behaviorist in both theory and practice, he carried his philosophical activities far beyond the confines of learned journals and scholarly books to the larger marketplace of ideas and action. For many decades, Dewey was widely regarded as an outstanding leader of political and social liberalism, progressive education, and uncompromising naturalistic humanism. His writings cover a span of more than half a century and deal with logic, epistemology, language, science, metaphysics, ethics, valuation, political and social philosophy, aesthetics, religion and education.

Dewey was born in Burlington, Vermont; he studied at the University of Vermont, and took his Ph.D. in 1884 at the newly founded Johns Hopkins University. He taught at the University of Michigan and the University of Chicago, and in his later years at Columbia University, retiring from active teaching in 1929.

The extent of his involvement in public affairs was great. He was a leader in liberal movements and was, for example, co-founder of the American Association of University Professors and of the New School for Social Research, and chairman of the unofficial commission that found Leon Trotsky innocent of the charges made by Stalin in the late nineteen thirties. The name of Dewey is synonymous with the liberating movement in progressive education—though Dewey cannot be identified with all of its supporters, as his many critics attempt to do. Dewey's influence was international. He visited and lectured in China, Turkey, Mexico, the U.S.S.R. and Japan, where many of his educational ideas were adopted.

Dewey's thought is the product of an early neo-Hegelianism, the Darwinian theory of evolution, the pragmatism of Peirce and the newer behavioral psychology. His own form of pragmatism stands midway between Peirce and James. With Peirce, he emphasized the laboratory and experimental verification of ideas, taking science as his model, but with James, he concentrated upon social and moral consequences. Broadly conceived, Dewey's philosophy is an attempt to apply the methods of science to all aspects of human experience, especially to the solution of problems of value. Dewey's conception of the role of philosophy was that it had a critical function to perform in civilization by helping to define and resolve conflicts. He believed that false dualisms and distinctions—between man and nature, theory and practice, mind and body, subject and object, means and ends, fact and value, individual and society, and so on—must be overcome.

Dewey thought that the historic

attempts by philosophers to create antecedent realities or transcendental fixities were mistaken. Philosophers must use empirical methods; all knowledge must be related to the immediate experiences of ordinary life, which are primary. Philosophic and intellectual distinctions are only secondary or derived. Much of this position is delivered in *Experience and Nature* (1929), Dewey's chief statement of his naturalism, the opening pages of which are reprinted below. Dewey also maintained that knowledge is tentative and provisional because nature is precarious and contingent, and change is a pervasive fact of the world that we encounter.

Man, Dewey asserted, is a biosocial animal transacting within a natural environment. Thinking is a natural activity (organic and social), and instrumental to the resolution of "indeterminate existential situations." In Dewey's last major work, *Logic: The Theory of Inquiry* (1938), a key section of which is reprinted below, Dewey argues that logical distinctions, forms, and principles grow out of the process of inquiry, and take on meaning only in relation to the situations in which they arise. The brief selection below, *What Pragmatism Means by the "Practical"* (1916), shows this instrumental and behavioristic interpretation of thinking and knowing. Dewey's definition of pragmatism here is brief and to the point: "pragmatism" is that outlook which refers all thinking "to *consequences* for final meaning and test."

Dewey was a stalwart defender of the method of science or intelligence, and he thought that the great challenge to contemporary man was to extend this method to all aspects of human life—politics, morality, religion, and value. Science, however, is continuous with common sense, and merely makes explicit what is already implicit in the way we think. In *The Logic of Judgments of Practice*, an early and frequently overlooked piece (1915), Dewey argues that judgments of practice (valuation judgments) are hypotheses, verifiable in principle in the same way as descriptive judgments. Indeed, Dewey believed that *all* judgments in a sense are prescriptive and practical in character, helping to resolve indeterminate situations. Valuation judgments in particular are part of a means-end continuum and are resolvable by reference to their instrumental functions in life activities.

Dewey's primary faith in intelligence had two basic social applications. First, in his theory of education, which had an enormous influence on the American system of democratic education, he maintained that the school should liberate the potentialities of children, develop their capacities for growth, and especially their critical intelligence, and enable them to share experiences. The development of habits is an important end of education, yet it must not be allowed to thwart creative impulse. In *Democracy and Education* (1916), Dewey's most important work in educational philosophy, the importance of creative growth and the democratic ideal are emphasized. Passages from this work are reprinted below.

A second application of pragmatic intelligence is Dewey's defense of liberalism. For Dewey, liberalism was first and foremost a method for the solution of social problems, not a platform or ideology. Dewey defended the liberal ideals of democracy and freedom. But his liberalism is not to be identified with either nineteenth-century individualism or

Marxism, even though it was influenced by both. It was a liberalism which attempted to avoid doctrinaire labels. Programs change from age to age, said Dewey, but liberalism is committed, whatever the age, to the application of freed intelligence to public problems. His article, *The Future of Liberalism* (1935), written at the height of the Great Depression of the nineteen-thirties, is reprinted below.

Dewey wrote many other works, too numerous to be listed here; but among the most important are *The Quest for Certainty* (1929), on metaphysics and theory of knowledge;

Knowing and the Known (1949), with A. Bentley, on semantics and epistemology; *A Common Faith* (1934), in which humanistic religious experience is defended; and *Art as Experience* (1934), an attempt to relate art to his own broad conception of experience.

No brief account can possibly do justice to the full measure and scope of the man. But with Dewey, perhaps more than with any other philosopher in the twentieth century, all of the qualities of American pragmatic intelligence seem to be most fully expressed.

EXPERIENCE AND NATURE [1]

EXPERIENCE AND PHILOSOPHIC METHOD

The title of this volume, *Experience and Nature*, is intended to signify that the philosophy here presented may be termed either empirical naturalism or naturalistic empiricism, or, taking "experience" in its usual signification, naturalistic humanism.

To many the associating of the two words will seem like talking of a round square, so engrained is the notion of the separation of man and experience from nature. Experience, they say, is important for those beings who have it, but is too casual and sporadic in its occurrence to carry with it any important implications regarding the nature of Nature. Nature, on the other hand, is said to be complete apart from experience. Indeed, according to some thinkers the case is even in worse plight: Experience to them is not only something extraneous which is occasionally superimposed upon nature, but it forms a veil or screen which shuts us off from nature, unless in some way it can be "transcended." So something non-natural by way of reason or intuition is introduced, something supra-empirical. According to an opposite school experience fares as badly, nature being thought to signify something wholly material and mechanistic; to frame a theory of experience in naturalistic terms is, accordingly,

[1] John Dewey, *Experience and Nature*, 1929 (2nd Edition). Chapter I, pp. 1–8, 38–39; Chapter II, pp. 46–48, 62–71.

to degrade and deny the noble and ideal values that characterize experience.

I know of no route by which dialectical argument can answer such objections. They arise from associations with words and cannot be dealt with argumentatively. One can only hope in the course of the whole discussion to disclose the meanings which are attached to "experience" and "nature," and thus insensibly produce, if one is fortunate, a change in the significations previously attached to them. This process of change may be hastened by calling attention to another context in which nature and experience get on harmoniously together—wherein experience presents itself as the method, and the only method, for getting at nature, penetrating its secrets, and wherein nature empirically disclosed (by the use of empirical method in natural science) deepens, enriches and directs the further development of experience.

In the natural sciences there is a union of experience and nature which is not greeted as a monstrosity; on the contrary, the inquirer must use empirical method if his findings are to be treated as genuinely scientific. The investigator assumes as a matter of course that experience, controlled in specifiable ways, is the avenue that leads to the facts and laws of nature. He uses reason and calculation freely; he could not get along without them. But he sees to it that ventures of this theoretical sort start from and terminate in directly experienced subject-matter. Theory may intervene in a long course of reasoning, many portions of which are remote from what is directly experienced. But the vine of pendant theory is attached at both ends to the pillars of observed subject-matter. And this experienced material is the same for the scientific man and the man in the street. The latter cannot follow the intervening reasoning without special preparation. But stars, rocks, trees, and creeping things are the same material of experience for both.

These commonplaces take on significance when the relation of experience to the formation of a philosophic theory of nature is in question. They indicate that experience, if scientific inquiry is justified, is no infinitesimally thin layer or foreground of nature, but that it penetrates into it, reaching down into its depths, and in such a way that its grasp is capable of expansion; it tunnels in all directions and in so doing brings to the surface things at first hidden—as miners pile high on the surface of the earth treasures brought from below. Unless we are prepared to deny all validity to scientific inquiry, these facts have a value that cannot be ignored for the general theory of the relation of nature and experience.

It is sometimes contended, for example, that since experience is a late comer in the history of our solar system and planet, and since these occupy a trivial place in the wide areas of celestial space, experience is at most a slight and insignificant incident in nature. No one with an honest respect for scientific conclusions can deny that experience as an existence is something that occurs only under highly specialized conditions, such as are found in a highly organized creature which in turn requires a specialized environment. There is no evidence that experience occurs everywhere and everywhen. But candid regard for scientific inquiry also compels the recognition that when experience does occur, no matter at what limited portion of time and space, it enters into possession of some portion of nature and in such a manner as to render other of its precincts accessible.

A geologist living in 1928 tells us about events that happened not only before he was born but millions of years before any human being came into existence on this earth. He does so by starting from things that are now the material of experience. Lyell revolutionized geology by perceiving that the sort of thing that can be experienced now in the operations of fire, water, pressure, is the sort of thing by which the earth took on its present structural forms. Visiting a natural history museum, one beholds a mass of rock and, reading a label, finds that it comes from a tree that grew, so it is affirmed, five million years ago. The geologist did not leap from the thing he can see and touch to some event in by-gone ages; he collated this observed thing with many others, of different kinds, found all over the globe; the results of his comparisons he then compared with data of other experiences, say, the astronomer's. He translates, that is, observed coexistences into non-observed, inferred sequences. Finally he dates his object, placing it in an order of events. By the same sort of method he predicts that at certain places some things not yet experienced will be observed, and then he takes pains to bring them within the scope of experience. The scientific conscience is, moreover, so sensitive with respect to the necessity of experience that when it reconstructs the past it is not fully satisfied with inferences drawn from even a large and cumulative mass of uncontradicted evidence; it sets to work to institute conditions of heat and pressure and moisture, etc., so as actually to reproduce in experiment that which he has inferred.

These commonplaces prove that experience is *of* as well as *in* nature. It is not experience which is experienced, but nature—stones, plants, animals, diseases, health, temperature, electricity, and so on. Things interacting in certain ways *are* experience; they are what is experienced. Linked in certain other ways with another natural object—the human organism—they are *how* things are experienced as well. Experience thus reaches down into nature; it has depth. It also has breadth and to an indefinitely elastic extent. It stretches. That stretch constitutes inference.

Dialectical difficulties, perplexities due to definitions given to the concepts that enter into the discussion, may be raised. It is said to be absurd that what is only a tiny part of nature should be competent to incorporate vast reaches of nature within itself. But even were it logically absurd one would be bound to cleave to it as a fact. Logic, however, is not put under a strain. The fact that something is an occurrence does not decide what kind of an occurrence it is; that can be found out only by examination. To argue from an experience "being an experience" to what it is of and about is warranted by no logic, even though modern thought has attempted it a thousand times. A bare event is no event at all; *something* happens. What that something is, is found out by actual study. This applies to seeing a flash of lightning and holds of the longer event called experience. The very existence of science is evidence that experience is such an occurrence that it penetrates into nature and expands without limit through it.

These remarks are not supposed to prove anything about experience and nature for philosophical doctrine; they are not supposed to settle anything about the worth of empirical naturalism. But they do show that in the case of natural science we habitually treat experience as starting-point, and as method for dealing with nature, and as the goal in which nature is disclosed for what it is. To realize this fact is at least to weaken those verbal associations which stand in the way of apprehending the force of empirical method in philosophy.

The same considerations apply to the other objection that was suggested: namely, that to view experience naturalistically is to reduce it to something materialistic, depriving it of all ideal significance. If experience actually presents esthetic and moral traits, then these traits may also be supposed to reach down into nature, and to testify to something that belongs to nature as truly as does the mechanical structure attributed to it in physical science. To rule out that possibility by some general reasoning is to forget that the very meaning and purport of empirical method is that things are to be studied on their own account, so as to find out what is revealed when they are experienced. The traits possessed by the subject-matters of experience are as genuine as the characteristics of sun and electron. They are *found*, experienced, and are not to be shoved out of being by some trick of logic. When found, their ideal qualities are as relevant to the philosophic theory of nature as are the traits found by physical inquiry.

To discover some of these general features of experienced things and to interpret their significance for a philosophic theory of the universe in which we live is the aim of this volume. From the point of view adopted, the theory of empirical method in philosophy does for experienced subject-matter on a liberal scale what it does for special sciences on a technical scale. It is this aspect of method with which we are especially concerned in the present chapter.

If the empirical method were universally or even generally adopted in philosophizing, there would be no need of referring to experience. The scientific inquirer talks and writes about particular observed events and qualities, about specific calculations and reasonings. He makes no allusion to experience; one would probably have to search a long time through reports of special researches in order to find the word. The reason is that everything designated by the word "experience" is so adequately incorporated into scientific procedures and subject-matter that to mention experience would be only to duplicate in a general term what is already covered in definite terms.

Yet this was not always so. Before the technique of empirical method was developed and generally adopted, it was necessary to dwell explicitly upon the importance of "experience" as a starting point and terminal point, as setting problems and as testing proposed solutions. We need not be content with the conventional allusion to Roger Bacon and Francis Bacon. The followers of Newton and the followers of the Cartesian school carried on a definite controversy as to the place occupied by experience and experiment in science as compared with intuitive concepts and with reasoning from them. The Cartesian school relegated experience to a secondary and almost accidental place, and only when the Galilean-Newtonian method had wholly triumphed did it cease to be necessary to mention the importance of experience. We may, if sufficiently hopeful, anticipate a similar outcome in philosophy. But the date does not appear to be close at hand; we are nearer in philosophic theory to the time of Roger Bacon than to that of Newton.

In short, it is the contrast of empirical method with other methods employed in philosophizing, together with the striking dissimilarity of results yielded by an empirical method and professed non-empirical methods that make the discussion of the methodological import of "experience" for philosophy pertinent and indeed indispensable.

This consideration of method may suitably begin with the contrast between gross, macroscopic, crude subject-matters in primary experience and the refined, derived objects of reflection. The distinction is one between what is experienced as the result of a minimum of incidental reflection and what is experienced in consequence of continued and regulated reflective inquiry. For derived and refined products are experienced only because of the intervention of systematic thinking. The objects of both science and philosophy obviously belong chiefly to the secondary and refined system. But at this point we come to a marked divergence between science and philosophy. For the natural sciences not only draw their material from primary experience, but they refer it back again for test. Darwin began with the pigeons, cattle and plants of breeders and gardeners. Some of the conclusions he reached were so contrary to accepted beliefs that they were condemned as absurd, contrary to common-sense, etc. But scientific men, whether they accepted his theories or not, employed his hypotheses as directive ideas for making new observations and experiments among the things of raw experience—just as the metallurgist who extracts refined metal from crude ore makes tools that are then set to work to control and use other crude materials. An Einstein working by highly elaborate methods of reflection, calculates theoretically certain results in the deflection of light by the presence of the sun. A technically equipped expedition is sent to South Africa so that by means of experiencing a thing—an eclipse—in crude, primary experience, observations can be secured to compare with, and test the theory implied in, the calculated result.

The facts are familiar enough. They are cited in order to invite attention to the relationship between the objects of primary and of secondary or reflective experience. That the subject-matter of primary experience sets the problems and furnishes the first data of the reflection which constructs the secondary objects is evident; it is also obvious that test and verification of the latter is secured only by return to things of crude or macroscopic experience—the sun, earth, plants and animals of common, every-day life. But just what rôle do the objects attained in reflection play? Where do they come in? They *explain* the primary objects, they enable us to grasp them with *understanding*, instead of just having sense-contact with them. But how?

Well, they define or lay out a path by which return to experienced things is of such a sort that the meaning, the significant content, of what is experienced gains an enriched and expanded force because of the path or method by which it was reached. Directly, in immediate contact it may be just what it was before—hard, colored, odorous, etc. But when the secondary objects, the refined objects, are employed as a method or road for coming at them, these qualities cease to be isolated details; they get the meaning contained in a whole system of related objects; they are rendered continuous with the rest of nature and take on the import of the things they are now seen to be continuous with. The phenomena observed in the eclipse tested and, as far as they went, confirmed Einstein's theory of deflection of light by mass. But that is far from being the whole story. The phenomena themselves got a far-reaching significance they did not previously have. Perhaps they would not even have been noticed if the theory had not been employed as a guide or road to observation of them. But even if they had been noticed, they would have been dismissed as of no importance, just as we daily drop from attention hundreds of perceived details for which we have no intellectual use. But approached by means of theory these lines of slight deflection take on a significance as large as that of the revolutionary theory that lead to their being experienced.

This empirical method I shall call the *denotative* method. That philosophy is a mode of reflection, often of a subtle and penetrating sort, goes without saying. The charge that is brought against the non-empirical method of philosophizing is not that it depends upon theorizing, but that it fails to use refined, secondary products as a path pointing and leading back to something in primary experience. The resulting failure is three-fold.

First, there is no verification, no effort even to test and check. What is even worse, secondly, is that the things of ordinary experience do not get enlargement and enrichment of meaning as they do when approached through the medium of scientific principles and reasonings. This lack of function reacts, in the third place, back upon the philosophic subject-matter in itself. Not tested by being employed to see what it leads to in ordinary experience and what new meanings it contributes, this subject-matter becomes arbitrary, aloof—what is called "abstract" when that word is used in a bad sense to designate something which exclusively occupies a realm of its own without contact with the things of ordinary experience.

As the net outcome of these three evils, we find that extraordinary phenomenon which accounts for the revulsion of many cultivated persons from any form of philosophy. The objects of reflection in philosophy, being reached by methods that seem to those who employ them rationally mandatory are taken to be "real" in and of themselves—and supremely real. Then it becomes an insoluble problem why the things of gross, primary experience, should be what they are, or indeed why they should be at all. The refined objects of reflection in the natural sciences, however, never end by rendering the subject-matter from which they are derived a problem; rather, when used to describe a path by which some goal in primary experience is designated or denoted, they solve perplexities to which that crude material gives rise but which it cannot resolve of itself. They become means of control, of enlarged use and enjoyment of ordinary things.

They may generate new problems, but these are problems of the same sort, to be dealt with by further use of the same methods of inquiry and experimentation. The problems to which empirical method gives rise afford, in a word, opportunities for more investigations yielding fruit in new and enriched experiences. But the problems to which non-empirical method gives rise in philosophy are blocks to inquiry, blind alleys; they are puzzles rather than problems, solved only by calling the original material of primary experience, "phenomenal," mere appearance, mere impressions, or by some other disparaging name.

Thus there is here supplied, I think, a first-rate test of the value of any philosophy which is offered us: Does it end in conclusions which, when they are referred back to ordinary life-experiences and their predicaments, render them more significant, more luminous to us, and make our dealings with them more fruitful? Or does it terminate in rendering the things of ordinary experience more opaque than they were before, and in depriving them of having in "reality" even the significance they had previously seemed to have? Does it yield the enrichment and increase of power of ordinary things which the results of physical science afford when applied in every-day affairs? Or does it become a mystery that these ordinary things should be what they are; and are philosophic concepts left to dwell in separation in some technical realm of their own? It is the fact, I repeat, that so many philosophies terminate in conclusions that make it necessary to disparage and condemn primary experience, leading those who hold them to measure the sublimity of their "realities" as philosophically defined by remoteness from the concerns of daily life, which leads cultivated common-sense to look askance at philosophy. . . .

. . . The most serious indictment to be brought against non-empirical philosophies is that they have cast a cloud over the things of ordinary experience. They have not been content to rectify them. They have discredited them at large. In casting aspersion upon the things of everyday experience, the things of action and affection and social intercourse, they have done something worse than fail to give these affairs the intelligent direction they so much need. It would not matter much if philosophy had been reserved as a luxury of only a few thinkers. We endure many luxuries. The serious matter is that philosophies have denied that common experience is capable of developing from within itself methods which will secure direction for itself and will create inherent standards of judgment and value. No one knows how many of the evils and deficiencies that are pointed to as reasons for flight from experience are themselves due to the disregard of experience shown by those peculiarly reflective. To waste of time and energy, to disillusionment with life that attends every deviation from concrete experience must be added the tragic failure to realize the value that intelligent search could reveal and mature among the things of ordinary experience. I cannot calculate how much of current cynicism, indifference and pessimism is due to these causes in the deflection of intelligence they have brought about. It has even become in many circles a sign of lack of sophistication to imagine that life is or can be a fountain of cheer and happiness. Philosophies no more than religions can be acquitted of responsibility for bringing this result to pass. The transcendental philosopher has probably done more than the professed sensualist and materialist to obscure the potentialities of daily experience for joy and for self-regulation. If what is written in these pages has no other result than creating and promoting a respect for concrete human experience and its potentialities, I shall be content.

EXISTENCE AS PRECARIOUS AND AS STABLE

Upon their surface, the reports of the world which form our different philosophies are various to the point of stark contrariness. They range from spiritualism to materialism, from absolutism to relativistic phenomenalism, from transcendentalism to positivism, from rationalism to sensationalism, from idealism to realism, from subjectivism to bald objectivism, from Platonic realism to nominalism. The array of contradictions is so imposing as to suggest to sceptics that the mind of man has tackled an impossible job, or that philosophers have abandoned themselves to vagary. These radical oppositions in philosophers suggest however another consideration. They suggest that all their different philosophies have a common premise, and that their diversity is due to acceptance of a common premise. Variant philosophies may be looked at as different ways of supplying recipes for denying to the universe the character of contingency which it possesses so integrally that its denial leaves the reflecting mind without a clew, and puts subsequent philosophising at the mercy of temperament, interest and local surroundings.

Quarrels among conflicting types of philosophy are thus family quarrels. They go on within the limits of a too domestic circle, and can be settled only by venturing further afield, and out of doors. Concerned with imputing complete, finished and sure character to the world of real existence, even if things have to be broken into two disconnected pieces in order to accomplish the result, the character desiderated can plausibly be found in reason or in mechanism; in rational conceptions like those of mathematics, or brute things like sensory data; in atoms or in essences; in consciousness or in a physical externality which forces and overrides consciousness.

As against this common identification of reality with what is sure, regular and finished, experience in unsophisticated forms gives evidence of a different world and points to a different metaphysics. We live in a world which is an impressive and irresistible mixture of sufficiencies, tight completenesses, order, recurrences which make possible prediction and control, and singularities, ambiguities, uncertain possibilities, processes going on to consequences as yet indeterminate. They are mixed not mechanically but vitally like the wheat and tares of the parable. We may recognize them separately but we cannot divide them, for unlike wheat and tares they grow from the same root. Qualities have defects as necessary conditions of their excellencies; the instrumentalities of truth are the causes of error; change gives meaning to permanence and recurrence makes novelty possible. A world that was wholly risky would be a world in which adventure is impossible, and only a living world can include death. Such facts have been celebrated by thinkers like Heracleitus and Laotze; they have been greeted by theologians as furnishing occasions for exercise of divine grace; they have been elaborately formulated by various schools under a principle of relativity, so defined as to become itself final and absolute. They have rarely been frankly recognized as fundamentally significant for the formation of a naturalistic metaphysics. . . .

The union of the hazardous and the stable, of the incomplete and the recurrent, is the condition of all experienced satisfaction as truly as of our predicaments and problems. While it is the source of ignorance, error and failure of expectation, it is the source of the delight which fulfillments bring. For if there were nothing in the way, if there were no deviations and resistances, fulfillment would be at once, and in so being would fulfill nothing, but merely be. It would not be in connection with desire or satisfaction. Moreover when a fulfillment comes and is pronounced good, it is *judged* good, distinguished and asserted, simply because it is in jeopardy, because it occurs amid indifferent and divergent things. Because of this mixture of the regular and that which cuts across stability, a good object once experienced acquires ideal quality and attracts demand and effort to itself. A particular ideal may be an illusion, but having ideals is no illusion. It embodies features of existence. Although imagination is often fantastic it is also an organ of nature; for it is the appropriate phase of indeterminate events moving toward eventualities that are now but possibilities. A purely stable world permits of no illusions, but neither is it clothed with ideals. It just exists. To be good is to be better than; and there can be no better except where there is shock and discord combined with enough assured order to make attainment of harmony possible. Better objects when brought into existence are existent not ideal; they retain ideal quality only retrospectively as commemorative of issue from prior conflict and prospectively, in contrast with forces which make for their destruction. Water that slakes thirst, or a conclusion that solves a problem have ideal character as long as thirst or problem persists in a way which qualifies the result. But water that is not a satisfaction of need has no more ideal quality than water running through pipes into a reservoir; a solution ceases to be a solution and becomes a bare incident of existence when its antecedent generating conditions of doubt, ambiguity and search are lost from its context. While the precarious nature of existence is indeed the source of all trouble, it is also an indispensable condition of ideality, becoming a sufficient condition when conjoined with the regular and assured.

We long, amid a troubled world, for perfect being. We forget that what gives meaning to the notion of perfection is the events that create longing, and that, apart from them, a "perfect" world would mean just an unchanging brute existential thing. The ideal significance of esthetic objects is no exception to this principle. Their satisfying quality, their power to compose while they arouse, is not dependent upon definite prior desire and effort as is the case with the ideally satisfying quality of practical and scientific objects. It is part of their peculiar satisfying quality to be gratuitous, not purchased by endeavor. The contrast to other things of this detachment from toil and labor in a world where most realizations have to be bought, as well as the contrast to trouble and uncertainty, give esthetic objects their peculiar traits. If all things came to us in the way our esthetic objects do, none of them would be a source of esthetic delight.

Some phases of recent philosophy have made much of need, desire and satisfaction. Critics have frequently held that the outcome is only recurrence to an older subjective empiricism, though with substitution of affections and volitional states for cognitive sensory states. But need and desire are exponents of natural being. They are, if we use Aristotelian phraseology, actualizations of its contingencies and incompletenesses; as such nature itself is wistful and pathetic, turbulent and passionate. Were it not, the existence of wants would be a miracle. In a world where everything is complete, nothing requires anything else for its completion. A world in which events can be carried to a finish only through the coinciding assistance of other transitory events, is already necessitous, a world of begging as well as of beggarly elements. If human experience is to express and reflect this world, it must be marked by needs; in becoming aware of the needful and needed quality of things it must project satisfactions or completions. For irrespective of whether a satisfaction is conscious, a satisfaction or non-satisfaction is an objective thing with objective conditions. It means fulfillment of the demands of objective factors. Happiness may *mark* an awareness of such satisfaction, and it may *be* its culminating form. But satisfaction is not subjective, private or personal: it is conditioned by objective partialities and defections and made real by objective situations and completions.

By the same logic, necessity implies the precarious and contingent. A world that was all necessity would not be a world of necessity; it would just be. For in its being, nothing would be necessary for anything else. But where some things are indigent, other things are necessary if demands are to be met. The common failure to note the fact that a world of complete being would be a world in which necessity is meaningless is due to a rapid shift from one universe of discourse to another. First we postulate a whole of Being; then we shift to a part; now since a "part" is logically dependent as such in its existence and its properties, it is necessitated by other parts. But we have unwittingly introduced contingency in the very fact of marking off something as just a part. If the logical implications of the original notion are held to firmly, a part is already a part-of-a-whole. Its being what it is, is not necessitated by the whole or by other parts: its being what it is, is just a name for the whole being what it is. Whole and parts alike are but names for existence there as just what it is. But wherever we can say *if* so-and-so, then something else, there is necessity, because partialities are implied which are not just parts-of-a-whole. A world of "ifs" is alone a world of "musts"—the "ifs" express real differences; the "musts" real connections. The stable and recurrent is needed for the fulfillment of the possible; the doubtful can be settled only through its adaptation to stable objects. The necessary is always necessary for, not necessary in and of itself; it is conditioned by the contingent, although itself a condition of the full determination of the latter.

One of the most striking phases of the history of philosophic thought is the recurrent grouping together of unity, permanence (or "the eternal"), completeness and rational thought, while upon another side full multiplicity, change and the temporal, the partial, defective, sense and desire. This division is obviously but another case of violent separation of the precarious and unsettled from the regular and determinate. One aspect of it however, is worthy of particular attention: the connection of thought and unity. Empirically, all reflection sets out from the problematic and confused. Its aim is to clarify and ascertain. When thinking is successful, its career closes in transforming the disordered into the orderly, the mixed-up into the distinguished or placed, the unclear and ambiguous into the defined and unequivocal, the disconnected into the systematized. It is empirically assured that the goal of thinking does not remain a mere ideal, but is attained often enough so as to render reasonable additional efforts to achieve it.

In these facts we have, I think, the empirical basis of the philosophic doctrines which assert that reality is really and truly a rational system, a coherent whole of relations that cannot be conceived otherwise than in terms of intellect. Reflective inquiry moves in each particular case from differences toward unity; from indeterminate and ambiguous position to clear determination, from confusion and disorder to system. When thought in a given case has reached its goal of organized totality, of definite relations of distinctly placed elements, its object is the accepted starting point, the defined subject matter, of further experiences; antecedent and outgrown conditions of darkness and of unreconciled differences are dismissed as a transitory state of ignorance and inadequate apprehensions. Retain connection of the goal with the thinking by which it is reached, and then identify it with true reality in contrast with the merely phenomenal, and the outline of the logic of rational and "objective" idealisms is before us. Thought like Being, has two forms, one real; the other phenomenal. It is compelled to take on *reflective* form, it involves doubt, inquiry and hypothesis, because it sets out from a subject-matter conditioned by sense, a fact which proves that thought, intellect, is not pure in man, but restricted by an animal organism that is but one part linked with other parts, of nature. But the conclusion of reflection affords us a pattern and guarantee of thought which is *constitutive*; one with the system of objective reality. Such in outline is the procedure of all ontological logics.

A philosophy which accepts the denotative or empirical method accepts at full value the fact that reflective thinking transforms confusion, ambiguity and discrepancy into illumination, definiteness and consistency. But it also points to the contextual situation in which thinking occurs. It notes that the starting point is the actually *problematic*, and that the problematic phase resides in some actual and specifiable situation.

It notes that the means of converting the dubious into the assured, and the incomplete into the determinate, is use of assured and established things, which are just as empirical and as indicative of the nature of experienced things as is the uncertain. It thus notes that thinking is no different in kind from the use of natural materials and energies, say fire and tools, to refine, re-order, and shape other natural materials, say ore. In both cases, there are matters which as they stand are unsatisfactory and there are also adequate agencies for dealing with them and connecting them. At no point or place is there any jump outside empirical, natural objects and their relations. Thought and reason are not specific powers. They consist of the procedures intentionally employed in the application to each other of the unsatisfactorily confused and indeterminate on one side and the regular and stable on the other. Generalizing from such observations, empirical philosophy perceives that thinking is a continuous process of temporal re-organization within one and the same world of experienced things, not a jump from the latter world into one of objects constituted once for all by thought. It discovers thereby the empirical basis of rational idealism, and the point at which it empirically goes astray. Idealism fails to take into account the specified or concrete character of the uncertain situation in which thought occurs; it fails to note the empirically concrete nature of the subject-matter, acts, and tools by which determination and consistency are reached; it fails to note that the conclusive eventual objects having the latter properties are themselves as many as the situations dealt with. The conversion of the logic of reflection into an ontology of rational being is thus due to arbitrary conversion of an eventual natural function of unification into a causal antecedent reality; this in turn is due to the tendency of the imagination working under the influence of emotion to carry unification from an actual, objective and experimental enterprise, limited to particular situations where it is needed, into an unrestricted, wholesale movement which ends in an all-absorbing dream.

The occurrence of reflection is crucial for dualistic metaphysics as well as for idealistic ontologies. Reflection occurs only in situations qualified by uncertainty, alternatives, questioning, search, hypotheses, tentative trials or experiments which test the worth of thinking. A naturalistic metaphysics is bound to consider reflection as itself a natural event occurring *within* nature because of traits of the latter. It is bound to inference from the empirical traits of thinking in precisely the same way as the sciences make inferences from the happening of suns, radio-activity, thunder-storms or any other natural event. Traits of reflection are as truly indicative or evidential of the traits of *other* things as are the traits of these events. A theory of the nature of the occurrence and career of a sun reached by denial of the obvious traits of the sun, or by denial that these traits are so connected with the traits of other natural events that they can be used as evidence concerning the nature of these other things, would hardly possess scientific standing. Yet philosophers, and strangely enough philosophers who call themselves realists, have constantly held that the traits which are characteristic of thinking, namely, uncertainty, ambiguity, alternatives, inquiring, search, selection, experimental reshaping of external conditions, do not possess the same existential character as do the objects of valid knowledge. They have denied that these traits are evidential of the character of the world within which thinking occurs. They have not, as realists, asserted that these traits are mere appearances; but they have often asserted and implied that such things are only personal or psychological in contrast with a world of objective nature. But the interests of empirical and denotative method and of naturalistic metaphysics wholly coincide. The world must actually be such as to generate ignorance and inquiry; doubt and hypothesis, trial and temporal conclusions; the latter being such that they develop out of existences which while wholly "real" are not as satisfactory, as good, or as significant, as those into which they are eventually re-organized. The ultimate evidence of genuine hazard, contingency, irregularity and indeterminateness in nature is thus found in the occurrence of thinking. The traits of natural existence which generate the fears and adorations of superstitious barbarians generate the scientific procedures of disciplined civilization. The superiority of the latter does not consist in the fact that they are based on "real" existence, while the former depend wholly upon a human nature different from nature in general. It consists in the fact that scientific inquiries reach *objects* which are better, because reached by method which controls them and which adds greater control to life itself, method which mitigates accident, turns contingency to account, and releases thought and other forms of endeavor.

The conjunction of problematic and determinate characters in nature renders every existence, as well as every idea and human act, an experiment in fact, even though not in design. To be intelligently experimental is but to be conscious of this intersection of natural conditions so as to profit by it instead of being at its mercy. The Christian idea of this world and this life as a probation is a kind of distorted recognition of the situation; distorted because it applied wholesale to one stretch of existence in contrast with another, regarded as original and final. But in truth anything which can exist at any place and at any time occurs subject to tests imposed upon it by surroundings, which are only in part compatible and reinforcing. These surroundings test its strength and measure its endurance. As we can discourse of change only in terms of velocity and acceleration which involve relations to other things, so assertion of the permanent and enduring is comparative. The stablest thing we can speak of is not free from conditions set to it by other things. That even the solid earth mountains, the emblems of constancy, appear and disappear like the clouds is an old theme of moralists and poets. The fixed and unchanged being of the Democritean atom is now reported by inquirers to possess some of the traits of his non-being, and to embody a temporary equilibrium in the economy of nature's compromises and adjustments. A thing may endure *secula seculorum* and yet not be everlasting; it will crumble before the gnawing tooth of time, as it exceeds a certain measure. Every existence is an event.

This fact is nothing at which to repine and nothing to gloat over. It is something to be noted and used. If it is discomfiting when applied to good things, to our friends, possessions and precious selves, it is consoling also to know that no evil endures forever; that the longest lane turns sometime, and that the memory of loss of nearest and dearest grows dim in time. The eventful character of all existences is no reason for consigning them to the realm of mere appearance any more than it is a reason for idealizing flux into a deity. . . .

WHAT PRAGMATISM MEANS BY THE "PRACTICAL" [2]

It is easier to start a legend than to prevent its continued circulation. No misconception of the instrumental logic has been more persistent than the belief that it makes knowledge merely a means to a practical end, or to the satisfaction of practical needs—practical being taken to signify some quite definite utilities of a material or bread-and-butter type. Habitual associations aroused by the word "pragmatic" have been stronger than the most explicit and emphatic statements which any pragmatist has been able to make. But I again affirm that the term "pragmatic" means only the rule of referring all thinking, all reflective considerations, to *consequences* for final meaning and test. Nothing is said about the nature of the consequences; they may be aesthetic, or moral, or political, or religious in quality—anything you please. All that the theory requires is that they be in some way consequences of thinking; not, indeed, of it alone, but of it acted upon in connection with other things. This is no after-thought inserted to lessen the force of objections. Mr. Peirce explained that he took the term "pragmatic" from Kant, in order to denote empirical consequences. When he refers to their practical character it is only

[2] From John Dewey, *Essays in Experimental Logic*, Chicago: U. of Chicago Press, 1916. Ch. XIII, pp. 330–334.

to indicate a criterion by which to avoid purely verbal disputes. Different consequences are alleged to constitute rival meanings of a term. Is a difference more than merely one of formulation? The way to get an answer is to ask whether, if realized, these consequences would exact of us different modes of behavior. If they do not make such a difference in conduct the difference between them is conventional. It is not that consequences are themselves practical, but that practical consequences from them may at times be appealed to in order to decide the specific question of whether two proposed meanings differ save in words. Mr. James says expressly that what is important is that the consequences should be specific, not that they should be active. When he said that general notions must "cash in," he meant of course that they must be translatable into verifiable specific things. But the words "cash in" were enough for some of his critics, who pride themselves upon a logical rigor unattainable by mere pragmatists.

In the logical version of pragmatism termed instrumentalism, action or practice does indeed play a fundamental rôle. But it concerns not the nature of consequences but the nature of knowing. To use a term which is now more fashionable (and surely to some extent in consequence of pragmatism) than it was earlier, instrumentalism means a behaviorist theory of thinking and knowing. It means that knowing is literally something which we do; that analysis is ultimately physical and active; that meanings in their logical quality are standpoints, attitudes, and methods of behaving toward facts, and that active experimentation is essential to verification. Put in another way it holds that thinking does not mean any transcendent states or acts suddenly introduced into a previously natural scene, but that the operations of knowing are (or are artfully derived from) natural responses of the organism, which constitute knowing in virtue of the situation of doubt in which they arise and in virtue of the uses of inquiry, reconstruction, and control to which they are put. There is no warrant in the doctrine for carrying over *this* practical quality into the consequences in which action culminates, and by which it is tested and corrected. A knowing as an act is instrumental to the resultant controlled and more significant situation; this does not imply anything about the intrinsic or the instrumental character of the consequent situation. That is whatever it may be in a given case.

There is nothing novel nor heterodox in the notion that thinking is instrumental. The very word is redolent of an *Organum*—whether *novum* or *veterum*. The term "instrumentality," applied to thinking, raises at once, however, the question of whether thinking as a tool falls within or without the subject-matter which it shapes into knowledge. The answer of formal logic (adopted moreover by Kant and followed in some way by all neo-Kantian logics) is unambiguous. To call logic "formal" means precisely that mind or thought supplies forms foreign to the original subject-matter, but yet required in order that it should have the appropriate form of knowledge. In this regard it deviates from the Aristotelian *Organon* which it professes to follow. For according to Aristotle, the processes of knowing—of teaching and learning—which lead up to knowledge are but the actualization through the potentialities of the human body of the *same* forms or natures which are previously actualized in Nature through the potentialities of extra-organic bodies. Thinking which is not instrumental to truth, which is merely formal in the modern sense, would have been a monstrosity inconceivable to him. But the discarding of the metaphysics of form and matter, of cyclic actualizations and eternal species, deprived the Aristotelian "thought" of any place within the scheme of things, and left it an activity with forms alien to subject-matter. To conceive of thinking as instrumental to truth or knowledge, and as a tool shaped out of the same subject-matter as that to which it is applied, is but to return to the Aristotelian tradition about logic. That the practice of science has in the meantime substituted a logic of experimental discovery (of which definition and classification are themselves but auxiliary tools) for a logic of arrangement and exposition of what is already known, necessitates, however, a very different sort of *Organon*. It makes necessary the conception that the object of knowledge is not something with which thinking sets out, but something with which it ends: something which the processes of inquiry and testing, that constitute thinking, themselves produce. Thus the object of knowledge is practical in the sense that it depends upon a specific kind of practice for its existence—for its existence as an object of knowledge. How practical it may be in any other sense than this is quite another story. The *object of knowledge* marks an achieved triumph, a secured control—that holds by the very nature of knowledge. What other uses it may have depends upon its own inherent character, not upon anything in the nature of knowledge. We do not know the origin and nature and the cure of malaria till we can both produce and eliminate malaria; the *value* of either the production or the removal depends upon the character of malaria in relation to other things. And so it is with mathematical knowledge, or with knowledge of politics or art. Their respective objects are not known till they are made in course of the process of experimental thinking. Their usefulness when made is whatever, from infinity to zero, experience may subsequently determine it to be.

LOGIC: THE THEORY OF INQUIRY [3]

. . . What is the *definition* of Inquiry? That is, what is the most highly generalized conception of inquiry which can be justifiably formulated? The definition that will be expanded, . . . is as follows: *Inquiry is the controlled or directed transformation of an indeterminate situation into one that is so determinate in its constituent distinctions and relations as to convert the elements of the original situation into a unified whole.*

The original indeterminate situation is not only "open" to inquiry, but it is open in the sense that its constituents do not hang together. The determinate situation on the other hand, *qua* outcome of inquiry, is a closed and, as it were, finished situation or "universe of experience." "Controlled or directed" in the above formula refers to the fact that inquiry is competent in any given case in the degree in which the operations involved in it actually do terminate in the establishment of an objectively unified existential situation. In the intermediate course of transition and transformation of the indeterminate situation, *discourse* through use of symbols is employed as means. In received logical terminology, propositions, or terms and the relations between them, are intrinsically involved.

I. THE ANTECEDENT CONDITIONS OF INQUIRY: THE INDETERMINATE
SITUATION

Inquiry and questioning, up to a certain point, are synonymous terms. We inquire when we question; and we inquire when we seek for whatever will provide an answer to a question asked. Thus it is of the very nature of the indeterminate situation which evokes inquiry to be *questionable;* or, in terms of actuality instead of potentiality, to be uncertain, unsettled, disturbed. The peculiar quality of what pervades the given materials, constituting them a situation, is not just uncertainty at large; it is a unique doubtfulness which makes that situation to be just and only the situation it is. It is this unique quality that not only evokes the particular inquiry engaged in but that exercises control over its special procedures. Otherwise, one procedure in inquiry would be as likely to occur and to be effective as any other. Unless a situation is uniquely qualified in its very indeterminateness, there is a condition of complete panic; response to it

[3] From John Dewey, *Logic: The Theory of Inquiry*, N. Y.: Holt, Rinehart and Winston, 1938. Selection taken from Chapter VI, "The Pattern of Inquiry," pp. 104–117.

takes the form of blind and wild overt activities. Stating the matter from the personal side, we have "lost our heads." A variety of names serves to characterize indeterminate situations. They are disturbed, troubled, ambiguous, confused, full of conflicting tendencies, obscure, etc.

It is the *situation* that has these traits. *We* are doubtful because the situation is inherently doubtful. Personal states of doubt that are not evoked by and are not relative to some existential situation are pathological; when they are extreme they constitute the mania of doubting. Consequently, situations that are disturbed and troubled, confused or obscure, cannot be straightened out, cleared up and put in order, by manipulation of our personal states of mind. The attempt to settle them by such manipulations involves what psychiatrists call "withdrawal from reality." Such an attempt is pathological as far as it goes, and when it goes far it is the source of some form of actual insanity. The habit of disposing of the doubtful as if it belonged only to *us* rather than to the existential situation in which we are caught and implicated is an inheritance from subjectivistic psychology. The biological antecedent conditions of an unsettled situation are involved in that state of imbalance in organic-environmental interactions which has already been described. Restoration of integration can be effected, in one case as in the other, only by operations which actually modify existing conditions, not by merely "mental" processes.

It is, accordingly, a mistake to suppose that a situation is doubtful only in a "subjective" sense. The notion that in actual existence everything is completely determinate has been rendered questionable by the progress of physical science itself. Even if it had not been, complete determination would not hold of existences as an *environment*. For Nature is an environment only as it is involved in interaction with an organism, or self, or whatever name be used.[4]

Every such interaction is a temporal process, not a momentary cross-sectional occurrence. The situation in which it occurs is indeterminate, therefore, with respect to its *issue*. If we call it *confused*, then it is meant that its outcome cannot be anticipated. It is called *obscure* when its course of movement permits of final consequences that cannot be clearly made out. It is called *conflicting* when it tends to evoke discordant responses. Even were existential conditions unqualifiedly determinate in and of themselves, they are indeterminate in *significance*: that is, in what they import and portend in

---

[4] Except of course a purely mentalistic name, like *consciousness*. The alleged problem of "interactionism" versus automatism, parallelism, etc., is a problem (and an insoluble one) because of the assumption involved in its statement—the assumption, namely, that the interaction in question is with something mental instead of with biological-cultural human beings.

their interaction with the organism. The organic responses that enter into the production of the state of affairs that is temporally later and sequential are just as existential as are environing conditions.

The immediate *locus* of the problem concerns, then, what kind of responses the organism shall make. It concerns the interaction of organic responses and environing conditions in their movement toward an existential issue. It is a commonplace that in any troubled state of affairs *things* will come out differently according to what is done. The farmer won't get grain unless he plants and tills; the general will win or lose the battle according to the way he conducts it, and so on. Neither the grain nor the tilling, neither the outcome of the battle nor the conduct of it, are "mental" events. Organic interaction becomes inquiry when existential consequences are anticipated; when environing conditions are examined with reference to their potentialities; and when responsive activities are selected and ordered with reference to actualization of some of the potentialities, rather than others, in a final existential situation. Resolution of the indeterminate situation is active and operational. If the inquiry is adequately directed, the final issue is the unified situation that has been mentioned.

II. INSTITUTION OF A PROBLEM

The unsettled or indeterminate situation might have been called a *problematic* situation. This name would have been, however, proleptic and anticipatory. The indeterminate situation becomes problematic in the very process of being subjected to inquiry. The indeterminate situation comes into existence from existential causes, just as does, say, the organic imbalance of hunger. There is nothing intellectual or cognitive in the existence of such situations, although they are the necessary condition of cognitive operations or inquiry. In themselves they are precognitive. The first result of evocation of inquiry is that the situation is taken, adjudged, to be problematic. To see that a situation requires inquiry is the initial step in inquiry.[5]

Qualification of a situation as problematic does not, however, carry inquiry far. It is but an initial step in institution of a problem. A problem is not a task to be performed which a person puts upon himself or that is placed upon him by others—like a so-called arithmetical "problem" in school work. A problem represents the partial transformation by inquiry of a problematic situation into a determinate

[5] If by "two-valued logic" is meant a logic that regards "true and false" as the sole logical values, then such a logic is necessarily so truncated that clearness and consistency in logical doctrine are impossible. Being the matter of a problem is a primary logical property.

situation. It is a familiar and significant saying that a problem well put is half-solved. To find out *what* the problem and problems are which a problematic situation presents to be inquired into, is to be well along in inquiry. To mistake the problem involved is to cause subsequent inquiry to be irrelevant or to go astray. Without a problem, there is blind groping in the dark. The way in which the problem is conceived decides what specific suggestions are entertained and which are dismissed; what data are selected and which rejected; it is the criterion for relevancy and irrelevancy of hypotheses and conceptual structures. On the other hand, to set up a problem that does not grow out of an actual situation is to start on a course of dead work, nonetheless dead because the work is "busy work." Problems that are self-set are mere excuses for seeming to do something intellectual, something that has the semblance but not the substance of scientific activity.

III. THE DETERMINATION OF A PROBLEM–SOLUTION

Statement of a problematic situation in terms of a problem has no meaning save as the problem instituted has, in the very terms of its statement, reference to a possible solution. Just because a problem well stated is on its way to solution, the determining of a genuine problem is a *progressive* inquiry; the cases in which a problem and its probable solution flash upon an inquirer are cases where much prior ingestion and digestion have occurred. If we assume, prematurely, that the problem involved is definite and clear, subsequent inquiry proceeds on the wrong track. Hence the question arises: How is the formation of a genuine problem so controlled that further inquiries will move toward a solution?

The first step in answering this question is to recognize that no situation which is *completely* indeterminate can possibly be converted into a problem having definite constituents. The first step then is to search out the *constituents* of a given situation which, as constituents, are settled. When an alarm of fire is sounded in a crowded assembly hall, there is much that is indeterminate as regards the activities that may produce a favorable issue. One may get out safely or one may be trampled and burned. The fire is characterized, however, by some settled traits. It is, for example, located *somewhere*. Then the aisles and exits are at fixed places. Since they are settled or determinate in *existence*, the first step in institution of a problem is to settle them in *observation*. There are other factors which, while they are not as temporally and spatially fixed, are yet observable constituents; for example, the behavior and movements of other members of the audience. All of these observed conditions taken together constitute "the facts of the case." They constitute the terms of the problem, because they are conditions that must be reckoned with or taken account of in any relevant solution that is proposed.

A *possible* relevant solution is then suggested by the determination of factual conditions which are secured by observation. The possible solution presents itself, therefore, as an *idea*, just as the terms of the problem (which are facts) are instituted by observation. Ideas are anticipated consequences (forecasts) of what will happen when certain operations are executed under and with respect to observed conditions.[6] Observation of facts and suggested meanings or ideas arise and develop in correspondence with each other. The more the facts of the case come to light in consequence of being subjected to observation, the clearer and more pertinent become the conceptions of the way the problem constituted by these facts is to be dealt with. On the other side, the clearer the idea, the more definite, as a truism, become the operations of observation and of execution that must be performed in order to resolve the situation.

An idea is first of all an anticipation of something that may happen; it marks a *possibility*. When it is said, as it sometimes is, that science is *prediction*, the anticipation that constitutes every idea an idea is grounded in a set of controlled observations and of regulated conceptual ways of interpreting them. Because inquiry is a progressive determination of a problem and its possible solution, ideas differ in grade according to the stage of inquiry reached. At first, save in highly familiar matters, they are vague. They occur at first simply as suggestions; suggestions just spring up, flash upon us, occur to us. They may then become stimuli to direct an overt activity but they have as yet no logical status. Every idea originates as a suggestion, but not every suggestion is an idea. The suggestion becomes an idea when it is examined with reference to its functional fitness; its capacity as a means of resolving the given situation.

This examination takes the form of reasoning, as a result of which we are able to appraise better than we were at the outset, the pertinency and weight of the meaning now entertained with respect to its functional capacity. But the final test of its possession of these properties is determined when it actually functions—that is, when

[6] The theory of *ideas* that has been held in psychology and epistemology since the time of Locke's successors is completely irrelevant and obstructive in logical theory. For in treating them as copies of perceptions or "impressions," it ignores the prospective and anticipatory character that defines *being* an idea. Failure to define ideas functionally, in the reference they have to a solution of a problem, is one reason they have been treated as merely "mental." The notion, on the other hand, that ideas are fantasies is a derivative. Fantasies arise when the function an idea performs is ruled out when it is entertained and developed.

it is put into operation so as to institute by means of observations facts not previously observed, and is then used to organize them with other facts into a coherent whole.

Because suggestions and ideas are of that which is not present in given existence, the meanings which they involve must be embodied in some symbol. Without some kind of symbol no idea; a meaning that is completely disembodied can not be entertained or used. Since an existence (which *is* an existence) is the support and vehicle of a meaning and is a symbol instead of a merely physical existence only in this respect, embodied meanings or ideas are capable of objective survey and development. To "look at an idea" is not a mere literary figure of speech.

"Suggestions" have received scant courtesy in logical theory. It is true that when they just "pop into our heads," because of the workings of the psycho-physical organism, they are not logical. But they are both the conditions and the primary stuff of logical ideas. The traditional empiristic theory reduced them, as has already been pointed out, to mental copies of physical things and assumed that they were *per se* identical with ideas. Consequently it ignored the function of ideas in directing observation and in ascertaining relevant facts. The rationalistic school, on the other hand, saw clearly that "facts" apart from ideas are trivial, that they acquire import and significance only in relation to ideas. But at the same time it failed to attend to the operative and functional nature of the latter. Hence, it treated ideas as equivalent to the ultimate structure of "Reality." The Kantian formula that apart from each other "perceptions are blind and conceptions empty" marks a profound logical insight. The insight, however, was radically distorted because perceptual and conceptual contents were supposed to originate from different sources and thus required a third activity, that of synthetic understanding, to bring them together. In logical fact, perceptual and conceptual materials are instituted in functional correlativity with each other, in such a manner that the former locates and describes the problem while the latter represents a possible method of solution. Both are determinations in and by inquiry of the original problematic situation whose pervasive quality controls their institution and their contents. Both are finally checked by their capacity to work together to introduce a resolved unified situation. As distinctions they represent logical divisions of labor.

IV. REASONING

The necessity of developing the meaning-contents of ideas in their relations to one another has been incidentally noted. This process, operating with symbols (constituting propositions) is reasoning in the sense of ratiocination or rational discourse.[7] When a suggested meaning is immediately accepted, inquiry is cut short. Hence the conclusion reached is not grounded, even if it happens to be correct. The check upon immediate acceptance is the examination of the meaning as a meaning. This examination consists in noting what the meaning in question implies in relation to other meanings in the system of which it is a member, the formulated relation constituting a proposition. If such and such a relation of meanings is accepted, then we are committed to such and such other relations of meanings because of their membership in the same system. Through a series of intermediate meanings, a meaning is finally reached which is more clearly *relevant* to the problem in hand than the originally suggested idea. It indicates operations which can be performed to test its applicability, whereas the original idea is usually too vague to determine crucial operations. In other words, the idea or meaning when developed in discourse directs the activities which, when executed, provide needed evidential material.

The point made can be most readily appreciated in connection with scientific reasoning. An hypothesis, once suggested and entertained, is developed in relation to other conceptual structures until it receives a form in which it can instigate and direct an experiment that will disclose precisely those conditions which have the maximum possible force in determining whether the hypothesis should be accepted or rejected. Or it may be that the experiment will indicate what modifications are required in the hypothesis so that it may be applicable, i.e., suited to interpret and organize the facts of the case. In many familiar situations, the meaning that is most relevant has been settled because of the eventuations of experiments in prior cases so that it is applicable almost immediately upon its occurrence. But, indirectly, if not directly, an idea or suggestion that is not developed in terms of the constellation of meanings to which it belongs can lead only to overt response. Since the latter terminates inquiry, there is then no adequate inquiry into the meaning that is used to settle the given situation, and the conclusion is in so far logically ungrounded.

V. THE OPERATIONAL CHARACTER OF FACTS—MEANINGS

It was stated that the observed facts of the case and the ideational contents expressed in ideas are related to each other, as, respectively,

[7] "Reasoning" is sometimes used to designate *inference* as well as ratiocination. When so used in logic the tendency is to identify inference and implication and thereby seriously to confuse logical theory.

a clarification of the problem involved and the proposal of some possible solution; that they are, accordingly, functional divisions in the work of inquiry. Observed facts in their office of locating and describing the problem are existential; ideational subject-matter is non-existential. How, then, do they cooperate with each other in the resolution of an existential situation? The problem is insoluble save as it is recognized that both observed facts and entertained ideas are operational. Ideas are operational in that they instigate and direct further operations of observation; they are proposals and plans for acting upon existing conditions to bring new facts to light and to organize all the selected facts into a coherent whole.

What is meant by calling facts operational? Upon the negative side what is meant is that they are not self-sufficient and complete in themselves. They are selected and described, as we have seen, for a purpose, namely statement of the problem involved in such a way that its material both indicates a meaning relevant to resolution of the difficulty and serves to test its worth and validity. In regulated inquiry facts are selected and arranged with the express intent of fulfilling this office. They are not merely *results* of operations of observation which are executed with the aid of bodily organs and auxiliary instruments of art, but they are the particular facts and kinds of facts that will link up with one another in the definite ways that are required to produce a definite end. Those not found to connect with others in furtherance of this end are dropped and others are sought for. Being functional, they are necessarily operational. Their function is to serve as evidence and their evidential quality is judged on the basis of their capacity to form an ordered whole in response to operations prescribed by the ideas they occasion and support. If "the facts of the case" were final and complete in themselves, if they did not have a special operative force in resolution of the problematic situation, they could not serve as evidence.

The operative force of facts is apparent when we consider that no fact in isolation has evidential potency. Facts are evidential and are tests of an idea in so far as they are capable of being organized with one another. The organization can be achieved only as they *interact* with one another. When the problematic situation is such as to require extensive inquiries to effect its resolution, a series of interactions intervenes. Some observed facts point to an idea that stands for a possible solution. This idea evokes more observations. Some of the newly observed facts link up with those previously observed and are such as to rule out other observed things with respect to their evidential function. The new order of facts suggests a modified idea (or hypothesis) which occasions new observations whose result again determines a new order of facts, and so on until the existing order is both unified and complete. In the course of this serial process, the ideas that represent possible solutions are tested or "proved."

Meantime, the orders of fact, which present themselves in consequence of the experimental observations the ideas call out and direct, are *trial* facts. They are provisional. They are "facts" if they are observed by sound organs and techniques. But they are not on that account the *facts of the case*. They are tested or "proved" with respect to their evidential function just as much as ideas (hypotheses) are tested with reference to their power to exercise the function of resolution. The operative force of both ideas and facts is thus practically recognized in the degree in which they are connected with *experiment*. Naming them "operational" is but a theoretical recognition of what is involved when inquiry satisfies the conditions imposed by the necessity for experiment.

I recur, in this connection, to what has been said about the necessity for symbols in inquiry. It is obvious, on the face of matters, that a possible mode of solution must be carried in symbolic form since it is a possibility, not an assured present existence. Observed facts, on the other hand, are existentially present. It might seem therefore, that symbols are not required for referring to them. But if they are not carried and treated by means of symbols, they lose their provisional character, and in losing this character they are categorically asserted and inquiry comes to an end. The carrying on of inquiry requires that the facts be taken as *re*presentative and not just as *pre*-sented. This demand is met by formulating them in propositions—that is, by means of symbols. Unless they are so represented they relapse into the total qualitative situation.

VI. COMMON SENSE AND SCIENTIFIC INQUIRY

The discussion up to this point has proceeded in general terms which recognizes no distinction between common sense and scientific inquiry. We have now reached a point where the community of pattern in these two distinctive modes of inquiry should receive explicit attention. It was said in earlier chapters that the difference between them resides in their respective subject-matters, not in their basic logical forms and relations; that the difference in subject-matters is due to the difference in the problems respectively involved; and, finally, that this difference sets up a difference in the ends or objective consequences they are concerned to achieve. Because common sense problems and inquiries have to do with the interactions into which living creatures enter in connection with environing conditions in order to establish objects of use and enjoyment, the symbols employed are those which have been determined in the habitual culture of a group. They form a system but the system is practical rather than intellectual. It is constituted by the traditions, occupations, techniques, interests, and established institutions of the group. The meanings that compose it are carried in the common everyday language of communication between members of the group. The meanings involved in this common language system determine what individuals of the group may and may not do in relation to physical objects and in relations to one another. They regulate *what* can be used and enjoyed and *how* use and enjoyment shall occur.

Because the symbol-meaning systems involved are connected directly with cultural life-activities and are related to each other in virtue of this connection, the specific meanings which are present have reference to the specific and limited environing conditions under which the group lives. Only those things of the environment that are taken, according to custom and tradition, as having connection with and bearing upon this life, enter into the meaning system. There is no such thing as disinterested intellectual concern with either physical or social matters. For, until the rise of science, there were no problems of common sense that called for such inquiry. Disinterestedness existed practically in the demand that group interests and concerns be put above private needs and interests. But there was no intellectual disinterestedness beyond the activities, interests and concerns of the group. In other words, there was no science as such, although, as was earlier pointed out, there did exist information and techniques which were available for the purposes of scientific inquiry and out of which the latter subsequently grew.

In scientific inquiry, then, meanings are related to one another on the ground of their character *as* meanings, freed from direct reference to the concerns of a limited group. Their intellectual abstractness is a product of this liberation, just as the "concrete" is practically identified by directness of connection with environmental interactions. Consequently a new language, a new system of symbols related together on a new basis, comes into existence, and in this new language semantic coherence, as such, is the controlling consideration. To repeat what has already been said, connection with problems of use and enjoyment is the source of the dominant role of qualities, sensible and moral, and of ends in common sense.

In science, since meanings are determined on the ground of their relation as meanings to one another, *relations* become the objects of inquiry and qualities are relegated to a secondary status, playing a part only as far as they assist in institution of relations. They are subordinate because they have an instrumental office, instead of being themselves, as in prescientific common sense, the matters of final importance. The enduring hold of common sense is testified to historically by the long time it took before it was seen that scientific objects are strictly relational. First tertiary qualities were eliminated; it was recognized that moral qualities are not agencies in determining the structure of nature. Then secondary qualities, the wet-dry, hot-cold, light-heavy, which were the explanatory principles of physical phenomena in Greek science, were ejected. But so-called primary qualities took their place, as with Newton and the Lockeian formulation of Newtonian existential postulates. It was not until the threshold of our time was reached that scientific inquiries perceived that their own problems and methods required an interpretation of "primary qualities" in terms of relations, such as position, motion and temporal span. In the structure of distinctively scientific objects these relations are indifferent to qualities.

The foregoing is intended to indicate that the different objectives of common sense and of scientific inquiry demand different subject-matters and that this difference in subject-matters is not incompatible with the existence of a common pattern in both types. There are, of course, secondary logical forms which reflect the distinction of properties involved in the change from qualitative and teleological subject-matter to non-qualitative and non-teleological relations. But they occur and operate within the described community of pattern. They are explicable, and explicable only, on the ground of the distinctive problems generated by scientific subject-matter. The independence of scientific objects from limited and fairly direct reference to the environment as a factor in activities of use and enjoyment, is equivalent, as has already been intimated, to their *abstract* character. It is also equivalent to their *general* character in the sense in which the generalizations of science are different from the generalizations with which common sense is familiar. The generality of *all* scientific subject-matter as such means that it is freed from restriction to conditions which present themselves at particular times and places. Their reference is to *any* set of time and place conditions—a statement which is not to be confused with the doctrine that they have no reference to actual existential occasions. Reference to time-place of existence is necessarily involved, but it is reference to whatever set of existences fulfils the general relations laid down in and by the constitution of the scientific object.

THE LOGIC OF JUDGMENTS OF PRACTICE [8]

In introducing the discussion, I shall first say a word to avoid possible misunderstandings. It may be objected that such a term as "practical judgment" is misleading; that the term "practical judgment" is a misnomer, and a dangerous one, since all judgments by their very nature are intellectual or theoretical. Consequently, there is a danger that the term will lead us to treat as judgment and knowledge something which is not really knowledge at all and thus start us on the road which ends in mysticism or obscurantism. All this is admitted. I do not mean by practical judgment a type of judgment having a different organ and source from other judgments. I mean simply a kind of judgment having a specific type of subject-matter. Propositions exist relating to *agenda*—to things to do or be done, judgments of a situation demanding action. There are, for example, propositions of the form: M. N. should do thus and so; it is better, wiser, more prudent, right, advisable, opportune, expedient, etc., to act thus and so. And this is the type of judgment I denote practical.

. . . Regarding them, we may say:

1. Their subject-matter implies an incomplete situation. . . .

2. Their subject-matter implies that the proposition is itself a factor in the completion of the situation, carrying it forward to its conclusion. . . .

3. The subject-matter implies that it makes a difference how the given is terminated: that one outcome is better than another, and that the proposition is to be a factor in securing (as far as may be) the better. In other words, there is something objectively at stake in the forming of the proposition. A right or wrong *descriptive* judgment (a judgment confined to the given, whether temporal, spatial, or subsistent) does not affect its subject-matter; it does not help or hinder its development, for by hypothesis it has no development. But a practical proposition affects the subject-matter for better or worse, for it is a judgment as to the condition (the thing to be done) of the existence of the complete subject-matter.

4. A practical proposition is binary. It is a judgment that the given is to be treated in a specified way; it is also a judgment that the given admits of such treatment, that it admits of a specified objective termination. It is a judgment, at the same stroke, of end—the result to be brought about—and of means. . . .

[8] From *The Journal of Philosophy, Psychology and Scientific Methods,* Vol. XII, No. 19 (Sept. 16, 1916), pp. 505–523.

5. The judgment of what is to be done implies, as we have just seen, a statement of what the given facts of the situation are, taken as indications of the course to pursue and of the means to be employed in its pursuit. . . . Logically, any factual proposition is a hypothetical proposition when it is made the basis of any inference.

6. The bearing of this remark upon the nature of the truth of practical judgments (including the judgment of what is given) is obvious. Their truth or falsity is constituted by the issue. The determination of end-means (constituting the terms and relations of the practical proposition) is hypothetical until the course of action indicated has been tried. The event or issue of such action *is* the truth or falsity of the judgment. This is an immediate conclusion from the fact that only the issue gives the complete subject-matter. In this case, at least, verification and truth completely coincide—unless there is some serious error in the prior analysis.

This completes the account, preliminary to a consideration of other matters. But the account suggests another and independent question with respect to which I shall make an excursus. How far is it possible and legitimate to extend or generalize the results reached to apply to all propositions of facts? That is to say, is it possible and legitimate to treat all scientific or descriptive statements of matters of fact as implying indirectly if not directly, something to be done, future possibilities to be realized in action? The question as to legitimacy is too complicated to be discussed in an incidental way. But it cannot be denied that there is a possibility of such application, nor that the possibility is worth careful examination. We may frame at least a hypothesis that all judgments of fact have reference to a determination of courses of action to be tried and to the discovery of means for their realization. In the sense already explained all propositions which state discoveries or ascertainments, all categorical propositions, would be hypothetical, and their truth would coincide with their tested consequences effected by intelligent action.

This theory may be called pragmatism. But it is a type of pragmatism quite free from dependence upon a voluntaristic psychology. It is not complicated by reference to emotional satisfactions or the play of desires.

JUDGMENTS OF VALUE

It is my purpose to apply the conclusions previously drawn as to the implications of practical judgment to the subject of judgments of value.

. . . A judgment of value is simply a case of a practical judgment, a judgment about the doing of something. This conflicts with the assumption that it is a judgment about a particular kind of existence independent of action, concerning which the main problem is whether it is subjective or objective. It conflicts with every tendency to make the determination of the right or wrong course of action (whether in morals, technology, or scientific inquiry) dependent upon an independent determination of some ghostly things called value-objects—whether their ghostly character is attributed to their existing in some transcendental eternal realm or in some realm called states of mind. It asserts that value-objects mean simply objects as judged to possess a certain *force* within a situation temporally developing toward a determinate result. To *find* a thing good is . . . to attribute or impute nothing to it. It is just to do something to it. But to consider *whether* it is good and how good it is, is to ask how it, *as if acted upon*, will operate in promoting a course of action.

Hence the great contrast which may exist between a good or an immediate experience and an evaluated or judged good. The rain may be most uncomfortable (just *be* it, as a man is more than five feet tall) and yet be "good" for growing crops—that is, favor or promote their movement in a given direction. This does not mean that two contrasting judgments of value are passed. It means that *no* judgment has yet taken place. If, however, I am moved to pass a value-judgment I should probably say that in spite of the disagreeableness of getting wet, the shower *is* a good thing. I am now judging it as a *means* in two contrasting situations, as a means with respect to two ends. I compare my discomfort as a *consequence* of the rain with the prospective crops as another consequence, and say "let the latter consequence be." I identify myself as agent with it, rather than with the immediate discomfort of the wetting. It is quite true that in this case I cannot do anything about it; my identification is, so to speak, sentimental rather than practical so far as stopping the rain or growing the crops is concerned. But in effect it is an assertion that one would not on account of the discomfort of the rain stop it; that one would, if one could, encourage its continuance. Go it, rain, one says.

The specific intervention of action is obvious enough in plenty of other cases. It occurs to me that this agreeable "food" which I am eating isn't a food for me; it brings on indigestion. It functions no longer as an *immediate* good; as something to be accepted. If I continue eating, it will be after I have deliberated. I have considered it as a means to two conflicting possible consequences, the present enjoyment of eating and the later state of health. One or other is possible, not both—though of course I may "solve" the problem by persuading myself that in this instance they are congruent. The value-object now means thing judged to be a means of procuring this or that end. As prizing, esteeming, holding dear denote ways of acting, so valuing denotes a passing judgment upon such acts with reference to their connection with other acts, or with respect to the continuum of behavior in which they fall. Valuation means change of mode of behavior from direct acceptance and welcoming to doubting and looking into—acts which involve postponement of direct (or so-called overt) action and which imply a future act having a different *meaning* from that just now occurring—for even if one decides to continue in the previous act its meaning-content is different when it is chosen after reflective examination.

A practical judgment has been defined as a judgment of what to do, or what is to be done: a judgment respecting the future termination of an incomplete and in so far indeterminate situation. To say that judgments of value fall within this field is to say two things: one, that the judgment of value is never complete in itself, but always in behalf of determining what is to be done; the other, that judgments of value (as distinct from the direct experience of something as good) imply that value is not anything previously given, but is something to be given by future action, itself conditioned upon (varying with) the judgment. This statement may appear to contradict the recent assertion that a value-object for knowledge means one investigated as a means to competing ends. For such a means it already is; the lobster *will* give me present enjoyment and future indigestion *if* I eat it. But as long as I judge, *value* is indeterminate. The question is not what the thing will do—I may be quite clear about that: it is whether to perform the act which will actualize its potentiality. What will I have the situation *become* as between alternatives? And that means what force shall the thing as means be given? Shall I take it as means to present enjoyment, or as a (negative) condition of future health? When its status in these respects is determined, its value is determined; judgment ceases, action goes on.

Practical judgments do not therefore primarily concern themselves with the value of *objects*; but with the course of action demanded to carry an incomplete situation to its fulfilment. The adequate control of such judgments may, however, be facilitated by judgment of the worth of objects which enter as ends and means into the action contemplated. For example, my primary (and ultimate) judgment has to do, say, with buying a suit of clothes: whether to buy and, if so, what? The question is of better and worse with respect to alternative courses of action, not with respect to various objects. But the judgment will be a judgment (and not a chance reaction) in the degree in which it takes for its intervening subject-matter the value-status of various objects. What are the prices of given suits? What are their styles in respect to current fashion? How do their patterns compare? What about their durability? How about their respective adaptability to the chief wearing use I have in mind? Relative, or comparative, durability, cheapness, suitability, style, aesthetic attractiveness constitute value traits. They are traits of objects not *per se*, but *as entering into a possible and foreseen completing of the situation*. Their value is their force in precisely this function. The decision of better and worse is the determination of their respective capacities and intensities *in this regard*. Apart from their status in this office, they have no traits of value for knowledge. A determination of better value as found in some one suit is equivalent to (has the force of) a decision as to what it is better to do. It provided the lacking stimulus so that action occurs, or passes from its indeterminate-indecisive-state into decision.

Reference to the terms "subjective" and "objective" will, perhaps, raise a cloud of ambiguities. But for this very reason it may be worth while to point out the ambiguous nature of the term objective as applied to valuations. Objective may be identified, quite erroneously, with qualities existing outside of and independently of the situation in which a decision as to a future course of action has to be reached. Or, objective may denote the status of qualities of an object *in respect* to the situation to be completed through judgment. Independently of the situation requiring practical judgment, clothes already have a given price, durability, pattern, etc. These traits are not affected by the judgment. They exist; they are given. But as given they are *not* determinate values. They are not *objects of* valuation; they are *data for* a valuation. We may have to take pains to discover what these given qualities are, but their discovery is in order that there may be a subsequent judgment of value. Were they already definite values, they would not be estimated; they would be stimuli to direct response. If a man had already decided that cheapness constituted value, he would simply take the cheapest suit offered. What he judges is the value of cheapness, and this depends upon its weight or importance in the situation requiring action, as compared with durability, style, adaptability, etc. Discovery of shoddy would not affect the *de facto* durability of the goods, but it would affect the value of cheapness—that is, *the weight assigned that trait in influencing judgment*—which it would not do, if cheapness already had a definite value. A value, in short, means a *consideration*, and a consideration does not mean an existence merely, but an existence having a claim upon judgment. Value judged is not existential quality noted, but is the influence attached by judgment to a given existential quality in determining judgment.

The conclusion is not that value is subjective, but that it is practical. The situation in which judgment of value is required is not mental, much less fanciful. I can but think that much of the recent discussion of the objectivity of value and of value-judgments rests upon a false psychological theory. It rests upon giving certain terms meanings that flow from an introspective psychology which accepts a realm of purely private states of consciousness, private not in a social sense (a sense implying courtesy or mayhap secrecy toward others), but existential independence and separateness. To refer value to choice or desire, for example, is in that case to say that value is sub-jectively conditioned. Quite otherwise, if we have steered clear from such a psychology. Choice, decision, means primarily a certain act, a piece of behavior on the part of a particular thing. That a horse chooses to eat hay means only that it eats hay; that the man chooses to steal means (at least) that he tries to steal. This trial may come, however, *after* an intervening act of reflection. It then has a certain intellectual or cognitive quality. But it may mean simply the bare fact of an action which is retrospectively called a choice: as a man, in spite of all temptation to belong to another nation, chooses to be born an Englishman, which, if it has any sense at all, signifies a choice to continue in a line adopted without choice. Taken in this latter sense (in which case, terms like choice and desire refer to ways of behavior), their use is only a specification of the general doctrine that all valuation has to do with the determination of a course of action. Choice, preference, is originally only a bias in a given direction, a bias which is no more subjective or psychical than is the fact that a ball thrown is swerving in a particular direction rather than in some other curve. It is just a name for the differential character of the action. But let continuance in a certain line of action become questionable, let, that is to say, it be regarded as a means to a future consequence, which consequence has alternatives, and then choice gets a logical or intellectual sense; a *mental* status if the term "mental" is reserved for acts having this intellectualized quality. Choice still means the fixing of a course of action; it means at least a *set* to be released as soon as physically possible. Otherwise man has not chosen, but has quieted himself into a belief that he has chosen in order to relieve himself of the strain of suspense.

Exactly the same analysis applies to desire. Diverse anticipated ends may provoke divided and competing present reactions; the or-ganism may be torn between different courses, each interfering with the completion of the other. This intra-organic pulling and hauling, this strife of active tendencies, is a genuine phenomenon. The pull in a given direction measures the immediate hold of an anticipated termination or end upon us, as compared with that of some other. If one asked after the mechanism of the valuing process, I have no doubt that the answer would be in terms of desires thus conceived.

But unless everything relating to the activity of a highly organized being is to be denominated subjective, I see no ground for calling it subjective. So far as I can make out, the emphasis upon a psychological treatment of value and valuation in a subjective sense is but a highly awkward and negative way of maintaining a positive truth: that value and valuation fall within the universe of *action*: that as welcoming, accepting, is an act, so valuation is a present act determining an act *to be* done, a present act taking place because the future act is uncertain and incomplete.

It does follow from this fact that valuation is not simply a *recognition* of the force or efficiency of a means with respect to continuing a process. For unless there is *question* about its continuation, about its termination, valuation will not occur. And there is no question save where activity is hesitant in direction because of conflict within it. Metaphorically we may say that rain is good to lay the dust, identifying force or efficiency with value. I do not believe that valuations occur and values are brought into being save in a continuing situation where things have potency for carrying forward processes. There is a close relationship between prevailing, valiancy, valency, and value. But the term "value" is not a mere reduplication of the term "efficiency": it adds something. When we are moving toward a result and at the same time are stimulated to move toward something else which is incompatible with it (as in the case of the lobster as a cause of both enjoyment and indigestion), a thing has a dual potency. Not until the end has been established is the value of the lobster settled, although there need be no doubt about its efficiencies. As was pointed out earlier, the practical judgment determines means and end at the same time. How then can value be given, as efficiency is given, until the end is chosen? The rain is (metaphorically) valuable for laying dust. Whether it is valuable for us to have the dust laid—and if so, how valuable—we shall never know until some activity of our own which is a factor in dust-laying comes into conflict with an incompatible activity. Its value is its force, indeed, but it is its force in moving us to one end *rather* than to another. Not every potency, in other words, but potency with the specific qualification of falling within judgment about future action, means value or valuable thing. Consequently there is no value save in situations where desires and the need of deliberation in order to choose are found, and yet this fact gives no excuse for regarding desire and deliberation and decision as subjective phenomena.

To use an Irish bull, as long as a man *knows* what he desires there is no desire; there is movement or endeavor in a given direction. Desire is desires, and simultaneous desires are incompatible; they mark, as we have noted, competing activities, movements in directions, which cannot both be extended. Reflection is a process of finding out what we want, what, as we say, we *really* want, and this means the formation of new desire, a new direction of action. In this process, things *get* values—something they did not possess before, although they had their efficiencies.

At whatever risk of shock, this doctrine should be exposed in all its nakedness. To judge value is to engage in instituting a determinate value where none is given. It is not necessary that antecedently given values should be the data of the valuation; and where they are given data they are only terms in the determination of a not yet existing value. When a man is ill and after deliberation concludes that it be well to see a doctor, the doctor doubtless exists antecedently. But it is not the doctor who is judged to be the good of the situation, but the *seeing* of the doctor: a thing which, by description, exists only because of an act dependent upon a judgment. Nor is the health the man antecedently possessed (or which somebody has) the thing which he judges to be a value; the thing judged to be a value is the restoring of health—something by description not yet existing. The results flowing from his past health will doubtless influence him in reaching his judgment that it will be a good to have restored health, but they do not constitute the good which forms his subject-matter and object of his judgment. He may judge that they *were* good without judging that they are now good, for to be judged now good means to be judged to be the object of a course of action still to be undertaken. And to *judge* that they were good (as distinct from merely recalling certain benefits which accrued from health) is to judge that *if* the situation had required a reflective determination of a course of action one would have judged health an existence to be attained or preserved by action. There are dialectic difficulties which may be raised about judgments of this sort. For they imply the seeming paradox of a judgment whose proper subject-matter is its own determinate formation. But nothing is gained by obscuring the fact that such is the nature of the practical judgment: it is a judgment of what and how to judge—of the weight to be assigned to various factors in the determination of judgment. . . .

From what has been said, it immediately follows, of course, that a determinate value is instituted as a decisive factor with respect to what is to be done. Wherever a determinate good exists, there is an adequate stimulus to action, and no judgment of what is to be done or of the value of an object is called for. It is frequently assumed, however, that valuation is a process of applying some fixed or determinate value to the various competing goods of a situation; that valuation implies a prior standard of value and consists in comparing various goods with the standard as the supreme value. This assumption requires examination. If it is sound it deprives the position which has been taken of any validity. For it renders the judgment of what to do a matter of applying a value existing ready-made, instead of making—as we have done—the valuation a determination within the practical judgment. The argument would run this way: Every practical judgment depends upon a judgment of the value of the end to be attained; this end may be such only proximately, but that implies something else judged to be good, and so, logically, till we have arrived at the judgment of a supreme good, a final end or *summum bonum*. If this statement correctly describes the state of the case there can be no doubt that a practical judgment depends upon a prior recognition of value; consequently the hypothesis upon which we have been proceeding reverses the actual facts.

The first thing by way of critical comment is to point out the ambiguity in the term "end." I should like to fall back upon what was said earlier about the thoroughly reciprocal character of means and end in the practical judgment. If this be admitted it is also admitted that only by a judgment of means—things having value in the carrying of an indeterminate situation to a completion—is the end determinately made out in judgment. But I fear I cannot count upon this as granted. So I will point out that "end" may mean either the *de facto* limit to judgment, which by definition does not enter into judgment at all, or it may mean the last and completing object of judgment, the conception of that object in which a transitive incompletely given situation would come to rest. Of end in the first sense, it is to be said that it is not a value at all; of end in the second sense, that it is identical with a finale of the kind we have just been discussing or that it is determined in judgment, not a value given by which to control the judgment. It may be asserted that in the illustration used some typical suit of clothes is the value which affords the standard of valuation of all the suits which are offered to the buyer; that he passes judgment on their value as compared with the standard suit as an end and supreme value. This statement brings out the ambiguity just referred to. The need of something to wear is the *stimulus* to the judgment of the value of suits offered, and possession of a suit puts an end *to* judgment. It is an end *of* judgment in the objective, not in the possessive, sense of the preposition "of"; it is an end not in the sense of aim, but in the sense of a terminating limit. When possession begins, judgment has already ceased. And if argument *ad veruecundiam* has any weight I may point out that this is the doctrine of Aristotle when he says we never deliberate about ends, but only about means. That is to say, in all deliberation (or practical judgment or inquiry) there is always something outside of judgment which fixes its beginning and end or terminus. And I would add that, according to Aristotle, deliberation always ceases when we have come to the "first link in the chain of causes, which is last in the order of discovery," and this means "when we have traced back the chain of causes [means] to ourselves." In other words, the last end-in-view is always that which operates as the direct or immediate means of setting our own powers in operation. The end-in-view upon which judgment of action settles down is simply the adequate or complete means to the doing of something.

We do deliberate, however, about *aims*, about ends-in-view—a fact which shows their radically different nature from ends as limits to deliberation. The aim in the present instance is not the suit of clothes, but the *getting of a proper* suit. That is what is precisely estimated or valuated; and I think I may claim to have shown that the determination of this aim is identical with the determination of the value of a suit through comparison of the values of cheapness, durability, style, pattern of different suits offered. Value is not determined by comparing various suits with an ideal model, but by comparing various suits with respect to cheapness, durability, adaptability *with one another*—involving, of course, reference also to length of purse, suits already possessed, etc., and other specific elements in the situation which demands that something be done. The purchaser may, of course, have settled upon something which serves as a model before he goes to buy; but that only means that his judging has been done beforehand; the model does not then function in judgment, but in his act as stimulus to immediate action. And there is a consideration here involved of the utmost importance as to practical judgments of the moral type: The more completely the notion of the model is formed outside and irrespective of the specific conditions which the situation of action presents, the less intelligent is the act. Most men might have their ideals of the model changed somewhat in the face of the actual offering, even in the case of buying clothes. The man who is not accessible to such change in the case of moral situations has ceased to be a moral agent and become a reacting machine. In short, the standard of valuation is formed in the process of practical judgment or valuation. It is not something taken from outside and applied within it—such application means there is no judgment.

Nothing has been said thus far about a standard. Yet the conception of a standard, or a measure, is so closely connected with valuation that its consideration affords a test of the conclusions reached. It must be admitted that the concept of the nature of a standard pointed to by the course of the prior discussion is not in conformity with current conceptions. For the argument points to a standard which is determined within the process of valuation, not outside of it, and hence not capable of being employed ready-made, therefore, to settle the valuing process. To many persons, this will seem absurd to the point of self-contradiction. The prevailing conception, however, has been adopted without examination; it is a preconception. If accepted, it deprives judgment and knowledge of all significant import in connection with moral action. If the standard is already given, all that remains is its mechanical application to the case in hand—as one would apply a yard rule to dry-goods. Genuine moral uncertainty is then impossible; where it seems to exist, it is only a name for a moral unwillingness, due to inherent viciousness, to recognize and apply the rules already made and provided, or else for a moral corruption which has enfeebled man's power of moral apprehension. When the doctrine of standards prior to and independent of moral judgments is accompanied by these other doctrines of original sin and corruption, one must respect the thoroughgoing logic of the doctrine. Such is not, however, the case with the modern theories which make the same assumption of standards preceding instead of resulting from moral judgments, and which ignore the question of uncertainty and error in their apprehension. Such considerations do not, indeed, decide anything, but they may serve to get a more unprejudiced hearing for a hypothesis which runs counter to current theories, since it but formulates the trend of current practices in their increasing tendency to make the act of intelligence the central factor in morals.

. . . The attempt to bring over from past objects the elements of a standard for valuing future consequences is a hopeless one. The express object of a valuation-judgment is to release factors which being new, cannot be measured on the basis of the past alone. This discussion of the analytic logic as applied in morals would, however, probably not be worth while did it not serve to throw into relief the significance of any appeal to fulfilment of a system or organization as *the* moral good—the standard. Such an appeal, if it is wary, is an appeal to the present situation as *undergoing that reorganization that will confer upon it the unification which it lacks;* to organization as something to be brought about, to be made. And it is clear that this appeal meets all the specifications of judgments of practice as they have been described. The organization which is to be fulfilled through action is an organization which, at the time of judging, is present in conception, in idea—in, that is, reflective inquiry as a phase of reorganizing activity. And since its presence in conception is both a condition of the organization aimed at *and* a function of the adequacy of the reflective inquiry, it is evident that there is here a confirmation of our statement that the practical judgment is a judgment of what and how to judge as an integral part of the completion of an incomplete temporal situation. More specifically, it also appears that the standard is a rule for conducting inquiry to its completion: it is a counsel to make examination of the operative factors complete, a warning against suppressing recognition of any of them. However a man may impose upon himself or upon others, a man's real measure of value is exhibited in what he *does*, not in what he consciously thinks or says. For the doing is the *actual* choice. It is the completed reflection.

It is comparatively easy at the present time in moral theory to slam both hedonism and apriorism. It is not so easy to see the logical implications of the alternative to them. The conception of an organization of interests or tendencies is often treated as if it were a conception which is definite in subject-matter as well as clear-cut in form. It is taken not as a rule for procedure in inquiry, a direction and a warning (which it is), but as something all of whose constituents are already given for *knowledge*, even though not given in fact. The act of fulfilling or realizing must then be treated as devoid of intellectual import. It is a mere doing, not a learning and a testing. But how can a situation which is incomplete in fact be completely known until it *is* complete? Short of the fulfilment of a conceived organization, how can the conception of the proposed organization be anything more than a working hypothesis, a method of treating the given elements in order to see what happens? Does not every notion which implies the possibility of an apprehension of knowledge of the end to be reached[9] also imply either an a priori revelation of the nature of that end, or else that organization is nothing but a whole composed of elementary parts already given— the logic of hedonism?

The logic of subsumption in the physical sciences meant that a given state of things could be compared with a ready-made concept as a model—the phenomena of the heavens with the implications of, say, the circle. The methods of experimental science broke down this motion; they substituted for an alleged regulative model a formula which was the integrated function of the particular phenomena themselves, a formula to be used as a method of further observations and experiments and thereby tested and developed. The unwillingness to believe that, in a similar fashion, moral standards or models can be trusted to develop out of the specific situations of action shows how little the general logical force of the method of science has been

[9] It must not be overlooked that a mere reminder of an end previously settled upon may operate as a sufficient stimulus to action. It is probably this act of calling the end to mind which the realist confuses with knowledge, and therefore terms apprehension. But there is nothing cognitive about it, any more than there is in pressing a button to give the signal for an act already decided upon.

grasped. Physical knowledge did not as matter of fact advance till
the dogma of models or forms as standards of knowledge had been
ousted. Yet we hang tenaciously to a like doctrine in morals for fear
of moral chaos. It once seemed to be impossible that the disordered
phenomena of perception could generate a knowledge of law and
order; it was supposed that independent principles of order must be
supplied and the phenomena measured by approach to or deviation
from the fixed models. The ordinary conception of a standard in
practical affairs is a precise analogue. Physical knowledge started on
a secure career when men had courage to start from the irregular
scene and to treat the suggestions to which it gave rise as methods
for instituting new observations and experiences. Acting upon the
suggested conceptions analyzed, extended, and ordered phenomena
and thus made improved conceptions—methods of inquiry—possible.
It is reasonable to believe that what holds moral knowledge back is
above all the conception that there are standards of good given to
knowledge apart from the work of reflection in constructing methods
of action. As the bringer of bad news gets a bad name, being made
to share in the production of the evil which he reports, so honest
acknowledgment of the uncertainty of the moral situation and of the
hypothetical character of all rules of moral mensuration prior to acting upon them, is treated as if it originated the uncertainty and
created the skepticism.

It may be contended, however, that all this does not justify the
earlier statement that the limiting situation which occasions and cuts
off judgment is not itself a value. Why, it will be asked, does a man
buy a suit of clothes unless that is a value, or at least a proximate
means to a further value? The answer is short and simple: Because
he has to; because the situation in which he lives demands it. The
answer probably seems too summary. But it may suggest that while
a man lives, he never is called upon to judge whether he shall act,
but simply *how* he shall act. A decision not to act is a decision to
act in a certain way; it is never a judgment not to act, unqualifiedly.
It is a judgment to do something else—to wait, for example. A judgment that the best thing to do is to retire from active life, to become
a Simon Stylites, is a judgment to act in a certain way, conditioned
upon the necessity that, irrespective of judging, a man will have to
act somehow anyway. A decision to commit suicide is not a decision
to be dead; it is a decision to perform a certain act. The act may
depend upon reaching the conclusion that life is not worth living.
But as a judgment, this is a conclusion to act in a way to terminate
the possibility of further situations requiring judgment and action.
And it does not imply that a judgment about life as a supreme value
and standard underlies all judgments as to how to live. More spe-

cifically, it is not a judgment upon the value of life *per se*, but a judgment that one does not find at hand the specific means of making life worth while. As an act to be done, it falls within and assumes life. As a judgment upon the value of life, by definition it evades the issue. No one ever influenced a person considering committing suicide by arguments concerning the value of life, but only by suggesting or supplying conditions and means which make life worth living; in other words, by furnishing *direct* stimuli to living.

However, I fear that all this argument may only obscure a point obvious without argument, namely, that all deliberation upon what to do is concerned with the completion and determination of a situation in some respect incomplete and so indeterminate. Every such situation is specific; it is not *merely* incomplete; the incompleteness is *of* a specific situation. Hence the situation sets limits to the reflective process; what is judged has reference to it and that which limits never is judged in the particular situation in which it is limiting. . . .

DEMOCRACY AND EDUCATION [11]

EDUCATION AS GROWTH

. . . In directing the activities of the young, society determines its own future in determining that of the young. Since the young at a given time will at some later date compose the society of that period, the latter's nature will largely turn upon the direction children's activities were given at an earlier period. This cumulative movement of action toward a later result is what is meant by growth. . . .

. . . When it is said that education is development, everything depends upon *how* development is conceived. Our net conclusion is that life is development, and that developing, growing, is life. Translated into its educational equivalents, this means *(i)* that the educational process has no end beyond itself; it is its own end; and that *(ii)* the educational process is one of continual reorganizing, reconstructing, transforming.

1. Development when it is interpreted in *comparative* terms, that is, with respect to the special traits of child and adult life, means the direction of power into special channels: the formation of habits involving executive skill, definiteness of interest, and specific objects of observation and thought. But the comparative view is not final. The child has specific powers; to ignore that fact is to stunt or dis-

[11] From John Dewey, *Democracy and Education,* N. Y.: Macmillan, 1916. Selections from Ch. IV, p. 49, pp. 59–62 and Ch. VII, pp. 94–96, 100–102.

tort the organs upon which his growth depends. The adult uses his powers to transform his environment, thereby occasioning new stimuli which redirect his powers and keep them developing. Ignoring this fact means arrested development, a passive accommodation. Normal child and normal adult alike, in other words, are engaged in growing. The difference between them is not the difference between growth and no growth, but between the modes of growth appropriate to different conditions. With respect to the development of powers devoted to coping with specific scientific and economic problems we may say the child should be growing in manhood. With respect to sympathetic curiosity, unbiased responsiveness, and openness of mind, we may say that the adult should be growing in childlikeness. One statement is as true as the other.

Three ideas which have been criticized, namely, the merely privative nature of immaturity, static adjustment to a fixed environment, and rigidity of habit, are all connected with a false idea of growth or development,—that it is a movement toward a fixed goal. Growth is regarded as *having* an end, instead of *being* an end. The educational counterparts of the three fallacious ideas are first, failure to take account of the instinctive or native powers of the young; secondly, failure to develop initiative in coping with novel situations; thirdly, an undue emphasis upon drill and other devices which secure automatic skill at the expense of personal perception. In all cases, the adult environment is accepted as a standard for the child. He is to be brought up *to* it.

Natural instincts are either disregarded or treated as nuisances—as obnoxious traits to be suppressed, or at all events to be brought into conformity with external standards. Since conformity is the aim, what is distinctively individual in a young person is brushed aside, or regarded as a source of mischief or anarchy. Conformity is made equivalent to uniformity. Consequently, there are induced lack of interest in the novel, aversion to progress, and dread of the uncertain and the unknown. Since the end of growth is outside of and beyond the process of growing, external agents have to be resorted to to induce movement towards it. Whenever a method of education is stigmatized as mechanical, we may be sure that external pressure is brought to bear to reach an external end.

2. Since in reality there is nothing to which growth is relative save more growth, there is nothing to which education is subordinate save more education. It is a commonplace to say that education should not cease when one leaves school. The point of this commonplace is that the purpose of school education is to insure the continuance of education by organizing the powers that insure growth. The inclination to learn from life itself and to make the conditions of life such

that all will learn in the process of living is the finest product of schooling.

When we abandon the attempt to define immaturity by means of fixed comparison with adult accomplishments, we are compelled to give up thinking of it as denoting lack of desired traits. Abandoning this notion, we are also forced to surrender our habit of thinking of instruction as a method of supplying this lack by pouring knowledge into a mental and moral hole which awaits filling. Since life means growth, a living creature lives as truly and positively at one stage as at another, with the same intrinsic fullness and the same absolute claims. Hence education means the enterprise of supplying the conditions which insure growth, or adequacy of life, irrespective of age. We first look with impatience upon immaturity, regarding it as something to be got over as rapidly as possible. Then the adult formed by such educative methods looks back with impatient regret upon childhood and youth as a scene of lost opportunities and wasted powers. This ironical situation will endure till it is recognized that living has its own intrinsic quality and that the business of education is with that quality.

Realization that life is growth protects us from that so-called idealizing of childhood which in effect is nothing but lazy indulgence. Life is not to be identified with every superficial act and interest. Even though it is not always easy to tell whether what appears to be mere surface fooling is a sign of some nascent as yet untrained power, we must remember that manifestations are not to be accepted as ends in themselves. They are signs of possible growth. They are to be turned into means of development, of carrying power forward, not indulged or cultivated for their own sake. Excessive attention to surface phenomena (even in the way of rebuke as well as of encouragement) may lead to their fixation and thus to arrested development. What impulses are moving toward, not what they have been, is the important thing for parent and teacher. The true principle of respect for immaturity cannot be better put than in the words of Emerson: "Respect the child. Be not too much his parent. Trespass not on his solitude. But I hear the outcry which replies to this suggestion: Would you verily throw up the reins of public and private discipline; would you leave the young child to the mad career of his own passions and whimsies, and call this anarchy a respect for the child's nature? I answer,—Respect the child, respect him to the end, but also respect yourself. . . . The two points in a boy's training are, to keep his *naturel* and train off all but that; to keep his *naturel*, but stop off his uproar, fooling, and horseplay; keep his nature *and arm it with knowledge in the very direction in which it points*." And as Emerson goes on to show this reverence for childhood and youth instead of opening up an easy and easy-going path to the instructors, "involves at once, immense claims on the time, the thought, on the life of the teacher. It requires time, use, insight, event, all the great lessons and assistances of God; and only to think of using it implies character and profoundness." ...

THE DEMOCRATIC CONCEPTION IN EDUCATION

... We have now to make explicit the differences in the spirit, material, and method of education as it operates in different types of community life. To say that education is a social function, securing direction and development in the immature through their participation in the life of the group to which they belong, is to say in effect that education will vary with the quality of life which prevails in a group. Particularly is it true that a society which not only changes but which has the ideal of such change as will improve it, will have different standards and methods of education from one which aims simply at the perpetuation of its own customs. To make the general ideas set forth applicable to our own educational practice, it is, therefore, necessary to come to closer quarters with the nature of present social life.

... Society is one word, but many things. Men associate together in all kinds of ways and for all kinds of purposes. One man is concerned in a multitude of diverse groups, in which his associates may be quite different. It often seems as if they had nothing in common except that they are modes of associated life. Within every larger social organization there are numerous minor groups: not only political subdivisions, but industrial, scientific, religious associations. There are political parties with differing aims, social sets, cliques, gangs, corporations, partnerships, groups bound closely together by ties of blood, and so in endless variety. In many modern states, and in some ancient, there is great diversity of populations, of varying languages, religions, moral codes, and traditions. From this standpoint, many a minor political unit, one of our large cities, for example, is a congeries of loosely associated societies, rather than an inclusive and permeating community of action and thought.

The terms society, community, are thus ambiguous. They have both a eulogistic or normative sense, and a descriptive sense; a meaning *de jure* and a meaning *de facto*. In social philosophy, the former connotation is almost always uppermost. Society is conceived as one by its very nature. The qualities which accompany this unity, praiseworthy community of purpose and welfare, loyalty to public ends, mutuality of sympathy, are emphasized. But when we look at the facts which the term *denotes* instead of confining our attention to its intrinsic *connotation*, we find not unity, but a plurality of societies, good and bad. Men banded together in a criminal conspiracy, business aggregations that prey upon the public while serving it, political machines held together by the interest of plunder, are included. If it is said that such organizations are not societies because they do not meet the ideal requirements of the notion of society, the answer, in part, is that the conception of society is then made so "ideal" as to be of no use, having no reference to facts; and in part, that each of these organizations, no matter how opposed to the interests of other groups, has something of the praiseworthy qualities of "Society" which hold it together. There is honor among thieves, and a band of robbers has a common interest as respects its members. Gangs are marked by fraternal feeling, and narrow cliques by intense loyalty to their own codes. Family life may be marked by exclusiveness, suspicion, and jealousy as to those without, and yet be a model of amity and mutual aid within. Any education given by a group tends to socialize its members, but the quality and value of socialization depends upon the habits and aims of the group.

Hence, once more, the need of a measure for the worth of any given mode of social life. In seeking this measure, we have to avoid two extremes. We cannot set up, out of our heads, something we regard as an ideal society. We must base our conception upon societies which actually exist, in order to have any assurance that our ideal is a practicable one. But, as we have just seen, the ideal cannot simply repeat the traits which are actually found. The problem is to extract the desirable traits of forms of community life which actually exist, and employ them to criticize undesirable features and suggest improvement. Now in any social group whatever, even in a gang of thieves, we find some interest held in common, and we find a certain amount of interaction and coöperative intercourse with other groups. From these two traits we derive our standard. How numerous and varied are the interests which are consciously shared? How full and free is the interplay with other forms of association? If we apply these considerations to, say, a criminal band, we find that the ties which consciously hold the members together are few in number, reducible almost to a common interest in plunder; and that they are of such a nature as to isolate the group from other groups with respect to give and take of the values of life. Hence, the education such a society gives is partial and distorted. If we take, on the other hand, the kind of family life which illustrates the standard, we find that there are material, intellectual, æsthetic interests in which all participate and that the progress of one member has worth for the experience of other members—it is readily communicable— and that the family is not an isolated whole, but enters intimately into relationships with business groups, with schools, with all the agencies of culture, as well as with other similar groups, and that it plays a due part in the political organization and in return receives support from it. In short, there are many interests consciously communicated and shared; and there are varied and free points of contact with other modes of association. . . .

The two elements in our criterion both point to democracy. The first signifies not only more numerous and more varied points of shared common interest, but greater reliance upon the recognition of mutual interests as a factor in social control. The second means not only freer interaction between social groups (once isolated so far as intention could keep up a separation) but change in social habit— its continuous readjustment through meeting the new situations produced by varied intercourse. And these two traits are precisely what characterize the democratically constituted society.

Upon the educational side, we note first that the realization of a form of social life in which interests are mutually interpenetrating, and where progress, or readjustment, is an important consideration, makes a democratic community more interested than other communities have cause to be in deliberate and systematic education. The devotion of democracy to education is a familiar fact. The superficial explanation is that a government resting upon popular suffrage cannot be successful unless those who elect and who obey their governors are educated. Since a democratic society repudiates the principle of external authority, it must find a substitute in voluntary disposition and interest; these can be created only by education. But there is a deeper explanation. A democracy is more than a form of government; it is primarily a mode of associated living, of conjoint communicated experience. The extension in space of the number of individuals who participate in an interest so that each has to refer his own action to that of others, and to consider the action of others to give point and direction to his own, is equivalent to the breaking down of those barriers of class, race, and national territory which kept men from perceiving the full import of their activity. These more numerous and more varied points of contact denote a greater diversity of stimuli to which an individual has to respond; they consequently put a premium on variation in his action. They secure a liberation of powers which remain suppressed as long as the incitations to action are partial, as they must be in a group which in its exclusiveness shuts out many interests.

The widening of the area of shared concerns, and the liberation of a greater diversity of personal capacities which characterize a democracy, are not of course the product of deliberation and conscious effort. On the contrary, they were caused by the development of modes of manufacture and commerce, travel, migration, and inter-communication which flowed from the command of science over natural energy. But after greater individualization on one hand, and a broader community of interest on the other have come into existence, it is a matter of deliberate effort to sustain and extend them. Obviously a society to which stratification into separate classes would be fatal, must see to it that intellectual opportunities are accessible to all on equable and easy terms. A society marked off into classes need be specially attentive only to the education of its ruling elements. A society which is mobile, which is full of channels for the distribution of a change occurring anywhere, must see to it that its members are educated to personal initiative and adaptability. Otherwise, they will be overwhelmed by the changes in which they are caught and whose significance or connections they do not perceive. The result will be a confusion in which a few will appropriate to themselves the results of the blind and externally directed activities of others. . . .

THE FUTURE OF LIBERALISM [10]

The emphasis of earlier liberalism upon individuality and liberty defines the focal points of discussion of the philosophy of liberalism today. This earlier liberalism was itself an outgrowth, in the late eighteenth and nineteenth centuries, of the earlier revolt against oligarchical government, one which came to its culmination in the "glorious revolution" of 1688. The latter was fundamentally a demand for freedom of the taxpayer from government arbitrary action in connection with a demand for confessional freedom in religion by the Protestant churches. In the liberalism, expressly so called, demand for liberty and individual freedom of action came primarily from the rising industrial and trading class and was directed against restrictions placed by government, in legislation, common law and judicial action, and other institutions having connection with the political state, upon freedom of economic enterprise. In both cases, governmental action and the desired freedom were placed in antithesis to each other. This way of conceiving liberty has persisted; it was strengthened in this country by the revolt of the colonies and by pioneer conditions.

Nineteenth-century philosophic liberalism added, more or less because of its dominant economic interest, the conception of natural laws to that of natural rights of the Whig movement. There are

[10] Reprinted from the *Journal of Philosophy*, Vol. 32, 1935, pp. 225–230.

natural laws, it held, in social matters as well as in physical, and these natural laws are economic in character. Political laws, on the other hand, are man-made and in that sense artificial. Governmental intervention in industry and exchange was thus regarded as a violation not only of inherent individual liberty but also of natural laws—of which supply and demand is a sample. The proper sphere of governmental action was simply to prevent and to secure redress for infringement by one, in the exercise of his liberty, of like and equal liberty of action on the part of others.

Nevertheless, the demand for freedom in initiation and conduct of business enterprise did not exhaust the content of earlier liberalism. In the minds of its chief promulgators there was included an equally strenuous demand for the liberty of mind, freedom of thought and its expression in speech, writing, print and assemblage. The earlier interest in confessional freedom was generalized, and thereby deepened as well as broadened. This demand was a product of the rational enlightenment of the eighteenth century and of the growing importance of science. The great tide of reaction that set in after the defeat of Napoleon, the demand for order and discipline, gave the agitation for freedom of thought and its expression plenty of cause and plenty of opportunity.

The earlier liberal philosophy rendered valiant service. It finally succeeded in sweeping away, especially in its home, Great Britain, an innumerable number of abuses and restrictions. The history of social reforms in the nineteenth century is almost one with the history of liberal social thought. It is not then from ingratitude that I shall emphasize its defects, for recognition of them is essential to an intelligent statement of the elements of liberal philosophy for the present and any nearby future. The fundamental defect was its lack of perception of historic relativity. This lack is expressed in the conception of the individual as something given, complete in itself, and of liberty as a ready-made possession of the individual, only needing the removal of external restrictions in order to manifest itself. The individual of earlier liberalism was a Newtonian atom having only external time and space relations to other individuals, save in that each social atom was equipped with inherent freedom. These ideas might not have been especially harmful if they had been merely a rallying cry for practical movements. But they formed part of a philosophy and of a philosophy in which these particular ideas of individuality and freedom were asserted to be absolute and eternal truths; good for all times and all places.

This absolutism, this ignoring and denial of temporal relativity is one great reason why the earlier liberalism degenerated so easily into pseudo-liberalism. For the sake of saving time, I shall identify what

I mean by this spurious liberalism, the kind of social ideas represented by the "Liberty League" and ex-President Hoover. I call it a pseudo-liberalism because it ossified and narrowed generous ideas and aspirations. Even when words remain the same, they mean something very different when they are uttered by a minority struggling against repressive measures and when expressed by a group that has attained power and then uses ideas that were once weapons of emancipation as instruments for keeping the power and wealth they have obtained. Ideas that at one time are means of producing social change assume another guise when they are used as means of preventing further social change. This fact is itself an illustration of historic relativity, and an evidence of the evil that lay in the assertion by earlier liberalism of the immutable and eternal character of their ideas. Because of this latter fact, the *laissez-faire* doctrine was held by the degenerate school of liberals to express the very order of nature itself. The outcome was the degradation of the idea of individuality until in the minds of many who are themselves struggling for a wider and fuller development of individuality, individualism has become a term of hissing and reproach, while many can see no remedy for the evils that have come from the use of socially unrestrained liberty in business enterprise, save change produced by violence. The historic tendency to conceive the whole question of liberty as a matter in which individual and government are opposed parties has borne bitter fruit. Born of despotic government, it has continued to influence thinking and action after government had become popular and *in theory* the servant of the people.

I pass now to what the philosophy of liberalism would be were its inheritance of absolutism eliminated. In the first place such liberalism knows that an individual is nothing fixed, given ready-made. It is something achieved, and achieved not in isolation, but with the aid and support of conditions, cultural and physical, including in "cultural" economic, legal and political institutions as well as science and art. Liberalism knows that social conditions may restrict, distort and almost prevent the development of individuality. It therefore takes an active interest in the working of social institutions that have a bearing, positive or negative, upon the growth of individuals who shall be rugged in fact and not merely in abstract theory. It is as much interested in the positive construction of favorable institutions, legal, political and economic, as it is in the work of removing abuses and overt oppressions.

In the second place, liberalism is committed to the idea of historic relativity. It knows that the content of the individual and freedom change with time; that this is as true of social change as it is of individual development from infancy to maturity. The positive counterpart of opposition to doctrinal absolutism is experimentalism. The connection between historic relativity and experimental method is intrinsic. Time signifies change. The significance of individuality with respect to social policies alters with change of the conditions in which individuals live. The earlier liberalism in being absolute was also unhistoric. Underlying it there was a philosophy of history which assumed that history, like time in the Newtonian scheme, means only modification of external relations; that it is quantitative, not qualitative and internal. The same thing is true of any theory that assumes, like the one usually attributed to Marx, that temporal changes in society are inevitable—that is to say, are governed by a law that is not itself historical. The fact is that the historicism and the evolutionism of nineteenth-century doctrine were only half-way doctrines. They assumed that historical and developmental processes were subject to some law or formula outside temporal processes.

The commitment of liberalism to experimental procedure carries with it the idea of continuous reconstruction of the ideas of individuality and of liberty in intimate connection with changes in social relations. It is enough to refer to the changes in productivity and distribution since the time when the earlier liberalism was formulated, and the effect of these transformations, due to science and technology, upon the terms on which men associate together. An experimental method is the recognition of this temporal change in ideas and policies so that the latter shall coordinate with the facts instead of being opposed to them. Any other view maintains a rigid conceptualism and implies that facts should conform to concepts that are framed independently of temporal or historical change.

The two things essential, then, to thorough-going social liberalism are, first, realistic study of existing conditions in their movement, and, secondly, leading ideas, in the form of policies for dealing with these conditions in the interest of development of increased individuality and liberty. The first requirement is so obviously implied that I shall not elaborate it. The second point needs some amplification. Experimental method is not just messing around nor doing a little of this and a little of that in the hope that things will improve. Just as in the physical sciences, it implies a coherent body of ideas, a theory, that gives direction to effort. What is implied, in contrast to every form of absolutism, is that the ideas and theory be taken as methods of action tested and continuously revised by the consequences they produce in actual social conditions. Since they are operational in nature, they modify conditions, while the first requirement, that of basing them upon realistic study of actual conditions, brings about their continuous reconstruction.

It follows, finally, that there is no opposition in principle between liberalism as social philosophy and radicalism in action, if by radicalism is signified the adoption of policies that bring about drastic instead of piecemeal social changes. It is all a question of what kind of procedures the intelligent study of changing conditions discloses. These changes have been so tremendous in the last century, yes, in the last forty years, that it looks to me as if radical methods were now necessary. But all that the argument here requires is recognition of the fact that there is nothing in the nature of liberalism that makes it a milk-water doctrine, committed to compromise and minor "reforms." It is worth noting that the earlier liberals were regarded in their day as subversive radicals.

What has been said should make it clear that the question of method in formation and execution of policies is the central thing in liberalism. The method indicated is that of maximum reliance upon intelligence. This fact determines its opposition to those forms of radicalism that place chief dependence upon violent overthrow of existing institutions as the method of effecting desired social change. A genuine liberal will emphasize as crucial the complete correlation between the means used and the consequences that follow. The same principle which makes him aware that the means employed by pseudo-liberalism only perpetuate and multiply the evils of existing conditions makes him aware also that dependence upon sheer massed force as the means of social change decides the kind of consequences that actually result. Doctrines, whether proceeding from Mussolini or from Marx, which assume that because certain ends are desirable therefore those ends and nothing else will result from the use of force to attain them is but another example of the limitations put upon intelligence by any absolute theory. In the degree in which mere force is resorted to, actual consequences are themselves so compromised that the ends originally in view have in fact to be worked out afterwards by the method of experimental intelligence.

In saying this, I do not wish to be understood as meaning that radicals of the type mentioned have any monopoly of the use of force. The contrary is the case. The reactionaries are in possession of force, in not only the army and police, but in the press and the schools. The only reason they do not advocate the use of force is the fact that they are already in possession of it, so their policy is to cover up its existence with idealistic phrases—of which their present use of individual initiative and liberty is a striking example.

These facts illustrate the essential evil of reliance upon sheer force. Action and reaction are equal and in opposite directions, and force as such is physical. Dependence upon force sooner or later calls out force on the other side. The whole problem of the relation of intelligence to force is much too large to go into here. I can only say that when the forces in possession are so blind and stubborn as to throw all their weight against the use of liberty of inquiry and of communication, of organization to effect social change, they not only encourage the use of force in those who want social change, but they give the latter the most justification they ever have. The emphasis of liberalism upon the method of intelligence does not commit it to unqualified pacifism, but to the unremitting use of every method of intelligence that conditions permit, and to search for all that are possible.

In conclusion, I wish to emphasize one point. . . . The question of the practical significance of liberty is much wider than that of the relation of government to the individual, to say nothing of the monstrosity of the doctrine that assumes that under all conditions governmental action and individual liberty are found in separate and independent spheres. Government is one factor and an important one. But it comes into the picture only in relation to other matters. At present, these other matters are economic and cultural. With respect to the first point, it is absurd to conceive liberty as that of the business entrepreneur and ignore the immense regimentation to which workers are subjected, intellectual as well as manual workers. As to the second point, the full freedom of the human spirit and of individuality can be achieved only as there is effective opportunity to share in the cultural resources of civilization. No economic state of affairs is merely economic. It has a profound effect upon the presence or absence of cultural freedom. Any liberalism that does not make full cultural freedom supreme and that does not see the relation between it and genuine industrial freedom as a way of life is degenerate and delusive liberalism.

BIBLIOGRAPHY

DEWEY, John. *The Influence of Darwin on Philosophy and Other Essays in Contemporary Thought.* N.Y.: Henry Holt, 1910.
———, *How We Think.* (1910, Rev. ed.) Boston: D. C. Heath, 1933.
———, *Democracy and Education.* N.Y.: Macmillan, 1916.
———, *Essays in Experimental Logic.* Chicago: U. of Chicago Press, 1916.
———, *Reconstruction in Philosophy.* N.Y.: Henry Holt, 1920.
———, *Human Nature and Conduct: An Introduction to Social Psychology.* N.Y.: Henry Holt, 1922.
———, *Experience and Nature.* Chicago: Open Court, 1925. (Revised Ed., 1929.)
———, *The Quest for Certainty.* N.Y.: Minton, Balch, 1929.
———, *Individualism, Old and New.* N.Y.: Minton, Balch, 1930.

———, *Philosophy and Civilization*. N.Y.: Minton, Balch, 1931.

———, *A Common Faith*. New Haven: Yale U. Press, 1934.

———, *Art as Experience*. N.Y.: Minton, Balch, 1934.

———, *Liberalism and Social Action*. N.Y.: G. P. Putnam's, 1935.

———, *Logic: The Theory of Inquiry*. N.Y.: Henry Holt, 1938.

———, *Freedom and Culture*. N.Y.: G. P. Putnam's, 1939.

———, *Theory of Valuation*. Chicago: The U. of Chicago Press, 1939.

———, *Education To-day*. (Joseph Ratner, ed.) N.Y.: G. P. Putnam's, 1940.

———, *Problems of Men*. N.Y.: Philosophical Library, 1946.

———, and James H. Tufts, *Ethics*. N.Y.: Henry Holt, 1908.

———, and Arthur F. Bentley, *Knowing and the Known*. Boston, Beacon Press, 1949.

———, and Arthur F. Bentley, *A Philosophical Correspondence, 1932–1951*. (Sidney Ratner, Jules Altman and James E. Wheeler, eds.) New Brunswick, N.J.: Rutgers University Press, 1964.

BLEWETT, John, ed. John Dewey: *His Thought and Influence*. N.Y.: Fordham U. Press, 1960.

CLAYTON, Alfred S., ed. *John Dewey in Perspective: Three Papers in Honor of John Dewey*. Bloomington: Indiana University School of Education Bulletin, 36. (1960).

CROSSER, Paul K. *The Nihilism of John Dewey*. N.Y.: Philosophical Library, 1955.

EDMAN, Irwin, ed. *John Dewey, His Contribution to the American Tradition*. Indianapolis: Bobbs-Merrill, 1955.

Essays in Honor of John Dewey, on the Occasion of His Seventieth Birthday. N.Y.: Henry Holt, 1929.

FELDMAN, William Taft. *The Philosophy of John Dewey: A Critical Analysis*. Baltimore: The Johns Hopkins Press, 1934.

GEIGER, George. *John Dewey in Perspective*. N.Y.: Oxford U. Press, 1958.

HENDEL, Charles W., ed. *John Dewey and the Experimental Spirit in Philosophy*. N.Y.: Liberal Arts Press, 1959.

HOOK, Sidney. *John Dewey: An Intellectual Portrait*. N.Y.: John Day, 1939.

———, ed. *John Dewey: Philosopher of Science and Freedom*. N.Y.: Dial Press, 1950.

HOWARD, Delton T. *John Dewey's Logical Theory*. N.Y.: Longmans, Green, 1918.

John Dewey, The Man and His Philosophy; Addresses Delivered in New York in Celebration of His Seventieth Birthday. Cambridge: Harvard U. Press, 1930.

LAMONT, Corliss, ed. *Dialogue on John Dewey*. N.Y.: Horizon Press, 1959.

LEVITT, Morton. *Freud and Dewey on the Nature of Man*. N.Y.: Philosophical Library, 1960.

MEAD, George Herbert. "The Philosophy of John Dewey," *International Journal of Ethics*, 46 (1935), pp. 64–81.

NATHANSON, Jerome. *John Dewey: The Reconstruction of the Democratic Life*. N.Y.: Charles Scribner's, 1951.

RATNER, Sidney, ed. *The Philosopher of the Common Man. Essays in Honor of John Dewey to Celebrate His Eightieth Birthday.* N.Y.: G. P. Putnam's, 1940.

SANTAYANA, George. "Dewey's Naturalistic Metaphysics" in *Obiter Scripta.* N.Y.: Charles Scribner's, 1936.

SCHILPP, Paul A., ed. *The Philosophy of John Dewey.* Evanston, Ill.: Northwestern U. Press, 1939.

THAYER, H. S. *The Logic of Pragmatism: An Examination of John Dewey's Logic.* N.Y.: Humanities Press, 1952.

THOMAS, Milton H., ed. *John Dewey, A Centennial Bibliography.* Chicago: U. of Chicago Press, 1962.

WHITE, Morton G. *The Origin of Dewey's Instrumentalism.* N.Y.: Columbia U. Press, 1943.

WOLSTEIN, Benjamin. *Experience and Valuation: A Study in John Dewey's Naturalism.* N.Y.: 1949.

George Santayana

[1863–1952]

Santayana was not an American by birth, family, background or temperament. In fact, he was a critic of American bustle and busyness and had little sympathy with American pressures of conformity. Born in Madrid of Spanish Catholic parents, he was brought to Boston at the age of nine. He was a graduate of the famous Boston Latin School, and a student under James and Royce at Harvard University, where he eventually became Professor of Philosophy. On the eve of the First World War, at the age of fifty, Santayana dramatically abandoned his teaching career and, like Henry James and T. S. Eliot, emigrated to Europe, first to England and then to Italy, where he remained the rest of his life. Here he produced a continuous flow of writings. Nonetheless, Santayana maintained that if he was to be counted at all, it would have to be as an American author.

In spite of the many "non-American" traits of the author, his writings expressed many qualities of the "American mind"; they have had an important influence on American shores, both in and out of philosophy. Being rich in poetic metaphor and literary device, and having both a personal and cosmopolitan appeal, Santayana's works have attracted a wide literary audience. But his ideas have also appealed to many professional philosophers.

Santayana's philosophy is a mixture of many influences: *naturalism* (man is part of nature); *skepticism* (we are related to the external world by animal faith); *materialism* (matter is primary); *Platonism* (there is a realm of essences). Santayana's naturalism, especially, served as an inspiration for many philosophers in America. It involved a criticism of transcendental illusions, an awareness of man's ultimate natural conditions, and a vigorous defense of the ideal possibilities of the life of reason.

Santayana's philosophical reputation was first established with the publication in 1905–06 of *The Life of Reason* (five volumes), the best statement of his naturalism. Here Santayana argued that the rational view of life is possible, and that the life of reason is a union of impulse and ideation and may be called an "art." Drawing upon Greek sources—Socrates, Plato and Aristotle—he followed the historic development and progress of reason through its postrational decline in Christianity and its renewal in Spinoza, to its place in the contemporary world. The different volumes trace the stages by which ideals manifest themselves in ordinary life, society, religion, art, morality and science. In *Reason in Common Sense* (a portion of which is reprinted below), Santayana shows how we first become aware of our ordinary impulses and ends, and how thought or consciousness is a natural instrument of the body fulfilling itself in ideal terms. In *Reason in Society*, he traces the growth of social institutions out of biological needs and ideal interests. *Reason in Religion* (partially reproduced below), shows how a rational religion would do away with superstition and magic, yet would allow for the poetic, imaginative and moral functions of religious symbols. *Reason in Art* (from which a selection is printed below) likewise illuminates the role of art in life, which, though practical, is of the highest human concern and a source of happiness. (*The Sense of Beauty*, published in 1896, which is probably Santayana's most important book on aesthetics, espouses the thesis that beauty is pleasure objectified.) In *Reason in Science* (from which extracts are reprinted below), Santayana considers science to be another symbolic system, although continuous with common sense. Science is a blend of physics and dialectic; it uses empirical observation and theory. Santayana also outlines the development of the stages of reason in morality: pre-rational morality (social mores and customs), rational ethics (the Socratic ideal), and post-rational morality (an ethic modified by disillusionment and detachment). He concludes with an appraisal of science's role in the life of reason and with a defense of its validity against its detractors.

Skepticism and Animal Faith (1923), part of which is reprinted below, is Santayana's chief epistemological work and his most highly developed defense of critical realism. Real objects, he says, exist independently of the knower. They are never known directly, but only by means of essences, which stand as signs of their existence. Belief in external objects does not depend upon inference alone, however, but upon the fact that we are actively involved in nature and that we manifest a kind of pragmatic animal faith in their real existence. Thus both the intuitive immediacy of essences and intent or purpose are to some extent present in knowledge.

The Realms of Being, the "Preface" (1927) of which is reprinted below, is Santayana's chief metaphysical account of the categories of being. *The Realm of Matter* and of substance is primary in nature (Santayana claimed to be the last materialist). *The Realm of Essence*, an expression of his Platonism, refers to the forms of everything actual and possible as directly given to "spirit" in perception or thought. *The Realm of Spirit* refers to the "mind" or "soul" which entertains essences. But spirit is an epiphenomenal generation, a reflection of matter, and it possesses no independent existence or causal efficacy of its own. *The Realm of Truth* refers to those essences which are signs of that which occurs in existence. Truth means "the sum of all assertions," the standard and comprehensive description of a fact in all of its relations. The true is "all things seen under the form of eternity." Readers of Santayana frequently find his language deceptive; his words are dipped in metaphorical and poetic honey. However, Santayana has made it clear that his "realms" are not mysterious entities; they are to be interpreted naturalistically, as "kinds or categories of things" which are worth distinguishing.

Santayana early felt the impact of pragmatism on his thinking. (Both thinking and art, for example, have an instrumental function). Yet his work as a whole, and particularly his later writings, attaches considerable importance to the contemplative ideal. Santayana is the detached ob-server, absorbed in the realm of imaginative essences, and indifferent to the practical causes that aroused the American colleagues he left behind.

THE LIFE OF REASON

REASON IN COMMON SENSE [1]

Introduction

Whatever forces may govern human life, if they are to be recognized by man, must betray themselves in human experience. Progress in science or religion, no less than in morals and art, is a dramatic episode in man's career, a welcome variation in his habit and state of mind; although this variation may often regard or propitiate things external, adjustment to which may be important for his welfare. The importance of these external things, as well as their existence, he can establish only by the function and utility which a recognition of them may have in his life. The entire history of progress is a moral drama, a tale man might unfold in a great autobiography, could his myriad heads and countless scintillas of consciousness conspire, like the seventy Alexandrian sages, in a single version of the truth committed to each for interpretation. What themes would prevail in such an examination of heart? In what order and with what emphasis would they be recounted? In which of its adventures would the human race, reviewing its whole experience, acknowledge a progress and a gain? To answer these questions, as they may be answered speculatively and provisionally by an individual, is the purpose of the following work.

A philosopher could hardly have a higher ambition than to make himself a mouth-piece for the memory and judgment of his race. Yet the most casual consideration of affairs already involves an attempt to do the same thing. Reflection is pregnant from the beginning with all the principles of synthesis and valuation needed in the most comprehensive criticism. So soon as man ceases to be wholly immersed in sense, he looks before and after, he regrets and desires; and the moments in which prospect or retrospect takes place constitute the reflective or representative part of his life, in contrast to the unmitigated flux of sensations in which nothing ulterior is regarded. Rep-

[1] From George Santayana, *Reason in Common Sense*, N. Y.: Scribner, 1905. Selections taken from the Introduction, and from Chapter 9, "How Thought is Practical."

resentation, however, can hardly remain idle and merely speculative. To the ideal function of envisaging the absent, memory and reflection will add (since they exist and constitute a new complication in being) the practical function of modifying the future. Vital impulse, however, when it is modified by reflection and veers in sympathy with judgments pronounced on the past, is properly called reason. Man's rational life consists in those moments in which reflection not only occurs but proves efficacious. What is absent then works in the present, and values are imputed where they cannot be felt. Such representation is so far from being merely speculative that its presence alone can raise bodily change to the dignity of action. Reflection gathers experiences together and perceives their relative worth; which is as much as to say that it expresses a new attitude of will in the presence of a world better understood and turned to some purpose. The limits of reflection mark those of concerted and rational action; they circumscribe the field of cumulative experience, or, what is the same thing, of profitable living.

Thus if we use the word life in a eulogistic sense to designate the happy maintenance against the world of some definite ideal interest, we may say with Aristotle that life is reason in operation. The *Life of Reason* will then be a name for that part of experience which perceives and pursues ideals—all conduct so controlled and all sense so interpreted as to perfect natural happiness.

Without reason, as without memory, there might still be pleasures and pains in existence. To increase those pleasures and reduce those pains would be to introduce an improvement into the sentient world, as if a devil suddenly died in hell or in heaven a new angel were created. Since the beings, however, in which these values would reside, would, by hypothesis, know nothing of one another, and since the betterment would take place unprayed-for and unnoticed, it could hardly be called a progress; and certainly not a progress in man, since man, without the ideal continuity given by memory and reason, would have no moral being. In human progress, therefore, reason is not a casual instrument, having its sole value in its service to sense; such a betterment in sentience would not be progress unless it were a progress in reason, and the increasing pleasure revealed some object that could please; for without a picture of the situation from which a heightened vitality might flow, the improvement could be neither remembered nor measured nor desired. The Life of Reason is accordingly neither a mere means nor a mere incident in human progress; it is the total and embodied progress itself, in which the pleasures of sense are included in so far as they can be intelligently enjoyed and pursued. To recount man's rational moments would be to take an inventory of all his goods; for he is not himself (as we say with unconscious accuracy) in the others. If he ever appropriates them in recollection or prophecy, it is only on the ground of some physical relation which they may have to his being.

Reason is as old as man and as prevalent as human nature; for we should not recognise an animal to be human unless his instincts were to some degree conscious of their ends and rendered his ideas in that measure relevant to conduct. Many sensations, or even a whole world of dreams, do not amount to intelligence until the images in the mind begin to represent in some way, however symbolic, the forces and realities confronted in action. There may well be intense consciousness in the total absence of rationality. Such consciousness is suggested in dreams, in madness, and may be found, for all we know, in the depths of universal nature. Minds peopled only by desultory visions and lusts would not have the dignity of human souls even if they seemed to pursue certain objects unerringly; for that pursuit would not be illumined by any vision of its goal. Reason and humanity begin with the union of instinct and ideation, when instinct becomes enlightened, establishes values in its objects, and is turned from a process into an art, while at the same time consciousness becomes practical and cognitive, beginning to contain some symbol or record of the co-ordinate realities among which it arises.

Reason accordingly requires the fusion of two types of life, commonly led in the world in well-nigh total separation, one a life of impulse expressed in affairs and social passions, the other a life reflection expressed in religion, science, and the imitative arts. In the Life of Reason, if it were brought to perfection, intelligence would be at once the universal method of practice and its continual reward. All reflection would then be applicable in action and all action fruitful in happiness. Though this be an ideal, yet everyone gives it from time to time a partial embodiment when he practises useful arts, when his passions happily lead him to enlightenment, or when his fancy breeds visions pertinent to his ultimate good. Everyone leads the Life of Reason in so far as he finds a steady light behind the world's glitter and a clear residuum of joy beneath pleasure or success. No experience not to be repented of falls without its sphere. Every solution to a doubt, in so far as it is not a new error, every practical achievement not neutralised by a second maladjustment consequent upon it, every consolation not the seed of another greater sorrow, may be gathered together and built into this edifice. The Life of Reason is the happy marriage of two elements—impulse and ideation—which if wholly divorced would reduce man to a brute or to a maniac. The rational animal is generated by the union of these two monsters. He is constituted by ideas which have ceased to be visionary and actions which have ceased to be vain.

Thus the Life of Reason is another name for what, in the widest sense of the word, might be called Art. Operations become arts when their purpose is conscious and their method teachable. In perfect art the whole idea is creative and exists only to be embodied, while every part of the product is rational and gives delightful expression to that idea. Like art, again, the Life of Reason is not a power but a result, the spontaneous expression of liberal genius in a favouring environment. Both art and reason have natural sources and meet with natural checks; but when a process is turned successfully into an art, so that its issues have value and the ideas that accompany it become practical and cognitive, reflection, finding little that it cannot in some way justify and understand, begins to boast that it directs and has created the world in which it finds itself so much at home. Thus if art could extend its sphere to include every activity in nature, reason, being everywhere exemplified, might easily think itself omnipotent. This ideal, far as it is from actual realisation, has so dazzled men, that in their religion and mythical philosophy they have often spoken as if it were already actual and efficient. This anticipation amounts, when taken seriously, to a confusion of purposes with facts and of functions with causes, a confusion which in the interests of wisdom and progress it is important to avoid; but these speculative fables, when we take them for what they are—poetic expressions of the ideal—help us to see how deeply rooted this ideal is in man's mind, and afford us a standard by which to measure his approaches to the rational perfection of which he dreams. For the Life of Reason, being the sphere of all human art, is man's imitation of divinity.

To study such an ideal, dimly expressed though it be in human existence, is no prophetic or visionary undertaking. Every genuine ideal has a natural basis; anyone may understand and safely interpret it who is attentive to the life from which it springs. To decipher the Life of Reason nothing is needed but an analytic spirit and a judicious love of man, a love quick to distinguish success from failure in his great and confused experiment of living. The historian of reason should not be a romantic poet, vibrating impotently to every impulse he finds afoot, without a criterion of excellence or a vision of perfection. Ideals are free, but they are neither more numerous nor more variable than the living natures that generate them. Ideals are legitimate, and each initially envisages a genuine and innocent good; but they are not realisable together, nor even singly when they have no deep roots in the world. Neither is the philosopher compelled by his somewhat judicial office to be a satirist or censor, without sympathy for those tentative and ingenuous passions out of which, after all, his own standards must arise. He is the chronicler of human progress, and to measure that progress he should be equally attentive to the impulses that give it direction and to the circumstances amid which it stumbles toward its natural goal. . . .

Here, then, is the programme of the following work: Starting with the immediate flux, in which all objects and impulses are given, to describe the Life of Reason; that is, to note what facts and purposes seem to be primary, to show how the conception of nature and gathers around them, and to point to the ideals of thought and action which are approached by this gradual mastering of experience by reason. A great task, which it would be beyond the powers of a writer in this age either to execute or to conceive, had not the Greeks drawn for us the outlines of an ideal culture at a time when life was simpler than at present and individual intelligence more resolute and free.

How Thought is Practical

Nothing is more natural or more congruous with all the analogies of experience than that animals should feel and think. The relation of mind to body, of reason to nature, seems to be actually this: when bodies have reached a certain complexity and vital equilibrium, a sense begins to inhabit them which is focussed upon the preservation of that body and on its reproduction. This sense, as it becomes reflective and expressive of physical welfare, points more and more to its own persistence and harmony, and generates the Life of Reason. Nature is reason's basis and theme; reason is nature's consciousness; and, from the point of view of that consciousness when it has arisen, reason is also nature's justification and goal.

To separate things so closely bound together as are mind and body, reason and nature, is consequently a violent and artificial divorce, and a man of judgment will instinctively discredit any philosophy in which it is decreed. But to avoid divorce it is well first to avoid unnatural unions, and not to attribute to our two elements, which must be partners for life, relations repugnant to their respective natures and offices. Now the body is an instrument, the mind its function, the witness and reward of its operation. Mind is the body's entelechy, a value which accrues to the body when it has reached a certain perfection, of which it would be a pity, so to speak, that it should remain unconscious; so that while the body feeds the mind the mind perfects the body, lifting it and all its natural relations and impulses into the moral world, into the sphere of interests and ideas.

No connection could be closer than this reciprocal involution, as nature and life reveal it; but the connection is natural, not dialectical.

The union will be denaturalised and, so far as philosophy goes, actually destroyed, if we seek to carry it on into logical equivalence. If we isolate the terms mind and body and study the inward implications of each apart, we shall never discover the other. That matter cannot, by transposition of its particles, *become* what we call consciousness, is an admitted truth; that mind cannot *become* its own occasions or determine its own march, though it be a truth not recognised by all philosophers, is in itself no less obvious. Matter, dialectically studied, makes consciousness seem a superfluous and unaccountable addendum; mind, studied in the same way, makes nature an embarrassing idea, a figment which ought to be subservient to conscious aims and perfectly transparent, but which remains opaque and overwhelming. In order to escape these sophistications, it suffices to revert to immediate observation and state the question in its proper terms: nature lives, and perception is a private echo and response to ambient motions. The soul is the voice of the body's interests; in watching them a man defines the world that sustains him and that conditions all his satisfactions. In discerning his origin he christens Nature by the eloquent name of mother, under which title she enters the universe of discourse. Simultaneously he discerns his own existence and marks off the inner region of his dreams. And it behooves him not to obliterate these discoveries. By trying to give his mind false points of attachment in nature he would disfigure not only nature but also that reason which is so much the essence of his life.

Consciousness, then, is the expression of bodily life and the seat of all its values. Its place in the natural world is like that of its own ideal products, art, religion, or science; it translates natural relations into synthetic and ideal symbols by which things are interpreted with reference to the interests of consciousness itself. This representation is also an existence and has its place along with all other existences in the bosom of nature. In this sense its connection with its organs, and with all that affects the body or that the body affects, is a natural connection. . . .

The conditions of consciousness, however, are far from being its only theme. As consciousness bears a transcendent relation to the dynamic world (for it is actual and spiritual, while the dynamic is potential and material) so it may be exuberant and irresponsibly rich. Although its elements, in point of distribution and derivation, are grounded in matter, as music is in vibrations, yet in point of character the result may be infinitely redundant. The complete musician would devote but a small part of his attention to the basis of music, its mechanism, psychology, or history. Long before he had represented to his mind the causes of his art, he would have proceeded to practise and enjoy it. So sense and imagination, passion and reason, may enrich the soil that breeds them and cover it with a maze of flowers.

The theme of consciousness is accordingly far more than the material world which constitutes its basis, though this also is one of its themes; thought is no less at home in various expressions and embroideries with which the material world can be overlaid in imagination. The material world is conceived by digging beneath experience to find its cause; it is the efficacious structure and skeleton of things. This is the subject of scientific retrospect and calculation. The forces disclosed by physical studies are of course not directed to producing a mind that might merely describe them. A force is expressed in many other ways than by being defined; it may be felt, resisted, embodied, transformed, or symbolised. Forces work; they are not, like mathematical concepts, exhausted in description. From that matter which might be describable in mechanical formulæ there issues notwithstanding all manner of forms and harmonies, visible, audible, imaginable, and passionately prized. Every phase of the ideal world emanates from the natural and loudly proclaims its origin by the interest it takes in natural existences, of which it gives a rational interpretation. Sense, art, religion, society, express nature exuberantly and in symbols long before science is added to represent, by a different abstraction, the mechanism which nature contains.

REASON IN RELIGION [2]

. . . What relation does this great business of the soul, which we call religion, bear to the Life of Reason? That the relation between the two is close seems clear from several circumstances. The Life of Reason is the seat of all ultimate values. Now the history of mankind will show us that whenever spirits at once lofty and intense have seemed to attain the highest joys, they have envisaged and attained them in religion. Religion would therefore seem to be a vehicle or a factor in rational life, since the ends of rational life are attained by it. Moreover, the Life of Reason is an ideal to which everything in the world should be subordinated; it establishes lines of moral cleavage everywhere and makes right eternally different from wrong. Religion does the same thing. It makes absolute moral decisions. It sanctions, unifies, and transforms ethics. Religion thus exercises a function of the Life of Reason. And a further function which is common to both

[2] From George Santayana, *Reason in Religion*, N. Y.: Scribner, 1905. Selection taken from Chapter 1, "How Religion May Be an Embodiment of Reason."

is that of emancipating man from his personal limitations. In different ways religions promise to transfer the soul to better conditions. A supernaturally favoured kingdom is to be established for posterity upon earth, or for all the faithful in heaven, or the soul is to be freed by repeated purgations from all taint and sorrow, or it is to be lost in the absolute, or it is to become an influence and an object of adoration in the places it once haunted or wherever the activities it once loved may be carried on by future generations of its kindred. Now reason in its way lays before us all these possibilities: it points to common objects, political and intellectual, in which an individual may lose what is mortal and accidental in himself and immortalise what is rational and human; it teaches us how sweet and fortunate death may be to those whose spirit can still live in their country and in their ideas; it reveals the radiating effects of action and the eternal objects of thought.

Yet the difference in tone and language must strike us, so soon as it is philosophy that speaks. That change should remind us that even if the function of religion and that of reason coincide, this function is performed in the two cases by very different organs. Religions are many, reason one. Religion consists of conscious ideas, hopes, enthusiasms, and objects of worship; it operates by grace and flourishes by prayer. Reason, on the other hand, is a mere principle or potential order, on which, indeed, we may come to reflect, but which exists in us ideally only, without variation or stress of any kind. We conform or do not conform to it; it does not urge or chide us, nor call for any emotions on our part other than those naturally aroused by the various objects which it unfolds in their true nature and proportion. Religion brings some order into life by weighting it with new materials. Reason adds to the natural materials only the perfect order which it introduces into them. Rationality is nothing but a form, an ideal constitution which experience may more or less embody. Religion is a part of experience itself, a mass of sentiments and ideas. The one is an inviolate principle, the other a changing and struggling force. And yet this struggling and changing force of religion seems to direct man toward something eternal. It seems to make for an ultimate harmony within the soul and for an ultimate harmony between the soul and all the soul depends upon. So that religion, in its intent, is a more conscious and direct pursuit of the Life of Reason than is society, science, or art. For these approach and fill out the ideal life tentatively and piecemeal, hardly regarding the goal or caring for the ultimate justification of their instinctive aims. Religion also has an instinctive and blind side, and bubbles up in all manner of chance practices and intuitions; soon, however, it feels its way toward the heart of things, and, from whatever quarter it may come, veers in the direction of the ultimate.

Nevertheless, we must confess that this religious pursuit of the Life of Reason has been singularly abortive. Those within the pale of each religion may prevail upon themselves to express satisfaction with its results, thanks to a fond partiality in reading the past and generous draughts of hope for the future; but any one regarding the various religions at once and comparing their achievements with what reason requires, must feel how terrible is the disappointment which they have one and all prepared for mankind. Their chief anxiety has been to offer imaginary remedies for mortal ills, some of which are incurable essentially, while others might have been really cured by well-directed effort. The Greek oracles, for instance, pretended to heal our natural ignorance, which has its appropriate though difficult cure, while the Christian vision of heaven pretended to be an antidote to our natural death, the inevitable correlate of birth and of a changing and conditioned existence. By methods of this sort little can be done for the real betterment of life. To confuse intelligence and dislocate sentiment by gratuitous fictions is a short-sighted way of pursuing happiness. Nature is soon avenged. An unhealthy exaltation and a one-sided morality have to be followed by regrettable reactions. When these come, the real rewards of life may seem vain to a relaxed vitality, and the very name of virtue may irritate young spirits untrained in any natural excellence. Thus religion too often debauches the morality it comes to sanction, and impedes the science it ought to fulfil.

What is the secret of this ineptitude? Why does religion, so near to rationality in its purpose, fall so far short of it in its texture and in its results? The answer is easy: Religion pursues rationality through the imagination. When it explains events or assigns causes, it is an imaginative substitute for science. When it gives precepts, insinuates ideals, or remoulds aspiration, it is an imaginative substitute for wisdom—I mean for the deliberate and impartial pursuit of all good. The conditions and the aims of life are both represented in religion poetically, but this poetry tends to arrogate to itself literal truth and moral authority, neither of which it possesses. Hence the depth and importance of religion become intelligible no less than its contradictions and practical disasters. Its object is the same as that of reason, but its method is to proceed by intuition and by unchecked poetical conceits. These are repeated and vulgarised in proportion to their original fineness and significance, till they pass for reports of objective truth and come to constitute a world of faith, superposed upon the world of experience and regarded as materially enveloping it, if not in space at least in time and in existence. The only truth of religion comes from its interpretation of life, from its symbolic rendering of that moral experience which it springs out of and which it seeks to elucidate. Its falsehood comes from the insidious misunderstanding which clings to it, to the effect that these poetic conceptions are not merely representations of experience as it is or should be, but are rather information about experience or reality elsewhere —an experience and reality which, strangely enough, supply just the defects betrayed by reality and experience here.

Thus religion has the same original relation to life that poetry has; only poetry, which never pretends to literal validity, adds a pure value to existence, the value of a liberal imaginative exercise. The poetic value of religion would initially be greater than that of poetry itself, because religion deals with higher and more practical themes, with sides of life which are in greater need of some imaginative touch and ideal interpretation than are those pleasant or pompous things which ordinary poetry dwells upon. But this initial advantage is neutralised in part by the abuse to which religion is subject, whenever its symbolic rightness is taken for scientific truth. Like poetry, it improves the world only by imagining it improved, but not content with making this addition to the mind's furniture—an addition which might be useful and ennobling—it thinks to confer a more radical benefit by persuading mankind that, in spite of appearances, the world is really such as that rather arbitrary idealisation has painted it. This spurious satisfaction is naturally the prelude to many a disappointment, and the soul has infinite trouble to emerge again from the artificial problems and sentiments into which it is thus plunged. The value of religion becomes equivocal. Religion remains an imaginative achievement, a symbolic representation of moral reality which may have a most important function in vitalising the mind and in transmitting, by way of parables, the lessons of experience. But it becomes at the same time a continuous incidental deception; and this deception, in proportion as it is strenuously denied to be such, can work indefinite harm in the world and in the conscience.

On the whole, however, religion should not be conceived as having taken the place of anything better, but rather as having come to relieve situations which, but for its presence, would have been infinitely worse. In the thick of active life, or in the monotony of practical slavery, there is more need to stimulate fancy than to control it. Natural instinct is not much disturbed in the human brain by what may happen in that thin superstratum of ideas which commonly overlays it. We must not blame religion for preventing the development of a moral and natural science which at any rate would seldom have appeared; we must rather thank it for the sensibility, the reverence, the speculative insight which it has introduced into the world.

We may therefore proceed to analyse the significance and the function which religion has had at its different stages, and, without disguising or in the least condoning its confusion with literal truth, we may allow ourselves to enter as sympathetically as possible into its various conceptions and emotions. They have made up the inner life of many sages, and of all those who without great genius or learning have lived steadfastly in the spirit. The feeling of reverence should itself be treated with reverence, although not at a sacrifice of truth, with which alone, in the end, reverence is compatible. Nor have we any reason to be intolerant of the partialities and contradictions which religions display. Were we dealing with a science, such contradictions would have to be instantly solved and removed; but when we are concerned with the poetic interpretation of experience, contradiction means only variety, and variety means spontaneity, wealth of resource, and a nearer approach to total adequacy.

If we hope to gain any understanding of these matters we must begin by taking them out of that heated and fanatical atmosphere in which the Hebrew tradition has enveloped them. The Jews had no philosophy, and when their national traditions came to be theoretically explicated and justified, they were made to issue in a puerile scholasticism and a rabid intolerance. The question of monotheism, for instance, was a terrible question to the Jews. Idolatry did not consist in worshipping a god who, not being ideal, might be unworthy of worship, but rather in recognising other gods than the one worshipped in Jerusalem. To the Greeks, on the contrary, whose philosophy was enlightened and ingenuous, monotheism and polytheism seemed perfectly innocent and compatible. To say God or the gods was only to use different expressions for the same influence, now viewed in its abstract unity and correlation with all existence, now viewed in its various manifestations in moral life, in nature, or in history. So that what in Plato, Aristotle, and the Stoics meets us at every step—the combination of monotheism with polytheism—is no contradiction, but merely an intelligent variation of phrase to indicate various aspects or functions in physical and moral things. When religion appears to us in this light its contradictions and controversies lose all their bitterness. Each doctrine will simply represent the moral plane on which they live who have devised or adopted it. Religions will thus be better or worse, never true or false. We shall be able to lend ourselves to each in turn, and seek to draw from it the secret of its inspiration.

REASON IN ART [3]

. . . Of all reason's embodiments art is . . . the most splendid and complete. Merely to attain categories by which inner experience may be articulated, or to feign analogies by which a universe may be conceived, would be but a visionary triumph if it remained ineffectual and went with no actual remodelling of the outer world, to render man's dwelling more appropriate and his mind better fed and more largely transmissible. Mind grows self-perpetuating only by its expression in matter. What makes progress possible is that rational action may leave traces in nature, such that nature in consequence furnishes a better basis for the Life of Reason; in other words progress is art bettering the conditions of existence. Until art arises, all achievement is internal to the brain, dies with the individual, and even in him spends itself without recovery, like music heard in a dream. Art, in establishing instruments for human life beyond the human body, and moulding outer things into sympathy with inner values, establishes a ground whence values may continually spring up; the thatch that protects from to-day's rain will last and keep out to-morrow's rain also; the sign that once expresses an idea will serve to recall it in the future.

Not only does the work of art . . . perpetuate its own function and produce a better experience, but the process of art also perpetuates itself, because it is teachable. Every animal learns something by living; if his offspring inherit only what he possessed at birth, they have to learn life's lessons over again from the beginning, with at best some vague help given by their parents' example. But when the fruits of experience exist in the common environment, when new instruments, unknown to nature, are offered to each individual for his better equipment, although he must still learn for himself how to live, he may learn in a humaner school, where artificial occasions are constantly open to him for expanding his powers. It is no longer merely hidden inner processes that he must reproduce to attain his predecessors' wisdom; he may acquire much of it more expeditiously by imitating their outward habit—an imitation which, furthermore, they have some means of exacting from him. Wherever there is art there is a possibility of training. A father who calls his idle sons from the jungle to help him hold the plough, not only inures them to labour but compels them to observe the earth upturned and refreshed, and to watch the germination there; their wandering thought,

---

[3] From George Santayana, *Reason in Art*, N. Y.: Scribner, 1905. Selections taken from Chapter 1, "The Basis of Art in Interest and Experience," and Chapter 11, "Art and Happiness."

their incipient rebellions, will be met by the hope of harvest; and it will not be impossible for them, when their father is dead, to follow the plough of their own initiative and for their own children's sake. So great is the sustained advance in rationality made possible by art which, being embodied in matter, is teachable and transmissible by training; for in art the values secured are recognised the more easily for having been first enjoyed when other people furnished the means to them; while the maintenance of these values is facilitated by an external tradition imposing itself contagiously or by force on each new generation.

Art is action which transcending the body makes the world a more congenial stimulus to the soul. All art is therefore useful and practical, and the notable aesthetic value which some works of art possess, for reasons flowing for the most part out of their moral significance, is itself one of the satisfactions which art offers to human nature as a whole. Between sensation and abstract discourse lies a region of deployed sensibility or synthetic representation, a region where more is seen at arm's length than in any one moment could be felt at close quarters, and yet where the remote parts of experience, which discourse reaches only through symbols, are recovered and recomposed in something like their native colours and experienced relation. This region, called imagination, has pleasures more airy and luminous than those of sense, more massive and rapturous than those of intelligence. The values inherent in imagination, in instant intuition, in sense endowed with form, are called aesthetic values; they are found mainly in nature and living beings, but often also in man's artificial works, in images evoked by language, and in the realm of sound.

Productions in which an aesthetic value is or is supposed to be prominent take the name of fine art; but the work of fine art so defined is almost always an abstraction from the actual object, which has many non-aesthetic functions and values. To separate the aesthetic element, abstract and dependent as it often is, is an artifice which is more misleading than helpful; for neither in the history of art nor in a rational estimate of its value can the aesthetic function of things be divorced from the practical and moral. What had to be done was, by imaginative races, done imaginatively; what had to be spoken or made, was spoken or made fitly, lovingly, beautifully. Or, to take the matter up on its psychological side, the ceaseless experimentation and ferment of ideas, in breeding what it had a propensity to breed, came sometimes on figments that gave it delightful pause; these beauties were the first knowledges and these arrests the first hints of real and useful things. The rose's grace could more easily be plucked from its petals than the beauty of art from its subject, occasion, and use. An aesthetic fragrance, indeed, all things may have, if in soliciting man's senses or reason they can awaken his imagination as well; but this middle zone is so mixed and nebulous, and its limits are so vague, that it cannot well be treated in theory otherwise than as it exists in fact—as a phase of man's sympathy with the world he moves in. If art is that element in the Life of Reason which consists in modifying its environment the better to attain its end, art may be expected to subserve all parts of the human ideal, to increase man's comfort, knowledge, and delight. And as nature, in her measure, is wont to satisfy these interests together, so art, in seeking to increase that satisfaction, will work simultaneously in every ideal direction. Nor will any of these directions be on the whole good, or tempt a well-trained will, if it leads to estrangement from all other interests. The aesthetic good will be accordingly hatched in the same nest with the others, and incapable of flying far in a different air.

. . . Happiness is the ultimate sanction of art, art in turn is the best instrument of happiness. In art more directly than in other activities man's self-expression is cumulative and finds an immediate reward; for it alters the material conditions of sentience so that sentience becomes at once more delightful and more significant. In industry man is still servile, preparing the materials he is to use in action. In action itself, though he is free, he exerts his influence on a living and treacherous medium and sees the issue at each moment drift farther and farther from his intent. In science he is an observer, preparing himself for action in another way, by studying its results and conditions. But in art he is at once competent and free; he is creative. He is not troubled by his materials, because he has assimilated them and may take them for granted; nor is he concerned with the chance complexion of affairs in the actual world, because he is making the world over, not merely considering how it grew or how it will consent to grow in future. Nothing, accordingly, could be more delightful than genuine art, nor more free from remorse and the sting of vanity. Art springs so completely from the heart of man that it makes everything speak to him in his own language; it reaches, nevertheless, so truly to the heart of nature that it co-operates with her, becomes a parcel of her creative material energy, and builds by her instinctive hand. If the various formative impulses afoot in the world never opposed stress to stress and made no havoc with one another, nature might be called an unconscious artist. In fact, just where such a formative impulse finds support from the environment, a consciousness supervenes. If that consciousness is adequate enough to be prophetic, an art arises. Thus the emergence of arts out of instincts is the token and exact measure of nature's success and of mortal happiness.

Rational Ethics

A truly rational morality, or social regimen, has never existed in the world and is hardly to be looked for. What guides men and nations in their practice is always some partial interest or some partial disillusion. A rational morality would imply perfect self-knowledge, so that no congenial good should be needlessly missed—least of all practical reason or justice itself; so that no good congenial to other creatures would be needlessly taken from them. The total value which everything had from the agent's point of view would need to be determined and felt efficaciously; and, among other things, the total value which this point of view, with the conduct it justified, would have for every foreign interest which it affected. Such knowledge, such definition of purpose, and such perfection of sympathy are clearly beyond man's reach. All that can be hoped for is that the advance of science and commerce, by fostering peace and a rational development of character, may bring some part of mankind nearer to that goal; but the goal lies, as every ultimate ideal should, at the limit of what is possible, and must serve rather to measure achievements than to prophesy them.

In lieu of a rational morality, however, we have rational ethics; and this mere idea of a rational morality is something valuable. While we wait for the sentiments, customs, and laws which should embody perfect humanity and perfect justice, we may observe the germinal principle of these ideal things; we may sketch the ground-plan of a true commonwealth. This sketch constitutes rational ethics, as founded by Socrates, glorified by Plato, and sobered and solidified by Aristotle. It sets forth the method of judgment and estimation which a rational morality would apply universally and express in practice. The method, being very simple, can be discovered and largely illustrated in advance, while the complete self-knowledge and sympathy are still wanting which might avail to embody that method in the concrete and to discover unequivocally where absolute duty and ultimate happiness may lie.

[4] From George Santayana, *Reason in Science*, N. Y.: Scribner, 1905. Selections taken from Chapter 9, "Rational Ethics"; Chapter 10, "Post-Rational Morality"; Chapter 11, "The Validity of Science," and Chapter 1, "Types and Aims of Science."

This method, the Socratic method, consists in accepting any estimation which any man may sincerely make, and in applying dialectic to it, so as to let the man see what he really esteems. What he really esteems is what ought to guide his conduct; for to suggest that a rational being ought to do what he feels to be wrong, or ought to pursue what he genuinely thinks is worthless, would be to impugn that man's rationality and to discredit one's own. With what face could any man or god say to another: Your duty is to do what you cannot know you ought to do; your function is to suffer what you cannot recognise to be worth suffering? Such an attitude amounts to imposture and excludes society; it is the attitude of a detestable tyrant, and any one who mistakes it for moral authority has not yet felt the first heart-throb of philosophy.

More even than natural philosophy, moral philosophy is something Greek: it is the appanage of freemen. The Socratic method is the soul of liberal conversation; it is compacted in equal measure of sincerity and courtesy. Each man is autonomous and all are respected; and nothing is brought forward except to be submitted to reason and accepted or rejected by the self-questioning heart. Indeed, when Socrates appeared in Athens mutual respect had passed into democracy and liberty into license; but the stalwart virtue of Socrates saved him from being a sophist, much as his method, when not honestly and sincerely used, might seem to countenance that moral anarchy which the sophists had expressed in their irresponsible doctrines. Their sophistry did not consist in the private *seat* which they assigned to judgment; for what judgment is there that is not somebody's judgment at some moment? The sophism consisted in ignoring the living moment's *intent*, and in suggesting that no judgment could refer to anything ulterior, and therefore that no judgment could be wrong: in other words that each man at each moment was the theme and standard, as well as the seat, of his judgment.

Socrates escaped this folly by force of honesty, which is what saves from folly in dialectic. He built his whole science precisely on that intent which the sophists ignored; he insisted that people should declare sincerely what they meant and what they wanted; and on that living rock he founded the persuasive and ideal sciences of logic and ethics, the necessity of which lies all in free insight and in actual will. This will and insight they render deliberate, profound, unshakable, and consistent. Socrates, by his genial mid-wifery, helped men to discover the truth and excellence to which they were naturally addressed. This circumstance rendered his doctrine at once moral and scientific; scientific because dialectical, moral because expressive of personal and living aspirations. His ethics was not like what has since passed under that name—a spurious physics, accompanied by commandments and threats. It was a pliant and liberal expression of ideals, inwardly grounded and spontaneously pursued. It was an exercise in self-knowledge.

Socrates' liberality was that of a free man ready to maintain his will and conscience, if need be, against the whole world. The sophists, on the contrary, were sycophants in their scepticism, and having inwardly abandoned the ideals of their race and nation—which Socrates defended with his homely irony—they dealt out their miscellaneous knowledge, or their talent in exposition, at the beck and for the convenience of others. Their theory was that each man having a right to pursue his own aims, skilful thinkers might, for money, furnish any fellow-mortal with instruments fitted to his purpose. Socrates, on the contrary, conceived that each man, to achieve his aims must first learn to distinguish them clearly; he demanded that rationality, in the form of an examination and clarification of purposes, should precede any selection of external instruments. For how should a man recognise anything useful unless he first had established the end to be subserved and thereby recognised the good? True science, then, was that which enabled a man to disentangle and attain his natural good; and such a science is also the art of life and the whole of virtue. . . .

Rational ethics is an embodiment of volition, not a description of it. It is the expression of living interest, preference, and categorical choice. It leaves to psychology and history a free field for the description of moral phenomena. It has no interest in slipping far-fetched and incredible myths beneath the facts of nature, so as to lend a non-natural origin to human aspirations. It even recognises, as an emanation of its own force, that uncompromising truthfulness with which science assigns all forms of moral life to their place in the mechanical system of nature. But the rational moralist is not on that account reduced to a mere spectator, a physicist acknowledging no interest except the interest in facts and in the laws of change. His own spirit, small by the material forces which it may stand for and express, is great by its prerogative of surveying and judging the universe; surveying it, of course, from a mortal point of view, and judging it only by its kindliness or cruelty to some actual interest, yet, even so, determining unequivocally a part of its constitution and excellence. The rational moralist represents a force energising in the world, discovering its affinities there and clinging to them to the exclusion of their hateful opposites. He represents, over against the chance facts, an ideal embodying the particular demands, possibilities, and satisfactions of a specific being. . . .

Now will, no less than that reason which avails to render will consistent and far-reaching, animates natural bodies and expresses their functions. It has a radical bias, a foregone, determinate direction, else it could not be a will nor a principle of preference. The knowledge of what other people desire does not abolish a man's own aims. Sympathy and justice are simply an expansion of the soul's interests, arising when we consider other men's lives so intently that something in us imitates and reenacts their experience, so that we move partly in unison with their movement, recognise the reality and initial legitimacy of their interests, and consequently regard their aims in our action, in so far as our own status and purposes have become identical with theirs. We are not less ourselves, nor less autonomous, for this assimilation, since we assimilate only what is in itself intelligible and congruous with our mind and obey only that authority which can impose itself on our reason. . . .

Rational ethics, then, resembles prerational precepts and half-systems in being founded on impulse. It formulates a natural morality. It is a settled method of achieving ends to which man is drawn by virtue of his physical and rational constitution. By this circumstance rational ethics is removed from the bad company of all artificial, verbal, and unjust systems of morality, which in absolving themselves from relevance to man's endowment and experience merely show how completely irrelevant they are to life. Once, no doubt, each of these arbitrary systems expressed (like the observance of the Sabbath) some practical interest or some not unnatural rite; but so narrow a basis of course has to be disowned when the precepts so originating have been swollen into universal tyrannical laws. A rational ethics reduces them at once to their slender representative rôle; and it surrounds and buttresses them on every side with all other natural ideals.

Rational ethics thus differs from the prerational in being complete. There is one impulse which intuitive moralists ignore: the impulse to reflect. Human instincts are ignorant, multitudinous, and contradictory. To satisfy them as they come is often impossible, and often disastrous, in that such satisfaction prevents the satisfaction of other instincts inherently no less fecund and legitimate. When we apply reason to life we immediately demand that life be consistent, complete, and satisfactory when reflected upon and viewed as a whole. This view, as it presents each moment in its relations, extends to all moments affected by the action or maxim under discussion; it has no more ground for stopping at the limits of what is called a single life than at the limits of a single adventure. To stop at selfishness is not particularly rational. The same principle that creates the ideal of a self creates the ideal of a family or an institution.

The conflict between selfishness and altruism is like that between any two ideal passions that in some particular may chance to be opposed; but such a conflict has no obstinate existence for reason. For reason the person itself has no obstinate existence. The *character* which a man achieves at the best moment of his life is indeed something ideal and significant; it justifies and consecrates all his coherent actions and preferences. But *the man's life*, the circle drawn by biographers around the career of a particular body, from the womb to the charnel-house, and around the mental flux that accompanies that career, is no significant unity. All the substances and efficient processes that figure within it come from elsewhere and continue beyond; while all the rational objects and interests to which it refers have a transpersonal status. Self-love itself is concerned with public opinion; and if a man concentrates his view on private pleasures, these may qualify the fleeting moments of his life with an intrinsic value, but they leave the life itself shapeless and infinite, as if sparks should play over a piece of burnt paper. . . .

If pleasure, because it is commonly a result of satisfied instinct, may by a figure of speech be called the aim of impulse, happiness, by a like figure, may be called the aim of reason. The direct aim of reason is harmony; yet harmony, when made to rule in life, gives reason a noble satisfaction which we call happiness. Happiness is impossible and even inconceivable to a mind without scope and without pause, a mind driven by craving, pleasure, and fear. The moralists who speak disparagingly of happiness are less sublime than they think. In truth their philosophy is too lightly ballasted, too much fed on prejudice and quibbles, for happiness to fall within its range. Happiness implies resource and security; it can be achieved only by discipline. Your intuitive moralist rejects discipline, at least discipline of the conscience; and he is punished by having no lien on wisdom. He trusts to the clash of blind forces in collision, being one of them himself. He demands that virtue should be partisan and unjust; and he dreams of crushing the adversary in some physical cataclysm.

Such groping enthusiasm is often innocent and romantic; it captivates us with its youthful spell. But it has no structure with which to resist the shocks of fortune, which it goes out so jauntily to meet. It turns only too often into vulgarity and worldliness. A snow-flake is soon a smudge, and there is a deeper purity in the diamond. Happiness is hidden from a free and casual will; it belongs rather to one chastened by a long education and unfolded in an atmosphere of sacred and perfected institutions. It is discipline that renders men rational and capable of happiness, by suppressing without hatred what needs to be suppressed to attain a beautiful naturalness. Discipline discredits the random pleasures of illusion, hope, and triumph, and substitutes those which are self-reproductive, perennial, and serene, because they express an equilibrium maintained with reality. So long as the result of endeavour is partly unforeseen and unintentional, so long as the will is partly blind, the Life of Reason is still swaddled in ignominy and the animal barks in the midst of human discourse. Wisdom and happiness consist in having recast natural energies in the furnace of experience. Nor is this experience merely a repressive force. It enshrines the successful expressions of spirit as well as the shocks and vetoes of circumstance; it enables a man to know himself in knowing the world and to discover his ideal by the very ring, true or false, of fortune's coin.

With this brief account we may leave the subject of rational ethics. Its development is impossible save in the concrete, when a legislator, starting from extant interests, considers what practices serve to render those interests vital and genuine, and what external alliances might lend them support and a more glorious expression. The difficulty in carrying rational policy very far comes partly from the refractory materials at hand, and partly from the narrow range within which moral science is usually confined. The materials are individual wills naturally far from unanimous, lost for the most part in frivolous pleasures, rivalries, and superstitions, and little inclined to listen to a law-giver that, like a new Lycurgus, should speak to them of unanimity, simplicity, discipline, and perfection. Devotion and singlemindedness, perhaps possible in the cloister, are hard to establish in the world; yet a rational morality requires that all lay activities, all sweet temptations, should have their voice in the conclave. Morality becomes rational precisely by refusing either to accept human nature, as it sprouts, altogether without harmony, or to mutilate it in the haste to make it harmonious. The condition, therefore, of making a beginning in good politics is to find a set of men with well-knit character and cogent traditions, so that there may be a firm soil to cultivate and that labour may not be wasted in ploughing the quicksands. . . .

Post-Rational Morality

When Socrates and his two great disciples composed a system of rational ethics they were hardly proposing practical legislation for mankind. One by his irony, another by his frank idealism, and the third by his preponderating interest in history and analysis, showed clearly enough how little they dared to hope. They were merely writing an eloquent epitaph on their country. They were publishing the principles of what had been its life, gathering piously its broken ideals, and interpreting its momentary achievement. The spirit of liberty and cooperation was already dead. The private citizen, debauched by the largesses and petty quarrels of his city, had become indolent and mean-spirited. He had begun to question the utility of religion, of patriotism, and of justice. Having allowed the organ for the ideal to atrophy in his soul, he could dream of finding some sullen sort of happiness in unreason. He felt that the austere glories of his country, as a Spartan regimen might have preserved them, would not benefit that baser part of him which alone remained. Political virtue seemed a useless tax on his material profit and freedom. The tedium and distrust proper to a disintegrated society began to drive him to artificial excitements and superstitions. Democracy had learned to regard as enemies the few in whom public interest was still represented, the few whose nobler temper and traditions still coincided with the general good. These last patriots were gradually banished or exterminated, and with them died the spirit that rational ethics had expressed. Philosophers were no longer suffered to have illusions about the state. Human activity on the public stage had shaken off all allegiance to art or reason.

The biographer of reason might well be tempted to ignore the subsequent attitudes into which moral life fell in the West, since they all embodied a more or less complete despair, and, having abandoned the effort to express the will honestly and dialectically, they could support no moral science. The point was merely to console or deceive the soul with some substitute for happiness. Life is older and more persistent than reason, and the failure of a first experiment in rationality does not deprive mankind of that mental and moral vegetation which they possessed for ages in a wild state before the advent of civilisation. They merely revert to their uncivil condition and espouse whatever imaginative ideal comes to hand, by which some semblance of meaning and beauty may be given to existence without the labour of building this meaning and beauty systematically out of its positive elements. . . .

Pessimism, and all the moralities founded on despair, are not pre-rational but post-rational. They are the work of men who more or less explicitly have conceived the Life of Reason, tried it at least imaginatively, and found it wanting. These systems are a refuge from an intolerable situation: they are experiments in redemption. As a matter of fact, animal instincts and natural standards of excellence are never eluded in them, for no moral experience has other terms; but the part of the natural ideal which remains active appears in opposition to all the rest and, by an intelligible illusion, seems to be no part of that natural ideal because, compared with the commoner passions on which it reacts, it represents some simpler or more attenuated hope—the appeal to some very humble or very much chastened satisfaction, or to an utter change in the conditions of life.

Post-rational morality thus constitutes, in intention if not in fact, a criticism of all experience. It thinks it is not, like pre-rational morality, an arbitrary selection from among co-ordinate precepts. It is an effort to subordinate all precepts to one, that points to some single eventual good. For it occurs to the founders of these systems that by estranging oneself from the world, or resting in the moment's pleasure, or mortifying the passions, or enduring all sufferings in patience, or studying a perfect conformity with the course of affairs, one may gain admission to some sort of residual mystical paradise; and this thought, once conceived, is published as a revelation and accepted as a panacea. It becomes in consequence (for such is the force of nature) the foundation of elaborate institutions and elaborate philosophies, into which the contents of the worldly life are gradually reintroduced. . . .

Post-rational systems . . . mark no real advance and offer no genuine solution to spiritual enigmas. The saving force each of them invokes is merely some remnant of that natural energy which animates the human animal. Faith in the supernatural is a desperate wager made by man at the lowest ebb of his fortunes; it is as far as possible from being the source of that normal vitality which subsequently, if his fortunes mend, he may gradually recover. Under the same religion, with the same posthumous alternatives and mystic harmonies hanging about them, different races, or the same race at different periods, will manifest the most opposite moral characteristics. Belief in a thousand hells and heavens will not lift the apathetic out of apathy or hold back the passionate from passion; while a newly planted and ungalled community, in blessed forgetfulness of rewards or punishments, of cosmic needs or celestial sanctions, will know how to live cheerily and virtuously for life's own sake, putting to shame those thin vaticinations. To hope for a second life, to be had gratis, merely because this life has lost its savour, or to dream of a different world, because nature seems too intricate and unfriendly, is in the end merely to play with words; since the supernatural has no permanent aspect or charm except in so far as it expresses man's natural situation and points to the satisfaction of his earthly interests. What keeps supernatural morality, in its better forms, within the limits of sanity is the fact that it reinstates in practice, under novel associations and for motives ostensibly different, the very natural virtues and hopes which, when seen to be merely natural, it had thrown over with contempt. The new dispensation itself, if treated in the same spirit, would be no less contemptible; and what makes it genuinely esteemed is the restored authority of those human ideals which it expresses in a fable. . . .

The value of post-rational morality, then, depends on a double conformity on its part with the Life of Reason. In the first place some natural impulse must be retained, some partial ideal must still be trusted and pursued by the prophet of redemption. In the second place the intuition thus gained and exclusively put forward must be made the starting-point for a restored natural morality. Otherwise the faith appealed to would be worthless in its operation, as well as fanciful in its basis, and it could never become a mould for thought or action in a civilised society.

The Validity of Science

The same despair or confusion which, when it overtakes human purposes, seeks relief in arbitrary schemes of salvation, when it overtakes human knowledge, may breed arbitrary substitutes for science. There are post-rational systems of nature as well as of duty. Most of these are myths hardly worth separating from the post-rational moralities they adorn . . . but a few aspire to be critical revisions of science, themselves scientific. It may be well, in bringing this book to a close, to review these proposed revisions. The validity of science is at stake, and with it the validity of that whole Life of Reason which science crowns, and justifies to reflection.

There are many degrees and kinds of this critical retractation. Science may be accepted bodily, while its present results are modified by suggesting speculatively what its ultimate results might be. This is natural philosophy or legitimate metaphysics. Or science may be accepted in part, and in part subjected to control by some other alleged vehicle of knowledge. This is traditional or intuitive theology. Or science may be retracted and withdrawn altogether, on the ground that it is but methodological fiction, its facts appearances merely, and its principles tendencies to feign. This is transcendentalism; whereupon a dilemma presents itself. We may be invited to abstain from all hypostasis or hearty belief in anything, and to dwell only on the consciousness of imaginative activity in a vacuum—which is radical idealism. Or we may be assured that, science being a dream, we may awake from it into another cosmos, built upon principles quite alien to those illustrated in nature or applicable in practice—which is idealism of the mythical sort. Finally it may occur to us that the criticism of science is an integral part of science itself, and that a transcendental method of survey, which marshals all things in the order of their discovery, far from invalidating knowledge can only serve to separate it from incidental errors and to disclose the relative importance of truths. Science would then be rehabilitated by criticism. The primary movement of the intellect would not be condemned by that subsequent reflection which it makes possible, and which collates its results. Science, purged of all needless realism and seen in its relation to human life, would continue to offer the only conception of reality which is pertinent or possible to the practical mind. . . .

The validity of science in general is . . . established merely by establishing the truth of its particular propositions, in dialectic on the authority of intent and in physics on that of experiment. It is impossible to base science on a deeper foundation or to override it by a higher knowledge. What is called metaphysics, if not an anticipation of natural science, is a confusion of it with dialectic or a mixture of it with myths. If we have the faculty of being utterly sincere and of disintegrating the conventions of language and religion, we must confess that knowledge is only a claim we put forth, a part of that unfathomable compulsion by force of which we live and hold our painted world together for a moment. If we have any insight into mind, or any eye for human history, we must confess at the same time that the oracular substitutes for knowledge to which, in our perplexities, we might be tempted to fly, are pathetic popular fables, having no other sanctity than that which they borrow from the natural impulses they play upon. To live by science requires intelligence and faith, but not to live by it is folly.

If science thus contains the sum total of our rational convictions and gives us the only picture of reality on which we should care to dwell we have but to consult the sciences in detail to ascertain, as far as that is possible, what sort of a universe we live in. The result is as yet far from satisfactory. The sciences have not joined hands and made their results coherent, showing nature to be, as it doubtless is, all of one piece. The moral sciences especially are a mass of confusion. Negative, I think, must be the attitude of reason, in the present state of science, upon any hypothesis far outrunning the recorded history and the visible habitat of the human race. Yet exactly the same habits and principles that have secured our present knowledge are still active within us, and promise further discoveries. It is more desirable to clarify our knowledge within these bounds than to extend it beyond them. For while the reward of action is contemplation or, in more modern phrase, experience and consciousness, there is nothing stable or interesting to contemplate except objects relevant to action—the natural world and the mind's ideals.

Both the conditions and the standards of action lie well within the territory which science, after a fashion, already dominates. But there remain unexplored jungles and monster-breeding lairs within our nominal jurisdiction which it is the immediate task of science to clear. The darkest spots are in man himself, in his fitful, irrational disposition. Could a better system prevail in our lives a better order would establish itself in our thinking. It has not been for want of keen senses, or personal genius, or a constant order in the outer world, that mankind have fallen back repeatedly into barbarism and superstition. It has been for want of good character, good example, and good government. There is a pathetic capacity in men to live nobly, if only they would give one another the chance. The ideal of political perfection, vague and remote as it yet seems, is certainly approachable, for it is as definite and constant as human nature. The knowledge of all relevant truth would be involved in that ideal, and no intellectual dissatisfaction would be felt with a system of ideas that should express and illumine a perfect life.

Types and Aims of Science

Science is so new a thing and so far from final, it seems to the layman so hopelessly accurate and extensive, that a moralist may well feel some diffidence in trying to estimate its achievements and promises at their human worth. The morrow may bring some great revolution in science, and is sure to bring many a correction and many a surprise. Religion and art have had their day; indeed a part of the faith they usually inspire is to believe that they have long ago revealed their secret. A critic may safely form a judgment concerning them; for even if he dissents from the orthodox opinion and ventures to hope that religion and art may assume in the future forms far nobler and more rational than any they have hitherto worn, still he must confess that art and religion have had several turns at the wheel; they have run their course through in various ages and climes with results which anybody is free to estimate if he has an open mind and sufficient interest in the subject. Science, on the contrary, which apparently cannot exist where intellectual freedom is denied, has flourished only twice in recorded times: once for some three hundred years in ancient Greece, and again for about the same period in modern Christendom. Its fruits have scarcely begun to appear; the lands it is discovering have not yet been circumnavigated, and there is no telling what its ultimate influence will be on human practice and feeling.

SCEPTICISM AND ANIMAL FAITH [5]

I have now reached the culminating point of my survey of evidence, and the entanglements I have left behind me and the habitable regions I am looking for lie spread out before me like opposite valleys. On the one hand I see now a sweeping reason for scepticism, over and above all particular contradictions or fancifulness of dogma. Nothing is ever present to me except some essence; so that nothing that I possess in intuition, or actually see, is ever *there*; it can never exist bodily, nor lie in that place or exert that power which belongs to the objects encountered in action. Therefore, if I regard my intuitions as knowledge of facts, all my experience is illusion, and life is a dream. At the same time I am now able to give a clearer meaning to this old adage; for life would not be a dream, and all experience would not be illusion, if I abstained from believing in them. The evidence of data is only obviousness; they give no evidence of anything else; they are not witnesses. If I am content to recognise them for pure essences, they cannot deceive me; they will be like works of literary fiction, more or less coherent, but without any claim to exist on their own account. If I hypostatise an essence into a fact, instinctively placing it in relations which are not given within it, I am putting my trust in animal faith, not in any evidence or implication of my actual experience. I turn to an assumed world about me, because I have organs for turning, just as I expect a future to reel itself out without interruption because I am wound up to go on myself. To such ulterior things no manifest essence can bear any testimony. They must justify themselves. If the ulterior fact is some intuition elsewhere, its existence, if it happens to exist, will justify that belief; but the fulfilment of my prophecy, in taking my present dream for testimony to that ulterior experience, will be found only in the realm of truth—a realm which is itself an object of belief, never by any possibility of intuition, human or divine. So too when the supposed fact is thought of as a substance, its existence, if it is found in the realm of nature, will justify that supposition; but the realm of nature is of course only another object of belief, more remote if possible from intuition than even the realm of truth. Intuition of essence, to which positive experience and certitude are confined, is therefore always illusion, if we allow our hypostatising impulse to take it for evidence of anything else.

In adopting this conclusion of so many great philosophers, that all

[5] From George Santayana, *Scepticism and Animal Faith*, N. Y., 1923. Selection taken from Chapter XI, "The Watershed of Criticism."

is illusion, I do so, however, with two qualifications. One is emotional and moral only, in that I do not mourn over this fatality, but on the contrary rather prefer speculation in the realm of essence—if it can be indulged without practical inconvenience—to alleged information about hard facts. It does not seem to me ignominious to be a poet, if nature has made one a poet unexpectedly. Unexpectedly nature lent us existence, and if she has made it a condition that we should be poets, she has not forbidden us to enjoy that art, or even to be proud of it. The other qualification is more austere: it consists in not allowing exceptions. I cannot admit that some particular essence—water, fire, being, atoms, or Brahma—is the intrinsic essence of all things, so that if I narrow my imagination to that one intuition I shall have intuited the heart and the whole of existence. Of course I do not deny that there is water and that there is being, the former in most things on earth, and the latter in everything anywhere; but these images or words of mine are not the things they designate, but only names for them. Desultory and partial propriety these names may have, but no metaphysical privilege. No more has the expedient of some modern critics who would take illusion as a whole and call it the universe; for in the first place they are probably reverting to belief in discourse, as conventionally conceived, so that their scepticism is halting; and in the second place, even if human experience could be admitted as known and vouched for, there would be an incredible arrogance in positing it as the whole of being, or as itself confined to the forms and limits which the critic assigns to it. The life of reason as I conceive it is a mere romance, and the life of nature a mere fable; such pictures have no metaphysical value, even if as sympathetic fictions they had some psychological truth.

The doctrine of essence thus renders my scepticism invincible and complete, while reconciling me with it emotionally.

If now I turn my face in the other direction and consider the prospect open to animal faith, I see that all this insecurity and inadequacy of alleged knowledge are almost irrelevant to the natural effort of the mind to describe natural things. The discouragement we may feel in science does not come from failure; it comes from a false conception of what would be success. Our worst difficulties arise from the assumption that knowledge of existences ought to be literal, whereas knowledge of existences has no need, no propensity, and no fitness to be literal. It is symbolic initially, when a sound, a smell, an indescribable feeling are signals to the animal of his dangers or chances; and it fulfils its function perfectly—I mean its moral function of enlightening us about our natural good—if it remains symbolic to the end. Can anything be more evident than that religion, language, patriotism, love, science itself speak in symbols? Given essences unify for intuition, in entirely adventitious human terms, the diffuse processes of nature; the æsthetic image—the sound, the colour, the expanse of space, the scent, taste, and sweet or cruel pressure of bodies—wears an aspect altogether unlike the mechanisms it stands for. Sensation and thought (between which there is no essential difference) work in a conventional medium, as do literature and music. The experience of essence is direct; the expression of natural facts through that medium is indirect. But this indirection is no obstacle to expression, rather its condition; and this vehicular manifestation of things may be knowledge of them, which intuition of essence is not. The theatre, for all its artifices, depicts life in a sense more truly than history, because the medium has a kindred movement to that of real life, though an artificial setting and form; and much in the same way the human medium of knowledge can perform its pertinent synthesis and make its pertinent report all the better when it frankly abandons the plane of its object and expresses in symbols what we need to know of it. The arts of expression would be impossible if they were not extensions of normal human perception. The Greeks recognised that astronomy and history were presided over by Muses, sisters of those of tragic and comic poetry; had they been as psychological as modern reflection has become, they might have had Muses of sight, hearing, and speech. I think they honoured, if they did not express, this complementary fact also, that all the Muses, even the most playful, are witnesses to the nature of things. The arts are evidences of wisdom, and sources of it; they include science. No Muse would be a humane influence, nor worthy of honour, if she did not studiously express the truth of nature with the liberty and grace appropriate to her special genius.

Philosophers would not have overlooked the fact that knowledge is, and ought to be, symbolical, if intuition did not exist also, giving them a taste of something which perhaps they think higher and more satisfying. Intuition, when it is placid and masterful enough to stand alone, free from anxiety or delusion about matters of fact, is a delightful exercise, like play; it employs our imaginative faculty without warping it, and lets us live without responsibility. The playful and godlike mind of philosophers has always been fascinated by intuition; philosophers—I mean the great ones—are the infant prodigies of reflection. They often take intuition of essence for their single ideal, and wish to impose it on the workaday thoughts of men; they make a play-world for themselves which it is glorious to dominate, much as other men of genius, prolonging the masterfulness of childhood, continue to play at this or at that in their politics and their religion. But knowledge of existence has an entirely different method and an entirely different ideal. It is playful too, because its terms are intuitive and its grammar or logic often very subjective. Perception, theory, hypothesis are rapid, pregnant, often humorous; they seize a fact by its skirts from some unexpected quarter, and give it a nick-name which it might be surprised to hear, such as the rainbow or the Great Bear. Yet in the investigation of facts all this play of mind is merely instrumental and indicative: the intent is practical, the watchfulness earnest, the spirit humble. The mind here knows that it is at school; and even its fancies are docile. Its nicknames for things and for their odd ways of behaving are like those which country people give to flowers; they often pointedly describe how things look or what they do to us. The ideas we have of things are not fair portraits; they are political caricatures made in the human interest; but in their partial way they may be masterpieces of char-acterisation and insight. Above all, they are obtained by labour, by investigating what is not given, and by correcting one impression by another, drawn from the same object—a thing impossible in the in-tuition of essences. They therefore conduce to wisdom, and in their perpetual tentativeness have a cumulative truth.

Consider the reason why, instead of cultivating congenial intui-tions, a man may be drawn to the study of nature at all. It is because things, by their impact, startle him into attention and a new thought. Such external objects interest him for what they do, not for what they are; and knowledge of them is significant, not for the essence it dis-plays to intuition (beautiful as this may be) but for the events it expresses or foreshadows. It matters little therefore to the pertinent knowledge of nature that the substance of things should remain recondite or unintelligible, if their movement and operation can be rightly determined on the plane of human perception. It matters lit-tle if their very existence is vouched for only by animal faith and presumption, so long as this faith posits existence where existence is, and this presumption expresses a prophetic preadaptation of animal instincts to the forces of the environment. The function of perception and natural science is, not to flatter the sense of omniscience in an absolute mind, but to dignify animal life by harmonising it, in action and in thought, with its conditions. It matters little if the news these methods can bring us of the world is fragmentary and is expressed rhetorically; what matters is that science should be integrated with art, and that the arts should substitute the dominion of man over circumstances, as far as this is possible, for the dominion of chance. In this there is no sacrifice of truth to utility; there is rather a wise direction of curiosity upon things on the human scale, and within the range of art. Speculation beyond those limits cannot be controlled, and is irresponsible; and the symbolic terms in which it must be car-ried on, even at close quarters, are the best possible indications for the facts in question. All these inadequacies and imperfections are proper to perfect signs, which should be brief and sharply distinguished.

Complete scepticism is accordingly not inconsistent with animal faith; the admission that nothing given exists is not incompatible with belief in things not given. I may yield to the suasion of instinct, and practise the arts with a humble confidence, without in the least disavowing the most rigorous criticism of knowledge or hypostatising any of the data of sense or fancy. And I need not do this with a bad conscience, as Parmenides and Plato and the Indians seem to have done, when they admitted illusion or opinion as an epilogue to their tight metaphysics, on the ground that otherwise they would miss their way home. It is precisely by *not* yielding to opinion and illusion, and by *not* delegating any favourite essences to be the substance of things, that I aspire to keep my cognitive conscience pure and my practical judgment sane; because in order to find my way home I am by no means compelled to yield ignominiously to any animal illusion; what guides me there is not illusion but habit; and the intuitions which accompany habit are normal signs for the circle of objects and forces by which that habit is sustained. The images of sense and science will not delude me if instead of hypostatising them, as those philosophers did the terms of their dialectic, I regard them as graphic symbols for home and for the way there. That such external things exist, that I exist myself, and live more or less prosperously in the midst of them, is a faith not founded on reason but precipitated in action, and in that intent, which is virtual action, involved in perception. This faith, which it would be dishonest not to confess that I share, does no violence to a sceptical analysis of experience; on the contrary, it takes advantage of that analysis to interpret this volatile experience as all animals do and must, as a set of symbols for existences that cannot enter experience, and which, since they are not elements in knowledge, no analysis of knowledge can touch—they are in another realm of being.

I propose now to consider what objects animal faith requires me to posit, and in what order; without for a moment forgetting that my assurance of their existence is only instinctive, and my description of their nature only symbolic. I may know them by intent, based on bodily reaction; I know them initially as whatever confronts me, whatever it may turn out to be, just as I know the future initially as whatever is coming, without knowing what will come. That something confronts me here, now, and from a specific quarter, is in itself a momentous discovery. The aspect this thing wears, as it first attracts my attention, though it may deceive me in some particulars, can hardly fail to be, in some respects, a telling indication of its nature in its relation to me. Signs identify their objects for discourse, and show us where to look for their undiscovered qualities. Further signs, catching other aspects of the same object, may help me to lay siege to it from all sides; but signs will never lead me into the citadel, and if its inner chambers are ever opened to me, it must be through sympathetic imagination. I might, by some happy unison between my imagination and its generative principles, intuit the essence which is actually the essence of that thing. In that case (which may often occur when the object is a sympathetic mind) knowledge of existence, without ceasing to be instinctive faith, will be as complete and adequate as knowledge can possibly be. The given essence will be the essence of the object meant; but knowledge will remain a claim, since the intuition is not satisfied to observe the given essence passively as a disembodied essence, but instinctively affirms it to be the essence of an existence confronting me, and beyond the range of my possible apprehension. Therefore the most perfect knowledge of fact is perfect only pictorially, not evidentially, and remains subject to the end to the insecurity inseparable from animal faith, and from life itself.

Animal faith being a sort of expectation and open-mouthedness, is earlier than intuition; intuitions come to help it out and lend it something to posit. It is more than ready to swallow any suggestion of sense or fancy; and perhaps primitive credulity, as in a dream, makes no bones of any contradiction or incongruity in successive convictions, but yields its whole soul to every image. Faith then hangs like a pendulum at rest; but when perplexity has caused that pendulum to swing more and more madly, it may for a moment stop quivering at a point of unstable equilibrium at the top; and this vertical station may be likened to universal scepticism. It is a more wonderful and a more promising equilibrium than the other, because it cannot be maintained; but before declining from the zenith and desisting from pointing vertically at zero, the pendulum of faith may hesitate for an instant which way to fall, if at that uncomfortable height it has really lost all animal momentum and all ancient prejudice. Before giving my reasons—which are but prejudices and human—for believing in events, in substances, and in the variegated truths which they involve, it may be well to have halted for breath at the apex of scepticism, and felt all the negative privileges of that position. The mere possibility of it in its purity is full of instruction; and although I have, for my own part, dwelt upon it only ironically, by a scruple of method, and intending presently to abandon it for common sense, many a greater philosopher has sought to maintain himself acrobatically at that altitude. They have not succeeded; but an impossible dwelling-place may afford, like a mountain-top, a good point of view in clear weather from which to map the land and choose a habitation.

REALMS OF BEING [6]

The world is old, and can have changed but little since man arose in it, else man himself would have perished. Why, then, should he still live without a sure and sufficient philosophy? The equivalent of such a philosophy is probably hereditary in sundry animals not much older than man. They have had time to take the measure of life, and have settled down to a routine of preferences and habits which keeps their heads, as a race, above water; and they are presumably visited at appropriate seasons by magic images, which are symbols to them for the world or for the cycles of their destiny. Among groups of men an equilibrium of this moral sort has been sometimes approached—in India, in China, under the Moslem or the Catholic regimens; and if socialist or other panaceas now exercise such a strange influence over men's hearts, it is perhaps because they are impatient of being so long the sport of divers ignorant dogmas and chance adventures, and aspire to live in a stable harmony with nature.

In fact, beneath these various complete systems which have professed but failed to be universal, there is actually a dumb human philosophy, incomplete but solid, prevalent among all civilized peoples. They all practise agriculture, commerce, and mechanical arts, with artificial instruments lately very much complicated; and they necessarily possess, with these arts, a modicum of sanity, morality, and science requisite for carrying them on, and tested by success in doing so. Is not this human competence philosophy enough? Is it not at least the nucleus of all sound philosophy? In spite of the superficial confusion reigning in the world, is not the universal wisdom of the future actually gathering about this human competence in engineering, in chemistry, in medicine, in war?

It might seem so, since the sort of knowledge involved in the arts, though it may not go very far, is compulsory so far as it goes, and being sanctioned by success, it ought to be permanent and progressive. There is indeed a circle of material events called nature, to which all minds belonging to the same society are responsive in common. Not to be responsive to these facts is simply to be stupid

[6] From George Santayana, *The Realm of Essence*, N. Y., 1927. Selection from Preface to *The Realms of Being*.

and backward in the arts; those who explore and master their environment cannot help learning what it is. In this direction competence involves enlightenment. Among minds forming a moral society, and able to compare their several opinions, this enlightenment in the expert is coercive over the layman also, because the same facts confront them both. Did not the same facts confront them, communication would be impossible between them, or if communication was reputed to exist by magic there would be no possible conflict or progress among their opinions, because they would not refer to the same events. Even if each declared himself competent and prosperous in his own world, he would know nothing of the world of his neighbors. Their several minds would simply be variously or similarly brilliant, like jewels signifying nothing to one another.

If any mind hopes to address another (or even itself) persuasively, as I now wish to address the reader and my own thoughts, it must assume a single system of events to which both minds are responsive, and which includes their respective bodies and actions. Assuming such a common world, it is easy to see how animals may acquire knowledge of it and may communicate it. Material events will arouse in them intuitions conformable to their several stations, faculties, and passions; and their active nature (since they are animals, not plants) will compel them to regard many of the essences so given in intuition as signs for the environment in which they move, modifying this environment and affected by it. This assumption justifies itself at every turn in practice, and establishes in the habits of all men, in proportion to their competence, an appropriate adjustment to the *Realm of Matter*, and in their imagination a suitable picture of the same.

Nevertheless, since the station, faculties, and passions of all men are not identical, these pictures will not be similar. Different observers may be addressed to different regions of nature, or sensitive to different elements in the same region; thus dwellers in distinct planets must evidently have distinct geographies, and the same battle in the clouds will be known to the deaf only as lightning and to the blind only as thunder, each responding to a different constituent of the total event, and not simultaneously. So an eclipse—itself but one aspect of a constellation of events in the heavens—may be known in various entirely different terms; by calculation before it occurs, by sense when it is occurring, by memory immediately afterward, and by reports to posterity. All these indications are entirely inadequate to the facts they reveal in the realm of matter, and qualitatively unlike those facts; they are a set of variegated symbols by which sensitive animals can designate them. Of course, the existence and use of such languages is an added fact in nature—a fact so important and close to the egotism of the animals themselves as perhaps to obscure all else in their eyes. Their instinct, indeed, keeps their attention stretched upon the material world that actually surrounds them; but sometimes sensation and language, instead of being passed over like the ticking of the telegraph, may become objects in themselves, in all their absolute musical insignificance; and then animals become idealists. The terms in which they describe things, unlike the things they meant to describe, are purely specious, arbitrary, and ideal; whether visual, tactile, auditory, or conceptual, these terms are essentially *words*. They possess intrinsically, in their own ontological plane, only logical or aesthetic being; and this contains no indication whatever of the material act of speaking, touching, or looking which causes them to appear. All possible terms in mental discourse are essences existing nowhere; visionary equally, whether the faculty that discovers them be sense or thought or the most fantastic fancy.

Such diversity in animal experience taken in itself exhibits sundry qualities or forms of being, a part of the infinite multitude of distinguishable ideal terms which (whether ever revealed to anybody or not) I call the *Realm of Essence*. Pure intuition, in its poetic ecstasy, would simply drink in such of these essences as happened to present themselves; but for a wakeful animal they are signals. They report to his spirit, in very summary and uncertain images, the material events which surround him and which concern his welfare. They may accordingly become terms in knowledge if interpreted judiciously, and if interpreted injudiciously they may become illusions.

The dumb philosophy of the human animal, by which he rears his family and practises the arts and finds his way home, might take definite shape and establish a healthy routine in all his dealings with matter (which includes society), and yet his imaginative experience might retain all its specious originality. The control which the environment exercises over the structure and conduct of animals is decidedly loose. They can live dragging a long chain of idle tricks, diseases, and obsolete organs; and even this loose control fails almost entirely in the case of alternative senses or languages, one of which may serve as well as another. Many species survive together, many rival endowments and customs and religions. And the same control fails altogether in regard to the immaterial essences which those senses or languages call up before the mind's eyes. Adaptation is physical, and it is only the material operation in sensation or speech that can possibly be implicated in the clockwork of nature. The choice of those visionary essences which meantime visit the mind, though regular, is free; they are the transcript of life into discourse, the rhetorical and emotional rendering of existence, which when deepened and purified becomes poetry or music. There can be no reason why differences in these spheres, even among men of the same race, should not be perpetual. It would be mere sluggishness and egotism to regret it. Such differences are not merely added like a vain luxury to a sane recognition, in other conscious terms, of the facts of nature. The "sane" response to nature is by action only and by an economy which nature can accept and weave into her own material economy; but as to the terms of sense and discourse, they are all from the very beginning equally arbitrary, poetical, and (if you choose) mad; yet all equally symptomatic. They vary initially and intangibly from mind to mind, even in expressing the same routine of nature. The imagination which eventually runs to fine art or religion is the same faculty which, under a more direct control of external events, yields vulgar perception. The promptings and the control exercised by matter are continuous in both cases; the dream requires a material dreamer as much as the waking sensation, and the latter is a transcript of his bodily condition just as directly as the dream. Poetic, creative, original fancy is not a secondary form of sensibility, but its first and only form. The same manual restlessness and knack which makes man a manufacturer of toys makes him, when by chance his toys prove useful, a manufacturer of implements. Fine art is thus older than servile labor, and the poetic quality of experience is more fundamental than its scientific value. Existence may revert at any moment to play, or may run down in idleness; but it is impossible that any work or discovery should ever come about without the accompaniment of pure contemplation, if there is consciousness at all; so that the inherent freedom of the spirit can never be stamped out, so long as spirit endures.

Nor is it safe to imagine that inspired people, because they dream awake in their philosophy, must come to grief in the real world. The great religious and political systems which I mentioned above have had brilliant careers. Their adepts have been far from making worse soldiers than sceptics make, or worse workmen than materialists; nor have they committed suicide or been locked up in the madhouse more often than exact philosophers. Nature drives with a loose rein, and vitality of any sort, even if expressed in fancy, can blunder through many a predicament in which reason would despair. And if the mythical systems decline at last, it is not so much by virtue of the maladjustments underlying their speculative errors—for their myths as a whole are wisely contrived—as because imagination in its freedom abandons these errors for others simply because the prevalent mood of mankind has changed, and it begins dreaming in a different key. Spirit bloweth where it listeth, and continually undoes its own work. This world of free expression, this drift of sensations, passions, and ideas, perpetually kindled and fading in the light of consciousness, I call the *Realm of Spirit*. It is only for the sake of this free life that material competence and knowledge of fact are worth attaining. Facts for a living creature are only instruments; his play-life is his true life. On his working days, when he is attentive to matter, he is only his own servant, preparing the feast. He becomes his own master in his holidays and in his sportive passions. Among these must be counted literature and philosophy, and so much of love, religion, and patriotism as is not an effort to survive materially. In such enthusiasms there is much asseveration; but what they attest is really not the character of the external facts concerned, but only the spiritual uses to which the spirit turns them.

A philosopher cannot wish to be deceived. His philosophy is a declaration of policy in the presence of the facts; and therefore his first care must be to ascertain and heartily to acknowledge all such facts as are relevant to his action or sentiment—not less, and not necessarily more. The pursuit of truth is a form of courage, and a philosopher may well love truth for its own sake, in that he is disposed to confront destiny, whatever it may be, with zest when possible, with resignation when necessary, and not seldom with amusement. The facts to which it is prudent and noble in him to bare his bosom are the morally relevant facts, such as touch his fortunes or his heart, or such as he can alter by his efforts; nor can he really discover other facts. Intuition, or absolute apprehension without media or doubt, is proper to spirit perusing essences; it is impossible to animals confronting facts. Animals know things by exploration, reaction, and prophetic fancy; they therefore can know only such parts and depths of nature as they explore materially and respond to vitally. The brave impulse to search may, indeed, become eager and may wish to recognize no limits; and there may be spirits so utterly practical and serious that the pursuit of material facts absorbs them altogether, to the exclusion of all play of mind. Yet such hectic exactitude is an expression of fear, and automatic rather than rational. Curiosity in an animal always has limits which it is foolish to transgress, because beyond them theory insensibly lapses into verbal myths, and if still taken for true knowledge defeats the honest curiosity that inspired it. What renders knowledge true is fidelity to the object; but in the conduct and fancy of an animal this fidelity can be only rough, summary, dramatic; too much refinement renders it subjective, as does too much haste. This is true of mathematical refinements no less than of verbal pedantries. The realm of matter can never be disclosed either to hypothesis or to sensation in its presumable inmost structure and ultimate extent: the garment of appearance must always fit it loosely and drape it in alien folds, because appearance is essentially an adaptation of facts to the scale and faculty of the observer.

There are also moral limits to seriousness and utter literalness in thought. The tragic compulsion to honor the facts is imposed on man by the destiny of his body, to which that of his mind is attached. But his destiny is not the only theme possible to his thought, nor the most congenial. The best part of this destiny is that he may often forget it; and existence would not be worth preserving if it had to be spent exclusively in anxiety about existence.

It follows from all this that knowledge of facts merely because they are facts cannot be the ultimate object of a philosopher, although he must wish to know the whole unvarnished truth about relevant matters. A liberal mind must live on its own terms, and think in them; it is not inferior to what surrounds it; fact-worship on its part would accordingly be a fault in taste and in morals. What is the function of philosophy? To disclose the absolute truth? But is it credible that the absolute truth should descend into the thoughts of a mortal creature, equipped with a few special senses and with a biased intellect, a man lost amidst millions of his fellows and a prey to the epidemic delusions of the race? Possession of the absolute truth is not merely by accident beyond the range of particular minds; it is incompatible with being alive, because it excludes any particular station, organ, interest, or date of survey: the absolute truth is undiscoverable just because it is not a perspective. Perspectives are essential to animal apprehension; an observer, himself a part of the world he observes, must have a particular station in it; he cannot be equally near to everything, nor internal to anything but himself; of the rest he can only take views, abstracted according to his sensibility and foreshortened according to his interests. Those animals which I was supposing endowed with an adequate philosophy surely do not possess the absolute truth. They read nature in their private idioms. Their imagination, like the human, is doubtless incapable of coping with all things at once, or even with the whole of anything natural. Mind was not created for the sake of discovering the absolute truth. The absolute truth has its own intangible reality, and scorns to be known. The function of mind is rather to increase the wealth of the universe in the spiritual dimension, by adding appearance to substance and passion to necessity, and by creating all those private perspectives, and those emotions of wonder, adventure, curiosity, and laughter which omniscience would exclude. If omniscience were alone respectable, creation would have been a mistake. The single duty of all creatures would then be to repair that creative error, by abolishing their several senses and desires and becoming indistinguishable from one another and from nothing at all; and if all creation could attain to this sort of salvation, the absolute substance, in whose honor all else had been abandoned, would become unconscious. The time will doubtless come for each of us, if not for the universe at large, to cease from care; but our passage through life will have added a marvellous episode to the tale of things; and our distinction and glory, as well as our sorrow, will have lain in being something in particular, and in knowing what it is.

Thus if there is a sense in which all special and separable existence is illusion, there is another sense in which illusion is itself a special and separable existence; and if this be condemned for not being absolute substance and for excluding knowledge of the absolute truth, it may also be prized for these very reasons. Sensation is true enough. All experience yields some acquaintance with the realm of essence, and some perspective of the material world; and this would always be a true perspective (since things seen at that angle and with that organ really look like that) if the appearance were not stretched to cover more than it covers in reality. Of such true perspectives the simplest and most violently foreshortened may be as good as the most complicated, the most poetical or pictorial as good as the most scientific, not only aesthetically but even cognitively; because it may report the things concerned on that human scale on which we need to measure them, and in this relation may report them correctly. Nor is the error which such very partial knowledge may breed, when inflated by precipitate judgments and vanity, altogether unavoidable. The variety of senses in man, the precarious rule of his instincts, and the range of his memory and fancy, give rise in him eventually to some sense of error and even of humor. He is almost able to pierce the illusions of his animal dogmatism, to surrender the claim to inspiration, and in one sense to transcend the relativity of his knowledge and the flightiness of his passions by acknowledging them with a good grace.

This relativity does not imply that there is no absolute truth. On the contrary, if there were no absolute truth, all-inclusive and eternal, the desultory views taken from time to time by individuals would themselves be absolute. They would be irrelevant to one another, and incomparable in point of truth, each being without any object but the essence which appeared in it. If views can be more or less correct, and perhaps complementary to one another, it is because they refer to the same system of nature, the complete description of which, covering the whole past and the whole future, would be the absolute truth. This absolute truth is no living view, no actual judgment, but merely that segment of the realm of essence which happens to be illustrated in existence. The question whether a given essence belongs to this segment or not—that is, whether a suggested idea is or is not true—has a tragic importance for an animal intent on discovering and describing what exists, or has existed, or is destined to exist in his world. He seldom has leisure to dwell on essences apart from their presumable truth; even their beauty and dialectical pattern seem to him rather trivial, unless they are significant of facts in the realm of matter, controlling human destiny. I therefore give a special name to this tragic segment of the realm of essence and call it the *Realm of Truth*.

The knowledge of relevant truth, while it has this fundamental moral importance, is far from being our only concern in the life of reason. It comes in only incidentally, in so far as a staunch and comprehensive knowledge of things makes a man master of things, and independent of them in a great measure. The business of a philosopher is rather to be a good shepherd of his thoughts. The share of attention and weight which he gives to physical speculation or to history or to psychology will express his race and disposition, or the spirit of his times; everyone is free to decide how far material arts and sciences are worth pursuing, and with what free creations they shall be surrounded. Young and ardent minds, and races without accumulated possessions, tend to poetry and metaphysics; they neglect or falsify the truth in the heat of their imaginative passion. Old men, and old nations, incline to mix their wine with larger dilutions of reality; and they prefer history, biography, politics, and humorous fictions; because in all these, while the facts are neither conceived nor tested scientifically, the savor of earth and of experience remains dominant.

By the philosopher, however, both the homeliest brew and the most meticulous science are only relished as food for the spirit. Even if defeated in the pursuit of truth, the spirit may be victorious in self-expression and self-knowledge; and if a philosopher could be nothing else, he might still be a moralist and a poet. He will do well to endow his vision of things with all the force, color, and scope of which his soul is capable. Then if he misses the truth of nature, as in many things is probable, he will at least have achieved a work of imagination. In such a case the universe, without being mapped as a whole in the fancy, will be enriched at one point, by the happy life enacted there, in one human focus of art and vision. The purer and more distinct the spirit which a philosopher can bring to light in his thoughts, the greater the intellectual achievement; and the greater the moral achievement also, if the policy so set forth is actually carried out in his whole life and conversation.

As for me, in stretching my canvas and taking up my palette and brush, I am not vexed that masters should have painted before me in styles which I have no power and no occasion to imitate; nor do

I expect future generations to be satisfied with always repainting my pictures. Agreement is sweet, being a form of friendship; it is also a stimulus to insight, and helpful, as contradiction is not; and I certainly hope to find agreement in some quarters. Yet I am not much concerned about the number of those who may be my friends in the spirit, nor do I care about their chronological distribution, being as much pleased to discover one intellectual kinsman in the past as to imagine two in the future. That in the world at large alien natures should prevail, innumerable and perhaps infinitely various, does not disturb me. On the contrary, I hope fate may manifest to them such objects as they need and can love; and although my sympathy with them cannot be so vivid as with men of my own mind, and in some cases may pass into antipathy, I do not conceive that they are wrong or inferior for being different from me, or from one another. If God and nature can put up with them, why should I raise an objection? But let them take care; for if they have sinned against the facts (as I suspect is often the case) and are kicking against the pricks of matter, they must expect to be brought to confusion on the day of doom, or earlier. Not only will their career be brief and troubled, which is the lot of all flesh, but their faith will be stultified by events, which is a needless and eternal ignominy for the spirit. But if somehow, in their chosen terms, they have balanced their accounts with nature, they are to be heartily congratulated on their moral diversity. It is pleasant to think that the fertility of spirit is inexhaustible, if matter only gives it a chance, and that the worst and most successful fanaticism cannot turn the moral world permanently into a desert.

The pity of it is only that contrary souls should often fight for the same bodies, natural or political, as if space and matter in the universe were inadequate (as on earth indeed they are) for every essence in its own time to see the sun. But existence is precipitate and blind; it cannot bide its time; and the seeds of form are often so wantonly and thickly scattered that they strangle one another, call one another weeds and tares, and can live only in the distracted effort to keep others from living. Seldom does any soul live through a single and lively summer in its native garden, suffered and content to bloom. Philosophers and nations cannot be happy unless separate; then they may be single-minded at home and tolerant abroad. If they have a spirit in them which is worth cultivating (which is not always the case) they need to entrench it in some consecrated citadel, where it may come to perfect expression. Human beings allowed to run loose are vowed to perdition, since they are too individual to agree and too gregarious to stand alone. Hence the rareness of any polity founded on wisdom, like that of which ancient Greece affords some glimpses, and the equal rareness of a pure and complete philosophy, such as that of Dante or of Spinoza, conceived in some moment of wonderful unanimity or of fortunate isolation.

My own philosophy, I venture to think, is well knit in the same sense, in spite of perhaps seeming eclectic and of leaving so many doors open both in physics and in morals. My eclecticism is not helplessness before sundry influences; it is detachment and firmness in taking each thing simply for what it is. Openness, too, is a form of architecture. The doctrine that all moralities equally are but expressions of animal life is a tremendous dogma, at once blessing and purging all mortal passions; and the conviction that there can be no knowledge save animal faith positing external facts, and that this natural science is but a human symbol for those facts, also has an immense finality: the renunciation and the assurance in it are both radical and both invincible.

In confessing that I have merely touched the hem of nature's garment, I feel that virtue from her has passed into me, and made me whole. There is no more bewitching moment in childhood than when the boy, to whom someone is slyly propounding some absurdity, suddenly looks up and smiles. The brat has understood. A thin deception was being practiced on him, in the hope that he might not be deceived, but by deriding it might prove he had attained to a man's stature and a man's wit. It was but banter prompted by love. So with this thin deception practiced upon me by nature. The great Sphinx in posing her riddle and looking so threatening and mysterious is secretly hoping that I may laugh. She is not a riddle but a fact; the words she whispers are not oracles but prattle. Why take her residual silence, which is inevitable, for a challenge or a menace? She does not know how to speak more plainly. Her secret is as great a secret to herself as to me. If I perceive it, and laugh, instantly she draws in her claws. A tremor runs through her enigmatical body; and if she were not of stone she would embrace her boyish discoverer, and yield herself to him altogether. It is so simple to exist, to be what one is for no reason, to engulf all questions and answers in the rush of being that sustains them. Henceforth nature and spirit can play together like mother and child, each marvellously pleasant to the other, yet deeply unintelligible; for as she created him she knew not how, merely by smiling in her dreams, so in awaking and smiling back he somehow understands her; at least he is all the understanding she has of herself.

BIBLIOGRAPHY

SANTAYANA, George. *The Sense of Beauty,* N.Y.: Scribner's, 1896.

————, *Interpretations of Poetry and Religion.* N.Y.: Scribner's, 1900.

————, *Lucifer, A Theological Tragedy.* Chicago & N.Y.: H.S. Stone & Co., 1899.

————, *The Life of Reason.* 5 vols. N.Y.: Scribner's, 1905–1906. Reprinted by Collier Books, 1962.

————, *Three Philosophical Poets.* N.Y.: Scribner's, 1910.

————, *Winds of Doctrine.* N.Y.: Scribner's, 1913.

————, *Egotism in German Philosophy.* N.Y.: Scribner's, 1916.

————, *Philosophical Opinion in America.* London: Oxford U. Press, 1918.

————, *Character and Opinion in the United States.* N.Y.: Scribner's, 1920.

————, *Soliloquies in England.* N.Y.: Scribner's, 1922.

————, *Scepticism and Animal Faith.* N.Y.: Scribner's, 1923.

————, *The Unknowable.* Oxford, Clarendon Press, 1923.

————, *Dialogues in Limbo.* N.Y.: Scribner's, 1926.

————, *Platonism and the Spiritual Life.* N.Y.: Scribner's, 1927.

————, *The Realm of Essence.* N.Y.: Scribner's, 1927.

————, *The Realm of Matter.* N.Y.: Scribner's, 1930.

————, *The Genteel Tradition at Bay.* N.Y.: Scribner's, 1931.

————, *Some Turns of Thought in Modern Philosophy.* Cambridge, England: The University Press, 1933; N.Y.: Scribner's, 1934.

————, *The Last Puritan.* N.Y.: Scribner's, 1936.

————, *Obiter Scripta: Lectures, Essays, and Reviews.* Justus Buchler and Benjamin Schwartz, eds. N.Y.: Scribner's, 1936.

————, *The Realm of Truth.* N.Y.: Scribner's, 1938.

————, *The Realm of Spirit.* N.Y.: Scribner's, 1940.

————, *Realms of Being,* one vol. ed. N.Y.: Scribner's, 1942.

————, *Persons and Places,* 3 vols. N.Y.: Scribner's, 1944–1953.

————, *The Idea of Christ in the Gospels.* N.Y.: Scribner's, 1946.

————, *Dominations and Powers: Reflections on Liberty, Society, and Government.* N.Y.: Scribner's, 1951.

————, *Letters.* Daniel Cory, ed. N.Y.: Scribner's, 1955.

ARNETT, W.E. *Santayana and the Sense of Beauty.* Bloomington: Indiana U. Press, 1955.

MUNITZ, Milton K. *The Moral Philosophy of George Santayana.* N.Y.: Columbia U. Press, 1939.

SCHLIPP, Paul Arthur, ed. *The Philosophy of Santayana.* Evanston and Chicago: Northwestern U. Press, 1940.

SINGER, Irving. *Santayana's Aesthetics: A Critical Introduction.* Cambridge: Harvard U. Press, 1957.

Alfred North Whitehead

[1861–1947]

Whitehead was born at Ramsgate, England. He was educated at Trinity College, Cambridge, and taught mathematics at Cambridge, the University College of London, and the Imperial College of Science and Technology in Kensington. He came to America at the age of 63, taught at Harvard from 1924 to 1937, and lived there after his retirement until his death in 1947, at the age of 87.

Whitehead's reputation was at first based on his contributions to mathematics and symbolic logic. He wrote several books in mathematics and he was co-author (with Bertrand Russell) of the famous *Principia Mathematica* (1910–12), which attempts to derive the fundamental concepts and principles of mathematics from formal logic.

By the end of the first World War, Whitehead had begun to publish in the field of philosophy, and this was the basis for his invitation to Harvard University as Professor of Philosophy. It was here that most of his mature philosophical writings were completed and published, and it was here that his major philosophical influence was felt. England had long since fallen under the sway of analytic, empirical and positivistic philosophy. By contrast, Whitehead indulged in speculative metaphysics to such an extent that his influence in England has to this day remained fairly limited. Through his writings and his lectures at Harvard, White-head inspired a group of disciples in America. For many, he ranks among the greatest Anglo-American metaphysicians of the twentieth century. Whereas a large number of Anglo-American philosophers abhorred speculative philosophy, Whitehead by contrast offered a comprehensive system of the universe. One reason his philosophy has been such anathema to many English and American analysts and positivists is the obfuscation they find in his metaphysics and his penchant for coining new technical terms. The selection *Speculative Philosophy*, reprinted below, is Chapter I of Whitehead's book *Process and Reality* (1929). It is perhaps the best statement of Whitehead's conception of the aims of speculative philosophy, and of the methods to be employed in building a metaphysical theory.

Whitehead's world view, with some qualifications, has appealed to a variety of thinkers: naturalistic metaphysicians (for its organismic approach), religious believers (for its sympathy to religious experience and its attempt to synthesize religion and science) and poets (for its Platonism and idealism). For Whitehead, the Newtonian concept of nature was in need of modification. He attacked the principles of "simple location" and "misplaced concretion," whereby bits of isolated matter and absolute space and time are abstracted and reified. Whitehead criticized the bifurcations of nature implicit in the mechanical world view, but he also attempted to modify aspects of Einstein's theory of relativity and to place them on more empirical foundations.

Many of Whitehead's critiques of scientific ideas were contained in three books published between 1919 and 1922, *An Enquiry Concerning the Principles of Natural Knowledge, The Concept of Nature,* and *The Principle of Relativity,* and in the first book he published in America, *Science and the Modern World* (1925). In these and in his later books, Whitehead was working toward a new cosmology, one which synthesized and made room for the sciences as well as for other aspects of human experience, including art and religion. The best description of his system is contained in his most ambitiously conceived work, *Process and Reality* (1929). Aspects of his system are also contained in *Adventures of Ideas* (1934), *Nature and Life* (1934), and *Modes of Thought* (1938). The two pieces reprinted below, *Nature Lifeless* and *Nature Alive,* offer excellent summaries of the main ideas of Whitehead's system, without excessively abstract terminology. In the first piece, Whitehead criticizes the limitations of the Newtonian universe, which was in his opinion devoid of life. In the second, we find a full statement of his view that nature is a domain of multiple actual occasions or events in process, each of which is an indivisible stretch of time, and that each appropriates to itself in a creative act everything else in the universe. For Whitehead organic life was fundamental to any metaphysical account of reality.

Although Whitehead was a speculative philosopher, much of his thought reflected the American scene, even pragmatism. In his influential work, *The Aims of Education* (1929), Whitehead maintained that education should be related to human purposes and attempt to achieve a kind of unity of life. Thus, Whitehead supported the characteristic American view that products of intellect should not be regarded as independent of life, but should seek to sustain and enhance it, and that in some sense the ultimate test of education is its relationship to actual living.

SPECULATIVE PHILOSOPHY [1]

SECTION I

. . . Speculative Philosophy is the endeavour to frame a coherent, logical, necessary system of general ideas in terms of which every element of our experience can be interpreted. By this notion of "interpretation" I mean that everything of which we are conscious, as enjoyed, perceived, willed, or thought, shall have the character of a

[1] From A. N. Whitehead, *Process and Reality: An Essay in Cosmology,* N. Y.: Macmillan, 1929, Chapter I, pp. 4–26.

particular instance of the general scheme. Thus the philosophical scheme should be coherent, logical, and, in respect to its interpretation, applicable and adequate. Here "applicable" means that some items of experience are thus interpretable, and "adequate" means that there are no items incapable of such interpretation.

"Coherence," as here employed, means that the fundamental ideas, in terms of which the scheme is developed, presuppose each other so that in isolation they are meaningless. This requirement does not mean that they are definable in terms of each other; it means that what is indefinable in one such notion cannot be abstracted from its relevance to the other notions. It is the ideal of speculative philosophy that its fundamental notions shall not seem capable of abstraction from each other. In other words, it is presupposed that no entity can be conceived in complete abstraction from the system of the universe, and that it is the business of speculative philosophy to exhibit this truth. This character is its coherence.

The term "logical" has its ordinary meaning, including "logical" consistency, or lack of contradiction, the definition of constructs in logical terms, the exemplification of general logical notions in specific instances, and the principles of inference. It will be observed that logical notions must themselves find their places in the scheme of philosophic notions.

It will also be noticed that this ideal of speculative philosophy has its rational side and its empirical side. The rational side is expressed by the terms "coherent" and "logical." The empirical side is expressed by the terms "applicable" and "adequate." But the two sides are bound together by clearing away an ambiguity which remains in the previous explanation of the term "adequate." The adequacy of the scheme over every item does not mean adequacy over such items as happen to have been considered. It means that the texture of observed experience, as illustrating the philosophic scheme, is such that all related experience must exhibit the same texture. Thus the philosophic scheme should be "necessary," in the sense of bearing in itself its own warrant of universality throughout all experience, provided that we confine ourselves to that which communicates with immediate matter of fact. But what does not so communicate is unknowable, and the unknowable is unknown;[2] and so this universality defined by "communication" can suffice.

This doctrine of necessity in universality means that there is an essence to the universe which forbids relationships beyond itself, as a violation of its rationality. Speculative philosophy seeks that essence.

[2] This doctrine is a paradox. Indulging in a species of false modesty, "cautious" philosophers undertake its definition.

Philosophers can never hope finally to formulate these metaphysical first principles. Weakness of insight and deficiencies of language stand in the way inexorably. Words and phrases must be stretched towards a generality foreign to their ordinary usage; and however such elements of language be stabilized as technicalities, they remain metaphors mutely appealing for an imaginative leap.

There is no first principle which is in itself unknowable, not to be captured by a flash of insight. But, putting aside the difficulties of language, deficiency in imaginative penetration forbids progress in any form other than that of an asymptotic approach to a scheme of principles, only definable in terms of the ideal which they should satisfy.

The difficulty has its seat in the empirical side of philosophy. Our datum is the actual world, including ourselves; and this actual world spreads itself for observation in the guise of the topic of our immediate experience. The elucidation of immediate experience is the sole justification for any thought; and the starting point for thought is the analytic observation of components of this experience. But we are not conscious of any clear-cut complete analysis of immediate experience, in terms of the various details which comprise its definiteness. We habitually observe by the method of difference. Sometimes we see an elephant, and sometimes we do not. The result is that an elephant, when present, is noticed. Facility of observation depends on the fact that the object observed is important when present, and sometimes is absent.

The metaphysical first principles can never fail of exemplification. We can never catch the actual world taking a holiday from their sway. Thus, for the discovery of metaphysics, the method of pinning down thought to the strict systematization of detailed discrimination, already effected by antecedent observation, breaks down. This collapse of the method of rigid empiricism is not confined to metaphysics. It occurs whenever we seek the larger generalities. In natural science this rigid method is the Baconian method of induction, a method which, if consistently pursued, would have left science where it found it. What Bacon omitted was the play of a free imagination, controlled by the requirements of coherence and logic. The true method of discovery is like the flight of an aeroplane. It starts from the ground of particular observation; it makes a flight in the thin air of imaginative generalization; and it again lands for renewed observation rendered acute by rational interpretation. The reason for the success of this method of imaginative rationalization is that, when the method of difference fails, factors which are constantly present may yet be observed under the influence of imaginative thought. Such thought supplies the differences which the direct observation lacks. It can even play with inconsistency; and can thus throw light on the consistent, and persistent, elements in experience by comparison with what in imagination is inconsistent with them. The negative judgment is the peak of mentality. But the conditions for the success of imaginative construction must be rigidly adhered to. In the first place, this construction must have its origin in the generalization of particular factors discerned in particular topics of human interest; for example, in physics, or in physiology, or in psychology, or in aesthetics, or in ethical beliefs, or in sociology, or in languages conceived as storehouses of human experience. In this way the prime requisite, that anyhow there shall be some important application, is secured. The success of the imaginative experiment is always to be tested by the applicability of its results beyond the restricted locus from which it originated. In default of such extended application, a generalization started from physics, for example, remains merely an alternative expression of notions applicable to physics. The partially successful philosophic generalization will, if derived from physics, find applications in fields of experience beyond physics. It will enlighten observation in those remote fields, so that general principles can be discerned as in process of illustration, which in the absence of the imaginative generalization are obscured by their persistent exemplification.

Thus the first requisite is to proceed by the method of generalization so that certainly there is some application; and the test of some success is application beyond the immediate origin. In other words, some synoptic vision has been gained.

In this description of philosophic method, the term "philosophic generalization" has meant "the utilization of specific notions, applying to a restricted group of facts, for the divination of the generic notions which apply to all facts."

In its use of this method natural science has shown a curious mixture of rationalism and irrationalism. Its prevalent tone of thought has been ardently rationalistic within its own borders, and dogmatically irrational beyond those borders. In practice such an attitude tends to become a dogmatic denial that there are any factors in the world not fully expressible in terms of its own primary notions devoid of further generalization. Such a denial is the self-denial of thought.

The second condition for the success of imaginative construction is unflinching pursuit of the two rationalistic ideals, coherence and logical perfection.

Logical perfection does not here require any detailed explanation. An example of its importance is afforded by the rôle of mathematics in the restricted field of natural science. The history of mathematics exhibits the generalization of special notions observed in particular instances. In any branches of mathematics, the notions presuppose each other. It is a remarkable characteristic of the history of thought that branches of mathematics developed under the pure imaginative impulse, thus controlled, finally receive their important application. Time may be wanted. Conic sections had to wait for eighteen hundred years. In more recent years, the theory of probability, the theory of tensors, the theory of matrices are cases in point.

The requirement of coherence is the great preservative of rationalistic sanity. But the validity of its criticism is not always admitted. If we consider philosophical controversies, we shall find that disputants tend to require coherence from their adversaries, and to grant dispensations to themselves. It has been remarked that a system of philosophy is never refuted; it is only abandoned. The reason is that logical contradictions, except as temporary slips of the mind— plentiful, though temporary—are the most gratuitous of errors; and usually they are trivial. Thus, after criticism, systems do not exhibit mere illogicalities. They suffer from inadequacy and incoherence. Failure to include some obvious elements of experience in the scope of the system is met by boldly denying the facts. Also while a philosophical system retains any charm of novelty, it enjoys a plenary indulgence for its failures in coherence. But after a system has acquired orthodoxy, and is taught with authority, it receives a sharper criticism. Its denials and its incoherences are found intolerable, and a reaction sets in.

Incoherence is the arbitrary disconnection of first principles. In modern philosophy Descartes' two kinds of substance, corporeal and mental, illustrate incoherence. There is, in Descartes' philosophy, no reason why there should not be a one-substance world, only corporeal, or a one-substance world, only mental. According to Descartes, a substantial individual "requires nothing but itself in order to exist." Thus this system makes a virtue of its incoherence. But on the other hand, the facts seem connected, while Descartes' system does not; for example, in the treatment of the body-mind problem. The Cartesian system obviously says something that is true. But its notions are too abstract to penetrate into the nature of things. . . .

SECTION III

. . . In its turn every philosophy will suffer a deposition. But the bundle of philosophic systems expresses a variety of general truths about the universe, awaiting co-ordination and assignment of their various spheres of validity. Such progress in co-ordination is provided by the advance of philosophy; and in this sense philosophy has advanced from Plato onwards. According to this account of the achievement of rationalism, the chief error in philosophy is overstatement. The aim at generalization is sound, but the estimate of success is exaggerated. There are two main forms of such overstatement. One form is what I have termed elsewhere,[3] the "fallacy of misplaced concreteness." This fallacy consists in neglecting the degree of abstraction involved when an actual entity is considered merely so far as it exemplifies certain categories of thought. There are aspects of actualities which are simply ignored so long as we restrict thought to these categories. Thus the success of a philosophy is to be measured by its comparative avoidance of this fallacy, when thought is restricted within its categories.

The other form of overstatement consists in a false estimate of logical procedure in respect to certainty, and in respect to premises. Philosophy has been haunted by the unfortunate notion that its method is dogmatically to indicate premises which are severally clear, distinct, and certain; and to erect upon those premises a deductive system of thought.

But the accurate expression of the final generalities is the goal of discussion and not its origin. Philosophy has been misled by the example of mathematics; and even in mathematics the statement of the ultimate logical principles is beset with difficulties, as yet insuperable.[4] The verification of a rationalistic scheme is to be sought in its general success, and not in the peculiar certainty, or initial clarity, of its first principles. In this connection the misuse of the *ex absurdo* argument has to be noted; much philosophical reasoning is vitiated by it. The only logical conclusion to be drawn, when a contradiction issues from a train of reasoning, is that at least one of the premises involved in the inference is false. It is rashly assumed without further question that the peccant premise can at once be located. In mathematics this assumption is often justified, and philosophers have been thereby misled. But in the absence of a well-defined categoreal scheme of entities, issuing in a satisfactory metaphysical system, every premise in a philosophical argument is under suspicion.

Philosophy will not regain its proper status until the gradual elaboration of categoreal schemes, definitely stated at each stage of prog-

---

[3] Cf. *Science and the Modern World*, Ch. III.

[4] Cf. *Principia Mathematica*, by Bertrand Russell and A. N. Whitehead, Vol. I, Introduction and Introduction to the Second Edition. These introductory discussions are practically due to Russell, and in the second edition wholly so.

ress, is recognized as its proper objective. There may be rival schemes, inconsistent among themselves; each with its own merits and its own failures. It will then be the purpose of research to conciliate the differences. Metaphysical categories are not dogmatic statements of the obvious; they are tentative formulations of the ultimate generalities.

If we consider any scheme of philosophic categories as one complex assertion, and apply to it the logician's alternative, true or false, the answer must be that the scheme is false. The same answer must be given to a like question respecting the existing formulated principles of any science.

The scheme is true with unformulated qualifications, exceptions, limitations, and new interpretations in terms of more general notions. We do not yet know how to recast the scheme into a logical truth. But the scheme is a matrix from which true propositions applicable to particular circumstances can be derived. We can at present only trust our trained instincts as to the discrimination of the circumstances in respect to which the scheme is valid.

The use of such a matrix is to argue from it boldly and with rigid logic. The scheme should therefore be stated with the utmost precision and definiteness, to allow of such argumentation. The conclusion of the argument should then be confronted with circumstances to which it should apply.

The primary advantage thus gained is that experience is not interrogated with the benumbing repression of common sense. The observation acquires an enhanced penetration by reason of the expectation evoked by the conclusion of the argument. The outcome from this procedure takes one of three forms: (i) the conclusion may agree with the observed facts; (ii) the conclusion may exhibit general agreement, with disagreement in detail; (iii) the conclusion may be in complete disagreement in the facts.

In the first case, the facts are known with more adequacy and the applicability of the system to the world has been elucidated. In the second case, criticisms of the observation of the facts and of the details of the scheme are both required. The history of thought shows that false interpretations of observed facts enter into the records of their observation. Thus both theory, and received notions as to fact, are in doubt. In the third case a fundamental reorganization of theory is required either by way of limiting it to some special province, or by way of entire abandonment of its main categories of thought.

After the initial basis of a rational life, with a civilized language, has been laid, all productive thought has proceeded either by the poetic insight of artists, or by the imaginative elaboration of schemes of thought capable of utilization as logical premises. In some measure or other, progress is always a transcendence of what is obvious.

Rationalism never shakes off its status of an experimental adventure. The combined influences of mathematics and religion, which have so greatly contributed to the rise of philosophy, have also had the unfortunate effect of yoking it with static dogmatism. Rationalism is an adventure in the clarification of thought, progressive and never final. But it is an adventure in which even partial success has importance.

SECTION IV

The field of a special science is confined to one genus of facts, in the sense that no statements are made respecting facts which lie outside that genus. The very circumstance that a science has naturally arisen concerning a set of facts secures that facts of that type have definite relations among themselves which are very obvious to all mankind. The common obviousness of things arises when their explicit apprehension carries immediate importance for purposes of survival, or of enjoyment—that is to say, for purposes of "being" and of "well-being." Elements in human experience, singled out in this way, are those elements concerning which language is copious and, within its limits, precise. The special sciences, therefore, deal with topics which lie open to easy inspection and are readily expressed by words.

The study of philosophy is a voyage towards the larger generalities. For this reason in the infancy of science, when the main stress lay in the discovery of the most general ideas usefully applicable to the subject-matter in question, philosophy was not sharply distinguished from science. To this day, a new science with any substantial novelty in its notions is considered to be in some way peculiarly philosophical. In their later stages, apart from occasional disturbances, most sciences accept without question the general notions in terms of which they develop. The main stress is laid on the adjustment and the direct verification of more special statements. In such periods scientists repudiate philosophy; Newton, justly satisfied with his physical principles, disclaimed metaphysics.

The fate of Newtonian physics warns us that there is a development in scientific first principles, and that their original forms can only be saved by interpretations of meaning and limitations of their field of application—interpretations and limitations unsuspected during the first period of successful employment. One chapter in the history of culture is concerned with the growth of generalities. In such a chapter it is seen that the older generalities, like the older hills, are worn down and diminished in height, surpassed by younger rivals.

Thus one aim of philosophy is to challenge the half-truths constituting the scientific first principles. The systematization of knowledge cannot be conducted in watertight compartments. All general truths condition each other; and the limits of their application cannot be adequately defined apart from their correlation by yet wider generalities. The criticism of principles must chiefly take the form of determining the proper meanings to be assigned to the fundamental notions of the various sciences, when these notions are considered in respect to their status relatively to each other. The determination of this status requires a generality transcending any special subject-matter.

If we may trust the Pythagorean tradition, the rise of European philosophy was largely promoted by the development of mathematics into a science of abstract generality. But in its subsequent development the method of philosophy has also been vitiated by the example of mathematics. The primary method of mathematics is deduction; the primary method of philosophy is descriptive generalization. Under the influence of mathematics, deduction has been foisted onto philosophy as its standard method, instead of taking its true place as an essential auxiliary mode of verification whereby to test the scope of generalities. This misapprehension of philosophic method has veiled the very considerable success of philosophy in providing generic notions which add lucidity to our apprehension of the facts of experience. The depositions of Plato, Aristotle, Thomas Aquinas, Descartes, Spinoza, Leibnitz, Locke, Berkeley, Hume, Kant, Hegel, merely mean that ideas which these men introduced into the philosophic tradition must be construed with limitations, adaptations, and inversions, either unknown to them, or even explicitly repudiated by them. A new idea introduces a new alternative; and we are not less indebted to a thinker when we adopt the alternative which he discarded. Philosophy never reverts to its old position after the shock of a great philosopher.

SECTION V

Every science must devise its own instruments. The tool required for philosophy is language. Thus philosophy redesigns language in the same way that, in a physical science, pre-existing appliances are redesigned. It is exactly at this point that the appeal to facts is a difficult operation. This appeal is not solely to the expression of the facts in current verbal statements. The adequacy of such sentences

is the main question at issue. It is true that the general agreement
of mankind as to experienced facts is best expressed in language.
But the language of literature breaks down precisely at the task of
expressing in explicit form the larger generalities—the very generalities which metaphysics seeks to express.

The point is that every proposition refers to a universe exhibiting
some general systematic metaphysical character. Apart from this
background, the separate entities which go to form the proposition,
and the proposition as a whole, are without determinate character.
Nothing has been defined, because every definite entity requires a
systematic universe to supply its requisite status. Thus every proposition proposing a fact must, in its complete analysis, propose the
general character of the universe required for that fact. There are
no self-sustained facts, floating in nonentity. This doctrine, of the
impossibility of tearing a proposition from its systematic context in
the actual world, is a direct consequence of the fourth and the
twentieth of the fundamental categoreal explanations which we shall
be engaged in expanding and illustrating. A proposition can embody
partial truth because it only demands a certain type of systematic
environment, which is presupposed in its meaning. It does not refer
to the universe in all its detail.

One practical aim of metaphysics is the accurate analysis of propositions; not merely of metaphysical propositions, but of quite ordinary propositions such as "There is beef for dinner today," and
"Socrates is mortal." The one genus of facts which constitutes the field
of some special science requires some common metaphysical presupposition respecting the universe. It is merely credulous to accept
verbal phrases as adequate statements of propositions. The distinction between verbal phrases and complete propositions is one of the
reasons why the logicians' rigid alternative, "true or false," is so largely
irrelevant for the pursuit of knowledge. . . .

For example, the word "Socrates," referring to the philosopher, in
one sentence may stand for an entity presupposing a more closely
defined background than the word "Socrates," with the same reference, in another sentence. The word "mortal" affords an analogous
possibility. A precise language must await a completed metaphysical
knowledge.

The technical language of philosophy represents attempts of various schools of thought to obtain explicit expression of general ideas
presupposed by the facts of experience. It follows that any novelty
in metaphysical doctrines exhibits some measure of disagreement
with statements of the facts to be found in current philosophical
literature. The extent of disagreement measures the extent of metaphysical divergence. It is, therefore, no valid criticism on one meta-

physical school to point out that its doctrines do not follow from the verbal expression of the facts accepted by another school. The whole contention is that the doctrines in question supply a closer approach to fully expressed propositions.

The truth itself is nothing else than how the composite natures of the organic actualities of the world obtain adequate representation in the divine nature. Such representations compose the "consequent nature" of God, which evolves in its relationship to the evolving world without derogation to the eternal completion of its primordial conceptual nature. In this way the "ontological principle" is maintained—since there can be no determinate truth, correlating impartially the partial experiences of many actual entities, apart from one actual entity to which it can be referred. . . .

Whatever is found in "practice" must lie within the scope of the metaphysical description. When the description fails to include the "practice," the metaphysics is inadequate and requires revision. There can be no appeal to practice to supplement metaphysics, so long as we remain contented with our metaphysical doctrines. Metaphysics is nothing but the description of the generalities which apply to all the details of practice.

No metaphysical system can hope entirely to satisfy these pragmatic tests. At the best such a system will remain only an approximation to the general truths which are sought. In particular, there are no precisely stated axiomatic certainties from which to start. There is not even the language in which to frame them. The only possible procedure is to start from verbal expressions which, when taken by themselves with the current meaning of their words, are ill-defined and ambiguous. These are not premises to be immediately reasoned from apart from elucidation by further discussion; they are endeavours to state general principles which will be exemplified in the subsequent description of the facts of experience. This subsequent elaboration should elucidate the meanings to be assigned to the words and phrases employed. Such meanings are incapable of accurate apprehension apart from a correspondingly accurate apprehension of the metaphysical background which the universe provides for them. But no language can be anything but elliptical, requiring a leap of the imagination to understand its meaning in its relevance to immediate experience. The position of metaphysics in the development of culture cannot be understood without remembering that no verbal statement is the adequate expression of a proposition.

An old established metaphysical system gains a false air of adequate precision from the fact that its words and phrases have passed into current literature. Thus propositions expressed in its language are more easily correlated to our flitting intuitions into metaphysical truth. When we trust these verbal statements and argue as though they adequately analysed meaning, we are led into difficulties which take the shape of negations of what in practice is presupposed. But when they are proposed as first principles they assume an unmerited air of sober obviousness. Their defect is that the true propositions which they do express lose their fundamental character when subjected to adequate expression. For example consider the type of propositions such as "The grass is green," and "The whale is big." This subject-predicate form of statement seems so simple, leading straight to a metaphysical first principle; and yet in these examples it conceals such complex, diverse meanings.

SECTION VI

It has been an objection to speculative philosophy that it is overambitious. Rationalism, it is admitted, is the method by which advance is made within the limits of particular sciences. It is, however, held that this limited success must not encourage attempts to frame ambitious schemes expressive of the general nature of things.

One alleged justification of this criticism is ill-success: European thought is represented as littered with metaphysical systems, abandoned and unreconciled.

Such an assertion tacitly fastens upon philosophy the old dogmatic test. The same criterion would fasten ill-success upon science. We no more retain the physics of the seventeenth century than we do the Cartesian philosophy of that century. Yet within limits, both systems express important truths. Also we are beginning to understand the wider categories which define their limits of correct application. Of course, in that century, dogmatic views held sway; so that the validity both of the physical notions, and of the Cartesian notions, was misconceived. Mankind never quite knows what it is after. When we survey the history of thought, and likewise the history of practice, we find that one idea after another is tried out, its limitations defined, and its core of truth elicited. In application to the instinct for the intellectual adventures demanded by particular epochs, there is much truth in Augustine's rhetorical phrase, *Securus judicat orbis terrarum*. At the very least, men do what they can in the way of systematization, and in the event achieve something. The proper test if not that of finality, but of progress.

But the main objection, dating from the sixteenth century and receiving final expression from Francis Bacon, is the uselessness of philosophic speculation. The position taken by this objection is that we ought to describe detailed matter of fact, and elicit the laws with a generality strictly limited to the systematization of these described details. General interpretation, it is held, has no bearing upon this procedure; and thus any system of general interpretation, be it true or false, remains intrinsically barren. Unfortunately for this objection, there are no brute, self-contained matters of fact, capable of being understood apart from interpretation as an element in a system. Whenever we attempt to express the matter of immediate experience, we find that its understanding leads us beyond itself, to its contemporaries, to its past, to its future, and to the universals in terms of which its definiteness is exhibited. But such universals, by their very character of universality, embody the potentiality of other facts with variant types of definiteness. Thus the understanding of the immediate brute fact requires its metaphysical interpretation as an item in a world with some systematic relation to it. When thought comes upon the scene, it finds the interpretations as matters of practice. Philosophy does not initiate interpretations. Its search for a rationalistic scheme is the search for more adequate criticism, and for more adequate justification, of the interpretations which we perforce employ. Our habitual experience is a complex of failure and success in the enterprise of interpretation. If we desire a record of uninterpreted experience, we must ask a stone to record its autobiography. Every scientific memoir in its record of the "facts" is shot through and through with interpretation. The methodology of rational interpretation is the product of the fitful vagueness of consciousness. Elements which shine with immediate distinctness, in some circumstances, retire into penumbral shadow in other circumstances, and into black darkness on other occasions. And yet all occasions proclaim themselves as actualities within the flux of a solid world, demanding a unity of interpretation.

Philosophy is the self-correction by consciousness of its own initial excess of subjectivity. Each actual occasion contributes to the circumstances of its origin additional formative elements deepening its own peculiar individuality. Consciousness is only the last and greatest of such elements by which the selective character of the individual obscures the external totality from which it originates and which it embodies. An actual individual, of such higher grade, has truck with the totality of things by reason of its sheer actuality; but it has attained its individual depth of being by a selective emphasis limited to its own purposes. The task of philosophy is to recover the totality obscured by the selection. It replaces in rational experience what has been submerged in the higher sensitive experience and has been sunk yet deeper by the initial operations of consciousness itself. The selectiveness of individual experience is moral so far as it conforms to the balance of importance disclosed in the rational vision; and conversely the conversion of the intellectual insight into an emotional force corrects the sensitive experience in the direction of morality. The correction is in proportion to the rationality of the insight.

Morality of outlook is inseparably conjoined with generality of outlook. The antithesis between the general good and the individual interest can be abolished only when the individual is such that its interest is the general good, thus exemplifying the loss of the minor intensities in order to find them again with finer composition in a wider sweep of interest.

Philosophy frees itself from the taint of ineffectiveness by its close relations with religion and with science, natural and sociological. It attains its chief importance by fusing the two, namely, religion and science, into one rational scheme of thought. Religion should connect the rational generality of philosophy with the emotions and purposes springing out of existence in a particular society, in a particular epoch, and conditioned by particular antecedents. Religion is the translation of general ideas into particular thoughts, particular emotions, and particular purposes; it is directed to the end of stretching individual interest beyond its self-defeating particularity. Philosophy finds religion, and modifies it; and conversely religion is among the data of experience which philosophy must weave into its own scheme. Religion is an ultimate craving to infuse into the insistent particularity of emotion that non-temporal generality which primarily belongs to conceptual thought alone. In the higher organisms the differences of tempo between the mere emotions and the conceptual experiences produce a life-tedium, unless this supreme fusion has been effected. The two sides of the organism require a reconciliation in which emotional experiences illustrate a conceptual justification, and conceptual experiences find an emotional illustration.

This demand for an intellectual justification of brute experience has also been the motive power in the advance of European science. In this sense scientific interest is only a variant form of religious interest. Any survey of the scientific devotion to "truth," as an ideal, will confirm this statement. There is, however, a grave divergence between science and religion in respect to the phases of individual experience with which they are concerned. Religion is centered upon the harmony of rational thought with the sensitive reaction to the percepta from which experience originates. Science is concerned with the harmony of rational thought with the percepta themselves. When science deals with emotions, the emotions in question are percepta and not immediate passions—other people's emotion and not our own; at least our own in recollection, and not in immediacy. Religion deals with the formation of the experiencing subject; whereas science deals with the objects, which are the data forming the primary phase in this experience. The subject originates from, and amid, given conditions; science conciliates thought with this primary matter of fact; and religion conciliates the thought involved in the process with the sensitive reaction involved in that same process. The process is nothing else than the experiencing subject itself. In this explanation it is presumed that an experiencing subject is one occasion of sensitive reaction to an actual world. Science finds religious experiences among its percepta; and religion finds scientific concepts among the conceptual experiences to be fused with particular sensitive reactions.

The conclusion of this discussion is, first, the assertion of the old doctrine that breadth of thought reacting with intensity of sensitive experience stands out as an ultimate claim of existence; secondly, the assertion that empirically the development of self-justifying thoughts has been achieved by the complex process of generalizing from particular topics, of imaginatively schematizing the generalizations, and finally by renewed comparison of the imagined scheme with the direct experience to which it should apply.

There is no justification for checking generalization at any particular stage. Each phase of generalization exhibits its own peculiar simplicities which stand out just at that stage, and at no other stage. There are simplicities connected with the motion of a bar of steel which are obscured if we refuse to abstract from the individual molecules; and there are certain simplicities concerning the behavior of men which are obscured if we refuse to abstract from the individual peculiarities of particular specimens. In the same way, there are certain general truths, about the actual things in the common world of activity, which will be obscured when attention is confined to some particular detailed mode of considering them. These general truths, involved in the meaning of every particular notion respecting the actions of things, are the subject matter for speculative philosophy.

Philosophy destroys its usefulness when it indulges in brilliant feats of explaining away. It is then trespassing with the wrong equipment upon the field of particular sciences. Its ultimate appeal is to the general consciousness of what in practice we experience. Whatever thread of presupposition characterizes social expression throughout the various epochs of rational society, must find its place in philosophic theory. Speculative boldness must be balanced by complete humility before logic, and before fact. It is a disease of philosophy when it is neither bold nor humble, but merely a reflection of the temperamental presuppositions of exceptional personalities.

Analogously, we do not trust any recasting of scientific theory depending upon a single performance of an aberrant experiment, unrepeated. The ultimate test is always widespread, recurrent experience;

and the more general the rationalistic scheme, the more important is this final appeal.

The useful function of philosophy is to promote the most general systematization of civilized thought. There is a constant reaction between specialism and common sense. It is the part of the special sciences to modify common sense. Philosophy is the welding of imagination and common sense into a restraint upon specialists, and also into an enlargement of their imaginations. By providing the generic notions philosophy should make it easier to conceive the infinite variety of specific instances which rest unrealized in the womb of nature.

NATURE LIFELESS [4a]

Philosophy is the product of wonder. The effort after the general characterization of the world around us is the romance of human thought. The correct statement seems so easy, so obvious, and yet it is always eluding us. We inherit the traditional doctrine: we can detect the oversights, the superstitions, the rash generalizations of the past ages. We know so well what we mean and yet we remain so curiously uncertain about the formulation of any detail of our knowledge. This word "detail" lies at the heart of the whole difficulty. You cannot talk vaguely about Nature in general. We must fix upon details within nature and discuss their essences and their types of inter-connection. The world around is complex, composed of details. We have to settle upon the primary types of detail in terms of which we endeavour to express our understanding of Nature. We have to analyse and to abstract, and to understand the natural status of our abstractions. At first sight there are sharp-cut classes within which we can sort the various types of things and characters of things which we find in Nature. Every age manages to find modes of classification which seem fundamental starting points for the researches of the special sciences. Each succeeding age discovers that the primary classifications of its predecessors will not work. In this way a doubt is thrown upon all formulations of Laws of Nature which assume these classifications as firm starting points. A problem arises. Philosophy is the search for the solution.

Our first step must be to define the term "nature" as here used.

[4a] From A. N. Whitehead, *Modes of Thought*, N. Y.: Macmillan, 1938, Lecture VII.

"Nature," in these chapters, means the world as interpreted by reliance on clear and distinct sensory experiences, visual, auditory, and tactile. Obviously, such an interpretation is of the highest importance for human understanding. These final chapters are concerned with the question,—How far does it take us?

For example, we can conceive nature as composed of permanent things, namely bits of matter, moving about in space which otherwise is empty. This way of thinking about nature has an obvious consonance with common-sense observation. There are chairs, tables, bits of rock, oceans, animal bodies, vegetable bodies, planets, and suns. The enduring self-identity of a house, of a farm, of an animal body, is a presupposition of social intercourse. It is assumed in legal theory. It lies at the base of all literature. A bit of matter is thus conceived as a passive fact, an individual reality which is the same at an instant, or throughout a second, an hour, or a year. Such a material, individual reality supports its various qualifications such as shape, locomotion, colour, or smell, etc. The occurrences of nature consist in the changes in these qualifications, and more particularly in the changes of motion. The connection between such bits of matter consists purely of spatial relations. Thus the importance of motion arises from its change of the sole mode of interconnection of material things. Mankind then proceeds to discuss these spatial relations and discovers Geometry. The geometrical character of space is conceived as the one way in which Nature imposes determinate relations upon all bits of matter which are the sole occupants of space. In itself, Space is conceived as unchanging from Eternity to Eternity, and as homogeneous from infinity to infinity. Thus we compose a straightforward characterization of Nature, which is consonant to common sense, and can be verified at each moment of our existence. We sit for hours in the same chair, in the same house, with the same animal body. The dimensions of the room are defined by its spatial relations. There are colours, sounds, scents, partly abiding and partly changing. Also the major facts of change are defined by locomotion of the animal bodies and of the inorganic furniture. Within this general concept of Nature, there have somehow to be interwoven the further concepts of Life and Mind.

I have been endeavouring to sketch the general common-sense notion of the Universe, which about the beginning of the sixteenth century, say in the year 1500 A.D., was in process of formation among the more progressive thinkers of the European population. It was partly an inheritance from Greek thought and from mediaeval thought. Partly it was based on the deliverance of direct observation, at any moment verified in the world around us. It was the presupposed support supplying the terms in which the answers to all further questions were found. Among these further questions, the most fundamental and the most obvious are those concerning the laws of locomotion, the meaning of life, the meaning of mentality, and the interrelations of matter, life, and mentality. When we examine the procedures of the great men in the sixteenth and seventeenth centuries, we find them presupposing this general common-sense notion of the Universe, and endeavouring to answer all questions in the terms it supplies.

I suggest that there can be no doubt but that this general notion expresses large, all-pervading truths about the world around us. The only question is as to how fundamental these truths may be. In other words, we have to ask what large features of the Universe cannot be expressed in these terms. We have also to ask whether we cannot find some other set of notions which will explain the importance of this common-sense notion, and will also explain its relations to those other features ignored by the common-sense notion.

When we survey the subsequent course of scientific thought throughout the seventeenth century up to the present day, two curious facts emerge. In the first place, the development of natural science has gradually discarded every single feature of the original common-sense notion. Nothing whatever remains of it, considered as expressing the primary features in terms of which the Universe is to be interpreted. The obvious common-sense notion has been entirely destroyed, so far as concerns its function as the basis for all interpretation. One by one, every item has been de-throned.

There is a second characteristic of subsequent thought which is equally prominent. This common-sense notion still reigns supreme in the work-a-day life of mankind. It dominates the market-place, the playgrounds, the Law Courts, and in fact the whole sociological intercourse of mankind. It is supreme in literature and is assumed in all the humanistic sciences. Thus the science of nature stands opposed to the presuppositions of humanism. Where some conciliation is attempted, it often assumes some sort of mysticism. But in general there is no conciliation.

Indeed, even when we confine attention to natural science, no special science ever is grounded upon the conciliation of presuppositions belonging to all the various sciences of nature. Each science confines itself to a fragment of the evidence and weaves its theories in terms of notions suggested by that fragment. Such a procedure is necessary by reason of the limitations of human ability. But its dangers should always be kept in mind. For example, the increasing departmentalization of universities during the last hundred years, however necessary for administrative purposes, tends to trivialize the mentality of the teaching profession. The result of this effective survival of two ways of thought is a patchwork procedure.

Presuppositions from the two points of view are interwoven sporadically. Every special science has to assume results from other sciences. For example, biology presupposes physics. It will usually be the case that these loans from one specialism to another really belong to the state of science thirty or forty years earlier. The presuppositions of the physics of my boyhood are today powerful influences in the mentality of physiologists. Indeed we do not need even to bring in the physiologists. The presuppositions of yesterday's physics remain in the minds of physicists, although their explicit doctrines taken in detail deny them. . . .

The state of modern thought is that every single item in this general doctrine is denied, but that the general conclusions from the doctrine as a whole are tenaciously retained. The result is a complete muddle in scientific thought, in philosophic cosmology, and in epistemology. But any doctrine which does not implicitly presuppose this point of view is assailed as unintelligible.

The first item to be abandoned was the set of qualifications which we distinguish in sense-perception, namely colour, sound, scent, and analogous qualifications. The transmission theories for light and sound introduced the doctrine of secondary qualities. The colour and the sound were no longer in nature. They are the mental reactions of the percipient to internal bodily locomotions. Thus nature is left with bits of matter, qualified by mass, spatial relations, and the change of such relations.

This loss of the secondary qualities was a severe restriction to Nature. For its value to the percipient was reduced to its function as a mere agent of excitement. Also the derived mental excitement was not primarily concerned with factors in nature. The colours and the sounds were secondary factors supplied by the mental reaction. But the curious fact remained that these secondary factors are perceived as related by the spatiality which is the grand substratum of nature. Hume was, I think, the first philosopher who explicitly pointed out this curious hybrid character of our perceptions, according to the current doctrine of the perception of secondary qualities. Though of course this hybrid characteristic was tacitly presupposed by Locke when he conceived colour as a *secondary* quality of the things in Nature. I believe that any cosmological doctrine which is faithful to the facts has to admit this artificial character of sense-perception. Namely, when we perceive the red rose we are associating our enjoyment of red derived from one source with our enjoyment of a spatial region derived from another source. The conclusion that I draw is that sense-perception for all its practical importance is very superficial in its disclosure of the nature of things. This conclusion is supported by the character of delusiveness—that is, of illusion—which persistently clings to sense-perception. For example, our perception of stars which years ago may have vanished, our perceptions of images in mirrors or by refraction, our double vision, our visions under the influence of drugs. My quarrel with modern Epistemology concerns its exclusive stress upon sense-perception for the provision of data respecting Nature. Sense-perception does not provide the data in terms of which we interpret it.

This conclusion that pure sense-perception does not provide the data for its own interpretation was the great discovery embodied in Hume's philosophy. This discovery is the reason why Hume's *Treatise* will remain as the irrefutable basis for all subsequent philosophic thought.

Another item in the common-sense doctrine concerns empty space and locomotion. In the first place, the transmission of light and sound shows that space apparently empty is the theatre of activities which we do not directly perceive. This conclusion was explained by the supposition of types of subtle matter, namely the ether, which we cannot directly perceive. In the second place, this conclusion, and the obvious behaviour of gross ordinary matter, show us that the motions of matter are in some way conditioned by the spatial relations of material bodies to each other. It was here that Newton supplied the great synthesis upon which science was based for more than two centuries. Newton's laws of motion provided a skeleton framework within which more particular laws for the inter-connection of bodily motions could be inserted. He also supplied one example of such a particular law in his great law of gravitation, which depended upon mutual distances.

Newton's methodology for physics was an overwhelming success. But the forces which he introduced left Nature still without meaning or value. In the essence of a material body—in its mass, motion, and shape—there was no reason for the law of gravitation. Even if the particular forces could be conceived as the accidents of a cosmic epoch, there was no reason in the Newtonian concepts of mass and motion why material bodies should be connected by any stress between them. Yet the notion of stresses, as essential connections between bodies, was a fundamental factor in the Newtonian concept of nature. What Newton left for empirical investigation was the determination of the particular stresses now existing. In this determination he made a magnificent beginning by isolating the stresses indicated by his law of gravitation. But he left no hint, why in the nature of things there should be any stresses at all. The arbitrary motions of the bodies were thus explained by the arbitrary stresses between material bodies, conjoined with their spatiality, their mass, and their initial states of motion. By introducing stresses—in particular the law of gravitation—instead of the welter of detailed transformations of motion, he greatly increased the systematic aspect of nature. But he left all the factors of the system—more particularly, mass and stress—in the position of detached facts devoid of any reason for their compresence. He thus illustrated a great philosophic truth, that a dead nature can give no reasons. All ultimate reasons are in terms of aim at value. A dead nature aims at nothing. It is the essence of life that it exists for its own sake, as the intrinsic reaping of value.

Thus for Newtonians, Nature yielded no reasons: it could yield no reasons. Combining Newton and Hume we obtain a barren concept, namely a field of perception devoid of any data for its own interpretation, and a system of interpretation, devoid of any reason for the concurrence of its factors. It is this situation that modern philosophy from Kant onwards has in its various ways sought to render intelligible. My own belief is that this situation is a *reductio ad absurdum*, and should not be accepted as the basis for philosophic speculation. Kant was the first philosopher who in this way combined Newton and Hume. He accepted them both, and his three Critiques were his endeavour to render intelligible this Hume-Newton situation. But the Hume-Newton situation is the primary presupposition for all modern philosophic thought. Any endeavour to go behind it is, in philosophic discussions, almost angrily rejected as unintelligible.

My aim in these lectures is briefly to point out how both Newton's contribution and Hume's contribution are, each in their way, gravely defective. They are right as far as they go. But they omit those aspects of the Universe as experienced, and of our modes of experiencing, which jointly lead to the more penetrating ways of understanding. . . . The Hume-Newton interpretation omits our intuitive modes of understanding.

I now pass on to the influence of modern science in discrediting the remaining items of the primary common-sense notion with which science in the sixteenth century started its career. But in the present-day reconstruction of physics fragments of the Newtonian concepts are stubbornly retained. The result is to reduce modern physics to a sort of mystic chant over an unintelligible Universe. This chant has the exact merits of the old magic ceremonies which flourished in ancient Mesopotamia and later in Europe. One of the earliest fragments of writing which has survived is a report from a Babylonian astrologer to the King, stating the favourable days to turn cattle into the fields, as deduced by his observations of the stars. This mystic relation of observation, theory, and practice, is exactly the present position of science in modern life, according to the prevalent scientific philosophy.

The notion of empty space, the mere vehicle of spatial interconnections, has been eliminated from recent science. The whole spatial universe is a field of force, or in other words, a field of incessant activity. The mathematical formulae of physics express the mathematical relations realized in this activity.

The unexpected result has been the elimination of bits of matter, as the self-identical supports for physical properties. . . .

Matter has been identified with energy, and energy is sheer activity; the passive substratum composed of self-identical enduring bits of matter has been abandoned, so far as concerns any fundamental description. Obviously this notion expresses an important derivative fact. But it has ceased to be the presupposed basis of theory. The modern point of view is expressed in terms of energy, activity, and the vibratory differentiations of space-time. Any local agitation shakes the whole universe. The distant effects are minute, but they are there. The concept of matter presupposed simple location. Each bit of matter was self-contained, localized in a region with a passive, static network of spatial relations, entwined in a uniform relational system from infinity to infinity and from eternity to eternity. But in the modern concept the group of agitations which we term matter is fused into its environment. There is no possibility of a detached, self-contained local existence. The environment enters into the nature of each thing. Some elements in the nature of a complete set of agitations may remain stable as those agitations are propelled through a changing environment. But such stability is only the case in a general, average way. This average fact is the reason why we find the same chair, the same rock, and the same planet, enduring for days, or for centuries, or for millions of years. In this average fact the time-factor takes the aspect of endurance, and change is a detail. The fundamental fact, according to the physics of the present day, is that the environment with its peculiarities seeps into the group-agitation which we term matter, and the group-agitations extend their character to the environment. In truth, the notion of the self-contained particle of matter, self-sufficient with its local habitation, is an abstraction. Now an abstraction is nothing else than the omission of part of the truth. The abstraction is well-founded when the conclusions drawn from it are not vitiated by the omitted truth.

This general deduction from the modern doctrine of physics vitiates many conclusions drawn from the applications of physics to other sciences, such as physiology, or even such as physics itself. For example, when geneticists conceive genes as the determinants of heredity. The analogy of the old concept of matter sometimes leads them to ignore the influence of the particular animal body in which they are functioning. They presuppose that a pellet of matter remains in all respects self-identical whatever be its changes of environment. So far as modern physics is concerned, any characteristics may, or may not, effect changes in the genes, changes which are as important in certain respects, though not in others. Thus no *a priori* argument as to the inheritance of characters can be drawn from the mere doctrine of genes. In fact recently physiologists have found that genes are modified in some respects by their environment. The presuppositions of the old common-sense view survive, even when the view itself has been abandoned as a fundamental description.

This survival of fragments of older doctrines is also exemplified in the modern use of the term space-time. The notion of space with its geometry is strictly coördinated to the notion of material bodies with simple location in space. A bit of matter is then conceived as self-sufficient with the simple location of the region which it occupies. It is just there, in that region where it is; and it can be described without reference to the goings-on in any other region of space. The empty space is the substratum for the passive geometrical relationships between material bodies. . . .

The new view is entirely different. The fundamental concepts are activity and process. Nature is divisible and thus extensive. But any division, including some activities and excluding others, also severs the patterns of process which extend beyond all boundaries. The mathematical formulae indicate a logical completeness about such patterns, a completeness which boundaries destroy. For example, half a wave tells only half the story. The notion of self-sufficient isolation is not exemplified in modern physics. There are no essentially self-contained activities within limited regions. These passive geometrical relationships between substrata passively occupying regions have passed out of the picture. Nature is a theatre for the interrelations of activities. All things change, the activities and their inter-relations. To this new concept, the notion of space with its passive, systematic, geometric relationship is entirely inappropriate. The fashionable notion that the new physics has reduced all physical laws to the statement of geometrical relations is quite ridiculous. It has done the opposite. In the place of the Aristotelian notion of the procession of forms, it has substituted the notion of the forms of process. It has thus swept away space and matter, and has substituted the study of the internal relations within a complex state of activity. This complex state is in one sense a unity. There is the whole universe of physical action extending to the remotest star-cluster. In another sense it is divisible into parts. We can trace interrelations within a selected group of activities, and ignore all other activities. By such an abstraction, we shall fail to explain those internal activities which are affected by changes in the external system which has been ignored. Also, in any fundamental sense, we shall fail to understand the retained activities. For these activities will depend upon a comparatively unchanging systematic environment.

In all discussions of nature we must remember the differences of scale, and in particular the differences of time-span. We are apt to take modes of observable functioning of the human body as setting an absolute scale. It is extremely rash to extend conclusions derived from observation far beyond the scale of magnitude to which observation was confined. For example, to exhibit apparent absence of change within a second of time tells nothing as to the change within a thousand years. Also no apparent change within a thousand years tells anything as to a million years; and no apparent change within a million years tells anything about a million million years. We can extend this progression indefinitely. There is no absolute standard of magnitude. Any term in this progression is large compared to its predecessor and is small compared to its successor.

Again, all special sciences presuppose certain fundamental types of things. Here I am using the word "thing" in its most general sense, which can include activities, colours and other sensa, and values. In this sense, "thing" is whatever we can talk about. A science is concerned with a limited set of various types of things. There is thus in the first place this variety of types. In the second place, there is the determination as to what types are exhibited in any indicated situation. For example, there is the singular proposition,—this is green; and the more general proposition,—all those things are green. This type of enquiry is what the traditional Aristotelian Logic takes care of. Undoubtedly such enquiries are essential in the initial stage of any science. But every science strives to get beyond it. Unfortunately, owing to the way in which for over two thousand years philosophic thought has been dominated by its background of Aristotelian Logic, all attempts to combine the set of special sciences into a philosophic cosmology, giving some understanding of the Universe—all these attempts are vitiated by an unconscious relapse into these Aristotelian forms as the sole mode of expression. The disease of philosophy is its itch to express itself in the forms, "Some S is P," or "All S is P."

Returning to the special sciences, the third step is the endeavour to obtain quantitative decisions. In this stage, the typical questions are, "How much P is involved in S" and "How many S's are P?" In other words, number, quantity, and measurement, have been introduced. A simple-minded handling of these quantitative notions can be just as misleading as undue trust in the Aristotelian forms for propositions.

The fourth stage in the development of the science is the introduction of the notion of pattern. Apart from attention to this concept of pattern, our understanding of Nature is crude in the extreme. For example, given an aggregate of carbon atoms and oxygen atoms, and given that the number of oxygen atoms and the number of carbon atoms are known, the properties of the mixture are unknown until the question of pattern is settled. How much free oxygen is there, —How much free carbon,—How much carbon monoxide,—How much carbon dioxide? The answers to some of these questions, with the total quantities of oxygen and of carbon presupposed, will determine the answer to the rest. But even allowing for this mutual determination, there will be an enormous number of alternative patterns for a mixture of any reasonable amount of carbon and oxygen. And even when the purely chemical pattern is settled, and when the region containing the mixture is given, there are an indefinite number of regional patterns for the distribution of the chemical substances within the containing region. Thus beyond all questions of quantity, there lie questions of pattern, which are essential for the understanding of nature. Apart from a presupposed pattern, quantity determines nothing. Indeed quantity itself is nothing other than analogy of functions within analogous patterns.

Also this example, involving mere chemical mixture, and chemical combination, and the seclusion of different substances in different subregions of the container, shows us that notion of pattern involves the concept of different modes of togetherness. This is obviously a fundamental concept which we ought to have thought of as soon as we started with the notion of various types of fundamental things. The danger of all these fundamental notions is that we are apt to assume them unconsciously. When we ask ourselves any question we will usually find that we are assuming certain types of entities involved, that we are assuming certain modes of togetherness of these entities, and that we are even assuming certain widely spread generalities of pattern. Our attention is concerned with details of pattern, and measurement, and proportionate magnitude. Thus the laws of nature are merely all-pervading patterns of behaviour, of which the shift and discontinuance lie beyond our ken. Again, the topic of every science is an abstraction from the full concrete happenings of nature. But every abstraction neglects the influx of the factors omitted into the factors retained. Thus a single pattern discerned by vision limited to the abstractions within a special science differentiates itself into a subordinate factor in an indefinite number of wider patterns when we consider its possibilities of relatedness to the omitted universe. Even within the circle of the special science we may find diversities of functioning not to be explained in terms of that science. But these diversities can be explained when we consider the variety of wider relationships of the pattern in question.

Today the attitude among many leaders in natural science is a vehement denial of the considerations which have here been put forward. Their attitude seems to me to be a touching example of baseless faith. This judgment is strengthened when we reflect that their position on the autonomy of the natural sciences has its origin in a concept of the world of nature, now discarded.

Finally, we are left with a fundamental question as yet undiscussed. What are those primary types of things in terms of which the process of the Universe is to be understood? Suppose we agree that Nature discloses to the scientific scrutiny merely activities and process. What does this mean? These activities fade into each other. They arise and then pass away. What is being enacted? What is effected? It cannot be that these are merely the formulae of the multiplication table— in the words of a great philosopher, merely a bloodless dance of categories. Nature is full-blooded. Real facts are happening. Physical Nature, as studied in Science, is to be looked upon as a complex of the more stable inter-relations between the real facts of the real universe.

This lecture has been confined to Nature under an abstraction in which all reference to life was suppressed. The effect of this abstraction has been that Dynamics, Physics, and Chemistry were the sciences which guided our gradual transition from the full common-sense notions of the sixteenth century to the concept of nature suggested by the speculative physics of the present day.

This change of view, occupying four centuries, may be characterized as the transition from Space and Matter as the fundamental notions to Process conceived as a complex of activity with internal relations between its various factors. The older point of view enables us to abstract from change and to conceive of the full reality of nature *at an instant*, in abstraction from any temporal duration and characterized as to its inter-relations solely by the instantaneous distribution of matter in space. According to the Newtonian view, what had thus been omitted was the change of distribution at neighbouring instants. But such change was, on this view, plainly irrelevant to the essential reality of the material universe at the instant considered. Locomotion, and change of relative distribution, were accidental and not essential.

Equally accidental was endurance. Nature at an instant is, in this view, equally real whether or no there be no nature at any other instant, or indeed whether or no there be any other instant. Descartes, who with Galileo and Newton, coöperated in the construction of the final Newtonian view, accepted this conclusion. For he explained endurance as perpetual re-creation at each instant. Thus the matter of fact was, for him, to be seen in the instant and not in the endurance. For him, endurance was a mere succession of instantaneous facts. There were other sides to Descartes' cosmology which might have led him to a greater emphasis on motion. For example, his doctrines of extension and vortices. But in fact, by anticipation, he drew the conclusion which fitted the Newtonian concepts.

There is a fatal contradiction inherent in the Newtonian cosmology. Only one mode of the occupancy of space is allowed for—namely, this bit of matter occupying this region at this durationless instant. This occupation of space is the final real fact, without reference to any other instant, or to any other piece of matter, or to any other region of space. Now assuming this Newtonian doctrine, we ask— What becomes of velocity, at an instant? Again we ask—What becomes of momentum at an instant? These notions are essential for Newtonian physics, and yet they are without any meaning for it. Velocity and momentum require the concept that the state of things at other times and other places enters into the essential character of the material occupancy of space at any selected instant. But the Newtonian concept allows for no such modification of the relation of occupancy. Thus the cosmological scheme is inherently inconsistent. The mathematical subtleties of the differential calculus afford no help for the removal of this difficulty. We can indeed phrase the point at issue in mathematical terms. The Newtonian notion of occupancy corresponds to the value of a function at a selected point. But the Newtonian physics requires solely the limit of the function at that point. And the Newtonian cosmology gives no hint why the bare fact which is the value should be replaced by the reference to other times and places which is the limit.

For the modern view process, activity, and change are the matter of fact. At an instant there is nothing. Each instant is only a way of grouping matters of fact. Thus since there are no instants, conceived as simple primary entities, there is no nature at an instant. Thus all the inter-relations of matters of fact must involve transition in their essence. All realization involves implication in the creative advance.

The discussion in this lecture is only the prolegomenon for the attempt to answer the fundamental question,—How do we add content to the notion of bare activity? Activity for what, producing what, Activity involving what?

The next lecture will introduce the concept of Life, and will thus enable us to conceive of Nature more concretely, without abstraction.

NATURE ALIVE [5]

The status of life in nature, as defined in the previous chapter, is the modern problem of philosophy and of science. Indeed it is the central meeting point of all the strains of systematic thought, humanistic, naturalistic, philosophic. The very meaning of life is in doubt. When we understand it, we shall also understand its status in the world. But its essence and its status are alike baffling.

After all, this conclusion is not very different from our conclusion respecting nature, considered in abstraction from the notion of life. We were left with the notion of an activity in which nothing is effected. Also this activity, thus considered, discloses no ground for its own coherence. There is merely a formula for succession. But there is an absence of understandable causation to give a reason for that formula for that succession. Of course it is always possible to work oneself into a state of complete contentment with an ultimate irrationality. The popular positivistic philosophy adopts this attitude.

The weakness of this positivism is the way in which we all welcome the detached fragments of explanation attained in our present stage of civilization. Suppose that a hundred thousand years ago our ancestors had been wise positivists. They sought for no reasons. What they had observed was sheer matter of fact. It was the development of no necessity. They would have searched for no reasons underlying facts immediately observed. Civilization would never have developed. Our varied powers of detailed observation of the world would have remained dormant. For the peculiarity of a reason is that the intellectual development of its consequences suggests consequences beyond the topics already observed. The extension of observation waits upon some dim apprehension of reasonable connection. For example, the observation of insects on flowers dimly suggests some congruity between the natures of insects and of flowers, and thus leads to a wealth of observation from which whole branches of science have developed. But a consistent positivist should be content with the observed facts, namely insects visiting flowers. It is a fact of charming simplicity. There is nothing further to be said upon the matter, according to the doctrine of a positivist. At present the scientific world is suffering from a bad attack of muddle-headed positivism, which arbitrarily applies its doctrine and arbitrarily escapes from it. The whole doctrine of life in nature has suffered from this positivist taint. We are told that there is the routine de-

[5] From A. N. Whitehead, *Modes of Thought*, N. Y.: Macmillan, 1938. Lecture VIII.

scribed in physical and chemical formulae, and that in the process of nature there is nothing else.

The origin of this persuasion is the dualism which gradually developed in European thought in respect to mind and nature. At the beginning of the modern period Descartes expresses this dualism with the utmost distinctness. For him, there are material substances with spatial relations, and mental substances. The mental substances are external to the material substances. Neither type requires the other type for the completion of its essence. Their unexplained interrelations are unnecessary for their respective existences. In truth, this formulation of the problem in terms of minds and matter is unfortunate. It omits the lower forms of life, such as vegetation and the lower animal types. These forms touch upon human mentality at their highest, and upon inorganic nature at their lowest.

The effect of this sharp division between nature and life has poisoned all subsequent philosophy. Even when the coördinate existence of the two types of actualities is abandoned, there is no proper fusion of the two in most modern schools of thought. For some, nature is mere appearance and mind is the sole reality. For others, physical nature is the sole reality and mind is an epiphenomenon. Here the phrases "mere appearance" and "epiphenomenon" obviously carry the implication of slight importance for the understanding of the final nature of things.

The doctrine that I am maintaining is that neither physical nature nor life can be understood unless we fuse them together as essential factors in the composition of "really real" things whose inter-connections and individual characters constitute the universe.

The first step in the argument must be to form some concept of what life can mean. Also we require that the deficiencies in our concept of physical nature should be supplied by its fusion with life. And we require that, on the other hand, the notion of life should involve the notion of physical nature.

Now as a first approximation the notion of life implies a certain absoluteness of self-enjoyment. This must mean a certain immediate individuality, which is a complex process of appropriating into a unity of existence the many data presented as relevant by the physical processes of nature. Life implies the absolute, individual self-enjoyment arising out of this process of appropriation. I have, in my recent writings, used the word "prehension" to express this process of appropriation. Also I have termed each individual act of immediate self-enjoyment an "occasion of experience." I hold that these unities of existence, these occasions of experience, are the really real things which in their collective unity compose the evolving universe, ever plunging into the creative advance.

But these are forward references to the issue of the argument. As a first approximation we have conceived life as implying absolute, individual self-enjoyment of a process of appropriation. The data appropriated are provided by the antecedent functioning of the universe. Thus the occasion of experience is absolute in respect to its immediate self-enjoyment. How it deals with its data is to be understood without reference to any other concurrent occasions. Thus the occasion, in reference to its internal process, requires no contemporary process in order to exist. In fact this mutual independence in the internal process of self-adjustment is the definition of contemporaneousness.

This concept of self-enjoyment does not exhaust that aspect of process here termed "life." Process for its intelligibility involves the notion of a creative activity belonging to the very essence of each occasion. It is the process of eliciting into actual being factors in the universe which antecedently to that process exist only in the mode of unrealized potentialities. The process of self-creation is the transformation of the potential into the actual, and the fact of such transformation includes the immediacy of self-enjoyment.

Thus in conceiving the function of life in an occasion of experience, we must discriminate the actualized data presented by the antecedent world, the non-actualized potentialities which lie ready to promote their fusion into a new unity of experience, and the immediacy of self-enjoyment which belongs to the creative fusion of those data with those potentialities. This is the doctrine of the creative advance whereby it belongs to the essence of the universe, that it passes into a future. It is nonsense to conceive of nature as a static fact, even for an instant devoid of duration. There is no nature apart from transition, and there is no transition apart from temporal duration. This is the reason why the notion of an instant of time, conceived as a primary simple fact, is nonsense.

But even yet we have not exhausted the notion of creation which is essential to the understanding of nature. We must add yet another character to our description of life. This missing characteristic is "aim." By this term "aim" is meant the exclusion of the boundless wealth of alternative potentiality, and the inclusion of that definite factor of novelty which constitutes the selected way of entertaining those data in that process of unification. The aim is at that complex of feeling which is the enjoyment of those data in that way. "That way of enjoyment" is selected from the boundless wealth of alternatives. It has been aimed at for actualization in that process.

Thus the characteristics of life are absolute self-enjoyment, creative activity, aim. Here "aim" evidently involves the entertainment of the purely ideal so as to be directive of the creative process. Also the enjoyment belongs to the process and is not a characteristic of any static result. The aim is at the enjoyment belonging to the process.

The question at once arises as to whether this factor of life in nature, as thus interpreted, corresponds to anything that we observe in nature. . . .

Science conceived as resting on mere sense-perception, with no other source of observation, is bankrupt, so far as concerns its claim to self-sufficiency. Science can find no individual enjoyment in nature: Science can find no aim in nature: Science can find no creativity in nature; it finds mere rules of succession. These negations are true of Natural Science. They are inherent in its methodology. The reason for this blindness of Physical Science lies in the fact that such Science only deals with half the evidence provided by human experience. It divides the seamless coat—or, to change the metaphor into a happier form, it examines the coat, which is superficial, and neglects the body which is fundamental.

The disastrous separation of body and mind which has been fixed on European thought by Descartes is responsible for this blindness of Science. In one sense the abstraction has been a happy one, in that it has allowed the simplest things to be considered first, for about ten generations. Now these simplest things are those widespread habits of nature that dominate the whole stretch of the universe within our remotest, vaguest observation. None of these Laws of Nature gives the slightest evidence of necessity. They are the modes of procedure which within the scale of our observations do in fact prevail. I mean, the fact that the extensiveness of the Universe is dimensional, the fact that the number of spatial dimensions is three, the spatial laws of geometry, the ultimate formulae for physical occurrences. There is no necessity in any of these ways of behaviour. They exist as average, regulative conditions because the majority of actualities are swaying each other to modes of interconnection exemplifying those laws. New modes of self-expression may be gaining ground. We cannot tell. But, to judge by all analogy, after a sufficient span of existence our present laws will fade into unimportance. New interests will dominate. In our present sense of the term, our spatio-physical epoch will pass into that background of the past, which conditions all things dimly and without evident effect on the decision of prominent relations.

These massive laws, at present prevailing, are the general physical laws of inorganic nature. At a certain scale of observation they are prevalent without hint of interference. The formation of suns, the motions of planets, the geologic changes on the earth, seem to proceed with a massive impetus which excludes any hint of modification by other agencies. To this extent sense-perception on which science relies discloses no aim in nature.

Yet it is untrue to state that the general observation of mankind, in which sense-perception is only one factor, discloses no aim. The exact contrary is the case. All explanations of the sociological functionings of mankind include "aim" as an essential factor in explanation. For example, in a criminal trial where the evidence is circumstantial the demonstration of motive is one chief reliance of the prosecution. In such a trial would the defence plead the doctrine that purpose could not direct the motions of the body, and that to indict the thief for stealing was analogous to indicting the sun for rising? Again no statesman can conduct international relations without some estimate —implicit or explicit in his consciousness—of the types of patriotism respectively prevalent in various nations and in the statesmen of these nations. A lost dog can be seen trying to find his master or trying to find his way home. In fact we are *directly* conscious of our purposes as *directive* of our actions. Apart from such direction no doctrine could in any sense be acted upon. The notions entertained mentally would have no effect upon bodily actions. Thus what happens would happen in complete indifference to the entertainment of such notions.

Scientific reasoning is completely dominated by the presupposition that mental functionings are not properly part of nature. Accordingly it disregards all those mental antecedents which mankind habitually presuppose as effective in guiding cosmological functionings. As a method this procedure is entirely justifiable, provided that we recognize the limitations involved. These limitations are both obvious and undefined. The gradual eliciting of their definition is the hope of philosophy.

The points that I would emphasize are, first that this sharp division between mentality and nature has no ground in our fundamental observation. We find ourselves living within nature. Secondly, I conclude that we should conceive mental operations as among the factors which make up the constitution of nature. Thirdly, that we should reject the notion of idle wheels in the process of nature. Every factor which emerges makes a difference, and that difference can only be expressed in terms of the individual character of that factor. Fourthly, that we have now the task of defining natural facts, so as to understand how mental occurrences are operative in conditioning the subsequent course of nature.

A rough division can be made of six types of occurrences in nature. The first type is human existence, body and mind. The second type includes all sorts of animal life, insects, the vertebrates, and other genera. In fact all the various types of animal life other than human. The third type includes all vegetable life. The fourth type consists of the single living cells. The fifth type consists of all large scale inorganic aggregates, on a scale comparable to the size of animal bodies, or larger. The sixth type is composed of the happenings on an infinitesimal scale, disclosed by the minute analysis of modern physics.

Now all these functionings of Nature influence each other, require each other, and lead on to each other. The list has purposely been made roughly, without any scientific pretension. The sharp-cut scientific classifications are essential for scientific method. But they are dangerous for philosophy. Such classification hides the truth that the different modes of natural existence shade off into each other. There is the animal life with its central direction of a society of cells, there is the vegetable life with its organized republic of cells, there is the cell life with its organized republic of molecules, there is the large-scale inorganic society of molecules with its passive acceptance of necessities derived from spatial relations, there is the infra-molecular activity which has lost all trace of the passivity of inorganic nature on a larger scale.

In this survey some main conclusions stand out. One conclusion is the diverse modes of functioning which are produced by diverse modes of organization. The second conclusion is the aspect of continuity between these different modes. There are border-line cases, which bridge the gaps. Often the border-line cases are unstable, and pass quickly. But span of existence is merely relative to our habits of human life. For infra-molecular occurrence, a second is a vast period of time. A third conclusion is the difference in the aspects of nature according as we change the scale of observation. Each scale of observation presents us with average effects proper to that scale.

Again, another consideration arises. How do we observe nature? Also, what is the proper analysis of an observation? The conventional answer to this question is that we perceive nature through our senses. Also in the analysis of sense-perception we are apt to concentrate upon its most clear-cut instance, namely sight. Now visual perception is the final product of evolution. It belongs to high grade animals— to vertebrates and to the more advanced type of insects. There are numberless living things which afford no evidence of possessing sight. Yet they show every sign of taking account of their environment in the way proper to living things. Also human beings shut off sight with peculiar ease, by closing our eyes or by the calamity of blindness. The information provided by mere sight is peculiarly barren—namely external regions disclosed as coloured. There is no necessary transition of colours, and no necessary selection of regions, and no necessary mutual adaptation of the display of colours. Sight at any instant merely provides the passive fact of regions variously coloured. If we have memories, we observe the transition of colours. But there is nothing intrinsic to the mere coloured regions which provides any hint of internal activity whereby change can be understood. It is from this experience that our conception of a spatial distribution of passive material substances arises. Nature is thus described as made up of vacuous bits of matter with no internal values, and merely hurrying through space.

But there are two accompaniments of this experience which should make us suspicious of accepting it at its face value as any direct disclosure of the metaphysical nature of things. In the first place, even in visual experience we are also aware of the intervention of the body. We know directly that we see *with our eyes*. That is a vague feeling, but extremely important. Secondly, every type of crucial experiment proves that what we see, and where we see it, depend entirely upon the physiological functioning of our body. Any method of making our body function internally in a given way, will provide us with an assigned visual sensation. The body is supremely indifferent to the happenings of nature a short way off, where it places its visual sensa.

Now the same is true of all other modes of sensation, only to a greater extent. All sense-perception is merely one outcome of the dependence of our experience upon bodily functionings. Thus if we wish to understand the relation of our personal experience to the activities of nature, the proper procedure is to examine the dependence of our personal experiences upon our personal bodies.

Let us ask about our overwhelming persuasions as to our own personal body-mind relation. In the first place, there is the claim to unity. The human individual is one fact, body and mind. This claim to unity is the fundamental fact, always presupposed, rarely explicitly formulated. I am experiencing and my body is mine. In the second place, the functioning of our body has a much wider influence than the mere production of sense-experience. We find ourselves in a healthy enjoyment of life by reason of the healthy functionings of our internal organs—heart, lungs, bowels, kidneys, etc. The emotional state arises just because they are not providing any sensa directly associated with themselves. Even in sight, we enjoy our vision because there is no eyestrain. Also we enjoy our general state of life, because we have no stomach-ache. I am insisting that the enjoyment of health, good or bad, is a positive feeling only casually associated with particular sensa. For example, you can enjoy the ease with which your eyes are functioning even when you are looking at a bad picture or a vulgar building. This direct feeling of the derivation of emotion from the body is among our fundamental experiences. There are emotions of various types—but every type of emotion is at least modified by derivation from the body. It is for physiologists to analyse in detail the modes of bodily functioning. For philosophy, the one fundamental fact is that the whole complexity of mental experience is either derived or modified by such functioning. Also our basic feeling is this sense of derivation, which leads to our claim for unity, body and mind.

But our immediate experience also claims derivation from another source, and equally claims a unity founded upon this alternative source of derivation. This second source is our own state of mind directly preceding the immediate present of our conscious experience. A quarter of a second ago, we were entertaining such and such ideas, we were enjoying such and such emotions, and we were making such and such observations of external fact. In our present state of mind, we are continuing that previous state. The word "continuing" states only half the truth. In one sense it is too weak, and in another sense it overstates. It is too weak, because we not only continue, but we claim absolute identity with our previous state. It was our very identical self in that state of mind, which is of course the basis of our present experience a quarter of a second later. In another sense the word "continuing" overstates. For we do not quite continue in our preceding state of experience. New elements have intervened. All of these new elements are provided by our bodily functionings. We fuse these new elements with the basic stuff of experience provided by our state of mind a quarter of a second ago. Also, as we have already agreed, we claim an identification with our body. Thus our experience in the present discloses its own nature as with two sources of derivation, namely, the body and the antecedent experiential functionings. Also there is a claim for identification with each of these sources. The body is mine, and the antecedent experience is mine. Still more, there is only one ego, to claim the body and to claim the stream of experience. I submit that we have here the fundamental basic persuasion on which we found the whole practice of our existence. While we exist, body and soul are inescapable elements in our being, each with the full reality of our own immediate self. But neither body nor soul possesses the sharp observational definition which at first sight we attribute to them. Our knowledge of the body places it as a complex unity of happenings within the larger field of nature. But its demarcation from the rest of nature is vague in the extreme. The body consists of the coördinated functionings of billions of molecules. It belongs to the structural essence of the body that, in an indefinite number of ways, it is always losing molecules and gaining molecules. When we consider the question with microscopic accuracy, there is no definite boundary to determine where the body begins and external nature ends. Again the body can lose whole limbs, and yet we claim identity with the same body. Also the vital functions of the cells in the amputated limb ebb slowly. Indeed the limb survives in separation from the body for an immense time compared to the internal vibratory periods of its molecules. Also apart from such catastrophes, the body requires the environment in order to exist. Thus there is a unity of the body with the environment, as well as a unity of body and soul into one person.

But in conceiving our personal identity we are apt to emphasize rather the soul than the body. The one individual is that coördinated stream of personal experiences, which is my thread of life or your thread of life. It is that succession of self-realization, each occasion with its direct memory of its past and with its anticipation of the future. That claim to enduring self-identity is our self-assertion of personal identity.

Yet when we examine this notion of the soul, it discloses itself as even vaguer than our definition of the body. First, the continuity of the soul—so far as concerns consciousness—has to leap gaps in time. We sleep or we are stunned. And yet it is the same person who recovers consciousness. We trust to memory, and we ground our trust on the continuity of the functionings of nature, more especially on the continuity of our body. Thus nature in general and the body in particular provide the stuff for the personal endurance of the soul. Again there is a curious variation in the vividness of the successive occasions of the soul's existence. We are living a full stretch with a keen observation of external occurrence; then external attention dies away and we are lost in meditation; the meditation gradually weakens in vivid presentation: we doze; we dream; we sleep with a total lapse of the stream of consciousness. These functionings of the soul are diverse, variable, and discontinuous. The claim to the unity of the soul is analogous to the claim to the unity of the body, and is analogous to the claim to the unity of body and soul, and is analogous to the claim to the community of the body with an external nature. It is the task of philosophic speculation to conceive the happenings of the universe so as to render understandable the outlook of physical science and to combine this outlook with these direct persuasions representing the basic facts upon which epistemology must build. The weakness of the epistemology of the eighteenth and nineteenth centuries was that it based itself purely upon a narrow formulation of sense-perception. Also among the various modes of sensation, visual experience was picked out as the typical example. The result was to exclude all the really fundamental factors constituting our experience.

In such an epistemology we are far from the complex data which philosophic speculation has to account for in a system rendering the whole understandable. Consider the types of community of body and soul, of body and nature, of soul and nature, or successive occasions of bodily existence, or the soul's existence. These fundamental interconnections have one very remarkable characteristic. Let us ask what is the function of the external world for the stream of experience which constitute the soul. This world, thus experienced, is the basic fact within those experiences. All the emotions, and purposes, and enjoyments, proper to the individual existence of the soul are nothing other than the soul's reactions to this experienced world which lies at the base of the soul's existence.

Thus in a sense, the experienced world is one complex factor in the composition of many factors constituting the essence of the soul. We can phrase this shortly by saying that in one sense the world is in the soul.

But there is an antithetical doctrine balancing this primary truth. Namely, our experience of the world involves the exhibition of the soul itself as one of the components within the world. Thus there is a dual aspect to the relationship of an occasion of experience as one relatum and the experienced world as another relatum. The world is included within the occasion in one sense, and the occasion is included in the world in another sense. For example, I am in the room, and the room is an item in my present experience. But my present experience is what I now am.

But this baffling antithetical relation extends to all the connections which we have been discussing. For example, consider the enduring self-identity of the soul. The soul is nothing else than the succession of my occasions of experience, extending from birth to the present moment. Now, at this instant, I am the complete person embodying all these occasions. They are mine. On the other hand it is equally true that my immediate occasion of experience, at the present moment, is only one among the stream of occasions which constitutes my soul. Again, the world for me is nothing else than how the functionings of my body present it for my experience. The world is thus wholly to be discerned within those functionings. Knowledge of the world is nothing else than an analysis of the functionings. And yet, on the other hand, the body is merely one society of functionings within the universal society of the world. We have to construe the world in terms of the bodily society, and the bodily society in terms of the general functionings of the world.

Thus, as disclosed in the fundamental essence of our experience, the togetherness of things involves some doctrine of mutual immanence. In some sense or other, this community of the actualities of the world means that each happening is a factor in the nature of every other happening. After all, this is the only way in which we can understand notions habitually employed in daily life. Consider our notion of "causation." How can one event be the cause of another? In the first place, no event can be wholly and solely the cause of another event. The whole antecedent world conspires to produce a new occasion. But some one occasion in an important way conditions the formation of a successor. How can we understand this process of conditioning?

The mere notion of transferring a quality is entirely unintelligible. Suppose that two occurrences may be in fact detached so that one of them is comprehensible without reference to the other. Then all notion of causation between them, or of conditioning, becomes unintelligible. There is—with this supposition—no reason why the possession of any quality by one of them should in any way influence the possession of that quality, or of any other quality, by the other. With such a doctrine the play and interplay of qualitative succession in the world becomes a blank fact from which no conclusions can be drawn as to past, present, or future, beyond the range of direct observation. Such a positivistic belief is quite self-consistent, provided that we do not include in it any hopes for the future or regrets for the past. Science is then without any importance. Also effort is foolish, because it determines nothing. The only intelligible doctrine of causation is founded on the doctrine of immanence. Each occasion presupposes the antecedent world as active in its own nature. This is the reason why events have a determinate status relatively to each other. Also it is the reason why the qualitative energies of the past are combined into a pattern of qualitative energies in each present occasion. This is the doctrine of causation. It is the reason why it belongs to the essence of each occasion that it is *where* it is. It is the reason for the transference of character from occasion to occasion. It is the reason for the relative stability of laws of nature, some laws for a wider environment, some laws for a narrower environment. It is the reason why—as we have already noted—in our direct apprehension of the world around us we find that curious habit of claiming a two-fold unity with the observed data. We are in the world and the world is in us. Our immediate occasion is in the society of occasions forming the soul, and our soul is in our present occasion. The body is ours, and we are an activity within our body. This fact of observation, vague but imperative, is the foundation of the connexity of the world, and of the transmission of its types of order.

In this survey of the observational data in terms of which our philosophic cosmology must be founded, we have brought together the conclusions of physical science, and those habitual persuasions dominating the sociological functionings of mankind. These persuasions also

guide the humanism of literature, of art, and of religion. Mere existence has never entered into the consciousness of man, except as the
remote terminus of an abstraction in thought. Descartes' "Cogito, ergo
sum" is wrongly translated, "I *think*, therefore I am." It is never bare
thought or bare existence that we are aware of. I find myself as essentially a unity of emotions, enjoyments, hopes, fears, regrets, valuations of alternatives, decisions—all of them subjective reactions to the
environment as active in my nature. My unity—which is Descartes' "I
am"—is my process of shaping this welter of material into a consistent pattern of feelings. The individual enjoyment is what I am in my
role of a natural activity, as I shape the activities of the environment
into a new creation, which is myself at this moment; and yet, as being
myself, it is a continuation of the antecedent world. If we stress the
role of the environment, this process is causation. If we stress the role
of my immediate pattern of active enjoyment, this process is self-
creation. If we stress the role of the conceptual anticipation of the
future whose existence is a necessity in the nature of the present,
this process is the teleological aim at some ideal in the future. This
aim, however, is not really beyond the present process. For the aim
at the future is an enjoyment in the present. It thus effectively conditions the immediate self-creation of the new creature.

We can now again ask the final question as put forward at the
close of the former lecture. Physical science has reduced nature to
activity, and has discovered abstract mathematical formulae which
are illustrated in these activities of Nature. But the fundamental question remains, How do we add content to the notion of bare activity?
This question can only be answered by fusing life with nature.

In the first place, we must distinguish life from mentality. Mentality involves conceptual experience, and is only one variable ingredient in life. The sort of functioning here termed "conceptual
experience" is the entertainment of possibilities for ideal realization
in abstraction from any sheer physical realization. The most obvious
example of conceptual experience is the entertainment of alternatives.
Life lies below this grade of mentality. Life is the enjoyment of emotion, derived from the past and aimed at the future. It is the enjoyment of emotion which was then, which is now, and which will be
then. This vector character is of the essence of such entertainment.

The emotion transcends the present in two ways. It issues from,
and it issues towards. It is received, it is enjoyed, and it is passed
along, from moment to moment. Each occasion is an activity of concern, in the Quaker sense of that term. It is the conjunction of
transcendence and immanence. The occasion is concerned, in the way
of feeling and aim, with things that in their own essence lie beyond
it; although these things in their present functions are factors in the

concern of that occasion. Thus each occasion, although engaged in its own immediate self-realization, is concerned with the universe.

The process is always a process of modification by reason of the numberless avenues of supply, and by reason of the numberless modes of qualitative texture. The unity of emotion, which is the unity of the present occasion, is a patterned texture of qualities, always shifting as it is passed into the future. The creative activity aims at preservation of intensity. The modifications of pattern, the dismissal into elimination, are in obedience to this aim.

In so far as conceptual mentality does not intervene, the grand patterns pervading the environment are passed on with the inherited modes of adjustment. Here we find the patterns of activity studied by the physicists and chemists. Mentality is merely latent in all these occasions as thus studied. In the case of inorganic nature any sporadic flashes are inoperative so far as our powers of discernment are concerned. The lowest stages of effective mentality, controlled by the inheritance of physical pattern, involves the faint direction of emphasis by unconscious ideal aim. The various examples of the higher forms of life exhibit the variety of grades of effectiveness of mentality. In the social habits of animals, there is evidence of flashes of mentality in the past which have degenerated into physical habits. Finally in the higher mammals and more particularly in mankind, we have clear evidence of mentality habitually effective. In our own experience, our knowledge consciously entertained and systematized can only mean such mentality, directly observed.

The qualities entertained as objects in conceptual activity are of the nature of catalytic agents, in the sense in which that phrase is used in chemistry. They modify the aesthetic process by which the occasion constitutes itself out of the many streams of feeling received from the past. It is not necessary to assume that conceptions introduce additional sources of measurable energy. They may do so; for the doctrine of the conservation of energy is not based upon exhaustive measurements. But the operation of mentality is primarily to be conceived as a diversion of the flow of energy.

In these lectures I have not entered upon systematic metaphysical cosmology. The object of the lectures is to indicate those elements in our experience in terms of which such a cosmology should be constructed. The key notion from which such construction should start is that the energetic activity considered in physics is the emotional intensity entertained in life. . . .

BIBLIOGRAPHY

WHITEHEAD, Alfred North (and Bertrand Russell). *Principia Mathematica.* 3 vols. Cambridge, England: Cambridge U. Press, 1910–1913.

————, *The Organization of Thought, Educational and Scientific.* London: Williams & Norgate, 1917.

————, *An Enquiry Concerning the Principles of Natural Knowledge.* Cambridge: Cambridge U. Press, 1919.

————, *The Concept of Nature.* Cambridge: Cambridge U. Press, 1920.

————, *The Principle of Relativity.* Cambridge: Cambridge U. Press, 1922.

————, *Science and the Modern World.* N.Y.: Macmillan, 1925.

————, *Religion in the Making.* N.Y.: Macmillan, 1926.

————, *Symbolism, Its Meaning and Effect.* N.Y.: Macmillan, 1927.

————, *Process and Reality.* N.Y.: Macmillan, 1929.

————, *The Function of Reason.* Princeton: Princeton U. Press, 1929.

————, *The Aims of Education and Other Essays.* N.Y.: Macmillan, 1929.

————, *Adventures of Ideas.* N.Y.: Macmillan, 1933.

————, *Nature and Life.* Chicago: U. of Chicago Press, 1934. (Reprinted in *Modes of Thought.*)

————, *Modes of Thought.* N.Y.: Macmillan, 1938.

————, *Essays in Science and Philosophy.* N.Y.: Philosophical Library, 1947.

————, *Alfred North Whitehead: An Anthology.* Ed. by F. S. C. Northrop & Mason W. Gross, N.Y.: Macmillan Co., 1953.

————, *Whitehead's American Essays in Social Philosophy.* A. H. Johnson, ed. N.Y.: Harper, 1959.

BLYTH, John W. *Whitehead's Theory of Knowledge.* Providence: Brown U. Press, 1941.

CHRISTIAN, William A. *An Interpretation of Whitehead's Metaphysics.* New Haven: Yale U. Press, 1959.

DAS, R. *The Philosophy of Whitehead.* London: J. Clarke, 1938.

ELY, S. L. *The Religious Availability of Whitehead's God.* Madison: U. of Wisconsin Press, 1942.

EMMET, Dorothy M. *Whitehead's Philosophy of Organism.* London: Macmillan, 1932.

HAMMERSCHMIDT, William W. *Whitehead's Philosophy of Time.* N.Y.: King's Crown Press, 1947.

JOHNSON, A. H. *Whitehead's Theory of Reality.* Boston: Beacon Press, 1952.

————, *Whitehead's Philosophy of Civilization.* Boston: Beacon Press, 1958.

LAWRENCE, Nathaniel. *Whitehead's Philosophical Development.* Berkeley: U. of California Press, 1956.

LECLERC, I., ed. *The Relevance of Whitehead.* London: Allen & Unwin, 1961.

LINTZ, E. J. *The Unity of the Universe According to Alfred North Whitehead.* Fribourg, Switzerland: U. of Fribourg Press, 1939; Baltimore: J. H. Furst, 1939.

LOWE, V., HARTSHORNE, C., JOHNSON, A.H., *Whitehead and the Modern World*. Boston: Beacon Press, 1950.

LOWE, Victor. *Understanding Whitehead*. Baltimore: Johns Hopkins Press, 1962.

MILLER, D.L. and GENTRY, G.V., *The Philosophy of A. N. Whitehead*. Minneapolis: Burgess Publ., 1938.

PALTER, R.M. *Whitehead's Philosophy of Science*. Chicago: U. of Chicago Press, 1960.

Philosophical Essays for Alfred North Whitehead. N.Y.: Longmans Green, 1936.

PRICE, Lucien. *Dialogues of Alfred North Whitehead*. Boston: Little, Brown, 1954.

SCHILPP, Paul Arthur, ed. *The Philosophy of Alfred North Whitehead*. Evanston and Chicago: Northwestern U. Press, 1941.

SHAHAN, Ewing P. *Whitehead's Theory of Experience*. N.Y.: King's Crown Press, 1950.

SHERBURNE, D. W. *A Whiteheadian Aesthetic*. New Haven: Yale U. Press, 1961.

WELLS, H. K. *Process and Unreality*. N.Y.: King's Crown Press, 1950.

George Herbert Mead

[*1863–1931*]

Dewey said in the nineteen-thirties that Mead was "the most original mind in philosophy in America of the last generation." Mead not only shared with Dewey and Peirce a pragmatic and behavioristic viewpoint, but he attempted to work out a comprehensive philosophical system. Unfortunately, this system was not complete at the time of his death, but was scattered in random articles, manuscripts and lecture notes, which his students helped to compile and to publish posthumously.

Mead was born in South Hadley, Massachusetts. He was a graduate of Oberlin College, and studied at Harvard, Leipzig and Berlin. He taught at the University of Michigan and from 1894 at the University of Chicago, where he came into contact with Dewey. He remained there for the rest of his life.

Mead's most important and daring contribution was his conception of social behaviorism, which avoided what he thought to be "subjectivistic" or "mentalistic" categories or "consciousness," and interpreted behavior in the context of fields of interaction. In his *Mind, Self, and Society* (1934), he argued that "mind," "self," and "I" and the "me" do not exist in isolated and discrete individuals, but emerge out of processes of social interaction. This is made possible because of certain neurological capacities, and appears especially when organisms begin to take the "role of the other." Language enables organisms to be related by means of vocal gestures and symbols, and the human animal acquires "mind" when it responds not merely to signs, but to significant symbols. Moreover, what we call "reason" develops when an organism appropriates into its own responses the attitudes possible to other organisms in the environment. The selection reprinted below is Mead's own "Summary and Conclusion" of *Mind, Self, and Society*.

Mead continued his behavioristic analysis in the posthumous work, *The Philosophy of the Act* (1938). Here Mead distinguished various stages of an act: impulse, perception, manipulation, and consummation. "Scientific objects" are considered to be abstractions from the manipulatory phase of the act, and they are instrumental in function. In *The Philosophy of the Present* (1932), Mead held that unpredictable novelties emerge in the present, and that the past must be reconstructed to account for them. Present and past thus have meaning in relation to "temporal perspectives"—all of which Mead thought to be consistent with contemporary physics. From this analysis of human experience, Mead was also led to a theory of emergent evolution. Although many of Mead's ideas are speculative, his behavioristic and social theory of mind has had an important influence on the social sciences, particularly social psychology.

MIND, SELF, AND SOCIETY
FROM THE STANDPOINT OF A SOCIAL BEHAVIORIST [1]

We have approached psychology from the standpoint of behaviorism; that is, we have undertaken to consider the conduct of the organism and to locate what is termed "intelligence," and in particular, "self-conscious intelligence," within this conduct. This position implies organisms which are in relationship to environments, and environments that are in some sense determined by the selection of the sensitivity of the form of the organism. It is the sensitivity of the organism that determines what its environment shall be, and in that sense we can speak of a form as determining its environment. The stimulus as such as found in the environment is that which sets free an impulse, a tendency to act in a certain fashion. We speak of this conduct as intelligent just in so far as it maintains or advances the interests of the form or the species to which it belongs. Intelligence is, then, a function of the relation of the form and its environment. The conduct that we study is always the action of the form in its commerce with the environment. Such intelligence we may find in plants or animals when the form in its reaction to the environment sets free its impulses through the stimuli that come from the environment.

Earlier psychologists—and many psychologists of the present time, for that matter—assume that at a certain point in the development of the organism consciousness as such arises. It is supposed to appear first of all in affective states, those of pleasure and pain; and it is assumed that through pleasure and pain the form controls its conduct. It is assumed that later consciousness finds its expression in the sensation of the antecedent stimulus process in the environment itself. But these sensations, from the point of view of our study, involve the statement of the environment itself; that is, we cannot state the environment in any other way than in terms of our sensations, if we accept such a definition of sensation as a consciousness that simply arises. If we try to define the environment within which sensation does arise, it is in terms of that which we see and feel and that which our observation assumes to be present. The suggestion I have made is that consciousness, as such, does not represent a separate substance or a separate something that is superinduced upon a form, but rather that the term "consciousness" (in one of its basic

<hr>

[1] From George H. Mead, *Mind, Self, and Society.* Chicago: U. of Chicago Press, 1934 (ed. C. W. Morris). Selection from Para. 42. "Summary and Conclusions," pp. 328–336.

usages) represents a certain sort of an environment in its relation to sensitive organisms.

Such a statement brings together two philosophic concepts, one of emergence and one of relativity. We may assume that certain types of characters arise at certain stages in the course of development. This may extend, of course, far below the range to which we are referring. Water, for example, arises out of a combination of hydrogen and oxygen; it is something over and above the atoms that make it up. When we speak, then, of such characters as sensations arising, emerging, we are really asking no more than when we ask the character of any organic compound. Anything that as a whole is more than the mere form of its parts has a nature that belongs to it that is not to be found in the elements out of which it is made.

Consciousness, in the widest sense, is not simply an emergent at a certain point, but a set of characters that is dependent upon the relationship of a thing to an organism. Color, for instance, may be conceived of as arising in relationship to an organism that has an organ of vision. In that case, there is a certain environment that belongs to a certain form and arises in relationship to that form. If we accept those two concepts of emergence and relativity, all I want to point out is that they do answer to what we term "consciousness," namely, a certain environment that exists in its relationship to the organism, and in which new characters can arise in virtue of the organism. I have not undertaken here[2] to defend this as a philosophic view, but simply to point out that it does answer to certain conscious characteristics which have been given to forms at certain points in evolution. On this view the characters do not belong to organisms as such but only in the relationship of the organism to its environment. They are characteristics of objects in the environment of the form. The objects are colored, odorous, pleasant or painful, hideous or beautiful, in their relationship to the organism. I have suggested that in the development of forms with environments that answer to them and that are regulated by the forms themselves there appear or emerge characters that are dependent on this relation between the form and its environment. In one sense of the term, such characters constitute the field of consciousness.

This is a conception which at times we use without any hesitancy. When an animal form appears, certain objects become food; and we recognize that those objects have become food because the animal has a certain sort of digestive apparatus. There are certain microorganisms that are dangerous to human beings, but they would not be dangerous unless there were individuals susceptible to the attack

[2] See *The Philosophy of the Present* and *The Philosophy of the Act* for such a defense.

of these germs. We do constantly refer to certain objects in the environment as existing there because of the relationship between the form and the environment. There are certain objects that are beautiful but that would not be beautiful if there were not individuals that have an appreciation of them. It is in that organic relation that beauty arises. In general, then, we do recognize that there are objective fields in the world dependent upon the relation of the environment to certain forms. I am suggesting the extension of that recognition to the field of consciousness. All that I aim to point out here is that with such a conception we have hold of what we term "consciousness," as such; we do not have to endow the form with consciousness as a certain spiritual substance if we utilize these conceptions, and, as I said, we do utilize them when we speak of such a thing as food emerging in the environment because of the relationship of an object with the form. We might just as well speak of color, sound, and so on, in the same way.

The psychical in that case answers to the peculiar character which the environment has for a particular organism. It comes back to the distinction which we made between the self in its universal character and in its individual character. The self is universal, it identifies itself with a universal "me." We put ourselves in the attitude of all, and that which we all see is that which is expressed in universal terms; but each has a different sensitivity, and one color is different to me from what it is to you. These are differences which are due to the peculiar character of the organism as over against that which answers to universality.

I want to keep in the field of psychological analysis; but it does seem to me that it is important to recognize the possibility of such a treatment of consciousness, because it takes us into a field where the psychologists have been working. It is important to determine whether experienced characters are states of consciousness or whether they belong to the surrounding world. If they are states of consciousness, a different orientation results than if so-called "conscious states" are recognized as the characters of the world in its relation to the individual. All I am asking is that we should make use of that conception as we do use it in other connections. It opens the door to a treatment of the conscious self in terms of a behaviorism which has been regarded as inadequate at that point. It avoids, for example, the criticism made by the configuration psychologists, that psychologists have to come back to certain conscious states which people have.

The "I" is of importance, and I have treated it in so far as it has relation to the definite field of psychology, without undertaking to consider or defend what metaphysical assumptions may be involved.

That limitation is justified, for the psychologist does not undertake to maintain a metaphysics as such. When he deals with the world about him, he just accepts it as it is. Of course, this attitude is shot through and through with metaphysical problems, but the approach is scientifically legitimate.

Further, what we term "mental images" (the last resort of consciousness as a substance) can exist in their relation to the organism without being lodged in a substantial consciousness. The mental image is a memory image. Such images which, as symbols, play so large a part in thinking, belong to the environment. The passage we read is made up from memory images, and the people we see about us we see very largely by the help of memory images. Very frequently we find that the thing we see and that we suppose answers to the character of an object is not really there; it was an image. The image is there in its relation to the individual who not only has sense organs but who also has certain past experiences. It is the organism that has had such experiences that has such imagery. In saying this we are taking an attitude which we are constantly using when we say we have read a certain thing; the memory image is there in its relationship to a certain organism with certain past experiences, with certain values also definitely there in relation to that particular environment as remembered.

Consciousness as such refers to both the organism and its environment and cannot be located simply in either. If we free the field in this sense, then we can proceed with a behavioristic treatment without having the difficulties in which Watson found himself in dealing with mental images. He denied there was any such thing, and then had to admit it, and then tried to minimize it. Of course, the same difficulty lies in dealing with experience regarded as states of consciousness. If we recognize that these characters of things do exist in relation to the organism, then we are free to approach the organism from the standpoint of behaviorism.

I do not regard consciousness as having selective power, in one current sense of "selection." What we term "consciousness" is just that relation of organism and environment in which selection takes place. Consciousness arises from the interrelation of the form and the environment, and it involves both of them. Hunger does not create food, nor is an object a food object without relation to hunger. When there is that relation between form and environment, then objects can appear which would not have been there otherwise; but the animal does not create the food in the sense that he makes an object out of nothing. Rather, when the form is put into such relation with the environment, then there emerges such a thing as food.

Wheat becomes food; just as water arises in the relation of hydrogen and oxygen. It is not simply cutting something out and holding it by itself (as the term "selection" seems to suggest), but in this process there appears or emerges something that was not there before. There is not, I say, anything about this view that impresses us as involving any sort of magic when we take it in the form of the evolution of certain other characters, and I want to insist that this conception does cover just that field which is referred to as consciousness.

Of course, when one goes back to such a conception of consciousness as early psychologists used, and everything experienced is lodged in consciousness, then one has to create another world outside and say that there is something out there answering to these experiences. I want to insist that it is possible to take the behavioristic view of the world without being troubled or tripped up by the conception of consciousness; there are certainly no more serious difficulties involved in such a view as has been proposed than there are in a conception of consciousness as a something that arises at a certain point in the history of physical forms and runs parallel in some way with specific nervous states. Try to state that conception in a form applicable to the work of the psychologist and you find yourself in all sorts of difficulties that are far greater than those in the conceptions of emergence and relativity. If you are willing to approach the world from the standpoint of these conceptions, then you can approach psychology from the behaviorist's point of view.

The other conception that I have brought out concerns the particular sort of intelligence that we ascribe to the human animal, so-called "rational intelligence," or consciousness in another sense of the term. If consciousness is a substance, it can be said that this consciousness is rational per se; and just by definition the problem of the appearance of what we call rationality is avoided. What I have attempted to do is to bring rationality back to a certain type of conduct, the type of conduct in which the individual puts himself in the attitude of the whole group to which he belongs. This implies that the whole group is involved in some organized activity and that in this organized activity the action of one calls for the action of all the others. What we term "reason" arises when one of the organisms takes into its own response the attitude of the other organisms involved. It is possible for the organism so to assume the attitudes of the group that are involved in its own act within this whole co-operative process. When it does so, it is what we term "a rational being." If its conduct has such universality, it has also necessity, that is, the sort of necessity involved in the whole act—if one acts in one way the others must act in another way. Now, if the individual can take the attitude of the others and control his action by these attitudes, and control their action through his own, then we have what we can term "rationality." Rationality is as large as the group which is involved; and that group could be, of course, functionally, potentially, as large as you like. It may include all beings speaking the same language.

Language as such is simply a process by means of which the individual who is engaged in co-operative activity can get the attitude of others involved in the same activity. Through gestures, that is, through the part of his act which calls out the response of others, he can arouse in himself the attitude of the others. Language as a set of significant symbols is simply the set of gestures which the organism employs in calling out the response of others. Those gestures primarily are nothing but parts of the act which do naturally stimulate others engaged in the co-operative process to carry out their parts. Rationality then can be stated in terms of such behavior if we recognize that the gesture can affect the individual as it affects others so as to call out the response which belongs to the other. Mind or reason presupposes social organization and co-operative activity in this social organization. Thinking is simply the reasoning of the individual, the carrying-on of a conversation between what I have termed the "I" and the "me."

In taking the attitude of the group, one has stimulated himself to respond in a certain fashion. His response, the "I," is the way in which he acts. If he acts in that way he is, so to speak, putting something up to the group, and changing the group. His gesture calls out then a gesture which will be slightly different. The self thus arises in the development of the behavior of the social form that is capable of taking the attitude of others involved in the same co-operative activity. The pre-condition of such behavior is the development of the nervous system which enables the individual to take the attitude of the others. He could not, of course, take the indefinite number of attitudes of others, even if all the nerve paths were present, if there were not an organized social activity going on such that the action of one may reproduce the action of an indefinite number of others doing the same thing. Given, however, such an organized activity, one can take the attitude of anyone in the group.

Such are the two conceptions of consciousness that I wanted to bring out, since they seem to me to make possible a development of behaviorism beyond the limits to which it has been carried, and to make it a very suitable approach to the objects of social psychology. With those key concepts one does not have to come back to certain conscious fields lodged inside the individual; one is dealing throughout with the relation of the conduct of the individual to the environment.

BIBLIOGRAPHY

MEAD, George H. *The Philosophy of the Present.* Chicago: Open Court, 1932.

———, *Mind, Self, and Society from the standpoint of a Social Behaviorist.* (Charles W. Morris, ed.) Chicago: U. of Chicago Press, 1934.

———, *Movements of Thought in the Nineteenth Century.* (Merritt H. Moore, ed.) Chicago: U. of Chicago Press, 1936.

———, *The Philosophy of the Act.* (Charles W. Morris, ed.) Chicago: U. of Chicago Press, 1938.

———, *The Social Psychology of George Herbert Mead.* (Anselm Strauss, ed.) Chicago: U. of Chicago Press, 1956.

AMES, Van Meter. *Zen and American Thought.* Honolulu: U. of Hawaii Press, 1962.

CLAYTON, Alfred S. *Emergent Mind and Education: A Study of George H. Mead's Bio-Social Behaviorism from an Educational Point of View.* N.Y.: Columbia U. Press, 1943.

HOLMES, Eugene C. *Social Philosophy and the Social Mind: A Study of the Genetic Methods of J. M. Baldwin, G. H. Mead, and J. E. Boodin.* N.Y.: Columbia U. Press, 1942.

LEE, Grace Chin. *George Herbert Mead: Philosophy of the Social Individual.* N.Y.: King's Crown Press, 1945.

NATANSON, Maurice. *The Social Dynamics of George H. Mead.* Washington, D.C.: Public Affairs Press, 1956.

PFUETZE, Paul. *Self, Society, Existence. Human Nature and Dialogue in the Thought of George Herbert Mead and Martin Buber.* (Revised ed.) N.Y.: Harpers, 1961.

New Realism

The realistic reaction against idealism reached a high point in the United States with the publication in *The Journal of Philosophy, Psychology and Scientific Methods* of "The Program and First Platform of the Six Realists." These realists looked upon philosophy as a cooperative inquiry, and they deplored the divorce between philosophy and science. Here was to be a first step in the progressive development of philosophical inquiry. The "new" realists hoped that they might articulate a doctrine free from the traditional objections to realism.

They began by attacking the prevailing idealism of the previous century, which they asserted was based upon an unclear use of the word "idea." They rejected the Absolute Idealism of Royce and Bradley, the doctrine of internal relations, and the subjectivism of Berkeley. "Reality" or "fact'" is an ultimate category, and the "truth" of a judgment means that the content asserted by it is a "reality" or "fact." In veridical perception or judgment, the "reals" are themselves the immediate content of consciousness. The realists maintained that at least some objects, physical things, logical and mathematical entities, other minds, etc., exist *independently* of a knowing consciousness. Moreover, things continue to exist unaltered when they are not known, and their reality is not dependent in any way on someone's experiencing or conceiving of them.

This newly won unity among philosophers proved to be only temporary, for aside from general agreement on some principles, the realists disagreed about many issues—the nature of error, the subsistence of mathematical and logical entities, the nature of the object known and so on. Their whole program was soon to be seriously criticized by the critical realists.

Of the six new realists, the most important were Ralph Barton Perry and William Pepperell Montague. Edwin B. Holt and Walter B. Pitkin eventually left philosophy for psychology.

RALPH BARTON PERRY (1876–1957). A biographical note appears on page 338.

WILLIAM PEPPERELL MONTAGUE (1873–1953) was born in Chelsea, Massachusetts. He was an enthusiastic and enlivening member of the realist group, vigorously combative in discussion, yet receptive to other points of view. He studied at Harvard, chiefly under Royce, where he took his Ph.D. His teaching career was spent at Barnard College and Columbia University (1903–1947). He was a President of the American Philosophical Association, Eastern Division (1929). Montague rejected the other new realists' notion that *all* perceptual appearances are part of the physical world. Error, illusion, and hallucination cannot be found, he said, in the existent world of space and time, but in the subsistent realm of Platonic essences. "Consciousness" was conceived by him to be a form of potential physical energy. Montague characterized his philosophy as "a spiritualistic or animistic materialism." Among his important works are *The Ways of Knowing* (1925), and his "Carus Lectures," *The Great Visions of Philosophy* (1950). In the latter, his attitude toward epistemological dualism was modified somewhat. He also favored what he took to be a scientifically warranted religion. Although Montague was a vigorous critic of the reigning philosophies of his day—behaviorism, pragmatism, logical positivism, and organicism—he found some elements of truth in many different points of view.

EDWIN B. HOLT (1875–1946) was born in Winchester, Massachusetts and studied at Columbia and Harvard. He took his Ph.D. at Harvard in 1901 and taught psychology there from 1901 to 1918 and later at Princeton (1926–36). Holt, an early champion of Freud, tried to state Freudian ideas within a behavioristic framework. His book, *The Concept of Consciousness* (1914) outlined

many of the ideas of the new behaviorism. His continuing interest in psychology also resulted in *The Freudian Wish in Psychology* (1915), and *Animal Drive and Learning Power* (1931).

EDWARD G. SPAULDING (1873–1939) was born in Burlington, Vermont. He studied at the University of Vermont, took his Ph.D. at Bonn (1900), and taught at City College of New York and Princeton. He was the author of *The New Rationalism* (1921).

WALTER T. MARVIN (1872–1944) was born in New York City. He took his B.A. at Columbia and his Ph.D. at Bonn (1898). He taught at Columbia, Adelbert College, Western Reserve, and Princeton. In 1910, he became Professor of Philosophy at Rutgers. Marvin published *A First Book in Metaphysics* (1912), which is realistic and pluralistic in viewpoint. In *The History of European Philosophy* (1917) he emphasized scientific thought to a greater degree than had his predecessors.

WALTER B. PITKIN (1878–1953) was born in Michigan. He taught at Columbia University, where he became Professor of Psychology and Journalism.

THE PROGRAM AND FIRST PLATFORM OF SIX REALISTS [1]
(1910)

Philosophy is famous for its disagreements, which have contributed not a little towards bringing it into disrepute as being unscientific, subjective, or temperamental. These disagreements are due in part, no doubt, to the subject-matter of philosophy, but chiefly to the lack

[1] Reprinted from *The Journal of Philosophy, Psychology and Scientific Methods,* Vol. VII, No. 15 (July 21, 1910), pp. 393–401.

of precision and uniformity in the use of words and to the lack of deliberate cooperation in research. In having these failings philosophy still differs widely from such sciences as physics and chemistry. They tend to make it seem mere opinion; for through the appearance of many figurative or loose expressions in the writings of isolated theorists, the impression is given that philosophical problems and their solutions are essentially personal. This impression is strengthened by the fact that philosophy concerns itself with emotions, temperaments, and taste. A conspicuous result of this lack of cooperation, common terminology, and a working agreement as to fundamental presuppositions is that genuine philosophical problems have been obscured, and real philosophical progress has been seriously hindered.

It is therefore with the hope that by cooperation genuine problems will be revealed, philosophical thought will be clarified, and a way opened for real progress, that the undersigned have come together, deliberated, and endeavored to reach an agreement. Such cooperation has three fairly distinct, though not necessarily successive stages: first, it seeks a statement of fundamental principles and doctrines; secondly, it aims at a program of constructive work following a method founded on these principles and doctrines; finally, it endeavors to obtain a system of axioms, methods, hypotheses, and facts, which have been so arrived at and formulated that at least those investigators who have cooperated can accept them as a whole.

After several conferences the undersigned have found that they hold certain doctrines in common. Some of these doctrines, which constitute a realistic platform, they herewith publish in the hope of carrying out further the program stated above. Each list has a different author, but has been discussed at length, revised, and agreed to by the other conferees. The six lists, therefore, though differently formulated, are held to represent the same doctrines.

By conferring on other topics, by interchange of ideas, and by systematic criticism of one another's phraseology, methods, and hypotheses, we hope to develop a common technique, a common terminology, and so finally a common doctrine which will enjoy some measure of that authority which the natural sciences possess. We shall have accomplished one of our purposes if our publications tempt other philosophers to form small cooperative groups with similar aims.

EDWIN B. HOLT, *Harvard University.*
WALTER T. MARVIN, *Rutgers College.*
W. P. MONTAGUE, *Columbia University.*
RALPH BARTON PERRY, *Harvard University.*
WALTER B. PITKIN, *Columbia University.*
E. G. SPAULDING, *Princeton University.*

I

1. The entities (objects, facts, *et cæt.*) under study in logic, mathematics, and the physical sciences are not mental in any usual or proper meaning of the word "mental."

2. The being and nature of these entities are in no sense conditioned by their being known.

3. The degree of unity, consistency, or connection subsisting among entities is a matter to be empirically ascertained.

4. In the present stage of our knowledge there is a presumption in favor of pluralism.

5. An entity subsisting in certain relations to other entities enters into new relations without necessarily negating or altering its already subsisting relations.

6. No self-consistent or satisfactory logic (or system of logic) so far invented countenances the "organic" theory of knowledge or the "internal" view of relations.

7. Those who assert this (anti-realistic) view, use in their exposition a logic which is inconsistent with their doctrine.

EDWIN B. HOLT

II

1. Epistemology is not logically fundamental.[2]

2. There are many existential, as well as non-existential, propositions which are logically prior to epistemology.[3]

[2] Some of the principles of logic are logically prior to any proposition that is deduced from other propositions. The theories of the nature of knowledge and of the relation of knowledge to its object are for this reason logically subsequent to the principles of logic. In short, logic is logically prior to any epistemological theory. Again, as theories of reality are deduced and are made to conform to the laws of logic they too are logically subsequent to logic; and in so far as logic is logically present in them it is itself a theory or part of a theory of reality.

[3] The terms knowledge, consciousness, and experience found in common sense and in psychology are not logically fundamental, but are logically subsequent to parts at least of a theory of reality that asserts the existence of terms and relations which are not consciousness or experience. *E.g.*, the psychical is distinguished from the physical and the physiological.

Now idealism has not shown that the terms knowledge, consciousness, and experience of its epistemology or of its theory of reality are logically fundamental or indefinable, nor has it succeeded in defining them without logically prior terms that are elsewhere explicitly excluded from its theory of reality. In short, idealistic epistemologists have borrowed the terms knowledge, consciousness, and experience from psychology, but have ignored or denied the propositions in psychology that are logically prior. In other words, epistemology has not thus far made itself logically independent of psychology nor has it freed itself logically from the common-sense dualism of psychology. On the contrary, epistemology from Locke until to-day has been and has remained, in part at least, a branch of psychology.

3. There are certain principles of logic which are logically prior to all scientific and metaphysical systems.

One of these is that which is usually called the external view of relations.

4. This view may be stated thus: In the proposition, "the term *a* is in the relation *R* to the term *b*," *aR* in no degree constitutes *b*, nor does *Rb* constitute *a*, nor does *R* constitute either *a* or *b*.

5. It is possible to add new propositions to some bodies of information without thereby requiring any modification of those bodies of information.

6. There are no propositions which are (accurately speaking) partly true and partly false, for all such instances can be logically analyzed into at least two propositions one of which is true and the other false. Thus as knowledge advances only two modifications of any proposition of the older knowledge are logically possible; it can be rejected as false or it can be analyzed into at least two propositions one of which is rejected.

As corollaries of the foregoing:

7. The nature of reality can not be inferred merely from the nature of knowledge.

8. The entities under study in logic, mathematics, physics, and many other sciences are not mental in any proper or usual meaning of the word mental.

9. The proposition, "This or that object is known," does not imply that such object is conditioned by the knowing. In other words, it does not force us to infer that such object is spiritual, that it exists only as the experiential content of some mind, or that it may not be ultimately real just as known.

WALTER T. MARVIN

III

§1. The Meaning of Realism

1. Realism holds that things known may continue to exist unaltered when they are not known, or that things may pass in and out of the cognitive relation without prejudice to their reality, or that the existence of a thing is not correlated with or dependent upon the fact that anybody experiences it, perceives it, conceives it, or is in any way aware of it.

2. Realism is opposed to subjectivism or epistemological idealism which denies that things can exist apart from an experience of them, or independently of the cognitive relation.

3. The point at issue between realism and idealism should not be confused with the points at issue between materialism and spiritualism, automatism and interactionism, empiricism and rationalism, or pluralism and absolutism.

§2. *The Opposition to Realism.*

Among the various classic refutations of realism the following fallacious assumptions and inferences are prominent.

1. THE PHYSIOLOGICAL ARGUMENT: The mind can have for its direct object only its own ideas or states, and external objects, if they exist at all, can only be known indirectly by a process of inference, of questionable validity and doubtful utility. This principle is fallacious because a knowing process is never its own object, but is rather the means by which some other object is known. The object thus known or referred to may be another mental state, a physical thing, or a merely logical entity.

2. THE INTUITIONAL ARGUMENT: This argument stands out most prominently in the philosophy of Berkeley. It has two forms. The first consists of a confused identification of a truism and an absurdity. The truism: *We can only know that objects exist, when they are known.* The absurdity: *We know that objects can only exist when they are known.* The second form of the arguments derives its force from a play upon the word idea, as follows: *Every "idea" (meaning a mental process or state) is incapable of existing apart from a mind; every known entity is an "idea" (meaning an object of thought); therefore, every known entity is incapable of existing apart from a mind.* It is to the failure to perceive these fallacies that idealism owes its supposedly axiomatic character.

3. THE PHYSIOLOGICAL ARGUMENT: Because the sensations we receive determine what objects we shall know, therefore the objects known are constructs or products of our perceptual experience. The fallacy here consists in arguing from the true premise that sensations are the *ratio cognoscendi* of the external world, to the false conclusion that they are therefore its *ratio fiendi* or *essendi*.

§3. *The Implications of Realism:*

1. Cognition is a peculiar type of relation which may subsist between a living being and any entity.

2. Cognition belongs to the same world as that of its objects. It has its place in the order of nature. There is nothing transcendental or supernatural about it.

3. The extent to which consciousness pervades nature, and the

conditions under which it may arise and persist, are questions which can be solved, if at all, only by the methods of empiricism and naturalism.

W. P. MONTAGUE

IV

1. The object or content of consciousness is any entity in so far as it is responded to by another entity in a specific manner exhibited by the reflex nervous system. Thus physical nature, for example, is, under certain circumstances, directly present in consciousness.

In its historical application, this means that Cartesian dualism and the representative theory are false; and that attempts to overcome these by reducing mind and nature to one another or to some third substance, are gratuitous.

2. The specific response which determines an entity to be content of consciousness, does not directly modify such entities otherwise than to endow them with this content status. In other words, consciousness selects from a field of entities which it does not create.

In its historical application, this implies the falsity of Berkeleyan and post-Berkeleyan idealism in so far as this asserts that consciousness is a general *ratio essendi*.

3. The response which determines an entity to be content, may itself be responded to and made content in like manner. In other words, the difference between subject and object of consciousness is not a difference of quality or substance, but a difference of office or place in a configuration.

In its historical application, this implies the falsity not only of the Cartesian dualism, but of all idealistic dualisms that, because they regard subject and object as non-interchangeable, conclude that the subject is either unknowable, or knowable only in some unique way such as intuitively or reflexively.

4. The same entity possesses both immanence, by virtue of its membership in one class, and also transcendence, by virtue of the fact that it may belong also to indefinitely many other classes. In other words, immanence and transcendence are compatible and not contradictory predicates.

In its historical application, this implies the falsity of the subjectivistic argument from the ego-centric predicament, *i.e.*, the argument that because entities are content of consciousness they can not also transcend consciousness; it also implies that, so far as based on such subjectivistic premises, the idealistic theory of a transcendent subjectivity is gratuitous.

5. An entity possesses some relations independently of one an-

other; and the ignorance or discovery of further relations does not invalidate a limited knowledge of relations.

In its historical applications, this implies the falsity of the contention of absolute idealism that it is necessary to know all of an entity's relations in order to know any of its relations, or that only the whole truth is wholly true.

6. The logical categories of unity, such as homogeneity, consistency, coherence, interrelation, etc., do not in any case imply a determinate degree of unity. Hence the degree of unity which the world possesses can not be determined logically, but only by assembling the results of the special branches of knowledge. On the basis of such evidence, there is a present presumption in favor of the hypothesis that the world as a whole is less unified than are certain of its parts.

In its historical application, this implies that the great speculative monisms, such as those of Plato, Spinoza, and certain modern idealists, are both dogmatic and contrary to the evidence.

RALPH BARTON PERRY

V

The realist holds that things known are not products of the knowing relation nor essentially dependent for their existence or behavior upon that relation. This doctrine has three claims upon your acceptance: first, it is the natural, instinctive belief of all men, and for this, if for no other reason, puts the burden of proof upon those who would discredit it; secondly, all refutations of it known to the present writer presuppose or even actually employ some of its exclusive implications; and, thirdly, it is logically demanded by all the observations and hypotheses of the natural sciences, including psychology.

Involved more or less intimately in a realistic view are the following:

1. One identical term may stand in many relations.

2. A term may change some of its relations to some other terms without thereby changing all its other relations to those same or to other terms.

3. What relations are changed by a given change of relation can not always be deduced merely from the nature of either the terms involved or their relation.

4. The hypothesis that "there can be no object without a subject" is pure tautology. It is confessedly a description of the cognitive situation only; and it says, in effect, that everything experienced is experienced. It becomes significant only by virtue of the wholly un-

warranted assumption that doctrines 1, 2, and 3, above given, are false. This assumption, however, is fatal to the idealist's supposed discovery, inasmuch as it means that there can be no true propositions. In conceding this, the idealist refutes himself.

5. In no body of knowledge, not even in evidences about the nature of the knowledge relation, can we discover that possible knowledge is limited or what its limits may be.

6. Entities are transcendent to the so-called "knowing mind" or "consciousness" only as a term is to the relations in which it may stand, viz., in two radically different manners: first, as the term is not identical with a particular relation in which it stands, so too a thing in the knowledge relation is not the relation itself; secondly, as the term may enter into or go out of a particular relation, without thereby being changed essentially or destroyed, so too can an object of knowledge exist prior to and after its entrance into or removed from the knowledge relation. Transcendence thus means, in the first place, distinctness and, in the second place, functional independence.

7. There may be axiomatic truths or intuitive truths. But the fact that a truth belongs to either of these classes does not make it fundamental or important for a theory of knowledge, much less for a theory of reality. Like all other truths, it too must be interpreted in the light of other relevant truths.

8. Though terms are not modified by being brought into new contexts, this does not imply that an existent can not be changed by another existent.

WALTER B. PITKIN

VI

1. Realism, while admitting the tautology that every entity which is known is in relation to knowing or experience or consciousness, holds that this knowing, etc., is eliminable, so that the entity is known as it would be if the knowing were not taking place. Briefly, the entity is, in its being, behavior, and character, independent of the knowing. This position agrees with common sense and with science in holding (1) that not all entities are mental, conscious, or spiritual, and (2) that entities are knowable without being known.

2. The fact that terms are in the cognitive relation does not imply that the terms are mutually dependent on, or capable of modifying, either each other or the relation, any more than this dependence, etc., is implied for any two terms in any other relation. The proposition that there is this dependence, etc., constitutes the "internal

---

[4] To hold the "internal view" means, in my opinion, to hold that, in order that a relation may relate, the relation must either (1) penetrate its terms, or (2) be

view" of relations.[4] Most of those systems which are opposed to realism can be shown to presuppose this "internal view," but this view can be shown to be self-contradictory and to presuppose the "external view."

3. That position which is based in part on the acceptance and the consistent use and development of the implications of those logical doctrines which are presupposed as a condition for any position being stated, argued, and held to be true has, thereby, a strong presumption created in favor of its truth.[5]

4. There is at least one logical doctrine and one principle which are ultimately presupposed by any system which is held to be true. That doctrine is the "external view" of relations, and the principle is that truth is independent of proof, although proof is not independent of truth. The first of these means, briefly:

5. (1) That both a term and a relation are (unchangeable) elements or entities; (2) that a term may stand in one or in many relations to one or many other terms; and (3) that any of these terms and that some of these relations could be absent or that other terms and relations could be present without there being any resulting modification, etc., of the remaining or already present terms or relations.

6. By this "external view" it is made logically possible that the knowing process and its object should be qualitatively dissimilar. (Cf. 1.)

7. The principle (see 4) means, that, while on the one hand no proposition is so certain that it can be regarded as exempt from examination, criticism, and the demand for proof, on the other hand, any proposition, if free from self-contradiction, may be true (in some system). In this sense every proposition is tentative, even those of this platform.

COROLLARY.—It is impossible to get a criterion, definition, theory, or content for the concept "absolute" by which it can be absolutely known or proved that any criterion, definition, theory, or content is absolutely true, *i.e.*, is more than tentative. The most that can be

---

mediated by an underlying (transcendent) reality. From the penetration there is deduced (*a*) modification, or (*b*) similarity, or (*c*) the generation of a contradiction. Cf. my paper, "The Logical Structure of Self-refuting Systems," *Phil. Review*, XIX., 3, pp. 277–282.

[5] Such a system *I hold* to be realism, its chief feature being the interpretation of the cognitive relation in accordance with the "external view." This "external view" can be held to be true quite consistently with itself, and is in this sense, I hold, self-consistent, as is also, in my opinion, realism. Accordingly I hold further that realism is not a merely dogmatic system, and that, as self-consistent, it refutes and does not merely contradict certain opposed systems which, as based on the "internal view," are self-refuting.

claimed for such a criterion, etc., is that it may be absolutely true, although not proved to be.

8. Any entity may be known as it really is in some respects without its being known in all respects and without the other entities to which it is related being known, so that knowledge can increase by *accretion.*

9. Knowing, consciousness, etc., are facts to be investigated only in the same way as are other facts, and are not necessarily more important than are other facts.

10. The position stated in this platform, which is a position concerning knowing as well as other things, can apply to itself, as a special instance of knowledge, all its own propositions about knowledge.[6]

EDWARD GLEASON SPAULDING

BIBLIOGRAPHY

For works dealing with New Realism the reader is referred to the General Bibliography, section 3.

[6] I hold that for this reason the position here stated is self-critical, and that it is this which distinguishes it from a large class of historical systems, notably phenomenalism, subjective and objective idealism, and absolutism.

Critical Realism

The critical realists, like the new realists, were interested in developing a cooperative approach to philosophical questions, and the book *Essays in Critical Realism* served as their platform and program. The critical realists were agreed on the general outline of their epistemological theories, though they differed in other areas. They accepted the new realists' criticism of idealism. With them, too, they asserted that there are real objects independent of the knower. But they dissented from the new realism on certain important points, especially in denying that the mind perceives or knows external objects immediately or directly. This latter contention they took to be a form of naïve realism, and they adopted the term "critical" in contrast to this "naïve" realism.

The critical realists asserted that there are at least three elements in knowledge: a) a subject, b) an external object, and c) a mediating "idea," "sensation" or "essence." The mind is directly confronted with "sense data" or "essences," on the basis of which it knows external objects. These material objects, however, are not identical with the data by which they are known. The critical realists were thus advocating a form of epistemological dualism reminiscent of Locke and Descartes. But the critical realists differed among themselves about the character of the dualism—the metaphysical import—of their theory.

What was the nature of "sense data"? They were variously interpreted as "psychical" or "mental existents," as "universal essences," as the identifiable "forms" of objects, or as their detached concrete "nature." If the new realists had difficulties in explaining error, the critical realists had difficulties in accounting for truth. Since it is the perceptual data and not the things themselves that are the *direct* objects of knowledge, how can we be sure the data truly represent external objects? Santayana, for example, in dealing with this problem, was led to a highly skeptical position in his *Skepticism and Animal Faith* (1923). Sellars, however, never doubted the possibility of knowledge and tried to avoid skepticism. In metaphysics, Sellars, Strong, Drake, and Santayana were naturalists. Strong and Drake supplemented this naturalism with a form of panpsychism, Sellars with materialism and emergent evolution, and Santayana with materialism and Platonism. Rogers was a skeptic, yet sympathetic to naturalism. Lovejoy and Pratt were dualists in psychophysics and epistemology. Lovejoy emphasized the significance of time in nature and mind and called his philosophy "temporalism." Pratt was sympathetic to Christian theism. Thus, although in agreement in the general outline of their realism, the critical realists differed on a variety of other points. The following is a brief description of the critical realists mentioned above:

GEORGE SANTAYANA (1863–1952). A biographical note appears on page 219.

ARTHUR O. LOVEJOY (1873–1962). A biographical note appears on page 354.

ROY WOOD SELLARS (1880–   ). A biographical note appears on page 363.

JAMES BISSETT PRATT (1875–1944) was born in Elmira, N. Y. He took his Ph.D. at Harvard in 1905, and spent most of his teaching career at Williams College. He was President of the American Philosophical Association, Eastern Division (1935). He devised a theory of knowledge, which he called "personal realism." He devoted much time to the study of religious consciousness and of the place of personality in the spiritual realm, and to Buddhism and the religions of India.

Pratt was a dualist who maintained that the self is a substance whose tool is the body with which it interacts. The continuity of thought, he held, is evidence for the independent existence of the self. In personality he recognized keys to the nature of the universe, which was organic and purposive. Among his important books are *The Psychology of Religious Belief* (1907), *What is Pragmatism?* (1909), *The Religious Consciousness* (1920), *Matter and Spirit* (1922), *Personal Realism* (1937), *Naturalism* (1939), *Reason in the Art of Living* (1950).

DURANT DRAKE (1878–1933) studied at Harvard and Columbia, and taught for many years at Vassar College. He considered himself to be a reformed "meliorist," opposed to needless unhappiness. Drake was a critic of both pragmatism and radical empiricism because of their anthropocentricism; he considered philosophy to be an objective and disinterested science. In *Mind and Its Place in Nature* (1925), and in later articles Drake expanded and modified his realism. He went on to accept a form of epistemological monism, agreeing with the neo-realists that the data of experience are the physical things that surround us, and that what we are aware of is not the cognitive state but outer objects. Drake opposed a mind-body dualism and even went so far as to claim the existence of mental states as primary in nature. Among his other works are *The Problem of Religion* (1916), *The Problem of Conduct* (1914) and *The New Morality* (1928).

CHARLES A. STRONG (1862–1940) began in philosophy, but later studied psychology at Harvard and in Germany before becoming Professor of Psychology at Columbia University. His main interests were the mind-body problem, the question of the origin of consciousness, and the nature of truth. Among his books are *Why the Mind Has a Body* (1903), *The Origin of Consciousness* (1918), *The Wisdom of the Beasts* (1921), *A Theory of Knowledge* (1923).

ARTHUR K. ROGERS (1868–1936) took his Ph.D. at the University of Chicago in 1898 and afterwards taught at Alfred University, Butler College, The University of Missouri, and Yale. Among his books are *The Religious Conception of The World*

(1907), *English and American Philosophy since 1800* (1922), *The Theory of Ethics* (1922), *What is Truth?* (1923), and *Morals in Review* (1927).

The following selection contains brief summarizing passages from the various pieces in *Essays in Critical Realism*.

ESSAYS IN CRITICAL REALISM [1]
(1920)

PREFACE

The doctrine here defended, while definitely realistic, is distinctly different from the "new" realism of the American group, whose volume, published in 1912, was a signal example of the value of co-operative effort in crystallizing and advertising a point of view in philosophy. Our realism is not a physically monistic realism, or a merely logical realism, and escapes the many difficulties which have prevented the general acceptance of the "new" realism. It is also free, we believe, from the errors and ambiguities of the older realism of Locke and his successors. To find an adjective that should connote the essential features of our brand of realism seemed chimerical, and we have contented ourselves with the vague, but accurate, phrase *critical realism*. Needless to say, the word "critical" has no reference to the Kantian philosophy, which should not be allowed to monopolize that excellent adjective. Our choice of this phrase was confirmed by the fact that several members of the group had already used it for their views—which, however divergent their expression, have been, we recognize, essentially the same. . . .

It should be added, however, that no agreement has been sought except on the epistemological problem with which this volume is concerned; and, actually, the members of our group hold somewhat different ontological views. Critics of the volume are asked to bear this in mind, and not to confuse the discussion of the epistemological solution here offered by the introduction of dissenting opinions upon irrelevant topics. We have found it entirely possible to isolate the problem of knowledge; and we believe that its solution lies along the lines that we have here indicated.

[1] From *Essays in Critical Realism*, by D. Drake, A. O. Lovejoy, J. B. Pratt, A. K. Rogers, G. Santayana, R. W. Sellars and C. A. Strong, N. Y. 1920.

THE APPROACH TO CRITICAL REALISM

The Justification of Realism

There are two familiar starting-points for knowledge, the objective and the subjective. The objectively-minded philosophers suppose that the data of perception are the very physical existents which we all practically believe to be surrounding and threatening our bodies. These physical objects themselves somehow get within experience, are directly apprehended; their surfaces constitute our visual and tactile data. The subjectively-minded philosophers suppose, on the contrary, that the data of perception are psychological existents, so many pulses or throbs of a stream of psychic life. At best they are merely copies or representatives of the outer objects. In so far, both approaches are realistic; but the subjectively-minded realist is, in a sense, shut in, according to his theory, to "ideas," *i.e.* to mental substitutes for outer objects, whereas the objectively-minded, or naïve, realist (for this seems to be the view of the plain man) believes that his experience extends beyond his body, and includes, in some of their aspects, those outer subjects. Whatever arguments are then adduced for "realistic epistemological monism" and "realistic epistemological dualism" respectively do little to shake the faith thus based upon an initial definition. An *impasse* exists here, and will exist until it is seen that *neither* starting-point, objective nor subjective, correctly describes what we have to start with, what is "given" (= what appears, what is apprehended) in immediate experience. It is the object of this paper, then, to expose the error in each of these views, and to point out a third view—we call it Critical Realism—which combines the insights of both these historic positions while free from the objections which can properly be raised to each.[2]

---

[2] In the above paragraph I have, for convenience, given the names *epistemological monism* and *epistemological dualism* to the two historic positions which we believe to be transcended by our analysis. There is, I should add, some doubt among us as to whether our position should be called a *dualism*.

On the one hand, in certain contexts it is desirable to emphasize the duality which we believe to exist between the cognitive state which is the vehicle of knowledge and the object known. By contrast with neo-realists, idealists, and believers in "pure experience," we are dualists.

On the other hand, the term "dualism" implies to most readers, probably, the notion that what we *know* is a mental state (or "idea"), an existent from which we have to infer the existence and character of the physical object. This notion, however, we repudiate. What we perceive, conceive, remember, think of, is the outer object itself (or, on occasion, the mental state introspected, remembered, or conceived), which is independent of the knowledge-process, and beyond which there is nothing else.

Before proceeding, however, to consider these two historic types of realism, it will be well to deal with the spectre of pure subjectivism, which is a likely, though not a logically necessary, deduction from the psychological starting-point. If we are shut in to our mental states, we can never know positively that anything exists beyond them. Perhaps, then, our experience (psychologically taken) = existence. It is doubtful, indeed, if any one practically believes this; for the content of our experience is very narrow, and we all really believe that many things exist, have existed, and will exist, that we, individually, and, for that matter, collectively, have never so much as thought of, and never will think of or know anything about. Moreover, those objects which we do think of, or perceive, are irresistibly believed to have an existence of their own, far more extensive, both as to nature and in time, than that of our evanescent and shallow experience. All who thus believe that existence is far wider than experience—that objects exist in or for themselves, apart from our experiencing them—are properly to be called realists. And we are now first to consider whether realism—any sort of realism—is philosophically indicated (as physicians say) as well as practically inevitable.

Now, as has been said above, it is the conviction of the authors of this volume that the psychological starting-point is as erroneous as the objective or physical. Our data—the character-complexes "given" in conscious experience—are simply character-complexes, essences, logical entities, which are irresistibly taken to be the characters of the existents perceived, or otherwise known. If this is true, it becomes necessary to ask what reason . . . we have for believing in the existence of physical objects. . . . The answer, in a word, is that our instinctive (and practically inevitable) belief in the existence of the physical world about us is pragmatically justifiable. . . .

DURANT DRAKE

Further, if the analysis is accepted (made in this essay, and, at greater length, in the concluding essay) which discriminates the "datum" in cases of knowledge from the mental state which is the vehicle of its givenness, we cannot say that the datum (what is "given" to the knower, what we start with in our epistemological inquiry) is an existent, representing the object. On the contrary, it is (in so far as knowledge is accurate) simply the essence or character (the *what*) of the object known. Professors Sellars, Lovejoy, and Pratt, however, maintain that although what is *given* is a mere character-complex, it is in reality *in toto* the character of the mental state of the moment, and so *is* an existent, in spite of the fact that its existence is not given; they may perhaps therefore be called dualistic by somewhat better right than the rest of us, although we all agree as to what the existential situation in knowledge is, and as to the fact that what we *know* is the independent object itself. Critics of our view are asked, therefore, not to label us simply as "dualists," but to recognize precisely what sort of duality we do and do not admit.

PRAGMATISM VERSUS THE PRAGMATIST

I shall in this essay inquire into the logical relations of the doctrine known as pragmatism to the principal philosophical problems under consideration in this volume. Does pragmatism imply the truth of realism, or of idealism, or of neither? If it is in any sense realistic, is it so in a monistic, or a dualistic, or in some third sense? Does it, expressly or by implication, affirm, or admit, or deny, the existence of "consciousness," of "mental states," or "psychical entities"? These are the questions to which answers are to be sought. . . .

I must be content with the results, in relation to the questions set down at the beginning, which have thus far been reached. And the most significant of those results may now be summed up in a sentence. *A consistent pragmatism must recognize:*

(a) *That all "instrumental" knowledge is, or at least includes and requires, "presentative" knowledge, a representation of not-present existents by present data;*

(b) *That, pragmatically considered, knowledge is thus necessarily and constantly conversant with entities which are existentially "transcendent" of the knowing experience, and frequently with entities which transcend the total experience of the knower;*

(c) *That, if a real physical world having the characteristics set forth by natural science is assumed, certain of the contents of experience, and specifically the contents of anticipation and retrospection, cannot be assigned to that world, and must therefore be called "psychical" (i.e. experienced but not physical) entities;*

(d) *That knowledge is mediated through such psychical existences, and would be impossible without them.*

ARTHUR O. LOVEJOY

CRITICAL REALISM AND THE POSSIBILITY OF KNOWLEDGE

. . . Percepts are simply my means of perceiving, and thoughts my means of thinking, just as the voice is my means of speaking. To insist that I cannot perceive a red house because I have to perceive it by means of my percept is like insisting that I cannot hear the organ because I can only hear its sound, or that I cannot say "Boo" because I have to say it with my voice. Critical realism, therefore, far from making of our ideas a prison-house, considers them a part of the necessary means of external reference and communication. And the criticism upon it . . . turns out to be in fact a demand that we should think without thoughts and perceive without perceptions.

But I should be doing injustice to both the critics and myself if I left the accusation of scepticism at this point. There is no denying the fact that the question how certain knowledge is possible is both crucial and difficult for every epistemological theory. And for my own part I am willing to go a long way with the critic and to confess that, on the theory which I am supporting, both what we human beings consider perception and what we consider knowledge in the more explicit and sophisticated sense are often misleading. Since on our view the mind's object is not its content, illusion may be taken for perception and error for knowledge, and the ultimate nature of reality in itself may be very difficult, or even impossible, to discover. To that extent I am forced to admit, with all humility, that critical realism is agnostic. But I would go on and ask the further question, Is not the fallible kind of perception and knowledge involved in critical realism exactly the kind of perception and knowledge which we really have? The situation which critical realism necessitates is admittedly undesirable; but does it not describe pretty well the actual state of affairs? If we could fashion the world over again more nearly to the heart's desire, very likely we should attempt to make perception "direct" (whatever that may mean!) and knowledge infallible; but the task of the epistemologist, as I understand it, is not to describe what we should like, but to expound the conditions of knowledge actually obtaining in the somewhat unsatisfactory world we have to live in. The agnostic elements (if such one wishes to call them) really involved in critical realism I would therefore regard as merits rather than the reverse. Like St. Paul, critical realism glories in its infirmities, since by means of them it is enabled to give a more exact rendering of the truth. In fact, it is the inability of either idealism, pragmatism, or neo-realism to find any room for the possibility of illusion and error that makes all of these systems quite untenable. They have been made to order with a view to "avoiding agnosticism," and the result is that, while they may fit some ideal world of gods or angels who are never mistaken, they completely fail to apply to such very fallible beings as we.

But while critical realism makes adequate provision for error and illusion, it also leaves plenty of room for the sort of veridical perception and of trustworthy knowledge that we mortals indubitably have. The critical realist does not pretend to the possession of a theory which will make all knowledge as completely demonstrable as mathematics, but he does maintain that by far the most reasonable construction of the facts of experience points to the three following conclusions: (1) that there are other minds or centres of experience beside his own, and that there are also existent physical entities independent of the minds that know them, but which stand in some sort of causal relation to these minds—in short, the general realistic view; (2) that we human beings are so coordinated with the rest of nature that when our psychophysical organisms are acting normally our percepts refer to and (in a pragmatic and functional sense) correspond with existent entities which are not part of our mental content; and (3) that we can make these various independent entities the objects of our thought, and by reasoning upon our experiences can come to conclusions about them which are true and which deserve the name of knowledge. . . .

JAMES BISSETT PRATT

THE PROBLEM OF ERROR

A definition of error, as I conceive that the theory represented by the present volume needs to view it, can be put very simply and briefly. It is no final refutation of a philosophy that, in order to find room for the possibility of some acknowledged kind of fact, it has to resort to extremely involved, laborious, and subtle considerations, about which its own adherents find difficulty in agreeing. But nevertheless it is not unreasonable to hold that this is a drawback, and that a more natural and obvious solution recommends in so far the point of view from which it follows. If, therefore . . . it can be made to appear that competing theories have in this particular matter of error no satisfactory account to give, and that they either land, when ambiguities are cleared away, in highly improbable constructions of reality, or else, to become intelligible, have to adopt the very position which they in terms repudiate, I shall consider such an outcome a real recommendation of the attitude here defended.

The definition which critical realism gives of error is briefly this: When we "know" an object, we are assigning a certain "essence"— a character or group of characters—to some reality existing independently of the knowledge-process. And as truth is the identity of this essence with the actual character of the reality referred to, so error stands for the lack of such agreement, and the ascribing of an ideal character to what we are mistaken in supposing to be real, or the ascribing to a reality of a wrong character instead of a right one. I regard it as a plain fact, that, on the level of ordinary discourse, such a statement has a perfectly intelligible sense, which corresponds moreover to what the ordinary man actually intends when he speaks of truth and error. . . .

ARTHUR K. ROGERS

Realism in regard to knowledge has various degrees. The minimum of realism is the presumption that there is such a thing as knowledge; in other words, that perception and thought refer to some object not the mere experience of perceiving and thinking. The maximum of realism would be the assurance that everything ever perceived or thought of existed apart from apprehension and exactly in the form in which it is believed to exist: in other words, that perception and conception are always direct and literal revelations, and that there is no such thing as error. If this is the range of realism, I think we may say that any reasonable theory of knowledge—any theory that does not abolish its own subject-matter—will occupy some point between these extremes, and will be more or less realistic.

The various degrees of realism, however, cannot be arranged in a single scale, for there are two distinct questions that may be answered more or less realistically: one, what measure of independence or separate existence shall be ascribed to the object? and the other, what degree of literalness and adequacy shall be claimed for knowledge? These two applications of realism by no means go hand in hand. The most decided realist in respect to the independence of objects may be a sceptic in respect to the accuracy of his ideas. He may be a believer in the unknowable, like Kant: or he may be a materialist, who thinks that most of the notions entertained by the human mind are either illusions or conventional symbols. On the other hand, the most imperturbed realist in respect to the accuracy of his ideas, who is sure that things are just what they seem, may for that very reason be tempted to drop the other strand of realism and to maintain that his experiences and their objects are identical. Then the only difference between him and an idealist will concern the genesis and duration he attributes to those neutral or epicene "facts of experience" which they both recognize: the naïve realist will deploy these objects naturalistically, in their own medium of space and continuous evolution, whereas the idealist will admit that they exist only intermittently and in single file, as perceptions in some mind. . . .

Realism . . . is the union of two instinctive assumptions, necessary to the validity of knowledge: first, that knowledge is *transitive*, so that self-existing things may become the chosen objects of a mind that identifies and indicates them; second, that knowledge is *relevant*, so that the thing indicated may have at least some of the qualities that the mind attributes to it. These two kinds of realism, though they may rise and fall reciprocally, like the pans of a balance, are like those pans necessary to each other: if either disappeared, the other would collapse. If relevance were wholly denied, it would be in vain hotly to assert the independence of the object; that independence would be undermined. An unknowable substance, even if it existed, could not be the object designated by a conception which, being by hypothesis wholly irrelevant to it, could not specify even its place, date, or relation to anything else. Similarly, if transcendence or transitiveness were wholly denied in its turn, so that the object could neither subsist when not known nor become the object of any other thought than the one which now knows it, relevance too would be eliminated; for the thought and its object would have become identical, and a thing cannot be relevant to itself. Knowledge in this case would perish by compression, by ceasing to aim at anything, as in the other case it would perish by futility, being condemned to aim always at an unattainable target. Some remnant, therefore, of each kind of realism must always persist, if knowledge is to be posited or to be actually valid at all: and the defender of realism, or of the possibility of genuine knowledge, has merely to show to what degree transcendence and relevance are achieved in particular instances. It is quite conceivable that the proportion of these two necessary ingredients should vary, as knowledge is addressed to various kinds of objects. I will attempt to show how the case stands in respect to three important spheres of knowledge: and the proof that in each our knowledge claims to be, and actually is, in some measure, both transitive and relevant, will be a triple demonstration of the truth of realism; though the exact force and scope of the demonstration will differ in each instance. . . .

GEORGE SANTAYANA

KNOWLEDGE AND ITS CATEGORIES

. . . The conception of knowledge which we have been suggesting can now be more precisely stated and defended. Knowledge is just the insight into the nature of the object that is made possible by the contents which reflect it in consciousness. Naïve realism makes the impossible claim to intuit the object, impossible because it would involve the leaping of spatial and temporal barriers in an unnatural fashion. Critical realism, on the other hand, is satisfied to admit the fact of causal mediation while yet proclaiming that the object affirmed and intended is known in terms of the content presented to the knowing self. The content has cognitive value. I believe that this is what my colleagues mean when they assert that (in so far as knowledge is accurate) the content given is the essence of the object. It is a way of saying that the content is relevant to the object, that it has a sort of revelatory identity with the object, that it contains its structure, position, and changes. The situation is so basic that it can hardly be further reduced. The content of knowledge offers us the fundamental categories, such as time, space, structure, relations, and behaviour, in terms of which we think the world. To postulate the validity of these categories is *ipso facto* to assert that knowledge-content gives us the constitution of the world. There is, of course, no sharp break between perception and propositional knowledge, for propositional knowledge is based upon perception, to which it must remain responsible. Scientific knowledge is clearly only a more explicit, more critical, and more developed form of knowledge than perception. Its conception of nature is based upon tested and interpreted data to the obtaining of which all the mental ingenuity of the ablest of men has been directed. The study of such knowledge is primarily the affair of logic, though there is and should be no conflict with the findings of psychology. . . .

The position at which we have arrived is realistic, and is as near natural realism as the conditions of knowledge permit. Physical things are the objects of knowledge, though they can be known only in terms of the data which they control within us. The postulate of knowledge is the cognitive or revelatory value of the idea taken as a content or character-complex and not as a mental existent. In other words, the content which we apprehend must have the property of reproducing something about the object, of conveying in its own medium the form of the object.

But a word like "form" is not a sufficient answer to the inevitable demand concerning the grasp of knowledge. Let me therefore explain what this term means to me. In the first place, I see no need to postulate a metaphysical dualism between form and matter. Matter is just as much of an abstraction as form. Reality is formed matter. Reality has structure and organization. It has a determinate nature. It is for this reason that our categories such as space, time, structure, and causality have validity. To the extent that Aristotelianism and scholasticism separated matter and form they were guilty of a vicious and unnecessary dualism. It is reality that is active and the seat of processes, not a form or a matter.

But if the object of knowledge is a formed matter, the question may next be raised, What about the object can be conveyed to mind? Obviously not the being but the "form." To convey the being is impossible, for the thing must remain outside the knowing mind. To know the thing is therefore not to *be* the thing. Nor is to know the thing to have a copy-like reproduction of the thing. What, then, is knowledge? It is the recognized possession by the mind of the "form" of the thing, that is, its position, size, structure, causal capacities, etc. It is the mediated grasp of those features of the thing which are reproducible. To know these is to know the thing.

But just because these features of the thing are alone grasped, there is the danger, on the one hand, of identifying reality with form, and on the other, of making reality unknowable, because only its form can be grasped. The proper limitations of knowledge are not realized. Critical realism is not agnostic, because it does not begin, as agnosticism usually does, with an unexamined notion of knowledge. It maintains, also, that reality, itself, is the object of human knowledge.

But there is another approach to the nature of reality with which I have very little concerned myself. I have felt it wiser to concentrate upon the problem of the knowledge of the physical world gained through external perception; for, until some agreement is reached upon this point, it seems difficult to travel far along other lines. And yet the contents of consciousness are real. Do we know the psychical adequately? Is the psychical an integral part of the pulse of the functioning brain, an expression of creative synthesis? Or is it the very stuff of the brain? These questions are fascinating, and indicate the line of investigation which must next be undertaken. But this is neither the time nor the place for this work. I shall be more than satisfied if I have helped to make clearer the nature and conditions of the knowledge of the physical world gained through the data of external perception.

ROY WOOD SELLARS

ON THE NATURE OF THE DATUM

The crucial question, in the problem of sense-perception, is as to the nature of the datum. By "datum" I mean what we are immediately conscious of. Six different views as to this have succeeded each other in the course of modern philosophy: (1) That the datum is the real thing; (2) that it is an ideal representative of the real thing; (3) that it is an ideal thing, psychological in its nature; (4) that it is an ideal thing, logical in its nature; (5) that it is a thing of psychological nature, but real; (6) that it is a thing of logical nature, but real—*naïve realism, representationism, psychological subjectivism, logical subjectivism, psychological objectivism, logical objectivism.* The view I shall try to recommend in this article, distinct from any of these, is (7) that the datum is the logical essence of the real thing. By "essence" I mean its *what* divorced from its *that*—its entire concrete nature, including its sensible character, but not its existence. To establish this, it will be necessary to show (1) that the things we are conscious of in sense-perception, as distinguished from the things we believe or affirm, are not the actual external existences; (2) that, on the other hand, they are not internal or psychical existences, either representative of the external ones or non-representative; (3) that, while they are logical entities—entities of the logical type—they are not identifiable with the things we perceive, but are only the detached concrete natures or "essences" of those things. . . .

C. A. STRONG

BIBLIOGRAPHY

For works dealing with Critical Realism the reader is referred to the General Bibliography, section 3.

Ralph Barton Perry

[1876–1957]

Perry was born in Poultney, Vermont. He studied at Princeton College, where McCosh's influence was still strong, and took his B.A. degree in 1896. During the Golden Age he studied at Harvard, where he took his Ph.D. Perry trained originally for the ministry, but later turned to a teaching career. He taught briefly at William and Smith College and returned to Harvard to become a professor in 1913. He was a President of the American Philosophical Association, Eastern Division (1920) and was decorated Chevalier of the Legion of Honor of France (1936). He delivered the Gifford Lectures at Glasgow (1946–48). Perry was married to Rachel Berenson, sister of Bernard Berenson, the famous art critic and historian.

Perry figured large in the attack on idealism and the formulation of the first program and platform of the New Realism; he was probably, indeed, its most effective exponent. His review of Royce's *The World and the Individual* in 1901 was an early and devastating criticism of Absolute Idealism. His influential article "The Ego-Centric Predicament" in *The Journal of Philosophy* (1910) was another such criticism. Idealism, Perry maintained, merely points to the epistemological difficulty that we can know nothing separate from the act of knowing or unrelated to the knower. The error of idealism is in reducing this "ego-centric predica-

ment" to a fundamental characteristic of reality and in equating being with being perceived. Perry maintained that it is necessary to go beyond this epistemological fact and instead describe the characteristics that objects have independently of the knower; for the ego-centric predicament applies only to thought, not to being. Perry's mature appraisal and restatement of realism, *Realism in Retrospect* (1930), written after the heat of battle had subsided, is reprinted below.

Perry's writings on value have been fairly influential. His *General Theory of Value* (1925) and later his *Realms of Value* (1954) were significant contributions to the development of a naturalistic theory of value. Perry defined "value" as "any-object of any interest." (A selection on this topic appears below.) His definition was both relational and realistic. Values were related to the interest that an organism has in an object, yet they were not subjective. Interests, which are motor-affective responses, and their objects, can be known like any other facts. In this way, Perry attempted to show that value might be amenable to empirical and scientific treatment.

Perry's efforts in value theory and ethics were not merely academic, and he devoted himself tirelessly to liberal causes and ideals. In *Puritanism and Democracy* (1944), he attempted to analyze the history and philosophical basis of American ideals, particularly democracy and civil rights. As a liberal international-ist, he was also an outspoken foe of fascism, and a devoted defender of world peace.

Perry was a student and colleague of William James, to whom he owed a great deal. He was the author of the Pulitzer Prize book, *The Thought and Character of William James* (1935), perhaps the most sensitive and eloquent biography that we have of an American philosopher. This work is an astute analysis of James the man and of his ideas, as well as an account of pragmatism and phi-losophy in America at the beginning of the twentieth century.

REALISM IN RETROSPECT [1]

THE CAMPAIGN AGAINST IDEALISM

. . . It was the controversial atmosphere of my early studies that led to my preoccupation with the shortcomings of idealism, and to my sustained interest in the classification of contemporary philosophi-cal tendencies.[2] European and American Philosophy, as I saw it at the close of the nineteenth century, was a dispute between the ex-travagant claims of the party of science (naturalism) and the equally extravagant claims of that post-Kantian idealistic philosophy, which, invigorated by its transplantation from Germany to a foreign soil, had become the bulwark of English-speaking Protestant piety.

It is unprofitable to quarrel over the diverse meanings of the term "idealism." That idealism which I went out to slay was born of the marriage of subjectivism and universalism. Its proof seemed to me then, as it seems to me still, to consist in an unseaworthy subjectivism rescued from the shipwreck of solipsism by the miraculous interven-tion of absolutism. The first premise is subjectivism, the doctrine, namely, that to be = to be perceived or thought. The second premise is universalism, the doctrine, namely, that being cannot be a product of human perception or thought, because man is a part of nature, and because the truth is a standard by which human perception and thought are themselves to be judged and corrected. The conclusion is absolute idealism, the doctrine, namely, that to be = to be per-ceived or thought (or willed, or felt, or otherwise manifested) by a

[1] From *Contemporary American Philosophy: Personal Statements*, ed. G. P. Adams and W. P. Montague, N. Y.: Macmillan, 1930. Vol. II, pp. 189–201.

[2] "Professor Royce's Refutation of Realism and Pluralism," *Monist*, 1902; *The Approach to Philosophy*, 1905; *Present Philosophical Tendencies*, 1912; *Present Conflict of Ideals*, 1918; *Philosophy of the Recent Past*, 1926.

transfinite, all-containing and infallible mind, commonly called *"the Absolute."*

The argument is dialectical and a priori, and its force depends on the truth of both premises. The critics of this reigning doctrine are readily divisible into two groups: those commonly called "realists," who have attacked the first premise; and those variously called "pragmatists," "instrumentalists," and "humanists," who have attacked the second premise. The former group being united by their rejection of subjectivism, are divided among themselves on the question of universalism; the latter, being united by their rejection of universalism, are divided on the issue of subjectivism. Both groups reject absolute idealism, but while one rejects this doctrine on the score of its idealism, the other rejects it on the score of its absolutism.

For the realist, then, the Absolute, construed as an individual mind or spirit, in which the imperfections of humanity are overcome and its prerogatives maximated—construed, in other words, as a being qualified to serve at one and the same time as the metaphysical reality, the moral standard and the object of worship—is the offspring of subjectivism. Such a being is not merely absolute: it is mind conceived as absolute. "I perceive," or "I judge," or "I will," or some similar act of conscious mind, is first supposed to be the inescapable form of reality; and since to identify this "I" with you or me or any or all finite creatures is palpably absurd, it is then inferred that there must be an "I" which is no creature at all, but the Creator. And, as Bradley has put it, what must be, is. Hence in so far as the realist refutes subjectivism he at the same time destroys the meaning and the ground of the Absolute in this idealistic sense.

An idealist of the post-Kantian school resents being called a "subjectivist," but this is because he takes the term to imply that the "subject" in question is the natural or psychological subject. If "subjectivism" be used to mean that all being is the dependent creation of *some* subject, or self, or mind, whether finite or absolute, then, I think, the term can be applied to the idealist without offence. In accordance with this usage absolute idealism is that species of subjectivism in which the unconditioned and all-conditioning subject has, over and above such properties as make it a subject, those other properties of infinity, perfection, and systematic unity, which the term "Absolute" is intended to convey. With this understanding I shall hereinafter use the terms "subjectivism" and "idealism" interchangeably.

The wide prevalence of subjectivism has always seemed to me to be due, in the first place, to excessive insistence on a relation which the reflective habits of the philosopher dispose him to magnify. Subjectivism exploits the relation, namely, which the world indubitably has to the human subject whenever he perceives it, or thinks about it, or otherwise concerns himself with it. He exploits this him-ward aspect of things *metaphysically*—that is, he construes it as fundamental, or takes it as affording the deepest insight. The realist, on the other hand, calls attention to the fact that this emphasis, natural as it is, may be misleading. Thus when Pistol says, "Why, then the world's mine oyster," we recognize that he is taking liberties with the world. It is true that the world is, among other things, Pistol's oyster, and Pistol is excusable for having mentioned the fact. But if, as a philosopher, one were interested in making the most significant possible statement about the world, it would scarcely be pertinent to remark that the world is that which is opened by Pistol's sword. This is not one of those central and pregnant characteristics of the world of which the metaphysician is in search. In the course of its career the world does meet Pistol, but this conjunction does not determine its orbit or destiny, nor does the bivalvular aspect which it presents to Pistol's sword afford the best clue to its essential structure.

In a sense that is at least superficially similar to Pistol's oyster, nature is Berkeley's percept and Kant's thought, or the idea of any philosopher who applies his mind to it. And it is not strange that sooner or later some philosopher should have taken this fact as the key to metaphysics. But the realist is one who is disposed, until more decisive evidence is advanced, to construe this indubitable relationship of the world to the mind that deals with it, as an accidental or subordinate aspect of the world. He refuses to assume[3] that knowing the world implies proprietorship. It is still open to him to suppose, with common sense, that the world *lends* itself to being known without surrendering itself wholly to that use. Such a view has its support in experiences that are no less authentic than Pistol's sense of ownership. If the idealist is justified in saying with Margaret Fuller, "I accept the universe," the realist is equally justified in remarking with Carlyle, "By gad, she'd better."

The question of the place of knowing mind in the universe, whether central or peripheral, is complicated by what I have called the "egocentric predicament."[4] This was a successful bit of phrase-making, if one is to judge by the frequency with which it has been misunderstood. My purpose in introducing the phrase was to call attention

[3] Arbitrarily to assign the leading rôle to a predicate merely because it happens to come first in the order of discovery or of discourse, has been called the "Fallacy of Initial Predication" (*The New Realism*, 1912, p. 15).

[4] "The Ego-Centric Predicament," *Journal of Philosophy, Psychology, and Scientific Methods*, 1910.

to the fact that idealists have used as an argument what is, in fact, only a difficulty. The difficulty or predicament consists in the fact that the extent to which knowledge conditions any situation in which it is present cannot be discovered by the simple and conclusive method of direct elimination. I cannot see what things look like when my eyes are shut, or judge the effect of extinguishing my thought. If I cognize *a* in any way, shape, or manner, I am not cognizing *a* in the absence of that way, shape, or manner of cognition. This is, of course, a truism, and in itself of no significance whatever. It does, however, bring to light the fact that the question which subjectivism raises is unique. In order that the question shall be *answered* at all, it is necessary to introduce the very factor, namely, the answering mind, which in examining this question it would be convenient to exclude. It follows that either the question must remain unanswered or that it must be attacked in some more indirect and perhaps less conclusive manner. If, for example, one can find out what the cognizing mind is and what it does, one can then discount its presence, or learn how much of the situation to ascribe to it.

Idealism has been guilty, historically, of arguing from what is only a methodological difficulty. It has created the appearance of a significant affirmation by concealing a redundancy. No one would think it worth while to say, "It is impossible for me to discover anything which is, when I discover it, undiscovered by me," or, "It is impossible that anything should remain totally unknown after it has become known;" but to say, "It is impossible to discover anything that is not thought," or, "It is impossible to find anything that is not known," has seemed to many idealists to be the beginning of philosophical wisdom—in spite of the fact that the self-evidence of the last two propositions consists entirely in the fact that "discover" and "thought," "find" and "known," are taken as meaning the same thing.

My contention has been, then, that the "ego-centric predicament" creates not the slightest presumption either for idealism or for realism. It is equally compatible with either alternative, although it has been, and still is, very generally supposed to nourish idealism and to stick in the crop of realism.

So far idealism is seen to rest on bias or ambiguity. The other arguments which have been advanced in its behalf are deserving of more respectful consideration, since they appeal to material facts for which any alternative theory must provide.

The oldest of the idealistic arguments are those which idealism shares with scepticism. Idealism has been held sometimes to *be* scepticism, sometimes to furnish the only authentic *escape* from it. Arguments of this general class may be summarily treated under the heads of "physiological relativism" and "psychological relativism."

Physiological relativism rests on the fact that sensation is doubly conditioned: externally, by a physical stimulus; and internally by the position, properties, and state of the organism. Sensation is then construed as the joint product or appearance created by these factors. At this point of the argument three alternatives diverge. The confirmed sceptic will hold that sensation, untrustworthy as it is, affords the only knowledge we possess, since thought is only its paler reflection. This is idealism of a sort, but a bankrupt, insolvent idealism—patently self-contradictory. The two remaining alternatives are realistic. The physico-chemical realist credits scientific thought as a way of escape from the subjective relativities of sensation. The agnostic realist, holding with the sceptic that physico-chemical concepts are only reproductions of sense-experience, and equally subjective, still credits the residual reflection that sense-experience is produced by the action *of* something he knows not how *upon* something he knows not what. It is clear that, whatever their validity, arguments from physiological relativism afford small comfort to the idealist.

Psychological relativism is a scepticism of thought rather than of sense; indeed, it is often used as an argument in support of sense. The argument rests on the fact of prejudice. Thought is held to be an effect of emotion, will, habit, imitation, historical development, or social *milieu*; and reality, as man thinks it, to be a mere projection of human bias. Here, again, three paths diverge. If, in the first place, one appeals from thought to sense on the ground that sense is externally controlled, one moves in the direction of the scepticisms and realisms already considered. The second alternative is to rest in the relativity of thought, or to accept psychological scepticism as the last word. This view, that the world is what man thinks it, and that man's thinking of it varies from individual to individual and from time to time, is a widespread doctrine in modern philosophy; but it is not that idealism with which I am here concerned. The third alternative, the absolute idealism which modern realism seeks to slay, is an idealism which has already slain and devoured scepticism, and which rests its claim to acceptance largely upon that conquest. Psychological relativism is held to be intolerable, because it gives equal credit to contradictory human assertions, and because, since it places nature inside of a mind which is itself inside of nature, it is viciously circular. Realism and absolute idealism here take the same ground, and both attribute to thought a power to recognize and transcend its own relativities. The difference lies in the nature of this corrective thought. For realism its nature lies in its more perfect fidelity to fact, or in its more dispassionate and colourless objectivity. For idealism its nature lies in its profounder and more authoritative subjectivity. For realism thinking truly is a conformity of mind to the given reality, while for idealism thinking truly is a conformity of the finite mind to a universal mind.[5]

This resort to absolute idealism as the way of escape from psychological relativism involves two steps, both of which the realist refuses to take. The first step is to discredit sense-perception. The relative passivity of this mode of experience, instead of being construed as a mark of cognitive superiority because it suggests a deference of the knowing mind to its objects, is construed as a mark of inferiority because the genius of the mind itself is too imperfectly manifested. Sense becomes a virtual, incipient, or degraded form of thought. The absolute idealist can usually be recognized by his insistence that pure sensation is a myth, but pure or impure he can hardly deny it, and it still remains as one of his most serious stumbling-blocks.

The second step is to construe thought as essentially creative. There is a widespread disposition (a disposition connected, no doubt, with the common-sense dogma that if things are not physical they must be mental) to suppose that the objects of thought, such as laws, mathematical quantities and forms, principles, categories, concepts, universals, necessities, possibilities, relations, and systematic unities, are the *creatures* of thought. Since the orderly structure of nature, as exhibited in the sciences, would fall to pieces without such connective tissue, this supposition is of decisive consequence, and is chiefly responsible for the hold of modern idealism upon those "tougher" minds which are not affected by its sentimental appeal.

Hence the rejection of a subjectivistic logic, and mathematics is one of the major arguments in the realistic polemic. Claiming the support of Socrates and Plato, and alliance with the whole stream of philosophical doctrine down through the Scholastics and Cartesians, modern realism distinguishes between the imaginative play of speculative thought, on the one hand, and, on the other hand, those moments of insight, acceptance, or contemplation in which the mind is confronted by a being not of its own making. Thought has moments in which its own caprice is superseded by specificities, connections, and consequences as intrusive and inexorable as the resistance of material bodies. One may think what one will, but having thought one finds oneself involved in natures and relations which have a way of their own, a way which must now be loyally followed if one is to think truly. The realms of mathematics and logic are not governed

[5] Since this universal mind may be itself governed by will or emotion, as well as by cold logic, absolute idealism does not necessarily imply the rejection of moral, æsthetic, or religious experiences as sources of metaphysical insight. Any idealizing activity of mind, in which man recognizes the gap between aspiration and present attainment, may be taken as a revelation of that standard spiritual being whose self-realization furnishes the motive force of creation.

by psychological laws, but by laws intrinsic to themselves. Idealists recognize this autonomy, and thereupon extend and exalt the meaning of mind to embrace the larger domain. But to confer the term "mind" upon the intelligible features of the world, whether viewed abstractedly in hierarchies of categories, or concretely in the systematic unity of nature, can serve no useful purpose. It adds nothing to our understanding of that specific mode of natural existence associated with animal bodies from which the term "mind" derives its original meaning, while at the same time it invests the intelligible features of the world with an aspect of complaisance to man, and thus flatters hopes that it does not really justify.

No summary of idealistic arguments would be complete without mention of that argument which idealism shares with spiritualism. The distinctive mark of modern idealism is, I believe, its annexation of the object to the act or state or mode of knowledge, whether in the Berkeleyan or in the Kantian manner. But modern idealism also absorbs and continues a strain of metaphysical speculation which is much older. According to this older or spiritualistic view, the metaphysical demand for a substantial being and an originating cause can be met only by self-consciousness, which, as intuitively apprehended, dissolves the dialectical difficulties which beset the time-worn topics of the "one and the many," "the thing and its qualities," "identity and difference," "freedom and necessity," and "infinity." Mind, so it is alleged, is superlatively and exclusively qualified for reality. This view rests, however, on the assumption that the nature of mind is self-evident. Modern realists, for the most part, reject this alleged revelation in the name of patient observation and rigorous analysis. They regard the nature of mind, not as the primal insight, but as a highly complicated and baffling problem which possesses in an eminent degree whatever difficulties beset the problem of reality in general.[6] The first personal pronoun is felt to resemble a question-mark more than an exclamation point.

To these counter-arguments, by which realism has disputed the claims of idealism, I should like to add the difference of philosophical method and attitude which has often divided these opposing schools. It was not an accident that realists should have formulated a platform and attempted collaboration. Anglo-American idealism, impregnated as it is with the romantic tradition, has encouraged the individual to

[6] I have argued that the idealist's position rests here upon a confusion between the apparent simplicity of the familiar or the innocence of the eye, and the objective simplicity which survives the effort to distinguish an internal multiplicity. I have termed this error "the fallacy of pseudo-simplicity." Cf. "Realism as a Polemic and Programme of Reform," *Journal of Philosophy*, Vol. VII (1910), p. 371.

regard himself as an authoritative organ of truth, or a fountain of lyric self-expression. To members of such a cult every attempt to define terms or to organize research must necessarily be abhorrent. Realists, on the other hand, cling to the naïve view that in the presence of common objects two philosophical minds should be able to find some area of agreement, or at least to localize and formulate their disagreement. The realist is baffled and annoyed by what seems to him the arrogant obscurity of idealism, which appears to claim the licence of poetry without assuming its artistic responsibilities. For the same reasons the realist is attracted by the use of the mathematical method, as a possible means of rendering philosophical discourse genuinely communicative, and philosophical discussion profitable and conclusive.

There is another incompatibility of temper which has divided idealists and realists. Idealistic metaphysics is essentially an a priori doctrine. Its central reality is inferred and not experienced. Indeed, the whole realm of human experience is disparaged as appearance. There is a tendency to solve problems in principle rather than in detail, or merely to read them by title. Since truth consists in the light shed by the whole on the part, since the Absolute is thus by definition the supreme solver of problems, and since all other minds are tainted with finitude, there is a temptation to rest cheerfully in the midst of unconquered difficulties, even when they are difficulties of the philosopher's own making. But pious resignation is not fruitful in philosophy. Whatever be the reasons, it seems to me in any case to be a fact that the idealist has contributed nothing to our understanding of infinity and continuity comparable with the contributions of the mathematical logician; and nothing to our understanding of the nature of consciousness, perception, matter, causality, or the relation of mind and body, comparable with the contributions made by their contemporaries of the pragmatist and realist schools. Idealists have been system-builders and have staked all on the monumental perfection of the whole. James, Bergson, Russell, and Whitehead, on the other hand, pay as they go. You do not have to be converted to their gospel in order to profit by them. They abound in suggestive hypothesis, shrewd observation, and delicate analysis which you can detach and build into your own thinking. The newer philosophy which has grown up in opposition to idealism, and which has set a fashion which even idealism is now adopting, has something of the fruitfulness of empirical science. It is achieving results which, because of their factual basis, may survive the decline of the systematic theories in which they are presently embodied.

Such, in brief, is the train of argument by which I have justified my own dissent from idealism, and in which for the most part I have been in agreement with those of my American colleagues who in 1910 formulated a "Programme and First Platform,"[7] and in 1912 wrote in collaboration the volume entitled *The New Realism*. The defence against the idealistic argument is only a part of the realistic polemic, but it is the most indispensable part—the declaration of independence, by which a new philosophy has sought to gain diplomatic recognition. This war of liberation has, it is true, been supported by an invasion of the enemy's territory. But here the chief weapon employed has been that charge of solipsism which is as familiar to idealists as to their opponents. Realism has, furthermore, been compelled in turn to consolidate and defend its own position. But the historic significance of the American movement at the opening of the present century will, I think, lie in its having revived and modernized a way of thinking which, in spite of its antiquity and its agreement both with science and with common sense, had at the close of the previous century been consigned to the obituary columns of the most authoritative philosophical organs.

Absolute idealism, at the very moment of its seeming triumph over naturalism, was attacked on both flanks: on the one by pragmatism, and on the other by the new realism. The former attack came first and had already lowered the morale of the idealistic forces when the realistic onslaught occurred. The issue of the battle is decisive only in the sense that the supremacy of idealism is destroyed. The hopes of naturalism, as well as of medieval scholasticism, have revived owing to assistance received from unexpected quarters. The idealists, though checked, have rallied. Pragmatists and realists have fallen afoul of one another at the point of their convergent attack. Former enemies are fraternizing. Ranks are broken and regimental colours are abandoned on the field. What have realists to contribute to the reconstruction that now promises to follow after war?

The answer to this question is too long and too recent a story to find a place in this brief retrospect. Furthermore, it does not belong, in any exclusive sense, to an account of realism. Still less does it belong to my own personal philosophical autobiography. Indeed, that which is most characteristic of the present moment in philosophy, as I understand it, is a confluence of currents which have hitherto run in separate channels. We are (and I am glad, as well as convinced, that it is so) less inclined than formerly to pride ourselves on partisan loyalties and polemical victories. A contemplative observer of the times would have great difficulty in describing its characteristic philosophical activity in terms of the doctrinal cleavages that were so well marked at the opening of the century. Its most conspicuous

---

[7] *Journal of Philosophy*, Vol. VII (1910), p. 393.

feature is, I think, an avoidance of the dualisms and disjunctions with which the influence of Descartes is associated. This attitude is due in part to recent changes in science, in part to a revival of interest in ancient and medieval philosophy, and in part to a growing sense of the inadequacy of any of the sharply antithetical alternatives which divided the thought of the last century. Conceptions such as "pattern," "aspect," "pure experience," "essence," "emergence," "event" owe their present vogue to the hope of healing the breach between mind and matter, soul and body, religion and science, teleology and mechanism, or substance and attribute. Viewed in the light of this conjunctive or reconciling motive, there is a recognizable strain of similarity in the thought of James, Bergson, Husserl, Alexander, Bosanquet, McTaggart, Stout, Whitehead, Russell, Broad, Dewey, Santayana, Strong, Montague, and Holt. It would be pretentious and unwarranted for realism to claim the credit for this tendency, but it would be blind to deny that the Anglo-American realism of the first decade of the century helped notably to prepare the way.

VALUE AS ANY OBJECT OF ANY INTEREST [8]

It is characteristic of living mind to be *for* some things and *against* others. This polarity is not reducible to that between "yes" and "no" in the logical or in the purely cognitive sense, because one can say "yes" with reluctance or be glad to say "no." To be "for" or "against" is to view with favor or disfavor; it is a bias of the subject toward or away from. It implies, as we shall see more clearly in the sequel, a tendency to create or conserve, or an opposite tendency to prevent or destroy. This duality appears in many forms, such as liking and disliking, desire and aversion, will and refusal, or seeking and avoiding. It is to this all-pervasive characteristic of the motor-affective life, this *state, act, attitude or disposition of favor or disfavor*, to which we propose to give the name of *"interest."*[9]

[8] From R. B. Perry, *General Theory of Value.* Cambridge, Mass.; Harvard U. Press, 1926, 1954.
[9] The term "interest" has been employed for technical purposes by various psychologists, but by none, I think, in the precise sense in which it is employed here. W. Mitchell, in his *Structure and Growth of Mind,* 1907, defines interest as our "feeling towards" an object, or, as how the object "strikes or affects us" (p. 64); whereas I propose to use the term to embrace desire and disposition as well. G. F. Stout, in his *Groundwork of Psychology,* 1903, uses the term for organized and permanent forms of the emotional life, such as sentiments [pp. 221 ff.]. More commonly "interest" is employed by psychology to mean *attention.*

   This, then, we take to be the original source and constant feature
of all value. That which is an object of interest is *eo ipso* invested
with value.[10] Any object, whatever it be, acquires value when any
interest, whatever it be, is taken in it; just as anything whatsoever
becomes a target when anyone whosoever aims at it. In other words,
Aristotle was fundamentally mistaken when he said, that as a thing's
"apparent good" makes it an object of appetite, so its real good
makes it the object of "rational desire."[11] By the same token Spinoza
was fundamentally correct when he said that

> in no case do we strive for, wish for, long for, or desire anything,
> because we deem it to be good, but on the other hand we deem a
> thing to be good, because we strive for it, wish for it, long for it, or
> desire it.[12]

   The view may otherwise be formulated in the equation: x is valuable $=$ interest is taken in x. Value is thus a specific relation into
which things possessing any ontological status whatsoever, whether
real or imaginary, may enter with interested subjects.
   This is value *simpliciter,*—value in the elementary, primordial and
generic sense. It follows that any variation of interest or of its object
will determine a variety of value; that any derivative of interest or
its object will determine value in a derived sense; and that any condition of interest or its object will determine a conditional value. In
short, interest being constitutive of value in the basic sense, theory
of value will take this as its point of departure and centre of reference; and will classify and systematize values in terms of the different
forms which interests and their objects may be found to assume.
   This view has rarely found a perfectly clear and consistent expression. It is, however, essentially conveyed in an early work of Mr.
George Santayana:

> Apart from ourselves, and our human bias, we can see in such a
> mechanical world no element of value whatever. In removing con-
> sciousness, we have removed the possibility of worth. But it is not
> only in the absence of all consciousness that value would be removed
> from the world; by a less violent abstraction from the totality of
> human experience, we might conceive beings of a purely intellectual
> cast, minds in which the transformations of nature were mirrored

[10] An object is valuable when *qualified* by an act of interest; relation to interest
assuming, in the experience or judgment of value, the rôle of adjective.

[11] *Metaphysica,* XII, Ch. 7, trans. by W. D. Ross, 1072a.

[12] *Ethics,* Part III, Prop. IX, Note trans. by R. H. M. Elwes, 1901. It is, of
course, possible to desire a thing because it is good, where its goodness consists in
its being desired by other subjects, or by some other interest on the same subject.
But *in the last analysis* good springs from desire and not desire from good.

without any emotion. . . . No event would be repulsive, no situation terrible. . . . In this case, as completely as if consciousness were absent altogether, all value and excellence would be gone. . . . Values spring from the immediate and inexplicable reaction of vital impulse, and from the irrational part of our nature. . . . The ideal of rationality is itself as arbitrary, as much dependent on the needs of a finite organization, as any other ideal.[13]

A more recent statement, and one more explicitly in accord with the view here proposed, is the following:

Anything is properly said to have value in case, and only in case, it is the object of the affective motor response which we call being *interested* in, positively or negatively. . . . The being liked, or disliked, of the object is its value. And since the being liked or disliked, is being the object of a motor-affective attitude in a subject, some sort of a subject is always requisite to there being value at all—not necessarily a *judging* subject, but a subject capable of at least motor-affective response. For the cat the cream has value, or better and more simply, the cat values the cream, or the warmth, or having her back scratched, quite regardless of her probable inability to conceive cream or to make judgments concerning warmth. . . .[14]

How is the view here proposed to be proved? What is the evidence upon which it rests?

In the first place, we have reached it by a process of systematic elimination. We have first examined and eliminated those views which affirm value to be indefinable, or to be definable independently of interest. If value cannot be successfully identified or defined without reference to interest, then we must incorporate interest into our definition. We have next examined those views which relate value to interest in some qualified and exclusive sense; first, those views which have proposed to qualify and limit the object of interest; second, those views which have proposed to qualify and limit the act or state of interest itself. The result has been to exhibit a variety of values all having the common generic character of being "object-of-interest." We have thus been led to define value as the peculiar relation between any interest and its object; or that special character of an object which consists in the fact that interest is taken in it. We are now justified in framing this hypothesis as a last remaining alterna-

[13] *The Sense of Beauty*, 1899, pp. 17–19. Cf. also William James: *"The essence of good is to satisfy demand"* (*Will to Believe*, etc., 1898, p. 201).

[14] D. W. Prall, *A Study in the Theory of Value*, Univ. of California Publications in Philosophy, Vol. 3, No. 2, 1921, pp. 215, 227. The present writer is in essential agreement with the whole of this admirable monograph.

tive. There is a certain presumption in favor of this remaining alternative not only because of the elimination of the others, but also because these have all betrayed a common tendency. They have not only through their failure left the field clear for our definition of value, but they have *pointed* to that definition and incidentally argued in its support.

A certain positive plausibility is given to this hypothesis by the fact that in order to create values where they did not exist before it seems to be sufficient to introduce an interest. The silence of the desert is without value, until some wanderer finds it lonely and terrifying; the cataract, until some human sensibility finds it sublime, or until it is harnessed to satisfy human needs. Natural substances or the by-products of manufacture are without value until a use is found for them, whereupon their value may increase to any degree of preciousness according to the eagerness with which they are coveted. There is no entity that can be named that does not, in the very naming of it, take on a certain value through the fact that it is selected by the cognitive purpose of some interested mind. As interests grow and expand, multiplying in number and extending their radius through experience and imagination, the store of cosmic values is enriched and diversified.

But it may be contended that such proof is redundant or verbal. It proves only that objects of interest appear whenever interest is taken in objects; or, it proves at most that what is added to a given situation when interests are introduced corresponds closely to what it is customary to *call* value. It does not add to our knowledge by demonstrating the existence of value where it was not suspected, or by resolving doubts as to what is *really* valuable.

This objection again brings to light the difference between the general definition of value and the solution of special questions of value. The doubts and perplexities of everyday life, as well as the limited theoretical problems of the several value-sciences, commonly assume a general definition of value, and turn upon some question of fact. Is this distant island worth annexing and defending? The answer depends upon the existence of mineral deposits or a good harbor, assuming that it is worth annexing if the satisfactions and utilities which it affords outweigh the sacrifices which it costs. Ought I to surrender my position for the sake of my scruples, or compromise temporarily in the hope of converting others to my way of thinking? The answer depends on certain probable trains of consequences following from each of the alternatives, assuming that the one or the other ought to be adopted in accordance with the principle of human happiness, broadly applied. Is recent American verse to be ranked as genuine poetry? The answer depends experimentally on the sort of feeling aroused in certain persons, such as the critic himself, by the prolonged and attentive reading of it, on the assumption that such a judgment of taste is decisive. Is the economic worth or the aesthetic superiority of a work of art dependent on its moral wholesomeness? The answer is assumed to depend on the record of market transactions, or the reported sentiments of connoisseurs.

Now the general definition of value does not directly answer any such question, because it does not ascertain the specific facts and probabilities upon which they turn. It concerns itself with the *assumption*, and must therefore always appear to deal with the obvious rather than the questionable. Its proper task is to make these assumptions explicit and consistent. By so doing it will inevitably affect the solution of such special questions, since it will prescribe the terms or the principle of their solution. But it has to do with the use which is to be made of evidence, rather than with the uncovering of new facts.

It follows that there can be no conclusive proof of a general definition of value, short of its success in facilitating the solution of all special questions of value. Such a definition is *an experiment in generalization.* If we adopt the fact of interest as our centre of reference, and view other facts of the surrounding field *in that relation* —if, in short, we take life *interest-wise*, as it can, in fact, be taken— do the data and the perplexities denoted by "good" and "evil," "right" and "wrong," "better" and "worse," or grouped within the special fields of morality, art, religion and kindred institutions, then fall into place and form a comprehensive system? It is evident that the only proof of which such a hypothesis is capable lies in its complete elaboration. . . .

BIBLIOGRAPHY

PERRY, Ralph Barton, *The Approach to Philosophy.* N.Y.: Scribner's, 1905.
————, *The Moral Economy.* N.Y.: Scribner's, 1909.
————, *Present Philosophical Tendencies.* N.Y.: Longmans, Green, 1912; revised ed., 1916.
————, *The Present Conflict of Ideals.* N.Y.: Longmans, Green, 1918.
————, *Philosophy of the Recent Past.* N.Y.: Scribner's, 1926.
————, *General Theory of Value. Its Meaning and Basic Principles Construed in Terms of Interest.* N.Y.: Longmans, Green, 1926.

————, *The Thought and Character of William James.* 2 vols., Boston: Little, Brown, 1935.

————, *In the Spirit of William James.* New Haven: Yale U. Press, 1938.

————, *Puritanism and Democracy.* N.Y.: Vanguard Press, 1944.

————, *Characteristically American.* N.Y.: Alfred A. Knopf, 1949.

————, *Realms of Value: A Critique of Human Civilization.* Cambridge: Harvard U. Press, 1954.

Arthur O. Lovejoy

[1873–1962]

Lovejoy was born in Berlin, the son of Rev. W. W. Lovejoy of Boston and Sara Oncken of Hamburg. Lovejoy took a B.A. degree at the University of California, where he studied with Howison, and did graduate work at Harvard and the University of Pennsylvania. Lovejoy began his teaching career at Stanford University (1899–1901). He taught at Washington University (St. Louis), Columbia University, and the University of Missouri. He went to Johns Hopkins University in 1910 and remained there for the rest of his teaching career, until 1938. He was one of the founders of the American Association of University Professors and was responsible for the first battle on behalf of academic freedom carried on by that organization (1915).

Lovejoy was an undeviating critical realist, effective in his rebuttals of both neo-realism and idealism. He was also a constant critic of pragmatism, behaviorism, and objective relativism. His Carus Lectures, *The Revolt Against Dualism* (1930), attempt to show the necessity of dualistic epistemology. He argued that anyone who believes in a real physical world must be a dualist and maintained: (a) that there are given in experience particular existents which are not parts of the world, and (b) that any knowledge we have of the real world is indirect or representative. The problem for Lovejoy was to defend epistemological dualism against possible criticisms, and to show how it is implied in all knowing. He tried to show, for example, that in memory and anticipation, as in perception, there is "a conscious intrinsic reference to a reality other than the content given." His own brand of critical realism, which he labeled "temporalistic realism," emphasized the temporal character of all experience. There is a time span, he argued, between the object which is perceived and the actual perception. Lovejoy claimed that perceptual and secondary qualities, which are necessary for knowledge and thought, are not part of the physical universe. They are psychically evolved emergents, which nonetheless have natural causes. We cannot prove beyond doubt that some of the properties of our ideas are also properties of the physical universe, but such is "a natural assumption which no one can prove to be false." The selection below from *The Revolt Against Dualism* (1930) contains Lovejoy's statement of critical realism.

Lovejoy was also a strong advocate of the history of ideas. He was instrumental in founding *The Journal of the History of Ideas* and was its first editor. His interest in this field may be seen as early as his monograph *The Dialectic of Bruno and Spinoza* (1904). It is seen again in *Essays in The History of Ideas* (1948), which brings together a number of papers in intellectual history. In these papers, Lovejoy examined general ideas—such as primitivism, romanticism, evolutionism, and naturalism—with erudition and insight. He traced the presence of such ideas in different areas of thought and in different periods of time, showing their different meanings and pointing out their ambiguities, if any.

Lovejoy's most important contribution to the history of ideas is probably *The Great Chain of Being* (1936). In this book he takes an idea first expressed by Plato in the *Timaeus,* that is, the creation myth: the demiurge wished the world to lack nothing; hence all possibilities must be realized. The realization of all possibilities is the "great chain of being," which rests upon the "principle of plenitude." Lovejoy traces these simple ideas in Christian theology, the cosmography of Bruno, Leibniz and Spinoza, to the biological speculation of the 18th century, showing finally how they received a temporal character. This work is characterized throughout by historical scholarship of the highest level.

THE REVOLT AGAINST DUALISM [1]

The hypothetical conclusion which we reached at the beginning of the preceding lecture was a conclusion pertinent only to the case of the physical realist. If you are to believe in a real physical world, then—so the argument ran—you must necessarily be a dualist in both senses of the term: you must hold (a) that there are given in experience particular existents which are not parts of that world, and you must hold (b) that whatever knowledge of real objects you have is indirect or representative, that the datum whereby you know any such object is not identical with the object known. Resuming our inquiry at this point—after some divagation into a collateral issue— we proceed to consider two further questions, relating exclusively to the second of these propositions. The first question is whether that proposition is valid not exclusively from the standpoint of the realist, but from any standpoint—in other words, whether epistemological dualism must be accepted by anyone, be he realist or idealist or phenomenalist or pragmatist, who believes that the phenomenon called knowing ever does actually occur. The second question is whether, in final analysis, epistemological dualism itself is tenable— whether the notion of the apprehension of an existent (whatever be its metaphysical nature) by means of the immediate presence in experience of *something other than itself* is psychologically intelligi-

[1] From A. O. Lovejoy, *The Revolt Against Dualism*, La Salle, Ill.: Open Court, 1930. Selection taken from Chapter 9, "The Nature of Knowing as a Natural Event," pp. 378–401.

ble, or even conceivable without self-contradiction. Our two questions, then, more briefly stated, are: (1) Is the mediate character of knowledge implied by idealism (or kindred doctrines) as well as by physical realism? (2) Is mediate knowledge possible—and if so, how? . . .

(1) We turn, then, to our first question. The answer to it is to be found in some very simple considerations already intimated. The idealist does, of course, avoid an admission of epistemological dualism with respect to the knowledge of the physical world, inasmuch as he denies that there is—in the sense in which we have been using the term—any physical world to be known. He is content (in this matter) with his private world of perceptual content. His sense-data have an indubitable, if transitory, existence; each of them is precisely what it is immediately experienced as being; and he seeks for nothing possessing similar generic characters beyond or behind them. The being of sensible things is simply their being sensed; and their true characters are therefore their sensed characters. And it is because he has, in dealing with the special problem of perception, thus contrived very easily and summarily to rid himself of the difficulty of understanding how things can be known indirectly, that the idealist has often supposed that he has avoided that difficulty altogether. But this is an illusion, and a very naïve and transparent one, arising chiefly from an excessive preoccupation of epistemologists in the past with the problem of perception.

For the type of cognitive—or putatively cognitive—experience with which a systematic epistemological inquiry ought to begin is not perception but retrospection, or, more specifically, remembrance. This is the primary mode of knowing, which must be presupposed, tacitly or explicitly, in any reflection upon the implications of what is sensibly given; and it is the kind of knowledge about the reality of which there is least disagreement. It is the one which involves the smallest transcendence of absolute skepticism, and from which it is improbable that the most resolutely subjectivistic of philosophers really dissents. Its thin end is of an exceeding thinness; it amounts to no more than the assumption that one was not born at this moment, that one has had experiences of which one now knows, though they are not the experiences which one is now having. If Descartes had been as critical and methodical in rebuilding his world as he was in shattering it, he would have seen that the existential proposition which, in his reconstruction, should have immediately followed the *cogito ergo sum* was *memini ergo fui*. He could not, indeed, have formally deduced this from the *cogito*; he could not, strictly speaking, have justified it by reasoning; but he could, by simply keeping his attention fixed upon his own consciousness, have, so to say, seen *cogito* transforming itself into *memini* before his eyes. Small as this step might have seemed, it would have altered the direction of Descartes' subsequent course of reasoning; and if he had taken it, the history of modern philosophy might well have been widely different from what it has been, and less involved in confusion.

For any belief in the possibility of true remembrance is not only a step out of subjectivism; it is also a step into epistemological dualism. Why this is true was briefly indicated in the first of these lectures; but it is perhaps advisable to recapitulate and complete the argument here. In memory and other retrospection there is a conscious and intrinsic reference to a reality other than the content given. The perceptual datum, as Berkeleian idealists and neo-realists both like to remind us, is not presented in unreflective experience as standing for an existent not itself; *merely* to perceive is not to be explicitly aware of a contrast between datum and *cognoscendum*. But merely to remember *is* to be aware of a contrast between the image presented and the event recalled. No man doubts that, when he recollects today the acts he performed yesterday, those acts are not occurring today and yet that something which somehow exhibits their character is an item in his experience today; or that when, for example, he brings to mind the look of a dog he owned when a boy, there is something of a canine sort immediately present to and therefore compresent with his consciousness, but that it is quite certainly not that dog in the flesh. Retrospection is thus a case in which the duality of the datum and the thing known is immediately manifest. . . .

Of the other form of intertemporal cognition, actual or supposed —that is, foreknowledge or expectation—the dualistic implications are, if possible, even more manifest; and thus those pragmatic philosophers who curiously tend to conceive of the future as the sole region upon which our interest and our intellection are directed must, not less certainly than the idealist, admit that the *cognoscendum* is not apprehended through actual possession. For such pragmatists knowledge is pre-presentative if not representative. Future events not only are not now being experienced, but they have never entered into experience nor into existence, *as* events; and upon them no sane mortal can suppose his cognitive grasp to be direct and assured. Yet unless we can truly be said in some sense to be capable of referring to and foreknowing some future events, all our other knowing is, not, indeed, spurious, but—as the pragmatist rightly enough insists—barren, and irrelevant to the occasions which chiefly makes knowledge needful to the expectant, purposive, and plan-devising creatures that we are.

Both retrospection and forecast, then, are crucial and undeniable examples of the fact that knowing—if there *is* any such phenomenon —may, and at least in certain cases must, consist in the apprehension of a particular existent through the presence in a given experience of some existent other than itself. . . .

(2) We pass now to our second question. It concerns the truth of the thesis—frequently maintained by philosophers who are themselves, as we have just seen, epistemological dualists—that any theory of indirect or representative knowledge is redundant and, in the last analysis, self-contradictory. . . .

The solution . . . of the supposed difficulty in the conception of knowing as mediate is evident. To claim knowledge of what is not temporally coexistent with the knowing, is *not* to have the intended object of knowledge *in propria persona* "before the mind"; and the epistemological dualist in expressing his thesis does not fall into the contradiction of asserting that he has that object before his mind and at the same time asserting that he knows it only through the presentation in his experience of something which is not that object. What his thesis means, or should mean, is that at the moment when any man believes himself to be, *e.g.*, remembering, there is before him both a particular concrete datum—usually an image—and the conception of a mode of relatedness in which mutually external existences, including this datum, may stand to one another; and that the character of the datum either is ascribed to a locus (in that relational order) conceived as other than that in which it is actually given (other, namely, than the here-and-now locus), or is at least regarded as capable of presence in that other locus. This ascription of the character to some locus of the not-present and not-given is not equivalent to, and is in knowledge—when, at least, it is at all reflective—not confused with, its veritable presence in such a locus; for it is as an externality in *existence* that the mutual externality of the loci is conceived. The notion of existence, which is so often treated as mysterious and incomprehensible, appears to be so only because it is fundamental in our thinking and irreducible; intelligence cannot take a single step without employing it. Those who think they have dispensed with it are transparently deceiving themselves. We are empirically acquainted with its meaning by ourselves being—and by the being, at any moment, of our present data. But we can, and must, and persistently do, extend it to objects and events to which we impute positions not our own in that order of temporal relations which we conceive as including and transcending our own position and that of our data. And when we do this we mean something more than the fact of our so extending it—more, that is, than the fact that those objects are now presented to us as so situated in that now presented frame. We mean, precisely, that that to which we extend it had, or will have, existence in its own position as truly as we and our data (including our concept of the temporal order of relations) now have existence; but in that order, the only part of which we are now *experiencing* the existence, and of which we can assert the present existence, is the part within which we and our data are situated. Thus it is that we can, at a given moment, contrast the reality of a not-present event with the givenness of the datum (whether percept or image) by which we apprehend it, and even with the givenness of the conceptual schema by means of which we are enabled to frame the distinction between the present and the not-present, the datum and the *cognoscendum*.

The "how" of mediate knowing being thus made intelligible primarily by a scrutiny of intertemporal knowledge, of which the mediate character is certain, the purely epistemological paradox supposed to inhere in any dualistic theory of perception disappears. . . .

We have been considering the knowing of particular existences from, so to say, the inside; we have been observing what it appears as to the knower. Accepting the results thus reached, we may now define the distinctive character and the rôle of knowledge in the economy of nature. Essentially, knowing is a phenomenon by which the simple location of things is circumvented without being annulled. Upon any metaphysical theory deserving of serious consideration reality is an aggregate of *partes extra partes*.[2] Every particular is in its own time, or its own place, or its own point-instant in space-time; or (for the idealist) it is an act of consciousness, or a subject of consciousness, or a presentation in the experience of some supposedly "windowless monad," each of these being numerically distinct from other entities of the same type. Existents, in short, whether they are physical or mental or both, are many; they are bounded, and the bounds of their being mean mutual exclusion. This is not equivalent to asserting that they are without relations, or that they do not causally interact, or even that they may not be mutually implicatory. But it is mere confusion of thought to suppose that any of these interconnections between particulars amount to a transcendence of the separateness and identity of the particulars. If things are said to be related, it is so much the more evident that they do not (with respect to any determinate mode of relation) escape from their reciprocal exclusiveness; for it is only where there are distinct terms that there can be said to be real relations. But though things exist in their own places and not elsewhere, they may get reported elsewhere; and the being-known of a thing is its getting-reported where it does not exist

---

[2] Among theories deserving of such consideration I should not include any Eleatic or Vedantic monism, or its modern counterparts.

—and its getting-reported there *as* existing at the locus or region in which it does exist. Any theory of knowledge which does not recognize both these distinctive peculiarities of the cognitive phenomenon, fails to provide either for actual knowledge or for possible error.

According to the contention of these lectures (with respect to the epistemological issue) this two-fold requirement for a thing's getting-reported is fulfilled, and can be fulfilled, only in one way—in the way, namely, of partial or symbolic reproduction in the awareness of a cognitive organism which is at the same time capable of thinking of some general scheme or order in which existences have separate and mutually exclusive situations, and of referring attributes of the data (*i.e.*, sensa or images) of which it is directly aware to external situations in that order. . . .

This account of knowing both accepts and qualifies, it will be seen, certain epistemological theses characteristic of idealism, of monistic realism, and of (in one sense of that ambiguous designation) pragmatism. Even the most subjective idealist is right in saying that, in a sense, we never in knowing "step outside the circle of our own ideas" or "transcend experience." For it is never the true *cognoscendum* as an existent that is present to us as an actual experienced datum. But the monistic realist is also right in saying that—in so far as we know at all—we always, in another sense, step outside the circle of our own ideas. For that which we apprehend through any particular idea must always be assigned in thought to a locus in some conceived order (temporal or other) which transcends the locus at which the idea as an existent is in fact situated. And the type of pragmatist who insists upon the necessity of postulation, of belief which outruns empirical evidence, is also, in an important sense, right. For since the externality of the *cognoscendum* to the idea of it is, in so far as it is now actually apprehended, externality within a scheme of relations which is, at any moment of cognition, also a present datum, a piece of schematic imagery now before me, the acceptance of it as valid and as trustworthy as a clue for action is an act of belief which goes beyond purely experiential proof. No judgment concerning a particular existent—other than the immediate and transient private datum, about which no act of judgment is necessary—can conceivably attain experiential verification in any literal sense; for the existent complex of ideas which is the content of the judgment can never, by any finite and temporal knower, be brought into the same locus with the existent to which it refers. Since our knowing is characteristically concerned with beyonds, we know by faith. But not all beyonds of which we can frame ideas are the objects of faiths for which we have motives equally persuasive, urgent, or irrepressible, equally deeply rooted in our cognitive constitution, and equally reconcilable with one another and with what—through our primary faiths in the reality of remembrance and in the existence of other knowers—we believe to have been the constant and common course of experience.

Upon realistic premises, the getting-reported of an existent at a locus not its own is, of course, dependent upon certain physical processes. In sense-perception there is, first, a series of causally-linked events, conforming to ordinary physical laws, temporally and spatially intervenient between the object and the peripheral nerve-terminus, and another series of such events within the nervous system; and there is, further, the wholly unique phenomenon of the production, as an effect of these neuro-cerebral processes, of certain nonphysical entities and events, *viz.*, sensa and the awareness of them. There are, in short, changes in certain physical structures which generate existents that are not physical in the sense in which those structures are; and these non-physical particulars are indispensable means to any knowledge of physical realities. Repellent as this conception still is to many scientific men, there is no conclusion of empirical science about the physical world—supposing that there in any sense *is* a physical world—which is better established; the proof of this is set forth in the first seven of these lectures. The getting-reported of a past experience of an organism in the subsequent experience of the same organism is likewise physically conditioned, first by certain purely physiological phenomena, and then by the cerebral events which generate images. But neither the processes which transmit certain physical effects of the action of the external object, or of the past event, nor even those which produce sensa and images, are equivalent to the getting-reported of that object or event. For that, there must arise—presumably at a late stage of organic evolution—as physically conditioned non-physical effects, at least two further functions; (a) a power to conceive of some realm or order of inter-related existents which includes but extends beyond the organism itself and the sensa and images which are immediately present to it; and (b) a propensity of the organism to think some of the characters of the immediately given as actually or potentially belonging to external situations in that order. This propensity is spontaneous, and in that sense instinctive, in the cognitive species of organism; but it is capable of extensive modification and control through experience and reflection. It could not be destroyed without destruction of the cognitive function itself.

BIBLIOGRAPHY

LOVEJOY, Arthur O., *Bergson and Romantic Evolutionism*. Berkeley: U. of California Press, 1914.

————, *The Revolt Against Dualism*. Chicago: W. W. Norton, 1930.

————, *The Great Chain of Being: A Study of the History of an Idea*. Cambridge: Harvard U. Press, 1936.

————, *Essays in the History of Ideas*. Baltimore: Johns Hopkins Press, 1948. (Contains a bibliography of Lovejoy's articles up through 1947.)

————, *Reflections on Human Nature*. Baltimore: Johns Hopkins Press, 1961.

————, *The Reason, the Understanding and Time*. Baltimore: Johns Hopkins Press, 1961.

————, *The Thirteen Pragmatisms and Other Essays*. Baltimore: Johns Hopkins Press, 1963.

————, with George Boas. *Primitivism and Related Ideas in Antiquity*. Baltimore: Johns Hopkins Press, 1935.

RECK, Andrew J., "The Philosophy of A. O. Lovejoy (1873–1962)," *The Review of Metaphysics,* Vol. XVII No. 2, Dec. 1963, pp. 257–85.

Roy Wood Sellars

[1880–   ]

Roy Wood Sellars was born in Ontario, Canada, and was raised in a pioneering community in Michigan. He took his A.B. degree at the University of Michigan in 1903 and his Ph.D. in 1908. He also studied at the Hartford Theological Seminary, the University of Wisconsin and the University of Chicago, and he spent a year in France and Germany. He began teaching at the University of Michigan in 1905, and remained there until his retirement in 1950. He is a former President of the Western Philosophical Association.

Sellars is a critical realist, an evolutionary naturalist, a materialist and a humanist. His contributions to critical realism are found in his book, *Critical Realism* (1916), in his article in *Essays in Critical Realism* (1920), and in many other pieces over the years. Sellars was opposed to a psychophysical dualism. In his book *Evolutionary Naturalism* (1922) he takes a naturalistic point of view and develops the doctrine of levels in nature. Sellars also helped to edit (with Farber and McGill) the collaborative volume *Philosophy for the Future; The Quest for Modern Materialism* (1949), in which he expressed his sympathy for materialism as a more forthright philosophy of nature than naturalism. His interest in humanism as an appropriate religious philosophy for our time is indicated by the fact that he helped to write *A Humanist Manifesto* (1933). The piece reprinted below, "Critical Realism" (1930), written a decade after the critical realists had published their position, represents Sellars' fully developed epistemological views.

CRITICAL REALISM [1]

The total act of perceiving with its beliefs, categories, and discriminations is the most elementary unit of knowing the external world. Reflection shows that this complex is mental and intrinsic to the active organism. I beg to point out that, when I use the word mental, I have in mind no dualistic assumption, but only the recognition that we have here a peculiar activity of the individual. In taking the act

[1] From *Contemporary American Philosophy: Personal Statements,* ed. G. P. Adams and W. P. Montague, N.Y.: Macmillan, 1930, Vol. II, pp. 269–273.

of knowing seriously, we must realize that we are on the inside of this act and that the logical discriminations used in it are not self-sufficient atoms to be called mental entities. We have here a structure which must be taken at its face value. The mind is interpreting an object in terms of characters. It is thinking the characteristics of the object. Shift the point of view quickly from a knowledge-claim to a survey of what is given in and to consciousness, and these characteristics of things become characters of a logical sort undoubtedly sustained by the mind. But then we are ceasing to claim to know external objects. The direction of the mind has altered.

How does this position differ from naïve realism? In three main ways. First, it is more aware of the conditions of knowing; second, it is ready to admit the mediate, or interpretative, nature of knowing; and, third, it holds that reflection must work within perceptual knowing to lift it to more adequate knowledge of the object. It sees that perception is dominated by practical interests and bodily perspective, and passes to science.

Let me summarize my results. In the first place, knowing is regarded as more than the awareness of abstracta to be called logical ideas. It is an interpretation of objects. Thus objective reference is intrinsic to the very nature of knowing whether perceptual or explicitly judgmental. This analysis rids us of the subjectivistic bias of traditional representative realism. In the second place, logical ideas are discriminations within a complex mental activity in which objects are selected and interpreted. We must not drop back to an atomistic psychology of sensations and images which ignores empirical facts. Our mental activity sustains for us an experienced structure in which we sense ourselves as interpreting objects in terms of predicates revealing their characteristics. This bit of redness, this instance of squareness, are logical characters enabling us to grasp the characteristics of the object. They are to be classed as mental only when we raise the question of their ultimate nature as related to the mental act of knowing to which they are intrinsic. In the act of knowing, it is their logical content which occupies our interest. We look through them at the object. Yet reflection, I believe, forces us to hold that the whole complex mental act to which they are intrinsic is a temporal affair expressive of the brain-mind. The only alternative is to hold them to be essences belonging to a realm of being other than that of physical existence. But this alternative theory seems to me less simple than the one I defend and more traditionalistic, more a reflection of Platonism.

The comment of the reader at this point may be somewhat as follows: Granted that the logic and psychology of this position is an advance upon Locke's and Kant's, due to the progress in both domains, does it not still hold that the characters held as predicates before the mind must resemble the qualities of the external thing? Yes and no. Sense-qualities fall away as we pass from naïve to critical claims and the appreciation of structure and relations increases. Now the structure conceived in the mind does, I believe, correspond to the structure of the object. It is because of this correspondence that the knowledge-claim is justified; the logical idea does reveal the characteristics of the object. These characteristics must not be conceived in the old fashion as properties inhering in an unknown substance, but as the nature of the physical system known. An object does weigh so much, is so large, has such and such a texture, will do certain things under certain conditions. We must simply move away from the literal assignment of passive sense-qualities.

A few words on a point which has been misunderstood are desirable. I was led to deny the reality of a cognitive relation. This did not mean that I did not supply what the cognitive relation stood for—reference to an object and the claim to know it. The expression "cognitive relation" was connected in my mind with the conflict between neo-realism and idealism. In the English form of the controversy, at least, there was assumed a sort of tenuous relation between the mind and the object called awareness. Was this internal or external? Now my own analysis forced me to maintain that a physical object known is never literally present in the field of consciousness; the mind makes no existential contact with it except through the sense-organs. Knowing is a claim and reference to an external object mediated by meanings in consciousness. It is a sort of mental pointing and not a literal transcendence. This fact but brings out more clearly the unique nature of knowing. This mental pointing, however, is founded on the attitude and response of the organism in perception and the reflection of this in consciousness. Conceptual pointing but carries on this structure and develops it in terms of frames of reference. Knowing handles objects through internal substitutes which are supposed to reveal the nature of the external object.

But, it may be replied, while you rightly avoid a gross interpretation of a cognitive relation by means of stress upon internal reference and claims attached to ideas, does it not remain a fact that the nature of the object is present to the mind? This query demands a reply. I do not think that, existentially, the nature of an object ever separates itself from the object. It can, however, be reproduced in the mind as an achieved abstractum and be held by that mind as a revelation of the nature of the object. We have here a logical, or better, a cognitive, identity between idea and object.

This problem brings out the fact that knowing is a kind of operation for which we can find no ordinary physical analogies. It depends upon the growth and use of distinctions, beliefs, and categories in consciousness. An object is cognitively present to the mind when it is known, but such knowledge does not involve the literal givenness of the object as an entity within the field of consciousness. Knowing is a looking at objects through the windows furnished by ideas. It is *sui generis*, though made possible by the situation and capacities of the organism.

In this very brief survey of some of the high points of epistemology we have now arrived at a stage which demands the discussion of truth. In order to secure clarity it will be better to limit ourselves to the question of what we mean by the trueness of a proposition. But, first of all, let me say that a proposition is to me a complex idea used in an act of knowing. It is a belief. Taken in this sense, a proposition seems to me to be called true when we consider it to give knowledge of its object, to reveal its object. Hence, I have always maintained that knowing is the basic idea which underlies truth. An idea which gives knowledge of its object is true. But, if this is the meaning of truth, what are the criteria or tests? It is often averred that critical realism has special difficulties here because of its doctrine of transcendence. How can you check up on the idea if the object is not given? And if the object is given, what need have you for ideas?

The proper approach is to ask what casts doubt on the truth-claim of a judgment. The doubt must be motivated and specific, otherwise we are merely doubting the ability of the human mind to know. When I come to analyse the situation, I find that the human mind begins in perception to interpret objects and that difficulties merely force a critical reinterpretation of this first interpretation. The basic postulate is the claim to know or, what amounts to the same thing at this level, the revelatory nature of our predicates. This postulate, if challenged, is confirmed by the success of our critical thinking. In other words, thought cures its own difficulties by showing how new distinctions satisfy old conflicts. The manner in which perceptual illusions are shown to result from our position and from the nature of our sense-organs illustrates what I mean. Critical thinking is the only remedy for specifically motivated doubt. And this success of critical thinking can be indicated under four headings: (1) the consilience of established facts; (2) the logical coherence of ideas; (3) agreement of investigators; and (4) guidance and control over nature. These headings have been so often discussed that there is no need to go into detail. It will be noted that I assign a place to both the logical and the larger pragmatic tests. But I am convinced that the very advance of thought rests on the belief that sense-perception is revelatory of nature and that the proper use of it enables us to penetrate into the characteristics of the world. The logic of science gives, I think, the proper use of sense-perception.

As conclusion of this summary account of critical realism, let me point out what I think is important about it as a direction of thought. It represents a deeper insight into the nature of human knowing and a greater awareness of its conditions. In place of knowing as a semi-magical intuition or compresence of mind and object, it grasps knowing as an achievement in which ideas function, ideas being distinctions within the field of consciousness used in accordance with slowly evolved meanings and beliefs. In this way it shows how organic activity flowers into knowing. It can be regarded more as a deepening of natural realism than its complete rejection. What, then, can we know about the external world? Essentially what science has worked out—structure, relative dimensions, relative mass, energy-content, behavior. Theory of knowledge does not so much dictate to science as interpret it.

BIBLIOGRAPHY

SELLARS, Roy Wood, *Critical Realism*. N.Y.: Rand, McNally, 1916.

———, *The Next Step in Democracy*. N.Y.: Macmillan, 1916.

———, *The Essentials of Logic*. Boston: Houghton, Mifflin, 1917.

———, *The Essentials of Philosophy*. N.Y.: Macmillan, 1917.

———, *The Next Step in Religion*. N.Y.: Macmillan, 1918.

———, *Evolutionary Naturalism*. Chicago: Open Court, 1922.

———, *The Principles and Problems of Philosophy*. N.Y.: Macmillan, 1926.

———, *Religion Coming of Age*. N.Y.: Macmillan, 1928.

———, *The Philosophy of Physical Realism*. N.Y.: Macmillan, 1932.

———, *Philosophy for the Future; The Quest of Modern Materialism*, (co-editor). N.Y.: Macmillan, 1949.

"A Symposium in Honor of Roy Wood Sellars," *Philosophy and Phenomenological Research*, Vol. XV, No. 1 (Sept. 1954), pp. 1–103. (Also contains a complete bibliography of his writings).

Humanism

The following piece provides an outline statement of the main principles of humanism. The first draft of this document was written by Roy Wood Sellars. It was subsequently signed by 34 people, including John Dewey, John H. Randall, Jr., Edwin A. Burtt, Harry E. Barnes, and Oliver L. Reiser. The Manifesto combines many of the features of naturalism, but it goes beyond a philosophical position by providing for a form of religious guidance. Although humanism is opposed to supernaturalism, it expresses a religious commitment to human values, particularly in its affirmation of life, individual and social, as the highest good. This piece was written during the liberal nineteen-thirties, but it continues to find support among a considerable number of American intellectuals.

A HUMANIST MANIFESTO [1]
(1933)

The time has come for widespread recognition of the radical changes in religious beliefs throughout the modern world. The time is past for mere revision of traditional attitudes. Science and economic change have disrupted the old beliefs. Religions the world over are under the necessity of coming to terms with new conditions created by a vastly increased knowledge and experience. In every field of human activity, the vital movement is now in the direction of a candid and explicit humanism. In order that religious humanism may be better understood we, the undersigned, desire to make certain affirmations which we believe the facts of our contemporary life demonstrate.

There is great danger of a final, and we believe fatal, identification of the word *religion* with doctrines and methods which have lost their significance and which are powerless to solve the problem of human living in the Twentieth Century. Religions have always been means for realizing the highest values of life. Their end has been accomplished through the interpretation of the total environing

[1] From *The New Humanist* (May–June, 1933), pp. 58–61.

situation (theology or world view), the sense of values resulting therefrom (goal or ideal), and the technique (cult), established for realizing the satisfactory life. A change in any of these factors results in alteration of the outward forms of religion. This fact explains the changefulness of religions through the centuries. But through all changes religion itself remains constant in its quest for abiding values, an inseparable feature of human life.

Today man's larger understanding of the universe, his scientific achievements, and his deeper appreciation of brotherhood, have created a situation which requires a new statement of the means and purposes of religion. Such a vital, fearless, and frank religion capable of furnishing adequate social goals and personal satisfactions may appear to many people as a complete break with the past. While this age does owe a vast debt to the traditional religions, it is none the less obvious that any religion that can hope to be a synthesizing and dynamic force for today must be shaped for the needs of this age. To establish such a religion is a major necessity of the present. It is a responsibility which rests upon this generation. We therefore affirm the following:

First: Religious humanists regard the universe as self-existing and not created.

Second: Humanism believes that man is a part of nature and that he has emerged as the result of a continuous process.

Third: Holding an organic view of life, humanists find that the traditional dualism of mind and body must be rejected.

Fourth: Humanism recognizes that man's religious culture and civilization, as clearly depicted by anthropology and history, are the product of a gradual development due to his interaction with his natural environment and with his social heritage. The individual born into a particular culture is largely molded by that culture.

Fifth: Humanism asserts that the nature of the universe depicted by modern science makes unacceptable any supernatural or cosmic guarantees of human values. Obviously humanism does not deny the possibility of realities as yet undiscovered, but it does insist that the way to determine the existence and value of any and all realities is by means of intelligent inquiry and by the assessment of their relations to human needs. Religion must formulate its hopes and plans in the light of the scientific spirit and method.

Sixth: We are convinced that the time has passed for theism, deism, modernism, and the several varieties of "new thought."

Seventh: Religion consists of those actions, purposes, and experiences which are humanly significant. Nothing human is alien to the religious. It includes labor, art, science, philosophy, love, friendship, recreation—all that is in its degree expressive of intelligently satisfying human living. The distinction between the sacred and the secular can no longer be maintained.

Eighth: Religious Humanism considers the complete realization of human personality to be the end of man's life and seeks its development and fulfillment in the here and now. This is the explanation of the humanist's social passion.

Ninth: In the place of the old attitudes involved in worship and prayer the humanist finds his religious emotions expressed in a heightened sense of personal life and in a co-operative effort to promote social well-being.

Tenth: It follows that there will be no uniquely religious emotions and attitudes of the kind hitherto associated with belief in the supernatural.

Eleventh: Man will learn to face the crises of life in terms of his knowledge of their naturalness and probability. Reasonable and manly attitudes will be fostered by education and supported by custom. We assume that humanism will take the path of social and mental hygiene and discourage sentimental and unreal hopes and wishful thinking.

Twelfth: Believing that religion must work increasingly for joy in living, religious humanists aim to foster the creative in man and to encourage achievements that add to the satisfactions of life.

Thirteenth: Religious humanism maintains that all associations and institutions exist for the fulfillment of human life. The intelligent evaluation, transformation, control, and direction of such associations and institutions with a view to the enhancement of human life is the purpose and program of humanism. Certainly religious institutions, their ritualistic forms, ecclesiastical methods, and communal activities must be reconstituted as rapidly as experience allows, in order to function effectively in the modern world.

Fourteenth: The humanists are firmly convinced that existing acquisitive and profit-motivated society has shown itself to be inadequate and that a radical change in methods, controls, and motives must be instituted. A socialized and co-operative economic order must be established to the end that the equitable distribution of the means of life be possible. The goal of humanism is a free and universal society in which people voluntarily and intelligently co-operate for the common good. Humanists demand a shared life in a shared world.

Fifteenth and last: We assert that humanism will: (a) affirm life rather than deny it; (b) seek to elicit the possibilities of life, not flee from it; and (c) endeavor to establish the conditons of a satisfactory life for all, not merely for a few. By this positive *morale* and intention humanism will be guided, and from this perspective and alignment the techniques and efforts of humanism will flow.

So stand the theses of religious humanism. Though we consider the religious forms and ideas of our fathers no longer adequate, the quest for the good life is still the central task for mankind. Man is at last becoming aware that he alone is responsible for the realization of the world of his dreams, that he has within himself the power for its achievement. He must set intelligence and will to the task.

(Signed) J. A. C. Fagginger Auer, E. Burdette Backus, Harry Elmer Barnes, L. M. Birkhead, Raymond B. Bragg, Edwin Arthur Burtt, Ernest Caldecott, A. J. Carlson, John Dewey, Albert C. Dieffenbach, John H. Dietrich, Bernard Fantus, William Floyd, F. H. Hankins, A. Eustace Haydon, Llewellyn Jones, Robert Morse Lovett, Harold P. Marley, R. Lester Mondale, Charles Francis Potter, John Herman Randall, Jr., Curtis W. Reese, Oliver L. Reiser, Roy Wood Sellars, Clinton Lee Scott, Maynard Shipley, W. Frank Swift, V. T. Thayer, Eldred C. Vanderlaan, Joseph Walker, Jacob J. Weinstein, Frank S. C. Wicks, David Rhys Williams, Edwin H. Wilson.

NOTE: *The Manifesto is a product of many minds. It was designed to represent a developing point of view, not a new creed. The individuals whose signatures appear, would, had they been writing individual statements, have stated the propositions in differing terms. The importance of the document is that more than thirty men have come to general agreement on matters of final concern and that these men are undoubtedly representative of a large number who are forging a new philosophy out of the materials of the modern world. It is obvious that many others might have been asked to sign the Manifesto had not the lack of time and the shortage of clerical assistance limited our ability to communicate with them.*

BIBLIOGRAPHY

For works dealing with Humanism, the reader is referred to the General Bibliography, section 6.

Morris R. Cohen

[1880–1947]

Cohen was born in Russia, came to the United States as a youth of twelve, and was brought up on New York's East Side. He graduated from the College of the City of New York and studied philosophy at Harvard, where he took his Ph.D. in 1906. From 1912 to 1938 he taught at City College, and later briefly at the University of Chicago. Cohen's influence as a teacher was very great. His keen logical and critical mind and his Socratic irony attracted many bright minds to philosophy.

Cohen's philosophy is difficult to classify. Like the pragmatists, he appreciated the role of ideas in action, but like the realists he considered that truth had an objective foundation in nature. He was a naturalist, in the sense that he opposed transcendental theories which claimed the existence of a "special" realm beyond that discovered by science, although he tended to criticize the excessive emphasis that naturalists were prone to place on experience. Cohen shared with Santayana the moral position expressed in *The Life of Reason,* but unlike Santayana he was a forthright liberal, committed to rational ethics in society. Cohen expressed a debt to Bertrand Russell's *Principles of Mathematics,* which helped him to forge instruments for acquiring intellectual independence—instruments he proceeded to employ with devastating effect upon the prevailing isms. He thought

of himself primarily as a logician, and logic was for him an obstinate attempt to think clearly.

What was perhaps distinctive in Cohen's philosophy was his defense of classical rationalism. Cohen described himself as a "rationalist" in believing that "reason is a genuine and significant phase of nature"— adding, however, that nature contains more than reason. He had a healthy respect for detailed facts and a profound faith in philosophy; sharpened by technique, philosophy was to provide us with "a contemplative vision." Cohen's defense of reason against obscurantism and irrationalism is contained in his major work, *Reason and Nature* (1931). Here Cohen maintained that science must not be interpreted too narrowly, for it goes beyond the data of experience to find the invariant properties and nature of things, and it uses deductive and conceptual methods to do so. Philosophy and metaphysics seek to provide us with the most general description of the nature of the world in which science operates. In the selection reprinted below from *Reason and Nature* Cohen relates philosophy to science and shows the significance of the "principle of sufficient reason." He suggests another key metaphysical idea, "the principle of polarity," which is a revised form of the Hegelian idea.

Cohen was greatly interested in political and social philosophy. His book, *The Faith of a Liberal* (1946), expressed his political convictions, and his *American Thought* (1954) contains incisive observations on American culture and thought. *The Meaning of Human History* (1947), his "Carus Lectures," was on the philosophy of history, a field to which he made considerable contributions.

Perhaps Cohen's most important practical influence was on legal thinking. He was a friend of Justices Holmes and Frankfurter, and attempted to revitalize concern for jurisprudence and the philosophy of law. Among his books on law were *Law and the Social Order* (1933) and *Reason and Law* (1950).

REASON AND NATURE [1]

THE METAPHYSICS OF REASON AND SCIENTIFIC METHOD

The Relation Between Philosophy and Science

Those who rank the truth-value of natural science very high and wish to utilize its results in their philosophy have followed one of three ways. They have tried to build a world-view either on the results, on the presuppositions, or on the method of science.

. . . Philosophy, seeking the most comprehensive vision, cannot ignore the insight gained by the sciences, but must go forward to envisage their possible synthesis. Though such synthesis is necessarily speculative it may be well to note: (1) that a certain speculative element is necessary for the substantial growth of science, and that the various sciences have in fact thus been nurtured by philosophy, and (2) that a scientific philosophy corrects the dangers of speculaiton by a rigorously logical analysis of fundamental concepts and assumptions, so that it should be aware of how much certainty can be attached to its wider speculative reaches. In recent years the work of the mathematical or neo-Leibnizian philosophers has remarkably clarified such traditional concepts as infinity and continuity, and the logical nature of inference and proof. We know better, thanks to the labors of Peirce, Frege, Whitehead, and Russell, what is requisite for rigorous proof, and we can be more honest in estimating the degree of probability that may attach to our various answers to the questions which science is not yet in a position to attack directly. In this respect philosophy is continuous with science in method. For, contrary to popular impression, science does not eschew speculative ventures into the unknown, though it is very cautious not to confuse anticipation with verification. The nature of number, matter, and life does

[1] From Morris R. Cohen, *Reason and Nature*, N. Y., 1931. Selections taken from Chapter IV, pp. 147–168.

not cease to be a concern of philosophy because definite light has been thrown upon these problems by modern logic, physics, and biology. But as the sciences grow by constantly correcting their content, it is the inescapable task of the philosopher to use the invariant principles of scientific method to go back to ever more rigorous analysis of the elements or rudiments of our knowledge, to examine the ideals which guide scientific effort, and to anticipate where possible what science *may* conquer in the future.

The Principle of Sufficient Reason

Scientific method, it is generally recognized, depends on the principle of causality. This, however, is only a special instance or application to temporal events of the wider principle of sufficient reason. The latter, as applied in mathematics, as well as in natural science, may be formulated as follows: *Everything is connected in definite ways with definite other things, so that its full nature is not revealed except by its position and relations within a system.* This is a familiar commonplace. Yet I venture to assert that its precise meaning is seldom justly appreciated in metaphysical discussion.

The Nature of Things

If we . . . take the principle of sufficient reason seriously we are justified in examining the nature of things without worrying about the ego-centric predicament of how we know that such knowledge is possible. The assumption of the critical philosophy that we can know only our own ideas is itself a dogmatism which involves an infinite regress. If the fact that I know a given entity does not determine any of its specific characteristics—and it is hard to see how it can determine any one known trait more than any other—then the fact of knowledge can be eliminated from the most general formula for the nature of things, though the existence of knowledge is itself a most important fact in our universe.

The fundamental metaphysical issue between rationalism and the various forms of anti-rationalism may be stated thus: Is the nature of things revealed most fully in developed rational science, or is it so well known in non-rational ways that we are justified in saying that science is a falsification or a merely practical device for dealing with dead things? Actually the various forms of anti-rationalism dogmatically assert the nature of things to be "really" individuality or continuous experience, spontaneity or practical experience, etc. But an attempt to justify any one of these formulae by evidence commits the anti-rationalist to the canons of scientific method.

The main metaphysical contention of anti-rationalism with its banal shibboleth about life, the organic, the dynamic, etc., is that things have no constant nature, that everything is pure change and nothing else. Historically we can understand the motive for this when we reflect how many of the old constancies have had to be abandoned in the progress of physics and biology. But though the principle of identity has undoubtedly been abused, the effort of the reaction to draw an account of the world without any element of identity in it is clearly self-defeating. Changes cannot have any definite character without repetition of identical patterns in different material. If the growth of science dissolves the eternity of the hills or the fixity of species, it is also discovering constant relations and order in changes which previously seemed chaotic and arbitrary. In daily life we find no difficulty in asserting that an individual or object maintains its character in the stream of change. Scientifically this constancy is expressed in the accurate language of mathematics by the concept of the *invariant*, not the isolated constant but that which remains identical amidst variation. We may say then that the nature of anything is the group of invariant characters.

From this point of view we are justified in making the ordinary distinction between the nature of anything and its manifestations. The fact that science seeks the invariant properties amidst the flux makes clear why science is never satisfied with empirical fact, and always seeks for explanation why things are constituted or behave in their particular way. The answer to the question *why*, is always a reason which puts the fact to be explained into a system, so that knowing the nature of the system and certain data (or given existences), we can deduce or form a rational account of the events to be explained. The fact that the abstract law makes the concrete particular intelligible does not, of course, prove that this law is less real or is more the product of our arbitrary fiat than the fact explained.

This view as to what is meant by the nature of things necessarily assigns a large and necessary rôle to the realm of possibility. If the actual is identified with the immediate, and the immediate with the sensuous, then the actual is certainly an infinitesimal portion of the wider world which it is found to presuppose. The sensuous vividness of the immediate may often be precisely what is meant by reality. But scientific reflection must and always does assume a larger world than that which is immediately before us or actual. Most of the sensuous material of the past, and of remote space, is beyond us and yet conditions the actuality before us. To be sure, the realm of possibility may be partly anticipated in actual imagination. But this is at best necessarily fragmentary. We may also denote by the word *actual* the historical order—all the things that have happened or will happen in all time and space, including men's dreams as themselves events. But shall we include in actuality the relations or implications of things which no one has perceived and which no one will, because of human limitations? Clearly we must distinguish here between knowledge by reference and knowledge by realized acquaintance. The totality of nature through all time and space is a limit which we can never attain and yet the idea of it is a necessity of scientific method. For the explanation of any part of the world always presupposes still other parts necessary to its complete determination. A completed rational system having nothing outside of it nor any possible alternative to it, is both presupposed and beyond the actual attainment of any one moment. It coincides in part with the Bradleyan Absolute, but it is an ideal limit rather than an actual experience. Unrealized possibilities are within it precisely to the extent that it contains endless time.

Rationalism, Naturalism and Supernaturalism

It is frequently asserted that the principle of scientific method cannot rule out in advance the possibility of any fact, no matter how strange or miraculous. This is true to the extent that science as a method of extending our knowledge must not let accepted views prevent us from discovering new facts that may seem to contradict our previous views. Actually, however, certain types of explanation cannot be admitted within the body of scientific knowledge. Any attempt, for instance, to explain physical phenomenon as directly due to providence or disembodied spirits, is incompatible with the principle of rational determinism. For the nature of these entities is not sufficiently determinate to enable us to deduce definite experimental consequences from them. The Will of Providence, for instance, will explain everything whether it happens one way or another. Hence, no experiment can possibly overthrow it. An hypothesis, however, which we cannot possibly refute cannot possibly be experimentally verified.

In thus ruling out ghostly, magical, and other supernatural influences, it would seem that scientific method impoverishes our view of the world. It is well, however, to remember that a world where no possibility is excluded is a world of chaos, about which no definite assertion can be made. Any world containing some order necessarily involves the elimination of certain abstract or ungrounded possibilities such as fill the minds of the insane.

From this point of view, what may be called the postulate of scientific materialism, viz. that all natural phenomena depend on material conditions, is not merely a well-supported generalization but the requirement of an orderly world, of a cosmos that is not a chaotic phantasmagoria.

As materialism has served as a sort of "bogey-man" to scare immature metaphysicians, it is well to make more explicit its relation to rational scientific method. If materialism means the denial of emotions, imaginings, thoughts, and other mental happenings, it is clearly not something worthy of serious consideration. It is contrary to facts of experience and clearly self-refuting. But this in no way disposes of the materialism of men like Democritus, Lucretius, Hobbes, or Spinoza, or of the assumption that every natural event must have a bodily or material basis.

The truth of the latter proposition is obscured by the popular confused concept of mental efficiency. Even technical discussion of the relation of mind and body is often vitiated by an inadequate analysis of the principle of rational determinism and a consequent misapprehension of the force of principles such as the conservation of energy. If, as it was contended before, scientific causality applies only to certain abstract aspects of entities, there is no reason why entities that determine each other in one way in a certain system may not be bound together in another way in another system. The presence of causal relation does not involve the denial of teleologic relations, while the assertion of the latter presupposes the former.

The principle of conservation of energy, for instance, leaves a wide realm of indetermination that other relations can make determinate. For the assertion that amidst all the transformations of a system the total amount of energy remains constant, is an assertion that clearly does not determine the character of the transformations other than in the one trait explicitly mentioned. The second law of thermodynamics does endeavor to indicate a general direction of phenomena, viz. towards a maximum of entropy. But this is largely problematic in certain regions, and in any case it often leaves room for all sorts of indetermination. Whether energy shall remain potential or be transformed into energy of motion is not completely determined by either principle, since either principle remains fulfilled whether the transformation takes place or not. Teleologic determinations are therefore not ruled out by the laws of energy.

Now the ordinary conception of mental efficiency combines elements of teleologic with strictly causal determination. We achieve certain purposes by taking advantage of natural mechanism. But this is in no way inconsistent with the proposition that every material change is correlated with a previous material condition in accordance with certain laws. What is inconsistent with scientific procedure is the argument that the existence of a mental motive makes the co-existence of a physical cause unnecessary.

Besides the objection from the existence of mental efficiency there is another line of arguments against materialism, viz. that matter is purely passive and cannot explain the activity of the world. Now it is doubtless true that the close connection between the notion of matter and that of mass or inertia leads to the view that matter by itself cannot explain the active processes of nature, and this leads to the introduction of forces which are the ghosts of spirits or of the volitions often connected with our own bodily movements. This argument, however, is based on a logical fallacy, taking the nature of matter to consist solely in its exclusive and passive aspect. But there is no valid reason against supposing that a purely material system without external influence can contain motion within it; and there is no conclusive argument against the view that under certain conditions material systems such as those which constitute the human body are capable of organic processes, feeling, etc.

The one serious objection to materialism from the point of view of the requisities of scientific method comes into play when materialism allies itself with sensationalistic empiricism and belittles the importance of relations and logical connection between things. The identification of empiricism with the scientific attitude is just a bit of natural complacency. The excessive worship of facts too often hides a disinclination to enter into a genuine inquiry as to whether they are so. A rationalism that is naturalistic must, of course, agree with empiricism in maintaining the factual or immediate aspect of existence. But scientific rationalism is incompatible with the complacent assumption that in sensations or in self-sufficient "facts" we have the only primary existences.

We do not have pure particulars any more than pure universals, to begin with. We begin with vague complexes which raise difficulties when we wish to give a rational or coherent account of them. It is scientific procedure itself which enables us to pass from vague impressions to definite propositions. Definite individuals are, therefore, the goals or limits rather than the data of scientific method. When we attain knowledge of particulars we see that their nature depends upon the universal connections which make them what they are.

To realize that the substance or nature of the individual consists of universals we must get rid of the Lockian confusion between matter and substance, and return to the Aristotelian distinction of ὕλη and οὐσία. Ὕλη or matter is a relative concept. Bricks are ὕλη for a building but are formed substances for one who makes them out of clay. Absolute primary ὕλη or matter is a limiting concept, not a starting point. The intelligible substance of things, however, is not pure formlessness or empty possibility, but the actual universals which, though arrived at as a result of inquiry, are conditions of what exists. Indeed, inquiry like all other forms of human effort must begin with the partial and can attain the whole or universal—if at all —only by seeing how the parts are conditioned.

The view that identifies the genuine substance of things with those relations or structures which are the objects of rational science is so opposed to the nominalistic tendency of our time, that a host of objections to it is naturally to be expected.

The most serious objection is one that cannot be answered—it is the habit which associates substance with reality and reality with the sensuously or psychologically vivid. But, however decisive the appeal to the subjectively vivid may be in practice, it is after all no evidence as to the objective constitution of the natural world.[2] More specific objections to our identification of the order of scientific ideas with the intrinsic order of things are the following: (a) Rational scientific method is devised for practical purposes only. Its fictional devices cannot give us truth. (b) The abstractions which science employs have no correspondence with or real existence in the natural world. (c) Reasoning supplies us only ground for belief not ground for existence.

FICTIONALISM. Philosophers as diverse as Bradley, Mach, and Bergson rely heavily on the so-called fictions of science, e.g. corpuscles of light, the ether, etc., which have proved useful, though not literally true. With regard to this we may observe that many of these so-called fictions, e.g. atoms, have turned out to be very much like other empirical entities. We count them, we weigh them and study their behavior—philosophers to the contrary notwithstanding. I have elsewhere tried to show that contrary to the contention of Vaihinger, none of the so-called fictions of science involve any contradiction.[3] If they did so, they could not be useful, since no consistent inferences could be drawn from them. Even when not completely true, they are analogies which offer useful suggestions just to the extent that they are true. To the extent that they fail they are subject to the process of correction.

CONCEPTUALISM. The form of reasoning to which science always seeks to attain is mathematics. But do the steps of a mathematical process correspond to anything in the objective world—even when the initial premises and final conclusions do? Mathematical physicists like Duhem and Mach categorically deny this. What have our equations, differentiations, and integrations to do with natural objects? If

[2] "If reality," argues Bradley, "consists in actual sequence of sensuous phenomena then our reasonings are all false because none of them are sensuous." To which we reply that if reality consists of sensuous material arranged in certain form or order then all the reasoning which is faithful to that form or order is true.

[3] See "The Logic of Fictions," *Journal of Philosophy*, Vol. XX (1923), p. 477.

the result of a mathematical calculation gives us a true account of objective nature, may not the mathematical process correspond to the sharpening of tools or to the mixing of colors, processes which surely do not correspond to the features which the artist wishes to represent? We must not however allow analogies to lead us away from the facts. Mathematical propositions do relate to the properties of all possible objects. Valid mathematical reasoning therefore deals with processes to which the objects before us are as subject as any others. It is often difficult to recognize these universal aspects in the particular, just as it may be difficult to recognize that an enemy is also a human being, yet truth requires the recognition of just such obvious general or universal aspects. Mathematical reasoning may indeed be too general for a specific situation (if we lack the proper data) but if true it always has objective meaning.

IRRATIONALISM. Bradley has argued that while reasoning determines the ground of our belief, it does not even pretend to determine the ground of existence. In our reasoning, he claims, some datum suffers alteration. Why assume that reality transforms itself in unison? This objection is largely based on the false suggestion of the word *transformation*. Logical reasoning does not produce any temporal change in the object reasoned about. The latter remains the same when we make progress in the recognition of its nature. But the ground of a true belief differs after all from the ground of a false belief precisely in this—that the former *is* connected (though not directly identical) with the ground of existence. For this purpose the most favorable example, for Bradley's objection, would be the case where I conclude that my idea of a given object is false. But even here the ground of existence and the ground of true belief are not independent. I begin in fact with an hypothesis as to the nature of the object. I consider what consequences it (with other things) has if it is true. I find the consequences are impossible because in conflict with actual existence, and I conclude that my original hypothesis is false. If my reasoning is valid it is because it has come into contact with actual facts and the transformation of the entities reasoned about does correspond to reality.

We conclude, then, that if the abstract is unreal, reality is of little moment. For what that is humanly interesting is not abstract? Mr. Bradley has gone through the whole gamut from qualities, relations, and things to our precious selves, and shown with a logic that is more readily ignored than refuted, that all these things are but abstract or detached parts of the absolute totality. But the conclusion that everything short of the absolute totality is appearance and not reality is a logical consequence of an arbitrary view of reality, which identifies it with purely immediate feeling or experience. But though the craving of the flesh for strong sensations and feelings is an important element of life, it is certainly not conclusive even as to the guidance of life. Even the hedonistic ideal cannot be realized except by organizing life on the basis of an intellectual recognition of our possibilities and the rational evaluation of the different factors which determine our happiness.

The contention that abstractions or logical relations form the very substance of things does not, according to the foregoing account, involve panlogism. Rationality does not exhaust existence. The relational form or pattern points to a non-rational or a logical element without which the former has no genuine meaning. For to deny the existence of any irrational elements is to make rationality itself a brute, contingent, alogical fact. The fact that we can rationally use terms like *irrational, alogical, inexpressible,* and the like has given rise to interesting paradoxes. These paradoxes, however, disappear if we recognize that a word may point to something which is not a word at all, and though the pointing is rationalized fact the thing pointed to may not be so. Rational distinctions and relations and all expression hold in the field of being which is thus presupposed but never fully described—just as the various lines on a blackboard may indicate the various objects represented on it but do not fully represent the blackboard itself which conditions them. If this doctrine that our universe thus contains something fundamental to which we may point but which we cannot fully describe be called mysticism, then mysticism is essential to all intellectual sanity. Language ceases to be significant if it cannot indicate something beyond language. But if we use the word *mysticism* to denote this faith in a universe that has ineffable and alogical elements, we cannot too sharply distinguish it from obscurantism. For the former denies our power to know the whole of reality, while the latter holds reality to be definitely revealed to us by non-rational processes. Rationalism does not deny that clear thoughts may begin as vague or obscure premonitions. But the essential difference between rationalism and obscurantism depends upon whether our guesses or obscure visions do or do not submit to the processes of critical examination and logical clarification. Our reason may be a pitiful candle light in the dark and boundless seas of being. But we have nothing better and woe to those who willfully try to put it out.

The Principle of Polarity

The foregoing considerations are all applications of a wider principle, viz. the principle of polarity. By this I mean that opposites such as immediacy and mediation, unity and plurality, the fixed and the flux, substance and function, ideal and real, actual and possible, etc., like the north (positive) and south (negative) poles of a magnet, all involve each other when applied to any significant entity. Familiar illustrations of this are: that physical action is not possible without resistance or reaction and that protoplasm, in the language of Huxley, cannot live except by continually dying. The idea is as old as philosophy. Anaximander expressed it in saying that determinate form arises out of the indefinite (τὸ ἄπειρον) with the emergence of opposities like hot and cold, dry and moist, etc. And Heraclitus insisted that strife was the father of all things and that the balancing of opposite forces, as in the string of the bow or lyre, gave form to things. The essential Hellenic wisdom of Socrates and Plato which viewed justice and the other virtues as conduct according to measure (Aristotle's mean) involves the idea of adjustment of opposite considerations. The relativity of form and matter, according to Aristotle, is determinative of all existence (save the divine essence).[4]

This principle of polarity seems to me to represent what is sound in the Hegelian dialectic without the indecent confusion at which we arrive if we violate the principle of contradiction and try to wipe out the distinctions of the understanding. The being and non-being of anything are always opposed and never identical, though all determination involves both affirmation and negation. Far from overriding the distinctions of the understanding the principle of polarity shows their necessity and proper use. Thus physical science employs this principle when it eliminates the vagueness and indetermination of popular categories like *high* and *low*, *hot* and *cold*, *large* and *small*, *far* and *near*, etc. It does so by substituting a definite determination such as a determinate number of yards or degrees of temperature. The indetermination and consequent inconclusiveness of metaphysical and of a good deal of sociologic discussion results from uncritically adhering to simple alternatives instead of resorting to the laborious

[4] The reading of Plato's *Parmenides* first impressed upon me the lesson taught to the young Socrates, viz. that it is impossible to arrive at sound philosophy without experience in tracing the diverse and opposed dialectic implications of such propositions as "unity exists" and thus learning to guard oneself against their pitfalls. Propositions are not bare tautologies but significant predications because non-being has being of a sort and *the one* is inseparable from, though not identical with, *the other*.

I am indebted to Professor Felix Adler for the figure of the scissors to denote the fact that the mind never operates effectively except by using both unity and plurality like the two blades which move in opposite directions. Professor Marshall, in his *Principles of Economics*, has used the same figure to express the mutual dependence of the two factors of supply and demand. We may, if we like, also use the figure of the pestle and mortar, of our jaws in mastication, or of applying brakes when going down a hill.

process of integrating opposite assertions by finding the proper distinctions and qualifications. . . .

This analysis puts us on guard against two opposite evil intellectual habits: on the one hand to regard real difficulties as absolute impossibilities, and on the other to belittle such difficulties by calling them false alternatives. Thus it is not sufficient to say that the old controversy between the claims of the active and those of the contemplative life represents a false alternative, and that we need both. It is in fact most frequently impossible to follow both and the actual problem of how much of one we need to sacrifice to the other often requires more knowledge than is at our disposal.

If it be urged that this after all is the essence of the Hegelian logic I should not object—provided it does not include Hegel's explicit identification of the historical and the logical, the real and the rational. The heart of Hegel's philosophy is, after all, the attempt at a synthesis calculated to do justice both to the classic rationalism of the Enlightenment and to the inspiring sweep of the romanticism of Fichte, Schelling, and their associates. Such a synthesis seems to me to be the great desideratum of our age. We cannot today accept Hegel's methods and results precisely because they are not—despite all their pretensions—sufficiently rational or logically rigorous. But his tremendous influence in law, art, and religion, as in the development of all the social sciences, shows that he grappled with a vital problem. If, as I think we should all admit, he was guilty of indecent haste due to intellectual ὕβρις, it is for us to face a similar task with greater patience and honest resoluteness not to minimize the obstacles to rational inquiry.

These suggestions of a possible metaphysics may be objected to either as commonplace, as unimportant, or as unjustified. Against the first objection we must note that sound metaphysic like science itself should begin—though it should not end—with the commonplace. As against the second and third objections we may urge that the full meaning, importance, and justification of a metaphysical doctrine can be seen only in its development. Towards this development the present chapter can offer only the barest hints.

BIBLIOGRAPHY

COHEN, Morris R., *Reason and Nature*. N.Y.: Harcourt, Brace & Co., 1931.
———, *Law and the Social Order*. N.Y.: Harcourt, Brace & Co., 1933.
———, (with Ernest Nagel), *An Introduction to Logic and Scientific Method*. N. Y.: Harcourt, Brace & Co., 1934.

————, *A Preface to Logic.* N.Y.: Henry Holt & Co., 1945.

————, *The Faith of a Liberal.* N.Y.: Henry Holt & Co., 1946.

————, *The Meaning of Human History.* La Salle, Ill.: Open Court Publishing Co., 1947.

————, *A Dreamer's Journey.* Boston: Beacon Press, 1949.

————, *Reason and Law: Studies in Juristic Philosophy.* Glencoe, Ill.: The Free Press, 1950.

————, *American Thought; A Critical Sketch.* (Felix S. Cohen, ed.) Glencoe, Ill.: The Free Press, 1954.

————, *A Source Book in Greek Science.* (with I. E. Drabkin). Cambridge: Harvard U. Press, 1958.

BARON, Salo and Nagel, Ernest. *Freedom and Reason: Essays in Honor of Morris R. Cohen.* Glencoe, Ill.: The Free Press, 1951.

ROSENFELD, Lenore Cohen. *Portrait of a Philosopher: Morris R. Cohen.* N.Y.: Harcourt, Brace & World, 1962.

PART TWO

The Contemporary Philosophical Scene

Clarence Irving Lewis

[1883–1964]

C. I. Lewis is a second-generation pragmatist who has attempted to refine and extend pragmatism, particularly in the light of symbolic logic. Lewis was born in Stoneham, Massachusetts. He studied at Harvard, received his Ph.D. in 1910, and taught there for the bulk of his career from 1921 to 1953. He also taught at Princeton, Stanford, and the University of California. At Harvard, Lewis was influenced by Royce's logical inquiries, if not by his metaphysics. He was also influenced by Peirce, James, Dewey and Kant, and by Russell and Whitehead's *Principia Mathematica.* Lewis' work in symbolic logic has been concerned with such problems as material implication, modal logic, the nature of analytic sentences, and the *a priori.*

Lewis has characterized himself as a "conceptual pragmatist." In *Mind and the World-Order* (1929), he pointed out that most pragmatists had restricted pragmatism to the empirical, but that he had found a pragmatic element in the *a priori*, in logic, and in that which is certifiable by analytic grounds alone. According to Lewis, the mind has some freedom of choice in defining its basic concepts, in stipulating and in applying them. The *a priori* is thus malleable to our purposes and responsive to our needs. Once our exact concepts have taken shape, however, we have no choice in deciding what follows logically from them, and analytic truths are

necessary. In regard to empirical knowledge, Lewis points to an intractable element, the given of presentation. Yet even here our experiences are conceptualized, structured and systematized, and hence have an *a priori* element. This, too, is pragmatic, in the sense that it is ordered by alternative categories supplied by us, and it is probable in the sense that it is dependent upon an unlimited set of future confirmatory predictions. The essence of Lewis' position is outlined in his succinct article "A Pragmatic Conception of the A Priori" (1923), which is reproduced below.

Lewis' pragmatic theory is further developed in his Carus Lectures, *An Analysis of Knowledge and Valuation* (1946). Here, in addition to offering theories about the nature of meaning and empirical knowledge, he proposes a theory of value and valuation. Lewis' main point is that valuation judgments are similar in their mode of verification to other empirical judgments. He distinguishes three types of empirical sentences—expressive, terminating, and non-terminating—to show their analogy to valuation judgments.

The pragmatic element in empirical knowledge is clearly seen in Lewis' treatment of "non-terminating" judgments. Like Peirce, Lewis argues that the meaning of such judgments is related to the predictive consequences which follow, though these are never final. Lewis' theory of value is intended to be an answer to the skepticism produced by the emotive theories concerning value judgments proposed by Stevenson, Carnap, and Ayer. He distinguishes between two main species of value, "intrinsic" value (the immediate quality of experience) and "inherent" value (the potentialities that objects have for leading to intrinsic value experiences). Lewis wishes to show that value judgments, in principle at least, are confirmable. His theory in this regard is naturalistic, like Dewey's and Perry's, though it differs from theirs in being an affective or hedonic theory. At the end of his study, however, Lewis makes it clear that his analysis applies primarily to value judgments ("the good"), if *not* to ethics ("the right"). He treated this latter topic later in his brief "Woodbridge Lectures," *The Ground and Nature of the Right* (1955). The second selection reprinted below is from *An Analysis of Knowledge and Valuation* and gives Lewis' view of the main similarities between empirical and valuational judgments.

A PRAGMATIC CONCEPTION OF THE *A PRIORI* [1]

The conception of the *a priori* points two problems which are perennial in philosophy; the part played in knowledge by the mind itself, and the possibility of "necessary truth" or of knowledge "independent of experience." But traditional conceptions of the *a priori* have proved untenable. That the mind approaches the flux of immediacy with some godlike foreknowledge of principles which are legislative for experience, that there is any natural light or any innate ideas, it is no longer possible to believe.

Nor shall we find the clue to the *a priori* in any compulsion of the mind to incontrovertible truth or any peculiar kind of demonstration which establishes first principles. All truth lays upon the rational mind the same compulsion to belief; as Mr. Bosanquet has pointed out, this character belongs to all propositions or judgments once their truth is established.

The difficulties of the conception are due, I believe, to two mistakes: whatever is *a priori* is necessary, but we have misconstrued the relation of necessary truth to mind. And the *a priori* is independent of experience, but in so taking it, we have misunderstood its relation to empirical fact. What is *a priori* is necessary truth not because it compels the mind's acceptance, but precisely because it does not. It is given experience, brute fact, the *a posteriori* element in knowledge which the mind must accept willy-nilly. The *a priori* represents

[1] From C. I. Lewis, "A Pragmatic Conception of the *A Priori*," *The Journal of Philosophy*, vol. XX (1923), pp. 169–77.

an attitude in some sense freely taken, a stipulation of the mind itself, and a stipulation which might be made in some other way if it suited our bent or need. Such truth is necessary as opposed to contingent, not as opposed to voluntary. And the *a priori* is independent of experience not because it prescribes a form which the data of sense must fit, or anticipates some preëstablished harmony of experience with the mind, but precisely because it prescribes nothing to experience. That is *a priori* which is true, *no matter what*. What it anticipates is not the given, but our attitude toward it: it concerns the uncompelled initiative of mind or, as Josiah Royce would say, our categorical ways of acting.

The traditional example of the *a priori* par excellence is the laws of logic. These can not be derived from experience since they must first be taken for granted in order to prove them. They make explicit our general modes of classification. And they impose upon experience no real limitation. Sometimes we are asked to tremble before the spectre of the "alogical," in order that we may thereafter rejoice that we are saved from this by the dependence of reality upon mind. But the "alogical" is pure bogey, a word without a meaning. What kind of experience could defy the principle that everything must either be or not be, that nothing can both be and not be, or that if x is y and y is z, then x is z? If anything imaginable or unimaginable could violate such laws, then the ever-present fact of change would do it every day. The laws of logic are purely formal; they forbid nothing but what concerns the use of terms and the corresponding modes of classification and analysis. The law of contradiction tells us that nothing can be both white and not-white, but it does not and can not tell us whether black is not-white, or soft or square is not-white. To discover *what contradicts what* we must always consult the character of experience. Similarly the law of the excluded middle formulates our decision that whatever is not designated by a certain term shall be designated by its negative. It declares our purpose to make, for every term, a complete dichotomy of experience, instead—as we might choose—of classifying on the basis of a tripartite division into opposites (as black and white) and the middle ground between the two. Our rejection of such tripartite division represents only our penchant for simplicity.

Further laws of logic are of similar significance. They are principles of procedure, the parliamentary rules of intelligent thought and speech. Such laws are independent of experience because they impose no limitations whatever upon it. They are legislative because they are addressed to ourselves—because definition, classification, and inference represent no operations of the objective world, but only our own categorical attitudes of mind.

And further, the ultimate criteria of the laws of logic are pragmatic. Those who suppose that there is, for example, *a* logic which everyone would agree to if he understood it and understood himself, are more optimistic than those versed in the history of logical discussion have a right to be. The fact is that there are several logics, markedly different, each self-consistent in its own terms and such that whoever, using it, avoids false premises, will never reach a false conclusion. Mr. Russell, for example, bases *his* logic on an implication relation such that if twenty sentences be cut from a newspaper and put in a hat, and then two of these be drawn at random, one of them will certainly imply the other, and it is an even bet that the implication will be mutual. Yet upon a foundation so remote from ordinary modes of inference the whole structure of *Principia Mathematica* is built. This logic—and there are others even more strange—is utterly consistent and the results of it entirely valid. Over and above all questions of consistency, there are issues of logic which can not be determined —nay, can not even be argued—except on pragmatic grounds of conformity to human bent and intellectual convenience. That we have been blind to this fact, itself reflects traditional errors in the conception of the *a priori.*

We may note in passing one less important illustration of the *a priori*—the proposition "true by definition." Definitions and their immediate consequences, analytic propositions generally, are necessarily true, true under all possible circumstances. Definition is legislative because it is in some sense arbitrary. Not only is the meaning assigned to words more or less a matter of choice—that consideration is relatively trivial—but the manner in which the precise classifications which definition embodies shall be effected, is something not dictated by experience. If experience were other than it is, the definition and its corresponding classification might be inconvenient, fantastic, or useless, but it could not be false. Mind makes classifications and determines meanings; in so doing it creates the *a priori* truth of analytic judgments. But that the manner of this creation responds to pragmatic considerations, is so obvious that it hardly needs pointing out.

If the illustrations so far given seem trivial or verbal, that impression may be corrected by turning to the place which the *a priori* has in mathematics and in natural science. Arithmetic, for example, depends *in toto* upon the operation of counting or correlating, a procedure which can be carried out at will in any world containing identifiable things—even identifiable ideas—regardless of the further characters of experience. Mill challenged this *a priori* character of arithmetic. He asked us to suppose a demon sufficiently powerful and maleficent so that every time two things were brought together with two other things, this demon should always introduce a fifth. The implication which he supposed to follow is that under such circumstances $2 + 2 = 5$ would be a universal law of arithmetic. But Mill was quite mistaken. In such a world we should be obliged to become a little clearer than is usual about the distinction between arithmetic and physics, that is all. If two black marbles were put in the same urn with two white ones, the demon could take his choice of colors, but it would be evident that there were more black marbles or more white ones than were put in. The same would be true of all objects in any wise identifiable. We should simply find ourselves in the presence of an extraordinary physical law, which we should recognize as universal in our world, that whenever two things were brought into proximity with two others, an additional and similar thing was always created by the process. Mill's world would be physically most extraordinary. The world's work would be enormously facilitated if hats or locomotives or tons of coal could be thus multiplied by anyone possessed originally of two pairs. But the laws of mathematics would remain unaltered. It is because this is true that arithmetic is *a priori*. Its laws prevent *nothing*; they are compatible with anything which happens or could conceivably happen in nature. They would be true in any possible world. Mathematical addition is not a physical transformation. Physical changes which result in an increase or decrease of the countable things involved are matters of everyday occurrence. Such physical processes present us with phenomena in which the purely mathematical has to be separated out by abstraction. Those laws and those laws only have necessary truth which we are prepared to maintain, no matter what. It is because we shall always separate out that part of the phenomenon not in conformity with arithmetic and designate it by some other category—physical change, chemical reaction, optical illusion—that arithmetic is *a priori*.

The *a priori* element in science and in natural law is greater than might be supposed. In the first place, all science is based upon definitive concepts. The formulation of these concepts is, indeed, a matter determined by the commerce between our intellectual or our pragmatic interests and the nature of experience. Definition is classification. The scientific search is for such classification as will make it possible to correlate appearance and behavior, to discover law, to penetrate to the "essential nature" of things in order that behavior may become predictable. In other words, if definition is unsuccessful, as early scientific definitions mostly have been, it is because the classification thus set up corresponds with no natural cleavage and does not correlate with any important uniformity of behavior. A name itself must represent *some* uniformity in experience or it names nothing. What does not repeat itself or recur in intelligible fashion is not a thing. Where the definitive uniformity is a clue to other uniformities, we have successful scientific definition. Other definitions can not be said to be false; they are merely useless. In scientific classification the search is, thus, for *things worth naming*. But the naming, classifying, defining activity is essentially prior to investigation. We can not interrogate experience in general. Until our meaning is definite and our classification correspondingly exact, experience can not conceivably answer our questions.

In the second place, the fundamental laws of any science—or those treated as fundamental—are *a priori* because they formulate just such definitive concepts or categorical tests by which alone investigation becomes possible. If the lightning strikes the railroad track at two places, A and B, how shall we tell whether these events are simultaneous? "We . . . require a definition of simultaneity such that this definition supplies us with the method by means of which . . . we can decide whether or not both the lightning strokes occurred simultaneously. As long as this requirement is not satisfied, I allow myself to be deceived as a physicist (and of course the same applies if I am not a physicist), when I imagine that I am able to attach a meaning to the statement of simultaneity. . . .

"After thinking the matter over for some time you then offer the following suggestion with which to test simultaneity. By measuring along the rails, the connecting line AB should be measured up and an observer placed at the mid-point M of the distance AB. This observer should be supplied with an arrangement (e.g., two mirrors inclined at 90°) which allows him visually to observe both places A and B at the same time. If the observer perceives the two flashes at the same time, then they are simultaneous.

"I am very pleased with this suggestion, but for all that I can not regard the matter as quite settled, because I feel constrained to raise the following objection: 'Your definition would certainly be right, if I only knew that the light by means of which the observer at M perceives the lightning flashes travels along the length A–M with the same velocity as along the length B–M. But an examination of this supposition would only be possible if we already had at our disposal the means of measuring time. It would thus appear as though we were moving here in a logical circle.'

"After further consideration you cast a somewhat disdainful glance at me—and rightly so—and you declare: 'I maintain my previous definition nevertheless, because in reality it assumes absolutely nothing about light. There is only *one* demand to be made of the definition of simultaneity, namely, that in every real case it must supply us with an empirical decision as to whether or not the conception which has to be defined is fulfilled. That light requires the same time to traverse the path *A—M* as for the path *B—M* is in reality *neither a sup-position nor a hypothesis* about the physical nature of light, but a *stipulation* which I can make of my own free-will in order to arrive at a definition of simultaneity.' . . . We are thus led also to a definition of 'time' in physics."[2]

As this example from the theory of relativity well illustrates, we can not even ask the questions which discovered law would answer until we have first by *a priori* stipulation formulated definitive criteria. Such concepts are not verbal definitions, nor classifications merely; they are themselves laws which prescribe a certain uniformity of behavior to whatever is thus named. Such definitive laws are *a priori*; only so can we enter upon the investigation by which further laws are sought. Yet it should also be pointed out that such *a priori* laws are subject to abandonment if the structure which is built upon them does not succeed in simplifying our interpretation of phenomena. If, in the illustration given, the relation "simultaneous with," as defined, should not prove transitive—if event *A* should prove simultaneous with *B*, and *B* with *C*, but not *A* with *C*—this definition would certainly be rejected.

And thirdly, there is that *a priori* element in science—as in other human affairs—which constitutes the criteria of the real as opposed to the unreal in experience. An object itself is a uniformity. Failure to behave in certain categorical ways marks it as unreal. Uniformities of the type called "natural law" are the clues to reality and unreality. A mouse which disappears where no hole is, is no real mouse; a landscape which recedes as we approach is but illusion. As the queen remarked in the episode of the wishing-carpet: "If this were real, then it would be a miracle. But miracles do not happen. Therefore I shall wake presently." That the uniformities of natural law are the only reliable criteria of the real, is inescapable. But such a criterion is *ipso facto a priori*. No conceivable experience could dictate the alteration of a law so long as failure to obey that law marked the content of experience as unreal.

This is one of the puzzles of empiricism. We deal with experience: what any reality may be which underlies experience, we have to learn. What we desire to discover is natural law, the formulation of those uniformities which obtain amongst the real. But experience as it comes to us contains not only the real but all the content of illusion, dream, hallucination, and mistake. The *given* contains both real and unreal, confusingly intermingled. If we ask for uniformities of this unsorted experience, we shall not find them. Laws which characterize all experience, of real and unreal both, are non-existent and

[2] Einstein, *Relativity*, pp. 26–8: italics are the author's.

would in any case be worthless. What we seek are the uniformities of the *real*; but *until we have such laws, we can not sift experience and segregate the real.*

The obvious solution is that the enrichment of experience, the separation of the real from the illusory or meaningless, and the formulation of natural law, all grow up together. If the criteria of the real are *a priori*, that is not to say that no conceivable character of experience would lead to alteration of them. For example, spirits can not be photographed. But if photographs of spiritistic phenomena, taken under properly guarded conditions, should become sufficiently frequent, this *a priori* dictum would be called in question. What we should do would be to redefine our terms. Whether "spook" was spirit or matter, whether the definition of "spirit" or of "matter" should be changed; all this would constitute one interrelated problem. We should reopen together the question of definition or classification, of criteria for this sort of real, and of natural law. And the solution of one of these would mean the solution of all. Nothing could *force* a redefinition of spirit or of matter. A sufficiently fundamental relation to human bent, to human interests, would guarantee continuance unaltered even in the face of unintelligible and baffling experiences. In such problems, the mind finds itself uncompelled save by its own purposes and needs. I *may* categorize experience as I will; but *what* categorical distinctions will best serve my interests and objectify my own intelligence? What the mixed and troubled experience shall be —that is beyond me. But what I shall do with it—that is my own question, when the character of experience is sufficiently before me. I am coerced only by my own need to understand.

It would indeed be inappropriate to characterize as *a priori* a law which we are wholly prepared to alter in the light of further experience, even though in an isolated case we should discard as illusory any experience which failed to conform. But the crux of the situation lies in this; beyond such principles as those of logic, which we seem fully prepared to maintain no matter what, there must be further and more particular criteria of the real prior to any investigation of nature whatever. We can not even interrogate experience without a network of categories and definitive concepts. And we must further be prepared to say what experimental findings will answer what questions, and how. Without tests which represent anterior principle, there is no question which experience could answer at all. Thus the most fundamental laws in any category—or those which we regard as most fundamental—are *a priori*, even though continued failure to render experience intelligible in such terms might result eventually in the abandonment of that category altogether. Matters so comparatively small as the behavior of Mercury and of starlight passing the sun's limb may, if there be persistent failure to bring them within the field of previously accepted modes of explanation, result in the abandonment of the independent categories of space and time. But without the definitions, fundamental principles, and tests, of the type which constitute such categories, no experience whatever could prove or disprove anything. And to that mind which should find independent space and time absolutely necessary conceptions, no possible experiment could prove the principles of relativity. "There must be some error in the experimental findings, or some law not yet discovered," represents an attitude which can never be rendered impossible. And the only sense in which it could be proved unreasonable would be the pragmatic one of comparison with another method of categorical analysis which more successfully reduced all such experience to order and law.

At the bottom of all science and all knowledge are categories and definitive concepts which represent fundamental habits of thought and deep-lying attitudes which the human mind has taken in the light of its total experience. But a new and wider experience may bring about some alteration of these attitudes, even though by themselves they dictate nothing as to the content of experience, and no experience can conceivably prove them invalid.

Perhaps some will object to this conception on the ground that only such principles should be designated *a priori* as the human mind *must* maintain, no matter what; that if, for example, it is shown possible to arrive at a consistent doctrine of physics in terms of relativity, even by the most arduous reconstruction of our fundamental notions, then the present conceptions are by that fact shown not to be *a priori*. Such objection is especially likely from those who would conceive the *a priori* in terms of an absolute mind or an absolutely universal human nature. We should readily agree that a decision by popular approval or a congress of scientists or anything short of such a test as would bring to bear the full weight of human capacity and interest, would be ill-considered as having to do with the *a priori*. But we wish to emphasize two facts: first, that in the field of those conceptions and principles which have altered in human history, there are those which could neither be proved nor disproved by any experience, but represent the uncompelled initiative of human thought—that without this uncompelled initiative no growth of science, nor any science at all, would be conceivable. And second, that the difference between such conceptions as are, for example, concerned in the decision of relativity versus absolute space and time, and those more permanent attitudes such as are vested in the laws of logic, there is only a difference of degree. The dividing line between the *a priori* and the *a posteriori* is that between principles and definitive concepts which *can* be maintained in the face of all experience and those genuinely empirical generalizations which *might* be proven flatly false. The thought which both rationalism and empiricism have missed is that there are principles, representing the initiative of mind, which impose upon experience no limitations whatever, but that such conceptions are still subject to alteration on pragmatic grounds when the expanding boundaries of experience reveal their infelicity as intellectual instruments.

Neither human experience nor the human mind has a character which is universal, fixed, and absolute. "The human mind" does not exist at all save in the sense that all humans are very much alike in fundamental respects, and that the language habit and the enormously important exchange of ideas has greatly increased our likeness in those respects which are here in question. Our categories and definitions are peculiarly social products, reached in the light of experiences which have much in common, and beaten out, like other pathways, by the coincidence of human purposes and the exigencies of human coöperation. Concerning the *a priori* there need be neither universal agreement nor complete historical continuity. Conceptions, such as those of logic, which are least likely to be affected by the opening of new ranges of experience, represent the most stable of our categories; but none of them is beyond the possibility of alteration.

Mind contributes to experience the element of order, of classification, categories, and definition. Without such, experience would be unintelligible. Our knowledge of the validity of these is simply consciousness of our own fundamental ways of acting and our own intellectual intent. Without this element, knowledge is impossible, and it is here that whatever truths are necessary and independent of experience must be found. But the commerce between our categorical ways of acting, our pragmatic interests, and the particular character of experience, is closer than we have realized. No explanation of any one of these can be complete without consideration of the other two.

Pragmatism has sometimes been charged with oscillating between two contrary notions; the one, that experience is "through and through malleable to our purpose," the other, that facts are "hard" and uncreated by the mind. We here offer a mediating conception: through all our knowledge runs the element of the *a priori*, which is indeed malleable to our purpose and responsive to our need. But throughout, there is also that other element of experience which is "hard," "independent," and unalterable to our will.

AN ANALYSIS OF KNOWLEDGE AND VALUATION

INTRODUCTION

Knowledge, Action, and Evaluation[3]

Knowledge, action, and evaluation are essentially connected. The primary and pervasive significance of knowledge lies in its guidance of action: knowing is for the sake of doing. And action, obviously, is rooted in evaluation. For a being which did not assign comparative values, deliberate action would be pointless; and for one which did not know, it would be impossible. Conversely, only an active being could have knowledge, and only such a being could assign values to anything beyond his own feelings. A creature which did not enter into the process of reality to alter in some part the future content of it, could apprehend a world only in the sense of intuitive or esthetic contemplation; and such contemplation would not possess the significance of knowledge but only that of enjoying and suffering.

The interest of action is not an interest in what is before us, on its own account, but an interest in what will be or may be. And the interest of that knowledge of the world which guides our action is the same. For the cognizing mind, something immediately presented —some item of direct experience—is a sign of something else, not so presented but likely to become realized or capable of being realized in further experience. Only so can what is said to be known be something capable of being verified; since obviously, to verify is to submit what is in question to the test of some experience, not given when the verification is called for but which may be given. Further; what an empirical cognition thus predicts as capable of being verified will, in the typical case if not in all cases, depend in some part on our action. If verification does not of itself and necessarily imply action, at least it is only where what is apprehended is conditional upon action that knowledge could be other than futile. A predicted future which should follow fatally upon what is presently given, is a future it would be pointless to foresee, since *ex hypothesi* nothing could be done about it. Knowledge which serves for the guidance of action must anticipate the future, but a future to which the action itself will make a possible difference.

Whether the action is performed or not, will depend upon evaluations made; will be determined by reference to anticipated possible

---

[3] From C. I. Lewis, *An Analysis of Knowledge and Valuation*, La Salle, Ill.: Open Court, 1946. Chapter I, pp. 3-5.

experience as something to be desired or something to be avoided. Action attempts to control future experience, so far as may be, in our own interest. It has its *terminus a quo* in the situation which is given; its *terminus ad quem* in some experience to which a positive value (or comparative value in relation to alternatives) is assigned. The principal function of empirical knowledge is that of an instrument enabling transition from the one to the other; from the actual present to a future which is desired and which the present is believed to signalize as possible. To know is to apprehend the future as qualified by values which action may realize; and empirical knowledge is essentially utilitarian and pragmatic.

If knowledge should seem to have a different significance, and one which is incompatible with these observations, then that appearance itself should challenge our attention; since plainly we shall not deny that the purport of knowledge is important for our choice of conduct. It may be said, for example, that what science predicts are future happenings which, just so far as they are predictable, are beyond our control; and that such categorical predictions are of the essence of knowledge at its best. But the difficulty which thus appears is apparent only. Let us grant that what science predicts—an explosion, perhaps—is unalterable future fact. Still no categorical prediction of any experience is necessarily contained in that. And the utility of this piece of information lies precisely in that fact. The point is that when the explosion occurs we may be elsewhere, or may make provision for confining the effects of it. The impact of the predicted event upon our experience, is one which still is conditional upon our possible action. And so in general: the utility of knowledge lies in the control it gives us, through appropriate action, over the quality of our future experience. And such control will be exercised in the interest of realizing that which we value, and of obviating or avoiding what is undesirable. Such considerations but serve to emphasize the essential relations between the knowledge we seek of objective facts, the values we hope to realize in experience, and the actions which, guided by the one, move toward the other. . . .

BOOK I
MEANING AND ANALYTIC TRUTH

The Modes of Meaning[4]

Every statement we know to be true is so known either by reason of experience or by reason of what the statement itself means. There are no other sources of knowledge than on the one hand data of

[4] *Ibid.*, Chapter III, pp. 35–38.

sense and on the other hand our own intended meanings. Empirical knowledge constitutes the one class; all that is knowable independently of sense experience—the *a priori* and the analytic—constitutes the other, and is determinable as true by reference to our meanings.

Traditionally a statement which can be certified by reference exclusively to defined or definable meanings is called *analytic*, what is non-analytic being called *synthetic*. And traditionally that knowledge whose correctness can be assured without reference to any particular experience of sense is called *a priori*, that which requires to be determined by sense experience being called *a posteriori*.

All analytic statements are, obviously, true *a priori*; whatever is determinable as true by reference exclusively to the meaning of expressions used, is independent of any empirical fact. That the converse relation also holds; that whatever is knowable *a priori*, including the principles of logic and all that logic can certify, is also analytic, is not so obvious. It has, of course, frequently been denied; most notably in the Kantian doctrine which makes *synthetic a priori* truth fundamental for mathematics and for principles of the knowledge of nature.

The thesis here put forward, that the *a priori* and the analytic coincide, has come to be a matter of fairly wide agreement amongst logicians in the last half-century. It is, however, by no means universal; and so far as it obtains, it is in part verbal only, since it has not been accompanied by any corresponding agreement concerning the nature of analytic truth, the nature of logic, and the ground on which, and sense in which, what logic assures is certifiable. The original and traditional conception of the analytic as that which may be known by reference to meanings (definable or connotational or intensional meanings) has in some part been lost sight of and displaced by conceptions more complex. In particular, there has appeared a tendency to regard the distinction between analytic and non-analytic as one which is relative—e.g., relative to vocabulary or to "language system"—and as linguistic or logico-procedural rather than epistemological in significance. If the implications of conceptions of this sort should be well worked out, it must appear that they are fatal to the thesis that what is *a priori* coincides with what is analytic; since the notion that what may be known true without recourse to sense experience, is relative to vocabulary or dependent on conventions of procedure, is not credible.

In order to approach such questions of the *a priori* and the analytic, it will be necessary to examine this traditional conception of analytic truth as that which is determinable by reference to meanings alone; and to isolate and clarify, if possible, the meaning of "meaning" which is here in question. . . .

The main conclusions concerning meaning and the analytic which will be reached in this first Book, may be set down summarily as follows.

(1) In general, the traditional conception of analytic truth as truth which is determined, explicitly or implicitly, by meanings alone, is justified and can be made adequate, and does not need to be displaced by any which is more complex.

(2) The requisite meaning of "meaning" can be arrived at by more precise specification of what is traditionally intended by "connotation" or "intension" and by developing the conception—traditionally omitted or inadequately treated—of the intension of propositions.

(3) Such intensional meaning can still be specified in alternative ways: as *linguistic meaning*, constituted by the pattern of definitive and other analytic relationships holding between linguistic expressions; or as *sense meaning*, constituted by the criterion in mind by which what is meant is to be recognized. It is sense meaning which is epistemologically the more important signification of "intension." Linguistic *expression* of what is meant and what is apprehended, is the dependent and derivative phenomenon: it is meaning and apprehension themselves which are the fundamental cognitive phenomena, and these are independent of any formulation in language.

(4) The principles of logic are analytic in this sense: their truth is certifiable by reference to intensional meanings involved in the statement of them.

(5) There is, however, no way of distinguishing fundamentally between principles of logic and other analytic truths. Such distinction is conventional, in the sense that it turns upon relative importance for the critique of inference, and upon comparative generality. There are, thus, alternative ways in which what is taken as belonging to logic may be marked off.

(6) There are no synthetic statements which can be known true *a priori*: what may appear to be such, must be regarded as representing some failure to elicit by analysis the criteria operative in the actual, or the ideally consistent, application of terms in question, or some failure to recognize implications which validly obtain. . . .

BOOK II
EMPIRICAL KNOWLEDGE

The Bases of Empirical Knowledge[5]

If the conclusions of the preceding discussion are to be accepted, then all knowledge has an eventual empirical significance in that all which is knowable or even significantly thinkable must have refer-

[5] *Ibid.*, Chapter VII, pp. 171–72, 182–85.

ence to meanings which are sense-representable. But this conception that even what is analytically true and knowable *a priori* is to be assured by reference to sense meanings, does not, of course, abrogate the distinction between what may be known independently of given data of sense and that which cannot be so known. Analytic statements assert some relation of meanings amongst themselves: non-analytic statements require relation of a meaning to what is found on particular occasions of experience. It is the latter class alone which may express empirical knowledge. They coincide with those the falsity of which is antecedently thinkable.

Empirical truth cannot be known except, finally, through presentations of sense. Most affirmations of empirical knowledge are to be justified, proximately, by others already accepted or believed: such justification involves a step or steps depending on logical truth. The classification as empirical will still be correct, however, if amongst such statements required to support the one in question, either deductively or inductively, there are some which cannot be assured by logic or analysis of meaning but only by reference to the content of a given experience. Our empirical knowledge rises as a structure of enormous complexity, most parts of which are stabilized in measure by their mutual support, but all of which rest, at bottom, on direct findings of sense. Unless there should be some statements, or rather something apprehensible and statable, whose truth is determined by given experience and is not determinable in any other way, there would be no non-analytic affirmation whose truth could be determined at all, and no such thing as empirical knowledge. But also there could be no empirical knowledge if there were not meanings capable of being entertained without dependence on particular occasions. No experience or set of experiences will determine truth of a statement or a belief unless, prior to such experience, we know what we mean; know what experiences will corroborate our affirmation or supposition and what experiences will discredit it. Apprehension of the criteria by which what we intend may be recognized, must be antecedent to any verification or disproof.

We shall find, however, that most empirical statements—all those ordinarily made, in fact—are such that no single experience could decisively prove them true; and it can be doubted that any experience would conclusively prove them false. . . .

. . . There are three classes of empirical statements. First, there are formulations of what is presently given in experience. Only infrequently are such statements of the given actually made: there is seldom need to formulate what is directly and indubitably presented. They are also difficult or—it might plausibly be said—impossible to state in ordinary language, which, as usually understood, carries implications of something more and further verifiable which *ipso facto* is not given. But this difficulty of formulating precisely and only a given content of experience, is a relatively inessential consideration for the analysis of knowledge. That which we should thus attempt to formulate plays the same role whether it is expressed, or could be precisely expressed, or not. Without such apprehensions of direct and indubitable content of experience, there could be no basis for any empirical judgment, and no verification of one.

To this there is no alternative. Even if one should wish to suppose that *all* empirical statements are affected by uncertainty; one could not—short of an absurd kind of skepticism—suppose them all to be doubtful in the same degree that they would be if there were no experience. And if there are some empirical statements not thus utterly doubtful, then there must be something which imparts to them this status of better-than-utterly-doubtful. And that something must be an apprehended fact, or facts, of experience. If facts of this order should not be clearly expressible in language, they would still be the absolutely essential bases of all empirical knowledge.

Those thinkers who approach all problems of analysis from the point of view of language, have raised numerous difficulties over this conception of the empirically given. We shall not pause to clear away all the irrelevant issues with which the point has thus been surrounded. That point is simply that there is such a thing as experience, the content of which we do not invent and cannot have as we will but merely find. And that this given is an element in perception but not the whole of perceptual cognition. Subtract, in what we say that we see, or hear, or otherwise learn from direct experience, *all that conceivably could be mistaken;* the remainder is the given content of the experience inducing this belief. If there were no such hard kernel in experience—e.g., what we *see* when we think we see a deer but there is no deer—then the word "experience" would have nothing to refer to.

It is essential to remember that in the statement or formulation of what is given (if such formulation be attempted), one uses language to *convey* this content, but what is *asserted* is what the language is intended to convey, not the correctness of the language used. If, for example, one says, "I see a red round something," one assumes but does *not* assert, "The words 'red' and 'round' correctly apply to something now given." This last is not a given fact of present experience but a generalization from past experience indicating the customary use of English words. But one does not have to know English in order to see red; and that the word "red" applies to this presently given appearance, is not a fact given in that experience.

Knowledge itself might well get on without the formulation of the immediately given: what is thus directly presented does not require verbalization. But the *discussion* of knowledge hardly can, since it must be able somehow to refer to such basic factualities of experience. If there should be no understood linguistic mode of telling what is given, the analysis of knowledge would have to invent one, if only by arbitrary figure of speech. But our situation is hardly so bad as that: such formulations can be made, in a manner the intent of which, at least, is recognizable by what we have called the expressive use of language, in which its reference is restricted to appearances—to what is given, as such.

Apprehensions of the given which such expressive statements formulate, are not judgments; and they are not here classed as knowledge, because they are not subject to any possible error. Statement of such apprehension is, however, true or false: there could be no doubt about the presented content of experience as such at the time when it is given, but it would be possible to tell lies about it.[6]

Second, there are terminating judgments, and statements of them. These represent some prediction of further possible experience. They find their cue in what is given: but what they state is something taken to be verifiable by some test which involves a way of acting. Thus terminating judgments are, in general, of the form, "If A then E," or "S being given, if A then E," where "A" represents some mode of action taken to be possible, "E" some expected consequent in experience, and "S" the sensory cue. The hypothesis "A" must here express something which, if made true by adopted action, will be *indubitably* true, and not, like a condition of my musculature in relation to the environment, an objective state of affairs only partially verified and not completely certain at the time. And the consequent "E" represents an eventuality of *experience*, directly and certainly recognizable in case it accrues; not a resultant objective event, whose factuality could have, and would call for, further verification. Thus both antecedent and consequent of this judgment, "If A then E," require to be formulated in expressive language; though we shall not call it an expressive

---

[6] It would be possible to take statements of the given as involving judgment of correspondence between the character of the given itself and a fixed (expressive) meaning of words. But a judgment, "What is given is what '——' expresses" is not expression of the given but of a relation between it and a certain form of words. There is such a 'judgment of formulation' in the case of *any* statable fact. Let 'P' be an empirical statement which says nothing about language. "This fact is correctly stated by 'P'" is then a different statement, stating a relation between the fact which 'P' asserts and the verbal formulation 'P'. Correlatively, it is always possible to make a mistake of formulation, even where there could be no possible error concerning what is formulated.

statement, reserving that phrase for formulations of the given. Also, unlike statements of the given, what such terminating judgments express is to be classed as knowledge: the prediction in question calls for verification, and is subject to possible error.

Third, there are non-terminating judgments which assert objective reality; some state of affairs as actual. These are so named because, while there is nothing in the import of such objective statements which is intrinsically unverifiable, and hence nothing included in them which is not expressible by some terminating judgment, nevertheless no limited set of particular predictions of empirical eventualities can completely exhaust the significance of such an objective statement. This is true of the simplest and most trivial, as much as of the most important. The statement that something is blue, for example, or is square—as contrasted with merely looking blue or appearing to be square—has, always, implications of further possible experience, beyond what should, at any particular time, have been found true. Theoretically complete and absolute verification of any objective judgment would be a never-ending task: any actual verification of them is no more then partial; and our assurance of them is always, theoretically, less than certain.

Non-terminating judgments represents an enormous class; they include, in fact, pretty much all the empirical statements we habitually make. They range in type from the simplest assertion of perceived fact—"There is a piece of white paper now before me"—to the most impressive of scientific generalizations—"The universe is expanding." In general, the more important an assertion of empirical objective fact, the more remote it is from its eventual grounds. The laws of science, for example, are arrived at by induction from inductions from inductions. . . . But objective judgments are all alike in being non-terminating, and in having no other eventual foundation than data of given experience.

The point of distinguishing expressive statements of given data of experience from predictive and verifiable statements of terminating judgments, and both of them from statements of objective fact, representing non-terminating judgments, is that without such distinctions it is almost impossible so to analyze empirical knowledge as to discover the grounds of it in experience, and the manner of its derivation from such grounds.

All empirical knowledge rests ultimately upon this kind of evidence and calls for the corroboration constituted by the facts of presentation. The cue to any statement of perceived actuality is in such presentation; and if there is to be any further confirmation of such statement, that can come about only through some further presentation. . . .

Knowing, Doing, and Valuing[7]

Evaluations are a form of empirical knowledge, not fundamentally different in what determines their truth or falsity, and what determines their validity or justification, from other kinds if empirical knowledge.

This fact has often been obscured by failure to distinguish mere apprehensions of good or ill in experience from predictions of the possible realizations of these qualities in particular empirical contexts, and from appraisals of the objective value-quality resident in existent things. The first of these—direct findings of value-quality in what is presented—are not judgments; and unless or until they become the basis of some further prediction, they are not cognitive. But predictions of a goodness or badness which will be disclosed in experience under certain circumstances and on particular occasions, are either true or false, and are capable of verification in the same manner as other terminating judgments, which predict accrual of other qualities than value. This kind of foresight represents one of the most essential of cognitive capacities: indeed, we might say it is the root of all practical wisdom. And evaluations of things; appraisals of their potentialities for good or ill; are likewise true or false, and must be justified as well as confirmed by reference to experience. The manner of their validation, and of their confirmation, does not differ, in general, from that of attributions of other properties to objects.

The contrary conception has, of course, been frequent. It has been held that value-apprehensions are subjective or relative in a sense which is incompatible with their genuinely cognitive significance. Or it has been maintained that value-predications are not matter of fact statements at all, being merely expressions of emotion and hence neither true nor false.

But this is one of the strangest aberrations ever to visit the mind of man. The denial to value-apprehensions in general of the character of truth or falsity and of knowledge, would imply both moral and practical cynicism. It would invalidate all action; because action becomes pointless unless there can be some measure of assurance of a valuable result which it may realize. And this negation, if it be carried out consistently, likewise invalidates all knowledge; both because believing is itself an active attitude which would have no point if it were not better to be right than wrong in what one believes,

---

[7] *Ibid.*, Chapter XII, pp. 365–66, 373–78, 390–392.

and because knowledge in general is for the sake of action. If action in general is pointless, then knowledge also is futile, and one belief is as good as another. . . .

Recognition of this fact that judgments of value represent an essential and basic form of knowledge has been impeded in a number of different ways. But particularly in two; by the failure to distinguish between fundamentally different types of value-predication, and by the attempt to define the goodness of all kinds of goods so as to secure the point that nothing can be a genuine and "objective" good which is to be attained through immoral action. In fact, the whole discussion of the validity of evaluations has often been characterized by a thorough entanglement of three matters which are, in their intrinsic nature, quite distinct: (1) the nature of ultimate or basic value; that kind of value from which the value of everything else correctly called valuable is derivative; (2) the question of the first-personality ("relativity," "subjectivity") or the impersonality ("community," "objectivity") of value-ascriptions; and (3) the question whether, and if so why, the possible realization of or possession of the valuable by other persons, legitimately lays claim to respect on one's own decisions of action.

The first of these is, of course, a fundamental question about evaluations. The second is itself a complex matter, but the root of it lies in considerations which are merely logical or have to do with our customary modes of speech. The third is a distinctive—perhaps *the* distinctive—question of ethics. The first two will demand of us lengthy consideration. The last is a separate topic outside the province of this book; though we shall make certain comments bearing on it.

We cannot make even a good beginning in the consideration of evaluations in general until we untangle the question what basic good is and what goods are derivative, from question of the subjectivity or objectivity of value-predications. And a first step here is to observe that there are three main types of value-predication, corresponding to the three main types of empirical statements in general.

First, there is expressive statement of a value-quality found in the directly experienced. One who says at the concert, "This is good," or who makes a similar remark at table, is presumably reporting a directly experienced character of the sensuously presented as such. He might, of course, have a quite different intention; he might be meaning to assert that the selection being played has a verifiably satisfactory character best attested by those endowed with musical discrimination and having long experience and training in music; or that the food verifiably meets all dietetic standards in high degree. In that case, the immediately experienced goodness would, presumably, provide the empirical cue to his judgment, but what is *judged* would be no more than partially verified in this directly apprehended quality of the given—which itself requires no judgment. Such judged and verifiable goodness of the musical selection or the viands, is an objective property, comparable to the objective roundness of a plate, or the objective frequency of vibrations in the surrounding atmosphere.

Directly experienced goodness or badness, like seen redness or felt hardness, may become, when attended, the matter of a formulation or report which intends nothing more than this apparent quality of what appears. There are any number of questions about value-quality as thus immediate, which will have to be discussed in the next chapter. But it will hardly be denied that there is what may be called "apparent value" or "felt goodness," as there is seen redness or heard shrillness. And while the intent to formulate just this apparent value-quality of what is given, without implication of anything further, encounters linguistic difficulties, surely it will not be denied that there are such immediate experiences of good and bad to be formulated. We shall probably agree also that without such direct value-apprehensions, there could be no determination of values, or of what is valuable, in any *other* sense, or any significance for value-terms at all. Without the experience of felt value and disvalue, evaluations in general would have no meaning.

Any such formulation or report of apparent value, taken by itself and divested of all further implication, is an expressive statement; self-verifying (for him who makes it) in the only sense in which it could be called verifiable, and subject to no possible error, unless merely linguistic error in the words chosen to express it. Such a statement is true or false, since we could tell lies about the quality of mediate experience; but the apprehension expressed is not a judgment, and is not to be classed as knowledge, in the sense in which we have used that word.

Second, there are evaluations which are terminating judgments; the prediction, in the circumstances as apprehended, or in other and similarly apprehensible circumstances, of the possible accrual of value-quality in experience—for example, of enjoyment or of pain—conditional upon adoption of a particular mode of action. If I taste what is before me, I shall enjoy it: if I touch this red-glowing metal, I shall feel pain. Such judgments may be put to the test by acting on them, and are then decisively and completely verified or found false. Being predictive—verifiable but not verified—and subject to possible error, they represent a form of knowledge.

Third, there is that most important and most frequent type of evaluation which is the ascription of the objective property of being valuable to an existent or possible existent; to an object, a situation, a state of affairs, or to some *kind* of such thing. Such objective judgments of value are, as we shall find, considerably more complex than objective judgments of other characters than value. There is also much diversity amongst them: "X is valuable," in this objective sense, is a form of statement covering a great variety of meanings, and subject to troublesome ambiguities by reason of the difficulty of distinguishing these. But they all possess the common character of being what we have called non-terminating judgments. They are not, at any given time, decisively and completely verified, but always retain a significance for further possible experience and are capable of further confirmation. Like other judgments of objective fact or of any objective property, determination of their truth or falsity can never be completed, and they are, theoretically, never more than probable, though often probable in the degree called "practically certain." Any particular confirmation of such a judgment comes by way of finding true some terminating judgment which is a consequence of it. And while there is no limit to the number of such terminating judgments, truth of which follows from the objective judgment of value, still there is nothing contained in the meaning of it which is not expressible by some terminating judgment or other. If, beyond what is thus expressible as some possible confirmation of it, the objective value-judgment should be supposed to have a further and different component of its significance, we should be unable to say or even to think to ourselves what this further component signified, or what conceivable difference the holding or not holding of it in fact would make to anybody under any thinkable circumstances.

Typically we should think of any such confirmation of the objective value of something as realization of some value-experience in connection with it. And there is question here—the question suggested, for example, by Mill's assertion that the only proof that a thing is desirable is its being desired[8]—whether objective value-judgments are not relative *exclusively* to the possibility of direct *value*-experience.

But a very little reflection reveals that such a conception would be unguarded: one may easily find evidence that a thing is valuable otherwise than through experiences of positive value. Just as one may find evidence that a thing is round or is hard in other ways than by seeing it round or feeling it hard, so too the objective value of a

[8] "The only proof capable of being given that a thing is visible, is that people actually see it. The only proof that a thing is audible, is that people hear it: and so of the other sources of our experience. In like manner, I apprehend, the sole evidence it is possible to produce that anything is desirable, is that people do actually desire it." *Utilitarianism,* Chap. IV, 3rd paragraph.

thing may be confirmed "indirectly" in other ways than by what would be called "experiencing the value of it."

For instance, judgment that my neighbor is a good musician may be confirmed by his rendition of difficult passages, though the selection he is presently at work on is one that leaves me cold, or even if I find his persistent exhibition of virtuosity an interruption to my train of thought and highly irritating. Or I may find evidence that my chisel is sharp, as a good chisel ought to be, through painfully cutting myself with it. We may still feel that in determination of any objective value, value-experiences occupy a privileged or peculiarly decisive place; but if so, this sense of their peculiar importance is elusive and will require to be probed. At least the conclusion would be ill-drawn, that a belief in objective value can be confirmed *only* through direct experiences of value.

Many of the puzzles which beset us about evaluation may be resolved or materially advanced by determining in which of these three senses the predication of value which is in question is to be taken. Does the statement made concern a value immediately found in experience? Then the matter lies outside any reasonable dispute: the finding of the subject of this experience is final; and concerning it there is no mistake that he can make. Any question about it concerns its evidential character as basis for some *different* evaluation; for judgment of *further* value-experiences derivable from the same thing, or judgment of some *objective* value-property of it; or else the question concerns merely the appropriateness of the language he uses for expressing what he finds in his experience.

Or is the value-predication in question intended to assert that under certain circumstances and by a certain procedure experience of a certain value-quality would accrue? It is then a terminating judgment; predictive, and verifiable or falsifiable. But it is *decisively* verifiable or falsifiable (in whatever sense the conditions of verification should be possible) by being put to the test. If or when it should be so tested, its truth or falsity will be absolutely determined, beyond any question or debate. But prior to such verification, at any time when, for example, it functions as a judgment of the desirability or undesirability of certain ways of acting, its believability rests upon inductive evidence drawn from past experience; and our assurance of it can be, theoretically, no better than probable.

Or does the value-predication signify the objective property of value or disvalue in some kind of existent? Its meaning is then translatable into some multiplicity of terminating judgments, each by itself decisively verifiable or falsifiable, and each representing some possible confirmation of this objective judgment. Such an affirmation

of objective value will have some probability or improbability on antecedent grounds, and this probability may be indefinitely increased or
diminished by the test of its confirmations; though always it will retain a further and as yet untested significance, because the number
of such possible confirmations of it will not be finitely exhaustible.
Also the evidence which we have or may obtain for it need not be
confined to direct disclosures of value or disvalue in the thing in
question, but may include other and indirect confirmations of its objective value.

. . . Although it would be agreed—with some measure of generality
at least—that the only *ultimately* good thing is such realization of
positive value-quality in experience, we all of us persistently speak
of objects of certain kinds as good in themselves. We say, for example, that the beauty of an art-object is intrinsic to that object; even
though we should be prepared to admit that if the object be such
that by no possibility could any human who should experience it
find satisfaction in it or by means of it, then this ascription of value
to it would be either meaningless or false.

What accounts for this frequent mode of speech may well be that,
in such cases, we are thinking exclusively of *objective* goodness. And
amongst objects, some are good only because they lead to others; but
some are good in a manner which does not depend upon their being
instrumental to any other *object*. As has been pointed out, those of
this latter class present a goodness found in the presence of that object to which it is attributed, and hence not depending on relation
to any other *object*, though it does depend on a relation, or at least
possible relation, of this object to some *subject*. Consonantly, when
we speak of an object as useful or as having utility, or having extrinsic value, it is by reason of a relation of the object in question
to some other object; if on occasion the beauty of a thing or its
pleasantness is called a utility of it, at least that manner of speech is
uncharacteristic.

If any should insist on repudiating our usage here of "*intrinsic
value*" and "*extrinsic value*," and reserving those terms for this distinction between that goodness of objects which may be realized in the
presence of them and that goodness which is realized in experience
only in the presence of something else, to which the object in question is instrumental, we should of course have no ground of quarrel
with that choice of terminology. Indeed, it is perhaps so well in-
trenched in customary usage that it should be respected; and we
would better have chosen some other set of terms for that different
distinction, which it is even more important to make, between what
is valued for its own sake and what is valued for the sake of some-

thing further. That kind of question is hardly worthy of debate. What we find it essential to point out here is that although the beauty of an art-object, for example, does not depend on relation to any other object, still this value does depend on relation to possible experience of subjects. What is *ultimately* desirable is not merely that this object and this property of it called its beauty should exist, but that this beauty of it should illuminate the experience of some beholder. And unless we remark this distinction between what represents our ultimate aim and that which is aimed at for the sake of it, we could not arrive at any clarity whatever concerning value-predications and the authentic facts which they intend to express. In particular, as has been pointed out, the distinction is essential in order to explain the difference between predications of value in general and predication to objects of other qualities than value; the difference which is evidenced by the fact that, for value-terms, their expressive meaning seems to rule the objective use of them, whereas for names of other properties, the expressive usage of them seems to be, on the whole, derivative from their objective meaning.

Furthermore, we do not overlook the other important distinction mentioned, which holds within the field of values in objects exclusively, between those objects which are good only by relation to others and those which are good without reference to any further object. Those values which are resident in objects in such wise that they are realizable in experience through presentation of the object itself to which they are attributed, we propose to call *inherent values*. And those values of things which consist in an instrumentality to some *other object*, in presentation of which a value is directly realizable in experience, we propose to call *instrumental values*.

This usage of the term "inherent" is meant to suggest that the value in question is one which is found or findable in the object itself to which the value is attributed, in the sense of being one which is disclosed or disclosable by observation of this object itself and not by examining some other object. But this must be distinguished from another meaning which "inherent" sometimes has, which it is *not* meant here to suggest; that meaning, namely, in which a quality is said to be inherent in a thing if and only if it is an essential character signified by the name by which the object in question is named. In this last sense—not here intended—the hardness and specific gravity of an emerald would be inherent properties, but the beauty of a particular emerald would not, since a stone may be correctly classifiable as emerald without being beautiful. In the sense we here adopt, the beauty of an emerald—or of anything else—would be an inherent value of that particular object, since it is a quality of it which is disclosed or disclosable in the presentation of the object in question, and not by observation of some other thing to which the object in question may be instrumental.

The Immediately Valuable[9]

The conception outlined . . . implies that there is one single kind of desideratum which is the ultimate concern in all valuations; since it takes all valuings to be either direct apprehensions of value-quality in the empirically presented, or predictions of such findings as possible, or judgments of a thing in question as capable of conducing to such realization of value-quality in experience. Prizings and disprizings of the presently given content of experience, are formulatable in expressive statements, the reference of which terminates in the immediate and phenomenal. With respect to these, the subject whose experience is in question can make no mistake, unless a verbal one in the manner of expressing what he finds. By the same token, such value-apprehensions of the given are not judgments and are not items of knowledge, though expression of them is true or false (since false report is possible). Valuations other than those which thus refer to a quality of the presently given, are value-judgments; and are either of the terminating sort which predict some value-quality as findable under certain conditions, or they are ascriptions to some actuality, or to some conceived entity, or to some *kind* of entity, of a potentiality for contributing a value-quality to experience. Thus the conception is that the only thing intrinsically valuable—valuable for its own sake—is a goodness immediately found or findable and unmistakable when disclosed: all values of any other sort, including all values attributable to objects, are extrinsic, and valued for the sake of their possible contribution to such realizations of the immediately good. . . .

Every such view might be called a naturalistic or humanistic conception of values; since it holds that the natural bent of the natural man stands in no need of correction in order validly to be the touchstone of *intrinsic* value. It repudiates the conception that with respect to intrinsic values we are natively incompetent, or born in sin, and can discern them justly only by some insight thaumaturgically acquired, or through some intimation of a proper vocation of man which runs athwart his natural bent. But in repudiating such redemptionist norms of the intrinsically valuable, such a naturalistic view does not wish to fall into the arms of a Protagorean relativism. It does not intend to put evaluations which the fool makes in his folly

[9] *Ibid.*, Chapter XIII, pp. 397–400.

on a par with those of the sage in his wisdom. Rather it would recognize that while the natural man does not need any change of heart or any more than natural insight in order to make just evaluations, still he does stand in need of all that can be learned from the experience of life in this natural world. Nor does such a naturalistic view wish to be confused with that neopositivism which, in the realm of values, is cynical or nihilistic, and denies all truth or falsity to valuations, classing them as expressions of feeling or emotion merely, and hence as having no criterion of determinable truth or falsity. In repudiating transcendental norms which would impose themselves as imperatives which must overrule our natural desires, it still does not mean to repudiate the normative significance for action which is implicit in all valuation, and is the reason for our interest in making correct judgments of value as against those which, upon trial, would prove to be mistaken. It intends to recognize a truth or falsity of valuations which is independent of our supposition or our wish, and which, like truth in general, has its imperative significance for belief and for sensibly taken action.

However, we shall not find any middle ground between transcendentalism on the one hand and Protagorean relativism on the other, unless we find a sense in which valuations—or *some* valuations—are judgments; are determinably true or false by reference to the natural consequences of acting in accordance with them; unless some value-predications are assertions which are confirmable but are not beyond the possibility of error when made; unless some things of which value is predicated have this predicated character in a manner not determined by immediate liking or desire or interest, but determined independently of what one may think or feel about them. And similarly, we can find no middle ground between the admission of norms in the sense of transcendental imperatives,[10] having extra-natural sanction, and that cynical repudiation of normative signifiances of every kind, unless we recognize that some value-statements affirm a kind of truth which experience may confirm, and which stands in need of such corroboration.

In order to be distinguished from transcendentalism, from Protagorean subjectivism, and from nihilism, all three, it is essential for a naturalistic conception of values to hold that some valuations have the significance of empirical cognition. But also it is essential for a naturalistic view to maintain that the quality or character by reference to which, ultimately, all things are to be judged valuable or disvaluable, is a quality unmistakably identifiable in the direct appre-

[10] The reference here is not to that ethical imperative which demands respect for others, but to an imperative which should find no adequate sanction by relation to the actual interests of anybody.

hension of it when disclosed in experience. It must hold that such immediately apprehensible value-quality or value-character constitutes the criterion by reference to which, eventually, those value-predications which are subject to possible error and need confirmation are to be attested. Thus such a naturalistic view can hardly attain to clarity and cogency unless the distinction be remarked between value-predications which are merely expressive statements of a value-quality immediately discovered, and those which attribute to some existent the objective property of conducing to such realization of the immediately valuable. . . .

BIBLIOGRAPHY

LEWIS, C.I., *A Survey of Symbolic Logic.* Berkeley: U. of Calif. Press, 1918.

———, *Mind and the World Order.* N.Y.: Charles Scribner's Sons, 1929.

———, (with C. H. Langford), *Symbolic Logic.* N.Y. and London: The Century Co., 1932.

———, *An Analysis of Knowledge and Valuation.* La Salle, Ill.: Open Court Publishing Co., 1946.

———, *The Ground and Nature of the Right.* N.Y.: Columbia U. Press, 1955.

———, *Our Social Inheritance.* Bloomington: Indiana U. Press, 1957.

MILMED, Bella. *Kant and Current Philosophical Issues: Some Current Modern Developments of His Theory of Knowledge.* N.Y.: New York U. Press, 1961.

Rudolf Carnap

[*1891–*]

Carnap was born in Wuppertal, Germany. He studied at the Universities of Jena and Freiburg, and received his Ph.D. from Jena in 1921. Carnap began his teaching career at the University of Vienna (1926–31), and taught at the German University of Prague (1931–35). From 1930 on he edited (together with Hans Reichenbach) *Erkenntnis,* the principal organ of the positivist movement. He came to America in 1935 and taught at the University of Chicago from 1936 to 1952. He was a member of the Institute for Advanced Study, Princeton (1952–54). Since 1954, he has been associated with the University of California at Los Angeles.

In 1928, Carnap's *Der Logische Aufbau der Welt (The Logical Structure of the World)* attempted to work out a rigorous phenomenalistic language for science, using the logical principles of *Principia Mathematica* and reducing all statements referring to physical objects to statements referring to classes of sensory data. By the middle 1930's, however, Carnap revised his position and defended physicalism (a form of radical behaviorism)—i.e., the view that words referring to physical objects and qualities could properly be taken as a basis for a rigorous scientific language. This shift avoided the need for reduction to sense-data language and the solipsistic subjectivism that went with it. Carnap maintained that

in basing scientific language on thing-words, he was simply following normal scientific practice in dealing with things encountered in the laboratory, and was not prescribing for science, nor presenting a doctrine of "metaphysical" realism.

Carnap's *The Logical Syntax of Language* (1934) was an early attempt to bring philosophy under the domain of logic. "Philosophy," he maintained, "is to be replaced by the logic of science—that is to say, by the logical analysis of the concepts and sentences of the sciences, for the logic of science is nothing other than the logical syntax of the language of science." (Foreword.) Eventually, however, Carnap moved away from a predominantly syntactical approach to language. This shift is recorded in his books *Introduction to Semantics* (1942) and *Meaning and Necessity* (1947).

Carnap, in his writings and as co-editor of the *International Encyclopedia of Unified Science,* has also helped to advance the "unity of science" movement by his efforts to develop a rigorous common language for all the sciences. His book *Logical Foundations of Probability* (1950) reflects his interest in the logic of science. Especially important in his philosophy of science is his extension of the verifiability criterion, which allows for theoretical as well as practical verification.

His article *Empiricism, Semantics,*

and Ontology (1950) is not, as is much of his recent writing, very specialized and technical, and is a good introduction to at least one aspect of Carnap's work. In the portion reprinted below, Carnap distinguishes between "internal" questions, which arise within a given conceptual framework, and "external questions," which concern the status and legitimacy of the framework itself. Carnap attempts to avoid ontological questions about "abstract entities," which he regards as metaphysical "pseudo-questions," but instead takes as his main task the rational reconstruction of a linguistic and conceptual system judged by its usefulness to the scientist. Although this essay comes relatively late in Carnap's development, it reflects a good deal of the temper and spirit of logical positivism.

EMPIRICISM, SEMANTICS, AND ONTOLOGY [1]

1. THE PROBLEM OF ABSTRACT ENTITIES

Empiricists are in general rather suspicious with respect to any kind of abstract entities like properties, classes, relations, numbers, propositions, etc. They usually feel much more in sympathy with nominalists than with realists (in the medieval sense). As fas as possible they try to avoid any reference to abstract entities and to restrict themselves to what is sometimes called a nominalistic language, i.e., one not containing such references. However, within certain scientific contexts it seems hardly possible to avoid them. In the case of mathematics, some empiricists try to find a way out by treating the whole of mathematics as a mere calculus, a formal system for which no interpretation is given or can be given. Accordingly, the mathematician is said to speak not about numbers, functions, and infinite classes, but merely about meaningless symbols and formulas manipulated according to given formal rules. In physics it is more difficult to shun the suspected entities, because the language of physics serves for the communication of reports and predictions and hence cannot be taken as a mere calculus. A physicist who is suspicious of abstract entities may perhaps try to declare a certain part of the language of physics as uninterpreted and uninterpretable, that part which refers to real numbers as space-time coordinates or as values of physical magnitudes, to functions, limits, etc. More probably he will just speak about all these things like anybody else but with an uneasy conscience, like a man who in his everyday life does with qualms many things which are not in accord with the high moral principles he professes on Sundays. Recently the problem of abstract entities has arisen again in connection with semantics, the theory of meaning and truth. Some semanticists say that certain expressions designate certain entities, and among these designated entities they include not only concrete material things but also abstract entities, e.g., properties as designated by predicates and propositions as designated by sentences.[2] Others object strongly to this procedure as violating the basic principles of empiricism and leading back to a metaphysical ontology of the Platonic kind.

It is the purpose of this article to clarify this controversial issue. The nature and implications of the acceptance of a language referring to abstract entities will first be discussed in general; it will be shown that using such a language does not imply embracing a Platonic ontology but is perfectly compatible with empiricism and strictly scientific thinking. Then the special question of the role of abstract entities in semantics will be discussed. It is hoped that the clarification of the issue will be useful to those who would like to accept abstract entities in their work in mathematics, physics, semantics, or any other field; it may help them to overcome nominalistic scruples.

2. FRAMEWORKS OF ENTITIES

Are there properties, classes, numbers, propositions? In order to understand more clearly the nature of these and related problems, it is above all necessary to recognize a fundamental distinction between two kinds of questions concerning the existence or reality of entities. If someone wishes to speak in his languge about a new kind of entities, he has to introduce a system of new ways of speaking, subject to new rules; we shall call this procedure the construction of a *framework* for the new entities in question. And now we must distinguish two kinds of questions of existence: first, questions of the existence of certain entities of the new kind *within the framework*; we call them *internal questions*; and second, questions concerning the existence or reality *of the framework itself*, called *external questions*. Internal questions and possible answers to them are formulated with the help of the new forms of expressions. The answers may be found either by purely logical methods or by empirical methods, depending upon whether the framework is a logical or a factual one. An external question is of a problematic character which is in need of closer examination.

THE WORLD OF THINGS. Let us consider as an example the simplest framework dealt with in the everyday language: the spatio-temporally ordered system of observable things and events. Once we have

---

[2] The terms "sentence" and "statement" are here used synonymously for declarative (indicative, propositional) sentences.

accepted this thing-language and thereby the framework of things, we can raise and answer internal questions, e.g., "Is there a white piece of paper on my desk?", "Did King Arthur actually live?", "Are unicorns and centaurs real or merely imaginary?", and the like. These questions are to be answered by empirical investigations. Results of observations are evaluated according to certain rules as confirming or disconfirming evidence for possible answers. (This evaluation is usually carried out, of course, as a matter of habit rather than a deliberate, rational procedure. But it is possible, in a rational reconstruction, to lay down explicit rules for the evaluation. This is one of the main tasks of a pure, as distinguished from a psychological, epistemology.) The concept of reality occurring in these internal questions is an empirical, scientific, non-metaphysical concept. To recognize something as a real thing or event means to succeed in incorporating it into the framework of things at a particular space-time position so that it fits together with the other things recognized as real, according to the rules of the framework.

From these questions we must distinguish the external question of the reality of the thing world itself. In contrast to the former questions, this question is raised neither by the man in the street nor by scientists, but only by philosophers. Realists give an affirmative answer, subjective idealists a negative one, and the controversy goes on for centuries without ever being solved. And it cannot be solved because it is framed in a wrong way. To be real in the scientific sense means to be an element of the framework; hence this concept cannot be meaningfully applied to the framework itself. Those who raise the question of the reality of the thing world itself have perhaps in mind not a theoretical question as their formulation seems to suggest, but rather a practical question, a matter of a practical decision concerning the structure of our language. We have to make the choice whether or not to accept and use the forms of expression for the framework in question.

In the case of this particular example, there is usually no deliberate choice because we all have accepted the thing language early in our lives as a matter of course. Nevertheless, we may regard it as a matter of decision in this sense: we are free to choose to continue using the thing language or not; in the latter case we could restrict ourselves to a language of sense-data and other "phenomenal" entities, or construct an alternative to the customary thing language with another structure, or, finally, we could refrain from speaking. If someone decides to accept the thing language, there is no objection against saying that he has accepted the world of things. But this must not be interpreted as if it meant his acceptance of a *belief* in the reality of the thing world; there is no such belief or assertion or assumption, because it is not a theoretical question. To accept the thing world means nothing more than to accept a certain form of language, in other words, to accept rules for forming statements and for testing, accepting, or rejecting them. Thus the acceptance of the thing language leads, on the basis of observations made, also to the acceptance, belief, and assertion of certain statements. But the thesis of the reality of the thing world cannot be among these statements, because it cannot be formulated in the thing language or, it seems, in any other theoretical language.

The decision of accepting the thing language, although itself not of a cognitive nature, will nevertheless usually be influenced by theoretical knowledge, just like any other deliberate decision concerning the acceptance of linguistic or other rules. The purposes for which the language is intended to be used, for instance, the purpose of communicating factual knowledge, will determine which factors are relevant for the decision. The efficiency, fruitfulness, and simplicity of the use of the thing language may be among the decisive factors. And the questions concerning these qualities are indeed of a theoretical nature. But these questions cannot be identified with the question of realism. They are not yes–no questions but questions of degree. The thing language in the customary form works indeed with a high degree of efficiency for most purposes of everyday life. This is a matter of fact, based upon the content of our experiences. However, it would be wrong to describe this situation by saying: "The fact of the efficiency of the thing language is confirming evidence for the reality of the thing world"; we should rather say instead: "This fact makes it advisable to accept the thing language."

THE SYSTEM OF NUMBERS. As an example of a framework which is of a logical rather than a factual nature let us take the system of natural numbers. This system is established by introducing into the language new expressions with suitable rules: (1) numerals like "five" and sentence forms like "there are five books on the table"; (2) the general term "number" for the new entities, and sentence forms like "five is a number"; (3) expressions for properties of numbers (e.g., "odd," "prime"), relations (e.g., "greater than"), and functions (e.g., "plus"), and sentence forms like "two plus three is five"; (4) numerical variables ("m," "n," etc.) and quantifiers for universal sentences ("for every n, . . .") and existential sentences ("there is an n such that . . .") with the customary deductive rules.

Here again there are internal questions, e.g., "Is there a prime number greater than hundred?" Here, however, the answers are found, not by empirical investigation based on observations, but by logical analysis based on the rules for the new expressions. Therefore the answers are here analytic, i.e., logically true.

What is now the nature of the philosophical question concerning the existence or reality of numbers? To begin with, there is the internal question which, together with the affirmative answer, can be formulated in the new terms, say, by "There are numbers" or, more explicitly, "There is an n such that n is a number." This statement follows from the analytic statement "five is a number" and is therefore itself analytic. Moreover, it is rather trivial (in contradistinction to a statement like "There is a prime number greater than a million," which is likewise analytic but far from trivial), because it does not say more than that the new system is not empty; but this is immediately seen from the rule which states that words like "five" are substitutable for the new variables. Therefore nobody who meant the question "Are there numbers?" in the internal sense would either assert or even seriously consider a negative answer. This makes it plausible to assume that those philosophers who treat the question of the existence of numbers as a serious philosophical problem and offer lengthy arguments on either side, do not have in mind the internal question. And, indeed, if we were to ask them: "Do you mean the question as to whether the system of numbers, *if* we were to accept it, would be found to be empty or not?", they would probably reply: "Not at all; we mean a question *prior* to the acceptance of the new framework." They might try to explain what they mean by saying that it is a question of the ontological status of numbers; the question whether or not numbers have a certain metaphysical characteristic called reality (but a kind of ideal reality, different from the material reality of the thing world) or subsistence or status of "independent entities." Unfortunately, these philosophers have so far not given a formulation of their question in terms of the common scientific language. Therefore our judgment must be that they have not succeeded in giving to the external question and to the possible answers any cognitive content. Unless and until they supply a clear cognitive interpretation, we are justified in our suspicion that their question is a pseudo-question, that is, one disguised in the form of a theoretical question while in fact it is non-theoretical; in the present case it is the practical problem whether or not to incorporate into the language the new linguistic forms which represent the framework of numbers.

THE FRAMEWORK OF PROPOSITIONS. New variables, "p," "q," etc., are introduced with a rule to the effect that any (declarative) sentence may be substituted for a variable of this kind; this includes, in addition to the sentences of the original thing language, also all general sentences with variables of any kind which may have been introduced into the language. Further, the general term "proposition" is introduced. "p is a proposition" may be defined by "p or not p" (or

by any other sentence form yielding only analytic sentences). Therefore, every sentence of the form ". . . is a proposition" (where any
sentence may stand in the place of the dots) is analytic. This holds,
for example, for the sentence:

(a) "Chicago is large is a proposition."

(We disregard here the fact that the rules of English grammar
require not a sentence but a that-clause as the subject of another
sentence; accordingly, instead of (a) we should have to say "That
Chicago is large is a proposition.") Predicates may be admitted whose
argument expressions are sentences; these predicates may be either
extensional (e.g., the customary truth-functional connectives) or not
(e.g., modal predicates like "possible," "necessary," etc.). With the
help of the new variables, general sentences may be formed, e.g.

(b) "For every p, either p or not-p."

(c) "There is a p such that p is not necessary and not-p is not
necessary."

(d) "There is a p such that p is a proposition."

(c) and (d) assert internal existence. The statement "There are
propositions" may be meant in the sense of (d); in this case it is
analytic (since it follows from (a)) and even trivial. If, however,
the statement is meant in an external sense, then it is non-cognitive.

It is important to notice that the system of rules for the linguistic
expressions of the propositional framework (of which only a few
rules have here been briefly indicated) is sufficient for the introduction of the framework. Any further explanations as to the nature of
the propositions (i.e., the elements of the framework indicated, the
values of the variables "p," "q," etc.) are theoretically unnecessary
because, if correct, they follow from the rules. For example, are propositions mental events (as in Russell's theory)? A look at the rules
shows us that they are not, because otherwise existential statements
would be of the form: "If the mental state of the person in question
fulfils such and such conditions, then there is a p such that . . .".
The fact that no references to mental conditions occur in existential
statements (like (c), (d), etc.) shows that propositions are not mental entities. Further, a statement of the existence of linguistic entities
(e.g., expressions, classes of expressions, etc.) must contain a reference to a language. The fact that no such reference occurs in the
existential statements here, shows that propositions are not linguistic
entities. The fact that in these statements no reference to a subject
(an observer or knower) occurs (nothing like: "There is a p which is
necessary for Mr. x"), shows that the propositions (and their properties, like necessity, etc.) are not subjective. Although characterizations of these or similar kinds are, strictly speaking, unnecessary, they
may nevertheless be practically useful. If they are given, they should

be understood, not as ingredient parts of the system, but merely as marginal notes with the purpose of supplying to the reader helpful hints or convenient pictorial associations which may make his learning of the use of the expressions easier than the bare system of the rules would do. Such a characterization is analogous to an extra-systematic explanation which a physicist sometimes gives to the beginner. He might, for example, tell him to imagine the atoms of a gas as small balls rushing around with great speed, or the electromagnetic field and its oscillations as quasi-elastic tensions and vibrations in an ether. In fact, however, all that can accurately be said about atoms or the field is implicitly contained in the physical laws of the theories in question.[3]

THE FRAMEWORK OF THING PROPERTIES. The thing language contains words like "red," "hard," "stone," "house," etc., which are used for describing what things are like. Now we may introduce new variables, say "f," "g," etc., for which those words are substitutable and furthermore the general term "property." New rules are laid down which admit sentences like "Red is a property," "Red is a color," "These two pieces of paper have at least one color in common" (i.e., "There is an f such that f is a color, and . . ."). The last sentence is an internal assertion. It is of an empirical, factual nature. However, the external statement, the philosophical statement of the reality of properties—a special case of the thesis of the reality of universals—is devoid of cognitive content.

[3] In my book *Meaning and Necessity* (Chicago, 1947) I have developed a semantical method which takes propositions as entities designated by sentences (more specifically, as intensions of sentences). In order to facilitate the understanding of the systematic development, I added some informal, extra-systematic explanations concerning the nature of propositions. I said that the term "proposition" "is used neither for a linguistic expression nor for a subjective, mental occurrence, but rather for something objective that may or may not be exemplified in nature . . . We apply the term 'proposition' to any entities of a certain logical type, namely, those that may be expressed by (declarative) sentences in a language" (p. 27). After some more detailed discussions concerning the relation between propositions and facts, and the nature of false propositions, I added: "It has been the purpose of the preceding remarks to facilitate the understanding of our conception of propositions. If, however, a reader should find these explanations more puzzling than clarifying, or even unacceptable, he may disregard them" (p. 31) (that is, disregard these extra-systematic explanations, not the whole theory of the propositions as intensions of sentences, as one reviewer understood). In spite of this warning, it seems that some of those readers who were puzzled by the explanations did not disregard them but thought that by raising objections against them they could refute the theory. This is analogous to the procedure of some laymen who by (correctly) criticizing the ether picture or other visualizations of physical theories, thought they had refuted those theories. Perhaps the discussions in the present paper will help in clarifying the role of the system of linguistic rules for the introduction of a framework of entities on the one hand, and that of extra-systematic explanations concerning the nature of the entities on the other.

THE FRAMEWORKS OF INTEGERS AND RATIONAL NUMBERS. Into a language containing the framework of natural numbers we may introduce first the (positive and negative) integers as relations among natural numbers and then the rational numbers as relations among integers. This involves introducing new types of variables, expressions substitutable for them and the general terms "integer" and "rational number."

THE FRAMEWORK OF REAL NUMBERS. On the basis of the rational numbers, the real numbers may be introduced as classes of a special kind (segments) of rational numbers (according to the method developed by Dedekind and Frege). Here again a new type of variables is introduced, expressions substitutable for them (e.g., "$\sqrt{2}$"), and the general term "real number."

THE FRAMEWORK OF A SPATIO-TEMPORAL COORDINATE SYSTEM FOR PHYSICS. The new entities are the space-time points. Each is an ordered quadruple of four real numbers, called its coordinates, consisting of three spatial and one temporal coordinates. The physical state of a spatio-temporal point or region is described either with the help of qualitative predicates (e.g., "hot") or by ascribing numbers as values of a physical magnitude (e.g., mass, temperature, and the like). The step from the framework of things (which does not contain space-time points but only extended objects with spatial and temporal relations between them) to the physical coordinate system is again a matter of decision. Our choice of certain features, although itself not theoretical, is suggested by theoretical knowledge, either logical or factual. For example, the choice of real numbers rather than rational numbers or integers as coordinates is not much influenced by the facts of experience but mainly due to considerations of mathematical simplicity. The restriction to rational coordinates would not be in conflict with any experimental knowledge we have, because the result of any measurement is a rational number. However, it would prevent the use of ordinary geometry (which says, e.g., that the diagonal of a square with the side 1 has the irrational value $\sqrt{2}$) and thus lead to great complications. On the other hand, the decision to use three rather than two or four spatial coordinates is strongly suggested, but still not forced upon us, by the result of common observations. If certain events allegedly observed in spiritualistic séances, e.g., a ball moving out of a sealed box, were confirmed beyond any reasonable doubt, it might seem advisable to use four spatial coordinates. Internal questions are here, in general, empirical questions to be answered by empirical investigations. On the other hand, the external questions of the reality of physical space and physical time are pseudo-questions. A question like "Are there (really) space-time points?" is ambiguous. It may be meant as an internal question; then the affirmative answer is, of course, analytic and trivial. Or it may be meant in the external sense: "Shall we introduce such and such forms into our language?"; in this case it is not a theoretical but a practical question, a matter of decision rather than assertion, and hence the proposed formulation would be misleading. Or finally, it may be meant in the following sense: "Are our experiences such that the use of the linguistic forms in question will be expedient and fruitful?" This is a theoretical question of a factual, empirical nature. But it concerns a matter of degree; therefore a formulation in the form "real or not?" would be inadequate.

3. WHAT DOES ACCEPTANCE OF A FRAMEWORK MEAN?

Let us now summarize the essential characteristics of situations involving the introduction of a new framework of entities, characteristics which are common to the various examples outlined above.

The acceptance of a framework of new entities is represented in the language by introduction of new forms of expressions to be used according to a new set of rules. There may be new names for particular entities of the kind in question; but some such names may already occur in the language before the introduction of the new framework. (Thus, for example, the thing language contains certainly words of the type of "blue" and "house" before the framework of properties is introduced; and it may contain words like "ten" in sentences of the form "I have ten fingers" before the framework of numbers is introduced.) The latter fact shows that the occurrence of constants of the type in question—regarded as names of entities of the new kind after the new framework is introduced—is not a sure sign of the acceptance of the framework. Therefore the introduction of such constants is not to be regarded as an essential step in the introduction of the framework. The two essential steps are rather the following. First, the introduction of a general term, a predicate of higher level, for the new kind of entities, permitting us to say of any particular entity that it belongs to this kind (e.g., "Red is a *property*," "Five is a *number*"). Second, the introduction of variables of the new type. The new entities are values of these variables; the constants (and the closed compound expressions, if any) are substitutable for the variables.[4] With the help of the variables, general sentences concerning the new entities can be formulated.

[4] W. V. Quine was the first to recognize the importance of the introduction of variables as indicating the acceptance of entities. "The ontology to which one's use of language commits him comprises simply the objects that he treats as falling . . . within the range of values of his variables" ("Notes on Existence and

After the new forms are introduced into the language, it is possible to formulate with their help internal questions and possible answers to them. A question of this kind may be either empirical or logical; accordingly a true answer is either factually true or analytic. From the internal questions we must clearly distinguish external questions, i.e., philosophical questions concerning the existence or reality of the framework itself. Many philosophers regard a question of this kind as an ontological question which must be raised and answered *before* the introduction of the new language forms. The latter introduction, they believe, is legitimate only if it can be justified by an ontological insight supplying an affirmative answer to the question of reality. In contrast to this view, we take the position that the introduction of the new ways of speaking does not need any theoretical justification because it does not imply any assertion of reality. We may still speak (and have done so) of "the acceptance of the framework" or "the acceptance of the new entities" since this form of speech is customary; but one must keep in mind that these phrases do not mean for us anything more than acceptance of the new linguistic forms. Above all, they must not be interpreted as referring to an assumption, belief, or assertion of "the reality of the entities." There is no such assertion. An alleged statement of the reality of the framework of entities is a pseudo-statement without cognitive content. To be sure, we have to face at this point an important question; but it is a practical, not a theoretical question; it is the question of whether or not to accept the new linguistic forms. The acceptance cannot be judged as being either true or false because it is not an assertion. It can only be judged as being more or less expedient, fruitful, conducive to the aim for which the language is intended. Judgments of this kind supply the motivation for the decision of accepting or rejecting the framework.[5]

Thus it is clear that the acceptance of a framework must not be regarded as implying a metaphysical doctrine concerning the reality of the entities in question. It seems to me due to a neglect of this important distinction that some contemporary nominalists label the admission of variables of abstract types as "Platonism."[6] This is, to say

---

Necessity," *Journal of Philosophy*, 40 (1943), pp. 113–127, see p. 118; compare also his "Designation and Existence," *ibid.*, 36 (1939), pp. 701–9, and "On Universals," *Journal of Symbolic Logic*, 12 (1947), pp. 74–84).

[5] For a closely related point of view on these questions see the detailed discussions in Herbert FEIGL, *Existential Hypotheses*, forthcoming in *Philosophy of Science*, 1950.

[6] Paul BERNAYS, *Sur le platonisme dans les mathématiques* (*L'Enseignement math.*, 34 (1935), pp. 52–69). W. V. QUINE, see footnote p. 65, and a recent paper *On What There Is*, (*Review of Metaphysics*, 2 (1948), pp. 21–38). Quine does

the least, an extremely misleading terminology. It leads to the absurd consequence, that the position of everybody who accepts the language of physics with its real number variables (as a language of communication, not merely as a calculus) would be called Platonistic, even if he is a strict empiricist who rejects Platonic metaphysics.

A brief historical remark may here be inserted. The non-cognitive character of the questions which we have called here external questions was recognized and emphasized already by the Vienna Circle under the leadership of Moritz Schlick, the group from which the movement of logical empiricism originated. Influenced by ideas of Ludwig Wittgenstein, the Circle rejected both the thesis of the reality of the external world and the thesis of its irreality as pseudo-statements;[7] the same was the case for both the thesis of the reality of universals (abstract entities, in our present terminology) and the nominalistic thesis that they are not real and that their alleged names are not names of anything but merely *flatus vocis*. (It is obvious that the apparent negation of a pseudo-statement must also be a pseudo-statement.) It is therefore not correct to classify the members of the Vienna Circle as nominalists, as is sometimes done. However, if we look at the basic anti-metaphysical and pro-scientific attitude of most nominalists (and the same holds for many materialists and realists in the modern sense), disregarding their occasional pseudo-theoretical formulations, then it is, of course, true to say that the Vienna Circle was much closer to those philosophers than to their opponents.

4. ABSTRACT ENTITIES IN SEMANTICS

The problem of the legitimacy and the status of abstract entities has recently again led to controversial discussions in connection with

---

not acknowledge the distinction which I emphasize above, because according to his general conception there are no sharp boundary lines between logical and factual truth, between questions of meaning and questions of fact, between the acceptance of a language structure and the acceptance of an assertion formulated in the language. This conception, which seems to deviate considerably from customary ways of thinking, will be explained in his forthcoming book, *Foundations of Logic*. When Quine in the article mentioned above classifies my logicistic conception of mathematics (derived from Frege and Russell) as "platonic realism" (p. 33), this is meant (according to a personal communication from him) not as ascribing to me agreement with Plato's metaphysical doctrine of universals, but merely as referring to the fact that I accept a language of mathematics containing variables of higher levels. With respect to the basic attitude to take in choosing a language form (an "ontology" in Quine's terminology, which seems to me misleading), there appears now to be agreement between us: "the obvious counsel is tolerance and an experimental spirit" (*op. cit.*, p. 38).

[7] See CARNAP, *Scheinprobleme in der Philosophie; das Fremdpsychische und der Realismusstreit*, Berlin, 1928. Moritz SCHLICK, *Positivismus und Realismus*, reprinted in *Gesammelte Aufsätze*, Vienna 1938.

semantics. In a semantical meaning analysis certain expressions in a language are often said to designate (or name or denote or signify or refer to) certain extra-linguistic entities.[8] As long as physical things or events (e.g., Chicago or Caesar's death) are taken as designata (entities designated), no serious doubts arise. But strong objections have been raised, especially by some empiricists, against abstract entities as designata, e.g., against semantical statements of the following kind:

(1) "The word 'red' designates a property of things;"
(2) "The word 'color' designates a property of properties of things;"
(3) "The word 'five' designates a number;"
(4) "The word 'odd' designates a property of numbers;"
(5) "The sentence 'Chicago is large' designates a proposition."

Those who criticize these statements do not, of course, reject the use of the expressions in question, like "red" or "five"; nor would they deny that these expressions are meaningful. But to be meaningful, they would say, is not the same as having a meaning in the sense of an entity designated. They reject the belief, which they regard as implicitly presupposed by those semantical statements, that to each expression of the types in question (adjectives like "red," numerals like "five," etc.) there is a particular real entity to which the expression stands in the relation of designation. This belief is rejected as incompatible with the basic principles of empiricism or of scientific thinking. Derogatory labels like "Platonic realism," "hypostatization," or " 'Fido'–Fido principle" are attached to it. The latter is the name given by Gilbert Ryle[9] to the criticized belief, which, in his view, arises by a naive inference of analogy: just as there is an entity well known to me, viz. my dog Fido, which is designated by the name "Fido," thus there must be for every meaningful expression a particular entity to which it stands in the relation of designation or naming, i.e., the relation exemplified by "Fido"-Fido. The belief criticized is thus a case of hypostatization, i.e., of treating as names expressions which are not names. While "Fido" is a name, expressions like "red," "five," etc. are said not to be names, not to designate anything.

Our previous discussions concerning the acceptance of frameworks enables us now to clarify the situation with respect to abstract entities as designata. Let us take as an example the statement:

[8] See *Introduction to Semantics*, Cambridge, Mass., 1942; *Meaning and Necessity*, Chicago, 1947. The distinction I have drawn in the latter book between the method of the name-relation and the method of intension and extension is not essential for our present discussion. The term "designation" is here used in a neutral way; it may be understood as referring to the name-relation or to the intension-relation or to the extension-relation or to any similar relations used in other semantical methods.

[9] G. Ryle, *Meaning and Necessity* (*Philosophy*, 24 (1949), pp. 69–76).

(a) " 'Five' designates a number."

The formulation of this statement presupposes that our language L contains the forms of expressions corresponding to what we have called the framework of numbers, in particular, numerical variables and the general term "number." If L contains these forms, the following is an analytic statement in L:

(b) "Five is a number."

Further, to make the statement (a) possible, L must contain an expression like "designates" or "is a name of" for the semantical relation of designation. If suitable rules for this term are laid down, the following is likewise analytic:

(c) " 'Five' designates five."

(Generally speaking, any expression of the form " '. . .' designates . . ." is an analytic statement provided the term ". . ." is a constant in an accepted framework. If the latter condition is not fulfilled, the expression is not a statement.) Since (a) follows from (c) and (b), (a) is likewise analytic.

Thus it is clear that *if* someone accepts the framework of numbers, then he must acknowledge (c) and (b) and hence (a) as true statements. Generally speaking, if someone accepts a framework of entities, then he is bound to admit its entities as possible designata. Thus the question of the admissibility of entities of a certain type or of abstract entities in general as designata is reduced to the question of the acceptability of those entities. Both the nominalistic critics, who refuse the status of designators or names to expressions like "red," "five," etc., because they deny the existence of abstract entities, and the skeptics, who express doubts concerning the existence and demand evidence for it, treat the question of existence as a theoretical question. They do, of course, not mean the internal question; the affirmative answer to *this* question is analytic and trivial and too obvious for doubt or denial, as we have seen. Their doubts refer rather to the framework itself; hence they mean the external question. They believe that only after making sure that there really are entities of the kinds in question are we justified in accepting the framework by incorporating the linguistic forms into our language. However, we have seen that the external question is not a theoretical question but rather the practical question whether or not to accept those linguistic forms. This acceptance is not in need of a theoretical justification (except with respect to expediency and fruitfulness), because it does not imply a belief or assertion. Ryle says that the "Fido"-Fido principle is "a grotesque theory." Grotesque or not, Ryle is wrong in calling it a theory. It is rather the practical decision to accept certain frameworks. Maybe Ryle is historically right with respect to those whom he mentions as previous representatives of the principle, viz. John Stuart Mill, Frege, and Russell. If these philosophers regarded the acceptance of a framework of entities as a theory, an assertion, they were victims of the same old, metaphysical confusion. But it is certainly wrong to regard *my* semantical method as involving a belief in the reality of abstract entities, since I reject a thesis of this kind as a metaphysical pseudo-statement.

The critics of the use of abstract entities in semantics overlook the fundamental difference between the acceptance of a framework of entities and an internal assertion, e.g., an assertion that there are elephants or electrons or prime numbers greater than a million. Whoever makes an internal assertion is certainly obliged to justify it by providing evidence, empirical evidence in the case of electrons, logical proof in the case of the prime numbers. The demand for a theoretical justification, correct in the case of internal assertions, is sometimes wrongly applied to the acceptance of a framework of entities. Thus, for example, Ernest Nagel[10] asks for "evidence relevant for affirming with warrant that there are such entities as infinitesimals or propositions." He characterizes the evidence required in these cases—in distinction to the empirical evidence in the case of electrons—as "in the broad sense logical and dialectical." Beyond this no hint is given as to what might be regarded as relevant evidence. Some nominalists regard the acceptance of abstract entities as a kind of superstition or myth, populating the world with fictitious or at least dubious entities, analogous to the belief in centaurs or demons. This shows again the confusion mentioned, because a superstition or myth is a false (or dubious) internal statement.

Let us take as example the natural numbers as cardinal numbers, i.e., in contexts like "Here are three books." The linguistic forms of the framework of numbers, including variables and the general term "number" are generally used in our common language of communication; and it is easy to formulate explicit rules for their use. Thus the logical characteristics of this framework are sufficiently clear (while many internal questions, i.e., arithmetical questions, are, of course, still open). In spite of this, the controversy concerning the external question of the ontological reality of numbers continues. Suppose that one philosopher says: "I believe that there are numbers as real entities. This gives me the right to use the linguistic forms of the numerical framework and to make semantical statements about numbers as designata of numerals." His nominalistic opponent replies: "You are wrong; there are no numbers. The numerals may still be used as meaningful expressions. But they are not names, there are no entities designated by them. Therefore the word 'number' and numerical

10 E. NAGEL, Review of Carnap, *Meaning and Necessity* (*Journal of Philosophy,* 45 (1948), pp. 467–72).

variables must not be used (unless a way were found to introduce them as merely abbreviating devices, a way of translating them into the nominalistic thing language)." I cannot think of any possible evidence that would be regarded as relevant by both philosophers, and therefore, if actually found, would decide the controversy or at least make one of the opposite theses more probable than the other. (To construe the numbers as classes or properties of the second level, according to the Frege-Russell method does, of course, not solve the controversy, because the first philosopher would affirm and the second deny the existence of classes or properties of the second level.) Therefore I feel compelled to regard the external question as a pseudo-question, until both parties to the controversy offer a common interpretation of the question as a cognitive question; this would involve an indication of possible evidence regarded as relevant by both sides.

There is a particular kind of misinterpretation of the acceptance of abstract entities in various fields of science and in semantics, that needs to be cleared up. Certain early British empiricists (e.g., Berkeley and Hume) denied the existence of abstract entities on the ground that immediate experience presents us only with particulars, not with universals, e.g., with this red patch, but not with Redness or Color-in-General; with this scalene triangle, but not with Scalene Triangularity or Triangularity-in-General. Only entities belonging to a type of which examples were to be found within immediate experience could be accepted as ultimate constituents of reality. Thus, according to this way of thinking, the existence of abstract entities could be asserted only if one could show either that some abstract entities fall within the given, or that abstract entities can be defined in terms of the types of entity which are given. Since these empiricists found no abstract entities within the realm of sense-data, they either denied their existence, or else made a futile attempt to define universals in terms of particulars. Some contemporary philosophers, especially English philosophers following Bertrand Russell, think in basically similar terms. They emphasize a distinction between the data (that which is immediately given in consciousness, e.g. sense-data, immediately past experiences, etc.) and the constructs based on the data. Existence or reality is ascribed only to the data; the constructs are not real entities; the corresponding linguistic expressions are merely ways of speech not actually designating anything (reminiscent of the nominalists' *flatus vocis*). We shall not criticize here this general conception. (As far as it is a principle of accepting certain entities and not accepting others, leaving aside any ontological, phenomenalistic and nominalistic pseudo-statements, there cannot be any theoretical objection to it.) But if this conception leads to the view that other philosophers or scientists who accept abstract entities thereby assert or imply their occurrence as immediate data, then such a view must be rejected as a misinterpretation. References to space-time points, the electromagnetic field, or electrons in physics, to real or complex numbers and their functions in mathematics, to the excitatory potential or unconscious complexes in psychology, to an inflationary trend in economics, and the like, do not imply the assertion that entities of these kinds occur as immediate data. And the same holds for references to abstract entities as designata in semantics. Some of the criticisms by English philosophers against such references give the impression that, probably due to the misinterpretation just indicated, they accuse the semanticist not so much of bad metaphysics (as some nominalists would do) but of bad psychology. The fact that they regard a semantical method involving abstract entities not merely as doubtful and perhaps wrong, but as manifestly absurd, preposterous and grotesque, and that they show a deep horror and indignation against this method, is perhaps to be explained by a misinterpretation of the kind described. In fact, of course, the semanticist does not in the least assert or imply that the abstract entities to which he refers can be experienced as immediately given either by sensation or by a kind of rational intuition. An assertion of this kind would indeed be very dubious psychology. The psychological question as to which kinds of entities do and which do not occur as immediate data is entirely irrelevant for semantics, just as it is for physics, mathematics, economics, etc., with respect to the examples mentioned above.[11]

5. CONCLUSION

For those who want to develop or use semantical methods, the decisive question is not the alleged ontological question of the existence of abstract entities but rather the question whether the use of abstract linguistic forms or, in technical terms, the use of variables beyond those for things (or phenomenal data), is expedient and fruitful for the purposes for which semantical analyses are made, viz. the analysis, interpretation, clarification, or construction of languages of communication, especially languages of science. This question is here neither decided nor even discussed. It is not a question simply of yes or no, but a matter of degree. Among those philosophers who have carried out semantical analyses and thought about suitable tools

[11] Wilfrid Sellars (*Acquaintance and Description Again*, in *Journal of Philosophy*, 46 (1949), pp. 496–504, see pp. 502 f.) analyzes clearly the roots of the mistake "of taking the designation relation of semantic theory to be a reconstruction of *being present to an experience*."

for this work, beginning with Plato and Aristotle and, in a more technical way on the basis of modern logic, with C. S. Peirce and Frege, a great majority accepted abstract entities. This does, of course, not prove the case. After all, semantics in the technical sense is still in the initial phases of its development, and we must be prepared for possible fundamental changes in methods. Let us therefore admit that the nominalistic critics may possibly be right. But if so, they will have to offer better arguments than they did so far. Appeal to ontological insight will not carry much weight. The critics will have to show that it is possible to construct a semantical method which avoids all references to abstract entities and achieves by simpler means essentially the same results as the other methods.

The acceptance or rejection of abstract linguistic forms, just as the acceptance or rejection of any other linguistic forms in any branch of science, will finally be decided by their efficiency as instruments, the ratio of the results achieved to the amount and complexity of the efforts required. To decree dogmatic prohibitions of certain linguistic forms instead of testing them by their success or failure in practical use, is worse than futile; it is positively harmful because it may obstruct scientific progress. The history of science shows examples of such prohibitions based on prejudices deriving from religious, mythological, metaphysical, or other irrational sources, which slowed up the developments for shorter or longer periods of time. Let us learn from the lessons of history. Let us grant to those who work in any special field of investigation the freedom to use any form of expression which seems useful to them; the work in the field will sooner or later lead to the elimination of those forms which have no useful function. *Let us be cautious in making assertions and critical in examining them, but tolerant in permitting linguistic forms.*

BIBLIOGRAPHY *

CARNAP, Rudolf, *Philosophy and Logical Syntax*. London: Kegan Paul, 1935.
———, *The Logical Syntax of Language*. N.Y.: Harcourt, Brace, 1937.
———, *The Unity of Science*. London: Routledge & Kegan Paul, 1938.
———, *Introduction to Semantics*. Cambridge: Harvard U. Press, 1942.
———, *Meaning and Necessity: A Study in Semantics and Modal Logic*. Chicago: U. of Chicago Press, 1947. (2nd ed., enlarged, 1956.)
———, *The Foundations of Logic and Mathematics*. International Encyclopedia of Unified Science, I., 3. Chicago: U. of Chicago Press, 1939.

* This Bibliography contains only books by or about Carnap published in English.

————, *Logical Foundations of Probability*. Chicago: U. of Chicago Press, 1950. (2nd edition, 1962.)

————, *Formalization of Logic: Studies in Semantics*. (Vol. II). Cambridge: Harvard U. Press, 1943.

————, "Testability and Meaning," *Philosophy of Science*, 3 (1936), pp. 419–71; 4 (1937), pp. 1–40.

————, *The Continuum of Inductive Methods*. Chicago: U. of Chicago Press, 1952.

————, *Introduction to Symbolic Logic and its Applications*. N.Y.: Dover, 1958.

SCHILLP, Paul A., ed. *The Philosophy of Rudolf Carnap*. La Salle, Ill.: Open Court, 1963.

Charles Leslie Stevenson

[*1908–*]

Stevenson was born in Cincinnati, Ohio. He studied at Yale University as an undergraduate, later at Cambridge, England, and took his Ph.D. at Harvard in 1935. He has taught at Harvard and Yale, and since 1946 has been at the University of Michigan, where he is Professor of Philosophy. He has been a Guggenheim Fellow and is a former President of the Western Division of the American Philosophical Association (1962).

Stevenson is the author of essays in ethics, aesthetics, and linguistic philosophy. His best known publication is the book *Ethics and Language* (1944). Stevenson worked out in great detail an emotive theory similar to that espoused by Ayer, Carnap, and other logical positivists. His position in this book was more qualified than the most extreme form of the emotive theory, which had reduced all ethical sentences to expressive and imperative utterances, and he tried to deal with critical objections to the emotive theory.

Stevenson maintained that the task of ethics is that of metaethics, i.e., the analyses of ethical terms and of the ways we resolve ethical disagreements. Ethical terms and predicates, he maintained, had an "emotive meaning," a "dynamic" or "magnetic" quality. Hence philosophical attempts to define terms such as "good" fell victim to the naturalistic fallacy, as G. E. Moore had shown, but not for the reasons he believed. Naturalistic definitions will not work because the descriptive expressions which are supposed to define ethical terms lack the emotive meaning characteristic of the latter. Stevenson devoted much thought to the nature of ethical disagreement. He distinguished two kinds of disagreement: disagreements in *belief,* which in principle were resolvable by reference to facts, and disagreements in *attitude,* which he claimed were not strictly resolvable by factual or scientific methods. Ethical disagreement, according to Stevenson, is fundamentally of the latter kind. This argument was a direct challenge to naturalists and objectivists in ethics, and particularly to the view that ethical judgments were descriptive in nature and ethical disputes resolvable by factual inquiry. The following article, *The Nature of Ethical Disagreement* (1947–1948), is an excellent summary of Stevenson's views on the nature of ethical disagreements.

THE NATURE OF ETHICAL DISAGREEMENT [1]

When people disagree about the value of something—one saying that it is good or right, and another that it is bad or wrong—by what methods of argument or inquiry can their disagreement be resolved? Can it be resolved by the methods of science, or does it require methods of some other kind, or is it open to no rational solution at all?

The question must be clarified before it can be answered. And the word that is particularly in need of clarification, as we shall see, is the word "disagreement."

Let us begin by noting that "disagreement" has two broad senses: In the first sense it refers to what I shall call "disagreement in belief." This occurs when Mr. A believes p, when Mr. B believes $not-p$, or something incompatible with p, and when neither is content to let the belief of the other remain unchallenged. Thus doctors may disagree in belief about the causes of an illness; and friends may disagree in belief about the exact date on which they last met.

In the second sense, the word refers to what I shall call "disagreement in attitude." This occurs when Mr. A has a favorable attitude to something, when Mr. B has an unfavorable or less favorable attitude to it, and when neither is content to let the other's attitude remain unchanged. The term "attitude" is here used in much the same sense that R. B. Perry uses "interest"; it designates any psychological disposition of being *for* or *against* something. Hence love and hate are relatively specific kinds of attitudes, as are approval and disapproval, and so on.

This second sense can be illustrated in this way: Two men are planning to have dinner together. One is particularly anxious to eat at a certain restaurant, but the other doesn't like it. Temporarily, then, the men cannot "agree" on where to dine. Their argument may be trivial, and perhaps only half serious; but in any case it represents a disagreement *in attitude*. The men have divergent preferences, and each is trying to redirect the preference of the other.

Further examples are readily found. Mrs. Smith wishes to cultivate only the four hundred; Mr. Smith is loyal to his old poker-playing friends. They accordingly disagree, in attitude, about whom to invite to their party. The progressive mayor wants modern school-buildings and large parks; the older citizens are against these "new-fangled" ways; so they disagree on civic policy. These cases differ

[1] From C. L. Stevenson, "The Nature of Ethical Disagreement," *Sigma*, Vols. 1-2 Nos. 8-9 (1947-48).

from the one about the restaurant only in that the clash of attitudes is more serious, and may lead to more vigorous argument.

The difference between the two senses of "disagreement" is essentially this: the first involves an opposition of beliefs, both of which cannot be true, and the second involves an opposition of attitudes, both of which cannot be satisfied.

Let us apply this distinction to a case that will sharpen it. Mr. A believes that most voters will favor a proposed tax, and Mr. B disagrees with him. The disagreement concerns attitudes—those of the voters—but note that A and B are *not* disagreeing in attitude. Their disagreement is *in belief about* attitudes. It is simply a special kind of disagreement in belief, differing from disagreement in belief about head colds only with regard to subject matter. It implies not an opposition of the actual attitudes of the speakers, but only of their beliefs about certain attitudes. Disagreement in attitude, on the other hand, implies that the very attitudes of the speakers are opposed. A and B may have opposed beliefs about attitudes without having opposed attitudes, just as they may have opposed beliefs about head colds without having opposed head colds. Hence we must not, from the fact that an argument is concerned with attitudes, infer that it necessarily involves disagreement *in* attitude.

We may now turn more directly to disagreement about values, with particular reference to normative ethics. When people argue about what is good, do they disagree in belief, or do they disagree in attitude? A long tradition of ethical theorists strongly suggest, whether they always intend to or not, that the disagreement is one *in belief*. Naturalistic theorists, for instance, identify an ethical judgment with some sort of scientific statement, and so make normative ethics a branch of science. Now a scientific argument typically exemplifies disagreement in belief, and if an ethical argument is simply a scientific one, then it too exemplifies disagreement in belief. The usual naturalistic theories of ethics that stress attitudes—such as those of Hume, Westermarck, Perry, Richards, and so many others—stress disagreement in belief no less than the rest. They imply, of course, that disagreement about what is good is disagreement *in belief* about attitudes; but we have seen that that is simply one sort of disagreement in belief, and by no means the same as disagreement *in* attitude. Analyses that stress disagreement *in* attitude are extremely rare.

If ethical arguments, as we encounter them in everyday life, involved disagreement in belief exclusively—whether the beliefs were about attitudes or about something else—then I should have no quarrel with the ordinary sort of naturalistic analysis. Normative judgments could be taken as scientific statements, and amenable to the usual scientific proof. But a moment's attention will readily show that disagreement in belief has not the exclusive role that theory has so repeatedly ascribed to it. It must be readily granted that ethical arguments usually involve disagreement in belief; but they *also* involve disagreement in attitude. And the conspicuous role of disagreement in attitude is what we usually take, whether we realize it or not, as the distinguishing feature of ethical arguments. For example:

Suppose that the representative of a union urges that the wage level in a given company ought to be higher—that it is only right that the workers receive more pay. The company representative urges in reply that the workers ought to receive no more than they get. Such an argument clearly represents a disagreement in attitude. The union is *for* higher wages; the company is *against* them, and neither is content to let the other's attitude remain unchanged. *In addition* to this disagreement in attitude, of course, the argument may represent no little disagreement in belief. Perhaps the parties disagree about how much the cost of living has risen, and how much the workers are suffering under the present wage scale. Or perhaps they disagree about the company's earnings, and the extent to which the company could raise wages and still operate at a profit. Like any typical ethical argument, then, this argument involves both disagreement in attitude and disagreement in belief.

It is easy to see, however, that the disagreement in attitude plays a unifying and predominating rôle in the argument. This is so in two ways:

In the first place, disagreement in attitude determines what beliefs are *relevant* to the argument. Suppose that the company affirms that the wage scale of fifty years ago was far lower than it is now. The union will immediately urge that this contention, even though true, is irrelevant. And it is irrelevant simply because information about the wage level of fifty years ago, maintained under totally different circumstances, is not likely to affect the present attitudes of either party. To be relevant, any belief that is introduced into the argument must be one that is likely to lead one side or the other to have a different attitude, and so reconcile disagreement in attitude. Attitudes are often functions of beliefs. We often change our attitudes to something when we change our beliefs about it; just as a child ceases to *want* to touch a live coal when he comes to *believe* that it will burn him. Thus in the present argument, any beliefs that are at all likely to alter attitudes, such as those about the increasing cost of living or the financial state of the company, will be considered by both sides to be relevant to the argument. Agreement in belief on these matters may lead to agreement in attitude toward the wage scale.

But beliefs that are likely to alter the attitudes of neither side will be declared irrelevant. They will have no bearing on the disagreement in attitude, with which both parties are primarily concerned.

In the second place, ethical argument usually terminates when disagreement in attitude terminates, even though a certain amount of disagreement in belief remains. Suppose, for instance, that the company and the union continue to disagree in belief about the increasing cost of living, but that the company, even so, ends by favoring the higher wage scale. The union will then be content to end the argument, and will cease to press its point about living costs. It may bring up that point again, in some future argument of the same sort, or in urging the righteousness of its victory to the newspaper columnists; but for the moment the fact that the company has agreed in attitude is sufficient to terminate the argument. On the other hand: suppose that both parties agreed on all beliefs that were introduced into the argument, but even so continued to disagree in attitude. In that case neither party would feel that their dispute had been successfully terminated. They might look for other beliefs that could be introduced into the argument. They might use words to play on each other's emotions. They might agree (in attitude) to submit the case to arbitration, both feeling that a decision, even if strongly adverse to one party or the other, would be preferable to a continued impasse. Or, perhaps, they might abandon hope of settling their dispute by any peaceable means.

In many other cases, of course, men discuss ethical topics without having the strong, uncompromising attitudes that the present example has illustrated. They are often as much concerned with redirecting their own attitudes, in the light of greater knowledge, as with redirecting the attitudes of others. And the attitudes involved are often altruistic, rather than selfish. Yet the above example will serve, so long as that is understood, to suggest the nature of ethical disagreement. Both disagreement in attitude and disagreement in belief are involved, but the former predominates in that (1) it determines what sort of disagreement in belief is relevantly disputed in a given ethical argument, and (2) it determines, by its continued presence or its resolution, whether or not the argument has been settled. We may see further how intimately the two sorts of disagreement are related: since attitudes are often functions of beliefs, an agreement in belief may lead people, as a matter of psychological fact, to agree in attitude.

Having discussed disagreement, we may turn to the broad question that was first mentioned, namely: By what methods or argument or inquiry may disagreement about matters of value be resolved?

It will be obvious that to whatever extent an argument involves disagreement in belief, it is open to the usual methods of the sciences. If these methods are the *only* rational methods for supporting beliefs—as I believe to be so, but cannot now take time to discuss— then scientific methods are the only rational methods for resolving the disagreement in *belief* that arguments about values may include.

But if science is granted an undisputed sway in reconciling beliefs, it does not thereby acquire, without qualification, an undisputed sway in reconciling attitudes. We have seen that arguments about values include disagreement in attitude, no less than disagreement in belief, and that in certain ways the disagreement in attitude predominates. By what methods shall the latter sort of disagreement be resolved?

The methods of science are still available for that purpose, but only in an indirect way. Initially, these methods have only to do with establishing agreement in belief. If they serve further to establish agreement in attitude, that will be due simply to the psychological fact that altered beliefs may cause altered attitudes. Hence scientific methods are conclusive in ending arguments about values only to the extent that their success in obtaining agreement in belief will in turn lead to agreement in attitude.

In other words: the extent to which scientific methods can bring about agreement on values depends on the extent to which a commonly accepted body of scientific beliefs would cause us to have a commonly accepted set of attitudes.

How much is the development of science likely to achieve, then, with regard to values? To what extent *would* common beliefs lead to common attitudes? It is, perhaps, a pardonable enthusiasm to *hope* that science will do everything—to hope that in some rosy future, when all men know the consequences of their acts, they will all have common aspirations, and live peaceably in complete moral accord. But if we speak not from our enthusiastic hopes, but from our present knowledge, the answer must be far less exciting. We usually *do not know*, at the beginning of any argument about values, whether an agreement in belief, scientifically established, will lead to an agreement in attitude or not. It is logically possible, at least, that two men should continue to disagree in attitude even though they had all their beliefs in common, and even though neither had made any logical or inductive error, or omitted any relevant evidence. Differences in temperament, or in early training, or in social status, might make the men retain different attitudes even though both were possessed of the complete scientific truth. Whether this logical possibility is an empirical likelihood I shall not presume to say; but it is unquestionably a possibility that must not be left out of account.

To say that science can always settle arguments about value, we have seen, is to make this assumption: Agreement in attitude will always be consequent upon complete agreement in belief, and science can always bring about the latter. Taken as purely heuristic, this assumption has its usefulness. It leads people to discover the discrepancies in their beliefs, and to prolong enlightening argument that *may* lead, as a matter of fact, from commonly accepted beliefs to commonly accepted attitudes. It leads people to reconcile their attitudes in a rational, permanent way, rather than by rhapsody or exhortation. But the assumption is *nothing more*, for present knowledge, than a heuristic maxim. It is wholly without any proper foundation of probability. I conclude, therefore, that scientific methods cannot be guaranteed the definite rôle in the so-called "normative sciences" that they may have in the natural sciences. Apart from a heuristic assumption to the contrary, it is possible that the growth of scientific knowledge may leave many disputes about values permanently unsolved. Should these disputes persist, there are non-rational methods for dealing with them, of course, such as impassioned, moving oratory. But the purely intellectual methods of science, and, indeed, *all* methods of reasoning, may be insufficient to settle disputes about values, even though they may greatly help to do so.

For the same reasons, I conclude that normative ethics is not a branch of any science. It deliberately deals with a type of disagreement that science deliberately avoids. Ethics is not psychology, for instance; for although psychologists may, of course, agree or disagree in belief about attitudes, they need not, as psychologists, be concerned with whether they agree or disagree with one another *in* attitude. Insofar as normative ethics draws from the sciences, in order to change attitudes *via* changing people's beliefs, it *draws* from *all* the sciences; but a moralist's peculiar aim—that of *redirecting* attitudes—is a type of activity, rather than knowledge, and falls within no science. Science may study that activity, and may help indirectly to forward it; but it is not *identical* with that activity.

I have only a moment to explain why the ethical terms, such as "good," "wrong," "ought," and so on, are so habitually used to deal with disagreement in attitude. On account of their repeated occurrence in emotional situations they have acquired a strong emotive meaning. This emotive meaning makes them serviceable in initiating changes in a hearer's attitudes. Sheer emotive impact is not likely, under many circumstances, to change attitudes in any permanent way; but it *begins* a process that can then be supported by other means.

There is no occasion for saying that the meaning of ethical terms is *purely* emotive, like that of "alas" or "hurrah." We have seen that ethical *arguments* include many expressions of *belief*; and the rough rules of ordinary language permit us to say that some of these beliefs are expressed by an ethical judgment itself. But the beliefs so expressed are by no means always the same. Ethical terms are notable for their ambiguity, and opponents in an argument may use them in different senses. Sometimes this leads to artificial issues; but it usually does not. So long as one person says "This is good" with emotive praise, and another says "No, it is bad," with emotive condemnation, a disagreement in attitude is manifest. Whether or not the beliefs that these statements express are logically incompatible may not be discovered until later in the argument; but even if they are actually compatible, disagreement in attitude will be preserved by emotive meaning; and this disagreement, so central to ethics, may lead to an argument that is certainly not artificial in its issues, so long as it is taken for what it is.

The many theorists who have refused to identify ethical statements with scientific ones have much to be said in their favor. They have seen that ethical judgments mold or alter attitudes, rather than describe them, and they have seen that ethical judgments can be guaranteed no definitive scientific support. But one need not, on that account, provide ethics with any extramundane, sui generis *subject matter*. The distinguishing features of an ethical judgment can be preserved by a recognition of emotive meaning and disagreement in attitude, rather than by some non-natural quality—and with far greater intelligibility. If an unique subject matter is *postulated*, as it usually is, to preserve the important distinction between normative ethics and science, it serves no purpose that is not served by the very simple analysis I have here suggested. Unless non-natural qualities can be defended by positive arguments, rather than as an "only resort" from the acknowledged weakness of ordinary forms of naturalism, they would seem nothing more than the invisible shadows cast by emotive meaning.

BIBLIOGRAPHY

STEVENSON, Charles L., *Ethics and Language.* New Haven: Yale U. Press, 1944.

——, *Facts and Values: Studies in Ethical Analysis.* New Haven: Yale U. Press, 1963.

——, "The Emotive Meaning of Ethical Terms," *Mind*, Vol. 46, 1937.

——, "Persuasive Definitions," *Mind*, Vol. 47, 1938.

———, "Ethical Judgments and Avoidability," *Mind*, Vol. 47, 1938.

———, "Moore's Arguments against Certain Forms of Ethical Naturalism," Essay 2 in Schilpp (ed.), *The Philosophy of G.E. Moore*, Evanston, Northwestern University Press, 1944.

———, "Relativism and Non-Relativism in the Theory of Value," in *Proceedings and Addresses of the American Philosophical Association*, Vol. XXXV, Yellow Springs, Ohio: The Antioch Press, October 1962.

Willard Van Orman Quine

[1908–   ]

Quine is one of the foremost of living logicians, combining the acumen of a symbolic logician with a general pragmatic outlook similar to that of C. I. Lewis, one of his predecessors at Harvard. Born in Akron, Ohio, he took his B.A. at Oberlin College (1930), M.A. (1931) and Ph.D. at Harvard (1932). Quine received a Sheldon Traveling Fellowship (1932–33), studied in Europe, and took an M.A. at Oxford. He has been teaching at Harvard since 1936, where he has been Edgar Pierce Professor of Philosophy since 1955. He was a Visiting Professor at the University of São Paulo, Brazil, and he has lectured at Oxford, the University of Tokyo, and the University of Adelaide, Australia. He was a Member of the Institute for Advanced Study, Princeton (1956–57), and a Fellow of the Center for Advanced Study in the Behavioral Sciences (1958–59). He is a former President of the Association for Symbolic Logic (1953–56) and of the American Philosophical Association, Eastern Division (1957).

In his collection of essays, *From a Logical Point of View* (1953), and especially in his two essays, "Two Dogmas of Empiricism" and "Truth by Convention," Quine asks for a revaluation of positivism, especially its distinctions between analytic and synthetic statements and between formal and empirical science. Specifically, his argument is based on the difficulties of establishing definite rules for analyticity (or synonymity). Broadly speaking, Quine's approach is pragmatic. All knowledge is a tool for coping with experience, and if there is a conflict with experience we change anything within the total body of knowledge, scientific, logical and mathematical, so as to restore the congruence. Logic is man-made; it has an instrumental role, and can be recast as scientific purposes require.

Quine (like Nelson Goodman, and unlike Carnap and other orthodox positivists) has dealt with questions of ontology, in particular with the question of how far one's choice of a language commits one to saying that certain things exist. He believes that such questions cannot be avoided by philosophers. Quine, as far as possible, wishes to be economical in the kind of "entities" that he will allow. And the question of what there is, he thinks, must also be settled on pragmatic grounds. He once suggested that the ontology to which we are committed by the language which we use is that "to be is to be the value of a variable."

In the article, *Speaking of Objects* (1957), reprinted below, Quine deals again with the question of abstract entities, attributes, classes, propositions, etc. He ends his genetic analysis by examining the possibility of the existence of "half entities." Quine's book *Word and Object*

(1960) continues the genetic inquiry into words. Interestingly, his general definition of meaning appears to be behavioristic: "The stimulus meaning of a sentence for a subject sums up his disposition to assent to or dissent from the sentence in response to present stimulation." (p. 34) Again he is concerned with questions of ontological commitment, which language uses entail.

SPEAKING OF OBJECTS [1]

I

We are prone to talk and think of objects. Physical objects are the obvious illustration when the illustrative mood is on us, but there are also all the abstract objects, or so there purport to be: the states and qualities, numbers, attributes, classes. We persist in breaking reality down somehow into a multiplicity of identifiable and discriminable objects, to be referred to by singular and general terms. We talk so inveterately of objects that to say we do so seems almost to say nothing at all; for how else is there to talk?

It is hard to say how else there is to talk, not because our objectifying pattern is an invariable trait of human nature, but because we are bound to adapt any alien pattern to our own in the very process of understanding or translating the alien sentences.

Imagine a newly discovered tribe whose language is without known affinities. The linguist has to learn the language directly by observing what the natives say under observed circumstances, encountered or contrived. He makes a first crude beginning by compiling native terms for environing objects; but here already he is really imposing his own patterns. Let me explain what I mean. I will grant that the linguist may establish inductively, beyond reasonable doubt, that a certain heathen expression is one to which natives can be prompted to assent by the presence of a rabbit, or reasonable *facsimile*, and not otherwise. The linguist is then warranted in according the native expression the cautious translation "There's a rabbit," "There we have a rabbit," "Lo! a rabbit," "Lo! rabbithood again," insofar as the differences among these English sentences are counted irrelevant. This much translation can be objective, however exotic the tribe. It rec-

---

[1] Presidential address delivered before the Fifty-fourth Annual Meeting of the Eastern Division of the American Philosophical Association at Harvard University, Cambridge, Massachusetts, Dec. 1957. From *Proceedings and Addresses*, Vol. XXXI. Yellow Springs, Ohio: The Antioch Press, 1957–58, pp. 5–22.

ognizes the native expression as in effect a rabbit-heralding sentence. But the linguist's bold further step, in which he imposes his own object-positing pattern without special warrant, is taken when he equates the native expression or any part of it with the *term* "rabbit."
It is easy to show that such appeal to an object category is unwarranted even though we cannot easily, in English, herald rabbits without objectification. For we can argue from indifference. Given that a native sentence says that a so-and-so is present, and given that the sentence is true when and only when a rabbit is present, it by no means follows that the so-and-so are rabbits. They might be all the various temporal segments of rabbits. They might be all the integral or undetached parts of rabbits. In order to decide among these alternatives we need to be able to ask more than whether a so-and-so is present. We need to be able to ask whether this is the same so-and-so as that, and whether one so-and-so is present or two. We need something like the apparatus of identity and quantification; hence far more than we are in a position to avail ourselves of in a language in which our high point as of even date is rabbit-announcing.
And the case is yet worse: we do not even have evidence for taking the native expression as of the form "A so-and-so is present"; it could as well be construed with an abstract singular term, as meaning that rabbithood is locally manifested. Better just "Rabbiteth," like "Raineth."
But if our linguist is going to be as cagey as all this, he will never translate more than these simple-minded announcements of observable current events. A cagey linguist is a caged linguist. What we want from the linguist as a serviceable finished product, after all, is no mere list of sentence-to-sentence equivalences, like the airline throwaways of useful Spanish phrases. We want a manual of instructions for custom-building a native sentence to roughly the purpose of any newly composed English sentence, within reason, and vice versa. The linguist has to resolve the potential infinity of native sentences into a manageably limited list of grammatical constructions and constituent linguistic forms, and then show how the business of each can be approximated in English; and vice versa. Sometimes perhaps he will translate a word or construction not directly but contextually, by systematic instructions for translating its containing sentences; but still he must make do with a limited lot of contextual definitions. Now once he has carried out this necessary job of lexicography, forwards and backwards, he has read our ontological point of view into the native language. He has decided what expressions to treat as referring to objects, and, within limits, what sorts of objects to treat them as referring to. He has had to decide, however arbi-

trarily, how to accommodate English idioms of identity and quantification in native translation.

The word "arbitrary" needs stressing, not because those decisions are wholly arbitrary, but because they are so much more so than one tends to suppose. For, what evidence does the linguist have? He started with what we may call native observation sentences, such as the rabbit announcement. These he can say how to translate into English, provided we impute no relevance to the differences between "Here a rabbit," "Here rabbithood," and the like. Also he can record further native sentences and settle whether various persons are prepared to affirm or deny them, though he find no rabbit movements or other currently observable events to tie them to. Among these untranslated sentences he may get an occasional hint of logical connections, by finding say that just the persons who are prepared to affirm A are prepared to affirm B and deny C. Thereafter his data leave off and his creativity sets in.

What he does in his creativity is attribute special and distinctive functions to component words, or conspicuously recurrent fragments, of the recorded sentences. The only ways one can appraise their attributions are as follows. One can see whether they add up to representing the rabbit sentence and the like as conforming to their previously detected truth conditions. One can see also how well they fit the available data on other sentences: sentences for which no truth conditions are known, but only the varying readiness of natives to affirm or deny them. Beyond this we can judge the attributions only on their simplicity and naturalness—to us.

Certainly the linguist will try out his theory on the natives, springing new sentences authorized by his theory, to see if they turn out right. This is a permuting of the time order: one frames the theory before all possible data are in, and then lets it guide one in the eliciting of additional data likeliest to matter. This is good scientific method, but it opens up no new kind of data. English general and singular terms, identity, quantification, and the whole bag of ontological tricks may be correlated with elements of the native language in any of various mutually incompatible ways, each compatible with all possible linguistic data, and none preferable to another save as favored by a rationalization of the native language that is simple and natural to us.

It makes no real difference that the linguist will turn bilingual and come to think as the natives do—whatever that means. For the arbitrariness of reading our objectifications into the heathen speech reflects not so much the inscrutability of the heathen mind, as that there is nothing to scrute. Even we who grew up together and learned English at the same knee, or adjacent ones, talk alike for no other reason than that society coached us alike in a pattern of verbal response to externally observable cues. We have been beaten into an outward conformity to an outward standard; and thus it is that when I correlate your sentences with mine by the simple rule of phonetic correspondence, I find that the public circumstances of your affirmations and denials agree pretty well with those of my own. If I conclude that you share my sort of conceptual scheme, I am not adding a supplementary conjecture so much as spurning unfathomable distinctions; for, what further criterion of sameness of conceptual scheme can be imagined? The case of a Frenchman, moreover, is the same except that I correlate his sentences with mine not by phonetic correspondence but according to a traditionally evolved dictionary.[2] The case of the linguist and his newly discovered heathen, finally, differs simply in that the linguist has to grope for a general sentence-to-sentence correlation that will make the public circumstances of the heathen's affirmations and denials match up tolerably with the circumstances of the linguist's own. If the linguist fails in this, or has a hard time of it, or succeeds only by dint of an ugly and complex mass of correlations, then he is entitled to say—in the only sense in which one *can* say it—that his heathens have a very different attitude toward reality from ours; and even so he cannot coherently suggest what their attitude is. Nor, in principle, is the natural bilingual any better off.

When we compare theories, doctrines, points of view, cultures, on the score of what sorts of objects there are said to be, we are comparing them in a respect which itself makes sense only provincially. It makes sense only as far afield as our efforts to translate our domestic idioms of identity and quantification bring encouragement in the way of simple and natural-looking correspondences. If we attend to business we are unlikely to find a very alien culture with a predilection for a very outlandish universe of discourse, just because the outlandishness of it would detract from our sense of patness of our dictionary of translation. There is a notion that our provincial ways of positing objects and conceiving nature may be best appreciated for what they are by standing off and seeing them against a cosmopolitan background of alien cultures; but the notion comes to nothing, for there is no ποῦ στῶ.[3]

[2] See Richard von Mises, *Positivism*, Cambridge: Harvard, 1951, pp. 46 ff.

[3] For a fuller development of the foregoing theme see my "Meaning and Translation" in Reuben Brower's anthology *On Translation*. For criticisms that have benefitted the above section of the present essay and ensuing portions I am grateful to Burton Dreben.

II

Yet, for all the difficulty of transcending our object-directed pattern of thought, we can examine it well enough from inside. Let us turn our attention from the heathen, who seemed to have a term for "rabbit," to our own child at home who seems to have just acquired his first few terms in our own language: "mama," "water," perhaps "red." To begin with, the case of the child resembles that of the heathen. For though we may fully satisfy ourselves that the child has learned the trick of using the utterances "mama" and "water" strictly in the appropriate presences, or as means of inducing the appropriate presences, still we have no right to construe these utterances in the child's mouth as terms, at first, for things or substances.

We in our maturity have come to look upon the child's mother as an integral body who, in an irregular closed orbit, revisits the child from time to time; and to look upon red in a radically different way, viz., as scattered about. Water, for us, is rather like red, but not quite; things can be red, but only stuff is water. But the mother, red, and water are for the infant all of a type: each is just a history of sporadic encounter, a scattered portion of what goes on. His first learning of the three words is uniformly a matter of learning how much of what goes on about him counts as the mother, or as red, or as water. It is not for the child to say in the first case "Hello! mama again," in the second case "Hello! another red thing," and in the third case "Hello! more water." They are all on a par: Hello! more mama, more red, more water. Even this last formula, which treats all three terms on the model of our provincial adult bulk term "water," is imperfect; for it unwarrantedly imputes an objectification of matter, even if only as stuff and not as bits.

Progressively, however, the child is seen to evolve a pattern of verbal behavior that finally comes to copy ours too closely for there to be any sense in questioning the general sameness of conceptual scheme. For perspective on our own objectifying apparatus we may consider what steps of development make the difference between the "mama"-babbling infant who cannot be said to be using terms for objects, and the older child who can.

It is only when the child has got on to the full and proper use of *individuative* terms like "apple" that he can properly be said to have taken to using terms as terms, and speaking of objects. Words like "apple," and not words like "mama" or "water" or "red," are the terms whose ontological involvement runs deep. To learn "apple" it is not sufficient to learn how much of what goes on counts as apple; we must learn how much counts as *an* apple, and how much as another. Such terms possess built-in modes of individuation.

Individuative terms are commonly made to double as bulk terms. Thus we may say "There is some apple in the salad," not meaning "some apple or other"; just as we may say "Mary had a little lamb" in either of two senses. Now we have appreciated that the child can learn the terms "mama," "red," and "water" quite well before he ever has mastered the ins and outs of our adult conceptual scheme of mobile enduring physical objects, identical from time to time and place to place; and in principle he might do the same for "apple," as a bulk term for uncut apple stuff. But he can never fully master "apple" in its individuative use, except as he gets on with the scheme of enduring and recurrent physical objects. He may come somewhat to grips with the individuative use of "apple" before quite mastering the comprehensive physical outlook, but his usage will be marred by misidentifications of distinct apples over time, or misdiscriminations of identical ones.

He has really got on to the individuative use, one is tempted to suppose, once he responds with the plural "apples" to a heap of apples. But not so. He may at that point have learned "apples" as another bulk term, applicable to just so much apple as is taken up in apple heaps. "Apples," for him, would be subordinated to "apple" as is "warm water" to "water," and "bright red" to "red."

The child might proceed to acquire "block" and "blocks," "ball" and "balls," as bulk terms in the same fashion. By the force of analogy among such pairs he might even come to apply the plural "-s" with seeming appropriateness to new words, and to drop it with seeming appropriateness from words first learned only with it. We might well not detect, for a while, his misconception: that "-s" just turns bulk terms into more specialized bulk terms connoting clumpiness.

A plausible variant misconception is this: "apple" bulkwise might cover just the apple stuff that is spaced off in lone apples, while "apples" still figures as last suggested. Then apples and apple would be mutually exclusive rather than subordinate the one to the other. This variant misconception could likewise be projected systematically to "block" and "blocks," "ball" and "balls," and long escape exposure.

How can we ever tell, then, whether the child has really got the trick of individuation? Only by engaging him in sophisticated discourse of "that apple," "not that apple," "an apple," "same apple," "another apple," "these apples." It is only at this level that a palpable difference emerges between genuinely individuative use and counterfeits lately imagined.

Doubtless the child gets the swing of these peculiar adjectives "same," "another," "an," "that," "not that," contextually: first he becomes attuned to various longer phrases or sentences that contain them, and then gradually he develops appropriate habits in relation to the component words as common parts and residues of those longer forms. His tentative acquisition of the plural "-s" lately speculated on, is itself a first primitive step of the kind. The contextual learning of these various particles goes on simultaneously, we may suppose, so that they are gradually adjusted to one another and a coherent pattern of usage is evolved matching that of one's elders. This is a major step in acquiring the conceptual scheme that we all know so well. For it is on achieving this step, and only then, that there can be any general talk of objects as such. Only at this stage does it begin to make sense to wonder whether the apple now in one's hand is the apple noticed yesterday.

Until individuation emerges, the child can scarcely be said to have general *or* singular terms, there being no express talk of objects. The pre-individuative term "mama," and likewise "water" and "red" (for children who happen to learn "water" and "red" before mastering individuation), hark back to a primitive phase to which the distinction between singular and general is irrelevant. Once the child has pulled through the individuative crisis, though, he is prepared to reassess prior terms. "Mama," in particular, gets set up retroactively as the name of a broad and recurrent but withal individual object, and thus as a singular term *par excellence*. Occasions eliciting "mama" being just as discontinuous as those eliciting "water," the two terms had been on a par; but with the advent of individuation the mother becomes integrated into a cohesive spatiotemporal convexity, while water remains scattered even in space-time. The two terms thus part company.

The mastery of individuation seems scarcely to affect people's attitude toward "water." For "water," "sugar," and the like the category of bulk terms remains, a survival of the pre-individuative phase, ill fitting the dichotomy into general and singular. But the philosophical mind sees its way to pressing this archaic category into the dichotomy. The bulk term "water" after the copula can usually be smoothly reconstrued as a general term true of each portion of water, while in other positions it is usually more simply construed as a singular term naming that spatio-temporally diffuse object which is the totality of the world's water.

III

I have urged that we could know the necessary and sufficient stimulatory conditions of every possible act of utterance, in a foreign language, and still not know how to determine what objects the speakers of that language believe in. Now if objective reference is so inaccessible to observation, who is to say on empirical grounds that belief in objects of one or another description is right or wrong? How can there ever be empirical evidence against existential statements? The answer is something like this. Grant that a knowledge of the appropriate stimulatory conditions of a sentence does not settle how to construe the sentence in terms of existence of objects. Still, it does tend to settle what is to count as empirical evidence for or against the truth of the sentence. If we then go on to assign the sentence some import in point of existence of objects, by arbitrary projection in the case of the heathen language or as a matter of course in the case of our own, thereupon what has already been counting as empirical evidence for or against the truth of the sentence comes to count as empirical evidence for or against the existence of the objects.

The opportunity for error in existential statements increases with one's mastery of the verbal apparatus of objective reference. In one's earliest phase of word-learning, terms like "mama" and "water" were learned which may be viewed retrospectively as names each of an observed spatiotemporal object. Each such term was learned by a process of reinforcement and extinction, whereby the spatiotemporal range of application of the term was gradually perfected. The object named is assuredly an observed one, in the sense that the reinforced stimuli proceeded pretty directly from it. Granted, this talk of name and object belongs to a later phase of language learning, even as does the talk of stimulation.

The second phase, marked by the advent of individuative terms, is where a proper notion of object emerges. Here we get general terms, each true of each of many objects. But the objects still are observable spatiotemporal objects. For these individuative terms, e.g. "apple," are learned still by the old method of reinforcement and extinction; they differ from their predecessors only in the added feature of internal individuation.

Demonstrative singular terms like "this apple" usher in a third phase, characterized by the fact that a singular term seriously used can now, through error, fail to name: the thing pointed to can turn out to be the mere facade of an apple, or maybe a tomato. But even at this stage anything that we do succeed in naming is still an observable spatiotemporal object.

A fourth phase comes with the joining of one general term to another in attributive position. Now for the first time we can get general terms which are not true of anything; thus "blue apple," "square ball." But when there are things at all of which the thus formed general terms are true, they are still nothing new; they are just some among the same old observables whereof the component terms are true.

It is a fifth phase that brings a new mode of understanding, giving access to new sorts of objects. When we form compounds by applying relative terms to singular terms, we get such compounds as "smaller than that speck." Whereas the non-existence of observable blue apples is tantamount to the non-existence of blue apples, the non-existence of observable objects smaller than that speck is not taken as tantamount to the non-existence of objects smaller than that speck. The notable feature of this fifth phase is not that it enables us to form meaningful singular terms devoid of reference, for that was already achieved on occasion with "this apple"; nor that it enables us to form meaningful general terms true of nothing, for that was already achieved with "blue apple"; but that it enables us, for the first time, to form terms whose references can be admitted to be forever unobservable without yet being repudiated, like blue apples, as non-existent.

Such applying of relative terms to singular terms is the simplest method of forming terms that purport to name unobservables, but there are also more flexible devices to much the same effect: the relative clause and description.

And there comes yet a sixth phase, when we break through to posits more drastically new still than the objects smaller than the smallest visible speck. For the objects smaller than the speck differ from observable objects only in a matter of degree, whereas the sixth phase ushers in abstract entities. This phase is marked by the advent of abstract singular terms like "redness," "roundness," "mankind," purported names of qualities, attributes, classes. Let us speculate on the mechanism of this new move.

One wedge is the bulk term. Such terms can be learned at the very first phase, we saw, on a par with "mama." We saw them diverge from "mama" at the second phase, simply on the score that the woman comes then to be appreciated as an integrated spatiotemporal thing while the world's water or red stuff ordinarily does not. For the child, thus, who is not on to the sophisticated idea of the scattered single object, the bulk term already has an air of generality about it, comparable to the individuative "apple"; and still it is much like the singular "mama" in form and function, having even been learned or learnable at the first phase on a par with "mama." So the bulk term already has rather the hybrid air of the abstract singular term. "Water" might, from the very advent of individuation, even be said to name a shared *attribute* of the sundry puddles and glassfuls rather than a scattered portion of the world *composed* of those puddles and glassfuls; for the child of course adopts neither position.

Moreover, there is a tricky point about color words that especially encourages the transition to abstract reference. "Red" can be learned as a bulk term, like "water," but in particular it applies to apples whose insides are white. Before mastering the conceptual scheme of individuation and enduring physical object, the child sees the uncut red apple, like tomato juice, simply as so much red exposure in the passing show, and, having no sense of physical identity, he sees the subsequently exposed white interior of the apple as irrelevant. When eventually he does master the conceptual scheme of individuation and enduring physical object, then, he has to come to terms with a pre-acquired use of "red" that has suddenly gone double: there is red stuff (tomato juice) and there are red things (apples) that are mostly white stuff. "Red" both remains a bulk term of the ancient vintage of "water" and "mama," and becomes a concrete general term like "round" or "apple." Since the child will still not clearly conceive of "red" as suddenly two words, we have him somehow infusing singularity into the concrete general; and such is the recipe, however unappetizing, for the abstract singular. The analogy then spreads to other general terms, that were in no such special predicament as "red," until they all deliver abstract singulars.

Another force for abstract terms, or for the positing of abstract objects, lies in abbreviated cross-reference. E.g., after an elaborate remark regarding President Eisenhower, someone says: "The same holds for Churchill." Or, by way of supporting some botanical identification, one says: "Both plants have the following attribute in common"—and proceeds with a double-purpose description. In such cases a laborious repetition is conveniently circumvented. Now the cross-reference in such cases is just to a form of words. But we have a stubborn tendency to reify the unrepeated matter by positing an attribute, instead of just talking of words.

There is indeed an archaic precedent for confusing sign and object; the earliest conditioning of the infant's babbling is ambiguous on the point. For suppose a baby is rewarded for happening to babble something like "mama" or "water" just as the mother or water is looming. The stimuli which are thus reinforced are bound to be two: there is not only the looming of the object, there is equally the word itself, heard by the child from his own lips. Confusion of sign and object is original sin, coeval with the word.

We have seen how the child might slip into the community's ontology of attributes by easy stages, from bulk terms onward. We have also seen how talk of attributes will continue to be encouraged, in the child and the community, by a certain convenience of cross-reference coupled with a confusion of sign and object. We have in these reflections some materials for speculation regarding the early beginnings of an ontology of attributes in the childhood of the race. There is room, as well, for alternative or supplementary conjectures; e.g., that the attributes are vestiges of the minor deities of some creed outworn.[4] In a general way such speculation is epistemologically relevant, as suggesting how organisms maturing and evolving in the physical environment we know might conceivably end up discoursing of abstract objects as we do. But the disreputability of origins is of itself no argument against preserving and prizing the abstract ontology. This conceptual scheme may well be, however accidental, a happy accident; just as the theory of electrons would be none the worse for having first occurred to its originator in the course of some absurd dream. At any rate the ontology of abstract objects is part of the ship which, in Neurath's figure, we are rebuilding at sea.[5] We may revise the scheme, but only in favor of some clearer or simpler and no less adequate over-all account of what goes on in the world.

IV

By finding out roughly which non-verbal stimulations tend to prompt assent to a given existential statement, we settle, to some degree, what is to count as empirical evidence for or against the existence of the objects in question. This I urged at the beginning of III. Statements, however, existential and otherwise, vary in the directness with which they are conditioned to non-verbal stimulation. Commonly a stimulation will trigger our verdict on a statement only because the statement is a strand in the verbal network of some elaborate theory, other strands of which are more directly conditioned to that stimulation. Most of our statements respond thus to reverberations across the fabric of intralinguistic associations, even when also directly conditioned to extralinguistic stimuli to some degree. Highly theoretical statements are statements whose connection with extralinguistic stimulation consists pretty exclusively in the reverberations across the fabric. Statements of the existence of various sorts of subvisible particles tend to be theoretical, in this sense; and, even more so, statements of the existence of certain abstract objects. Commonly such statements are scarcely to be judged otherwise than by coherence, or by considerations of over-all simplicity of a theory whose ultimate contacts with experience are remote as can be from the statements in question. Yet, remarkably enough, there are abstract existence statements that do succumb to such considerations. We have had the wit to posit an ontology massive enough to crumble of its own weight.

For there are the paradoxes of classes. These paradoxes are usually stated for classes because classes are a relatively simple kind of ab-

---

[4] Thus Ernst Cassirer, *Language and Myth*, pp. 95 ff.
[5] Otto Neurath, "Protokollsätze," *Erkenntnis*, vol. 3 (1932), p. 206.

stract object to talk about, and also because classes, being more innocent on the face of them than attributes, are more fun to discredit. In any event, as is both well known and obvious, the paradoxes of classes go through *pari passu* for attributes, and again for relations.

The moral to draw from the paradoxes is not necessarily nominalism, but certainly that we must tighten our ontological belts a few holes. The law of attributes that was implicit in our language habits or that fitted in with them most easily was that *every* statement that mentions a thing attributes an attribute to it; and this cultural heritage, however venerable, must go. Some judicious *ad hoc* excisions are required at least.

Systematic considerations can press not only for repudiating certain objects, and so declaring certain *terms* irreferential; they can also press for declaring certain *occurrences* of terms irreferential, while other occurrences continue to refer. This point is essentially Frege's,[6] and an example is provided by the sentence "Tom believes that Tully wrote the *Ars Magna*." If we assert this on the strength of Tom's confusion of Tully with Lully, and in full appreciation of Tom's appreciation that Cicero did not write the *Ars Magna*, then we are not giving the term "Tully" purely referential occurrence in our sentence "Tom believes that Tully wrote the *Ars Magna*"; our sentence is not squarely about Tully. If it were, it would have to be true of Cicero, who *is* Tully.

It was only after somehow deciding what heathen locutions to construe as identity and the like that our linguist could begin to say which heathen words serve as terms and what objects they refer to. It was only after getting the knack of identity and kindred devices that our own child could reasonably be said to be talking in terms and to be talking of objects. And it is to the demands of identity still, specifically the substitutivity of identity, that the adult speaker of our language remains answerable as long as he may be said to be using terms to refer.

We are free so to use the verb "believes" as to allow ensuing terms full referential status after all. To do so is to deny "Tom believes that Tully wrote the *Ars Magna*" in the light of Tom's knowledge of Cicero and despite his confusion of names. The fact is that we can and do use "believes" both ways: one way when we say that Tom believes that Tully wrote the *Ars Magna*, and the other way when we deny this, or when, resorting to quantification, we say just that there is *someone* whom Tom believes to have done thus and so. Parallel

[6] See Frege, "On sense and reference," translated in *Philosophical Writings of Gottlob Frege* (Geach and Black, eds.), Oxford: Blackwell, 1952, and in *Readings in Philosophical Analysis* (Feigl and Sellars, eds.), New York: Appleton, 1949. See also my *From a Logical Point of View*, Cambridge: Harvard, 1953, Essay 8.

remarks are suited also to others of the *propositional attitudes*, as Russell calls them: thus doubting, wishing, striving, along with believing.

Man in a state of nature is not aware of the doubleness of these usages of his, nor of the strings attached to each; just as he is not aware of the paradoxical consequences of a naïve ontology of classes or attributes. Now yet another ontological weakness that we are likewise unaware of until, philosophically minded, we start looking to coherence considerations, has to do with the individuation of attributes.

The positing of attributes is accompanied by no clue as to the circumstances under which attributes may be said to be the same or different. This is perverse, considering that the very use of terms and the very positing of objects are unrecognizable to begin with except as keyed in with idioms of sameness and difference. What happens is that at first we learn general patterns of term-talk and thing-talk with help of the necessary adjuncts of identity; afterward we project these well-learned grammaticial forms to attributes, without settling identity for them. We understand the forms as referential just because they are grammatically analogous to ones that we learned earlier, for physical objects, with full dependence on the identity aspect.

The lack of a proper identity concept for attributes is a lack that philosophers feel impelled to supply; for, what sense is there in saying that there are attributes when there is no sense in saying when there is one attribute and when two? Carnap and others have proposed this principle for identifying attributes: two sentences about x attribute the *same* attribute to x if and only if the two sentences are not merely alike in truth value for each choice of x, but necessarily and analytically so, by sameness of meaning.[7]

However, this formulation depends on a questionable notion, that of sameness of meaning. For let us not slip back into the fantasy of a gallery of ideas and labels. Let us remember rather our field lexicographer's predicament: how arbitrary his projection of analogies from known languages. Can an empiricist speak seriously of sameness of meaning of two conditions upon an object x, one stated in the heathen language and one in ours, when even the singling out of an object x as object at all for the heathen language is so hopelessly arbitrary?

We could skip the heathen language and try talking of sameness of meaning just within our own language. This would degrade the ontology of attributes; identity of attributes would be predicated on frankly provincial traits of English usage, ill fitting the objectivity of true objects. Nor let it be said in extenuation that all talk of objects,

[7] Rudolf Carnap, *Meaning and Necessity*, Chicago, 1947, p. 23.

physical ones included, is in a way provincial too; for the way is differ-ent. Our physics is provincial only in that there is no universal basis for translating it into remote languages; it would still never condone defining physical identity in terms of verbal behavior. If we rest the identity of attributes on an admittedly local relation of English syn-onymy, then we count attributes secondary to language in a way that physical objects are not.

Shall we just let attributes be thus secondary to language in a way that physical objects are not? But our troubles do not end here; for the fact is that I see no hope of making reasonable sense of sameness of meaning even for English. The difficulty is one that I have enlarged on elsewhere.[8] English expressions are supposed to mean the same if, vaguely speaking, you can use one for the other in any situation and any English context without *relevant* difference of effect; and the essential difficulty comes in delimiting the required sense of relevant.

V

There is no denying the access of power that accrues to our con-ceptual scheme through the positing of abstract objects. Most of what is gained by positing attributes, however, is gained equally by positing classes. Classes are on a par with attributes on the score of abstract-ness or universality, and they serve the purposes of attributes so far as mathematics and certainly most of science are concerned; and they enjoy, unlike attributes, a crystal-clear identity concept. No wonder that in mathematics the murky intensionality of attributes tends to give way to the limpid extensionality of classes; and likewise in other sciences, roughly in proportion to the rigor and austerity of their systematization.

For attributes one might still claim this advantage over classes: they help in systematizing what we may call the *attributary attitudes* —hunting, wanting, fearing, lacking, and the like. For, take hunting. Lion-hunting is not, like lion-catching, a transaction between men and individual lions; for it requires no lions. We analyze lion-catching, rabbit-catching, etc. as having a catching relation in common and varying only in the individuals caught; but what of lion-hunting, rabbit-hunting, etc.? If any common relation is to be recognized here, the varying objects of the relation must evidently be taken not as

---

[8] "Two dogmas of empiricism," *Philosophical Review*, vol. 60 (1951), pp. 20–43; reprinted in my *From a Logical Point of View*. See further my "Carnap e la verità logica," *Rivista di Filosofia*, vol. 48 (1957), pp. 3–29, which is a translation of an essay part of which has appeared also in the original English under the title "Logical Truth" in *American Philosophers at Work* (Sidney Hook, ed.), New York: Criterion, 1956.

individuals but as kinds. Yet not kinds in the sense of classes, for then unicorn-hunting would cease to differ from griffin-hunting. Kinds rather in the sense of attributes.

Some further supposed abstract objects that are like attributes, with respect to the identity problem, are the *propositions*—in the sense of entities that somehow correspond to sentences as attributes correspond to predicates. Now if attributes clamor for recognition as objects of the attributary attitudes, so do propositions as objects of the propositional attitudes: believing, wishing, and the rest.[9]

Overwhelmed by the problem of identity of attributes and of propositions, however, one may choose to make a clean sweep of the lot, and undertake to manage the attributary and propositional attitudes somehow without them. Philosophers who take this austere line will perhaps resort to actual linguistic forms, sentences, instead of propositions, as objects of the propositional attitudes; and to actual linguistic forms, predicates, instead of attributes, as objects of the attributary attitudes.

Against such resort to linguistic forms one hears the following objection, due to Church and Langford.[10] If what are believed are mere sentences, then "Edwin believes the English sentence S" goes correctly into German as "Edwin glaubt den englischen Staz S," with S unchanged. But it also goes correctly into German as "Edwin glaubt" followed by a German translation of S in indirect discourse. These two German reports, one quoting the English sentence and the other using German indirect discourse, must then be equivalent. But they are not, it is argued, since a German ignorant of English cannot equate them. Now I am not altogether satisfied with this argument. It rests on the notion of linguistic equivalence, or sameness of meaning; and this has seemed dubious as a tool of philosophical analysis. There is, however, another objection to taking linguistic forms as objects of the attributary and propositional attitudes; viz., simply that that course is discouragingly artificial. With this objection I sympathize.

Perhaps, after all, we should be more receptive to the first and least premeditated of the alternatives. We might keep attributes and propositions after all, but just not try to cope with the problem of their individuation. We might deliberately acquiesce in the old unregenerate positing of attributes and propositions without hint of a standard of identity. The precept "No entity without identity" might simply

[9] See my "Quantifiers and propositional attitudes," *Journal of Philosophy*, vol. 53 (1956), pp. 177–187.

[10] Alonzo Church, "On Carnap's analysis of statements of assertion and belief, *Analysis*, vol. 10 (1950), pp. 97–99. Reprinted in *Philosophy and Analysis* (Margaret Macdonald, ed.), Oxford and New York: Blackwell and Philosophical Library, 1954.

be relaxed. Certainly the positing of first objects makes no sense except as keyed to identity; but those patterns of thing talk, once firmly inculcated, have in fact enabled us to talk of attributes and propositions in partial grammatical analogy, without an accompanying standard of identity for them. Why not just accept them thus, as twilight half-entities to which the identity concept is not to apply?[11] If the disreputability of their origins is undeniable, still bastardy, to the enlightened mind, is no disgrace. This liberal line accords with the Oxford philosophy of ordinary language, much though I should regret, by my sympathetic reference, to cause any twinge of sorrow to my revered predecessor in this presidential chair.[12]

What might properly count against countenancing such half-entities, inaccessible to identity, is a certain disruption of logic. For, if we are to tolerate the half-entities without abdication of philosophical responsibility, we must adjust the logic of our conceptual scheme to receive them, and then weigh any resulting complexity against the benefits of the half-entities in connection with propositional and attributary attitudes and elsewhere.

But I am not sure that even philosophical responsibility requires settling for one all-purpose system.[13] Propositional and attributary attitudes belong to daily discourse of hopes, fears, and purposes; causal science gets on well without them. The fact that science has shunned them and fared so well could perhaps encourage a philosopher of sanguine temper to try to include that erstwhile dim domain within an overhauled universal system, science-worthy throughout. But a reasonable if less ambitious alternative would be to keep a relatively simple and austere conceptual scheme, free of half-entities, for official scientific business, and then accommodate the half-entities in a second-grade system.

In any event the idea of accommodating half-entities without identity illustrates how the individuative, object-oriented conceptual scheme so natural to us could conceivably begin to evolve away.

It seemed in our reflections on the child that the category of bulk terms was a survival of a pre-individuative phase. We were thinking ontogenetically, but the phylogenetic parallel is plausible too: we may have in the bulk term a relic, half vestigial and half adapted, of a pre-individuative phase in the evolution of our conceptual scheme. And some day, correspondingly, something of our present individuative

---

[11] Frege did so in *Grundgesetze der Arithmetik*, where he was at pains not to subject *Begriffe* to identity. See also Peter Geach, "Class and concept," *Philosophical Review*, vol. 64 (1955), pp. 561–570.

[12] John H. Randall, Jr.

[13] See James B. Conant, *Modern Science and Modern Man*, New York: Columbia University, 1952, pp. 98 ff.

talk may in turn end up, half vestigial and half adapted, within a new and as yet unimagined pattern beyond individuation.

Transition to some such radically new pattern could occur either through a conscious philosophical enterprise or by slow and unreasoned development along lines of least resistance. A combination of both factors is likeliest; and anyway the two differ mainly in degree of deliberateness. Our patterns of thought or language have been evolving, under pressure of inherent inadequacies and changing needs, since the dawn of language; and, whether we help guide it or not, we may confidently look forward to more of the same.

Translation of our remote past or future discourse into the terms we now know could be about as tenuous and arbitrary a projection as translation of the heathen language was seen to be. Conversely, even to speak of that remote medium as radically different from ours is, as remarked in the case of the heathen language, to say no more than that the translations do not come smoothly. We have, to be sure, a mode of access to future stages of our own evolution that is denied us in the case of the heathen language: we can sit and evolve. But even those historical gradations, if somehow traced down the ages and used as clues to translation between widely separated evolutionary stages, would still be gradations only, and in no sense clues to fixed ideas beneath the flux of language. For the obstacle to correlating conceptual schemes is not that there is anything ineffable about language or culture, near or remote. The whole truth about the most outlandish linguistic behavior is just as accessible to us, in our current Western conceptual scheme, as are other chapters of zoology. The obstacle is only that any one intercultural correlation of words and phrases, and hence of theories, will be just one among various empirically admissible correlations, whether it is suggested by historical gradations or by unaided analogy; there is nothing for such a correlation to be uniquely right or wrong about. In saying this I philosophize from the vantage point only of our own provincial conceptual scheme and scientific epoch, true; but I know no better.

BIBLIOGRAPHY

QUINE, Willard V. O., *A System of Logistic*. Cambridge: Harvard U. Press, 1934.

———, *Elementary Logic*. N.Y.: Ginn, 1941.

———, *Mathematical Logic*. N.Y.: W. W. Norton, 1940. Rev. Ed., 1951.

———, *Methods of Logic*. N.Y.: Holt, 1950.

_____, *From a Logical Point of View: Nine Logico–Philosophical Essays*. Cambridge: Harvard U. Press, 1953.

_____, *Word and Object*. N.Y.: John Wiley, 1960.

_____, *Set Theory and Its Logic*. Cambridge: Harvard U. Press, 1964.

_____, co-editor, *Philosophical Essays for Alfred North Whitehead*, N.Y.: Longmans Green, 1936.

Max Black

[*1909*–   ]

Max Black was born in Russia. He took his B.A. at Cambridge, studied at the University of Göttingen, and received his Ph.D. from the University of London in 1939. Black came to America in 1940, has taught at the University of Illinois (1940–46), and since 1946 at Cornell, where he is also one of the editors of *The Philosophical Review.* Formerly a co-editor of the *Journal of Symbolic Logic,* he has also taught for a year at the University of Washington (1951–52), and has been a Guggenheim Fellow. Black is a former President of the American Philosophical Association, Eastern Division (1958), and a member of the International Institute of Philosophy.

Black's main work has been in the area of philosophical analysis. He represents, perhaps better than anyone else, the recent influence in America of British "ordinary language" philosophy and of the later Wittgenstein. He is a caustic critic of rival philosophic positions, and he attempts to resolve philosophical puzzles by the method of logical and linguistic clarification. Through his many articles and collected essays, in books such as *Language and Philosophy* (1949), *Problems of Analysis* (1954), and *Models and Metaphors* (1962), he explicates and affirms this approach to philosophy.

In "Language and Reality" (1958), reprinted below, Black discusses (like Carnap and Quine) the problem of the relation of language to ontology. In his view, we should not look to language as a mirror of reality, but would do well instead to classify words and expressions by their uses and functions. Language, moreover, should not be treated as a logical calculus, as though it were subject to simple and determinate rules. Rather, the analysis of the flexible informal rules and vagaries of ordinary language is, he maintains, the more useful philosophical approach.

LANGUAGE AND REALITY [1]

Bertrand Russell once said, "The study of grammar, in my opinion, is capable of throwing far more light on philosophical questions than is commonly supposed by philosophers. Although a grammatical dis-

[1] Presidential address delivered before the Fifty-fifth Annual Meeting of the Eastern Division of the American Philosophical Association at the University of Vermont, December 27–29, 1958. From *Proceedings and Addresses*, Vol. XXXII, Yellow Springs, Ohio: The Antioch Press, 1958–59, pp. 5–17.

tinction cannot be uncritically assumed to correspond to a genuine philosophical difference, yet the one is *primâ facie* evidence of the other, and may often be most usefully employed as a source of discovery" (*The Principles of Mathematics*, 1903, p. 42).

The grammatical distinctions that Russell proceeds to use as guides to philosophical discoveries are the familiar ones between nouns, adjectives, and verbs. But he says that he hopes for "a classification, not of words, but of ideas" (*loc cit.*) and adds, "I shall therefore call adjectives or predicates all notions which are capable of being such, even in a form in which grammar would call them substantives" (*ibid.*). If we are ready to call adjectives nouns, in defiance of grammar, we can hardly expect the grammatical distinction between the two parts of speech to guide us towards what Russell calls a "correct logic" (*ibid.*). If grammar is to teach us anything of philosophical importance, it must be treated with more respect.

My object in this paper is to clarify the character of philosophical inferences from grammar. By "grammar" I shall understand a classification of meaningful units of speech (*i.e.*, "morphology"), together with rules for the correct arrangement of such units in sentences (*i.e.*, "syntax"). The conclusions of the kinds of inferences I have in mind will be propositions commonly called "ontological"; they will be metaphysical statements about "the ultimate nature of reality," like "Relations exist," or "The World is the totality of facts, not of things," or "There exists one and only one substance."

I

In seeking ontological conclusions from linguistic premises, our starting point must be the grammar of some actual language, whether living or dead. From the standpoint of a language's capacity to express what is or what might be the case, it contains much that is superfluous, in grammar as well as in vocabulary. Grammatical propriety requires a German child to be indicated by a neuter expression ("*das* Kind"), a liability from which French children are exempt. If we are willing to speak ungrammatical German or French, so long as the fact-stating resources of the language are unimpaired, we can dispense with indications of gender. For to be told that the word "*Kind*" is neuter is to be told nothing about children that would have been the case had the German language never existed. The indifference of the English language to the gender of nouns sufficiently demonstrates the superfluity of this particular grammatical feature. For the purpose of eventual metaphysical inference, gender is an accidental, a nonessential, grammatical category.

In order to have any prospects of validity, positive philosophical inferences from grammar must be based upon essential, non-acciden-tal, grammatical features, that is to say on features whose deletion would impair or render impossible the fact-stating functions of lan-guage. The essential grammatical features, if there are any, must therefore be present in all actual or possible languages that have the same fact-stating powers. They must be invariant under all possible transformations of a given language that conserve fact-stating re-sources. The system of all such invariant grammatical features would constitute a universal or philosophical grammar. Metaphysical infer-ences from grammar must be founded upon the constitution of a hypothetical universal grammar, in abstraction from the idiomatic peculiarities of the grammars of given languages.

There is little reason to suppose that the universal grammar, if there is such a thing, will closely resemble any conventional grammar. Contemporary linguists have made plain the "formal" character of conventional grammatical classifications and the "arbitrariness" of con-ventional rules of syntax. We shall need something other than gram-marians' tools to uncover the universal grammar.

I assume, however, that philosophical grammar will still resemble conventional grammar in consisting of a morphology together with a syntax. I shall suppose throughout that we are considering the pros-pects of a certain kind of classification, coupled with a system of rules for admissible combinations of the things classified. I shall use the conveniently non-committal expression, "linguistic features," to refer to the things classified.

Were it possible to construct a philosophical grammar, or any frag-ment of it, it would be very tempting to say that something would thereby have been revealed about the nature of ultimate reality. For what could be the reason for the presence of some grammatical fea-ture in all conceivable fact-stating languages except the correspond-ence of every such language with reality? There is an inclination to say with the author of the *Tractatus* that the essence of language must be "the essence of the World" (*Tractatus*, 5.4711). Or, with a more recent writer, "The universe is not a vain capricious customer of ours. If the shoe fits, this is a good clue to the size of the foot. If a language is adequate to describe it, this indicates something about its structure" (I. M. Copi, in *The Review of Metaphysics*, vol. 4 [1951], p. 436).

Of course, if metaphysical inferences from grammar are not to be circular, the construction of a universal grammar must proceed with-out prior ontological commitments We shall need to consider whether the search for a universal grammar can be undertaken from a position of ontological neutrality.

It is obviously easier to show that some linguistic feature does not belong to universal grammar than the reverse; most of the examples I shall consider will have this negative character, that is to say, will be instances in which we argue that some feature of a given language is not essential to the fact-stating powers of the language. The corresponding ontological inference is the negative one that nothing in ultimate reality corresponds to the rejected linguistic feature.

II

In the *Tractatus*, Wittgenstein says, "In the proposition there must be exactly as much distinguishable (*gleich soviel zu unterscheiden*) as in the state of affairs that it represents" (4.04). Let us read this to mean: "In the particular utterance, there must be exactly as many different symbols as there are constituents in the state of affairs represented." Following Wittgenstein, I shall assign two physically similar word-tokens to different symbols, when they have different senses or references.

Let us try to apply this plausible principle of invariance of the number of constituents to a concrete instance. Suppose I am riding in an automobile with somebody who is learning to drive, and I need some pre-arranged signals to tell him to start the car or to stop it. It is natural, and adequate, to use the words "Stop" and "Go"; but, of course, a tap on the shoulder would do just as well. Here we have a system of orders, not statements of fact; but similar considerations will apply in both cases, since the logical structure of the orders will be the same as that of the factual statements specifying the actions performed in response to those orders. An adherent of Wittgenstein's principle of isomorphism might point out that here the two actions to be performed are represented by exactly the same number of distinct symbols, "Stop" and "Go." He might add that it would be logically impossible for the learner–driver to understand the two different orders, unless he were supplied with different and distinct symbols for the two cases. And he might add that every set of symbols that could serve the same purpose would necessarily exhibit the same duality. Whether the instructor spoke German, or Swahili, or anything else, he must necessarily use two symbols: here seems to be a perfect example of an essential feature, necessarily manifested in all the mutually equivalent notations.

But suppose the instructor used a whistle to signal "Start" as well as to signal "Stop." This device would be just as effective as the conventional words, and we need not suppose the whistle blasts to be substitutes for the English sounds: their meanings might have been taught directly, by demonstration and training. Have we not here an exception to Wittgenstein's principle—one symbol (the blown whistle), but two represented actions?

The retort is obvious: A whistle blown when the car is at rest means one thing ("Go"), but means another ("Stop") when the car is in motion. So the full symbol is whistle-plus-condition-of-car: there are two relevant states of the car, hence two symbols after all. But is this conclusive? Surely it would be just as easy to argue as follows: The whistle is one symbol, not two; but it also represents one action, not two: each time it means a *change-of-state*, whether from motion to rest or *vice versa*. To be consistent, an advocate of this view must be willing to say that the familiar orders "Stop" and "Go" mean one and the same thing; but a determined searcher for a depth grammar must accept consequences at least as strange as this.

In order to determine whether Wittgenstein's principle applies to the case in hand, we need criteria of identity for actions and criteria of identity for the corresponding symbols. We have to say whether starting the car and stopping it are to count as the same or as different actions; and we have to say whether blowing the whistle is to count as having the same or different meanings on various occasions. There are no definite criteria for identity in these cases. In ordinary life, in a particular setting, we might understand sufficiently well a request to say something different, or to do something different; but here we are not in an ordinary setting. We want to know whether there are *really* two actions and two symbols, and have no way of finding out. We are free to decide whether the symbols are the same or different; the relevant fragment of philosophical grammar must be stipulated. The philosophical questions lack determinate sense and depend for their answers upon how we choose to describe the relevant utterances.

It may be said that this disappointing outcome arises from the artificiality of the example. I shall therefore turn to other cases having greater intrinsic interest.

III

Nowadays, it is often said that the copula, that figures so prominently in traditional logic, is superfluous. Listen to this, for instance: "There might certainly be various relations that the copula stood for, if it stood for any relation at all. But in fact no link is needed to join subject and predicate . . . The grammatical copula is logically significant only when it serves as a sign of tense" (P. T. Geach, in *Mind*, vol 59 [1950], p. 464).

But here is a traditionalist speaking: "The mode of connection of the subject and the predicate is symbolized in the standard formula-

tion by the word 'is,' which is called the 'copula' because it links subject and predicate together . . . some mode of connection requires
symbolization, and this function is performed by the copula" (C. A.
Mace, *The Principles of Logic*, 1933, pp. 77–78).

The dispute is clearly about philosophical grammar: the question is
whether the copula is, or is not, an essential feature of language. On
the one side, a strong case can be presented for the dispensability of
the copula. There are languages, like Hebrew or Japanese, which
manage very well without a copula; and we ourselves do without it
in such constructions as "Peter loves Mary," in which the predicate,
"loves Mary," is attached to its subject, "Peter," without benefit of any
verbal link. Strongest of all is the argument that we could jettison the
copula without in any way impairing the fact-stating resources of our
language. Were we to say, "Peter happy," as the Chinese are said to
do, we would lose nothing in expressive and descriptive power. In any
case, *some* words and expressions must be able to "hang together" in a
sentence without a symbolic link, for otherwise no completed sentence
would be possible. So why not dispense with the copula altogether?

A defender of the copula's significance might reply as follows: "You
are right in claiming that we don't need the *word* 'is' or any other
word between the subject and the predicate of a sentence. But this is
trivial and was never in dispute. Consider the pidgin English sentence, 'Peter happy,' that you offered as an adequate substitute for
the conventional form. What is significant in this sentence is not
merely the occurrence of the word-tokens, 'Peter' and 'happy,' but
the *relationship* between them. Separating the two words by others or
by a sufficiently wide interval will disintegrate your sentence. It is the
relationship of juxtaposition that here performs the function of linking
subject and predicate. Similarly, in the conventional form, 'Peter is
happy,' the union is effected by a relationship generated by writing
the three words in correct order and in sufficiently close proximity.
What is essential to the copula is not at all deleted by the translation
into pidgin English. *Floreat copula!*"

What are we to say of this rebuttal? Its plausibility is undeniable,
yet once again nothing compels us to accept it. For one thing, we may
feel some reluctance to recognize "juxtaposition" as a genuine relation.
Do we really need to *bring* the words into any relationship? Isn't it
enough that we use them both in making the statement in question?
Here again, consideration of some non-verbal notation might rid us
of certain initial prejudices. Could we not, perhaps, use a red disk to
mean that Peter is happy, with the disk standing for the man and its
color for his condition of felicity? And what then would become of
the alleged relationship between subject and predicate? Somebody
might still insist, like A. E. Johnson in his *Logic*, that there would

have to be a *characterizing relation* between the disk and its color. But anybody who can confidently assert this must already be in a position to analyze reality directly, and has no need of the detour through language.

But indeed, an advocate of the no copula view can reaffirm his position without invoking a hypothetical notation of qualified objects. *His* analysis of the sentence-fact, "Peter happy," might well be in terms of an "object," the word-token, "Peter," qualified by a certain property, that of having the word-token "happy" in immediate proximity. If he conceives of properties as "incomplete," *i.e.*, as having the power to unite with objects without need of intermediaries, he will *see* the linguistic predicate in the same light. For such a neo-Fregean, learning how to *use* a predicate *is* learning how to attach it to subjects in complete statements, and there is no separate rule to be learned about the symbolic significance of the alleged relation of juxtaposition. For such a philosopher, a question about the relationship between subject and predicate of a statement is as otiose as a question about the relationship between a hand and the object it points at. Specification of the hand and the object indicated defines the gesture, without need for further specification; similarly, choice of a subject and an appropriate predicate uniquely determines a statement, without need for a further choice of a relationship between them.

Once again, we have a dispute which is inconclusive and threatens to be undecidable. What turns on the outcome? What difference will it make whether or not we recognize a characterizing relation? Well, a relation is conceived to hold between *terms*, so the traditional recognition of the copula goes with a classification of properties as special kinds of *things*. Admission of a characterizing relation allows questions to be asked about properties, so that predicates or their surrogates are sometimes permitted to function as subjects. The opposite point of view, that treats properties and their representing predicates as incomplete, forbids questions and assertions to be made about properties as subjects. The dispute about the copula, trifling as it may seem at first sight, is a focus of contention for full-blown alternative grammars.

IV

I pass on now to consider whether the ancient distinction between subject and predicate should be regarded as an essential feature of language that belongs to universal grammar.

How do we identify the subject and predicate of a given statement? A contemporary answers as follows: "A predicate is an expression that gives us an assertion about something if we attach it to another ex-

pression that stands for what we are making the assertion about"
(P. T. Geach, *Mind*, vol. 59 [1950], pp. 461–462).

In order to apply this prescription to a particular instance, we have
first to determine what a given assertion is "about." Should the assertion contain an expression standing for what the assertion is about,
that expression will be the subject. According to the prescription, the
remainder of the sentence will be the attached predicate.

This works well when applied to such a sentence as "Peter is
happy," in which there is reference to a person. It is natural to say
that a statement using that sentence is about Peter; hence the word
"Peter" may be said to be a subject standing for Peter, and the remainder of the sentence, the expression, "is happy," counts as the
predicate.

But even in this paradigm case of the application of the distinction,
an objection can be lodged. It may be plausibly argued that the statement in question is about happiness, no less than about Peter: the assertion, some would say, can be understood as a claim that happiness
is instantiated in Peter. If it is permissible to say that the word
"happy" stands for happiness, the rule we have adopted would lead
us to say that "happy" is the subject and "Peter is" the predicate. The
philosopher who formulated the rule I have cited would want to reject
this inference.

Or, take the case of the statement, "Happiness is desired by all
men." Here, it is still more plausible to say that the statement is about
happiness, referred to by the word "happiness." But the author of our
rule refuses to recognize "happiness" as a subject, preferring to construe the sentence in question as being composed of two predicates.

I do not wish to suggest that a preference for this mode of analysis
is willful or capricious; yet I believe there is no rational method for
persuading somebody who rejects it. The dispute, like others already
reported in this paper, can be resolved only by fiat. It is an error to
suppose that we can determine what a statement is "about" by inspection of some extra-linguistic realm. No amount of observation or reflection about non-verbal "things" will show whether a given statement
is about a person or about a quality. The answer must be sought in
language itself.

We know that the statement "Peter is happy" is about Peter, because we recognize "Peter" as a proper name, without knowing
whether there is such a person as Peter. The starting point of the
intended philosophical distinction between subject and predicate is
conventional grammar, relying only upon formal criteria. But conventional grammar leaves us in the lurch as soon as we are asked to decide whether a statement using the word "happiness" is "really" about
happiness.

V

I propose now to test the thesis of the universality of the subject-predicate form, by applying it to the report of a move in chess. The case may be thought to have special peculiarities, but will serve to reveal the chief points in dispute.

A full verbal report of a chess move, such as might be found in nineteenth century manuals, has the form, "The King's pawn moved to the King's fourth square." Here, there is no difficulty in identifying the grammatical subject, *i.e.*, the expression, "The King's pawn." Hence, the remainder of the formula, the expression, "moved to the King's fourth square," must be the predicate, and the report can be certified as being of the subject-predicate form.

Nowadays, English-speaking chess players commonly use the concise notation, "*P-K4*." Reading this as a conventional abbreviation of the full English sentence previously cited, it is easy enough to discern a subject and a predicate in this fragment of symbolism: we might say that in "*P-K4*" the "*P*" is the subject, and the rest of the formula the predicate.

But other and equally adequate notations are in common use. In the so-called "Continental notation," a move is specified by giving only coordinates of the initial and terminal squares; thus the move already cited would be reported as "*e2-e4*." In this version, there is no component homologous with the subject recognized in the other form of report. A last-ditch defender of the omnipresence of the subject-predicate form might still argue that in the formula "*e2-e4*" the first complex symbol, "*e2*," indirectly specifies the chessman moved. However, it would be equally correct to treat the initial symbol, "*P*," of the English notation as being "really" an indirect specification of the square from which the move started. Somebody familiar only with the Continental notation can treat the English notations as having the square-to-square structure of his own paradigm; while a devotee of the English notation can treat the alternative symbolism as a disguised version of his own.

It becomes progressively harder to perceive the subject-predicate form in every conceivable chess notation as alternative notations are imagined. A given chess move might be represented by drawing a line on a square divided into 64 compartments, or by a set of two integers between 1 and 64, or by a single number less than 4096 ($= 64^2$), or by Morse code, or by suitably modulated electrical waves. Some of these possibilities might be handled by human beings, others might perhaps serve only to inform chess-playing computers; but all alike would have the requisite structure for representing every possible move in a game of chess. All of them, to use Wittgenstein's word,

would have the same "multiplicity" (*Tractatus*, 4.04). Now a determination to view all of these equivalent symbolic forms as having the
subject-predicate structure would be quixotic in the extreme. Absurd
loyalty to a preconception about logical form would be needed in
order to view a line drawn on a chessboard as having a subject and a
predicate. Long before this point was reached, most of us would
prefer to abandon the dogma of the omnipresence of subject-predicate
form.

The example may prepare us to expect similar conclusions about
languages that are not restricted to the representation of an invented
game. We are told, on good authority, that "Chinese, which is fully
equipped for every sort of civilized communication, makes no use of
the formal categories devised for the Indo-European languages" (W. J.
Entwistle, *Aspects of Language*, 1953, p. 162). Another writer, after
surveying the variety of grammars known to contemporary linguists,
concludes that "No grammatical concept seems to be *per se* sacred or
universal, far less indispensable" (Mario Pei, *The Story of Language*,
1949, p. 129). In some languages, we are told, "An isolated word is a
sentence; a sequence of such sentence words is like a compound sentence . . . [and] the terms verb and noun in such a language are
meaningless" (B. L. Whorf, *Language, Thought and Reality*, 1956,
pp. 98–99). If Whorf was right, the hope of finding the subject-
predicate distinction exemplified in such "polysynthetic" languages is
doomed to frustration. For that distinction presupposes a way of distinguishing between nouns and other parts of speech. Yet "polysynthetic" languages may be just as rich in fact-stating resources as our
own relatively analytical English. I conclude that the subject-predicate distinction, valuable as it may be for analyzing Indo-European
languages, ought to find no place in a universal philosophical grammar.

VI

The three examples I have discussed sufficiently illustrate the difficulties that beset any serious effort to construct a universal grammar.
We are now in a position to diagnose the source of these difficulties.
In each case, we were assuming that the logical structure of certain
statements ("Stop," "Go," "Peter is happy") must be identical with the
structure of the situations or states-of-affairs represented. The search
for what is presumed to be invariant in all statements having the
same meaning, that is to say, those representing the same state of affairs, is a search for some way of presenting the common logical structure. In order to do this, we must be able to do at least the following:
decide which perceptible features of words or other signs can be
treated as non-significant, recognize one and the same symbol behind

its alternative manifestations (that is to say, recognize when signs mean the same thing), and assign different symbols to the same logical category or type, on the basis of identity of function. In order for the procedure to provide any ground for ontological inference, such recognition, individuation, and classification of symbols must be performed without recourse to ontological premises, or to methods assuming the truth of such premises.

The chief difficulty arose from the need to count non-linguistic contextual features of statements as significant. So long as we confine ourselves to analysis of conventional verbal statements, in isolation from their settings, traditional grammar provides us with means of segmentation and classification that can subsequently be elaborated and refined in the service of philosophical insight. There is no question but that "Stop" and "Go" are different words; "Peter" is clearly a noun and a grammatical subject in "Peter is happy." But immediately we recognize the non-verbal setting in which the words are pronounced as significant, we face formidable difficulties in identifying, distinguishing, counting and classifying the symbols that interest us. Are the situations in which a car is at rest and in motion to count as the same or as different? Are the actions of stopping and starting a car the same or different? These are not questions to be answered by looking at cars or their drivers. They are questions of philosophical grammar for which there are no decision procedures. We have criteria for deciding whether words are to be treated as the same or different; for rules to this end (superficial rules of grammar) are part of the language we speak and understand. But there are no adequate criteria for deciding whether contextual situations are to be counted as the same or different, for the purpose of determining identities and differences of meaning. It might be thought that we ought to examine the semantical *rules* governing the sounds and written marks in question. But this maneuver achieves nothing. Were we assured that the rule governing "Stop" must count as different from the rule governing "Go," we would be entitled to conclude that there were indeed *two* symbols in question. But since the word "Stop" and "Go" or their synonyms will occur in the expressions of those semantical rules, individuation of the rules will raise the same troublesome questions. Nor will the case be altered by speaking about "uses" instead of about "rules." For the purposes of philosophical grammar, descriptions in terms of "symbols," "rules," and "uses" are mutually equivalent and generate the same problems. We can choose as we please, and our decisions about the points of philosophical grammar at issue will be determined by the choices we have made, not by any imposed analysis of the statements inspected.

Similarly in our illustrations of the copula and the subject-predicate form. At the level of surface grammar, there are crude criteria for deciding whether an expression is expendable without loss of meaning. But when we try to push on to a would-be "deeper" level of analysis, we are embarrassed again by lack of criteria. Is the *relation* between "Peter" and "happy" "really" significant? Is there "really" a relationship there at all? It all depends upon how you choose to look at the statement. Nothing imposes an answer except the determination of the philosophical analyst to adhere to one mode of logical parsing rather than another. Seen through one pair of grammatical spectacles, there plainly is a significant relation of juxtaposition between subject and predicate; but we can wear another pair of lenses, and see nothing but subject and predicate, "hanging in one another like the links of a chain."

When we recognize that the fact-stating functions of language can be adequately performed by non-verbal symbolisms, the problems of detecting invariant logical structure become insuperable. If we represent states of affairs by configurations of physical objects, the task of discerning logical structure demands a capacity to determine the logical structure of certain physical facts. But if we can ever do this, we don't need the detour via language. If we can analyze a fact, we can in principle discover the logical structure of reality without prior recourse to language. On the other hand, if we face some obstacle of principle in dissecting reality, we shall meet the very same difficulties in trying to dissect language. For language, though it represents reality, is also a part of reality.

VII

In the light of the foregoing considerations, the prospects for a universal philosophical grammar seem most unpromising. I believe the hope of finding *the* essential grammar to be as illusory as that of finding the single true coördinate system for the representation of space. We can pass from one systematic mode of spatial representation to another by means of rules for transforming coördinates, and we can pass from one language to another having the same fact-stating resources by means of rules of translation. But rules for transformation of coördinates yield no information about space; and translation rules for sets of languages tell us nothing about the ultimate nature of reality.

It might perhaps be said that common logical structure is shown in an invariant web of entailment relations. It is certainly part of our concept of synonymity that statements of the same meaning shall have parallel consequences: if one statement has an entailment that is not synonymous with some entailment of a second statement, that proves that the two original statements have different meanings. To put the matter differently, we shall not regard two languages as having the same fact-stating resources unless we can trace corresponding patterns of transformation rules in both. But we shall never arrive at a philosophical grammar by this road: correspondence of sets of entailments is compatible with the widest divergences of morphology and of syntax.

If we abandon the vain hope of finding the true philosophical grammar, we may still hope to use its by-products. Schoolroom grammar is coarse-grained for philosophical purposes, and the refinements of latter-day linguists are impressive without being philosophically useful. We shall do well to continue classifying words and expressions according to their uses and functions, inventing whatever labels will help us to remember our discoveries. It is not my intention to deprecate the received grammatical categories of "quality," "relation," "function," "class" and the rest, or the finer classifications invented by contemporaries. I would urge, however, that our attitude to such grammatical sieves should be pragmatic. If reality leaves us free to choose our grammars as convenience and utility dictate, we shall properly regard them as speculative instruments to be sharpened, improved, and, where necessary, discarded when they have served their turn.

To anybody who still feels that there *must* be an identity of logical form between language and reality, I can only plead that the conception of language as a mirror of reality is radically mistaken. We find out soon enough that the universe is not capricious: the child who learns that fire burns and knife-edges cut knows that there are inexorable limits set upon his desires. Language must conform to the discovered regularities and irregularities of experience. But in order to do so, it is enough that it should be apt for the expression of everything that is or might be the case. To be content with less would be to be satisfied to be inarticulate; to ask for more is to desire the impossible. No roads lead from grammar to metaphysics.

BIBLIOGRAPHY

BLACK, Max, *The Nature of Mathematics: a Critical Survey*. N.Y.: Harcourt, Brace, 1933.
———, *Language and Philosophy: Studies in Method*. Ithaca: Cornell U. Press, 1949.
———, *Critical Thinking; An Introduction to Logic and Scientific Method*. N.Y.: Prentice-Hall, 1946. (Rev. ed., 1952).

————, *Problems of Analysis: Philosophical Essays.* Ithaca: Cornell U. Press, 1954.

————, *Models and Metaphors.* Ithaca: Cornell U. Press, 1962.

————, *A Companion to Wittgenstein's Tractatus.* Ithaca, N.Y.: Cornell U. Press, 1964.

————, (ed.) *The Social Theories of Talcott Parsons; a Critical Examination.* Englewood Cliffs, N.J.: Prentice-Hall, 1961.

————, (ed.) *Philosophical Analysis, A Collection of Essays.* Ithaca: Cornell U. Press, 1950.

————, (ed.) *The Importance of Language.* Englewood Cliffs, N.J.: Prentice-Hall, 1962.

————, (with P.T. Geach). *Translations from the Philosophical Writings of Gottlob Frege.* N.Y.: Philosophical Library, 1952.

Brand Blanshard

[*1892–*]

Brand Blanshard is probably the outstanding defender of classical rationalism in America today. Born in Fredericksburg, Ohio, he took his B.A. at the University of Michigan (1914), his M.A. at Columbia (1918), where he was a student of John Dewey, a B.S.C. at Oxford (1920), and a Ph.D. at Harvard (1921). Blanshard was a Rhodes Scholar (1913–15, 1919–20) and a Guggenheim Fellow. He has taught at the University of Michigan, Swarthmore, Columbia, and since 1945 at Yale, where he was Chairman of the Department of Philosophy. Blanshard is a past President of the American Theological Society (1955–56) and of the American Philosophical Association, Eastern Division (1942–44). He delivered the Gifford Lectures (1952–53) and the Carus Lectures (1959).

Early in his career, Blanshard was influenced by the absolute idealism that prevailed during the early part of the century (British and Roycean), and particularly by its rationalism. A rationalist, according to Blanshard, is one who holds that there are truths apprehended through the intellect, that these are the most certain truths we possess, and that they reveal in some measure an intelligible structure in the world. He suggests that "reason" is the faculty and function of grasping "necessary connections," laws or principles. Such grasping is intellectual, and not a matter of sense perception. Moreover, the principles understood are held to be universally and objectively valid quite apart from our grasp of them.

The Nature of Thought (1939), in which Blanshard undertakes a detailed analysis of thought, stands midway between psychology and metaphysics. Here he restates the idealistic position in response to the criticisms of realism, pragmatism and behaviorism. The rationalist throughout, Blanshard finds, even at the level of perception, elements of judgment and thought. Blanshard defends a coherence theory of truth, causal and logical necessities, and the doctrine of internal relations. The end of thought is understanding, and the ideal is an all-inclusive and intelligible system in which the universe of all existing things is internally related.

In *Reason and Goodness* (1961), Blanshard extends his analysis of reason to the domain of practical wisdom and ethics. He is particularly interested in rebutting emotive and subjective theories of ethics and politics, and in defending the classical view that moral judgments express knowledge. His theory has a naturalistic aspect, since ethics is related to human nature, and "the good" in the sense of ethical end is "the most comprehensive possible fulfillment of satisfaction of impulse–desire."

In *Reason and Analysis* (1962),

Blanshard offers a sustained examination and attack on analytic philosophy and logical positivism, as they have developed in the past forty years. Finding these viewpoints symptomatic of the generalized contemporary revolt against reason, he once again explains and defends classical rationalism. The following selection from *Reason and Analysis* is pivotal to Blanshard's whole philosophical position. Blanshard criticizes the influential Humean idea of causation as constant conjunction, not necessary connection, and the logical positivist claim that all *a priori* statements are merely consequences of linguistic conventions and say nothing about the world. Among the many kinds of "necessary connections" Blanshard discovers in the world are logical and mathematical laws (which reveal the nature of things), connections between properties and attributes, and necessary connections in ethics and value. In the remainder of the book, he suggests still other more fundamental connections.

REASON AND ANALYSIS [1]

NECESSITIES IN NATURE

§1.

We have held that the prime office of reason was the discovery of necessary connections. The tendency of recent thought has been to restrict this office by confining necessity within increasingly narrow limits. It is insisted, first, in the spirit of Hume, that necessity never links existents, but only our own meanings. It is then added that not all meanings admit of such linkage, but only those that can stand as terms in propositions, simple or compound. Next propositions themselves are scrutinized, and many that were thought to be necessary are excluded; only analytic propositions are admitted to the inner fold. Finally, many even of these are questioned, on the ground that they contain empirical elements. "All bachelors are unmarried" is analytic, of course, but the content of its terms is drawn from experience, and, strictly speaking, empirical contents are never linked by necessity. So we are left in the end with such luminous assertions as "*a* is *a*," or "*a* is not non-*a*," or $p \supset \cdot p \vee q$ as the most characteristic achievements of reason.

In the minds of many philosophers there is a rising revolt against all this. They feel that the retreat of reason has gone too far, that it is time to call a halt and to start reclaiming territory needlessly sur-

---

[1] From Brand Blanshard, *Reason and Analysis*, LaSalle, Ill.: Open Court, 1962. Selections taken from Chapter X, pp. 422–443.

rendered. This retreat seems to them to evince a strange failure of nerve. Philosophy has suffered from a creeping palsy of suspicion that reason, its chief weapon, is not much more than a toy, of use only in playing "language games" or arranging symbols in arbitrary patterns.

It is possible, to be sure, that the philosophers from Plato downwards who have relied upon reason to provide knowledge of the nature and structure of the world were uniformly mistaken. A skeptical inquiry into their procedure must at all times be welcomed, and indeed the findings of recent years have shown that with regard to both the terms and the connections of our so-called rational knowledge, earlier philosophies were unduly complacent. They floated a paper currency of terms only part of which could be redeemed in coin, and they often indulged lavishly in a priori argumentation without any clear view of its true nature and limits. It is therefore conceivable that their whole speculative enterprise was an uncritical dream. Contemporary analytic philosophers have alleged that it was, and have brought particularly severe charges against the traditional employment of reason. Necessary knowledge, they insist, is not knowledge in the strict sense at all. The connections it reveals, if not always purely formal, are at any rate conventional, and provide us merely with the rules of our linguistic practice. Of nature it tells us nothing. And even if it did, what it said would be tautologous, containing only what a clear enough eye could see in that which was already before us.

We have examined these contentions in our discussion of a priori knowledge, finding in them some truth, but not a little also that was superficial and confused. We found no good ground whatever for regarding necessity as arbitrary or conventional or linguistic, nor again as analytic merely. And if these charges fail, there is no good ground, either, for saying that necessary judgments can tell us nothing of nature.

Let us suppose now that reason is acquitted of these charges. How much light on nature may be hoped for from its exercise? Have we any intimations that nature is governed by necessity, either as a whole or in any considerable part? Even if necessity does hold among existent characters and things, it may hold in so small an area that the fullest success we could hope for would bring little illumination. Our best course would seem to be to make an inventory of such necessities as we have already in possession, and then to raise the further question how far we may legitimately hope that such knowledge may be extended. Our first question, then, must be: How large a capital of necessary knowledge do we now have?

§2.

(1) First, we have logical law. The assumption that at least the law of contradiction holds of the real world was the basis of a famous "metaphysical essay" by Bradley. "To think is to judge, and to judge is to criticize, and to criticize is to use a criterion of reality . . . in rejecting the inconsistent as appearance, we are applying a positive knowledge of the ultimate nature of things. Ultimate reality is such that it does not contradict itself; here is an absolute criterion. And it is proved absolute by the fact that, either in endeavouring to deny it, or even in attempting to doubt it, we tacitly assume its validity."[2] Nearly three-quarters of a century have passed since Bradley wrote these words, and philosophy has taken directions that he could not have foreseen. Has it effectively belied these words of his? I do not think so. The chief developments that might have affected it are the appearance of a linguistic theory of a priori statements, of a conventionalism that would justify logical rules pragmatically as means to desired ends, and of "alternative systems" of logic. We have inquired into these developments, and have found nothing to render it plausible that such logical laws as $\frown(p.\frown p)$ apply exclusively to thought or language rather than to things. The issue here is so important that we must briefly return to it.

Professor Popper has pointed out that there are "three main views on the nature of logic."[3] It is worth seeing that on all of these views logical laws must be interpreted as asserting about the world. The three are (A) that such laws are laws of thought which either (a) describe how we actually think, or (b) tell us how we ought to think; (B) that they report about the constitution of all actual and possible objects; (C) that they are rules for the use of words and sentences.

§3.

When theory (A*a*) says that these laws describe how we actually think, it is pointing out that in a sense we always think logically, that we cannot violate a law of logic if we try. We can say both that Caesar did, and that he did not ride a three-toed horse, but in a sense we cannot *think* both. But in *what* sense? Is it in the sense that we cannot *believe* both, or that we cannot *see* or *understand* how both could be true, or that we can see that both *cannot* be true? Not the first, certainly, because we often do in fact accept contradictory beliefs. The second sense, that we cannot in fact see both sides to be

---

[2] *Appearance and Reality*, 120.

[3] In a symposium on 'Why are the Calculuses of Logic and Arithmetic Applicable to Reality?', *Proc. of the Arist. Soc.*, Sup. Vol. 20 (1946), 48.

true, is undoubtedly correct, but it does not content us as a final answer, for we are at once moved to ask the further question, *Why* can we not see both sides to be true? Is it because of the limitations of our own thought or because we can see of the real that it *could not* be self-contradictory? The view that logic gives us laws of thought only would take the first line. It would presumably say that though we cannot conceive how Caesar could both ride and not ride a three-toed horse, he might in fact have done so. But if this latter statement has any meaning for us, then we *are* conceiving of his both doing and not doing it, which is precisely what was declared inconceivable, and we have contradicted ourselves. The statement that the laws of logic are laws of thought only, and not of things, cannot be coherently stated.

The second form of the first theory (A*b*), to the effect that these laws are normative and tell us how we ought to think, seems more promising. In saying that we ought to think in accordance with them, it assumes that we can also break them. And in a sense we plainly can; most of us have surprising gifts for believing contradictory things. But granting that we can do this, why should we seek to avoid it? The answer seems clear enough. It is because if we do not think in accordance with logical law, we shall not think in accordance with fact. The "ought" is a hypothetical imperative; it tells us that we must avoid thinking illogically if we want to think truly. And this implies that the reality of which our thought is true is itself governed by logic. If contradictory assertions cannot both be true, it is because the reality of which they are asserted does not admit contradictory characteristics.

§4.

Leaping next to the third view (C), that logical laws are linguistic rules, we may content ourselves with adding a consideration or two to the many that have been mentioned earlier.

If a logical law is a rule of usage, we may always legitimately ask why this rule has been adopted rather than some alternative. Suppose, for example, we adopt *ponendo ponens* as a rule, that is, we decide so to regulate our thought and speech that when we have asserted sentence S^1 and the further sentence "S^1 implies S^2" we should go on to assert S^2. How should we justify this procedure? Those who take the linguistic line do not generally hold this rule to be purely arbitrary, and to do so would certainly not be plausible. They ordinarily fall back on a statement of the calculus of propositions, namely $(p.(p \supset q)) \supset q$, and show by the truth-table method that this is necessarily because a tautology. But to say that it is a tautology means that the *truth* of q is among the assertions already made by $(p.(p \supset q))$.

The rule of language is adopted because of a set of relations holding among the *truth*-values of propositions expressed by that language. It may be said that a relation among truth-values, for example that p and $\sim p$ are not both true, is itself a rule of language. But (1) the linguistic logicians never so interpret it. They would think it absurd to accept $(p.\sim p)$ as a rule of procedure, though if $\sim(p.\sim p)$ is only such a rule, we should be at liberty to do so. (2) If it is only such a rule, we may again legitimately ask how to justify it. Why should we shrink from saying that p and its contradictory, that this crow is black and that it is not black, are both true? To which the simple and sufficient answer is: Because the crow itself cannot have incompatible attributes, and we see that it cannot.

We shall indicate one more way in which the rule theory negates itself, a difficulty that Arthur Pap takes as "perhaps the most decisive objection against the theory that the laws of logic are not propositions, but rules of symbolism. Briefly, the objection is that whatever rules one may have initially stipulated, and however arbitrary such stipulations may be, one will thereafter have to *find out* what these rules entail, and the statement that such and such is entailed by the rules could hardly be characterized as itself a rule."[4] Take as an example *ponendo ponens* again. It is not now asserted to be true; it simply reports part of what we propose to mean by deducing one proposition from another. We apply it to the axioms of some system, and in the course of so applying it we make a new discovery. In such a case "it will be perfectly proper to say . . . 'now I *know* that this is a theorem in the system, i.e. that this formula is entailed by the axioms.' But that formula F_1 entails formula F_2 . . . is itself a logical truth, and it would be simply nonsense to characterize it as a *rule*."[5] Suppose, to take a rough parallel, that I make it a rule to get up with the sun. The adoption of this rule entails that I shall never see what the world looks like just before dawn. But that my adoption of it does entail this is not itself a proposal or rule of procedure. It is a true proposition apprehended by a cognitive act. Sooner or later the logician who starts with logical rules is bound to develop their implications, and when he does so, he is moving over into the sphere of logical truths. And if a "truth" is not true of reality, what else is it true of?

§5.

We are left with position (B), namely that logical law tells us something about the actual structure of things. This has been the view of all the rationalist philosophers, and it has been defended in recent

[4] *Semantics and Necessary Truth*, 184.
[5] *Ibid.*

times by Bertrand Russell in Britain,[6] by Morris Cohen in America,[7] and by Ferdinand Gonseth in Europe.[8] The view has been brushed aside in a sentence by Wittgenstein on the ground that while "it is raining" gives us information about fact, "it is either raining or not raining" gives us none.[9] And obviously enough it gives us none if the only things counting as information are ruled beforehand to be items verifiable in sense. But we have found no ground for this dogma. And the fact that a logical law applies necessarily and to everything does not show that it says nothing. Nor does the fact of its being empirically irrefutable. To say this would commit one to saying also that nothing a logician or mathematician said was true, for how could it be true without saying anything? And we have found no plausible alternative to the position that such laws are true. That the desk I am writing on is either a desk or not may be admitted to be a most unhelpful truth and one in which nobody but a philosopher would take the slightest interest. Does it say something true, however? Try to deny it and see. Does it say something about this particular desk? Yes, and this is not controverted by pointing out that what it says holds equally of all desks, clouds, and lamp-posts. We must repeat that a statement does not say nothing simply because it applies to everything.

§6.

(2) In apprehending logical law, then, we know something about the nature of things. Do we have other rational insights of the kind? In descending order of abstractness the next step is to arithmetic. The multiplication table has generally been taken as offering prime examples of propositions which are at once necessary and true, and there is no good reason to deny this. Their applicability to nature, however, is a curiously treacherous matter and has often been mis-understood. Mill thought that it was guaranteed by our having found them to hold with unbroken regularity among experienced things. If this is true, they are not really necessities apprehended by reason, but connections that have so impressed themselves on our minds as to have induced fixed habits of expectation. Laws thus empirically arrived at should be capable of empirical confirmation or disproof. But the evident truth is that we never seriously resort to either. Would it occur to us that a bank teller, because he counts money all day long, knows with more certainty than the rest of us that 5 and 5=10?

---

[6] *Problems of Philosophy,* Ch. VII–VIII.
[7] *Reason and Nature,* 202–205; *Preface to Logic,* 53–56.
[8] *Qu'est-ce que la Logique?* Chap. 7–9 (1937).
[9] *Tractatus,* 4.461.

And can we think of an instance in which any sort of perceptual experience would make us doubt the truth of this proposition? Someone may, indeed, put 5 drops and 5 more drops of water into a dry pitcher and challenge us to get 10 out; he may put 5 rabbits and 5 more in a hutch and find 20 when he comes back; and he may then say triumphantly that in the first case 5 and 5 make less than 10, and in the second case more. Should we be ready, in the light of such cases, to say that, after all, 5 and 5 sometimes fail to make 10? Obviously not. We are far more certain that they do than we are of the validity of any alleged exceptions. We can usually see by a moment's reflection that these are not exceptions at all. The multiplication table says nothing about what will *causally* ensue if we put drops in a pitcher or rabbits in a hutch; it leaves out everything that characterizes any of its units as opposed to any other, and interests itself only in units as units, that is as entities regarded simply as distinguishable. It says: Take any set of 5 units, of which, for the present purpose, we know nothing except that they are distinct, add to them in thought 5 other such units, and you *must* have 10. If one see this *must*, one will not be shaken by suggestions that in this or that queer instance an exception has turned up. One will merely start hunting for the fallacy that led anyone to suppose he has found such an exception.

§7.

Now does this fact that in arithmetic the appeal to empirical confirmation is needless show that arithmetic is not true of the empirical order? I do not see that it does. The assertion seems to rest on two confusions. (a) The first is the now familiar confusion of supposing that because a statement says nothing about this rather than that, it says nothing at all. What arithmetic says is that so far as things are regarded merely as classes of units, certain necessary relations will be found among these classes. Now things *can* be so regarded. One may abstract in a set of ten clothespins from everything about them— everything that they have in common and everything that differentiates them—except that here are ten somethings distinguishable from each other. We know that to this group of ten X's all the properties applying to the number ten will also apply. We know, further, that all actual and possible groups, because their members are distinguishable somethings, will have arithmetical properties, and that every thing and quality will be a member of many such groups. Thus our knowledge of the multiplication table supplies us, so far as it goes, with knowledge of the world. As Whitehead says, "the first noticeable fact about arithmetic is that it applies to everything, to tastes and sounds, to apples and angels, to the ideas of the mind and to the bones of the body."[10]

(b) A second source of the error that arithmetic tells us nothing of the real is a confusion about form and content. It is supposed that form would still be significant if there were nothing it could apply to, and that when we talk logic or mathematics, we are saying something not only without reference to this or that thing, but without reference to any possible content. This is not true. In a world that lacked distinguishable things, numbers would be meaningless, like "up" with no "down," or "out" with no "in." Number means number *of* something. Where there is nothing numerable, there is no number. Not that the numerable things need be of any specified type; numerical statements do not have to wait for what is called "interpretation" in order to become meaningful. They are of the highly abstract but important kind that says something about all that is.

§8.

There is something very odd in having to defend the view that mathematical statements give us light about the world at a time when natural science is scoring its greatest triumphs with the aid of mathematics. There is also something paradoxical in having to defend it against the very philosophers—the logical empiricists—who think that science gives us our only reliable knowledge. These philosophers draw the sharpest possible line between the necessary statements of mathematics, which are alleged to say nothing about nature, and these statements as "interpreted," which are then taken as empirical generalizations to be tested by sense experience. Starting from this sharp division, they naturally find it a problem how the propositions of the multiplication table can be true of empirical things. Professor Hempel writes: "the propositions of mathematics are devoid of all factual content; they convey no information whatever on any empirical subject matter." This he says as a logical empiricist. But he immediately adds, as a physical scientist, "This result seems to be irreconcilable with the fact that after all mathematics has proved to be eminently applicable to empirical subject matter, and that indeed the greater part of present-day scientific knowledge has been reached only through continual reliance on and application of the propositions of mathematics."[11] His way out of the impasse is a simple one. It is to distinguish within a proposition of applied mathematics a part that is

[10] *An Introduction to Mathematics*, 2.

[11] "On the Nature of Mathematical Truth," Feigl and Sellars, *Readings in Philosophical Analysis*, 234. See his equally good article that follows on 'Geometry and Empirical Science.'

purely formal, which is admitted to be necessary, and another part that is empirical and without necessity. While agreeing that 5+5=10, he would, if I follow him, deny that "5 apples and 5 apples are 10 apples" is a necessary statement on the grounds (a) that whether the formal concepts do apply, whether the groups before us do number 5, 5, and 10 respectively, is an empirical matter, in which we might be mistaken, and (b) that anything said about *apples*, which are known only empirically, is likewise fallible and subject to empirical check. Now this doctrine seems to imply that we can never be sure that any mathematical "truth" (whatever that now means) has any applications anywhere, since any possible example would be open to both these objections. But the doctrine implies more: it implies that instead of being "eminently applicable," as Mr. Hempel suggests, mathematics never will or can apply anywhere. For to say that it applies is to say just such things as that 5 and 5 apples make 10 apples; and so far as this proposition is mathematical, it has nothing to do with apples, while so far as it concerns apples, it is not mathematics. It would thus appear that the real tendency of positivist doctrine is not to exalt exact science but to depreciate it by making "the queen of the sciences" sterile of any knowledge of the world.

§9.

Our own way out of the impasse is to deny both (a) and (b) in their unqualified forms. (a) It is true that we determine the number of an aggregate by counting, and that our result may be mistaken. But (i) the likelihood of such error is often negligible. If we can never be sure that we have five apples before us rather than four or six, there is little or nothing of which we can be sure. (ii) Even if we err in counting, there is a curious fact about such error. Though we may be mistaken as to the particular number of things we are trying to count, we cannot be mistaken in our report that there are countable things, or, therefore, that things exist to which number applies. If we mistake six things for five things, we have at least found a numerable aggregate of distinct things in the world, and if there is a numerable aggregate, arithmetic applies to it. The objection might be offered that it is theoretically possible to think one has found a plurality where no plurality exists. I do not think this even theoretically possible. For if the plurality counted is an illusion, at least the plurality in the acts of distinction in which the counting consists can hardly be an illusion. Furthermore, to deny plurality is to say that this is true rather than that; this admits *two* distinguishable entities; and with the number two, carrying all other numbers in its train, arithmetic steals back into the picture.

(b) In the proposition "5 apples + 5 apples = 10 apples," is it true that the mathematical part says nothing about apples, and that so far as anything is said about apples, it is empirical merely? The division seems to me too sharp. The logical and the empirical are more intimately united than this. We may grant that whether what is before us is an apple, whether it is red or round or hard, must be determined empirically, and that arithmetic has nothing to do with apples or reds as such. But we must remember also that the simplest recognition of an apple is logically complex. It is not only the identification of this apple as opposed to other apples, or of apples as opposed to other kinds of thing, but of what is more abstract still, a something distinct from something else. And such abstract *distincta* are precisely what arithmetic deals with. In counting five apples, even if every identification is mistaken, it remains true that we have arrived at five somethings-or-other which in this abstraction constitute numerical units. Is our achievement of such units an empirical or an intellectual affair? Such either-ors are hardly in place here. It is both. The successive objects of our sensation would no doubt be called empirical, and perhaps also the successive strokes of our attention; but each of these objects and acts has implicit in it that character of a *distinction* which makes it amenable to arithmetical handling; and the explicit apprehension of this character, or of the number of the instances in the case before us, is presumably an intellectual act. Reason and sense work so closely together here that to mark off their contributions sharply is impracticable. They work in interdependence.

§*10.*

(3) We have seen that logic and arithmetic supply us with their own highly abstract truth about things and classes. Can we say the same of geometry? There are three different questions here, corresponding to the three levels of abstractness on which geometry may be pursued. Pure geometry starts from primitive terms and propositions so abstract that the ordinary connotations of "point," "straight line," and "surface" are not involved, and there may be nothing to indicate that one is dealing with spatial relations at all. Such geometry does not advance beyond the kind of knowledge we have been discussing. Secondly, Euclidean and non-Euclidean geometries do go beyond this and deal with space, but each with its own kind of space, defined by its special postulates, and with no assumption that its space is that of the actual world. Euclid's space, for example, is that in which, if one starts with a straight line, one can draw through a point outside that line only one parallel line; Lobachevsky's space is one in which a variety of such parallels can be drawn; and Rie-

mann's is one in which none can be drawn. Each system is valid, and each tells us, therefore, what would be true in a space constructed according to its postulates. But none of them, as developed by modern geometers, offers itself as an account of relations in physical space. Thirdly, at a lower level of abstraction than either of these types, stands physical geometry. It is this that particularly interests the philosopher, since what it seeks is a geometrical knowledge of nature. Is there really any such thing? Does it make sense to speak of a *rational* knowledge of actual spatial relations?

That we do possess such knowledge was for many centuries taken for granted; Euclid had supplied it and Newton's physics assumed that he had. But a very simple reflection is enough to call the assumption in question. The points, lines, and planes of which Euclid was speaking were not empirical things at all. A geometrical point, for example, was supposed to be without parts and without magnitude, and it is obvious that what has no size would be invisible; we can see nothing smaller than a dot. Further, a line is supposed to be a continuous series of points; but if a point is really without size, you cannot produce something that does have size by putting a great many points side by side; indeed they have no sides. Thus the lines of the geometer are as far removed from chalk lines on a blackboard as his points are from dots. Again geometrical surfaces are made up of an infinite number of lines drawn side by side, and geometrical solids of an infinite series of stratified surfaces; but neither sort of entity has ever been felt or seen. If it is such remote and fictional things as these that geometry deals with, what reason have we to say that it tells us anything about nature at all? The logical positivist would say quite simply that it tells us nothing, and that our knowledge of actual space is purely empirical. But in view of the confident and successful use of geometrical theorems in the building of bridges, the construction of tennis courts, and the guidance of rockets, this is a paradox. "It is surely not insignificant to ask whether there may be constructed with ruler and compass a circle equal in area to a given square."[12] Does the geometrical demonstration that this is impossible tell us nothing about what we may expect in actual experience?

§11.

At least two suggestions have been made in recent years that help us to bridge the gap between the ideal figures of geometry and the actual ones of experience. One comes from C. D. Broad.[13] Broad

---

[12] M. R. Cohen, *Preface to Logic*, 54.
[13] *Examination of McTaggart's Philosophy*, I, 42–45.

points out that empirical series may be of different kinds: we can see of some of them a priori that they have no limits, and of others that they have. If we take a series of increasing hotnesses, for example, we can see that there is nothing in the series to require a halt at any point; when we had reached the hotness of boiling water, we could go on to that of a furnace, and from there to the heat of the sun, and so on apparently without limit. On the other hand, suppose we take first a very jagged line, like that of the edge of a cross-cut saw, and then a less jagged one like the edge of a carpenter's saw, and proceed to decrease the jaggedness at each step; is this series without limit? No; we can see a priori that there is a limit to it; when we have reached zero jaggedness, we have a straight line, beyond which the continuation of the series is logically impossible. Now if this suggestion is correct, we have a priori knowledge about empirical fact, in the sense that of some empirical series we can see a priori that they have a certain kind of limit. Even if no line that we ever see is perfectly straight, we can still say of a given line that it belongs to an imaginable series whose limit would be a line of a certain kind, and we can talk of that line with the aid of any member of the series. Similarly of the arc of the moon or a rocket or a rainbow in relation to the perfect geometrical circle. Actual figures may always fall short of geometrical ones, and still be related to them necessarily. Such a theory, instead of having Platonic figures "laid up in heaven," builds an intelligible bridge to them from the figures of actual space.

§12.

Another pregnant suggestion was made by Whitehead in his "principle of extensive abstraction." He proposed to regard a point, or a line, or a surface, not as the limit of a series, but as the series itself. This is a welcome suggestion to those who are averse to Euclidean points and Platonic figures. Suppose one holds, for example, that the Euclidean point, something with position but no parts or magnitude, is unreal and inconceivable; is geometry therefore to be bereft of meaning? Not at all, says Whitehead. For even if there is no such thing as this shadowy point, we can still conceive the series of volumes that would ordinarily be said to converge upon it. We can conceive of a series of Chinese boxes one inside the other, or a series of concentric spheres growing smaller and smaller. Whitehead's discovery was that for geometrical purposes, the series of these concentric volumes had all the properties traditionally assigned to points while at the same time requiring us to deal only with finite and verifiable magnitudes, and that lines, surfaces, and other mathematical entities could be dealt with in the same way.

It might be objected that volumes are different in kind from points, and that one is not solving the problem of their relation by substituting the one for the other. There are two answers. First, in mathematics a thing is defined by its properties, and if, for all purposes of the science, the properties of the converging series of volumes are the same as those of the original points, the two concepts are interchangeable. Secondly, even if one sticks to points, the new notion can be made to approximate to the old within any desired degree. One of the functions of a pair of points, for example, is to determine the connection between them which we call a straight line. If we substitute basketballs for these points, the line that connects them, being an imaginary cable as thick as the balls themselves, will hardly be accepted as a line at all. But substitute billiard balls for the basketballs, marbles for the billiard balls, and birdshot for the marbles, and the terms will come closer and closer to defining your notion of a line; and the series provides for making the line as gossamer as you please. The older geometry would have it that the line talked about is the line of zero thickness forming the limit of this series. Whitehead held that for all purposes of the physical geometer this line could be dismissed as an airy nothing in favor of the series of converging volumes, and geometry would retain all its validity. We can conceive of any actual dot or ball as enclosed in such a series, and base on the latter our geometrical deductions. We shall thus have a genuinely geometrical knowledge of the physical world.[14]

§13.

Broad's suggestion differs from Whitehead's; one, as I understand it, would still have physical geometry deal with the limit of an empirical series, the other with the series itself. But they agree that such geometry is more than a compound of tautology and sensory report. It supplies us with necessary knowledge about actual things. This answers to an old conviction of common sense, which has found a persistent and at times a passionate expression in both speculative rationalism and physical science. "God forever geometrizes," said the Plato recorded by Plutarch. "Nature's great book," said Galileo, "is written in mathematical language." "What a deep conviction of the rationality of the universe," Einstein exclaimed, "and what a yearning to understand, were it but a feeble reflection of the mind revealed in this world, Kepler and Newton must have had to enable them to spend years of solitary labour in disentangling the principles of celes-

---

[14] Whitehead's explanation of extensive abstraction is given in *The Concept of Nature*, Ch. IV, and *The Principles of Natural Knowledge*, Pt. III. There is a brief and clear account of it also in Broad's *Scientific Thought*, 38–52.

tial mechanics!"[15] This attitude has largely remained in the new scientific era that Einstein ushered in. It may be that Sir James Jeans was going beyond his scientific brief, as Professor Stebbing alleged, when he said that "the universe can best be pictured, although still very imperfectly and inadequately, as consisting of pure thought, the thought of what, for want of a wider word, we must describe as a mathematical thinker."[16] But he was not exceeding his knowledge as an astronomer when he said that "nature seems very conversant with the rules of pure mathematics."[17] It has sometimes been thought that quantum mechanics is inconsistent with such a view. An event of such dimensions that we can perceive it is composed of minute and invisible events of whose behavior singly nothing is known; we must study their behavior in masses or great aggregates, and when we do so, we find that the laws governing it express probabilities only. But then probability itself, if quantitative, must be formulated in mathematical terms, and laws do not become less open to such formulation when they become statistical.

Working scientists like Jeans, Eddington, and Einstein are sometimes charged by persons not conspicuously qualified to do so with mere romancing when they talk about the mathematical framework of the universe. And it must be admitted that actual masses, velocities, and distances have no place among the terms of pure mathematics. "By 'pure mathematics' is meant those departments of mathematics which are creations of pure thought, of reason operating solely within her own sphere, as contrasted with 'applied mathematics' which reasons about the external world, after first taking some supposed property of the external world as its raw material."[18] To let the mathematical x stand for any actual mass or velocity always involves a venture in the dark which may come to nothing. On the other hand, it may strike a spark or a flash which suddenly illuminates the structure of things. Suppose you have two x's possessed respectively of properties M^1 and M^2 and of a mutual and quantitative relation R. And suppose you form the hypothesis that there is a second relation between them, G, which varies with the quantity $M^1 \times M^2$ and inversely with the quantity R^2. Suppose that with this precise but barren formula in mind, you introduce substitutions. You let the two x's be the earth and the moon, let M^1 and M^2 stand respectively for their masses, assumed to be concentrated at their centers, let R be

[15] *The World As I See It*, 27.
[16] *The Mysterious Universe*, 2nd ed., 124. For Miss Stebbing's criticism, which is perhaps unduly severe, see her *Philosophy and the Physicists*, Ch. II.
[17] *Op. cit.*, 113.
[18] Jeans, *op. cit.*, 113–114.

the distance between these centers, and G stand for gravitational force. Then suppose that, based on these substitutions, you make a dozen or a hundred predictions as to the course the moon will follow, and find with the closest observable accuracy that it does follow that course. Next suppose that for the variables of the formula you go on to substitute other masses at random—including tides and apples, the sun and the planets—and find that their behavior answers to the predictions required by your formula. When such things have been successfully done, is it visionary to say, as Newton did, that one has found a mathematical framework in nature? We suggest that he was amply entitled to say so. But what if some bodies, or even all bodies, are found to diverge slightly from the formula? Would not this be enough to destroy the notion of a mathematical order in nature? No, not at all, if the divergences are themselves found capable of formulation and prediction. The predictions based on inserting into our formulas gross masses and crudely measured distances are perhaps never quite precise; but "although there is always a remainder, we can still maintain the ideal of mathematical analysis, always looking in the deviations of our theories for those mathematical threads of identity which bind new laws and new fields of experience to our problem."[19]

§14.

(4) Further chains of necessary connections in which all existing things are bound are those of *serial order*. Some types of order, such as those of ordinal numbers and of points on a line, may be fairly thought to belong among the arithmetical and geometrical relations already considered, but the orders of degree, of temporal succession, and of the series that lead to the infinitely large and infinitely small may well have separate mention.

When an order is called "serial," it is usually assumed to have a direction, so that A is not related to B as B is to A. But where these relations are the same—in technical usage "symmetrical"—the type of order remains unchanged, however the terms are re-disposed. The order of quality is an example. Necessity enters into this order in the sense that things equal to the same thing are necessarily all equal to each other. Of course the equality must be in the same respect. A is equal to B in height or weight or speed, and B to C in the same respect; hence in that respect A and C are equal. Are such insights purely formal, or can we see them to hold of actual things? Where the respect in which things are declared equal is numerical, we can

[19] M. R. Cohen, *Reason and Nature*, 204.

often reason thus with a certainty that it would be merely captious to question. If the graces equal the muses in number, and the muses equal the team that the New York Yankees now have on the field, then it must be conceded, however surprising, that in one respect the Yankees equal the graces. Where the respect in which equality is ascribed is height, weight, or speed, the principle of the inference is still certain, but whether the conclusion is true will depend on the material truth of the premises, and this in turn on the exactitude of our measurements. Exact equality in any respect would be identity in that respect, as we have argued earlier, and there is no reason to deny that such identities occur in nature. But even where they do, the best we can assert in fact will as a rule be similarity.

The term "order," however, is usually reserved for series in which one cannot move indifferently forward or backward. Such series are asymmetrical; if A precedes B, B cannot also precede A; they are often transitive also, in the sense, for example, that if A precedes B, and B, C, then A precedes C. Now the beads of our particular experiences are strung on a large number of such serial threads, each of them constituting lines of necessary relation. As Kant pointed out, every quality we ever sense is on the same scale of intensity with every other of the same kind; everything that is hot or hard, sweet or sour, bright or loud, sharp or heavy, rough or large, is related, and necessarily related, to all other things possessing a quality falling under the same "determinable." "When one term does, by virtue of one and the same point in it, stand in a relation of degree with two or more other terms, then these others are also related in degree."[20] Of anything that is visible we may say a priori not merely that it is identical with or similar to everything else that is visible in respect to having brightness, but also that if it differs in brightness from B in the same way as B differs from C, then it differs itself in the same way from C. Such a priori knowledge of serial order does not apply to intensities only. It applies to length of lines and acuteness of angles, to sizes, masses, and velocities; and it is the basis of every variety of a fortiori argument. Perhaps its most obvious application is to times, for we are arguing constantly that if A comes before B, it will also precede anything contemporary with or subsequent to B. Sometimes we intertwine several strands of serial reasoning together. If General Wolfe died in 1759, Macaulay in 1859, and G. E. Moore in 1959, if Moore was a better philosopher than Macaulay and Macaulay than Wolfe, and if Wolfe was a better soldier than Macaulay and Macaulay than Moore, then there died, two centuries after another, a man who was a worse soldier but a better philosopher.

[20] Bradley, *Principles of Logic*, I, 266.

§15.

It has already been pointed out that empirical series may be seen a priori to have certain properties, for example, the property of having a certain kind of limit. It seems also to be the case that some can be seen to be endless, and this raises at once the question of external and internal infinities. An external infinity is one determined by the extension of a series beyond given limits, an internal infinity one determined by the continued division of a whole into smaller parts. Consider, for example, the extension of the series of moments in time, either into the past or into the future. Is there any reason for saying that the series had a beginning or will have an end? Apparently not. There is nothing in the constitution of the series that calls for a first or last term, and to halt the progression at any moment, no matter how far away, is arbitrary. Indeed a beginning or end of the temporal series seems strictly unthinkable. If one carries one's thought back to a certain moment selected as the first, one places this moment within the temporal series by contrasting it not only with the moments that follow it but also implicitly with the moments that precede it. One cannot think of a moment preceded by eternity or by nothing at all, not even empty time. And there is a like difficulty for anyone who would bring the series to an end.

What of internal infinities? Are we to say of any segment of the temporal series that it may be divided endlessly? Again this seems to be a necessity in the very nature of time. When an hour is divided into minutes, and a minute into seconds, and a second into shorter components, we soon reach a point where our power to distinguish still shorter durations ceases, but there is no reason to suppose that such durations do not exist merely because we cannot perceive them; in principle any duration, however short, may be divided and subdivided without end.

§16.

(5) Differing attributes and even categories may be so connected that we can see that whatever has one must also have another. Shape and size are different attributes, but if a thing has shape it must have size also. Colour is not the same attribute as extension, but if we know that something is coloured, we need not wait till we inspect it to assure ourselves that it covers some extent in space. If we know that a sound has some pitch, is it a matter of probability only that it will also have some degree of loudness? Clearly not. We can see that, different as they are, the first character could not occur without the other. Once more, according to Aristotle and others who have

drawn up lists of categories, qualities are ultimately different from relations. But could qualities exist without relations? Obviously qualities in the plural could not, since they would be connected at least by the relation of difference. Could a *single* quality exist in a world where there were no relations at all? It could not exist in time, for if it did, an earlier phase of it would be related to a later phase. Nor could it exist in space, since if it occupied space, its parts would be spatially related, and if it existed somehow at a point, the point would have to be somewhere, and this "somewhere" again implies relations. Even in a world in which space and time were done away—if such a world can be conceived—a single scent, for example, could be what it was only by being different from other possible qualities; in short, to be at all is to be this rather than that, and the rather-than-that is an inseparable adjunct of being this.

Not only can we see at times that if something has a certain character, it must also have another; we can often see that if something is of a certain kind, it *cannot* belong to certain other kinds. There is necessary exclusion as well as necessary accompaniment. Joseph proposed as a necessary judgment, "Thought is not laryngeal motion." I agree, and can only suppose that if behaviorists do not, there is radical confusion on one side or on the other. Husserl offered "A judgment cannot be colored." Descartes suggested, "Unity is not a quantity." Other similar insights are "Number is not the thing that is counted," and "The difference between two degrees of quality is not itself a quality." These are all exclusions, and apparently necessary ones, that cross categorical lines.

§17.

(6) There are similar relations of necessity that link, both positively and negatively, the determinates of the same determinable. Consider the inter-relation of colors. There have been many attempts in recent years to show that statements of color relation are merely empirical. No doubt the statements that this patch of grass is green and that patch of sky is blue are, so far as present insight goes, empirical purely. Is this also true of the statement that in the table of color affinities, orange is between red and yellow, or the statement that it is nearer to yellow than to blue? Is it true of the statement that purple is more closely related to blue and red than it is to green? No answers I have seen have effectively challenged what seems to be the position of common sense on these points. If one asked the ordinary man, who had just remarked that a given orange shade fell between given shades of red and yellow whether it would also fall between them in other instances where the shades were the same, he would

think the question a silly one; of course they would, for if the relation is really between the colors, it must hold wherever the colors are the same. As Isaiah Berlin puts it, "invited to conceive of a world in which the shades we call pink, red, black, occurred in some order other than that presented in ours, we must say that we cannot do so: not because of a failure of imagination, but because it is inconceivable: the invitation is itself nonsensical."[21]

Thus determinates of the same determinable may be necessarily linked with each other. There is also a negative linkage: they exclude each other necessarily when asserted of the same subject. A surface that is pure red cannot, at the same time and to the same observer, be pure green. It has been alleged that this is an analytic statement, that it says only that the two colors are different, which is already involved in their being two. But the statement clearly goes beyond this. A color and a shape are different, but they can belong at once to the same surface; what our statement tells us is not merely that the colors are different, but that in the same subject they are exclusive of each other. Again, being exclusive of green, though it is entailed by being red, is hardly part of what we *mean* by being red, nor not-being-red part of what we mean by being green. Nor is there any *formal* contradiction in saying that what is red is also green, any more than in saying that what is red is also square. The *must* arises from the content; it is in virtue of the special character of being red, in distinction for example from being square, that the red excludes the green. What we have is a particular kind of incompatibility, based not on the form of the propositions but on the nature of the predicates.

§18.

(7) There has been a stubborn tradition in western philosophy that necessity is to be found also in the sphere of values. This has been challenged of late years by an ethical theory which holds that judgments of good or evil, right or wrong, are not judgments at all, but imperatives or expressions of feeling. If we say that Plato's wisdom was good and the suffering of Bruno's martyrdom evil, we are, to be sure, implying matters of fact, namely that Plato was wise and Bruno a martyr; but the value words in our statements assert nothing whatever; they are not even *reports* of our own attitudes; they are rather exclamations expressive of these, like "ouch!" or "cheers!". If this is true, all statements of value would seem to be removed from the sphere of necessity at one stroke. Necessity links characters or the propositions that ascribe them; but values are not characters, nor are value statements propositions. And the attempt to prove or refute a

21 *Proc. of the Arist. Soc.*, Supplementary Vol. 16 (1937), 77.

feeling by reason is inept, as if, when you said "cheers!", I said, "Nay not so, and on the following grounds."

I do not think that this attempt to reduce value statements to expressions of attitude has succeeded.[22] To say that when we call Plato's wisdom good or suffering evil we mean nothing that held of these things at the time they existed, but are expressing only our present feelings about them, remains very unconvincing. However hard it may be to bring to light and define what we mean here by "good" and "evil," we do mean something by them, and something that does not come and go with our fluctuating attention. If such words refer to characters in the object, are these characters linked to fact and to each other by relations of necessity? I do not myself know how to deny it. The judgment that intense suffering as such is evil—intrinsically as opposed to instrumentally evil—is not a merely empirical one like "grass is green" or "snow is white." We know that grass is often in fact not green, and that snow could conceivably be other than white. But that a given pain should be bad as felt by one man, and that a pain of precisely the same kind and intensity as felt by another should be good—this I think we can see to be inconsistent and absurd. Again, when we say that Plato's wisdom is intrinsically good, our ultimate meaning, I am inclined to hold, is that such wisdom fulfills and satisfies human nature;[23] and the perception that, given the desires and capacities of our nature, such wisdom would partially fulfill these seems to me more than a merely contingent insight. Still again, the perception that one value, for example that of clear understanding, is intrinsically better than another, for example that of ignorance or confusion, may be a necessary one. I say *may* be, for claims to necessary insight in ethics may be as mistaken as they sometimes are in mathematics. But if the fact that they are sometimes mistaken in mathematics does not imply that they are always so, neither should it in ethics.

§19.

Necessity appears also at other points in ethical thinking. To say that I *can* do something is not the same as to say that I *ought* to do it, and clearly does not entail this: but if I ought to do it, it does follow, and follow necessarily, that I can do it. Once more, if Jones, a landlord, has a right to the payment of rent by his tenant, Smith, Jones's right is not the same fact, or at least not the same aspect of the same fact, as Smith's duty to pay; but it does entail or necessitate this duty.

[22] For one statement of the case, see my *Reason and Goodness*, Ch. VIII and IX.
[23] Cf. *Reason and Goodness*, Chap. XI–XIII.

Many moralists have sought to find in ordinary rules of truth-telling, promise-keeping, etc., statements that were necessarily true. The attempt has usually foundered on the consideration that what is necessary must be also universal, and that there are no rules of this intermediate level that seem to hold without exception. It was shown, however, by that most judicial of moralists, Sidgwick, that the claim to necessary ethical principles could be made good at a higher level of generality. He pointed to certain propositions in ethics which were genuine axioms in the older sense of that term, principles which, though undemonstrable, were necessary and exceptionless. There were at least three of these—the axioms of prudence, benevolence, and equity.[24] "It does on reflection strike us as self-evident," says Rashdall in summarizing them, "that I ought to promote my own good on the whole (where no one else's good is affected), that I ought to regard a larger good for society in general as of more intrinsic value than a smaller good, and that one man's good is (other things being equal) of as much intrinsic value as any other man's."[25] These principles may be so stated as to be tautologies merely, but as actually used in moral reflection Sidgwick did not consider them so. I agree.

If what we have said about value judgments is true, ethical reflection is shot through with rational insight. The inference that a certain action will produce consequences of a certain kind is indeed based upon experience and may have no seen necessity about it. But the insights that a certain consequence would be good, that it would be better than a certain alternative consequence, and that the good to be produced should be distributed in certain ways—all these are, or may be, genuine apprehensions of necessity. And if they are, the pursuit of morality is a rational pursuit. The good life, as the three great Greeks maintained, is the life of reason, not in the sense that it consists of thinking merely, though Aristotle at times suggested this, but in the sense that the judgments most essential for the guidance of life are rational judgments, open only to minds that can grasp necessities in the field of value.

§20.

This chapter began with a reminder of the current revolt against reason as a means of knowing nature. It is alleged that so far as reason deals with necessities, it is confined to the conventions of our own minds and can tell us nothing of necessities in the world of things and events. We have reviewed seven fields of experience in which the

[24] Sidgwick, *The Methods of Ethics*, Bk. III, Ch. 13, Sec. 3.
[25] *The Theory of Good and Evil*, I, 90–91.

knowledge of necessity seems clearly present, not as a convention but as a discovery, not as a relation among meanings only but as linking the attributes of things and persons. The notion that the world is a gigantic ragbag of loose ends, in which nothing is connected intelligibly with anything else, will not stand even a cursory examination. The world as we know it is shot through and through with lines of necessity, and there is every reason to believe that if we knew it better, we should see those lines to be more numerous and far-ramified than at present they seem. Even now we must take the world as a consistent whole; it is at least governed by the law of non-contradiction; thought must start with that, not as a rule of usage merely, but as governing the structure of things. We saw that numerical and geometrical thinking, rightly interpreted, also applies to the existent. We found, again, that qualities come to us in serial orders such that in a given order all the members are necessarily connected with each other. We found that there are bridges of necessity from one quality to others of different kinds, that there are necessities linking the determinates of a determinable, that necessities seem to abound even in our thought about value.

No claim for exhaustiveness is made for this review, and no doubt many other types of necessity could be brought to light. But fragmentary as it is, the list makes a massive demurrer against the claim that reason reveals no necessities in nature. The resolute rationalist would of course go much further. He would point out that these, after all, are only scattered threads of necessity tying abstractions together, and that they are bound to raise two further questions about the range of necessity in the world. First, does necessity link universals only, or does it also link things and events? Again, does it supply the warp of nature without its woof; does it link some items and not others; or is its network all-involving? The first question raises the issue whether the main link between events, causation, is itself a necessary relation. The second asks whether the cosmos itself may, with any ground, be regarded as an intelligible whole. . . .

BIBLIOGRAPHY

BLANSHARD, Brand, *The Nature of Thought.* 2 vols. N.Y.: Macmillan, 1939.
_____, *Philosophy in American Education.* N.Y.: Harpers, 1945.
_____, *On Philosophical Style.* Bloomington: Indiana U. Press, 1954.
_____, *The Impasse in Ethics and a Way Out.* Berkeley: U. of California Press, 1955.

_____, (ed.) *Education in the Age of Science*. N.Y.: Basic Books, 1959.

_____, *Reason and Goodness*. N.Y.: Macmillan, 1961.

_____, *Reason and Analysis*. London: Allen & Unwin, 1962.

_____, *Preface To Philosophy*. (With W. Hocking, C. Hendel and J. H. Randall, Jr.) N.Y.: Macmillan, 1946.

_____, "The Philosophy of Analysis," *Proceedings of the British Academy,* XXXVIII, 1952, pp. 39–69.

Materialism

The "Foreword" to a book of selections on materialism, edited by Roy Wood Sellars, Marvin Farber, and V. J. McGill, is reprinted below because it summarizes one aspect of twentieth-century materialism. Materialism has had a long career in Western thought, from the Greek philosophers, through the Newtonian period and Marxism, down to the present day. There are many variations on the same basic theme: matter is in some way primary, and the findings of science are the most reliable guide to the nature of the universe. One point of dispute, however, among materialists and their critics, concerns the issue of reductionism. Can all the laws of the various sciences be reduced to those of physics and chemistry, or are there levels of explanation? The selection below suggests that a theory of levels is perfectly consistent with materialism. The editors maintain that many naturalists are not forthright enough in their commitment to a world view, and accordingly they recommend the materialist position.

Roy Wood Sellars (1880–). See biographical note on page 363.

Marvin Farber (1901–). Although Farber is sympathetic to materialistic and naturalistic points of view, he is best known for his writings on phenomenology. Farber took his B.A. and Ph.D. (1925) at Harvard. He also studied with Husserl and his group at Freiburg. He has been a member of the Department of Philosophy at the State University of New York at Buffalo for many years. Farber is the founder and editor of the journal, *Philosophy and Phenomenological Research* (since 1940) and President of the International Phenomenological Society. He was a Guggenheim Fellow and a President of the American Philosophical Association, Eastern Division (1963). Among his important books are: *The Foundation of Phenomenology* (1943), and *Naturalism and Subjectivism* (1959).

V. J. McGill (1897–). McGill has had interests in both Marxism and psychology. He took his Ph.D. at Harvard in 1925, and also studied at Cambridge and Freiburg. He taught for many years at Hunter College. Recently he has been associated with the Institute for Philosophical Research. A former editor of *Science and Society,* he is the author of biographical studies of Strindberg and Schopenhauer and a book of philosophical–literary essays.

THE QUEST OF MODERN MATERIALISM [1]
(1949)

The growth of science and technology, the advance of medicine, universal education, and general enlightenment have greatly increased the valid authority of science. Any number of social questions which were once the exclusive prerogative of religion and conventional morality are now recognized as falling within the sphere of the social sciences. Sex and family relations are examples. Virtue and wickedness have largely given way to personality adjustment and maladjustment; and crime is traced in considerable measure to social causes. The schoolboy is no longer beaten as inherently bad or lazy because he neglects his studies. Nutritional, medical, personality factors are, instead, investigated, and the home life and associates of the boy are searched for contributing causes. In this shift from moral condemnation to technical remedies, we see the concurrent rise of science and humaneness. This kind of progress has resulted in an increasingly materialist outlook. But, as we shall see, it is a more subtle and adequate kind of materialism. . . .

The early Greeks wrote the first chapter of materialism, but many more are still to be added. . . . Modern materialism, as we understand it, asserts the following. The inorganic pattern of matter is prior to living, minded and purposive organisms, which arise gradually and only as a result of a complex evolutionary development. With the advent of organic life, new, biological laws begin to operate. The principles of physics and chemistry necessarily apply, but are not by themselves sufficient to the biological level. Thus mechanism or the theory that physicochemical explanation is adequate to all levels, is emphatically rejected. If a thing can be explained by physics and chemistry, however, it must be so explained, and there is no justification for adverting to any other level of the organization of matter. The inorganic and organic constitute distinctive levels, which can be referred to as lower and higher, in the sense that organic material systems are more highly organized and more complex, exhibiting new behavior traits. There are also many subsidiary levels, gradients, and resonances within the inorganic and organic. Within the organic, for example, we have cell, tissue, organ, organ system, organism, and population. Each level except the first contains all lower levels within it. For example, the tissue contains cells, which in turn have chemical components. The cell within a tissue, however, does not behave just

[1] From *Philosophy for the Future* (eds. R. W. Sellars, V. J. McGill, M. Farber), N.Y.: Macmillan, 1949. Selections from "Foreword," pp. v–xi.

as it does outside the tissue. Chemistry within the cell, too, is altered by the envelope which contains it. The one-floor plan of the classical biological mechanism is thus superseded by a modern structure displaying many diverse stories. The top stories, however, are always supported by the lower floors; and all floors must rest upon the ground floor studied by physics and chemistry. The diverse stories, the modern materialist insists, can be easily confirmed by scientific methods. Organized matter reveals integrative levels of organization characterized by distinctive laws.

As to the nature of matter, the materialist as a philosopher has nothing factual to add to the account of the scientists, although scientists may sometimes use "matter" in a limited sense (interpreting light, for example, as matter if it is corpuscular, but not if it is of wave form). The materialist holds that philosophers cannot improve upon the descriptive concepts of matter supplied by the working scientists of his time. He accepts what the physicist, chemist, biologist, histologist, etc. say as the best approximation at any given time. But he should be able to add considerable epistemological clarification along with semantic and categorial analysis. History shows this is also needed.

The theory of integrative levels turns its back upon any crude mechanism, much as recent science is doing, but also guards against new and subtle forms of Vitalism. In conformity with the findings of the biological sciences, purpose, intention, plan are confined to the top reaches of the phylogenetic scale. General teleology is therefore excluded. The modern materialist forgoes the comfort, unless it be in poetic reverie, of imagining that the order of nature is attuned to his purposes, or endowed with sensitivity and beneficence. Such longings have yielded myths in all ages, but are scarcely appropriate for a scientific era like our own. The materialist makes himself at home in the world, not by investing Nature with purpose, but by transforming it to meet his needs. The vast strides already accomplished by science in controlling and utilizing and molding nature are an earnest of the advances to be worked for and achieved in the future. Modern materialism is thus marked by an effective, working optimism.

Modern materialism is hospitable to every effective method of the sciences, and excludes no procedure which is likely to yield understanding or prediction. It characteristically emphasizes explanation in terms of causal and genetic relations, in contrast to idealism, which makes the relations of ideas primary, and explains the course of the world in terms of abstractions. While insisting on the indispensability of highly specialized, detached studies of various subject matters, the modern materialist recognizes the equal importance of integrating special departmental studies into a comprehensive world view. He thus emphasizes, in contrast to many other philosophical tendencies, the interrelatedness of things. Materialism does not doubt the possibility of satisfying man's need for a comprehensive picture of the universe, and asserts the capacity of scientific methods eventually to cope with basic human problems. It therefore combats agnosticism, skepticism, and all irrational confessions of defeat.

Thought and symbolism have a strategic role in the material world at the human level, but always in close connection with brain events and brain traces. No mental process occurs without its appropriate neural patterns. In the behavior of the organism, the psychic and biological are fused. The movement of an animal is not merely transposition in space but also movement to escape, for example, or movement for food. Movement is psychobiological. There are not two processes that satisfy basic needs and desires—one mental, the other physical—but rather one psychobiological process. The study of behavior is the only scientific approach to the understanding of mind; but this does not rule out hypotheses as to the contents of other minds, that is, reconstructions of mental states of others, on the basis of behavior. Language is here of primary import. Introspection is, of course, a valid method, but the final test of it is behavioral. Obviously excluded by our position are dualisms, parallelisms, and simple or reductionist identity views of mental and bodily processes.

The psychobiological individual must be understood in his development and relations. Personality is conditioned by society and can only be comprehended in its historical context. The alleged conflict between the individual and society as such is artificial, for a human being is highly socialized. Conflicts which arise are concrete and historical. In accounting for the development of societies and their members, increasing importance has been assigned to economic factors, such as natural resources, technology, and ownership relationships; but it is necessary to recognize likewise the interweaving of other factors, such as education, art, and morals. The latter themselves, however, are not independent of economic conditions. To be rejected, in our view, are historical idealism, extreme economic determinism, and romantic pluralism, that is, the view that no systematic empirical account of history is possible.

The advance of science, technology, industrial organization, and rationality opens up the opportunity of a far fuller servicing of human needs than has ever been possible before. It is the socio-economic organization of men which lags behind, and prevents the full realization of human values inherent in our industrial and scientific efficiency.

Because modern materialism recognizes that cultural values must, in general, wait upon the servicing of vital needs, it favors forms of social organization which release the productive forces of the economy, so that men, living in some leisure and dignity, can express their genius, their intellectual and artistic bent. It demands a society which organizes full production for the maximum benefit of all its members. There is no evidence meanwhile that, with security and basic needs supplied, man will not make good use of his additional leisure and abundance, realizing indefinite potentialities.

Like naturalism, modern materialism is opposed to any other criterion of human value and policy than human needs and aspirations. It combats all forms of authoritarianism in morals and arts, opposes reduction of ethics to mere formalism, and rejects the appeal to any supposed extranatural source of experience. With the removal of a supernatural perspective, man must stand consciously on his own feet. Let him rise to his full stature and dignity.

The term "naturalism" has been defined by R. B. Perry as "the philosophical generalization of the sciences," and it has been determined with respect both to the content and to the method of the sciences. Unfortunately, the historical forms of naturalism have often been distinguished by their readiness to compromise, or cautiously to set limits to the use of scientific method. Thus, the naturalism of Spencer was tempered by his agnosticism; and the same may be said of Huxley. Added to this fact is the further circumstance that the evolutionary movement eventuated in what may be called a "pseudo-evolutionary" social philosophy, often referred to as "social Darwinism," in which there was a dangerous confusion of biological and social concepts. It is a notorious fact that writers such as Pearson and Kidd extolled or apologized for social conflicts in the name of biological values. The general term "naturalist" has been applied not only to such types, but also to the pantheistic Haeckel, to some emergent evolutionists with their natural piety and theistic acknowledgments, and to the contemporary group influenced by Dewey. In the recent volume *Naturalism and the Human Spirit* (edited by Y. H. Krikorian) the reader is informed that "contemporary naturalism recognizes much more clearly than did the tradition from which it stems that its distinction from other philosophical positions lies in the postulates and procedures which it criticizes and rejects rather than in any positive tenets of its own about the cosmos."

This passage will serve clearly to distinguish current naturalism from the frank materialism described above. Whereas this type of naturalism is reluctant to commit itself to a positive theory of the world, materialism endeavors to set forth a synoptic view of man and the universe implicit in the sciences at their present stage of development.

Realism, the view that matter is independent of cognition, is essential to materialism. The Realists, both the New and the Critical, did yeoman service against persisting forms of idealism. In so far as the New Realists were faithful to their realism, and did not resolve matter into sense-data or so-called neutral stuff, their thesis resembles a main tenet of materialism. On the whole critical realism is closer to materialism. Both schools, however, were myopic, restricting their interest to a few epistemological and metaphysical questions, whereas the gamut of materialist theory goes far beyond.

Just as realism and naturalism have taken many forms, there are also varieties of materialism. A number of these are listed in the fairly classical summaries of materialism in English, American, German, and French dictionaries and encyclopedias. There is *cosmological,* and *ontological materialism,* whose dominant motive is a comprehensive world-scheme. There is *medical materialism,* directed by the bias of physicians in favor of physiological causes for disease. There is *scientific materialism,* expressive of the methodology of science and opposed to dualistic vitalism. And there is *historical materialism,* begun as a protest against the speculative and idealistic approach to history. It held that economic and class relations were the main, though not the only, determinants of social development. And in all this we must be on guard against emotional transfers, such as moral materialism, and question-begging assumptions.

Materialism has had a long history, reflecting scientific climates and clashing cultural currents. Hobbes turned materialism to defense of secular power against the claims of the Church, and to the undermining of superstition. The spirit of the Enlightenment continues in the writings of Diderot, La Mettrie, Holbach, and Cabanis. The ideas of peace, progress, indefinite perfectibility and equality were impressed upon men's minds. Physiological interest grew. The brain came in for ever more consideration as something of its powers was guessed. In literature, this mode of thought maintained itself with Stendhal beyond the romantic reaction, to Balzac and Zola. The next wave of materialism appeared in Germany, largely as a challenge to speculative idealism. Here Feuerbach played a crucial part in a transition from Hegelian idealism to the dialectical materialism of Marx and Engels. Parallel to this development was the popular materialistic literature of Vogt, Moleschott, and Büchner. Despite crudities and confusions, they were instrumental for a short period in disseminating materialistic ideas and perspectives. Dialectical materialism, on the other hand, has continued its development, and today exerts enormous influence. . . .

Almost simultaneously with the understanding of social development came the theory of organic evolution. Now, for the first time, massive evidence was given for the view already suggested by ancient materialists, that man is inseparable from nature, and is the product of a long and continuous development from simpler forms of life.

"Materialism" has been used as a term of opprobrium for so long that numerous scholars who might well identify themselves with it, at least as a broad tendency, have chosen to use other names, and have carefully justified that action by repudiating "crude" forms of materialism in the past. But is it more justifiable to renounce "materialism" because of its crude and partially antiquated beginnings than to repudiate science because so many epochmaking changes in concepts and methods have come only in recent decades? The use of a particular term is not important in itself. The avoidance of a term or designation may, however, be important. It would not take long for a truly critical naturalism to become an object of condemnation in fideistic and conservative quarters, just as forthright materialism is today. The broad, programmatic, and self-corrective character of modern materialism makes unreserved endorsement possible to scholars who wish to preserve their birthright of independence, and the ideal of following wherever the facts may lead, in all fields of inquiry. . . .

BIBLIOGRAPHY

For works dealing with Materialism, the reader is referred to the General Bibliography, section 5.

Paul J. Tillich

[1886–   ]

Paul J. Tillich was born in Prussia, the son of a Protestant pastor. He was a chaplain in the German army in the First World War. Tillich received his Ph.D. from Breslau, and he taught philosophy and theology at Berlin, Marburg, Dresden, Leipzig and Frankfurt. As a leader and spokesman of the Christian Socialist Party, he espoused a religious socialism that was derived to a great extent from Marx' analysis of bourgeois society, though he claimed that he was not a Marxist in its strict political or economic sense. Soon after the Nazis came to power in Germany, Tillich was removed from the Chair of Philosophy of the University of Frankfurt, and in 1933 he was invited to Union Theological Seminary at Columbia University where he remained until 1955. He has also taught at Harvard (1955–62). More recently he joined the faculty of the Divinity School at the University of Chicago.

Tillich has had a profound effect upon American Protestant thought. Many consider him to be the greatest Protestant theologian in America, because he seems to provide a new interpretation and justification of religion, and because he is receptive to and uses existentialist and psychoanalytic ideas. But he has also appealed to a wide audience outside of Protestantism. Liberals have been attracted to his socialism. Many naturalists have found much in his work

that they can accept, for his interpretation of religion appears to be humanistic rather than transcendental.

Tillich has claimed that the Christian message must be reinterpreted in every age. He is an existentialist in his criticism of the equation of reality with rational thought or essence, and he relates reality to men's immediate experiences in actual living. Like other existentialists, particularly Heidegger, Tillich finds the problem of Being, and the human predicament in the face of non-being, central. Religion, Tillich affirms, is man's "ultimate concern" whatever its specific nature, and is the expression of the "depths of our being." He stresses the existential involvement of the subject in knowledge and the fragmentary and dynamic character of truth and human fulfillment. In a sense, this is similar to what many American thinkers, such as Dewey, have done. Tillich, however, is a critic of what he considers the exclusively "finite" character of instrumentalism and of other systems that underestimate the conditional, the irrational, and the tragic in human experience. Among Tillich's most important philosophical books published in America have been *Systematic Theology* (1951–63) and *The Courage to Be* (1952).

The article reprinted below, *Existential Philosophy* (1944), shows the influence of existentialism on

Tillich's thought. Here Tillich describes existentialism as seen from German eyes. The article was written before the post-War French revival of existentialism, so that it is not influenced by Sartre and Camus; nonetheless, it outlines some of ex-istentialism's main ideas (as Tillich views them), particularly the distinction between "essence" and "existence," and the concepts of "subjectivity," "finitude," "estrangement," and "anxiety."

EXISTENTIAL PHILOSOPHY [1]

The distinctive way of philosophizing which today calls itself *Existenzphilosophie* or "existential philosophy" emerged as one of the major currents of German thought under the Weimar Republic, counting among its leaders such men as Heidegger and Jaspers. But its history goes back at least a century, to the decade of the 1840's, when its main contentions were formulated by thinkers like Schelling, Kierkegaard, and Marx, in sharp criticism of the reigning "rationalism" or panlogism of the Hegelians; and in the next generation Nietzsche and Dilthey were among its protagonists. Its roots are still more ancient, deeply embedded in the pre-Cartesian German tradition of supra-rationalism and *Innerlichkeit* represented by Böhme.

Existential philosophy thus seems a specifically German creation. It sprang originally from the tensions of the German intellectual situation in the early nineteenth century. It has been strongly influenced by the political and spiritual catastrophes of the Germans in our own generation. Its terminology has been largely determined by the genius and often by the demon of the German language—a fact which makes the translation of Heidegger's *Sein und Zeit* so difficult.

But when we come to understand the import of the name and the basic critical drive of Existential philosophy, we realize that it is part of a more general philosophical movement which counts its representatives in France, England, and America as well as in Germany. For in calling men back to "existence," these German thinkers are criticizing the identification of Reality or Being with Reality-as-known, with the object of Reason or thought.

Starting from the traditional distinction between "essence" and "existence," they insist that Reality or Being in its concreteness and fullness is not "essence." It is not the object of cognitive experience, but rather "existence" is Reality as immediately experienced, with the accent on the inner and personal character of man's immediate experi-

[1] From *Journal of the History of Ideas,* vol. V, no. 1 (Jan. 1944), pp. 44–70.

ence. Like Bergson, Bradley, James, and Dewey, the Existential philosophers are appealing from the conclusions of rationalistic thinking which equates Reality with the object of thought, with relations or "essence," to Reality as men experience it immediately in their actual living. They consequently take their place with all those who have regarded man's "immediate experience" as revealing more completely the nature and traits of Reality than man's cognitive experience. The philosophy of Existence is hence one version of that widespread appeal to immediate experience which has been so marked a feature of recent thought. . . .

The Methodological Foundations of The Existential Philosophy

The Distinction Between Essentia *and* Existentia *in the Philosophical Tradition*

The philosophy of Existence derives its name and its way of formulating its critical opposition to rationalistic views of Reality from the traditional distinction between "essence" and "existence." "Existence" —which comes from *existere*, meaning "emerge"—designates its root meaning "being" within the totality of Being, in distinction from "not being." *Dasein*, a word which has received a pregnant meaning in Heidegger's *Sein und Zeit*, adds the concrete element of "being in a special place," being *da* or "there." The scholastic distinction between *essentia* and *existentia* was the first step toward giving a more significant meaning to the word "existence." In the distinction, "essence" signifies the What, the τί ἐστιν or *quid est* of a thing; "existence" signifies the That, the ὅτι ἔστιν or *quod est. Essentia* thus designates what a thing is *known* to be, the non-temporal object of knowledge in a temporal and changing thing, the οὐσία of that thing which makes it possible. But whether a thing is real or not is not implied in its essence: we do not know whether there is such a thing by knowing its "essence" alone. This must be decided by an existential proposition.

The assertion of the scholastics that in God essence and existence are identical is the second step in the development of the meaning of "existence." The Unconditioned cannot be conditioned by a difference between its essence and its existence. In absolute Being there is no possibility which is not an actuality: it is pure actuality. In all finite beings, on the other hand, this difference is present; in them existence as something separated from essence is the mark of finitude.

The third step in the enrichment of the term "existence" came from the discussion of the ontological argument, from its criticism by Kant and its re-establishment in a changed and broadened form by

Hegel. This discussion brought out the fundamental fallacy involved. The ontological argument relies on the sound principle of the identity of Being and thinking, which all thinking presupposes: this identity is the "*Unvordenkliche*" (that principle prior to which thought cannot take place, the *Prius* of all thinking), as Schelling called it. But the argument surreptitiously transforms this principle into a highest Being, for the existence or non-existence of which demonstrations can be advanced. Kant's criticism of this interpretation is valid, but it does not touch the principle itself. On the contrary, Kant himself, in a powerful passage, describes the *Unvordenklichkeit* of Being-as-such from the point of view of an imagined highest Being who asks himself: Whence do I come? Hegel not only re-establishes the ontological argument in a purified form, he extends the principle of the identity of Being and thought to the whole of Being in so far as it is the "self-actualization of the Absolute." In this way he tries to overcome the separation of existence from essence in finite beings: for him, the finite is infinite both in its essence *and* in its existence.

Hegel's Doctrine of Essence and Existence

The post-Hegelian attack on Hegel's dialectical system is directed against his attempt to absorb the whole of reality, not only in its essential but also in its existential and especially in its historical aspect, into the dialectical movement of "pure thought." The logical expression of this attempt is found in statements like these concerning essence and existence: "Essence *necessarily* appears." It transforms itself into existence. Existence is the being of essence, and therefore existence can be called "essential being." Essence *is* existence, it is not distinguished from its existence.[2]

It is in the light of these definitions that certain familiar propositions of Hegel's *Philosophy of Right* must be understood. If existence is essential being, reason is real and reality is rational. And therefore: "It is the task of philosophy to understand what is; for what is, is Reason . . . If philosophy builds a world as it ought to be, such a world can indeed be realized, but only in imagination, a plastic material on which anything can be impressed."[3] The task of philosophy is not to sketch an ideal world; on the contrary, we must say: the task of philosophy is "the reconciliation with reality." In contrast to this statement, it can be said: the task of Existential philoso-

---

[2] Hegel, *Logik*, ed. Lasson, ii, 103, 105.
[3] Hegel, *Philosophie des Rechts*, ed. Lasson, 14, 15.

phy was first of all to destroy this Hegelian "reconciliation," which was merely conceptual, and left existence itself unreconciled. . . .

The Existential Thinker

The approach to Existence or Reality through immediate personal experience leads to the idea of the "Existential thinker," a term coined by Kierkegaard but applicable to all Existential philosophers. "The way of objective reflexion makes the subject accidental and thereby transforms his Existence into something impersonal—truth also becomes impersonal, and this impersonal character is precisely its objective validity; for all interest, like all decision, is rooted in personal experience."[4]

The Existential thinker is the interested or passionate thinker. Although Hegel applies the words "interest" and "passion" to those driving forces in history which the "cunning Idea" uses for its purposes, there is for him no problem of Existential thinking, because individuals are but the agents of the objective dialectical process. It is chiefly Marx who uses the term "interest" in this connection, though it is not lacking in Kierkegaard also. According to Marx, the Idea always fails when it is divorced from interest.[5] When united with interest, it can be either ideology or truth. It is "ideology" if, while claiming to represent society as a whole, it expresses merely the interest of a partial group. It is "true" if the partial group whose interest it expresses represents by its very nature the interest of the entire society. For Marx, in the period of capitalism this group is the proletariat. In this way he tries to unite universal validity with the concrete situation of the Existential thinker.

Feuerbach and Kierkegaard prefer the term "passion" for the attitude of the Existential thinker. In his beautifully written *Grundsätze der Philosophie der Zukunft*, Feuerbach says: "Do not wish to be a philosopher in contrast to being a man . . . do not think as a thinker . . . think as a living, real being . . . think in Existence."[6] "Love is passion, and only passion is the mark of Existence."[7] In order to unite this attitude with the demand for objectivity, he says: "Only what is an object of passion—really is."[8] The passionately living man knows the true nature of man and life.

Kierkegaard's famous definition of truth reads, "An objective un-

[4] Kierkegaard, *Concluding Unscientific Postscript*, 173.
[5] Marx, *Der Historische Materialismus*, I, 379.
[6] Feuerbach, *Grundsätze der Philosophie der Zukunft* (Zürich, 1843), 78.
[7] *Ibid.*, 60.
[8] *Ibid.*, 60.

certainty held fast in the most passionate personal experience is the truth, the highest truth attainable for an Existing individual."[9] This, he continues, is the definition of faith. Such a view seems to exclude any objective validity, and can hardly be considered the basis for an Existential philosophy. But Kierkegaard tries to show through the example of Socrates that the Existential thinker can be a philosopher. "The Socratic ignorance which Socrates held fast with the entire passion of his personal experience was thus an expression of the principle that the eternal truth is related to an existing individual."[10] The validity of the truth which appears in a passionate personal experience is based on the relation of the Eternal to the Existing individual.

The Existential thinker cannot have pupils in the ordinary sense. He cannot communicate any ideas, because *they* are *not* the truth he wants to teach. He can only create in his pupil by indirect communication that "Existential state" or personal experience out of which the pupil may think and act. Kierkegaard carries out this interpretation for Socrates. But all Existential philosophers have made similar statements—naturally, for if the approach to Existence is through personal experience, the only possibility of educating is to bring the pupil by indirect methods to a personal experience of his own Existence.

Interest, passion, indirect communication—all these qualities of the Existential thinker are forcefully expressed in Nietzsche. In no respect is he more obviously a philosopher of experienced Existence than in his description of Existential thinking. None of the later Existential philosophers has approached him in this, though they all hold the same attitude. While in Marx objective validity is united with "Existential" personal experience because of the special situation of the proletariat, in Nietzsche it is the Master-man in general and his prophet in particular who stand in the favored place where validity and Existence coincide.

The Existential thinker needs special forms of expression, because personal Existence cannot be expressed in terms of objective experience. So Schelling uses the traditional religious symbols, Kierkegaard uses paradox, irony, and the pseudonym, Nietzsche the oracle, Bergson images and fluid concepts, Heidegger a mixture of psychological and ontological terms, Jaspers uses what he calls "ciphers," and the Religious Socialist uses concepts oscillating between immanence and transcendence. They all wrestle with the problem of personal or "non-objective" thinking and its expression—this is the calamity of the Existential thinker.

[9] Kierkegaard, *Postscript*, 182.
[10] *Ibid.*, 180.

Ontological Problems of The Existential Philosophy

Existential Immediacy and The Subject-object Distinction

The thinking of the Existential thinker is based on his immediate personal and inner experience. It is rooted in an interpretation of Being or Reality which does *not* identify Reality with "objective being." But it would be equally misleading to say that it identifies Reality with "Subjective being," with "consciousness" or feeling. Such a view would still leave the meaning of "subjective" determined by its contrast with "objective," and this is just the contrary of what the Existential philosophy is aiming at. Like many other appeals to immediate experience, it is trying to find a level on which the contrast between "subject" and "object" has not arisen. It aims to cut under the "subject-object distinction" and to reach that stratum of Being which Jaspers, for instance, calls the "*Ursprung*" or "Source." But in order to penetrate to this stratum we must leave the sphere of "objective" things and pass through the corresponding "subjective" inner experience, until we arrive at the immediate creative experience or "Source." " 'Existence' is something that can never become a mere object; it is the 'Source' whence springs my thinking and acting."[11] Schelling follows Hegel in emphasizing the "subject" and its freedom against Substance and its necessity. But while in Hegel the "subject" is immediately identified with the *thinking* subject, in Schelling it becomes rather the "*existing*" or immediately experiencing subject.

All the Existential philosophers reject any identification of Being or Reality with the objects of thought, which they feel is the great threat to personal human Existence in our period. . . .

. . . The meaning of this desperate refusal to identify Reality with the world of objects is clearly brought out by Nietzsche when he says: "When we have reached the inevitable universal economic administration of the earth, then mankind as a machine can find its meaning in the service of this monstrous mechanism of smaller and smaller cogs adapted to the whole."[12] No one any longer knows the significance of this huge process. Mankind demands a new aim, a new meaning for life. In these words anxiety about the social character of the "objective world" is clearly revealed as the motive for the fight of the philosophers of personal Existence against "objectivation," against the transformation of men into impersonal objects.

---

[11] Jaspers, *Philosophie*, I, 15.
[12] Nietzsche, *Wille zur Macht*, *Werke*, x, 114.

Psychological and Ontological Concepts

The principle of personal Existence or "Existential Subjectivity" demands a special type of concept in which to describe this immediate personal experience. These concepts must be "non-objectivating"; they must not transform men into things, but at the same time they must not be merely "subjective." In the light of this double demand we can understand the choice of psychological notions with a non-psychological connotation.

If the philosophy of personal Existence is right in maintaining that immediate experience is the door to the creative "Source" of Being, it is necessary for the concepts describing immediate experience to be at the same time descriptive of the structure of Being itself. The so-called "affects" are then not mere subjective emotions with no ontological significance; they are half-symbolic, half-realistic indications of the structure of Reality itself. It is in this way that Heidegger and many other philosophers of personal Existence are to be understood. Heidegger fills his book *Sein und Zeit* not with definitions of *Sein*-as-such or *Zeit*-as-such, but with descriptions of what he calls *Dasein* and *Zeitlichkeit*, temporal or finite Existence. In these descriptions he speaks of *Sorge* (care) as the general character of Existence, or of *Angst* (anxiety) as the relation of man to nothingness, or of fear of death, conscience, guilt, despair, daily life, loneliness, etc. But he insists again and again that these characterizations are not "ontic," describing merely a particular being, Man, but are rather "ontological," describing the very structure of Being itself. He denies that their negative character, their seemingly pessimistic connotations, have anything to do with actual pessimism. They all point to human finitude, the real theme of the philosophy of personal Existence. It remains, of course, an open question how the psychological meaning of these concepts can be distinguished from their ontological meaning. Most of the criticism directed against Heidegger deals with this problem; and it appears that Heidegger has implicitly admitted that he was unable to explain the difference clearly, and that he himself has increasingly emphasized human nature as the starting-point of the Existential ontology. . . .

The Principle of Finitude

While an ontology which claims to have knowledge of Being *a priori* is arrogant, an ontology which restricts itself to the structure of finitude is possible.[13] Such an ontology can be called a doctrine of

---

[13] Feuerbach, *Grundsätze*, p. 118.

human nature, but not in the sense of giving any special knowledge of the human race. An ontological doctrine of man develops the structure of finitude as man finds it in himself as the center of his own personal Existence. He alone of all finite beings is aware of his own finitude; therefore the way to ontology passes through the doctrine of man. But of course, in traveling this way he cannot escape his finitude. The way to finitude is itself finite and cannot claim finality: such is the limit set upon the Existential thinker. Heidegger concludes his analysis with the statement that the fight against Kant's doctrine of the *Ding-an-sich* was a fight against the acknowledgment of the finitude of our human experience in knowing. . . .

The Ethical Attitude of The Existential Philosophy

History Viewed in The Light of The Future

All the Existential philosophers agree on the historical character of immediate personal experience. But the fact that man has a fundamentally "historical Existence" does not mean merely that he has a theoretical interest in the past; his Existence is not directed toward the past at all. It is the attitude not of the detached spectator, but of the actor who must face the future and make personal decisions. . . .

Finitude and Estrangement

The description of man's "Existential situation" or present estate as finitude is usually connected with the contrast between man's present estate and what he is "essentially," and therefore ought to be. Ever since Schelling's *On Human Freedom*, the world we are living in, including Nature, has been described as a disrupted unity, as fragments and ruins. In accord with Kant's half-mythological and genuinely "Existential" doctrine of radical evil, Schelling speaks of the transcendent Fall of Man as the "presupposition of the tragic nature of Existence." Kierkegaard's famous work on *Angst*, in which he interprets the transition from essence to existence, is his psychological masterpiece: the *Angst* of finitude drives man to action and at the same time to an alienation from his essential being and to the profounder *Angst* of guilt and despair. . . .

Finitude and Loneliness

Every personal Existence is unique, says Jaspers: "We are completely irreplaceable. We are not merely cases of universal Being."[14]

---

[14] Jaspers, *Vernunft und Existenz* (Groningen, 1935), 19.

Heidegger speaks of the *Jemeinigkeit* of personal Existence, its belonging to me and nobody else.[15] Men usually live in the common experiences of daily life, covering over with talk and action their real inner personal experience. But conscience, guilt, having to die, come home to the individual only in his inner loneliness. The death of another as an objective event has nothing to do with our personal attitude toward our own death. Nietzsche praises the higher type of man who is lonely and cut off not only from the masses but also from others like himself. Nietzsche's estimate of the average man is exactly that of Heidegger and Jaspers. Kierkegaard goes even beyond them in emphasizing man's inner experience of loneliness before God. Anything objective and universal has no other meaning for him than an escape from the ethical decision each individual has to make. . . .

Conclusion—The Significance of The Existential Philosophy

We have considered a large group of Existential philosophers, covering a period of about a hundred years. They represent many different and even contradictory tendencies in philosophic thought, and they had many different and even contradictory effects on religion and politics. Do they all exhibit some common trait which justifies calling them all "Existential philosophers"? If the above analysis is correct, there can be no doubt that they display a very fundamental unity. This unity can be described in both negative and positive terms: all the philosophers of Existence share a common opposition to a common foe, and all have a common aim, though they try to attain it in very different ways.

What all philosophers of Existence oppose is the "rational" system of thought and life developed by Western industrial society and its philosophic representatives. During the last hundred years the implications of this system have become increasingly clear: a logical or naturalistic mechanism which seemed to destroy individual freedom, personal decision, and organic community; an analytic rationalism which saps the vital forces of life and transforms everything, including man himself, into an object of calculation and control; a secularized humanism which cuts man and the world off from the creative Source and the ultimate mystery of existence. The Existential philosophers, supported by poets and artists in every European country, were consciously or subconsciously aware of the approach of this self-estranged form of life. They tried to resist it in a desperate struggle

[15] Heidegger, *Sein und Zeit*, 42.

which drove them often to mental self-destruction and made their utterances extremely aggressive, passionate, paradoxical, fragmentary, revolutionary, prophetic, and ecstatic. But this did not prevent them from achieving fundamental insights into the sociological structure of modern society and the psychological dynamics of modern man, into the originality and spontaneity of life, into the paradoxical character of religion and the Existential roots of knowledge. They immensely enriched philosophy, if it be taken as man's interpretation of his own existence, and they worked out intellectual tools and spiritual symbols for the European revolution of the twentieth century.

To understand the fundamental drive and function of Existential philosophy, it is necessary to view it against the background of what was happening in the nineteenth-century religious situation, especially in Germany, for all the groups that appeared after 1830 had to face a common problem, the problem created by the breakdown of the religious tradition under the impact of enlightenment, social revolution, and bourgeois liberalism. First among the educated classes, then increasingly in the mass of industrial workers, religion lost its "immediacy," it ceased to offer an unquestioned sense of direction and relevance to human living. What was lost in immediacy Hegel tried to restore by conscious reinterpretation. But this mediating reinterpretation was attacked and dissolved from both sides by a revived theology on the one hand and by philosophical positivism on the other. The Existential philosophers were trying to discover an ultimate meaning of life beyond the reach of reinterpretation, revived theologies, or positivism. In their search they passionately rejected the "estranged" objective world with its religious radicals, reactionaries, and mediators. They turned toward man's immediate experience, toward "subjectivity," not as something opposed to "objectivity," but as that living experience in which both objectivity and subjectivity are rooted. They turned toward Reality as men experience it immediately in their actual living, to *Innerlichkeit* or inward experience. They tried to discover the creative realm of being which is prior to and beyond the distinction between objectivity and subjectivity.

If the experience of this level of living is "mystical," Existential philosophy can be called the attempt to reconquer the meaning of life in "mystical" terms after it had been lost in ecclesiastical as well as in positivistic terms. It is however necessary to redefine "mystical" if we are to apply it to Existential philosophy. In this context the term does not indicate a mystical union with the transcendent Absolute; it signifies rather a venture of faith toward union with the depths of life, whether made by an individual or a group. There is more of the Protestant than the Catholic heritage in this kind of "mysticism";

but it *is* mysticism in trying to transcend the estranged "objectivity" as well as the empty "subjectivity" of the present epoch. Historically speaking, Existential philosophy attempts to return to a pre-Cartesian attitude, to an attitude in which the sharp gulf between the subjective and the objective "realms" had not yet been created, and the essence of objectivity could be found in the depth of subjectivity— in which God could be best approached through the soul.

This problem and this solution are in some respects peculiar to the German situation, in others common to all European culture. It is the desperate struggle to find a new meaning of life in a reality from which men have been estranged, in a cultural situation in which two great traditions, the Christian and the humanistic, have lost their comprehensive character and their convincing power. The turning towards *Innerlichkeit*, or more precisely, toward the creative sources of life in the depth of man's experience, occurred throughout Europe. For sociological reasons it was in Germany more philosophical and more radical than in other lands. There it became that quasi-religious power which had transformed society, first in Russia and then in other parts of Europe, during the first half of the twentieth century.

In understanding Existential philosophy a comparison with the situation in England may be helpful. England is the only European country in which the Existential problem of finding a new meaning for life had no significance, because there positivism and the religious tradition lived on side by side, united by a social conformism which prevented radical questions about the meaning of human "Existence." It is important to note that the one country without an Existential philosophy is that in which during the period from 1830 to 1930 the religious tradition remained strongest. This illustrates once more the dependence of the Existential philosophy on the problems created by the breakdown of the religious tradition on the European continent.

In their struggle against the meaninglessness of modern technological civilization, the several philosophers of Existence used very different methods and had very different aims. In all of them the Existential emphasis was only one factor among others, more or less controlling. Schelling shared the belief of German Romanticism that a new philosophy, and in particular a new interpretation of religion, could produce a new reality. But this assumption was wrong; and his immediate influence remained very limited, restricted to the theology of the restoration period. Feuerbach's significance for Existential thinking lies more in his destruction of Hegel's reconciliation of Christianity with modern philosophy than in his metaphysical materialism, which indeed considerably strengthened the bourgeois-mechanistic interpretation of nature and man.

Kierkegaard represents the religious wing of Existential philosophy. He himself did not claim to be a philosopher, and those who find in him the classic type of Existential thinking often assert that a genuinely Existential thinker cannot be one. But Kierkegaard's actual work reveals a much more intimate connection. As a religious thinker he encountered the obstacle of a church which had become "bourgeois" in both theory and practice, and he was able to maintain his own radical Christianity only in terms of an absolute paradox and of a passionately personal devotion. As a philosophical thinker, however, he produced a "dialectical" psychology which has contributed greatly to an anti-rationalistic and anti-mechanistic interpretation of human nature.

If we call Marx an Existential thinker, this can obviously apply only to certain particular strains of his thought: to his struggle against the self-estrangement of man under capitalism, against any theory that merely interprets the world without changing it, against the assumption that knowledge is quite independent of the social situation in which it is sought. Like Kierkegaard, Marx did not want to be a philosopher: he pronounced the end of all philosophy and its transformation into a revolutionary sociology. But the impulse he gave to the interpretation of history, his doctrine of "ideology," his introduction of sociological analysis into economics, made him a powerful force in the philosophic discussion of the end of the nineteenth and the beginning of the twentieth centuries, long before he became the greatest political force in the fight of the twentieth century against the traditions of the nineteenth.

Like Marx, Nietzsche and the "*Lebensphilosophen*" are Existential philosophers only in certain of their views. Nietzsche's attack on "European nihilism," his biological interpretation of the categories of knowledge, his fragmentary and prophetic style, his eschatological passion; Dilthey's problem of the Existential roots of the different interpretations of life; Bergson's attack on spatial rationality in the name of creative vitality; the primacy of life as over against its products in Simmel and Scheler—all these ideas reveal their Existential character. But just as Marx never called into question natural science, economic theory, and dialectical reason, so Nietzsche and the "*Lebensphilosophen*" always presupposed the scientific method and an ontology of life. Heidegger, and less emphatically Jaspers, returned to the Kierkegaardian type of Existential philosophy, and in particular to the dialectical psychology of Kierkegaard. They reintroduced the term "Existential" to designate a philosophy that appealed to immediate personal experience, and they cooperated with a theology that was profoundly influenced by Kierkegaard, especially by his attack on the secularized bourgeois churches. But with the help of Aristotle and the *"Lebensphilosophie,"* Heidegger transformed the dialectical psychology into a new ontology, radically rejecting the religious implications of the Existential attitude, and replacing it with the unchecked resoluteness of the tragic and heroic individual.

It is a dramatic picture that Existential philosophy presents: the polarity between the Existential attitude and its philosophic expression dominates the whole movement. At times the Existential element prevails, at times the philosophical—even in the same thinker. In all of them the critical interest is predominant. All of them are reacting—in theory and practice—against an historical destiny the fulfilment of which they are furthering by their very reaction against it. They are the expression of the great revolution within and against Western industrial society which was prepared in the nineteenth century and is being carried out in the twentieth.

BIBLIOGRAPHY*

TILLICH, Paul, *The Religious Situation,* trans. H. Richard Niebuhr. N.Y.: Meridian Books, 1932, 1956.

————, *The Interpretation of History,* trans. N. A. Rasetzki and E. L. Talmey. N.Y.: Scribner's, 1936.

————, *The Protestant Era,* trans. James L. Adams, Chicago: U. of Chicago Press, 1948.

————, *The Shaking of the Foundations.* N. Y.: Scribner's, 1948.

————, *Systematic Theology,* 3 vols. Chicago: U. of Chicago Press, 1951–1963.

————, *A History of Christian Thought,* recorded and edited by Peter H. John. Providence, R.I., 1953.

————, *The Courage To Be.* New Haven: Yale U. Press, 1952.

————, *Love, Power, and Justice. Ontological Analyses and Ethical Applications.* N.Y.: Oxford U. Press, 1954.

————, *New Being.* N.Y.: Scribner's, 1955.

————, *Biblical Religion and the Search for Ultimate Reality.* Chicago: U. of Chicago Press, 1955.

————, *Dynamics of Faith.* N.Y.: Harpers, 1957.

————, *Theology of Culture,* ed. by Robert C. Kimball. N.Y.: Oxford U. Press, 1959.

KILLEN, R. *The Ontological Theology of Paul Tillich.* Kampen: J. H. Kok, 1956.

KEGLEY, Charles W. and BRETALL, Robert W., (eds.) *The Theology of Paul Tillich.* N.Y.: Macmillan, 1956.

* Contains only books published in or translated into English.

LEIBRECHT, Walter, (ed.) *Religion and Culture: Essays in Honor of Paul Tillich.* N.Y.: Harpers, 1959.

MARTIN, Bernard. *The Existentialist Theology of Paul Tillich.* N.Y.: Twayne, 1962.

MURPHY, Carol R. *A Deeper Faith; The Thought of Paul Tillich.* Wallingford, Pa.: Pendle Hill, 1958.

Sidney Hook

[*1902–*]

Sidney Hook is among the foremost spokesmen for the pragmatic temper in America today. A left-wing disciple of John Dewey, he has done much to expound and further develop Dewey's philosophy, especially in regard to political, social, ethical and educational questions.

Hook early came under the influence of Marxism, finding in it important parallels with pragmatism. His sympathies have consistently been with democratic socialism. Hook was among the first of American intellectuals to become disenchanted with communism, and today he is regarded as an intellectual leader in the ideological battle against the Leninist–Stalinist variety of Marxism. His efforts in this connection have had a wide impact outside of scholarly circles. As a philosophical naturalist, Hook has been opposed to the metaphysical quest for Being. Throughout his writings, he has attempted to use the methods of pragmatic reason and the techniques of logical analysis. He has a wide reputation as a keen critic and polemicist.

Hook was born in New York City and educated at City College, where he studied under Morris R. Cohen. He took his Ph.D. at Columbia University in 1927. He is presently the Chairman of the Department of Philosophy at Washington Square College, New York University. He has been a Guggenheim Fellow and a Fellow of the Center for Advanced

Study in the Behavioral Sciences. He has been instrumental in founding the Conference on Methods in Philosophy and Science, the Congress for Cultural Freedom, the New York University Institute of Philosophy, and other organizations. He is a past President of the American Philosophical Association, Eastern Division (1959). Among his most important works are *The Metaphysics of Pragmatism* (1927), *From Hegel to Marx* (1936), *Reason, Social Myths and Democracy* (1940), *The Hero in History* (1943), *Education for Modern Man* (1946), *The Quest for Being* (1961) and *The Paradoxes of Freedom* (1962).

In the selection reprinted below, "Pragmatism and the Tragic Sense of Life" (1959), Hook defends the pragmatic view of life against the criticism and pessimism of existentialist, Asian, and other anti-naturalistic philosophies. Pragmatism, he asserts, is not insensitive to the tragic, which flows primarily from the conflict of moral ideals. Indeed, a degree of awareness of the tragic enables man to live in a world of inescapable tragedy. If the conflicts of moral ideals are taken seriously, and if rational methods are applied, many, if not all, human problems can be solved and most conflicts can be negotiated.

The second selection, taken from Hook's article, "Naturalism and First Principles" (1956), is an attempt to answer the charge that naturalism's argument for first principles is circular. This critique, however, is applicable to *all* philosophical first principles. Naturalism's basic meth- odological principles, Hook maintains, are justifiable by reference to the actual methods encountered in common experience and ordinary life.

PRAGMATISM AND THE TRAGIC SENSE OF LIFE [1]

. . . The juxaposition of the expressions "pragmatism" and "the tragic sense of life" may appear bewildering to those who understand pragmatism as a narrow theory of meaning and "the tragic sense of life" as the hysterical lament that man is not immortal—the theme song of Unamuno's book of that title. . . .

By the tragic sense of life I do not understand merely sensitivity to the presence of evil or suffering in the world although all tragic situations to some degree involve one or the other. . . . The presence of the evils in the world which led Buddha to surrender his Kingdom in order to seek salvation for himself and mankind are not to me the realities fundamental to the tragic sense of life. There were three things in Buddha's experience, reflection upon which led him to a renunciation of his princely lot and a quest for liberation from desire and incarnate existence—sickness, old age and death. One can very well understand why in the world in which he lived and for many centuries thereafter until our own, these phenomena loomed so large in the over-populated and poverty-stricken areas of Asia. Nonetheless if we are to distinguish between the sense of the *pitiful* and the sense of the *tragic*—sickness, old age and even many forms of death, despite their numbing effect upon human sensibility, are not necessarily to be classified as tragic.

First, given the rapidly expanding horizons of knowledge in our age, there is nothing in the nature of things which requires that the sick, any more than the poor, must always be with us. If scientific medicine develops at the same pace in the next few hundred years as it has in the last century, it is not shallow optimism to anticipate that the most serious forms of sickness will disappear and not be replaced by others. Even where sickness is present it may be the occasion of tragedy but by itself is not an illustration of it. In relation to the forces of nature man's lot may appear pitiful. The tragic is a moral phenomenon.

[1] Presidential address delivered before the Fifty-sixth Annual Meeting of the Eastern Division of the American Philosophical Association at Columbia University, Dec. 1959. From *Proceedings and Addresses*, Vol. XXXIII. Yellow Springs, Ohio: The Antioch Press, 1959–60, pp. 10–26.

What is true of sickness is true of old age. The aged arouse our compassion because of their feebleness and fragility—and the multiplicity of their aches and pains. When these are absent—and this, too, is a concern of scientific medicine—there is a chance for serenity, wisdom and beauty of spirit to manifest themselves. There is sometimes a grandeur and stateliness about an old tree which aged persons do not possess because the processes of physical degeneration, and the consequent weakening of the vital powers, make man pitiful. There is no tragedy in growing old biologically but only sorrow; the element of the tragic enters in the defeat of plans or hopes, in the realization that in much grief there is not much wisdom, and that we cannot count merely upon the passage of time alone to diminish our stupidities and cruelties.

But what of death—Buddha's third appalling discovery—preoccupation with which has become so fashionable today among some European existentialist philosophers that their philosophy seems to be more a meditation upon death than upon life? Is not death the ultimate source of whatever is tragic in life? I cannot bring myself to think so. Nor can I convince myself that its nature and significance in life waited to be discovered by Kierkegaard and Heidegger and their modern disciples.

It is the reflective attitude towards death, not the popular attitude or the one displayed by those in its last agonies, which throws light on its nature and place in life. The attitude exhibited by Socrates in facing it seems wiser than that expressed by the contemnors of the rational life who, not content with talking about what they find when they look into themselves, inflate it into a universal trait of the human psyche. So Tolstoy who is quoted by existentialist writers, writes: "If a man has learned to think, no matter what he may think about, he is always thinking of his own death. All philosophers are like that. And what truth can there be, if there is death?" Logically, of course, this makes no more sense than the even more extreme statement of Sartre that "if we must die then our life has no meaning," which to those who solve some problems in life and therefore find some meaning, might be taken as a premise in a new short proof of human immortality. All this it seems to me expresses little more than a fear of death and a craving for immortality. It is a commonplace observation, however, that most human beings who desire immortality desire not unending life but unending youth or other desirable qualities which life makes possible. The fable of Juno and her lover in which Juno petitions the Gods to take back the gift of eternal life they had conferred upon a mortal indicates that the Greeks knew that a life without end could be a dubious blessing. In this respect the Hellenes were wiser than the Hebrews whose God drives Adam from

Paradise after he had eaten of the fruit of the tree of knowledge to prevent him from eating of the fruit of the tree of eternal life. Agony over death strikes me as one of the unloveliest features of the intellectual life of our philosophic times—and certainly unworthy of any philosophy which conceives itself as a quest for wisdom. It has never been clear to me why those who are nauseated by life, not by this or that kind of life but any kind of life, should be so fearful of death.

Wisdom is knowledge of the uses of life and death. The uses of life are to be found in the consummatory experiences of vision and delight, of love, understanding, art, friendship and creative activity. That is why in a contingent world of finite men, vulnerable to powers they cannot control which sometimes robs them of the possibility of any justifying consummations, death has its uses, too. For it gives us some assurance that no evil or suffering lasts forever. To anyone aware of the multitude of infamies and injustices which men have endured, of the broken bodies and tortured minds of the victims of these cruelties, of the multiple dimensions of pain in which millions live on mattress graves or with minds shrouded in darkness, death must sometimes appear as a beneficent release not an inconsolable affliction. It washes the earth clean of what cannot be cleansed in any other way. Not all the bright promises of a future free of these stains of horror can redeem by one iota the lot of those who will not live to see the dawn of the new day.

It is nobler to exist and struggle in a world in which there is always a vital option to live or die. The fear of death, the desire to survive at any cost or price in human degradation, has been the greatest ally of tyranny, past and present. "There are times," says Woodbridge, "when a man ought to be more afraid of living than dying." And we may add, there are situations in which because of the conditions of survival, the worst thing we can know of anyone is that he has survived. We have known such times and situations. They may come again.

Even in a world in which all injustices, cruelties and physical anguish have disappeared, the possibility of withdrawing from it makes the world insofar forth a better and a freer world. So long as we retain possession of our faculties, our decision to remain in the world indicates a participating responsibility on our part for those events within it which our continuance affects. If human beings were unable to die they would to that extent be unfree. Man shares a *conatus sui esse perservare* with everything else in the world or at least with all other sentient beings. But just because he can on rational grounds give up his being, choose not to be, he differentiates himself most strikingly from his fellow creatures in nature. I conclude therefore that death as such is not a tragic phenomenon and that its presence does not make the world and our experience within it tragic. It would be truer to call tragic a world in which men wanted to die but couldn't.

What, then, do I mean by the tragic sense of life and what is its relevance to pragmatism? I mean by the tragic sense a very simple thing which is rooted in the very nature of the moral experience and the phenomenon of moral choice. Every genuine experience of moral doubt and perplexity in which we ask: "What should I do?" takes place in a situation where good conflicts with good. If we already know what is evil the moral inquiry is over, or it never really begins. "The worse or evil," says Dewey, "is the rejected good," but until we reject it, the situation is one in which apparent good opposes apparent good. "All the serious perplexities of life come back to the genuine difficulty of forming a judgment as to the values of a situation: they come back to a conflict of goods." No matter how we resolve the opposition some good will be sacrificed, some interest, whose immediate craving for satisfaction may be every whit as intense and authentic as its fellows, will be modified, frustrated or even suppressed. Where the goods involved are of a relatively low order, like decisions about what to eat, where to live, where to go, the choice is unimportant except to the mind of a child. There are small tragedies as there are small deaths. At any level the conflict of values must become momentous to oneself or others to convey adequately the tragic quality. Where the choice is between goods that are complex in structure and consequential for the future, the tragic quality of the moral dilemma emerges more clearly. And when it involves basic choices of love, friendship, vocations, the quality becomes poignant. The very nature of the self as expressed in habits, dispositions and character is to some extent altered by these decisions. If, as Hobbes observes, "Hell is truth seen too late," all of us must live in it. No matter how justified in smug retrospect our moral decisions seem to have been, only the unimaginative will fail to see the possible selves we have sacrificed to become what we are. Grant that all regrets are vain, that any other choice would have been equally or more regretted, the selves we might have been are eloquent witnesses of values we failed to enjoy. If we have played it safe and made our existence apparently secure, the fascinating experience of a life of adventure and experience can never be ours, and every thought of a good fight missed will be accompanied by a pang. It is a poor spirit William James reminds us who does not sense the chagrin of the tardy Crillon, who arriving when the battle is over is greeted by Henry IV with the words: "Hang yourself, brave Crillon! We fought at Arques, and you were not there!" On the other hand, if we have scorned to put down our roots, hugged our liberty tightly to ourselves by refusing to give hostages to fortune, become crusaders or martyrs for lost causes, we have thrust from ourselves the warmth of sustained affection, and the comforting regularities which can best heal the bruised spirit.

There is a conflict not only between the good and the good but between the good and the right where the good is a generic term for all the values in a situation and the right for all the obligations. The *concepts* of good and right are irreducible to each other in ordinary use. We are often convinced we must fulfill a certain duty even when we are far from convinced to the same degree that the action or the rule it exemplifies will achieve the greatest good. The "good" is related to the reflective satisfaction of an interest: "the right" to the fulfillment of a binding demand or rule of the community. There is no moral problem when in doing the right thing we can see that it *also* leads to the greatest good or when striving for the greatest good conforms to our sense of what is right. But the acute ethical problems arise when in the pursuit of the good we do things which appear not to be right, as e.g., when in order to avoid the dangers of war a nation repudiates its treaty obligations or when in order to win a war non-combatants are punished who are in no way responsible for the actions of others. They also arise when in doing what is right our actions result in evil consequences, as e.g., when a dangerous criminal, set free on a legal technicality, kills again or when the refusal to surrender to the unjust claims of an aggressor results in wholesale slaughter. Many have been the attempts made to escape the antinomies between the right and the good by defining the good as the object of right or the right merely as the means to the good. All have failed. To act upon the right no matter what its consequences for human weal or woe seems inhuman, at times insane. The thirst for righteousness has too often been an angry thirst satisfied if at all by long draughts of blood. On the other hand, the attempt to do good by *any* means no matter how unjust, is subhuman and usually irrational.

As compared to traditional ethical doctrines, ideal utilitarianism reaches farthest in our quest for an adequate ethics but in the end it, too, must be rejected. And it was the pragmatist and pluralist, William James, long before Prichard and Ross, who indicated why in the famous question he asked: "If the hypothesis were offered us of a world in which Messrs. Fourier's and Bellamy's and Morris' Utopia should all be outdone, and millions be kept permanently happy on the one simple condition that a certain lost soul on the far off edge of things should lead a life of lonely torture, what except a specifical and independent sort of emotion can it be which would make us immediately feel . . . how hideous a thing would be its enjoyment when deliberately accepted as the fruit of such a bargain?" The situation is unaltered if we recognize that there are other goods besides happiness and that justice is itself a good, because in that case the conflict breaks out again between good and good. In this connection I would venture the statement that it is the failure to see the radical pluralism in the nature of the goods which are reckoned in the consequences of an action which accounts both for Moore's view that it is self-evident that it can *never* be right knowingly to approve an action that would make the world as a whole worse than some alternative action and for Kant's view that there are some duties that it would *always* be right to perform, even if the consequences of the action resulted in a worse world or in no world at all. No specific rule can be laid down as absolutely binding in advance either way. Nothing can take the place of intelligence; the better or the lesser evil in each situation can be best defined as the object of reflective choice. Even the decision in the stock illustration of the text-books whether to execute an innocent man or turn him over to be tortured in order to save the community from destruction—would depend upon a complex of circumstances. It is perfectly conceivable that an unjust act will sometimes produce the greater good or the lesser evil. It is sometimes necessary to burn down a house to save a village. Although when applied to human beings the logic seems damnable, few are prepared to take the position of Kant in those agonizing moral predicaments that are not uncommon in history, especially the history of oppressed minority peoples, in which the survival of the group can be purchased only at the price of the pain, degradation and death of the innocent. No matter how we choose, we must either betray the ideal of the greater good or the ideal of right or justice. In this lies the agony of the choice.

Many have been the attempts to escape the guilt of that choice. I cite one from the past. During the Middle Ages, Maimonides writing on the Laws of the Torah to guide his people discusses what a community is to do when it is beset by enemies who demand the life of one man with the threat to kill all if he be not turned over to them. Maimonides teaches that they are to refuse to turn over any man even if all must die in consequence, except if their enemies call out the name of a specific person. I had heard this teaching defended on the ground that if the community itself had to make the decision who was to die, it would be taking the guilt of an innocent man's death upon itself, which is impermissible. But if the enemy names the man, then he can be turned over because the guilt and sin fall now on *their* heads. By this miserable evasion it was thought that the tragic choice could be avoided. But it turns out that Maimonides has been misread. What Maimonides really taught is that only if the name of the person who has been called out is of one already under the death sentence for his crimes should he be surrendered. But never an innocent man. "Never," however, is a long time. It is problematic whether the Jews would have survived if they had always abided by Maimonides' injunction.

If anything, human beings are more readily inclined to sacrifice the right to the good than the good to the right, especially in revolutionary situations which have developed because of grievances too long unmet. It can easily be shown that it was Lenin's conception of Communist ethics which implicitly defined the right action as consisting in doing *anything*—literally anything that would bring victory in the class struggle—which explains the transformation of a whole generation of idealists into hangmen. In fact the health of the revolution whether in the times of Robespierre or Castro never really requires the holocaust of victims offered up to it. But no revolution including our own has ever been achieved without injustice to someone. However the conflict between the principles of right and the values of good be theoretically resolved, in every concrete situation it leads to some abridgement of principle or some diminution of value.

The most dramatic of all moral conflicts is not between good and good, or between good and right, but between right and right. This in its starkest form is the theme of Sophoclean tragedy, but the primary locus of the tragic situation is not in a play but in life, in law, and in history. Innocence in personal matters consists in overlooking the conflict of moral duties and obligations. Innocence in political matters, the characteristic of ritualistic liberalism, consists in failing to see the conflicts of rights in our Bill of Rights and the necessity of their intelligent adjustment. In our own country we have witnessed again and again the antinomy of rights revealed in divided loyalties, in the conflict between allegiance to the laws of the state and allegiance to what is called divine law or natural law or the dictates of conscience. On the international scene it is expressed in the conflict of incompatible national claims, each with *some* measure of justification, as in the Israeli-Arab impasse.

One of the noteworthy features of moral intuitionism as illustrated in the doctrines of Ross is this recognition that *prima facie* duties conflict and that every important moral act exhibits at the same time characteristics which tend to make it both *prima facie* right and *prima facie* wrong so that although we may claim certainty about these *prima facie* duties, any particular moral judgment or action is at best only probable or contingent. As Ross says, "There is therefore much truth in the description of the right act as a fortunate act." From this the conclusion to be drawn, it seems to me, is that the most important *prima facie* duty of all in a situation requiring moral decision is that of *conscientiousness*, or reflective assessment of all the relevant factors involved, and the searching exploration of our own hearts to determine what we sincerely want, whether we really wish to do what is right in a situation or to get our own scheming way come what may. As much if not more evil results from confusion of our purposes and ignorance of our motives than from ruthless and clear-eyed resolve to ignore everyone's interests but one's own. This emphasis on the importance of reflective inquiry into the features of the situation which bear on the rightness of an action seems to me to be more important than Ross' conception or interpretation of the intuitive apprehension of our *prima facie* duties. It is easier to doubt that we have this faculty of infallible intuition than that our intelligence has the power to discover our conflicts and mediate between them.

Irony is compounded with tragedy in the fact that many of the rights we presently enjoy we owe to our ancestors who in the process of winning them for us deprived others of their rights. In some regions of the world the very ground on which people stand was expropriated by force and fraud from others by their ancestors. Yet as a rule it would be a new injustice to seek to redress the original injustice by depriving those of their possessions who hold present title to them. Every just demand for reparations against an aggressor country is an unjust demand on the descendants of its citizens who as infants were not responsible for the deeds of aggression. That is why history is the arena of the profoundest moral conflicts in which some legitimate right had always been sacrificed, sometimes on the altars of the God of War.

The Christian and especially the Buddhist ethics of purity which seeks to transcend this conflict and avoid guilt by refusal to violate anyone's right in such situations, can only do so by withdrawing from the plane of the ethical altogether. This may succeed in God's eyes but not in man's. The Buddhist saint or any other who out of respect for the right to life of man or beast refuses ever to use force, or to kill, even when this is the only method, as it sometimes is, that will save multitudes from suffering and death, makes himself responsible for the greater evil, all the more so because he claims to be acting out of compassion. He cannot avoid guilt whether we regard him as more than man or less than man. No more than we does he escape the tragic decision.

There are three generic approaches to the tragic conflicts of life. The first approach is that of history. The second is that of love. The third is that of creative intelligence in quest for ways of mediation which I call here the pragmatic.

The approach of history is best typified by Hegel precisely because he tries to put a gloss of reason over the terrible events which constitute so much of the historical process. Its upshot is woefully inept to its intent. It suggests not only that whatever cause wins and *however* it wins, is more just than the cause which is defeated, but that the loser is the more wicked and not merely the weaker. Further, it calls into question the very fact of tragic conflict from which it so perceptively starts. No one has seen more profoundly into the nature of the tragic situation than Hegel and its stark clash of equally legitimate rights. But his solution, expressed in Schiller's dictum *Die Weltgeschichte ist das Weltgericht,* as Hegel develops it, makes the philosophy of history a theodicy. It thereby vulgarizes tragedy. For it attempts to console man with a dialectical proof that his agony and defeat are not really evils but necessary elements in the goodness of the whole. The position is essentially religious. No monotheistic religion which conceives of God as both omnipotent and benevolent, no metaphysics which asserts that the world is rational, necessary and good has any room for genuine tragedy.

The approach of love is incomplete and ambiguous. It is incomplete because if love is more than a feeling of diffused sympathy but is expressed in action no *man* can love everyone or identify himself with every interest. Empirically love has produced as much disunity as unity in the world—not only in Troy but in Jerusalem. Injustice is often born of love, not only of self-love but of love of some rather than others. Love is not only incomplete but ambiguous. There are various kinds of love and the actions to which they lead may be incompatible. An order of distinction is required. A man's love for his family must be discriminatory: his love of mankind not. He cannot love both in the same way without denying one or the other. The quality of love is altered with the range of its generalization. In one sense love always shows a bias which reinforces some conflicting interest; in another it gives all conflicting values its blessing without indicating any specific mode of action by which conflict can be mediated. Love may enable a person to live with the burden of guilt which he assumes when he sacrifices one right to another. But it is no guide to social conflict as the last two thousand years have shown. Because the Lord loves man equally nothing follows logically about the equality of man before the Law, "The *Agape* quality of love," says Tillich, "sees man as God sees him." But what *man* can tell us how *God* sees man? "*Agape,*" continues Tillich, "loves in everybody and through everybody love itself." Karl Barth speaks more simply and intelligibly, and with a basic brutality which is the clue to his crude neutralism, when he claims that such love has no bearing whatever for the organization of any human society.

Finally there is the method of creative intelligence. It, too, tries to make it possible for men to live with the tragic conflict of goods and rights and duties, to mediate not by arbitrary fiat but through informed and responsible decision. Whoever uses this method must find his way among all the conflicting claims. He must therefore give each one of them and the interests it represents tongue or voice. Every claimant therefore has a right to be heard. The hope is that as much as possible of each claim may be incorporated in some inclusive or shared interest which is accepted because the alternatives are less satisfactory. To this end we investigate every relevant feature about it, the conditions under which it emerged, its proximate causes and consequences, the costs of gratifying it, the available alternatives and *their* costs. Every mediation entails some sacrifice. The quest for the unique good of the situation, for what is to be done here and now, may point to what is better than anything else available but what it points to is also a lesser evil. It is a lesser evil whether found in a compromise or in moderating the demand of a just claim or in learning to live peacefully with one's differences on the same general principle which tells us that a divorce is better for all parties concerned than a murder. In every case the rules, the wisdom, the lessons of the past are to be applied but they have presumptive, not final, validity because they may be challenged by new presumptions. "The pragmatic import of the logic of individualized situations," says Dewey, "is to transfer the attention of theory from pre-occupation with general conceptions to the problem of developing effective methods of inquiry," and applying them. It is a logic which does not preach solutions but explores the suggestions which emerge from the analyses of problems. Its categorical imperative is to inquire, to reason together, to seek in every crisis the creative devices and inventions that will not only make life fuller and richer but tragedy bearable. William James makes essentially the same point as Dewey in the language of ideals. Since in the struggles between ideals "victory and defeat there must be, the victory to be philosophically prayed for is that of the more inclusive side—of the side which even in the hour of triumph will to some degree do *justice* to the ideals in which the vanquished interests lay. . . ." But prayer is not enough. He goes on: "*Invent some manner* of realizing your own ideals which will also satisfy the alien demands—that and that only is the path of peace." To which we must add, provided there is a reciprocal will to peace in the matter. And even then, your own or the alien demands or both must be curtailed.

As you may have gathered by this time, I have been concerned to show that this pragmatic approach to the moral problem can not only be squared with the recognition of tragic conflicts, of troubles, minor and grave, which dog the life of man in a precarious world, but that it gets its chief justification from this recognition. Intelligence may be optimistic when it deals with the control of things but the moral life by its very nature forbids the levity and superficiality which has often been attributed to the pragmatic approach by its unimaginative critics.

Indeed I make bold to claim that the pragmatic approach to tragedy is more serious, even more heroic, than any other approach because it doesn't resign itself to the bare fact of tragedy or take easy ways out at the price of truth. Where death does not result from the tragic situation, there are always consequences for continued living which it takes responsibly without yielding to despair. It does not conceive of tragedy as a pre-ordained doom, but as one in which the plot to some extent depends upon us, so that we become the creators of our own tragic history. We cannot then palm off altogether the tragic outcome upon the universe in the same way as we can with a natural disaster.

Contrast this attitude towards tragedy with the Hegelian fetishism of history which in the end is but the rationalization of cruelty. Contrast it with the Judaic-Christian conception which offers at the price of truth, the hope that the felicities of salvation will both explain and recompense human suffering. Contrast it with the attitude of Unamuno whose hunger for immortality is so intense that he sees in intelligence or reason the chief enemy of life, both in time and eternity. For him the joy and delight of life is the conflict of value and value no matter what the cost. "The very essence of tragedy," he tells us, "is the combat of life with reason." And since the Inquisitor is concerned with the eternal life of his victim's soul, the potential victim must defend the Inquisitor's place in society and regard him as far superior to the merchant who merely ministers to his needs. "There is much more humanity in the Inquisitor," he says. Crazed by this thirst for the infinite, Unamuno glorifies war as the best means of spreading love and knowledge. He illustrates the dialectic of total absurdity and caprice in thought which often prepares the way for atrocity in life. Here is no quest for the better, for the extension of reasonable controls in life and society, for peace in action.

To be sure, Unamuno is so horrified by the flux of things in which all things are ultimately liquefied that he expresses pity for the very "star-strewn heavens" whose light will some day be quenched. But this cosmic sentimentality is disdainful of the vexatious, unheroic daily tasks of mediating differences, even of mitigating the consequences of irreconcilable conflicts, of devising ways to limit human suffering whose ubiquitous presence is the alleged cause of spiritual agony.

No two thinkers seem so far removed from each other as Miguel de Unamuno and Bertrand Russell—and as philosophers they are indeed related as a foothill to a Himalayan peak. But this makes all the more significant the similarity of their attitude towards the arts of social control which require the extension of man's power over nature. For Russell, any philosophy, and particularly one like Dewey's, which interprets ideas as implicit guides to activity and behavior, and knowledge as dependent upon experimental reconstructive activity in the situation which provokes it, exhibits "the danger of what may be called cosmic impiety." It is an arrogant power-philosophy whose insolence towards the universe is hardly less objectionable when it stresses social power than individual power.

It is fortunate that Russell's attitude—in which he is not always consistent—towards scientific power and control of our natural environment has not prevailed, otherwise the whole of modern civilization including modern medicine would never have developed. The charge of megalomania against any view of knowledge just because it is not a pure spectator view is absurd. For the pragmatic view accepts the Spinozistic dictum that nature can be changed only by nature's means. The problem is to discover or devise these means. This cannot be intelligently done without experimental activity. According to Russell's own position, power itself is neither good nor bad but only the uses and ends of power. But since he also tells us that there is no such thing as a rational or irrational end, that intelligence or reason is helpless in determining what we should do with our power, one can argue with much better warrant that it is *his* view, *if acted upon*, that increases "the danger of vast social disaster" than the pragmatic view which believes that by changing nature and society, men can to some extent change themselves in the light of rationally determined ends. No humane person can read history without being moved more by man's failures to use the knowledge he has had to remove the evils and sufferings which were remedial than by his attempt to achieve too great a control or power over nature. It was not science which was responsible for the use of the atomic bomb. It was politics—a failure of politics to understand the true situation. The pitiful disparity at any particular time between what we know and what we don't know is sufficient to inspire a sense of humility in the most intellectually ambitious. But it is only in the most vulgarized sense of the term "pragmatism," a sense which Russell helped to popularize by flagrant misunderstandings, that the adequacy of a theory of knowledge, which regards activity or experiment as integral to the achievement of knowledge of fact, can be judged by its alleged social consequences.

I am more interested tonight in stating a position than establishing it. As I understand the pragmatic perspective on life, it is an attempt to make it possible for men to live in a world of inescapable tragedy, —a tragedy which flows from the conflict of moral ideals,—without lamentation, defiance or make-believe. According to this perspective even in the best of human worlds there will be tragedy—tragedy perhaps without bloodshed but certainly not without tears. It focuses its analysis on problems of normative social inquiry in order to reduce the costs of tragedy. Its view of man is therefore melioristic, not optimistic. Some philosophers belittle man by asking him to look at the immensities without: others belittle him by asking him to look at the perversities and selfishness within. Pragmatism denies nothing about the world or men which one truly finds in them but it sees in men something which is at once, to use the Sophoclean phrase, more wonderful and more terrible than anything else in the universe, viz., the power to make themselves and the world around them better or worse. In this way pragmatic meliorism avoids the romantic pessimism of Russell's free man, shaking his fist in defiance of a malignant universe, and the grandiose optimism of Niebuhr's redeemed man with his delusions of a cosmic purpose which he knows is there but knows in a way in which neither he nor anyone else can possible understand.

To the meliorist the recognition of the gamut of tragic possibilities is what feeds his desire to find some method of negotiating conflicts of value by intelligence rather than war, or brute force. But this is not as simple as it sounds. There is no substitute for intelligence. But intelligence may not be enough. It may not be enough because of limitations of our knowledge, because of the limited reach of our powers of control. It may not be enough because of the recalcitrance of will —not merely the recalcitrance of will to act upon goods already known and not in dispute, but because of unwillingness to find out what the maximizing good in the situation is. And although we are seeking to settle conflicts of value by the use of intelligence rather than by force, is it not true that sometimes intelligence requires the use of force?

Let us take this last question first. Faced by a momentous conflict of values in which some value must give way if the situation is to be resolved, the rational approach is to find some encompassing value on the basis of some shared interest. This, as we have seen, involves willingness to negotiate—to negotiate honestly. The grim fact, however, is that there is sometimes no desire to reason, no wish to negotiate except as a holding action to accumulate strategic power, nothing but the reliance of one party or the other upon brute force even when other alternatives may exist. In such cases the moral onus rests clearly upon those who invoke force. Their victory no more establishes their claim to be right than a vandal's destruction of a scientists' instruments of inquiry has any bearing on the validity of his assertions, evidence for or against which could have been gathered by the instrument destroyed. The intelligent use of force to *prevent* or crush the use of force where a healthy democratic process, equitable laws and traditions and customs of freedom make it possible to vent differences in a rational and orderly way, is therefore justifiable even if on prudential grounds one may forego such action. This means that tolerance always has limits—it cannot tolerate what is itself actively intolerant.

There is a tendency in modern philosophical thought which, in rejecting too sweeping claims for the role of intelligence in human affairs, settles for too little even when it does not embrace a wholesale skepticism. Of course, a man may know what is right and not do it just as he may know what is true and not publicly assert it. In neither case is this a ground for maintaining that we cannot know what action is more justified than another or what assertion is more warranted than another. The *refusal* to follow a rational method, to give good reasons is one thing: the claim that there are different rational methods, different *kinds* of good reasons each with its own built-in modes of validity, is something else again—and to me unintelligible. To be sure, the acceptance of rational method is not enough. Men must have some non-rational element in common. Hume is on unquestionably solid ground in asserting that reason must always *serve* a human need, interest or passion. But his mistake outweighed his insight when he contended that rational method could only be a servant or slave of what it served and that needs, interests and passions could not be changed or transformed by the use of intelligence. In our flights into space if we encounter other sentient creatures capable of communicating with us, it is more likely that their logical and mathematical judgment will be the same as ours than their ethical judgments, because we can more readily conceive creatures of different needs than of different minds.

At any rate the world we live in is one in which men do not share all their needs and interests and yet it is one in which they have sufficient needs and interests in common to make possible their further extension, and to give intelligence a purchase, so to speak, in its inquiry.

The most difficult of all situations is one in which even the common use of methods of inquiry seem to lead to conclusions which are incompatible with each other although each is objectively justified. There is always an open possibility of ultimate disagreement no matter how far and long we pursue rational inquiry. We can conceive it happening. In such situations we must resign ourselves to living with our divergences. Otherwise we must fight or surrender. But it is simply a non-sequitur to maintain that because no guarantee can be given that there will not be ultimate disagreement, penultimate agreements cannot be validly reached and justified.

In any case we cannot in advance determine the limits of reason or intelligence in *human* affairs. So long as we don't know where it lies, it is sensible to press on, at the same time devising the means to curb the effects of the refusal to reason when it manifests itself. Above all, we must avoid oversimplifying the choice of evils and encouraging the hope that to be unreasonable will pay dividends.

We are moving into another period of history in which freedom once more is being readied for sacrifice on the altars of survival. The Munichmen of the spirit are at work again. The stakes are now for the entire world. Our task as philosophers is not to heed partisan and excited calls for action, but rather to think through the problems of freedom and survival afresh. In a famous pronouncement two years ago Bertrand Russell declared that if the Kremlin refused to accept reasonable proposals of disarmament, the West should disarm unilaterally "even if it means the horrors of Communist domination." Although he no longer believes this, there are many others who do. I know that common sense is at a discount in philosophy but in ethics it should not be lightly disregarded. A position like this obviously can have only one effect, viz., to encourage the intransigeance of those who wish to destroy the free world without which there cannot be a free philosophy. You cannot negotiate successfully by proclaiming in advance that you will capitulate if the other side persists in being unreasonable. Our alternatives are not limited to surrender and extinction of freedom, on the one hand, and war and the danger of human extermination on the other. There are other alternatives to be explored—all tragic in their costs but not equally extreme. The very willingness, if necessary, to go down fighting in defense of freedom may be the greatest force for peace when facing an opponent who makes a fetish of historical survival. On pragmatic grounds, the willingness to act on a position like Kant's *fiat justitia, pereat mundus* may sometimes—I repeat—sometimes—be the best way of preserving a just and free world—just as the best way of saving one's life is sometimes to be prepared to lose it. The uneasy peace we currently enjoy as a result of "the balance of terror" is tragic. But it may turn out that it is less so than any feasible alternative today. If it endures long enough and it becomes clear to the enemies of freedom that they cannot themselves survive war, they may accept the moral equivalents of war in the making. The pragmatic program is always to find moral equivalents for the expression of natural impulses which threaten the structure of our values.

I have perhaps overstressed the sense of the tragic in human life in an effort to compensate for the distortions to which pragmatism has been subject. There is more in life than the sense of the tragic. There is laughter and joy and the sustaining discipline of work. There are other dimensions of experience besides the moral. There is art and science and religion. There are other uses for intelligence besides the resolution of human difficulties. There is intellectual play and adventure. But until men become Gods—which will never be—they will live with the sense of the tragic in their hearts as they go in quest for wisdom. Pragmatism, as I interpret it, is the theory and practice of enlarging human freedom in a precarious and tragic world by the arts of intelligent social control. It may be a lost cause. I do not know of a better one. And it may not be lost if we can summon the courage and intelligence to support our faith in freedom—and enjoy the blessings of a little luck.

NATURALISM AND FIRST PRINCIPLES [2]

That first principles must be justified before we can achieve assured knowledge is a view seemingly held by some philosophers but rarely by anyone else. Scientists, for example, have satisfactorily solved problem after problem without feeling called upon to solve the problem of justifying their first principles. Not only scientists but people of ordinary affairs generally know when something is truer than something else without knowing, or even claiming to know, what is *absolutely* true. To say that we do not have to know what is ultimately or absolutely true or good in order to know what is truer or better, sounds dialectically impossible. But I submit that this is actually the way common sense and science operate. Even the most rationalist of philosophers in their nonprofessional capacity make effective use of everyday knowledge long before they reach their uncertain conclusions about the validity of first principles. It isn't necessary to assert that we know what is absolutely true about the cause of tuberculosis to know that a certain germ has more to do with it than climate. Similarly, few people know what their "ultimate" values are, and yet almost everyone will claim to know that it is better for human beings to do productive labor for a living than to be recipients of charity. Deny propositions of this sort and insist that declarations of the truer or better must wait upon knowledge of *the* true or *the* good, and the whole of human inquiry anywhere would come to a halt.

This is not to assert that there is no problem concerning the justification of first principles or of those rules of procedure which we follow when we reach the knowledge about which there is a maximum of agreement among human beings. What I am asserting is that the justification of rules of procedure in inquiry is not of a different logical order, possessing so to speak another or higher type of necessity

[2] From Sidney Hook, *American Philosophers at Work*. N.Y.: Criterion Books, 1956, pp. 238–241.

than the actions of which they are the rule. More specifically what I am asserting is that there is no such thing as strictly logical justification of first principles in science or common sense since proof by definition involves the reduction of all statements to indefinable terms and undemonstrable propositions or to propositions themselves so reducible. And secondly, what I am further asserting is that in the sense in which justification of first principles is an intelligible question—as when someone asks me why I regard naturalism as a truer or more adequate doctrine than its rivals—the answer will take the same *general* form of the answers given by those who do the world's work—the cobblers, the carpenters and gardeners—when they are asked to justify one set of procedures rather than alternative ones.

In other words I am saying somewhat differently what William James observed in *The Problems of Philosophy* although it is alleged he sometimes sinned against the meaning of his own words. "Philosophy," he there says, "taken as something distinct from science or human affairs, follows no method peculiar to itself. All our thinking today has evolved gradually out of primitive human thought, and the only really important changes that have come over its manner (as distinguished from the matters in which it believes) are a *greater* hesitancy in asserting its convictions, and the *habit* of seeking verification for them when it can." [my italics]

Such an approach, as I understand it, is the only one that can consistently be advanced by naturalists in justifying their first principles. This has provoked the retort that it is essentially question-begging, that since the methods and categories of common day activity and science—upon which naturalism relies—are designed to take note only of the existence of certain things, the existence of other things like immaterial entities, cosmic purposes, Gods, and disembodied souls are ruled out *a priori*. The assertion of their existence on the naturalist's view must therefore be assumed to be not merely false but meaningless or contradictory. Since we are concerned here with questions of existential fact, the naturalist who naïvely believes himself to be imbued with a spirit of natural piety for a world he has not created, is taxed with the ironic charge of legislating for all existence.

Before evaluating the charge of circularity it is important to realize that if valid, it holds for *every* philosophical position. We cannot break out of this circularity by invoking only the law of contradiction, unless we are prepared to hold that all knowledge is analytic and that the differences between nature and history, with all their contingency, and mathematics and logic, disappear. Certainly, whatever falls outside the scope of the basic explanatory categories of any philosophical position cannot be recognized. This is a tautology. That these categories are restrictive follows from their claim to be meaningful since a necessary condition of a meaningful statement is that it should be incompatible with its opposite. The only legitimate question here is whether they are narrowly restrictive, whether there are matters of knowledge in common experience which they exclude or whose existence they make unintelligible.

Since every philosophic position must start somewhere and make some preliminary or initial assumptions that can be challenged at least verbally by other philosophers, it is always possible to level the charge of circularity. But what shall we therefore conclude? That these assumptions are mere stipulations or arbitrary postulations which express nothing but the *resolutions* of philosophers? This would be voluntarism gone mad. Philosophers might just as well close up shop insofar as they claim for their position some objective validity in reporting or interpreting the facts of experience. For even voluntarism could not sustain itself against the charge of circularity.

The naturalist does not despair because he cannot demonstrate what is by definition indemonstrable. Nor can he rely upon intuitions or revealed dogmas because of their irreducible plurality. He believes he can show that although not demonstrable, his assumptions can be made reasonable to "reasonable" men. And the mark of a "reasonable" man is his willingness to take responsibility for his actions, to explain why he proceeds to do one thing rather than another, and to recognize that it is his conduct, insofar as it is voluntary, which commits him to a principle or belief rather than any form of words where the two seem at odds with each other. The naturalist does not speak, as one of its critics does, in large terms of "justifying philosophical categories as rationally and comprehensively as possible," and then fail to tell us in what specific ways philosophical rationality and comprehensiveness differ from scientific rationality and comprehensiveness. Are the laws of logic and the canons of evidence and relevance any different in philosophy from what they are in science and common sense?

To every critic of naturalism who has charged it with circularity I propose the following. Consider someone who comes to you and proclaims on the basis of some special personal experience that an all-pervasive R substance exists. It is neither physical nor psychical nor social, neither natural nor divine, nor can it be identified by, defined in, or reduced, in any sense of reduction, to any physical, psychical, or social terms. It is subject, so you are told, to no material conditions of determination whatsoever. The very request that these conditions be indicated is brushed aside as revealing a constitutional incapacity or blindness to grasp this unique entity to which all sorts of edifying qualities are attributed in an analogical sense, including a triune gender. It is granted by the believer in R that its existence cannot be logically inferred from whatever *else* is experienced, but he is quick to add that its existence cannot be logically *disproved* without assuming a question-begging philosophical position which rules out the possibility of this unique cosmic process. The next day he reports personal contact with another presence which he calls the analogical father, and the day after, the analogical grandfather, and so on, until even the most fervent supernaturalist finds himself confronted with an embarrassment of supernatural riches.

Embroider the fancy as you will. It is obvious that he can repeat almost word for word the points in the indictment of those who charge naturalists with circular reasoning.

Even if all philosophical positions are *au fond* question begging, there would still remain the task, pursued by all philosophers, of determining which of all question-begging positions is more adequate to the facts of experience. Every philosopher who seriously attempts an answer does assume *in fact* that there is some common method of determining when a position is adequate to the facts of experience and when not. The contention of the naturalist is that this common method is in principle continuous with the method which we ordinarily use to hold individuals to responsible utterance about the existence of things in the world—a method which is pre-eminently illustrated in the ways in which men everywhere solve the problem of adaptation of material means to ends.

BIBLIOGRAPHY

HOOK, Sidney, *The Metaphysics of Pragmatism*. Chicago: Open Court, 1927.
_____, *Towards the Understanding of Karl Marx; a Revolutionary Interpretation*. N.Y.: John Day, 1933.
_____, *From Hegel to Marx*. N.Y.: Reynal & Hitchcock, 1936.
_____, *John Dewey: An Intellectual Portrait*. N.Y.: John Day, 1939.
_____, *Reason, Social Myths, and Democracy*. N.Y.: John Day, 1940.
_____, *The Hero in History: A Study in Limitations and Possibility*. N.Y.: John Day, 1943.
_____, *Education for Modern Man*. N.Y.: Dial, 1946.
_____, *Heresy, Yes—Conspiracy, No*. N.Y.: John Day, 1953.
_____, *Marx and the Marxists: The Ambiguous Legacy*. Princeton: Van Nostrand, 1955.
_____, *Political Power and Personal Freedom*. N.Y.: Criterion, 1959.
_____, *The Quest for Being*. N. Y.: St. Martin's Press, 1961.
_____, *The Paradoxes of Freedom*. Berkeley: U. of California Press, 1962.
_____ (ed.), *John Dewey, Philosopher of Science and Freedom: a Symposium*. N.Y.: Dial Press, 1950.

_____ (ed.), *American Philosophers at Work: the Philosophic Scene in the United States*. N.Y.: Criterion, 1956.

_____ (ed.), *Determinism and Freedom in the Age of Modern Science*. N.Y.: New York U. Press, 1958.

_____ (ed.), *Psychoanalysis, Scientific Method and Philosophy*, N.Y.: New York U. Press, 1959.

_____ (ed.), *Dimensions of Mind*. N.Y.: New York U. Press, 1960.

_____ (ed.), *Religious Experience and Truth*. N.Y.: New York U. Press, 1961.

_____ (ed.), *Philosophy and History*. N.Y.: New York U. Press, 1962.

_____ (ed.), *Law and Philosophy*. N.Y.: New York U. Press, 1964.

KONVITZ, Milton R. "Sidney Hook, Thinker in Action," *The New Leader*, No. 51, 1952. (Bibliography.)

Ernest Nagel

[*1901*–   ]

Ernest Nagel is a logician and outstanding philosopher of science who has been influenced by pragmatism, naturalism, logical positivism, and philosophical analysis. Throughout his writings Nagel displays a rare critical acument, especially as regards problems concerning the logic of science. His most important work in the philosophy of science is *The Structure of Science* (1961). Nagel's interests, unlike those of many other philosophers of science, extend beyond physics to biology and the social sciences; and he has also been deeply concerned with broader ethical and social questions.

Nagel was born in Czechoslovakia, but he came to the United States at the age of ten. He received his B.A. in 1923 from City College, where he studied under Morris R. Cohen, and his Ph.D. in 1931 from Columbia University, where he was a student of John Dewey. He has taught in the New York Public Schools, City College, and has been professor of philosophy for many years at Columbia University. He was on the editorial boards of *The Journal of Symbolic Logic* (1939–45), *The Journal of Philosophy* (1940–56), and *Philosophy of Science* (1956–59). He has held fellowships from the Guggenheim Foundation, the Center for Advanced Study in the Behavioral Sciences, and the American Council of Learned Societies. He is a former Chairman of the Conference on Methods in Philosophy and the Sciences (1946–47), and a former President of the Association for Symbolic Logic (1947–49) and of the American Philosophical Association, Eastern Division (1954).

Nagel is primarily a critical philosopher and has been highly dubious of metaphysical speculation, as traditionally conceived. His rejection of speculative philosophy does not, however, preclude the formulation of comprehensive assumptions about the scope of human reason, the world, and man's place in it. Philosophers should on occasion make clear what their general ground rules are. The selection reprinted below, "Naturalism Reconsidered" (1954), is Nagel's own careful statement of a general naturalistic position. Nagel maintains that naturalism supports two theses about nature: (1) "the existential and causal primacy of organized matter" and (2) "the manifest plurality and variety of things," their "qualities" and "functions." He finds that the career and destiny of man is part of nature, though human materials are *human* in quality and significance. Like other naturalists, Nagel supports the methods of scientific reason, and he is intent equally on answering the claims of pessimists who seek to demean human aspirations, and of transcendentalists who attempt to give man a privileged place in the universe.

NATURALISM RECONSIDERED [1]

It is surely not the highest reach for a philosopher to be a com-
batant in the perennial wars between standardized "isms" which fill
conventional handbooks of philosophy. Philosophy at its best is a critical commentary upon existence and upon our claims to have knowledge of it; and its mission is to help illuminate what is obscure in
experience and its objects, rather than to profess creeds or to repeat
the battle-cries of philosophical schools aiming at intellectual hege-
mony. The conception of philosophy as a struggle between competing
systems is especially sterile when the "ism" defended or attacked
covers as miscellaneous an assortment of not always congruous views
as fly the banner of naturalism. The number of distinguishable doctrines for which the word "naturalism" has been a counter in the
history of thought, is notorious. Even among contemporaries who proclaim themselves to be naturalists in philosophy, there are not only
important differences in stress and perspective, but also in specific
doctrines professed and in intellectual methods used to support commitments made. I am aware, therefore, that in taking naturalism as
my subject this evening, I run the risk of becoming involved in futile
polemics—a risk made graver by the fact that although the stated title
of my address may have aroused different expectations, it is not my
intention to recant and to confess past errors. I must explain why,
notwithstanding the hazards of my theme, I have elected to discuss it.

The past quarter century has been for philosophy in many parts of
the world a period of acute self-questioning, engendered in no small
measure by developments in scientific and logical thought, and in part
no doubt by fundamental changes in the social order. In any event,
there has come about a general loss of confidence in the competence
of philosophy to provide by way of a distinctive intellectual method
a basic ground-plan of the cosmos, or for that matter to contribute to
knowledge of any primary subject-matter except by becoming a specialized positive science and subjecting itself to the discipline of
empirical inquiry. Although the abysses of human ignorance are undeniably profound, it has also become apparent that ignorance, like
actual knowledge, is of many special and heterogeneous things; and
we have come to think, like the fox and unlike the hedgehog of

[1] Presidential address delivered before the annual meeting of the Eastern Division
of the American Philosophical Association at Goucher College, Baltimore, Mary-
land, Dec. 1954. From *Proceedings and Addresses*, Vol. XXVIII. Yellow Springs,
Ohio: The Antioch Press, 1954–55, pp. 5–17.

whom Mr. Isaiah Berlin has recently reminded us, that there are a great many things which are already known or remain to be discovered, but that there is no one "big thing" which, if known, would make everything else coherent and unlock the mystery of creation. In consequence, many of us have ceased to emulate the great system-builders in the history of philosophy. In partial imitation of the strategy of modern science, and in the hope of achieving responsibly held conclusions about matters concerning which we could acquire genuine competence, we have tended to become specialists in our professional activities. We have come to direct our best energies to the resolution of limited problems and puzzles that emerge in the analysis of scientific and ordinary discourse, in the evaluation of claims to knowledge, in the interpretation and validation of ethical and esthetic judgments, and in the assessment of types of human experience. I hope I shall not be regarded as offensive in stating my impression that the majority of the best minds among us have turned away from the conception of the philosopher as the spectator of all time and existence, and have concentrated on restricted but manageable questions, with almost deliberate unconcern for the bearing of their often minute investigations upon an inclusive view of nature and man.

Some of us, I know, are distressed by the widespread skepticism of the traditional claims for a *philosopia perennis*, and have dismissed as utterly trivial most if not all the products of various current forms of analytical philosophy. I do not share this distress, nor do I think the dismissal is uniformly perspicacious and warranted. For in my judgment, the skepticism which many deplore is well-founded. Even though a fair-sized portion of recent analytical literature seems inconsequential also to me, analytical philosophy in our own day is the continuation of a major philosophic tradition, and can count substantial feats of clarification among its assets. Concentration on limited and determinate problems has yielded valuable fruits, not least in the form of an increased and refreshing sensitivity to the demands of responsible discourse.

On the other hand, philosophers like other men conduct their lives within the framework of certain comprehensive if not always explicit assumptions about the world they inhabit. These assumptions color evaluations of major ideals and proposed policies. I also suspect that the directions taken by analyses of specific intellectual problems are frequently if subtly controlled by the expressed or tacit beliefs philosophers hold concerning the over-all nature of things, by their views on human destiny, and by their conceptions of the scope of human reason. But conversely, resolutions of special problems made plausible by recent philosophical analysis, as well as by the findings of various positive sciences, seem to me to support certain broad generalizations about the cosmos and to disconfirm others. It is clearly desirable that such basic intellectual commitments, which are at once the matrix and the outcome of inquiries into specific problems, be made as explicit as possible. A philosopher who is a reflective man by profession, certainly owes it to himself to articulate, if only occasionally, what sort of world he thinks he inhabits, and to make clear to himself where approximately lies the center of his convictions.

The discharge of the important obligation which is mine this evening, seems to me an appropriate occasion for stating as simply and as succinctly as I can the substance of those intellectual commitments I like to call "naturalism." The label itself is of no importance, but I use it partly because of its historical associations, and partly because it is a reminder that the doctrines for which it is a name are neither new nor untried. With Santayana, I prefer not to accept in philosophic debate what I do not believe when I am not arguing; and naturalism as I construe it merely formulates what centuries of human experience have repeatedly confirmed. At any rate, naturalism seems to me a sound generalized account of the world encountered in practice and in critical reflection, and a just perspective upon the human scene. I wish to state briefly and hence with little supporting argument what I take to be its major tenets, and to defend it against some recent criticisms.

Claims to knowledge cannot ultimately be divorced from an evaluation of the intellectual methods used to support those claims. It is nevertheless unfortunate that in recent years naturalists in philosophy have so frequently permitted their allegiance to a dependable method of inquiry to obscure their substantive views on things in general. For it is the inclusive intellectual image of nature and man which naturalism supplies that sets it off from other comprehensive philosophies. In my conception of it, at any rate, naturalism embraces a generalized account of the cosmic scheme and of man's place in it, as well as a logic of inquiry.

I hasten to add, however, that naturalism does not offer a theory of nature in the sense that Newtonian mechanics, for example, provides a theory of motion. Naturalism does not, like the latter, specify a set of substantive principles with the help of which the detailed course of concrete happenings can be explained or understood. Moreover, the principles affirmed by naturalism are not proposed as competitors or underpinnings for any of the special theories which the positive sciences assert. Nor, finally, does naturalism offer its general view of nature and man as the product of some special philosophical mode of knowing. The account of things proposed by naturalism is a distillation from knowledge acquired in the usual way in daily encounters with the world or in specialized scientific inquiry. Naturalism articulates features of the world which, because they have become so obvious, are rarely mentioned in discussions of special subject-matter, but which distinguish our actual world from other conceivable worlds. The major affirmations of naturalism are accordingly meager in content; but the principles affirmed are nevertheless effective guides in responsible criticism and evaluation.

Two theses seem to me central to naturalism as I conceive it. The first is the existential and causal primacy of organized matter in the executive order of nature. This is the assumption that the occurrence of events, qualities and processes, and the characteristic behaviors of various individuals, are contingent on the organization of spatio-temporally located bodies, whose internal structures and external relations determine and limit the appearance and disappearance of everything that happens. That this is so, is one of the best-tested conclusions of experience. We are frequently ignorant of the special conditions under which things come into being or pass away; but we have also found repeatedly that when we look closely, we eventually ascertain at least the approximate and gross conditions under which events occur, and we discover that those conditions invariably consist of some more or less complex organization of material substances. Naturalism does not maintain that only what is material exists, since many things noted in experience, for example, modes of action, relations of meaning, dreams, joys, plans, aspirations, are not as such material bodies or organizations of material bodies. What naturalism does assert as a truth about nature is that though *forms* of behavior or *functions* of material systems are indefeasibly parts of nature, forms and functions are not themselves agents in their own realization or in the realization of anything else. In the conception of nature's processes which naturalism affirms, there is no place for the operation of disembodied forces, no place for an immaterial spirit directing the course of events, no place for the survival of personality after the corruption of the body which exhibits it.

The second major contention of naturalism is that the manifest plurality and variety of things, of their qualities and their functions, are an irreducible feature of the cosmos, not a deceptive appearance cloaking some more homogeneous "ultimate reality" or transempirical substance, and that the sequential orders in which events occur or the manifold relations of dependence in which things exist are *contingent* connections, not the embodiments of a fixed and unified pattern of logically necessary links. The existential primacy of organized matter does not make illusory either the relatively permanent or the comparatively transient characters and forms which special configurations of bodies may possess. In particular, although the continued existence of the human scene is precarious and is dependent on a balance of forces that doubtless will not endure indefinitely, and even though its distinctive traits are not pervasive throughout space, it is nonetheless as much a part of the "ultimate" furniture of the world, and is as genuine a sample of what "really" exists, as are atoms and stars. There undoubtedly occur integrated systems of bodies, such as biological organisms, which have the capacity because of their material organization to maintain themselves and the direction of their characteristic activities. But there is no positive evidence, and much negative evidence, for the supposition that all existential structures are teleological systems in this sense, or for the view that whatever occurs is a phase in a unitary, teleologically organized, and all-inclusive process or system. Modern physical cosmology does indeed supply some evidence for definite patterns of evolutionary development of stars, galactic systems, and even of the entire physical universe; and it is quite possible that the stage of cosmic evolution reached at any given time causally limits the types of things which can occur during that period. On the other hand, the patterns of change investigated in physical cosmogony are not patterns that are exhaustive of everything that happens; and nothing in these current physical speculations requires the conclusion that changes in one star or galaxy are related by inherent necessity to every action of biological organisms in some remote planet. Even admittedly teleological systems contain parts and processes which are causally irrelevant to some of the activities maintained by those systems; and the causal dependencies known to hold between the parts of any system, teleological or not, have never been successfully established as forms of logically necessary relations. In brief, if naturalism is true, irreducible variety and logical contingency are fundamental traits of the world we actually inhabit. The orders and connections of things are all accessible to rational inquiry; but these orders and connections are not all derivable by deductive methods from any set of premises that deductive reason can certify.

It is in this framework of general ideas that naturalism envisages the career and destiny of man. Naturalism views the emergence and the continuance of human society as dependent on physical and physiological conditions that have not always obtained, and that will not permanently endure. But it does not in consequence regard man and his works as intrusions into nature, any more than it construes as intrusions the presence of heavenly bodies or of terrestrial protozoa. The stars are no more foreign to the cosmos than are men, even if the conditions for the existence of both stars and men are realized only occasionally or only in a few regions. Indeed, the conception of human life as a war with nature, as a struggle with an implacable foe that has doomed man to extinction, is but an inverted theology, with a malicious Devil in the seat of Omnipotence. It is a conception that is immodest as well as anthropomorphic in the importance it imputes to man in the scheme of things.

On the other hand, the affirmation that nature is man's "home" as much as it is the "home" of anything else, and the denial that cosmic forces are *intent* on destroying the human scene, do not warrant the interpretation that every sector of nature is explicable in terms of traits known to characterize only human individuals and human actions. Man undoubtedly possesses characteristics which are shared by everything that exists; but he also manifests traits and capacities that appear to be distinctive of him. Is anything gained but confusion when all forms of dependence between things, whether animate or inanimate, and all types of behaviors they display, are subsumed under distinctions that have an identifiable content only in reference to the human psyche? Measured by the illumination they bring, there is nothing to differentiate the thesis that human traits are nothing but the properties of bodies which can be formulated exclusively in the language of current physical theory, from the view that every change and every mode of operation, in whatever sector of the cosmos it may be encountered, is simply an illustration of some category pertinent to the description of human behavior.

Indeed, even some professed naturalists sometimes appear to promote the confusion when they make a fetish of continuity. Naturalists usually stress the emergence of novel forms in physical and biological evolution, thereby emphasizing the fact that human traits are not identical with the traits from which they emerge. Nevertheless, some distinguished contemporary naturalists also insist, occasionally with overtones of anxiety, that there is a "continuity" between the typically human on the one hand, and the physical and biological on the other. But is man's foothold in the scheme of things really made more secure by showing that his distinctive traits are in some sense "continuous" with features pervasive in nature, and would man's place in nature be less secure if such continuity did not obtain? The actual evidence for a continuity of development is conclusive in some instances of human traits, however it may be in others. But I sometimes suspect that the cardinal importance philosophers assign to the alleged universality of such continuity is a lingering survival of that ancient conception, according to which things are intelligible only when seen as teleological systems producing definite ends, so that nature itself is properly understood only when construed as the habitat of human society. In any event, a naturalism that is not provincial in its outlook will not accept the intellectual incorporation of man into nature at the price of reading into all the processes of the cosmos the passions, the strivings, the defeats and the glories of human life, and then exhibiting man as the most adequate, because most representative, expression of nature's inherent constitution. No, a mature naturalism seeks to understand what man is, not in terms of a discovered or postulated continuity between what is distinctive of him and what is pervasive in all things. Without denying that even the most distinctive human traits are dependent on things which are non-human, a mature naturalism attempts to assess man's nature in the light of *his* actions and achievements, *his* aspirations and capacities, *his* limitations and tragic failures, and *his* splendid works of ingenuity and imagination.

Human nature and history, in short, are *human* nature and history, not the history and nature of anything else, however much knowledge of other things contributes to a just appraisal of what man is. In particular, the adequacy of proposed ideals for human life must be judged, not in terms of their causes and origins, but in reference to how the pursuit and possible realization of ideals contribute to the organization and release of *human* energies. Men are animated by many springs of action, no one of which is intrinsically good or evil; and a moral ideal is the imagined satisfaction of some complex of impulses, desires, and needs. When ideals are handled responsibly, they therefore function as hypotheses for achieving a balanced exercise of human powers. Moral ideals are not self-certifying, any more than are the theories of the physical sciences; and evidence drawn from experienced satisfactions is required to validate them, however difficult may be the process of sifting and weighing the available data. Moral problems arise from a conflict of specific impulses and interests. They cannot, however, be effectively resolved by invoking standards derived from the study of non-human nature, or of what is allegedly beyond nature. If moral problems can be resolved at all, they can be resolved only in the light of specific human capacities, historical circumstance and acquired skills, and the opportunities (revealed by an imagination disciplined by knowledge) for altering the physical and social environment and for redirecting habitual behaviors. Moreover, since human virtues are in part the products of the society in which human powers are matured, a naturalistic moral theory is at the same time a critique of civilization, that is, a critique of the institutions that channel human energies, so as to exhibit the possibilities and limitations of various forms and arrangements of society for bringing enduring satisfactions to individual human careers.

These are the central tenets of what I take to be philosophical naturalism. They are tenets which are supported by compelling empirical evidence, rather than dicta based on dogmatic preference. In my view of it, naturalism does not dismiss every other differing conception of the scheme of things as logically impossible; and it does not rule out all alternatives to itself on a priori grounds. It is possible, I think, to conceive without logical inconsistency a world in which disembodied forces are dynamic agents, or in which whatever happens is a manifestation of an unfolding logical pattern. In such possible worlds it would be an error to be a naturalist. But philosophy is not identical with pure mathematics, and its ultimate concern is with the actual world, even though philosophy must take cognizance of the fact that the actual world contains creatures who can envisage possible worlds and who employ different logical procedures for deciding which hypothetical world is the actual one. It is partly for this reason that contemporary naturalists devote so much attention to methods of evaluating evidence. When naturalists give their allegiance to the method of intelligence commonly designated as the method of modern empirical science, they do so because that method appears to be the most assured way of achieving reliable knowledge.

As judged by that method, the evidence in my opinion is at present conclusive for the truth of naturalism, and it is tempting to suppose that no one familiar with the evidence can fail to acknowledge that philosophy. Indeed, some commentators there are who assert that all philosophies are at bottom only expressions in different idioms of the same conceptions about the nature of things, so that the strife of philosophic systems is mainly a conflict over essentially linguistic matters. Yet many thinkers for whom I have a profound respect explicitly reject naturalism, and their espousal of contrary views seems to me incompatible with the irenic claim that we really are in agreement on fundamentals.

Although I do not have the time this evening to consider systematically the criticisms currently made of naturalism, I do wish to examine briefly two repeatedly voiced objections which, if valid, would in my opinion seriously jeopardize the integrity and adequacy of naturalism as a philosophy. Stated summarily, the first objection is that in relying exclusively on the logico-empirical method of modern science for establishing cognitive claims, naturalists are in effect stacking the cards in their own favor, since thereby all alternative philosophies are antecedently disqualified. It is maintained, for example, that naturalism rejects any hypothesis about trans-empirical causes or time-transcending spiritual substances as factors in the order of things, not because such hypotheses are actually shown to be false, but simply because the logic of proof adopted dismisses as irrelevant any evidence which might establish them.

This criticism does not seem to me to have merit: the logico-empirical method of evaluating cognitive claims to which naturalists subscribe does not eliminate by fiat any hypothesis about existence for which evidence can be procured, that is, evidence that in the last resort can be obtained through sensory or introspective observation. Thus, anyone who asserts a hypothesis postulating a trans-empirical ground for all existence, presumably seeks to understand in terms of that ground the actual occurrences in nature, and to account thereby for what actually happens as distinct from what is merely imagined to happen. There must therefore be some connection between the postulated character of the hypothetical trans-empirical ground, and the empirically observable traits in the world around us; for otherwise the hypothesis is otiose, and not relevant to the spatio-temporal processes of nature. This does not mean, as some critics of naturalism suppose the latter to maintain, that the hypothetical trans-empirical ground must be characterized exclusively in terms of the observable properties of the world, any more than that the sub-microscopic particles and processes which current physical theory postulates must be logical constructions out of the observable traits of macroscopic objects. But it does mean that unless the hypothesis implies, even if only by a circuitous route, some statements about empirical data, it is not adequate to the task for which it is proposed. If naturalists reject hypotheses about trans-empirical substances, they do not do so arbitrarily. They reject such hypotheses either because their relevance to the going concerns of nature is not established, or because, though their relevance is not in question, the actual evidence does not support them.

Nor does naturalism dismiss as unimportant and without consideration experiences such as of the holy, of divine illumination, or of mystical ecstasy, experiences which are of the greatest moment in the lives of many men, and which are often taken to signify the presence and operation of some purely spiritual reality. Such experiences have dimensions of meaning for those who have undergone them, that are admittedly not on par with the import of more common experiences like those of physical hunger, general well-being, or feelings of remorse and guilt. Yet such experiences are nonetheless events among other events; and though they may be evidence for something, their sheer occurrence does not certify *what* they are evidence for, any more than the sheer occurrence of dreams, hopes, and delusions authenticates the actual existence of their ostensible objects. In particular, whether the experience labelled as an experience of divine illumination is evidence for the existence of a divinity, is a question to be settled by inquiry, not by dogmatic affirmations or denials. When naturalists refuse to acknowledge, merely on the strength of such experiences, the operation or presence of a divine power, they do so not because their commitment to a logical method prevents them from treating it seriously, but because independent inquiry fails to confirm it. Knowledge is knowledge, and cannot without confusion be identified with intuitive insight or with the vivid immediacy of profoundly moving experiences. Claims to knowledge must be capable of being tested; and the testing must be conducted by eventual reference to such evidence as counts in the responsible conduct of everyday affairs as well as of systematic inquiry in the sciences. Naturalists are therefore not engaged in question-begging when, through the use of the logic of scientific intelligence, they judge non-naturalistic accounts of the order of things to be unfounded.

There is, however, a further objection to naturalism, to the effect that in committing itself to the logic of scientific proof, it is quite analogous to religious belief in resting on unsupported and indemonstrable faith. For that logic allegedly involves assumptions like the uniformity of nature or similar principles which transcend experience, cannot be justified empirically, and yet provide the premises that constitute the ultimate warrant for the conclusions of empirical inquiry. But if naturalism is thus based on unprovable articles of faith, on what cogent grounds can it reject a different conception of the true order of governance of events which rests on a different faith?

I cannot here deal adequately with the complex issues raised by this objection. Its point is not satisfactorily turned by claiming, as some have done, that instead of being articles of faith, the alleged indemonstrable postulates of scientific method are simply rules of the scientific game which *define* what in that game is to be understood by the words "knowledge" and "evidence." As I see it, however, the objection has force only for those whose ideal of reason is demonstration, and who therefore refuse to dignify anything as genuine knowledge unless it is demonstrable from self-luminous and self-evident premises. But if, as I also think, that ideal is not universally appropriate, and if, furthermore, a *wholesale* justification for knowledge and its methods is an unreasonable demand and a misplaced effort, the objection appears as quite pointless. The warrant for a proposition about some specific inter-relations of events does not derive from a faith in the uniformity of nature or in other principles with a cosmic scope. The warrant derives exclusively from the specific evidence available for that proposition, and from the contingent historical fact that the special ways employed in obtaining and appraising the evidence have been generally effective in yielding reliable knowledge. Subsequent inquiry may show that we were mistaken in accepting a proposition on the evidence available earlier; and further inquiry may also reveal that a given inductive policy, despite a record of successful past performance, requires correction if not total rejection. Fortunately, however, we are not always mistaken in accepting various propositions or in employing certain inductive policies, even though we are unable to demonstrate that we shall never fall into error. Accordingly, though many of our hopes for the stability of beliefs in the face of fresh experience may turn out to be baseless, and though no guarantees can be given that our most assured claims to knowledge may not eventually need revision, in adopting scientific method as the instrument for evaluating claims to knowledge, naturalists are not subscribing to an indemonstrable faith.

The bitter years of cataclysmic wars and social upheavals through which our generation has been passing have also witnessed a general decline of earlier hopes in the possibilities of modern science for achieving a liberal and humane civilization. Indeed, as is well known, many men have become convinced that the progress and spread of science, and the consequent secularization of society, are the prime sources of our present ills; and a not inconsiderable number of thinkers have made widely popular various revived forms of older religious and irrationalistic philosophies as guides to human salvation. Moreover, since naturalists have not abandoned their firm adherence to the method of scientific intelligence, naturalism has been repeatedly charged with insensitivity toward spiritual values, with a shallow optimism toward science as an instrument for ennobling the human estate, and with a philistine blindness toward the ineradicable miseries of human existence. I want to conclude with a few brief comments on these allegations.

It is almost painful to have to make a point of the elementary fact that whatever may happen to be the range of special interests and sensibilities of individual naturalists, there is no incompatibility, whether logical or psychological, between maintaining that warranted knowledge is secured only through the use of a definite logical method, and recognizing that the world can be experienced in many other ways than by knowing it. It is a matter of record that outstanding exponents of naturalism, in our own time as well as in the past, have exhibited an unequaled and tender sensitivity to the esthetic and moral dimensions of human experience; and they have been not only movingly eloquent celebrants of the role of moral idealism and of intellectual and esthetic contemplation in human life, but also vigorous defenders of the distinctive character of these values against facile attempts to reduce them to something else.

It seems to me singularly inept, moreover, to indict naturalism as a philosophy without a sense for the tragic aspects of life. For unlike many world-views, naturalism offers no cosmic consolation for the unmerited defeats and undeserved sufferings which all men experience in one form or another. It has never sought to conceal its view of human destiny as an episode between two oblivions. To be sure, naturalism is not a philosophy of despair. For one facet in its radical pluralism is the truth that a human good is nonetheless a good, despite its transitory existence. There doubtless are foolish optimists among those professing naturalism, though naturalism has no monopoly in this respect, and it is from other quarters that one usually receives glad tidings of a universal nostrum. But in any event, neither the pluralism so central to naturalism, nor its cultivation of scientific reason, is compatible with any dogmatic assumption to the effect that men can be liberated from *all* the sorrows and evils to which they are now heirs, through the eventual advances of science and the institution of appropriate physical and social innovations. Indeed, why suppose that a philosophy which is wedded to the use of the sober logic of scientific intelligence, should thereby be committed to the dogma that there are no irremediable evils? On the contrary, human reason is potent only against evils that are *remediable*. At the same time, since it is impossible to decide responsibly, *antecedent* to inquiry, *which* of the many human ills can be mitigated if not eradicated by extending the operations of scientific reason into human affairs, naturalism is not a philosophy of *general* renunciation, even though it recognizes that it is the better part of wisdom to be equably resigned to what, in the light of available evidence, cannot be avoided. Human reason is not an omnipotent instrument for the achievement of human goods; but it is the only instrument we do possess, and it is not a contemptible one. Although naturalism is acutely sensitive to the actual limitations of rational effort, those limitations do not warrant a romantic philosophy of general despair, and they do not blind naturalism to the possibilities implicit in the exercise of disciplined reason for realizing human excellence.

BIBLIOGRAPHY

NAGEL, Ernest, *On the Logic of Measurement.* N.Y.: 1930. Thesis (Ph.D.) Columbia U., 1931.
———, *Principles of The Theory of Probability.* Chicago: U. of Chicago Press, 1939.
———, *Logic Without Metaphysics and Other Essays in the Philosophy of Science.* Glencoe, Ill.: Free Press, 1954.
———, *Sovereign Reason.* Glencoe, Ill.: Free Press, 1954.
———, *The Structure of Science. Problems in the Logic of Scientific Explanation.* N.Y.: Harcourt Brace & World, 1961.

_____ (with Morris R. Cohen), *An Introduction to Logic and Scientific Method.* N.Y.: Harcourt Brace, 1934.

_____ (with S. Baron, eds.), *Freedom and Reason: Essays in Honor of Morris R. Cohen.* Glencoe, Ill.: The Free Press, 1951.

_____ (with J. R. Newman), *Gödel's Proof.* N.Y.: New York U. Press, 1958.

_____ (with P. Suppes and A. Tarski, eds.), *Logic, Methodology and Philosophy of Science.* Stanford: Stanford U. Press, 1962.

General Bibliography[1]

1. REFERENCE WORKS

ADAMS, G.P. and MONTAGUE, W.P., ed. *Contemporary American Philosophy*, 2 vols., N.Y.: Macmillan, 1930.

ALSTON, William and NAKHNIKIAN, George, eds. *Twentieth Century Philosophy*. N.Y.: The Free Press, 1963.

ANDERSON, Paul Russell and FISCH, Max Harold. *Philosophy in America, From the Puritans to James, With Representative Selections*. N.Y.: Appleton-Century, 1939.

BARRETT, William and AIKEN, Henry D., eds. *Philosophy in the Twentieth Century*, Vol. One. N.Y.: Random House, 1962.

Bibliotheca Americana: A Dictionary of Books Relating to America, from its Discovery to the Present Time, 29 Vols. N.Y.: Bibliographical Society of America, 1868–1936.

BLAU, Joseph. *Men and Movements in American Philosophy*. N.Y.: Prentice-Hall, 1952.

COHEN, Morris R. *American Thought, A Critical Sketch*, ed. Felix S. Cohen. Glencoe, Ill.: The Free Press, 1954.

COMMAGER, Henry S. *The American Mind*. New Haven: Yale U. Press, 1950.

CURTI, Merle. *The Growth of American Thought*. 2nd ed. N.Y.: Harpers, 1950.

Dictionary of American Biography, ed. Allen Johnson, 20 vols., N.Y.: Charles Scribner's, 1928–37.

Dictionary of Philosophy and Psychology, ed. J.M. Baldwin, 3 vols. N.Y.: Macmillan, 1901–05.

Encyclopedia of Philosophy, ed. Paul Edwards, 10 vols. N.Y.: Macmillan, forthcoming, Articles on American Philosophy.

FARBER, Marvin, ed. *Philosophic Thought in France and the United States*. Buffalo: U. of Buffalo Press, 1950.

FERM, Vergilius, ed. *A History of Philosophical Systems*. N.Y.: Philosophical Library, 1950.

FISCH, Max H., ed. *Classic American Philosophers: Peirce, James, Royce, Santayana, Dewey, Whitehead*. N.Y.: Appleton-Century-Crofts, 1951.

FRANKEL, Charles, ed. *The Golden Age of American Philosophy*. N.Y.: Braziller, 1960.

GETTELL, R.D. *History of American Political Thought*. N.Y.: Century, 1929.

HOOK, Sidney, ed. *American Philosophers at Work*. N.Y.: Criterion, 1956.

JACOBSON, J. Mark. *The Development of American Political Thought*. N.Y.: Appleton-Century, 1932.

---

[1] *Note*: This General Bibliography contains additional books usually not listed under the separate author Bibliographies.

JARRETT, J. L. and MC MURRIN, S. M., eds. *Contemporary Philosophy. A Book of Readings.* N.Y.: Holt, 1954.

Journal of Philosophy, 50-year index (1904–1953.)

KALLEN, Horace M. and HOOK, Sidney, eds. *American Philosophy Today and Tomorrow.* N.Y.: Lee Furman, 1935.

KRIKORIAN, Yervant H. and EDEL, Abraham, eds. *Contemporary Philosophic Problems.* N.Y.: Macmillan, 1959.

MUELDER, Walter G., SEARS, Laurence, SCHLABACH, Anne V., eds. *The Development of American Philosophy. A Book of Readings,* (2nd ed.) Boston: Houghton, Mifflin, 1960.

MAYER, Frederick. *A History of American Thought: an Introduction.* Dubuque, Iowa: Wm. C. Brown, 1951.

PARRINGTON, V.L. *Main Currents in American Thought.* 3 vols., N.Y.: Harcourt, Brace, 1927–30.

PERRY, Ralph Barton. *Present Philosophical Tendencies.* (Rev. ed.) N.Y.: Longmans, Green, 1929.

PERSONS, Stow. *American Minds: A History of Ideas.* N.Y.: Holt, 1958.

RECK, Andrew. *Recent American Philosophy.* N.Y.: Random House, 1964.

RILEY, I.W. *American Thought from Puritanism to Pragmatism and Beyond.* 2nd ed. N.Y.: Holt, 1923.

RUNES, Dazobert, ed. *Twentieth Century Philosophy.* N.Y.: Philosophical Library, 1947.

SANTAYANA, George. *Character and Opinion in the United States.* N.Y.: Scribner's, 1920.

SCHNEIDER, Herbert W. *A History of American Philosophy.* N.Y.: Columbia U. Press, 1946; 2nd Ed., 1963.

SMITH, John E. *The Spirit of American Philosophy.* N.Y.: Oxford U. Press, 1963.

TAYLOR, Walter F. *A History of American Letters.* Atlanta: American Book Co., 1936.

TOWNSEND, H.G. *Philosophical Ideas in the United States.* N.Y.: American Book Co., 1934.

TRENT, William P., ERSKINE, John, SHERMAN, Stuart P., VAN DOREN, Carl, eds. *The Cambridge History of American Literature.* 4 vols., N.Y.: G.P. Putnam's, 1917–21.

WERKMEISTER, W.H. *A History of Philosophical Ideas in America.* N.Y.: The Ronald Press, 1949.

WHITE, Morton. *Social Thought in America.* (2nd ed.) Boston: Beacon Press, 1957.

2. PRAGMATISM

ABEL, Reuben. *The Pragmatic Humanism of F. C. S. Schiller.* N.Y.: King's Crown Press, 1955.

BAUMGARTEN, Eduard. *Der Pragmatismus: R. W. Emerson, W. James, J. Dewey.* Frankfurt A.M.: V. Klostermann, 1938.

BAWDEN, H. Heath. *The Principles of Pragmatism.* Boston: Houghton, Mifflin, 1910.

BENJAMIN, A.C. *Operationism*. Springfield, Ill.: Thomas, 1955.

BRIDGMAN, Percy W. *The Logic of Modern Physics*. N.Y.: Macmillan, 1927.

BENTLEY, Arthur F. *Behavior, Knowledge, Fact*. Bloomington, Ind.: The Principia Press, 1935.

_____. *Inquiry into Inquiries*, ed. Sidney Ratner. Boston: Beacon Press, 1954.

CALDWELL, William. *Pragmatism and Idealism*. London: Adam and Charles Black, 1913.

CHILDS, John Lawrence. *American Pragmatism and Education: An Interpretation and Criticism*. N.Y.: Holt, 1956.

CHURCHMAN, C. West. *Theory of Experimental Inference*. N.Y.: Macmillan, 1948.

_____. *Prediction and Optimal Decision*. Englewood Cliffs, N.J.: Prentice-Hall, 1961.

DEWEY, John, ed. *Creative Intelligence: Essays in the Pragmatic Attitude*. N.Y.: Holt, 1917.

_____, "The Development of American Pragmatism," in *Studies in the History of Ideas*. N.Y.: Columbia U. Press, 1925.

HOFSTADTER, Richard. *Social Darwinism in American Thought: 1860–1915*. Philadelphia: U. of Pennsylvania Press, 1945.

KALLEN, Horace M. *Individualism: An American Way of Life*. N.Y.: Liveright, 1933.

KENNEDY, Gail, ed. *Pragmatism and American Culture*. Boston: Heath, 1950.

KONVITZ, Milton R. and KENNEDY, Gail, eds. *The American Pragmatists, Selected Writings*. N.Y.: Meridian Books, 1960.

LARRABEE, Harold A. *Reliable Knowledge*. Boston: Houghton, Mifflin, 1945.

LOVEJOY, Arthur O. "The Thirteen Pragmatisms," *Journal of Philosophy, Psychology, and Scientific Methods*, Vol. 5 (1908), pp. 6–12, 29–39.

MADDEN, Edward H. *Chauncey Wright and the Foundations of Pragmatism*. Seattle: U. of Washington Press, 1963.

MEAD, George H. "The Philosophies of Royce, James, and Dewey in Their American Setting," *International Journal of Ethics*, XL (1930), pp. 211–31.

MOORE, Ernest C. *American Pragmatism: Peirce, James, and Dewey*. N.Y.: Columbia U. Press, 1961.

MOORE, Addison W. *Pragmatism and Its Critics*. Chicago: U. of Chicago Press, 1910.

MORRIS, Charles W. *Logical Positivism, Pragmatism, and Scientific Empiricism*. Paris: Hermann, 1937.

_____, *Signs, Language, and Behavior*. N.Y.: Prentice-Hall, 1946.

MONTAGUE, William P. "The Method of Pragmatism," in *Ways of Knowing*. London: Allen & Unwin, 1925. pp. 131–72.

OTTO, Max C. *Things and Ideals*. N. Y.: Holt, 1924.

PRATT, James B. *What Is Pragmatism?* N. Y.: Macmillan, 1909.

PERSONS, Stow, ed. *Evolutionary Thought in America*. New Haven: Yale U. Press, 1950.

RATNER, Sidney, ed. *Vision and Action: Essays in Honor of Horace M. Kallen on his 70th Birthday*. New Brunswick: Rutgers U. Press, 1953.

TAYLOR, Richard W., ed. *Life, Language, Law: Essays in Honor of Arthur F. Bentley*. Yellow Springs: Antioch Press, 1957.

WAHL, Jean A. The *Pluralist Philosophies of England and America*, (trans. F. Rothwell). London: Open Court, 1925.

THAYER, H.S. *The Logic of Pragmatism*. N.Y.: Humanities Press, 1952.

WHITE, Morton G. *Social Thought in America*. N.Y.: Viking Press, 1949.

WIENER, Philip P. *Evolution and the Founders of Pragmatism*. Cambridge: Harvard U. Press, 1949.

3. REALISM

BOWMAN, Lars. *Criticism and Construction in the Philosophy of the American New Realism*. Stockholm: Almquest and Wiksell, 1955.

CHISHOLM, Roderick M., ed. *Realism and the Background of Phenomenology*. Glencoe, Ill.: Free Press, 1960.

COSTELLO, Harry T. *A Philosophy of the Real and the Possible*. N.Y.: Columbia U. Press, 1954.

FEIBLEMAN, J. *The Revival of Realism*. Chapel Hill: U. of N. Carolina Press, 1946.

HARLOW, V.E. *A Bibliography and Genetic Study of American Realism*. Oklahoma City: Harlow Publ. Co., 1931.

MONTAGUE, William P. "The Story of American Realism," *Philosophy*, Vol. 12 (1937), pp. 140–50, 155–61.

REINHARDT, Kurt. *Realistic Philosophy*. Milwaukee: Bruce, 1944.

STACE, W.T. "The Refutation of Realism," *Mind*, XLIII (1934), pp. 145–55.

WEISS, Paul. *Reality*. Princeton: Princeton U. Press, 1938.

URBAN, Wilbur M. *Beyond Realism and Idealism*. London: Allen & Unwin, 1949.

VEATCH, Henry. *Realism and Nominalism Revisited*. Milwaukee: Marquette U. Press, 1954.

WILD, John D. *Introduction to Realistic Philosophy*. N.Y.: Harper, 1948.

4. NATURALISM

BUCHLER, Justus. *Toward a General Theory of Human Judgment*. N.Y.: Columbia U. Press, 1951.

———, *Nature and Judgment*. N.Y.: Columbia U. Press, 1955.

———, *Concept of Method*. N.Y.: Columbia U. Press, 1961.

EDEL, Abraham. *Ethical Judgment*. Glencoe, Ill.: Free Press, 1955.

———, *Science and the Structure of Ethics*. Chicago: U. of Chicago Press, 1961.

KRIKORIAN, Yervant H., ed. *Naturalism and the Human Spirit*. N.Y.: Columbia U. Press, 1944.

KURTZ, Paul W. *The Problems of Value Theory*. N.Y.: Eagle Press, 1952.

———, *Decision and the Condition of Man*. Seattle: U. of Washington Press, 1965.

LEPLEY, Ray, ed. *Value: A Cooperative Inquiry*. N.Y.: Columbia U. Press, 1949.

————, *Verifiability of Value.* N.Y.: Columbia U. Press, 1944.

————, ed. *The Language of Value.* N.Y.: Columbia U. Press, 1957.

PEPPER, Stephen C. *World Hypotheses: A Study in Evidence.* Berkeley: U. of California Press, 1942.

————, *Sources of Value.* Berkeley: U. of California Press, 1958.

PRATT, James B. *Naturalism.* New Haven: Yale U. Press, 1939.

RANDALL, John Herman, Jr. *Nature and Historical Experience.* N.Y.: Columbia U. Press, 1958.

ROMANELL, Patrick. *Towards a Critical Naturalism: Reflection on Contemporary American Philosophy.* N.Y.: Macmillan, 1958.

SCHNEIDER, Herbert W. *Ways of Being; Elements of Analytic Ontology.* N.Y.: Columbia U. Press, 1962.

WHITE, Edward A. *Science and Religion in American Thought: The Impact of Naturalism.* Stanford: Stanford U. Press, 1952.

WOODBRIDGE, F. J. E. *Nature and Mind.* N.Y.: Columbia U. Press, 1937.

————. *The Purpose of History.* N.Y.: Columbia U. Press, 1939.

————. *An Essay on Nature.* N.Y.: Columbia U. Press, 1940.

5. MATERIALISM

HOLT, Edwin B. *Animal Drive and Learning Process; An Essay Toward Radical Empiricism.* N.Y.: Holt, 1931.

HOOK, Sidney. "What is Materialism?", *Journal of Philosophy,* Vol. 31, 1934, pp. 235–42.

MONTAGUE, William P. "Confessions of an Animistic Materialist," in *Contemporary American Philosophy,* ed. Adams and Montague. N. Y.: Macmillan, 1930, Vol. II.

MAYER, Charles L. *Man: Mind or Matter?,* translated with a Preface by Harold A. Larrabee. Boston: Beacon Press, 1951.

OTTO, Max. *The Human Enterprise: An Attempt to Relate Philosophy to Daily Life.* N.Y.: Crofts, 1940.

PERRY, Ralph Barton. *Present Philosophical Tendencies* (rev. ed.). N.Y.: Longmans, Green, 1929. (Part II on "Naturalism.")

PRATT, James B. *Matter and Spirit.* N.Y.: Macmillan, 1922.

6. HUMANISM

BURKHARDT, Frederick H., ed. *The Cleavage in Our Culture: Studies in Scientific Humanism in Honor of Max Otto.* Boston: Beacon Press, 1952.

BURTT, Edwin A. *Types of Religious Philosophy.* N.Y.: Harpers, 1939.

FROMM, Erich. *Man for Himself.* N.Y.: Rinehart, 1947.

KALLEN, Horace M., ed. *Freedom in the Modern World.* N.Y.: Coward-McCann, 1928.

KEYSER, C.J., *Humanism and Science.* N.Y.: Columbia U. Press, 1931.

KUENZLI, Alfred E., ed. *Reconstruction in Religion.* Boston: Beacon Press, 1961.

LAMONT, Corliss. *Humanism as a Philosophy.* N.Y.: Philosophical Library, 1949.

————, *The Illusion of Immortality*. N.Y.: Putnam, 1935.

OTTO, Max C. *The Human Enterprise*. N.Y.: Crofts, 1940.

POTTER, Charles F. *Humanism: A New Religion*. N.Y.: Simon & Schuster, 1930.

REESE, Curtis W. *The Meaning of Humanism*. Boston: Beacon Press, 1945.

REISER, Oliver L. *The Promise of Scientific Humanism*. N.Y.: Piest, 1940.

RANDALL, John Herman, Jr. *The Role of Knowledge in Western Religion*. Boston: Beacon Press, 1958.

SCHILLER, F.C.S. *Humanism*. (2nd ed.). London: Macmillan, 1912.

SCHNEIDER, Herbert W. *Religion in Twentieth Century America*. Cambridge: Harvard U. Press, 1952.

7. IDEALISM [2]

BARRETT, Clifford, ed. *Contemporary Idealism in America*. N. Y.: Macmillan, 1932.

BERTOCCI, P., NEWHALL, J. and BRIGHTMAN, E.S., eds. *Person and Reality*. N.Y.: Ronald Press, 1958.

BRIGHTMAN, E.S. *Religious Values*. N.Y.: Abingdon Press, 1925.

————, *A Philosophy of Ideals*. N.Y.: Henry Holt, 1928.

————, *The Problem of God*. N.Y.: Abingdon Press, 1930.

————, *The Finding of God*. N.Y.: Abingdon Press, 1931.

————, *Moral Laws*. N.Y.: Abingdon Press, 1933.

————, *Personality and Religion*. N.Y.: Abingdon Press, 1934.

————, *A Philosophy of Religion*. N.Y.: Prentice-Hall, 1940.

————, *The Spiritual Life*. N.Y.: Abingdon Press, 1942.

————, *Nature and Values*. N.Y.: Abingdon Press, 1945.

CREIGHTON, James E. *Studies in Speculative Philosophy*, ed. H.R. Smart. N.Y.: Macmillan, 1925.

CUNNINGHAM, G.W. *The Idealistic Argument in Recent British and American Philosophy*. N.Y.: Century, 1933.

EWING, A.C., ed. *The Idealist Tradition*. Glencoe, Ill.: Free Press, 1957.

FITE, Warner. *The Living Mind; Essays on the Significance of Consciousness*. N.Y.: Dial Press, 1930.

HOCKING, W.E. *The Meaning of God in Human Experience*. New Haven: Yale U. Press, 1912.

————, *The Self—Its Body and Freedom*. New Haven: Yale U. Press, 1928.

————, *Types of Philosophy*. N.Y.: Scribner's, 1959 (3rd ed.).

————, *Thoughts on Death and Life*. N.Y.: Harpers, 1937.

————, *Living Religions and a World Faith*. London: Allen & Unwin, 1940.

————, *Science and the Idea of God*. Chapel Hill: U. of N. Carolina Press, 1944.

KNUDSON, A.C. *The Philosophy of Personalism*. N.Y.: Abingdon Press, 1927.

MUIRHEAD, John H. *The Platonic Tradition in Anglo-Saxon Philosophy*. N.Y.: Macmillan, 1931.

[2] Note: This list of books supplements a Bibliography on pre-twentieth century Idealism in the companion volume, *American Thought Before 1900*.

PARKER, De Witt H. *Experience and Substance*. Ann Arbor: U. of Michigan Press, 1941.

SABINE, George H., ed. *Philosophical Essays in Honor of James Edwin Creighton*, N.Y.: Macmillan, 1917.

SHELDON, Wilman H., *Process and Polarity*. N.Y.: Columbia U. Press, 1944.

URBAN, Wilbur M. *The Intelligible World*. N.Y.: Macmillan, 1929.

————, *Beyond Realism and Idealism*. London: Allen & Unwin, 1949.

————, *Humanity and Deity*. London: Allen & Unwin, 1951.

————, *Language and Reality*. London: Allen & Unwin, 1951.

8. RATIONALISM

BOAS, George. *Rationalism in Greek Philosophy*. Baltimore: Johns Hopkins Press, 1961.

HARTSHORNE, Charles. *The Logic of Perfection and Other Essays in Neo-Classical Metaphysics*. LaSalle: Open Court, 1962.

LOWENBERG, Jacob. *Reason and the Nature of Things*. LaSalle: Open Court, 1959.

SANTILLANA, George. *Aspects of Scientific Rationalism in the Nineteenth Century*. Chicago: U. of Chicago Press, 1941.

———— and ZILSEL, Edgar. *The Development of Rationalism and Empiricism*. Chicago: U. of Chicago Press, 1941.

SPAULDING, Edward G. *The New Rationalism*. N.Y.: Holt, 1918.

WEISS, Paul. *Modes of Being*. Carbondale, Ill.: Southern Illinois U. Press, 1958.

9. PHILOSOPHICAL ANALYSIS: LOGICAL POSITIVISM AND LINGUISTIC PHILOSOPHY

AYER, A.J., ed. *Logical Positivism*. Glencoe, Ill.: The Free Press, 1959.

BERGMANN, Gustav. *The Metaphysics of Logical Positivism*. London: Longmans, Green, 1954.

————, *Philosophy of Science*. Madison: U. of Wisconsin Press, 1957.

CHISHOLM, R. M. *Perceiving: A Philosophical Study*. Ithaca: Cornell U. Press, 1957.

FEIGL, Herbert and SELLARS, Wilfrid, eds. *Readings in Philosophical Analysis*. N.Y.: Appleton-Century-Crofts, 1949.

FEIGL, Herbert and BRODBECK, M., eds. *Readings in the Philosophy of Science*. N.Y.: Appleton-Century-Crofts, 1953.

FEIGL, Herbert and BRODBECK, M., eds. *Readings in the Philosophy of Science*. Minneapolis: U. of Minnesota Press. Vol. I, 1956; Vol. II, 1958; Vol. III, 1962.

FRANK, Philip. *Philosophy of Science*. Englewood Cliffs: Prentice-Hall, 1957.

GOODMAN, Nelson. *The Structure of Appearance*. Cambridge: Harvard U. Press, 1951.

————, *Fact, Fiction, and Forecast*. Cambridge: Harvard U. Press, 1955.

564   GENERAL BIBLIOGRAPHY

HANSON, Norwood R. *Patterns of Discovery.* Cambridge: Harvard U. Press, 1958.

HEMPEL, Carl. *Fundamentals of Concept Formation in Empirical Sciences.* Chicago: U. of Chicago Press, 1952. (Intl. Encycl. of Unified Science).

HOSPERS, John. *An Introduction to Philosophical Analysis.* N.Y.: Prentice-Hall, 1953.

International Encyclopedia of Unified Science, ed. by O. Neurath and others. Chicago: U. of Chicago Press, 1938 and continuing.

LAZEROWITZ, Morris. *The Structure of Metaphysics.* London: Routledge and Kegan Paul, 1955.

LEAN, Martin. *Sense Perception and Matter.* London. Routledge and Kegan Paul, 1953.

LINSKY, Leonard, ed. *Semantics and the Philosophy of Language.* Urbana: U. of Illinois Press, 1952.

MALCOLM, Norman. *Ludwig Wittgenstein: A Memoir.* N.Y.: Oxford U. Press, 1958.

_____, *Dreaming.* N.Y.: Humanities Press, 1959.

MARTIN, R.M. *Truth and Denotation: A Study in Semantical Theory.* Chicago: U. of Chicago Press, 1958.

NEURATH, Otto. *Foundations of the Social Sciences.* Chicago: U. of Chicago Press, 1944. (International Encycl. of Unified Science).

PAP, Arthur. *The A Priori in Physical Theory.* N.Y.: King's Crown Press, 1946.

_____, *Elements of Analytic Philosophy.* N.Y.: Macmillan, 1949.

_____, *Semantics and Necessary Truth.* New Haven: Yale U. Press, 1958.

_____, *In Introduction to the Philosophy of Science.* N.Y.: Free Press, 1962.

REICHENBACH, Hans. *Experience and Prediction.* Chicago: U. of Chicago Press, 1938.

_____, *Philosophic Foundations of Quantum Mechanics.* Berkeley: U. of California Press, 1944.

_____, *Elements of Symbolic Logic.* N.Y.: Macmillan, 1947.

_____, *The Rise of Scientific Philosophy.* Berkeley: U. of California Press, 1951.

_____, *Nomological Statements and Admissible Operations.* Amsterdam: North Holland Pub. Co., 1954.

_____, *The Direction of Time,* ed. M. Reichenbach. Berkeley: U. of California Press, 1956.

SELLARS, Wilfred and HOSPERS, John, eds. *Readings in Ethical Theory.* N.Y.: Appleton-Century-Crofts, 1952.

TARSKI, A. *Logic, Semantics, Meta-Mathematics.* Oxford: Clarendon Press, 1956.

WEINBERG, Julius R. *An Examination of Logical Positivism.* N.Y.: Harcourt, Brace, 1936.

WHITE, Morton G. *Toward Reunion in Philosophy.* Cambridge: Harvard U. Press, 1956.

WIENER, Philip, ed. *Readings in Philosophy of Science.* N.Y.: Scribner's, 1953.

10. MARXISM

FROMM, Erich. *Marx's Concept of Man*. N.Y.: Ungar, 1961.

MARCUSE, Herbert. *Reason and Revolution: Hegel and the Rise of Social Theory*. N.Y.: Oxford U. Press, 1941.

————, *Soviet Marxism: A Critical Analysis*. N.Y.: Columbia U. Press, 1958.

SABINE, George. *Marxism*. Ithaca: Cornell U. Press, 1958.

SOMERVILLE, John. *Soviet Philosophy: A Study of Theory and Practice*. N.Y.: Philosophical Library, 1946.

SELSAM, Howard. *Philosophy in Revolution*. N.Y.: Intl. Publ., 1957.

TAYLOR, Overton H. *The Classical Liberalism, Marxism and the Twentieth Century*. Cambridge: Harvard U. Press, 1960.

VENABLE, Vernon. *Human Nature: The Marxian View*. N.Y.: Knopf, 1946.

WELLS, Harry K. *Pragmatism: Philosophy of Imperialism*. N.Y.: Intl. Publ., 1954.

11. NEO-THOMISM

ADLER, Mortimer J. *St. Thomas and the Gentiles*. Milwaukee: Marquette U. Press, 1958.

ANDERSON, James F. *The Bond of Being: An Essay on Analogy and Existence*. St. Louis: Herder, 1949.

————, *The Cause of Being*. St. Louis: Herder, 1952.

BOURKE, Vernon J. *A Thomistic Bibliography, 1920–40*. (The Modern Schoolman, suppl. to vol. XXI) St. Louis, Mo., 1945.

BRENNAN, R. E., ed. *Essays in Thomism*. N.Y.: Sheed & Ward, 1942.

COLLINS, James D. *God in Modern Philosophy*. Chicago: Henry Regnery, 1959.

GALLAGHER, D. A. and I. *The Achievement of Jacques and Räissa Maritain, 1906–1961*. N.Y.: Doubleday, 1962.

HART, C.A., ed. *Aspects of the New Scholastic Philosophy*, N.Y.: Benziger Bros., 1932.

————, *Thomistic Metaphysics*. Englewood Cliffs, N.J.: Prentice-Hall, 1959.

KLOCKER, Harry. *Thomism and Modern Thought*. N.Y.: Appleton, 1962.

KLUBERTANZ, George. *St. Thomas Aquinas on Analogy*. Chicago: Loyola U. Press, 1960.

MARITAIN, Jacques. *St. Thomas Aquinas*. London: Sheed & Ward, 1933.

————, *Scholasticism and Politics*. N.Y.: Macmillan, 1940.

————, *Education at the Crossroads*. New Haven: Yale U. Press, 1943.

————, *The Person and the Common Good*. N.Y.: Scribner's, 1947.

————, *Christianity and Democracy*. N.Y.: Scribner's, 1950.

————, *Man and the State*. Chicago: U. of Chicago Press, 1951.

————, *Philosophy of Nature*. N.Y.: Philosophical Library, 1951.

————, *The Range of Reason*. N.Y.: Scribner's, 1952.

————, *Creative Intuition in Art and Poetry*. N.Y.: Pantheon, 1953.

————, *Approaches to God.* N.Y.: Harpers, 1954.

————, *On the Philosophy of History.* N.Y.: Scribner's, 1957.

————, *Reflections on America.* N.Y.: Scribner's, 1958.

————, *Art and Scholasticism.* N.Y.: Scribner's, 1962.

OWENS, Joseph. *St. Thomas and the Future of Metaphysics.* Milwaukee: Marquette U. Press, 1957.

REGIS, L. M. *Epistemology.* N.Y.: Macmillan, 1959.

SIMON, Y. *The Nature and Functions of Authority.* Milwaukee: Marquette U. Press, 1940.

————, *Philosophy of Democratic Government.* Chicago: U. of Chicago Press, 1951.

————, *General Theory of Authority.* Notre Dame, Ind.: U. of Notre Dame Press, 1962.

ZYBURA, J. S., ed. *Present-day Thinkers and the New Scholasticism.* St. Louis: Herder, 1927.

12. PHENOMENOLOGY

CHISHOLM, Roderick, ed. *Realism and the Background of Phenomenology.* Glencoe, Ill.: Free Press, 1960.

FARBER, Marvin. *The Foundation of Phenomenology: Edmund Husserl and the Quest for a Rigorous Science of Philosophy.* Cambridge: Harvard U. Press, 1943. (Second Ed., 1962.)

————, ed. *Philosophical Essays in Memory of Edmund Husserl.* Cambridge: Harvard U. Press, 1940.

————. *Naturalism and Subjectivism.* Springfield, Ill.: C. C. Thomas, 1959.

LAUER, Quentin J. *The Triumph of Subjectivity: An Introduction to Transcendental Phenomenology.* N.Y.: Fordham U. Press, 1958.

OSBORN, A. D. *Edmund Husserl and His Logical Investigations.* (2nd ed.) Cambridge, Mass.: 1949.

SPIEGELBERG, Herbert. *The Phenomenological Movement. A Historical Introduction.* The Hague: Nijhoff, 1960.

WELCH, E. P. *Edmund Husserl's Phenomenology.* Los Angeles: U. of So. California Press, 1949.

WILD, John. *Existence and the World of Freedom.* Englewood Cliffs, N.J.: Prentice-Hall, 1963.

13. EXISTENTIALISM

ALLERS, Rudolf. *Existentialism and Psychiatry.* Springfield, Ill.: C. C. Thomas, 1961.

ARENDT, Hannah. *The Human Condition.* Chicago: U. of Chicago Press, 1958.

BARRETT, William. *Irrational Man.* N.Y.: Doubleday, 1958.

BREISACH, Ernst. *Introduction to Modern Existentialism.* N.Y.: Grove Press, 1962.

COLLINS, James. *Existentialists: A Critical Study.* Chicago: Henry Regnery, 1952.

DESAN, Wilfred. *The Tragic Finale: An Essay on the Philosophy of Jean-Paul Sartre.* Cambridge: Harvard U. Press, 1954.

KAELIN, Eugene F. *An Existentialist Aesthetic: The Theories of Sartre and Merleau-Ponty.* Madison: U. of Wisconsin Press, 1962.

KAUFMANN, Walter, ed. *Existentialism from Dostoevski to Sartre.* N.Y.: Meridian Books, 1956.

LOWRIE, Walter. *Kierkegaard.* N.Y.: Oxford U. Press, 1938.

OLSON, Robert G. *An Introduction to Existentialism.* N.Y.: Dover, 1962.

WILD, John. *The Challenge of Existentialism.* Bloomington: Indiana U. Press, 1955.

14. PHILOSOPHY EAST-WEST

AMES, Van Meter. *Zen and American Thought.* Honolulu: U. of Hawaii Press, 1962.

MOORE, Charles A., ed. *Philosophy East and West.* Princeton: Princeton U. Press, 1944.

————, ed. *Essays in East-West Philosophy: An Attempt at World Philosophical Synthesis.* Honolulu: U. of Hawaii Press, 1951.

————, ed. *Philosophy and Culture—East and West: East–West Philosophy in Practical Perspective.* Honolulu: U. of Hawaii Press, 1962.

NORTHROP, F. S. C. *Meeting of East and West: An Inquiry Concerning World Understanding.* N.Y.: Macmillan, 1946.

PRATT, James B. *India and Its Faiths.* Boston: Houghton Mifflin, 1915.

————, *The Pilgrimage of Buddhism and a Buddhist Pilgrimage.* N.Y.: Macmillan, 1928.

RIEPE, Dale. *The Naturalistic Tradition in Indian Thought.* Seattle: U. of Washington Press, 1960.

STACE, W.T. *Mysticism and Philosophy.* Phila.: Lippincott, 1960.

————. *The Teachings of the Mystics.* N.Y.: New American Library, 1960.

SUZUKI, D.T. *The Essentials of Zen Buddhism,* ed. Bernard Phillips. N.Y.: Dutton, 1962.

Index of Authors and Selections Included in this Volume